# COMMAND OF THE SEA

# Clark G. Reynolds
# COMMAND

By Clark G. Reynolds

*Command of the Sea:*
The History and Strategy of Maritime Empires

*The Fast Carriers:*
The Forging of an Air Navy

With Admiral J. J. "Jocko" Clark, USN
*Carrier Admiral*

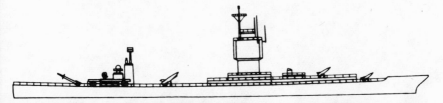

# OF THE SEA

## The History and Strategy of Maritime Empires

*Maps by Richard D. Kelly, Jr.*

William Morrow & Company, Inc.

New York 1974

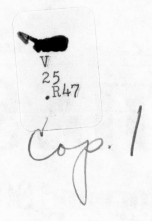
BOOK DESIGN BY HELEN ROBERTS

PRINTED IN THE UNITED STATES OF AMERICA.

1 2 3 4 5 78 77 76 75 74

**Library of Congress Cataloging in Publication Data**

Reynolds, Clark G
  Command of the sea.

  Bibliography: p.
  1. Sea-power.  2. Naval strategy.  3. Naval
history.  I. Title.
V25.R47     359′.03′09     73-19809
ISBN 0-688-00267-6

*To my parents,*
*who made everything possible*

# Acknowledgments

*Study of the workings of the minds of the proved strategists stimu-
lates, if it does not actually procreate, ideas. It opens up one's mental
vision, it widens one's strategic horizon. . . . We see, in history, how
the Masters of War have tackled their problems. Would it not be
something approaching impudence to pretend that we can learn
nothing from them, that we are self-sufficient in ourselves?*

—SIR HERBERT RICHMOND, *c.* 1928

Just as any book of history should represent the cumulative knowledge of all relevant previous historical writers and evidence at the
moment of going to press, so the present work is indebted to most available superior scholarship in naval and maritime history, especially that
in English, to the middle of 1973. Of particular note are several scholars,
mentors and colleagues of the present century (some now deceased)
upon whose diligent research and perceptive insights the writer has relied, especially Robert G. Albion, Roger C. Anderson, Charles R. Boxer,
Lionel Casson, Sir Julian Corbett, Gerald S. Graham, A. R. Lewis,
Michael Lewis, William H. McNeill, Alfred Thayer Mahan, Arthur
Marder, Samuel Eliot Morison, J. H. Parry, Theodore Ropp, Herbert
Rosinski and Stephen Roskill.

No less important have been the virtually innumerable other scholars
who must await notice with their fine but very specialized works in the
bibliography. Mention, however, must be made of other historians who
assisted in some way in the completion of this particular book: John F.
Battick, Robert E. Beitzell, Robert W. Daly, Robert W. Herrick, Ralph
O. Hjelm, Neville T. Kirk, Robert M. Langdon, Philip K. Lundeberg,
Spyridon Marinatos, Peter O'M. Pierson, E. B. Potter, William H. Russell, Howard B. Schonberger and Robert Seager II. Not least deserving
of credit in helping the writer to mature his thoughts have been several
of his students, midshipmen of the United States Naval Academy classes
of 1965 to 1968 and undergraduates and graduate students at the University of Maine from 1968 through 1973.

In addition to historical scholarship, other persons and agencies contributed materially to the completion of this work. A University of

Maine Summer Research Grant provided essential partial funding for the purchase of books and other materials. A number of translators helped the writer to utilize important non-English sources: R. W. Daly (Russian), Marie T. Haag (German), Charles W. Petersen (Swedish and Danish), Michael Poirier (French) and Diane Potter (Italian). My typist, Dorothea Beeuwkes, did her own excellent translating of my longhand draft.

To my wife, Connie, I owe deep appreciation, not only for valuable assistance in proofreading but most importantly for her constant and crucial moral and logistical support that only a devoted wife can furnish a writer if his work is ever to be completed. And to my editor, Howard Cady, goes my heartfelt thanks for his continuing patience and encouragement.

The writer can only hope that the final product of his synthesizing efforts will both satisfy the above persons and act as a point of departure for the current generation of scholars, sailors and laymen concerned with the eternal importance of navies.

C.G.R.

# Contents

# Introduction

*From the days when we humans first began to use the seas, the great lesson of history is that the enemy who is confined to a land strategy is in the end defeated.*

—MONTGOMERY OF ALAMEIN, 1958

"Sea power is indeed a great thing," Thucydides reminds us from his histories of that golden age of Greek learning from which Western civilization directly evolved. Why was it great then, during such an intellectually dynamic era? What were the political, economic and military dimensions of Greek commercial and war shipping? What considerations of strategy underlay the Athenian Empire and the employment of its navy? Indeed, how—if at all—did command of the sea make possible and even stimulate the monumental Greek art and thought of the fifth century B.C.? Upon what historical precedents did the thalassocracy of Athens build, and what legacies did that state leave for future nations that would be founded upon the sea?

Such questions are immense, but so important that they must be answered—the intent of the present work. Not only ancient Greece, but all maritime states and non-maritime-centered peoples who have plied the sea must be analyzed historically and strategically if sea power is to be appreciated, understood and applied in the future. The task is not a simple one, for it involves two methodological ingredients traditionally avoided by most historians: generalization and subjectivity. Historians, like other professionals, feel most secure in their own areas of specialization, and they jealously guard their specialties from generalizing pirates. Nevertheless, this writer believes that the painstaking labors behind a great many specialized studies can be synthesized into a meaningful overview of naval history. In contrast, strategists, by trade and definition, must analyze in order to understand principles, trends and any patterns in strategic thought and practice, which requires a large measure of subjective but informed opinion. Historical objectivity must then yield to such analysis if the notion of command of the sea is to have any real meaning.

This book consequently seeks to discover the strategic alternatives and constants governing navies and empires throughout the continuum of history by raising hypotheses to be tested by historical examination and by future action. It therefore examines the natural factors such as geography and topography, the political and economic aspects of empire building, the cultural and intellectual manifestations, technology and the tactical evolution of naval forces. Together, these elements define the concept of sea power—in the twentieth century A.D. as well as in the twentieth century B.C. Sea power, when applied to command of the major waterways of the world, indeed emerges as "a great thing"—in the past, today and for the foreseeable future.

*The council [sic] which Themistocles gave to Athens—Pompey to Rome —Cromwell to England—DeWitt to Holland—and Colbert to France . . . That as the great questions of commerce between nations and empires must be decided by a military marine, and war or peace are determined by sea, all reasonable encouragement should be given to a navy. The trident of Neptune is the sceptre of the world.*

—JOHN ADAMS, 1802

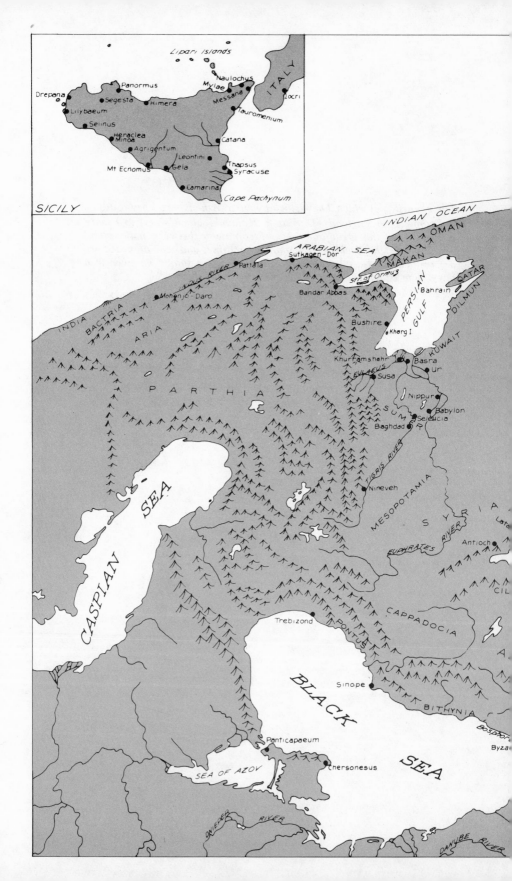

SICILY

Lipari Islands

ITALY

Panormus · Naulochus
Segesta · · Himera · Mylae
Drepana · Messana
Lilybaeum · Locri
Selinus · Tauromenium
Heraclea
Minoa · Catana
Agrigentum
Leontini
Mt Ecnomus · Gela · Thapsus
Camarina · Syracuse
Cape Pachynum

INDIAN OCEAN

OMAN

ARABIAN SEA

MAKAN

Sutkagen-Dor

INDUS RIVER · Pattala

St. of Ormuz

PERSIAN GULF

QATAR

INDIA

BACTRIA

Mohenjo-Daro

Bandar Abbas

Bahrain

DILMUN

ARIA

Bushire

KUWAIT

Kharg I.

PARTHIA

Khurramshahr

Basra

EULAEUS

Susa

Ur

SUMER

Nippur

Babylon

Baghdad

Seleucia

TIGRIS RIVER

Nineveh

MESOPOTAMIA

SYRIA

EUPHRATES RIVER

Lara

CASPIAN SEA

Antioch

CIL

CAPPADOCIA

Trebizond

PONTUS

A.

BLACK

Sinope

BITHYNIA

BOSPHOR

Byza

Panticapaeum

SEA

SEA OF AZOV

Chersonesus

DNIEPER RIVER

DANUBE RIVER

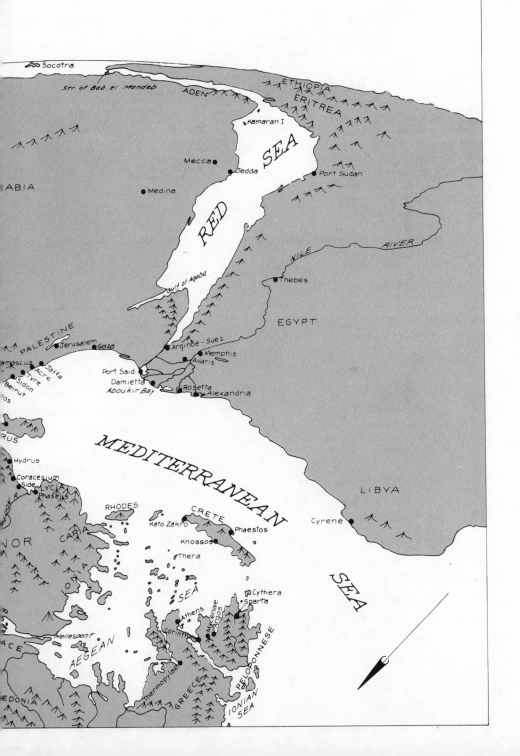

# THE MEDITERRANEAN

NORWAY

NORTH SEA

SWEDEN

FINLAND

Oslo

Helsinki

BALTIC SEA

Leningrad

Glasgow

Liverpool

Copenhagen

Heligoland

Texel

Lowestoft

ELBE

VISTULA

ENGLAND

Zuyder Zee

GERMANY

Berlin

Warsaw

Bristol

London

Damme

ZEELAND

Antwerp

Lizard Head

ENGLISH CHANNEL

Str of Dover

Ostend

Bruges

Boulogne

RHINE

Prague

Ushant

Brest

La Hogue

SOMME

RHINE

Le Havre

Paris

Vienna

St Malo

FRANCE

Munich

Lorient

LOIRE

Bay of Biscay

Oléran

Rochefort

Lyon

RHONE

Milan

Lake Garda

Trieste

Bordeaux

Padua

Venice

Pola

GARONNE

Genoa

Patras

Corunna

Ferrol

Santander

Marseille

Villefranche

Leghorn

Florence

Pontevedra

Toulon

CORSICA

ETRURIA

RIVER

Rapallo

DUERO

SPAIN

EBRO

Maddalena

MONDEGO

Madrid

Barcelona

SARDINIA

DOURO

TAGUS RIVER

Tarraco

TYRRHE

Balearic Is.

Minorca

Lisbon

Saguntum

Port Mahon

PORTUGAL

Valencia

Majorca

Lagos Bay

Algarve

Alicante

MEDITERRANEAN

Cape St Vincent

Sagres

Seville

Cartagena

Rota

Ameria

Cadiz

Malaga

Algiers

Bougie

Bo

Cape Trafalgar

Marbella

Alboran I.

Str of Gibraltar

Mers-el-Kebir

Tangier

Ceuta

Oran

Melilla

Tlemcen

ALGERIA

ATLANTIC OCEAN

Fez

Casablanca

MOROCCO

Agadir

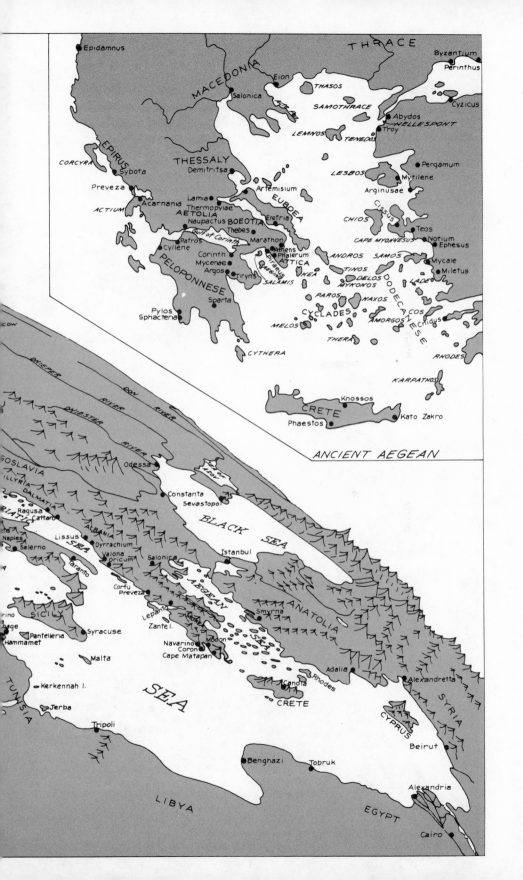

ANCIENT AEGEAN

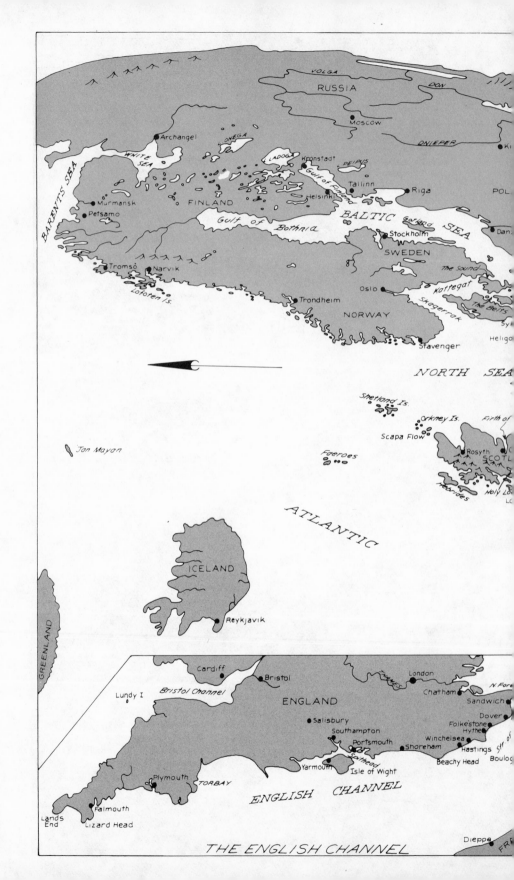

# THE BOTTLENECK OF EUROPE

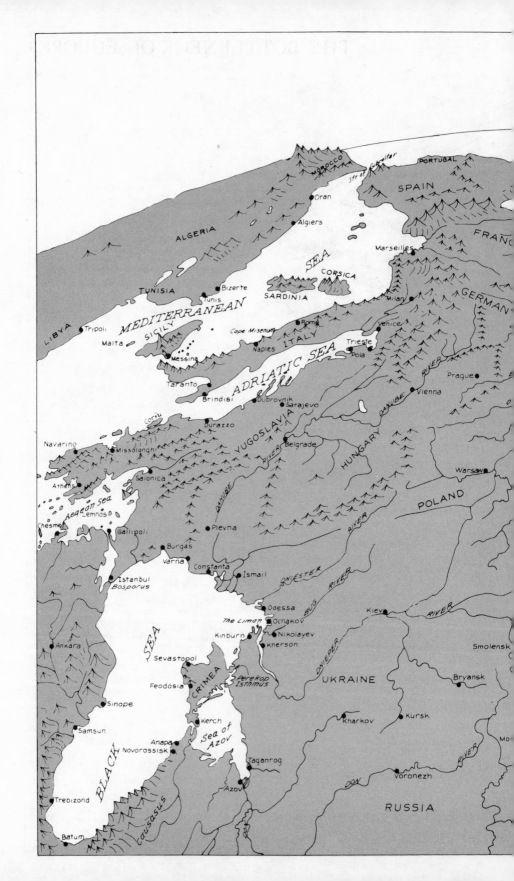

# THE EUROPEAN PENINSULA

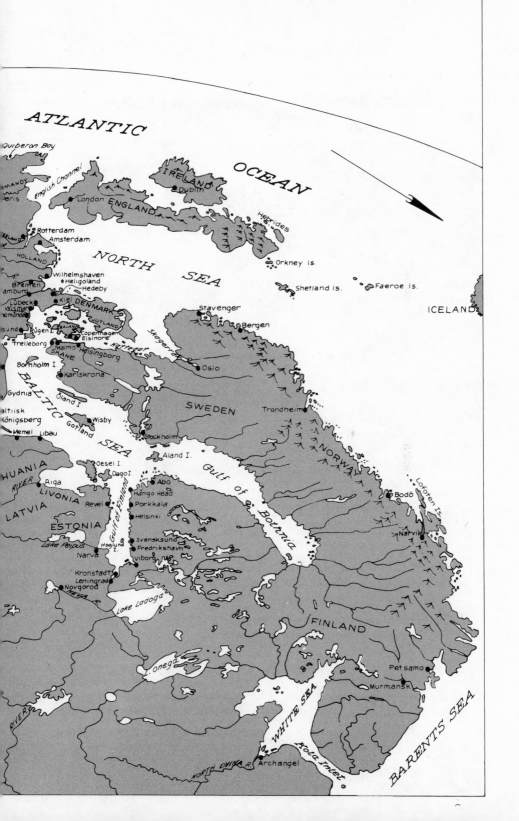

ATLANTIC OCEAN

Quiberon Bay

NORMANDY

Paris

English Channel

IRELAND
Dublin

London ENGLAND

Hebrides

HOLLAND Rotterdam
Amsterdam

NORTH SEA

Orkney Is.

Shetland Is.

Faeroe Is.

ICELAND

Wilhelmshaven
Heligoland
Bremen Hedeby
Hamburg
Lübeck Kiel DENMARK
Wismar
Swinemünde JUTLAND
Stralsund Rügen I. Copenhagen
Trelleborg ZEALAND Elsinore
Bornholm I. SKANE Malmö Helsingborg
Karlskrona
Gydnia Öland I.
Baltiisk
Königsberg Gotland Wisby
Memel Libau

Stavenger

Bergen

Skagerrak

Kattegat

Osio

SWEDEN

Trondheim

Stockholm

Åland I.

BALTIC SEA

LITHUANIA
RIVER Riga
LIVONIA
LATVIA Revel
ESTONIA
Lake Peipus
Narva

Oesel I.
DagoI
Abo
Hango Head
Porkkala
Helsinki

Gulf of Finland

Svensksund
Hoglund I.
Fredrikshavn
Viborg

Kronstadt
Leningrad
Novgorod
NEVA R.

Lake Ladoga

Gulf of Bothnia

NORWAY

Bodö

Lofoten Is.

Narvik

FINLAND

Petsamo

L. Onega

Murmansk

RIVER

WHITE SEA

Kola Inlet

BARENTS SEA

NORTH DVINA R. Archangel

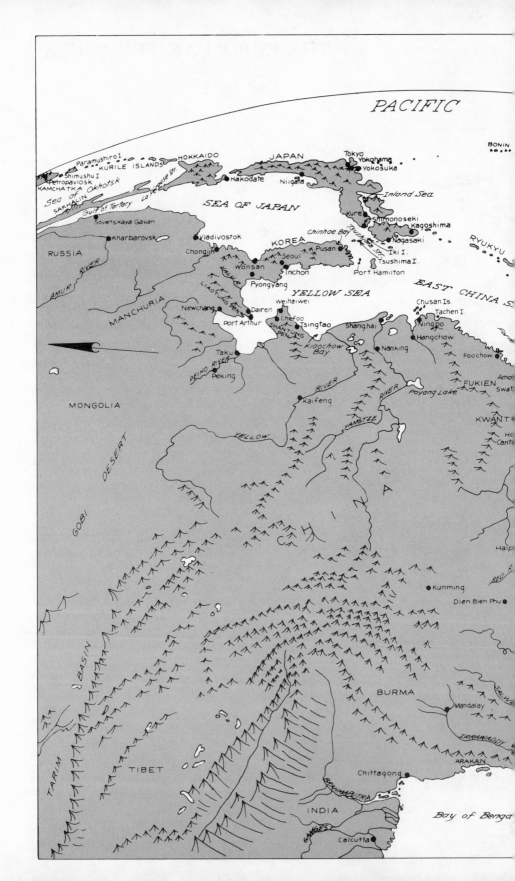

# THE PERIPHERY OF ASIA

OCEAN

MARIANAS
• • • •
•Saipan
•Tinian
ISLANDS •Guam

CAROLINE
• Truk
• • •
ISLANDS
•
PHILIPPINE SEA
— Palau Is.

SOLOMON IS.
Rabaul •
Admiralty New Britain
Is. •

Batan Is.
PHILIPPINE ISLANDS
NEW GUINEA
·res I.
San Bernardino Str.
LUZON Leyte ·Surigao Str.
Lingayen •Manila Sibuyan Sea
Samar
Mindoro MINDANAO
HALMAHERA
CELEBES SEA
Ternate
Banda I.
MOLUCCA IS.
·chow Bay
SULU SEA
Amboina
HAINAN
SOUTH PALAWAN

CHINA
Tarakan
Str. of Macassar
of Tonkin
Brunei
CELEBES
Hué •Da Nang
Spratly Is.
SEA
·NAM
Camranh Bay
Balikpapan
MEKONG
SARAWAK
RIVER Saigon
·hang Vung Tau
CAMBODIA
BORNEO
·AND Tonle Sap Pnom Penh
Natuna I.
JAVA SEA
Bangkok
Anambas Is.
Soerabaja
Gulf of Siam
EAST INDIES
Kra Isthmus MALAYA
Singapore
ANDAMAN
Batavia
Penang I.
Malacca Str.
SEA
Palembang
·daman Is.
SUMATRA
Nicobar Is.
Bencoolen

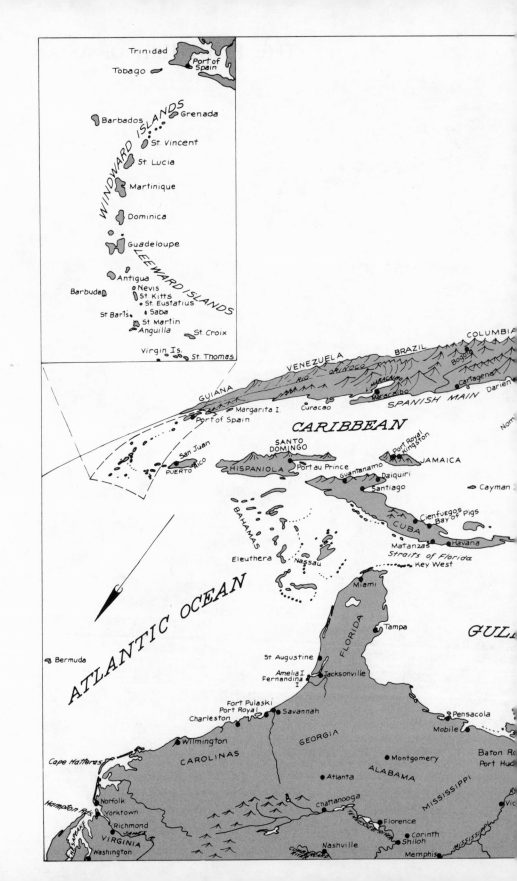

QUITO
PERU
ECUADOR
Lima
Callao

GALAPAGOS

P A C I F I C   O C E A N

ytown
COSTA RICA
San Jose
NICARAGUA
Managua
HONDURAS
EL SALVADOR
San Salvador
Guatemala
Belize
GUATEMALA
YUCATAN
Merida
Campeche
Carmen
TABASCO
Frontera

Bay of Campeche
San Juan de Ulua
Veracruz
Acapulco
MEXICO
Tuxpan
Mexico City
Tampico
Soto la Marina
Manzanillo
Matamoros
Brownsville
MEXICO
Galveston
RIO GRANDE
RIVER
Corpus Christi
TEXAS
Mazatlan

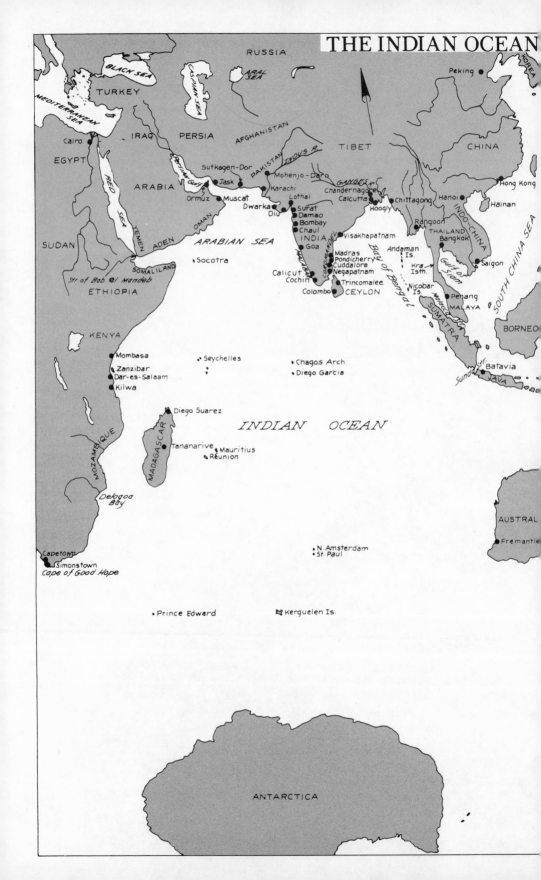

THE INDIAN OCEAN

# BOOK ONE

## Command of the Sea—
## and the Alternatives

*. . . a vague feeling of contempt for the past, supposed to be obsolete, combines with natural indolence to blind men even to those permanent strategic lessons which lie close to the surface of naval history.*

—ALFRED THAYER MAHAN

*The primary aim of naval war is the command of the sea. Any other aim is an acceptance of the position of the inferior naval power, and the abnegation of all hopes of ultimate success.*

—P. H. COLOMB

The sea covers 71 percent of the earth's surface; the remaining 29 percent is mostly land mass, generally occupied by human groupings in areas readily accessible either to the great saltwater oceans or to the many inland fresh-waterways, the major lakes and rivers. The sea-borne communications between these settlements have often been a dominant force in the history of great nations. Thus, command of the sea and inland waterways has remained a key political and strategic concern of seagoing peoples throughout history.

Geography is the major determining factor in any nation's ability to utilize the sea commercially and to defend its political and economic

1

integrity from overseas attack. Thus, each nation tends to orient its political, economic and military life around the advantages of its geographical position vis-à-vis other nations. And history reveals that this orientation has usually favored either the ocean-maritime element or the continental. No nation has yet been able to afford the sheer expense of sustaining both a large army to control its continental frontiers and a large navy to maintain control over vast areas of water.

While immediately adjacent waters have been of constant concern to every nation, the specific waterways politically disputed throughout history have changed in emphasis with the growth and reach of Western civilization.

In the ancient and medieval periods of history, the Mediterranean Sea enclosed the areas of major political dispute. These were the Eastern Mediterranean, from the Aegean Sea and the Dardanelles in the north, to Cyprus and Crete islands in the center, to the Phoenician coast and Nile Delta in the south; the Central Mediterranean, from the Adriatic Sea and Italy in the north, to the Ionian and Tyrrhenian seas and Sicily in the center, to Carthage and Malta in the south; and the Western Mediterranean, the clockwise circle of southern France, Corsica, Sardinia, North Africa, Gibraltar, the Balearic Islands (Majorca and Minorca) and the Iberian peninsula.

In the modern period, roughly 1500 to 1900, maritime relations between nations were geographically governed by the so-called funnel of Europe, the sea lanes of the North Atlantic Ocean that passed through the narrow Strait of Dover and English Channel, connecting the North Sea nations with France, Spain and Portugal to the south. At the focus of this activity lay England, around which the major maritime events of this period revolved. Flanking this center of maritime activity and international rivalry were three virtual overseas lakes, all linked to the ever-lengthening European trade routes: the Baltic Sea to the north, the Mediterranean to the south and the Caribbean to the west. Secondary areas in this period were the South Atlantic, Indian and Pacific oceans, and the Black Sea.

In the contemporary period, the twentieth century, the rise of non-European powers has made the two great oceans, the Atlantic and Pacific, of equal importance. All the other oceans, seas, lakes and rivers are secondary in importance, although it must be recognized that international rivalry upon the seas has become global in this period.

Throughout history, the chances of a nation becoming a dominant power upon the sea, with a large merchant marine, overseas colonies and a strong navy to protect both, has been determined always by favorable geographic conditions. Insularity is of prime importance. Without land frontiers to defend, a maritime nation may minimize its army for home defense and simultaneously be able to project its commercial and naval strength overseas. Placed in the dominant geographic position relative to rival land powers, oceanic states such as ancient Athens, modern Great Britain or the contemporary United States have been able to emerge as dominant maritime nations. And their strategies have rested upon their ability to command the sea.

Nature must be kind to aspiring maritime nations by also providing them with many good bays and inlets, protected from storms and extreme tides, adverse winds and weather, yet deep enough and large enough to harbor many large ships. In the ancient period, smooth coastal waters were essential for the operation of rowed galleys between these harbors. In the modern period, favorable prevailing winds were essential to propel sailing ships from these ports. In addition, long and wide rivers with sizable outlets, deltas or bays opened oceanic trade and naval operations to and from the interior.

Without these strategic geographical assets, no nation has ever been able to achieve a lasting political and economic dominion over the seas. Continental powers so limited have had to adopt special measures or alternatives to compensate for their inherent geographical shortcomings. As a result, two separate strategic policies recur throughout history as great maritime and continental powers have confronted one another.

## EMPIRES, NAVIES AND STRATEGY

Great powers have evolved to the height of their political prestige and might by becoming imperial nations, though they may not choose to accept this label. Though the meaning is forever debated among historians, *empire* may be generally defined as the supreme authority of a large and powerful nation over considerable territory beyond its immediate borders. *Imperialism* is the policy of extending that authority further, by acquiring colonies or dependencies. Though any sprawling nation may be (and many have been) considered *imperial,* common usage throughout history has tended to regard mostly those nations with overseas holdings as truly deserving of the label *imperial.* Nevertheless, landed rulers have often preferred the grandiose title of *emperor,* and occasionally they have deserved it in the political context of having far-flung subject peoples. But for purposes of convenience, historical accuracy and strategic analysis, real imperial powers may be considered as those great nations in history which have based their national political and economic policies and strategies chiefly on *maritime* activities: commercial trade, overseas possessions or dependencies, and naval forces. The other great powers, non-maritime by nature, may be simply labeled as continental, relying chiefly upon the produce and manufactures of the national homeland and whatever political or economic advantage it can gain from its continental neighbors. Lesser nations may vary in their orientations between livelihood on the sea and the soil, but their larger destinies are usually subject to the actions of the great *maritime/ imperial* and/or *continental* powers.

Maritime powers, vulnerable to external pressures on their food supply, raw materials and power sources and thus primarily interested in maintaining their economic wealth through overseas trade, have therefore sought to enforce a reasonable state of international order on the high seas, so that the economic lifeblood of their merchant economy should not be interrupted or threatened. They have consequently depended upon their navies to maintain that order by policing both the trade routes to their overseas markets and also the oceans of the world wherever their merchant vessels ply. The national interest of maritime powers has generally dictated a policy of either monopoly or the free use of the seas, whichever best profited their own economies. In addition, uninterrupted sea-borne communication among such a maritime people has tended to bind them politically and culturally as well as economically.

Domination of the seas by a great maritime power in the cause of economic and thus political stability has resulted in protracted periods of seeming "peace." Each so-called *Pax—Romana, Britannica* and *Americana*—has really been naval peace, where supremacy at sea provides a major deterrent against serious challenge by unfriendly opponents. In reality, *pax* or peace has been a misnomer, as true peace can exist only within a political vacuum. And political vacuums are—sad to say for "peace"-loving peoples—a virtual impossibility. Rather, periods of international stability and political orderliness are made possible by a precarious balance of tensions between two or more great powers. That the prolonged maintenance of such balances is difficult is evident in the multitude of "policing actions" and wars fought in the name of maintaining some balance of the great powers.

If one needs a working definition of the balance of power, it is the distribution of nearly equal political-military power between two competing nations or groupings of nations so that normal economic intercourse remains unrestrained—or, so that relations between nations remain "peaceful."

Maritime empires have been expensive to protect. A large navy is necessary to patrol the colonies and trade routes of the empire and, if necessary, the seas beyond them. Also required are police-type (pacification) ground forces to enforce internal order within the overseas possessions. But the biggest expense is ships, which are costly to build, arm, supply, man, keep up, repair and eventually replace. Still, the investment in a navy is an investment in political and economic security. Ignorance of this fact has led to strong internal political opposition to large naval budgets in all nations having warships. So necessary are the navy and constabulary troops to the welfare of a maritime empire that one may generalize that the stability, loyalty and trustworthiness of overseas colonies and dependencies are directly proportional to the strength of the mother navy.

Just as the navy helps to determine the political and economic destiny of great maritime nations, so too is it a dynamic force in the cultural and social aspects of the national life, for maritime nations or thalassocracies have two important social advantages over continental powers, stemming from the natural accident of their geographic location.

First, since maritime nations are usually insular, they enjoy what might be called national privacy. With no unfriendly powers poised on their borders, they enjoy something which continental peoples have always considered a luxury—no large standing army or national psychosis of impending attack. If maritime peoples can rely upon a formidable navy operating literally out of sight of their homeland to insure their insularity, they can ignore such culturally inhibiting forces as military frontiers and forts, military strongmen and despots, standing alliances, frequent invasions and wars, and the whole mosaic of problems involved in counterattacking, occupying, defeating and reconstructing an enemy nation. Such countries have had the advantage of *time* over their constantly embattled peers on the continents, time in which to develop their institutions and industries in relative peace. Maritime insularity, then, has been a key ingredient in intellectual ferment, the growth of applied technology, and the fostering of democracy. Isolated and thereby well-defended men have tended to be free men, free to think and to apply their ideas to machinery and to government.

The other advantage of the maritime nations over the continental, and closely related to this tendency of isolated peoples to promote free thought, is that by the very nature of their economic life such nations have placed a high premium on the worth and skills of the individual. Merchant traders on land or sea are an independent lot anyway, yet the growth of the merchant class has been more rapid and pronounced in countries that depend on overseas trade. Continental states have taken decades longer than their maritime counterparts to bridge or close the great gap between aristocracy and peasant class. Equally if not more significant has been the individual sailor. Life at sea is a high adventure, involving the wisdom and raw stamina of men against not only an enemy in battle but against nature. The spirit of great maritime peoples has been embodied in their naval heroes and their tireless explorers, who in the past conquered unknown frontiers overseas and in the contemporary period have been mastering the poles, the ocean depths, the skies and space beyond.

Navies especially have been a bedrock of individualism, while the naval profession nurtures this individualism by demanding the very qualities that shape great peoples—discipline, creativity and a high degree of practical intelligence. Discipline at sea is more than abiding by the orders issued from a rigid hierarchy of authority; it is also the self-discipline of the individual seaman in the face of constant danger. Practical common sense and the ability to improvise when short on doctrine or material are equally essential for survival at sea. Rugged and outspoken when in their own element, sailors have always possessed a large measure of tolerance and yet a keen sense of justice and fair play. They respect authority, but can be pushed to rebel against unreasonable commanders.

This thalassocratic individualism has remained an essential ingredient not only of effective navies but of great maritime nations. Small wonder, then, that such nations place such value on their seamen, merchant as well as naval. At one with the sea, which he must eternally battle to control in the struggle between man and the elements, the individual sailor develops a self-confidence and pride of service seldom equaled in armies. Relatively unaffected by shifting political winds ashore, the sailor fashions a hardened sense of duty and loyalty to his ship and his profession. Hence navies have usually been among the least political and most stable of institutions in maritime nations. A vital component of the democratic spirit, navies have remained a pillar in the support of free institutions, socially as well as strategically.

Politically, however, navies have always been weak in asserting themselves overtly. Sailors learn their professional skills at sea among a small ship's company, where administrative and political considerations are minimal. They are technical experts, skilled in the technology of service at sea and sensitive to the inherent fragility of their machines. And seamanship knows no politics. By contrast, land-oriented officers deal with vast administrative organizations of many men and large tracts of territory and are in constant physical association with the political organs of government. These army men are the most skilled administrators in any military operation involving both land and sea forces.

Naval officers have therefore lacked the political polish of the generals and have tended to remain aloof from politics or to adopt a seemingly safer, conservative approach. Even in political revolutions, navies tend to remain as nonparticipants. Broadly speaking, sea power works slowly and subtly, whereas generals, politicians and the people at large are impatient for direct, immediately apparent results, as with armies on the march. These elements of society therefore tend to view expensive navies with suspicion when confronted with often short-term or superficially more pressing domestic and diplomatic concerns. Resisting "liberals" out to cut the fleet, admirals tend to oppose changes to their service from which recovery will be difficult when the national mood again suddenly reverts to a frantic awareness of actual naval requirements. Thus sensitive to criticism by politicians and their constituents, flag officers usually fare rather badly when embroiled in broad political disputes.

Strategically, then, as well as politically, navies and their admirals tend to favor the *status quo*. They need *time* for their exercise of command over the seas to be felt, and they require an economically superior government to support their own needs for a superior fleet. Unlike armies, whose strength is built on manpower, navies depend more on the technology of their ships and weapons, which are infinitely more costly than the raising of armies. Furthermore, navies are intolerant of forces aimed at disrupting the order they enforce. Consequently, they have tended to regard interlopers into their imperial system as illegal enemies. Most outstanding of their "outlaw" foes throughout history have been rebels, smugglers and pirates.

Colonial settlers or subject peoples sooner or later develop a desire to share with the mother country the fruits of their labors. But if such empires persist in exploiting these areas and not sharing their wealth with such indigenous folk, they will likely be faced with revolt. The navy is then charged with the task of reestablishing order in the colonies, an expensive task that requires considerable effort and diversion of naval material from other pressing strategic activities. The rebels must be isolated from outside help, thus requiring warships to police the seas in the troubled area. Imperial troops must be sealifted to the place, then supported logistically by the navy and merchant marine. And once suppressed, the rebellious possession must then be closely watched by a garrison and the navy, which is dependent upon the area for its advanced base of operations. Thus navies, like their governments, regard any political upheaval as dangerous to imperial stability. Rebels cannot be tolerated if order (or "peace") is to prevail.

Pirates have generally been considered to be outlaws preying upon merchant shipping and the colonies. In the early ancient and early modern periods, before the advent of maritime empires based upon far-flung political and economic order, piracy and privateering (commissioned private raiders by an enemy) were considered to be more or less respectable professions. As civilization became more rigid and erected legal safeguards to protect the economic wealth of the nation-state, the pirate appeared increasingly as a violator of civilized international law upon the high seas. A "barbarian" (*i.e.*, uncivilized), this outlaw became such an outrage to imperial nations that he was effectively eliminated by them before the end of the modern period. In their role of policing the oceans of the realm, navies have always had to be able to suppress piracy effectively on the high seas. Without navies, pirates flourish.

Therefore, to maintain political and economic stability upon the oceans of the world and throughout their own empires, maritime nations have depended upon their navies. Their strategies have thus embodied the ability to deter rival powers from interfering with their own maritime activities, to suppress pirates and to police the trade routes and overseas possessions of their own empires. To do these things, such navies must be able to command the seas. Opponents of major maritime nations have been the competing maritime nations, major continental powers, or a combination of both.

Continental powers have been governed by very different geographical considerations, the result being that the naval or maritime aspects of these nations have generally been secondary in political and strategic importance. A systematic analysis of great land powers is not within the scope of this study, except as such nations have attempted to utilize waterborne economic power and military force in the face of strong maritime rivals. Generally speaking, continental powers have depended upon overland communications for their economic wealth and upon large armies and fortifications for their political and military security. Constantly exposed to and threatened by overland invasion, such nations have reduced their armies only at their peril. Agriculturally (and later industrially) based, these nations have depended mostly on manpower for defense—the mobilizing, disciplining and administration of large armies. The effect has been a general tendency toward authoritarian government, national regimentation and a servile population. In general, whereas the independent merchant class has typified maritime societies, a powerful landed aristocracy has dominated the life styles of continental powers until very recent times. Their political base has literally been the land. And their political goals have usually been obvious—defense against the invader—as opposed to nations which depend on more subtle goals to be gained through the application of sea power.

The attempt of continental powers to operate navies has consequently been frustrated not only by geographic limitations but by related political, cultural and social contradictions. Politically, the ruling landed aristocracy (or industrial managers in the contemporary period) is preoccupied with defending the *status quo* at home, preserving the government from internal upheaval and external attack. Such a class has little appreciation for expensive overseas enterprises and tends to be too rigid to adopt the techniques and innovations of the maritime powers.

So it invests primarily in the army, subordinating the navy to these continental objectives. Culturally and socially, such nations do not generally enjoy the spirit of individualism engendered by maritime adventurers, but rely rather upon their people as a mass. When in fact such land powers have attempted to create a maritime empire replete with a navy, as some have, their merchant mariners usually have emerged profitably, but the navy soon discovered itself outside the mainstream of internal politics and national life. This apolitical trait is consistent with the naval politics of maritime nations, except that eventually the continental navy finds itself manipulated into virtual extinction by the dominant army-supported class.

History indicates that the most viable solution a continental power can seek in its quest for a naval presence is—in addition to its own small navy—alliance with a maritime nation. Depending upon such an ally has proved risky, for obvious reasons, but alliance has probably been the most workable compromise solution to meet an otherwise almost impossible need.

So, strategically there have been great maritime nations and great continental nations. One type has shaped its strategy largely around the overseas thrust of its navy. The other has depended strategically upon the defensive stance and occasional offensive thrust of the standing army (and later, land-based air forces) overland. Despite exceptions throughout history, these distinctions between land and sea powers have generally held true for major peoples and nations.

## STRATEGIC HISTORY

The history and strategy of maritime empires have been shaped not only by geography and men but by naval technology as well. Indeed, the fact that a navy exists is a sure indication of civilization and its growing technology. A full understanding of the technological element is thus crucial, because the misunderstanding of dominant weapons and other technical aspects of defense policy has often led historians and strategic analysts alike astray from the essential lasting principles of maritime power.

More so than armies, navies have required many years to evolve, due to the technological nature of their relatively more sophisticated equipment. Ships must be designed to incorporate the latest innovations in naval architecture and weaponry, then constructed over a number of years—up to four years for the largest warships of the modern and contemporary periods. These latter, often called capital ships, have usually been the yardstick of naval power, the ship-type around which the tactics of a fleet are formulated. Essential to evaluating the actual strength of such vessels, however, is an understanding of their cruising characteristics, the propulsion system and operating range, main and secondary armaments, defensive protection, signals communications and control over the ship's operation. Smaller vessels deserve equal attention as seagoing machinery. And the whole weapon (or weapons system, in recent parlance) depends on the skill and well-being of its operators. The officers and crew fashion the merchant ship and the vessel of war, so that a given naval technology is only as good as the training, experience, clothing, feeding, health and morale of the seagoing technicians.

Furthermore, naval technology and weaponry are utterly useless if the techniques of employing them prove wanting. Unfortunately, the inferior employment of potentially superior weapons has been an all too frequently repeated mistake of maritime and continental powers alike throughout history. This has been due largely to the very human assumption that the dominant weapon should determine the strategy and tactics of a given period. Often this has proved to be a sound assumption. But just as often, strategic and tactical realities change, rendering the apparently dominant weapon less effective or even downright obsolete.

This difficult strategic problem, of weighing the weapons technology of a given period against historical experience, has no simple solution. Indeed, strategic thought has tended to polarize into two general schools in the industrial nations of the late modern and contemporary periods. They are the material and historical schools of strategic analysis.

The *material* school rests upon the assumption that the dominant military hardware or weapon—the material strength—at a given time creates such an overwhelming superiority that it alone generally satisfies the nation's defense needs. This line of thinking is usually concerned primarily with waging or deterring *total war* between superpowers. It further includes a recognition that a technological ceiling has been reached, creating not only superior weaponry but perhaps also national superiority in overall technology, political and economic systems and culture. Such a weapons superiority in the Western world has given certain nations the power to dictate the course of international affairs or to balance off the weaponry of an equally strong power in a strategic stalemate. In either case, such a nation assumes the position of controlling the balance of political power. In the industrial and scientific environment since the early nineteenth century, such technological determinism has tended to dominate strategic thinking.

The *historical* school of strategy rejects this determinism by examining the past conduct of competing nations in order to understand all historical forces at work and thus the various alternative approaches to strategic problems. Along with the problems of waging or deterring total wars, historical strategists are also concerned with *limited war,* with the diplomatic and legal aspects and alternatives to conflict, and with the problems of combating primitive or undeveloped peoples who do not honor the technological assumptions of advanced Western nations.

In the search for simple solutions and panaceas in strategy, both schools of analysis have erred in overstating their respective cases. Many material strategists have viewed superweapons as a panacea, while strategic historians have often expected history to repeat itself, thus committing the folly of depending completely on the proverbial dead hand of precedent. The overconfidence of both groups has frequently led to unfortunate consequences throughout history.

The difficulty of adequately combining the military principles and ideas of both history and advanced technology in order to formulate strategy has been due partly to the sheer chance of historical timing. Until the mid-nineteenth century, each nation-state had been generally governed by the same constant factors—agricultural wealth, land-based aristocratic political institutions, and the extent of territory and raw materials under its control. The generally constant level of technology tended to limit the size of armies and navies, therefore making the strategic options open to great maritime and continental powers fairly predictable. Indeed, by the 1880s, the Old World seemed to have reached a state of eternal peace, or at least a political stability in which only limited wars could occur. At that time, however, a number of brilliant maritime-oriented strategic historians emerged to examine systematically the forces that had shaped their world. The leaders of this intellectual ferment were the American Mahan and the Britons Corbett and Richmond. Their penetrating questions, ideas and writings epitomized the historical school of strategy.

However, the pinnacle reached by the Old World and its strategic analysts was accompanied by the end of the modern period. With the advent of the twentieth century came advanced scientific thought, systematically applied to the new weapons of unprecedented power. In 1914, the Old World figuratively vanished as these weapons of the new technology were unleashed on the battlefields of Europe. Limited war and the relative peace also seemed to disappear in the new era of total technological war. So blinding was the new technology in its destructiveness that the Old World and its historical lessons were all but forgotten. In their place arose the material strategists such as the Italian Douhet, the Briton Trenchard and the American Mitchell who envisioned military success in the aerial superweapons of mass destruction. The events of this contemporary era, with its world wars, airborne nuclear weapons and resultant technological determinism, have dominated strategic thinking to the present. In fact, though, the efficacy of this school was finally revealed as wholly inadequate by the Cuban missile confrontation of 1962.

Indeed, by the 1970s, mankind has certainly reached a major historical watershed in all its activities—political relationships, communications, social habits, medicine, the need for control of unchecked technology, population and pollution—and in sheer scientific advancement, symbolized most dramatically by the landings on the Moon. Surely the time has come for new hypotheses and a fresh synthesis in strategic thinking as in the other aspects of human relations.

## STRATEGIC APPLICATIONS OF NAVAL POWER

The examination of the strategic history of navies and maritime empires requires not only the analysis of evolving strategic principles of naval warfare but of the long and often slow development of tactics, logistics (supply), command and administrative control, communications, ships, weapons and other aspects of naval life and technology. Through studying the flow of history and navies in history, it is possible to discover both the impact of sea power upon history and the impact of historical forces upon navies, empires and strategy. Finally, along with the successful application of the strategic doctrine of command of the sea, an appreciation is possible of the strategic alternatives to such a policy.

As guidelines to this examination, a list of theoretical strategic applications of naval power is useful. Since no one type of nation has existed throughout history, however, there has been no one type of navy or naval strategy. The guidelines of applied naval power, therefore, are aimed at understanding three different types of navies, that of maritime or "blue-water" nations, that of continental nations and that of small nations.

For *maritime* nations, the navy has been the main strategic arm of the nation's defensive structure, dominating the defensive policies of the home government, maintaining a generally *offensive* stance, and operating mainly on the "blue water" of the high seas. The army of such a nation is usually small by contrast, so that for large-scale land operations, the maritime nation usually must depend upon a large continental ally. This navy has several functions, all of them geared to the principle of achieving *command of the sea:*

1. Maintain a superior fighting fleet either a) to seize command of the sea, or b) to deter an enemy from attempting to control the sea. In wartime, this fleet is used as the *active* force to seize, exercise and maintain control over disputed waters. The waters in question are usually the open ocean, but may also include coastal areas, lakes and rivers. In

periods when no declared war exists, this fleet acts as a *passive* force by demonstrating to competitor nations that it has the ability to dominate the seas; in this way, it deters aggression by its threat of seaborne retaliation.

2. Defend against invasion. A defensive requirement, this task calls upon the fleet to protect the shores of the home country either by destroying or otherwise neutralizing the enemy fleet in wartime or in "peacetime" by threatening a competitor navy with destruction.

3. Protect maritime commerce. Also a defensive need, this requires the fleet to keep open its own sea lanes for its merchant ships. It may utilize overseas bases and its own mobility either to escort merchant vessels or to clear the seas of enemy raiders, pirates or other interlopers.

4. Blockade the enemy coast. An offensive requirement of the fleet, the seas around the enemy coast must be denied the enemy for the use of his merchant marine, for neutral vessels trading with him and for his own vessels of war. As long as the enemy fleet survives, the blockade is generally *naval;* after the enemy fleet is destroyed or otherwise neutralized, the blockade is primarily *commercial,* aimed at stopping enemy trade. In either case, it may be a *direct* blockade, with the fleet actually remaining on station off the enemy ports, or it may be *indirect,* the fleet observing and thwarting enemy ship movements from a considerable distance away.

5. Engage in combined operations. Either in offensive or defensive situations, the blue-water fleet must be able to sealift ground forces, army and marines, to and from a disputed area, the goal being invasion and capture of an enemy's overseas possessions and bases. The fleet must be ready and able to invade the enemy's home country, in the event that a successful commercial blockade does not compel the enemy to submit. In all such amphibious landings, the fleet provides tactical bombardment to cover the assault, then logistical support of the beachhead. In such *sealift* and *support* operations, the navy cooperates with the ground forces (which in recent times have included land-based air forces) by keeping open their lines of communications, by policing coastal and inland waters, and by commanding the sea (and the air, in recent times).

6. Provide strategic bombardment. The ultimate expression of naval superiority comes when naval power can be projected inland against the vitals of the enemy homeland. This function is not always required, as an enemy may sue for peace or may surrender to the naval and commercial blockade first, or the army (and strategic air forces) may be better equipped for this task, which belongs essentially to a continental strategy. Nevertheless, recent technology has given the blue-water navy the capability to project its firepower well beyond the enemy coastline.

For *continental* powers, the army (and lately, in combination with the land-based air force) has been the main strategic arm of the nation's defense. For blue-water operations of a broad offensive nature, this nation will best rely upon an allied maritime power. Its own navy usually maintains a *defensive* strategic stance, governing its operations to enhance the strategic advantages of the army. This navy has several functions, all dictated by strategic needs on the continent:

1. Defend against invasion. This navy must augment coastal defenses to help repel an enemy fleet from the continental periphery, adjacent lakes and rivers, and overseas possessions for the purpose of not allowing the enemy to establish a bridgehead on the coast for an invasion or for small-scale raids.

2. Engage in combined operations. In *support* of the main strategic arm, the army, the continental navy may gain command of the sea by default, that is, by the combined effort of army and navy in capturing enemy ports mainly by overland attack, thus depriving the enemy fleet of its crucial bases. To do this, this navy should have a limited *sealift* capability, for transporting troops over short stretches of local waters. The magnitude of such offensive amphibious operations may vary from small raids to an actual mass expeditionary force invasion. But a major difficulty of such operations is that a continental navy usually lacks both command of the seas to carry out the assault and a sophisticated amphibious doctrine due to its lack of experience. The continental navy may also provide a complementary offensive capability by combining, in recent times, with the army or air force to project its firepower into the enemy interior. But such strategic bombardment remains under the control of the senior services, as it is still part of the continental strategy.

3. Attack enemy commerce. Using the technique of what the French call *guerre de course,* the continental navy operates small squadrons or single ship units to prey upon enemy commerce. If utilized in overwhelming strength, this offensive function may assume the proportions of an effective commercial *counterblockade,* preventing vital war supplies from reaching the maritime enemy's homeland.

4. Maintain an efficient second-class fighting fleet either a) to restrict enemy offensive action, or b) to deter an enemy from attempting to dominate local waters. These closely related objectives may be achieved by the construction of a force of sophisticated naval vessels, ship-for-ship at least slightly superior to their individual counterparts in the enemy navy. Such excellent warships deploying singly for sporadic operations can force their maritime adversary to deploy a significant number of his own ships to deal with them. Or such superior single units can be combined to present the appearance of a formidable fleet capable of blue-water operations. Loosely defined as a *fleet-in-being,* it can deter a maritime power from aggressive action, or in actual war it can tie down

the enemy blue-water fleet from other vital pursuits in order to keep track of its movements. (Correctly, however, a fleet-in-being seeks to hold the defensive until it is able to assume the offensive, a concept practiced more by hard-pressed maritime nations than continental ones.) A well-handled continental navy of superior vessels, though inferior quantitatively, can thus have a pronounced effect on restricting the actions of a blue-water navy against the continent. In the contemporary period, the possible use of such vessels for projecting their firepower strategically into the enemy homeland further increases their prestige in any continental strategy.

Thus, if such an effective continental navy is directed by enlightened leaders in the government and is blessed with a generally bungling blue-water adversary, it can win command of the sea vicariously. If such conditions are just right, it can in some measure neutralize the enemy fleet by keeping it off balance, cutting supply lanes to the enemy homeland with a counterblockade, and thus protecting its own coast and merchant marine. It can sealift ground forces over limited distances and possibly provide some measure of tactical and strategical bombardment. But as long as the enemy blue-water fleet exists in any real strength, the continental navy can never maintain control over the blue-waterways. Whatever brief command of the sea it may enjoy, that command is only temporary and must be exploited quickly in order to serve the ends of the continental strategy.

For *small* powers, armies and navies alike can usually only hope for major success by allying with a great continental or maritime power and adopting its particular strategy—that is to say, unless they are fighting an equally minor power, in which case their strategy is dictated by the strengths and weaknesses of their adversary, emphasizing appropriate ground or naval forces. In any case, the minor navy must concentrate on three immediate tasks:

1. Defend against invasion. Inshore craft and naval weapons can be used to augment the national army and allied navy to help thwart an overseas or overland enemy attack.

2. Police local waters. Inshore and river craft and occasional large cruisers are necessary to check pirates and high-handed maritime competitors in time of relative peace. In war, these forces are combined with the larger ally. Without such an ally, however, they have no hope for long-term success.

3. Attack enemy commerce. Utilizing their few cruisers as commerce raiders, small navies can impress major powers with their fighting prowess, but without a major ally they cannot hope seriously to alter the outcome of an open conflict by this technique.

These strategic guidelines for the application of naval power are admittedly broad and theoretical. But they represent the questions raised by nations throughout history aspiring to use navies. By utilizing these hypotheses based on the advantage of historical hindsight, we may arrive at a basis for understanding the strategic history of navies in all times. Without such guidelines, the roles of naval forces are obscured both for layman and naval professional alike, giving naval matters an aura of mystery, which is not only unnecessary but potentially dangerous.

# BOOK TWO

## The Early Thalassocracies

*With our own Macedonian ships and the Phoenician, and . . . with ships from Cyprus too, we shall then have command of the sea, and so the conquest of Egypt will present no difficulty.*

—ALEXANDER THE GREAT

Just as the sea hides many secrets of our own times such as the fate of disappearing ships and airplanes, so too does it yield up ever so reluctantly many of the sunken artifacts upon which contemporary man can reconstruct the broad historical outlines of the earliest seafaring peoples. The long period of recorded history of the five millennia from about 3500 B.C. to A.D. 1500 remains only partly understood, but archeologists, scientists and historians are gradually adding light to these years (and, indeed, to times even more remote). Not least among such individuals have been the last of the seagoing adventurers who have shown just how much earliest man was capable of doing upon the waters; witness the voyages of Thor Heyerdahl from Peru to the South Seas in the balsa raft *Kon-Tiki* in 1947 and from Morocco to the West Indies in the papyrus reed boat *Ra II* in 1970.

Many of the earliest peoples who mastered and depended upon the seas not only plied their own waters, but traded widely and extensively along the lengthy coasts of Europe, exploring as far as the coastal waters of tropical Africa, the Far East and apparently even the Americas. Yet, only when the proper mix of geographical and cultural factors combined at propitious times in history did several of these seagoing peoples de-

**17**

velop into sophisticated maritime states with merchant marines, navies and imperial holdings. Such thalassocracies then burgeoned into superior high cultures and political states, battling jealous continental rivals as well as the excesses of affluence that bred internal laxity and decay. The sum legacy of these earliest thalassocrats, however, lay in the precedents and foundations they established for the modern world.

## PRIMITIVE MAN

Primitive peoples, dating from the eighth millennium B.C., exhibited great genius when the need and desire arose for travel upon the water. In construction, they produced lake, river and coastal craft that grew until large enough to keep to the open sea for extended voyages: inflated-skin floats, dugouts, wicker basket boats, wooden and pot rafts, skin and wicker coracles, kayaks, reed boats, bark canoes, wooden-framed curraghs, sewn-plank boats, catamaran outriggers, early junks and sampans. In navigation, simple observation of tides, flooding and celestial motions provided the data to primitive men for finding their way afloat. Literally any individual was—and is—capable of learning the art of seamanship, with adequate training, exposure to and experience on the water. But the crucial broader elements of social evolution to a higher culture determined whether water craft would progress beyond their primitive state into large bulk-carrying transports and merchantmen. Such progress also determined whether an organized system of maritime trade would develop concurrently, along with improved navigational instruments and finally specialized craft for fighting.

Such things are indicative of civilized peoples whose towns and cities lie upon major watercourses, but not all primitive peoples escaped their rudimentary Stone Age condition to deserve the designation of being called civilized. Simple techniques of bartering from primitive boats have survived among aboriginal peoples down to the present, although actual waterborne combat with aggregations of primitive craft generally disappeared in the onslaught of Western civilization. For example, Cortez encountered great numbers of war canoes on the lakes during his conquest of Mexico during the sixteenth century; New England settlers battled canoe-borne Indians of Maine and Nova Scotia throughout the seventeenth and early eighteenth centuries; late eighteenth-century explorers witnessed King Kamehameha's unification of the Hawaiian Islands with a large fleet of war canoes; and imperialists in Nigerian West Africa during the nineteenth century encountered Yoruba natives warring on the waters of the Lagos Lagoon.

Civilization emerged when some primitive peoples began to manipulate the life-giving elements of their water environments. Irrigation from flooding and rainfall made possible the first high civilizations, converting nomadic hunting tribes into communal, agricultural societies; these communities eventually learned also to harness the water by dams and irrigation canals and to exchange their harvested grains for other goods by transporting these items for exchange over their rivers, canals and coastal waters in enlarged boats. Accumulated wealth led to urban power centers dominated by a ruling class which controlled the primitive economy, supported a state religion, erected great palaces and ceremonial structures, fashioned land and naval forces to protect it all and fostered the use of writing to streamline the economic processes built upon trade. In this way did the first high civilizations of Mesopotamia and Egypt emerge by the beginning of the fifth millennium B.C.

Another type of society also arose when its meager agricultural subsistence could be augmented by the trade of foodstuffs, Bronze Age metals and rudimentary handcrafted implements: the maritime community. First evolving in the Aegean area during the third millennium B.C., these peoples developed coastal urban centers, palaces and ruling classes, but were much looser and freer in their political, social, economic and defensive arrangements than their continental counterparts along the rivers. Such seafaring peoples tended to act as catalysts of thought, innovation and material growth among non-maritime peoples with whom they came in contact, thanks to their physical mastery of the sea, the invention and use of writing for trade and their general cosmopolitan habits. Between both types of civilizations, mankind passed from its primitive state between the fifth millennium B.C. and the first millennium A.D.

## THE EARLY RIVER CIVILIZATIONS

Whence civilization originated first and most importantly seems to have been in Mesopotamia around the city-state of Sumer, but scholars continue to dispute the extent to which that first culture actively influenced the emergence and growth of similar cultures east and west of it during the fourth, third and second millennia B.C. Suffice it to say that five general centers of civilization did emerge around major watercourses: the Mesopotamian in the "fertile crescent" of the Tigris and Euphrates rivers, the Egyptian in the valley of the Nile River, the Indus River culture, the Chinese in the plain of the Yellow River and the Minoan in the Aegean Sea region. Save for China, all these cultures enjoyed early mutual contacts which were gradually strengthened through intermediary seafaring peoples within the Persian Gulf and along the Levantine coast of Canaan. The early Chinese expanded southward from the Yellow River to create a broadly continental civilization that embraced the Yangtze River valley, the two great rivers finally being connected in the fifth century B.C. by a canal. The peoples of the Aegean generally remained within their own sea, plying between its many islands, mainland Greece and Asia Minor until coming under the broad maritime domination of the Minoans from Crete late in the third millennium. The other cultures grew around their respective rivers, canals and coastal waters, stimulated by the metallurgical discoveries of the Bronze Age from the beginning of the third millennium.

The Mesopotamians, though culturally united, remained politically divided into separate city-states which only occasionally came under the single rule of one conqueror. However, the cities typified by Ur, Lagash, Nippur, Babylon and Akkad (or Agade) found common economic ties by boating along the Tigris and Euphrates rivers and over an elaborate system of canals that they constructed during the third millennium. Needless to say, their high-prow and high-stern river boats provided platforms for battle as well as transportation for troops and goods. At least one conqueror, Sargon of Akkad, in the twenty-fourth century B.C. consolidated the entire region under one dynasty and reached the shores of the Eastern Mediterranean at the Canaanite port cities of Ugarit and Byblos, from which Mesopotamian goods were ferried over water at least as far as Cyprus and the delta of the Nile. In the opposite direction, Mesopotamian trading vessels passed into the Persian Gulf en route to the delta of the Indus. They traded and replenished at the Persian Gulf kingdoms of the Sealand (later Bit-Iakin) along the northwest Arabian shore, Dilmun farther along the coast between present-day Kuwait and Bahrain Island, and Magan, which was probably centered along the Oman but also controlling both shores of the Strait of Ormuz opening out into the Arabian Sea. Sargon also conquered this entire coast and enjoyed the fruits of the extensive maritime trade with the emerging Indus civilization and the east coast of Africa. Sargon's successors used naval vessels as part of their internal control over the Gulf, but political upheavals and outside invasions destroyed the Akkadian Empire and much of the Gulf trade before the end of the millennium. The Babylonian conquest of Mesopotamia by Hammurabi in the late eighteenth century briefly restored political and commercial unity on the rivers and canals, but this collapsed thereafter before the Kassite invasion of the southern regions and the pressure of the Hittites from the north.

The Indus River civilization (maybe known as Meluhha) appeared about the mid-third millennium B.C., possibly from Mesopotamian migrants who still used Sumerian-shaped boats and depended upon the riverborne commerce between such great inland cities as Mohenjo-Daro and Harappa and the coastal entrepôts facing the Arabian Sea and Indian Ocean. The Indus coastal settlements stretched from the large port city of Lothal on the Gulf of Cambay on the east and the western frontier port of Sutkagen-Dor on the sea route to Magan, Dilmun and Ur of the Persian Gulf-Euphrates River trading complex. This western trade began to decline near the end of the millennium, while internal flooding and external invasions led to the demise of the Indus civilization by the mid-eighteenth century. Several coastal enclaves like Lothal managed to survive longer, and early in the first millennium a new inland urban culture grew up along the banks of the Ganges River. But such Eastern cultures of India, China and Mesopotamia—save for the brief maritime interludes of Alexander the Great and Rome—remained essentially continental throughout this period until the arrival of Westerners in the middle of the second millennium A.D.

Egypt, thanks to the natural barriers of the Sinai and African deserts and Mediterranean Sea, evolved along the Nile River relatively secure from outside invaders. Politically unified by the beginning of the third millennium B.C., "Old Kingdom" Egypt utilized both square sail and rowed (and poled) reed and planked low crescent-shaped cargo boats to ply the Nile and to cruise down the Red Sea to the land of Punt (probably Somaliland). The latter trading vessels were more than likely prefabricated, carried overland and then reassembled for operations on the Red Sea. Enlarged Nile craft might have been suitable for coastal cruising, but the pharaohs probably relied upon the large (500 tons?) vessels of Canaan to transport cedars of Lebanon to Egypt and for other purposes. At least one overseas military expedition reached Syria in the twenty-fifth century, while naval patrols surely policed the desert-river frontier of Upper Egypt. About 2200 B.C internal warring erupted, with a northern army from Memphis being ferried up the Nile to land and defeat the army and vessels of the rebellious city of Thebes. The struggle persisted between the two factions until the Theban river fleet and army took Memphis and reunified Egypt late in the twenty-second century. This "Middle Kingdom" generally continued earlier patterns of waterborne trafficking, especially maritime contacts with Canaan and Crete, and even constructed a canal across the desert from the Nile to Suez on the Red Sea. But from the eighteenth century Egypt fragmented and declined through internal conflict and the overland conquest of the delta region by the invading Asian Hyksos, which continued the same trading patterns. As resistance was again developing in Thebes, Egyptian emigrés may well have fled across the Mediterranean to Crete.

Though not a river civilization, the Minoans (possibly known as Keftiu or Caphtor, Crete) evolved during the third millennium B.C. into the first real seafaring culture in history and the root of all subsequent Western European civilization, probably due partly to contacts with the river and coastal civilizations of Mesopotamia, Canaan and Egypt. From the Cyclades Islands, mainland Greece and Crete the Aegean peoples of the early Bronze Age during this millennium developed into separate seafaring communities which shared common interests of trade and defense. To barter raw and worked metals, olive oil, wines and other goods, the Aegean shipwrights created the rowed longship, which over the centuries evolved into a slender rounded hull with a single square sail in addition to perhaps ten to fifteen oars on a side. Not only did this revolutionary vessel stimulate intra-Aegean trade, but it encouraged piracy, with the result that most of the early settlements were consciously located inland and fortified with walls. The growth of new wealth from farming and trade, however, kept the Aegean peoples established fairly close to the sea, and the recurring pirate threat from island dwellers led to the need for protective countermeasures. Around the year 2000 B.C., therefore, at a time when Aegean maritime contacts with the Near East and Egypt were growing, the independent communities of Crete and the Aegean began to rely upon the protection of a navy fashioned by one of several kings named Minos. This new strategic security thus encouraged the founding of new settlements directly on the coasts and large centers with no fortifications at all on Crete, where "Minoan" power was centered. With piracy being checked, trade and wealth flourishing, and contacts between the Eastern Mediterranean cultures increasing, the Minoans became an energetic force early in the second millennium.

The importance of these early civilizations lies in the foundations they laid not only for the future of the human race but especially for the maritime empires of the ensuing three and half millennia. In no respect is this legacy more striking than in the modes and habits of oceanic communications.

## SHIPS AND SEAFARING

The arts and techniques of ancient seafaring may be said to have been established by the end of the second millennium B.C., with the large sailing and rowed vessels reaching their technological ceilings early in the first millennium; except for larger sizes and new details, these tools of seafaring remained basically unchanged until the fifteenth century A.D. Ancient seamen did most of their voyaging during the day and then only during the summer months. To navigate, though they no doubt understood the night sky and celestial motions, these ancients needed to determine their daily positions in relation to familiar topographical landmarks on the shore. This could be done only in clear daylight, which meant, in the Mediterranean world, the fog-, mist-, storm- and cloud-free days from May to September (often extended from early March to early

November). By dead reckoning, knowledge of the winds, currents and tides (the latter two virtually negligible in the middle sea), and familiarity with the motions of the sun and stars, ancient mariners plied the coastal waters of the Mediterranean and points beyond. Only the application of the magnetic compass in these waters about the twelfth century A.D. gave open-ocean voyaging any navigational certainty. The other factor requiring proximity to the shore was logistical. The large-crewed rowed galleys, especially, needed to be beached each evening for cooking, provisioning, general rest and sleep, and for water, which could not be preserved effectively in the ceramic jars or pitch-lined wooden chests then in use. A night encampment also had to be guarded by an armed watch or, in the case of fleets, by a friendly army. Crews in antiquity enjoyed general good health, being exposed to the open balmy air of the Mediterranean summers.

Both types of ships during antiquity—the sailing vessel and rowed galley—shared merchant and military functions, though the galley comprised the major fighting fleets. Aside from the large poled, single-sail river barges that ferried great stone obelisks and blocks for the pyramids in the river civilizations, the rowed craft first evolved as the standard merchant and fighting vessel of the Aegean and Eastern Mediterranean seas. The auxiliary square sail gave added speed, and in time the pure sailer evolved as the most efficient cargo ship. When both, during the course of the second millennium, began to receive internal bracing with ribs, they became true seafaring craft. Throughout antiquity, pirates favored small, single-banked and highly maneuverable galleys of some thirty oarsmen to overhaul merchantmen, and the ancient navies responded with like vessels to deal with them; by the mid-fifteenth century war galleys had up to forty-two oars (actually paddles) for distant expeditions. The method of fighting during the third and second millennia was simple missile fire with spears and arrows, followed by grappling and hand-to-hand combat between ships or during a landing. Then, about 1000 B.C., with the advent of the Iron Age, iron rams could be fitted to the low, sleek galleys for a puncturing blow just below the waterline.

Beginning with the Greeks and then the Phoenicians, the galley ram grew into larger multi-decked vessels of two or three banks of oars that lasted in varied forms down into modern times. With strengthened hulls and high-platformed bow and stern fighting palisades, the galley came to be known by various designations. Most successful and common, the Greek trireme *(trieres)* evolved from the early single-bank thirty-oar triaconter and fifty-oar penteconter (some double-banked) and the eighth-century B.C. two-banked bireme ram into the sixth-century standard fighting ship of three superimposed banks of oars worked by 170 rowers. Triremes could be used as troop and horse transports, but served primarily as battle ships, being modified with fewer oars but with two or more men to the oar into quadriremes ("four"), quinqueremes ("five") and even larger polyremes ("six" to "sixteen"); two large galleys linked by a large platform briefly served as a catamaran supergalley ("twenty" to "forty"). But the trireme size remained optimum in the three-banked *triemiolia* of Rhodes and two-banked *liburnian* of Rome, *dromon* of Byzantium, *karabos* of the Arabs, and the large single-banked *a zenzile* of Venice. Unlike the galley, with its limitations imposed by oars and crews, the rounded sailing vessel ranged in size from 70 tons up to 500 tons, with fore-and-aft rigs (especially the lateen) being occasionally added for auxiliary power to the main mast very late in the first millennium. With favorable winds, the individual ancient ship under sail averaged four to six knots speed over open water, against the wind about two knots. A fleet of galleys, its speed restricted by the slowest vessel, did well if it averaged three knots.

The galley led to two types of naval tactics that found varying favor in the navies of antiquity—ramming and boarding. In both, skilled seamanship and fighting prowess were essential, so that usually only free citizens, professionals or hired mercenaries were employed as rowers and marines, sometimes doubling in either capacity. Except on privately owned merchantmen, therefore, slaves were virtually never used to crew warships—or, if so, they did so only at the price of gaining their freedom; the first "galley slaves" were not employed until the mid-fifteenth century A.D. Three to five officers led each Greek trireme, 170 men rowed, ten marines guarded against boarding, four archers provided missile fire and several ratings rounded out the ship's complement of 200. Ramming tactics dictated such an emphasis on rowers. Boarding tactics required a broader, bulkier galley to carry more marines and missilemen for a virtual infantry-battle-at-sea, a type of warfare promoted by the Phoenicians. Catapults and grapnels thus found a prominent place on later Hellenistic vessels, while the invention of "Greek fire" led much later to the employment of several flamethrowing devices on Byzantine ships. Through it all, the pirate craft depended on the small twenty- or thirty-oared fast galley to run down and board merchant ships.

With naval architecture, technology and tactics thus standardized over these several millennia, the fortunes of naval warfare and imperial policing depended upon superior uses of strategy.

# 1

# Empires of the Eastern Mediterranean, 2000–200 B.C.

*Seamanship . . . is an art. It is not something that can be picked up and studied in one's spare time; indeed, it allows one no spare time for anything else. . . .*

—PERICLES

## EGYPT AND THE MINOANS

During the first half of the second millennium B.C. the dynamic cultures of the Eastern Mediterranean—Egypt, the Minoans and the Levantine Canaanites—joined in mutual trade and prosperity and military operations against the aggressive Hittites of Asia Minor. The vehicles of such international contacts were the ships of the latter two peoples and a third, the Mycenaeans, who emerged during this period of dynamic growth. Continental Egypt alone among them enjoyed any sort of real political unification, the seafaring peoples instead maintaining a stubborn characteristic of independence in separate city-states—as they did down to the appearance of the modern nation-state. Systems of overseas trade therefore remained equally loose and decentralized, depending on the enterprise of private traders as well as of local princes or kings. As such, extended international commerce was not great, with Egyptians and Minoans alike usually accepting imports from the outside for their flourishing agricultural palace states passively. The Aegean remained fairly isolated, as did Egypt, with the Canaanites and later the Mycenaeans acting as mutual carriers. In this arrangement, the "empires" of the second millennium could better be interpreted as spheres of influence typified by the free dependence of smaller cities on the protection of stronger ones against pirates. Colonies were actually coastal trading enclaves; navies were merely small collections of armed merchant craft.

The common purpose of Egypt, "Minoa" and Canaan between the

eighteenth and fifteenth centuries developed from dynamic internal
events within Egypt and Crete, from the mutual desire for prosperous
trade and from the threat posed by the continental Hittite Empire. From
Thebes in Upper Egypt, rebellious native Egyptians undermined Hyksos
rule until Ahmose laid siege to their last stronghold at Avaris by land
and river and drove them out of Egypt in the 1570s. Proclaiming himself pharaoh of the "New Kingdom" Eighteenth Dynasty, Ahmose pursued the Hyksos forces into Palestine, where his army destroyed them
and consolidated Egyptian hegemony over much of the Levantine coast,
threatening Ugarit and other Canaanite port cities. His successor, Thutmose I, even pressed on to the banks of the Euphrates, while the more
peaceful Queen Hatshepsut increased maritime contacts with especially
large ships down the Red Sea to Punt early in the fifteenth century.

Meanwhile, Minoan civilization was flourishing around several city-
states, especially Knossos on the north coast of Crete and Phaistos on
the south. Minoan traders established stations in mainland Greece, the
coast of Asia Minor, the islands of Rhodes and Karpathos and especially
at the great port cities of Canaan, entrepôt to the East, and possibly
even outposts as far away as the Western Mediterranean. In addition,
Minoan colonial settlements were planted on such Aegean and Cyclades
islands as Samos, Kythera, Melos, Kea (Keos) and Kallista (modern
Thera), while trade with Egypt flourished. Contacts with Egypt and
Mesopotamia seem to have stimulated Minoan technical skills to an ex-
cellence beyond even those from whom they were originally borrowed.
In the other direction, the Greek mainland, Minoan trade and cultural
impact provided a major catalyst for the sudden growth of the hitherto
fairly primitive Mycenaean city-states. To ward off coastal pirate peoples
such as the Lycians and Ionians of Asia Minor, the Minoans established
a major naval base at Kato Zakro (modern name; possibly ancient
Dikta) on the east coast of Crete, from which its armed merchant vessels could operate, probably cooperating with Canaanite warships between there and Ugarit. Minoan rowing craft were too light to use the
ram, so boarding tactics undoubtedly remained standard practice.

The three cultures seem to have come together in close physical contact during the fifteenth century when Pharaoh Thutmose III determined
to consolidate Egyptian control over the entire Levantine coast and thus
establish a frontier against the Hittites and other Asiatic tribes. Thutmose
probably recruited Minoan vessels in his successful campaigns against
the Levantine coast and inland Syria early in the century. Four annual
offensives into Syria convinced Thutmose that unless he captured the
northern Canaanite port cities his communications would be threatened,
so he mobilized a great fleet, probably of new Egyptian, hired Minoan
and requisitioned Syrian vessels under his admiral Nibamon to achieve

this objective. His fifth campaign thus took an adjacent small port with its ships, with which he augmented his navy for the seizure of the larger ports of Arvad and Ullaza. With such a mercenary fleet of Canaanites (who occasionally used their new position to plunder cities under Egyptian control), Thutmose conducted annual expeditions to subdue rebellious cities along the coast and inland, with the coastal peoples supplying ships and crews to the Egyptian navy as tribute. By mid-century, after *eighteen* successive annual campaigns which had taken Thutmose's army even across the Euphrates, Egypt had won hegemony over the Levant; the local enemy Mitanni accepted Egyptian authority over all Canaan and Syria in return for their independence as a buffer state against the Hittites. After Thutmose's death in the 1430s, his successors continued to fight the Hittites—who overran the Mitanni—for control of Syria, while Canaanite shippers established trading stations in Egypt and provided the ships for most Egyptian naval and maritime activities, in contrast to the Minoans, whose influence virtually disappeared.

Minoan civilization reached its zenith during the fifteenth century, then succumbed to a combination of natural disasters and the outburst of Mycenaean seafaring activity. A particularly powerful dynasty ruled in Knossos by 1500, which in its creation of a *Pax Minoica* over the Aegean may have overextended itself by the naval operations off Canaan, military expeditions into some Aegean islands, to Libya, and an apparent lengthy and unsuccessful one to Sicily, not to mention stiff competition from the Mycenaeans. But any such external difficulties, including possible invasions of Crete itself, alone could not have ended the dynamic Minoan civilization. The major trouble came from inside the bowels of the earth, specifically the activity of the restless Santorini volcano on Kallista (Thera), the major Minoan colony in the Cyclades Islands. The geologically active Aegean basin had already caused severe earthquakes that toppled the large Minoan palaces about 1700 B.C. and damaged the rebuilt ones over a century later, and about 1500 the Santorini cone spewed out enough pumice to force the temporary abandonment of Kallista.

Then, at some moment, probably between 1490 and 1450, this volcano unleashed a fierce earthquake that again destroyed the palaces of Crete, partly through fires, before blowing off its own cone in a colossal eruption that obliterated Kallista, caused tidal waves which surely overwhelmed any offshore shipping on any coast in their path, and finally blanketed central and eastern Crete with thick layers of volcanic ash that stifled agricultural fertility. Thus was the Minoan economy disrupted, its shipping and port cities—notably the naval station at Zakro—destroyed and its vibrant thalassocracy brought to an abrupt end. Only Knossos seems to have recovered, but the rest of eastern Crete was abandoned in favor of the western half and the Mycenaean Peloponnesus mainland.

By mid-century, these dislocations were complete, exposing Minoan overseas settlements and the Eastern Mediterranean as far as the delta of the Nile to enemy and pirate attacks. Though the central government at Knossos seems to have survived, it had finally fallen to Mycenaean invaders by 1380, by which time also most Minoan trading enclaves abroad had been abandoned. Minos passed into history, and into legend as the possible basis for the Atlantis empire that sank beneath the sea.

The Minoan-Egyptian-Canaanite hegemony over the Eastern Mediterranean dissolved during the fourteenth century B.C. as new, warlike and basically non-maritime peoples combined with seafaring pirates to initiate an era of fragmentation and upheaval. The fortified mainland Greek cities of Mycenae, Tiryns and Pylos tried to fill the vacuum left by the Minoans, drawing upon the latter's culture, refugees and seafaring example to extend their trade across the Mediterranean and Aegean from Italy to Egypt, including trading settlements at Ugarit, Cyprus, Rhodes and along the Asia Minor coast. But the Mycenaeans could not stem the outburst of Lydian and Ionian pirates who raided far south to the Nile delta early in the century, forcing the Egyptians to create a special marine police. Egypt, itself beset by internal changes and the drive of the Hittites into Syria, retreated back to its original frontier. The Hittites under Kings Supiluliumash I and II engulfed Ugarit and the coast of Canaan where they promoted continuing maritime trade with Mycenae and Egypt and even used the considerable Canaanite navy to suppress rebellious subjects and pirates. But Canaanite merchant activities, based at Ugarit and three other ports, rested in the hands of private owners rather than under a centralized naval authority. The Hittites thus coexisted with both the peoples of the Aegean and the Nile, intriguing, however, in their internal affairs and those of neighboring border states. One of these was Troy, near the entrance to the Hellespont (Dardanelles), invested by the amphibious forces of the city of Mycenae under King Agamemnon, probably during a two-year siege about 1250. The coexistence with Egypt was broken by Pharaoh Rameses II, who followed Thutmose III's steps by reconquering Palestine in the 1280s and sealing this frontier by a treaty with the Hittites in 1269. This truce came of necessity, for everywhere fresh migrations threatened both Egyptian and Hittite security and destroyed the Mycenaean civilization altogether.

The "Peoples of the Sea" represented the final dislocations caused by the migrations of ironworking Indo-European tribes into Greece, Asia Minor and Mesopotamia during the late thirteenth and twelfth centuries B.C. Mycenaean stability weakened internally from the advance of the Dorians, then collapsed, probably from their overland drive and flanking attacks by sea. Some minor cities such as Athens seem to have survived, at the sufferance of the invader, though most Mycenaeans apparently fled eastward to Cyprus and other points, joined in their flight by refugees from Crete, Sardinia and Asia Minor. Simultaneously, Phrygians, Assyrians and other tribes thrust into the Hittite Empire, adding to the massive exodus southward, just as the Egyptians were expelling the Jews from the Nile basin and repelling Libyan attacks from the west. Joined in common cause for their safety and food, the (probably Aegean) Philistines and other elements comprising the Sea Peoples swept all in their path even in spite of occasional defeats in pitched battle. For example, although Pharaoh Merenptah repelled a combined attack by Sea Peoples and Libyans on the delta in 1221, another thrust of Sea Peoples shortly destroyed Ugarit and the last remnants of the Hittite Empire before pressing on down the Canaanite coast toward Egypt. The new pharaoh, Rameses III, met them head-on with a great army and fleet on the Syrian coast in 1190, defeated their army, then used his archers on the shore in combination with others on board his ships to virtually annihilate the fleet of the Sea Peoples in the first recorded naval battle in history. Rameses also insured Egypt's western border by repelling another thrust from another desert tribe there. But Rameses could not stem the nonmilitary infiltration of the maritime nomads into Palestine, and after his death in 1167 his successors even integrated Philistine officers into their army to help defend their frontiers.

By the middle of the following century, both Egypt and Greece had entered into dark ages, with the lands in between being dominated by successive warrior empires and the final settlers of the once restless Sea Peoples and Hebrews. Indeed, particularly the Philistines brought with them Aegean influences and picked up those of Canaan to develop as a dynamic people in Palestine alongside the Jews. But the real benefactors of the several upheavals were the growing Phoenician port cities of the Canaanite coast which managed to build upon the ruins of the older cities.

## PHOENICIANS AND GREEKS

From the ruins of the great late-Bronze Age second-millennium states and empires arose successor Iron Age continental powers, first Assyria and then Persia, and a multitude of city-states that both served and helped to undermine them. During the first half of the new millennium, the Phoenicians and then the Greeks took to the seas as brilliant traders and naval warriors, established colonies the length of the Mediterranean and sailed outside it, built upon Minoan-Mycenaean-Canaanite-Mesopotamian languages to create the phonetic alphabet and a brilliant literary tradition thereafter, and fought tenaciously with one another. Though the Phoenicians seem to have preceded the maritime Greeks in many such achievements, cross-fertilization of influences was strong enough to make new developments in naval architecture like the ram almost simultaneous. Greco-Phoenician maritime achievements also stimulated Etrurians, Jews and ultimately Romans to imitate them upon the seas and the continental empires to depend upon them for maritime support.

Phoenicia embraced the coast of the former Canaanites and Syro-Palestinians who had battled the Sea Peoples and probably included descendants of all these groups. Dominated by the emerging port cities of Sidon, Tyre and to a lesser extent Byblos and Arvad (later Aradus), the Phoenicians from the twelfth century B.C. fashioned strong island-coastal city-states by undertaking extensive overseas trading activities and by accommodating successive continental conquerors. They founded colonies throughout the Mediterranean, notably Carthage, and enjoyed exceedingly close relations with Cyprus, but they never organized an integrated political-imperial system. First and foremost merchants, they engaged in political action only when their home cities faced an external threat. Thus they paid tribute to several Assyrian kings from the early eleventh century and rebelled only occasionally and unsuccessfully against the great Assyrian warrior state thereafter. The neighboring Philistines and Israelites presented another matter altogether, and the Phoenicians found common purpose with David and Solomon of Israel to destroy Philistine power in the tenth century. Solomon cemented economic relations with King Hiram I of Tyre to break the Egyptian monopoly in the northern Red Sea, built a base there and cruised thereon to trade with Ophir (probably Yemen or maybe India). But the breakup of the Israeli state after Solomon's death and civil war enabled the Egyptians to regain their hold on the Red Sea and destroy the new base. And when the new southern Jewish state of Judah attempted to restore a maritime presence on the Red Sea in the ninth century, a severe storm destroyed the new fleet before it could even sortie. The northern state of Israel maintained closer relations with Phoenicia, whose merchants, however, soon eliminated—through competition—the last vestiges of the brief Jewish maritime enterprise.

Far more serious to the Phoenicians was the growing cruelty of the Assyrian Empire, which in the eighth century reduced the independence of the Phoenician cities through conquest. Though the other cities offered no resistance, insular Tyre profited from Assyria's lack of a navy and survived several sieges from the nearby coast. Thus threatened, however, from the ninth century on, Tyre and the subjected Phoenician cities gave increasing attention to their far-flung colonies in the Western Mediterranean: Carthage, Utica, Malta, Motya on Sicily, several sites on Sardinia, the Balearic Islands (Ibiza), Cadiz (Gades) and Tarshish (or

Tartessos) in southern Spain, and the Atlantic coast on both sides of the Pillars of Hercules (Strait of Gibraltar).

Phoenician-Carthaginian (Punic) settlement in the Western Mediterranean during the ninth, eighth and seventh centuries B.C. coincided with the simultaneous appearance of the Greeks in that region, both having a marked influence on the maritime splendor of the Etruscans. Greece and the Aegean islands, isolated and disrupted by the Mycenaean collapse, many migrations and piratic wars, stagnated in a dark age until the ninth century when fresh activities on land and sea reopened Greek contacts with the Levant via Cyprus. By 800 a Greek trading station flourished at coastal Al Mina near the ruins of Ugarit, soon leading to strong Eastern influences on the Greeks, especially that of the Phoenician alphabet, which they readily adopted. Greek trading colonies grew up along the Black Sea and Asia Minor coasts (Ionia) and adjacent offshore islands, and Greek mercenaries and traders journeyed on to Egypt and along the Libyan coast. These contacts did much to hasten the birth of classical Greek culture, which soon surpassed that of the Eastern teachers and was imported to new Greek colonies in Sicily, notably Syracuse, and southern Italy. By the late 700s, this culture had transformed that of the natives of Etruria in northwest Italy. The Etruscans extended their authority over much of the Italian mainland, placing several kings on the throne of the small state of Rome in the late seventh and early sixth centuries B.C., and utilized a fleet to dominate the Tyrrhenian Sea. Greco-Phoenician-Etruscan Western Mediterranean culture and trade intermingled throughout these years, but the Greeks could not hope to challenge the growing might of the opposing navies. By the end of the seventh century, therefore, the Etruscans controlled northwestern Mediterranean waters, while Carthage took over Phoenician supremacy in the southwest as political strife enveloped the Levant.

The maritime-naval confrontation of Phoenicians and Greeks emanated ultimately from the rise and fall of three successive great continental empires in the Middle East in the seventh and sixth centuries. Assyria consolidated its control over rebellious subjects in the Persian Gulf by using Phoenician shipwrights to build a fleet at Nineveh and man it in a river-gulf expedition to subdue the insurgents early in the seventh century. The Assyrians then put down the Phoenicians themselves during the revolts of Sidon in 677 and of Tyre in 671. But a new and powerful rival in Babylon arose to replace Assyrian rule late in the century, whereupon Pharaoh Necho of Egypt's Twenty-sixth Dynasty attempted to revive the Egyptian Empire by mounting an overland offensive to the Euphrates. With merchant and war fleets provided again by the subject Phoenicians on the Mediterranean and Red seas, Necho enjoyed a brief reign before being crushed by the Babylonians in 605.

Non-maritime Babylon suppressed Phoenician (except for Tyre) resistance in the 580s and 570s, but did not last much longer, for in mid-century the Persians swept out of the Iranian plateau to conquer the entire Middle East from Asia Minor to Egypt to the Indus River by the year 525. Persian Emperor Darius I had the Suez canal redug and sent a fleet from the Nile through it and the Red Sea to the Persian Gulf, another traveling down the Indus and around Arabia to Egypt. Again Phoenicians provided the bulk of Persian sealift, though Greeks were also employed. As the new Persian Empire threatened to engulf the known world, the Greek city-states began to challenge each other as well as the Phoenicians upon the waters, both using the first ram galleys as instruments of war.

The Greek city-states matured rapidly throughout the seventh and sixth centuries in culture, trade, politics and war either as thalassocracies like Corinth and Athens or as warrior-centered states like Sparta. With their penteconters and triremes, the maritime states defended their own trade from pirates, attacked Phoenician vessels as a legitimate (Greek) practice, established colonies abroad and warred against rival Greek states. Corinth, favored by its central geographic location, dominated overland and overseas commerce during the seventh century and used new galleys to battle piracy and defeat the rebellious colony of Corcyra in a great naval battle about 680. New Greek colonies joined Syracuse in Sicily to face those of Phoenician Carthage, where recurrent fighting developed between the settlers. The Phocaean Greeks migrating from Asia Minor entered Etruscan waters to found Massilia (Marseilles) and defeated a Carthaginian fleet which tried to prevent settlement about 600.

To protect her sea lanes from the Greeks across the Western Mediterranean, Carthage strengthened her position in Sicily and allied with Etruria, especially against the Phocaeans trying to settle Corsica. To check Phocaean piracy, a Punic-Etruscan fleet of one hundred penteconters attacked sixty Phocaean penteconters at their east Corsican base of Alalia in 535 and were defeated, but Phocaean losses were too great to sustain the victory. The Phocaeans withdrew to settle in southern Italy, followed by the Etruscans, who were repulsed there in an attack on Cumae in 524. Active Greek galleys continued to weaken the Etruscans, as did internal revolts and the rise of neighboring Rome, which recognized Carthaginian maritime supremacy in a treaty in 509. These anti-Greek coalitions fed strengthened ties between Carthage and the Phoenician homeland, especially after the latter came under Persian control. Phoenicians throughout the middle sea were only too happy to combine against the Greeks, their arch maritime rivals.

The Aegean Sea had never been dominated by an Eastern power, so that the Persian-Phoenician penetration to the west coast of Asia Minor during the second half of the sixth century gave the constantly warring Greek maritime states a new enemy. To protect the important grain route to the Black Sea, Athens in about 600 seized the approaches to the Hellespont from Aeolian and Phocaean Greeks and fought a protracted war throughout the century to hold these strategic points. Other maritime states policed their own local waters, but none attempted to consolidate political power over the Ionian coast and islands until Samos under Polykrates used its successful pirate fleet of one hundred penteconters to do it in 533. During the summer of 530 Polykrates' penteconters challenged the Persian encroachment into the Aegean by giving battle to two Greek Ionian states that had been pressed into Persian service. The Samian fleet defeated and captured the thirty triremes of the Miletus navy and destroyed altogether the fleet of Lesbos, extending its control as far as Rhodes. Alert to the new strategic realities of Persian domination over the East, however, Polykrates in 526–525 broke his alliance agreement with Egypt and accepted Persian Emperor Cambyses' demand that he supply his thirty triremes for the conquest of Egypt. But the crews of these vessels mutinied and then defeated the home fleet, landed on Samos but were repulsed, going thence to Sparta on the Peloponnesian mainland. With Samian naval power thus shattered, Sparta and Corinth carried out an amphibious expedition and siege of Samos in 524, but unsuccessfully. The Samian mutineers meanwhile settled in Kydonia, where local enemies defeated them and destroyed their triremes in 518.

In the meantime Cambyses used Phoenician vessels to help him subdue Egypt in 525, though they refused to join him for the conquest of kindred Carthage, so that was never attempted. His successor, Darius ("the Great"), then used Ionian Greeks to throw a pontoon bridge across the Bosporus for his army's advance into Thrace in 516 and to support an unsuccessful campaign into the Black Sea and another bridge for a drive up the Danube River against the Scythians in 512. Having thus severed Athenian and other Greek grain routes, causing the Greeks to seek alternate sources in the Adriatic, Darius forced the Greeks to reconsider their own differences in the face of a common threat.

The first challenge of Greeks to any Eastern empire came as the consequence of Persia's rule over the Ionian Greek states of the Asia Minor coast and led to a general Persian invasion of the Greek world. By the time of Darius' thrust into Europe, Athens and Sparta had risen to prominence among the Greeks as champions of democracy and oligarchy respectively and thus came into repeated conflict. Both had navies, as did Corinth, Naxos and Eretria, but the Athenian fleet had become the largest and most important within the Aegean world. When several

Ionian cities revolted against Persia in 510, they failed for lack of any outside help, and Spartans even captured Athens in 507 in one of their interminable quarrels. But when the Ionian city of Miletus revolted again in 499 and asked for assistance from other Greeks, Athens and Eretria sent twenty and five galleys respectively. After serious reverses on land, the Ionian cities of Chios, Lesbos, Miletus and Samos with the allied Athenian-Eretrian ships gathered a fleet of over 350 triremes and penteconters, all commanded by the brilliant Phocaean naval tactician Dionysius, at the island of Lade in order to relieve the Persian siege of Miletus.

The Persians mobilized an even larger fleet of subject Phoenician, Egyptian and Cypriot galleys to win command of the seas and thus cut Miletus' communications with Greece. Dionysius developed special ramming tactics to break the enemy battle line with his triremes, but at the great naval battle of Lade in 494 many of his ships quit the action early, leaving the remaining Chians to be overwhelmed by the Persian imperial fleet. Miletus then fell, and the Ionian revolt collapsed. Dionysius and the others who managed to escape with him turned to a life of piracy, and Darius demanded tribute from the mainland city-states of Greece. When Athens and Sparta refused, Darius determined to coerce them into submission.

With the victorious imperial fleet built around the Phoenicians with their broader and heavier galleys for boarding tactics, Darius made two attempts to use his supremacy at sea to conquer Greece—but in vain. Because the army and navy needed to be mutually supporting—the army to protect the shore for the fleet's night encampments, the navy to protect the army's seaborne communications—the expedition of 492 followed the coastal route across the Hellespont (ferried across) into Thrace to the Acte peninsula. When the fleet rounded the peninsula, however, a great storm struck and smashed perhaps 300 imperial vessels against the rocks, drowning some 20,000 men. Deprived of its naval support, the army had to retrace its steps back into Persia, with but a few Phoenician ships left for recrossing the Hellespont.

From his vast empire Darius hastily mustered a new fleet of 600 vessels (a third of them triremes) for another try. This time, however, he used a strategy of island-hopping across the Aegean. In 490, this force departed the Cilician coast near Cyprus, captured Naxos, the sacred island of Delos, Aegina and Eretria on the island of Euboea, ending the naval contributions any of these small thalassocracies could have made to a joint defense. As matters stood, even Athens and Sparta did not coordinate any collective response, leaving Athens with but fifty triremes to deal with the Persian landing in 490 on the beach at Marathon, overland from Athens, alone. But superior Greek infantry tactics defeated the Persians in the Battle of Marathon, and a swift overland march back to Athens frustrated the descent thence by the Phoenician vessels. Again, Darius had to recall his punitive expedition, though he left subject Aegina to carry out naval raids against Athenian shipping and made plans for another attempt. The taxes raised for this caused Egypt to revolt against Persian rule, but in 485 Darius died, and the Egyptians had to be suppressed by his successor, Xerxes.

To insure the integrity of the Persian Empire, internally as well as externally, Xerxes resolved to conquer all Greece, leaving the defenders no choice but to cooperate for their survival. Xerxes planned to follow Darius' original course across the Hellespont on a double-pontoon bridge, down the Thracian coast, avoiding the dreaded Acte promontory by cutting a canal across the peninsula, and into Macedonia, utilizing supply depots established along the route ahead of his vast army of over 200,000 men. The huge imperial fleet of Phoenician, Egyptian, Cypriot, Ionian and other vessels numbered some 650 triremes organized into three equal squadrons and a light squadron; hundreds of other craft acted as horse transports and supply ships. The strategic difficulty lay in the fact that from the Acte canal to Euboea Island, no one harbor could enable this vast armada to be concentrated, while the coast in general was open and dangerously exposed to winds all the way to the Bay of Phalerum facing the Athenian waterfront. Tactically, a continuous storming bridge ran the length of each Phoenician trireme, upon which thirty marines could fight the traditional infantry-battle-at-sea but which made the vessel heavier and less maneuverable for employing the ram. Logistically, Xerxes' supply routes were so long that from Macedonia southward his army would have to live off the land.

The Greeks in the late 480s buried their differences in the face of this Eastern horde, and even enemy Aegina threw off the Persian yoke to join the new Panhellenic League. Strategically, powerful Sparta preferred to use its fine army at the Isthmus of Corinth, thus abandoning Athens and other Attican cities to the invader. But under the inspired leadership of the Athenian Themistocles, a maritime defensive strategy prevailed. Themistocles developed the natural three-harbor port of Piraeüs near Athens into an imposing naval base and shipyard at which he directed the construction of 200 new triremes, in addition to the 50 older ones, to be reinforced by 124 more from the Hellenic alliance. Tactically, Themistocles built on the experiences of Phoenicians and Ionians alike to practice galley-ram tactics: the *diekplous* in line-ahead column to drive in the flank of the enemy formation arrayed in line-abreast; the *periplous* to encircle the enemy fleet and drive it in from all sides; and the *kyklos,* forming a prows-out defensive circle. The ram would thus make a Persian-Phoenician infantry-battle-at-sea impossible, so that the Greek galleys had no large marine contingent embarked. By the time that Xerxes' great army crossed the Hellespont in the spring of 480, Greek preparations were nearly complete.

To neutralize the great numbers of imperial Persian troops and warships, the Greeks masterfully maneuvered their opponents into restricted areas, forcing them to fight either on an even-numbered basis or to crowd together in confusion. Though the Spartan admiral Eurybiades held overall fleet command of the over 350 Greek galleys by virtue of Sparta's superior strength on land, Themistocles generally directed strategic and tactical dispositions because he controlled the 250 galleys of Athens and understood naval operations better than did Eurybiades. Leaving perhaps 150 ships to guard the eastward approaches to Athens near Salamis Island, the Greek commanders in late July sortied with 271 galleys to Artemisium, the narrow strait off the north end of Euboea through which the Persians must pass. On the adjacent land, a Spartan contingent and others held the pass at Thermopylae, forty miles away.

Then, in mid-August, Xerxes' combined forces approached these positions, only to be ravaged by a three-day storm that wrecked some 200 triremes against the exposed coast while the Greeks stayed under the sheltered lee shore of Artemisium. Soon after, Themistocles formed into the circular *kyklos* for an attack which succeeded in taking some 30 enemy vessels. Xerxes had sent about 200 of his surviving 500 galleys in an end run around Euboea to trap the Greek fleet and now unleashed his army against Thermopylae. But the Spartans bludgeoned this series of assaults on land, while another storm struck, destroying many more imperial vessels and forcing the return of the battered flanking force. A 53-ship Athenian squadron raced north to join Themistocles, who sallied forth to hit and hurt the Persians again. Then, on August 20, Xerxes launched simultaneous attacks on the Greeks at Thermopylae and Artemisium, finally overrunning the pass, but being fought to a standstill in a bloody general naval battle in which both fleets—totaling perhaps 450 Persian and 300 Greek ships—suffered heavy losses in ships and men. Outflanked on land, however, Themistocles had no choice but to abandon his position at Artemisium and retire to Attica.

The issue could only be decided by battle at sea, for vulnerable Athens had to be evacuated, while the Spartan-Peloponnesian retirement behind a new wall at the Corinthian isthmus for a stand there would surely be outflanked by sea. Violating the Panhellenic League's orders to retire behind the isthmus, Themistocles therefore took the Greek fleet into the sheltered waters of Salamis Island near Athens—where his reserve squadrons brought his strength to just over 300 triremes—and overcame the pessimistic objections of his allies. By ruse and careful arguments, he kept the fleet there for battle in the narrow strait between Salamis

and the mainland rather than be exposed to Xerxes' larger squadrons in
the open sea off the isthmus. As for Xerxes, his army could not reach
the isthmus before his navy won command of the sea by destroying the
Greek fleet at Salamis; basing at Phalerum late in August his reinforced
fleet of over 400 triremes prepared to force the issue.

During the night of September 19–20 the four imperial squadrons
sealed off all Greek escape routes, no doubt tiring their own rowers, and
at dawn moved into the strait in line-abreast for a boarding battle,
Phoenicians on the right, Ionian Greeks on the left, Cilicians and Cypriots in the center. Jammed into a strait less than a thousand feet across,
Persian superiority was completely neutralized. The Greeks in perfect
discipline sallied out to meet them, and when the Phoenicians backed
water to improve their position a stiff morning breeze combined with the
Greek attack to throw their heavier ships into confusion, opening a gap
in the Persian right. Into this Themistocles used a deadly *diekplous* that
fell on the flank of the exposed center and turned it. The Ionians held
the Persian left as long as possible, but the mass confusion created by the
Athenian thrust soon turned onto their flank and rear. The Phoenicians
had all but quit the battle, leading to a general Persian retreat amid the
slaughter. Having lost perhaps forty galleys to the Persian loss of maybe
two hundred, the Greeks had regained command of their seas. Xerxes
had no choice but to order retreat from Greece.

The Greek victory at the Battle of Salamis marked the general repulse
of the Persian-Phoenician attack on the Greeks throughout the Mediterranean. In the West, sensitive to the valuable grain routes to the Adriatic,
the Greeks had continued to harass Phoenician shipping, while the rise
of Gelon as dictator of Greek Syracuse prompted Carthage to take punitive measures against the Greeks in Sicily and Italy. The Persians coordinated Carthaginian preparations with their own, so that the 200 new
Punic galleys could neutralize the 200 belonging to Gelon before he
could go to the aid of the Panhellenic League during Xerxes' invasion.
The Carthaginian fleet crossed from Africa to Panormus harbor in the
summer of 480 but lost most of its transports to a storm; the galleys then
moved eastward along the coast, the army on the adjacent land, to invest
Himera. As the siege began, the Carthaginians beached their triremes—
the common practice during extended operations. Into this situation, on
virtually the same day as the Battle of Salamis, Gelon executed a brilliant
ruse whereby his own cavalry acted as pro-Carthaginian decoys to enter
the Punic lines and set fire to the beached vessels. The conflagration
destroyed fleet and army alike, and the 20-ship squadron on offshore
patrol escaped only to be destroyed by a storm at sea. Carthage immediately sued for peace.

In the East, Xerxes left a rearguard army in Greece as his surviving warships ferried the retreating main army back across the Hellespont. In 479 Greek arms destroyed the rear guard at the battle of Plataea, while a Greek amphibious expeditionary force crossed over to Samos and crushed the Persians at the battle of Mycale, burning their ships and thus liberating the Ionian city-states. When the Spartan warships left this allied fleet to return home, however, the Athenians went on to besiege and take the Persian garrison defending the Hellespont throughout the winter of 479–478. The Greeks had preserved their independence by defeating the Phoenicians of Persia and Carthage, and when Gelon's navy later defeated the Etruscans in the battle of Cumae off southern Italy in 474 Greek maritime communications became secure throughout the Mediterranean.

## ATHENS AND SPARTA

Although the repulse of the Persians in the Aegean did not end hostilities, it provided the catalyst that elevated Greek culture and society to unprecedented heights, creating the Golden Age of Athens. Supported by a vast commercial system and a most formidable navy which commanded the Aegean and adjacent waters, Athens from the early fifth to the mid-fourth centuries became the focus of urban Western thalassocratic activities, a magnet which attracted learned and ambitious Greeks from everywhere. A partial list of thinkers and artists who reflected this dynamic society (from the sixth century) is stunning in its brilliance: in poetry Pindar, in painting Polygnotus, in drama Aeschylus, Sophocles, Euripides and Aristophanes, in history Herodotus and Thucydides, in rhetoric Isocrates, in philosophy and physics Pythagoras, Parmenides, Heraclitus, Zeno, Thales, Anaximenes, Anaximander, Anaxagoras, Socrates, Protagoras, Plato, Democritus, and such later universal characters as Xenophon and Aristotle. Like the high Minoan civilization before it, however, the Athenian maritime-centered state of the Aegean rested not on political tranquillity but on perpetual tension—first from the continuing external threat of Persia, then that of Sparta and from the directly related internal divisiveness of the peoples and states made subject to the fifth-century Athenian Empire. Although the endless wars of these times would sap the wealth and power of Athens, its intellectual vigor would eventually conquer and Hellenize the entire Western world.

Formed as a voluntary anti-Persian defensive and offensive alliance in 478, the Delian League of Ionian islands and coastal cities followed Athenian leadership in the spirit of Marathon and Salamis to rid the Aegean of the Persians and Phoenicians altogether. From the beginning, however, Spartan refusal to join and Athenian demands for Panhellenic cooperation and tribute brought resentment and revolts by several city-states that had to be coerced back into the alliance. In that very summer of 478 the Greeks improved their strategic position by sending naval expeditions to support a successful revolt against Persian rule over the island of Cyprus and to seize Byzantium, which commanded the approaches to the Black Sea, thus restoring the grain route thence. Two years later another force captured Eion in Thrace, ending Persian influence there and convincing nearby islands to submit to Athenian rule. But other cities, especially Naxos and Thasos, resisted or seceded and over the next ten years were forced to submit, losing their autonomy as a penalty. Under the leadership of Themistocles, until his dismissal for overambitious tendencies, Athens annually added 10 to 20 new triremes to its 200-vessel war fleet and depended upon naval vessels also from several major subject allies. Utilizing a new and stronger type trireme that could carry more troops, the Athenian admiral Cimon crossed the Aegean with 200 triremes in 466, crushed and destroyed the Persian fleet of equal size at the Eurymedon River in southern Asia Minor, then turned to destroy a reinforcing squadron off Hydrus.

The back of Persian sea power thus shattered and the Empire in chaos since the death of Xerxes in 465, Athens in 460 mounted a naval offensive throughout the Eastern Mediterranean which brought on the consternation of the League members who felt Athens had exceeded the original intent of the alliance. Powerful Aegina and Corinth, encouraged and occasionally assisted by both Persia and Sparta, revolted in 459, so that Athens had to fight a two-front war—in the Aegean and in the Eastern Mediterranean. With consummate skill, Athenian vessels crushed the Aeginetan fleet and took 70 vessels in a naval battle in 458 and raided the Peloponnesus; ground forces battled the Spartans and Corinthians and conquered Boeotia; and a League fleet cruised to Egypt via Cyprus to assist the Egyptian revolt against Persia. Moving up the Nile, the Greeks brushed aside a Persian squadron and took Memphis, only to be defeated during a Persian counteroffensive in 455–454. This reverse ended Greek aspirations in the Eastern Mediterranean and encouraged more Ionian revolts, which the Athenians suppressed in the late 450s. In 451 Cimon used his 200 triremes again to attack the delta of the Nile and then to destroy a major Persian fleet of Phoenicians and Cilicians at the beach of Salamis in Cyprus, though Cimon died during the campaign. By the end of the year Athens, able to conclude favorable peace treaties with Persia and Sparta, stood at the pinnacle of her power.

The end of the hostilities with Persia heralded an acceleration of Athenian culture and overseas trade and the institution of a *Pax Atheniana* over the Aegean and Black seas—the greatest stability over these waters since the days of Minos. The architect of this period of Athenian Empire was Pericles, an experienced naval commander who directed

Athenian naval-maritime policies and codified them in Athenian laws and the Constitution of 432. At the heart of Periclean strategy lay the notion of command of the sea over real and potential rivals: Phoenician and Greek pirates, restless subject states like Samos, and the Spartan-led Peloponnesian League. Extending the walls of Athens to include the port of Piraeus, Pericles garrisoned troops in the overseas possessions and drew upon a great fleet of 300 triremes (plus another 100 in reserve) to police Athenian trade routes, keeping a permanent squadron of 60 ships at sea on maneuvers eight months out of every year. Continuing strife and reverses in mainland Boeotia, fed by Spartan intervention, convinced Pericles to abandon any continental pretensions in 446 and to rely totally on Athens' insular position—the final cornerstone in his logical maritime strategy.

A long-term peace treaty between Athens and Sparta in 445 proved illusory, though, for as Pericles put down several revolts within the empire he alarmed the Spartans. In 440–439, for instance, Samos revolted and received some aid from Persia, only to be crushed in an eight-month blockade and siege by Pericles and his reinforced fleet of 160 triremes of Athens and another 55 from Chios and Lesbos. As penalties, Samos lost her autonomy and navy altogether. Then, in 435, war broke out on the Adriatic coast—Corinth of the Peloponnesian League and Epidamnus (later Dyrrachium, modern Durazzo) against Corcyra (Corfu)—during which, the next year, the Corcyran fleet destroyed or captured 75 Corinthian triremes in a naval battle off Actium, then blockaded and captured Epidamnus. Angered by this reverse, Corinth created a 150-trireme fleet of new and allied Peloponnesian vessels, whereupon Athens gave support—10 triremes—to Corcyra. In the naval battle off the Sybota Islands in 433 Corinth claimed 60 Corcyran ships, but was checked from finishing the job by the Athenian intervention.

Athens' brief war against a Spartan ally, Corinth, now precipitated the general Peloponnesian War in 431 between the two major powers of the Greek world—already mutually suspicious competitors. For ten years Athens pitted her maritime strategy against the armies of continental Sparta. Aided by allied vessels from Chios and Lesbos, the Athenians used their navy to blockade and raid the Peloponnesus, the Ionian coast of Asia Minor and the Gulf of Corinth, while Spartan and Boeotian armies ravaged the Attican countryside, leading to a strategic stalemate. When, in 429, a Corinthian-Spartan fleet of 47 and then 77 triremes attempted to wrest command of the Gulf of Corinth from an Athenian squadron of 20 galleys under Phormio, he routed it in two successive engagements at Chalcis and Naupactus (Lepanto). However, the cramped conditions of insular, walled-in Athens gave rise to a disastrous plague which claimed the life of the brilliant Pericles in 429. His successors, notably Cleon and Demosthenes, continued his strategy by suppressing revolts in Lesbos and Corcyra in 427, but began to overextend Athenian energies by carrying the war overland into Boeotia and overseas into Sicily.

Then, in 425, Demosthenes brought the war home to Sparta by taking the coastal city of Pylos and offshore Sphacteria by amphibious operations, capturing a Spartan fleet in the process. Athenian warships also occupied the island of Kythera to further strangle Peloponnesian overseas communications, and the theater of active fighting shifted northward to mainland Boeotia and Thrace, where the Spartans tried to cut the Athenian grain routes to the Black Sea. Refusing to make peace following the success at Pylos, Athens suffered sufficiently in the north—where Cleon met his death—to accept a settlement in 421.

But Athens had become so aggressive, particularly under the new leadership of Alcibiades, that cold war ensued throughout the Aegean and finally grew into a full-blown world war. While Sparta crushed a revolt by Argos and other cities, Alcibiades used 30 triremes to virtually annihilate the small island state of Melos in 416 and then to extend the Athenian Empire west to Sicily. Little had happened there until 415 when the cities of Segesta and Leontini appealed to Athens for help against Syracuse, ally of Corinth. The next year Alcibiades and Nicias led a fleet of 136 galleys to Catana, Sicily, followed later by reinforcements under Demosthenes. Alcibiades fled his political enemies by defecting to Sparta, which now rallied to the side of Syracuse and again declared open war on Athens.

An Athenian blockade of Syracuse was broken by a skirmish with a Spartan-Corinthian squadron in 413, thus opening maritime communications between Syracuse, Sparta and Corinth. Athens tried to disrupt these connections by stationing a 33-ship squadron off the Gulf of Corinth, only to have it ravaged by 25 Corinthian triremes equipped with a new, reinforced prow for bows-on ramming. Then the Syracusans blocked the 115 Athenian triremes returning to the blockade in the harbor of Syracuse by sinking several hulks at the harbor entrance. There, after several skirmishes, on September 9, 74 Syracusan triremes —all reinforced with the new Corinthian prow—pressed in on the cautious Nicias and aggressive Demosthenes. In cramped waters that prevented the use of their *diekplous* and *periplous* maneuvers, the Athenian fleet was roundly defeated, losing 50 triremes sunk to 30 of Syracuse. Trapped, the Athenians scuttled their surviving craft and attempted to escape overland, only to be pursued and captured, Nicias and Demosthenes being executed. Still, the loss of 200 triremes did not deter Athens from raising another fleet and conniving successfully to get Alcibiades back from Sparta to command it. More colonies revolted, Persia intervened on the side of Sparta, and long-quiescent Carthage became involved in the Sicilian theater. The Peloponnesian War had become general.

Because of the remarkable Athenian ability to recover from the disaster in Syracuse and retain command of the Aegean, the issue would have to be settled at sea—for which non-maritime Sparta only slowly and with great difficulty prepared itself. A general Ionian revolt against Athens in 412 resulted from the news from Syracuse, but under the inspired political and naval leadership of Alcibiades between 411 and 407 Athens so isolated rebellious Lesbos, Chios, Thasos and Euboea by his naval and amphibious victories that pro-Athenian parties managed to return to power throughout the Aegean, with Samos being restored as the staunchest of Athenian allies and main naval base in the eastern Aegean. Sparta developed a fleet to cut Athenian supply routes to the Black Sea, but its various inexperienced commanders suffered disastrous defeats at the hands of Alcibiades, in 411 at Cynossema and Abydos and in 410 at Cyzicus, where the main Spartan fleet was wiped out. Alcibiades restored Athenian control over the Hellespont, only to be removed from command by his political enemies in 407.

Sparta built another fleet of 170 triremes, a contingent of which under Lysander won a small engagement at Notium in Asia Minor, and then moved against Lesbos under Callicratidas. This fleet trapped 70 Athenian triremes under Conon in the roadstead of Mytilene, only to be attacked and defeated by a relieving force of 150 triremes from Athens off Arginusae which sank or took 70 ships and killed Callicratidas. By now, the Athenian thalassocracy had degenerated into a military despotism which executed six admirals, allegedly for their poor performance at the battle. By contrast, Sparta placed its fortunes in the hands of Lysander, who cemented relations with Persia and took the offensive at sea with yet another fleet. The Athenian fleet of 180 ships under Conon moved to Aegospotami near the Hellespont to guard the supply route and in 405 was there surprised at anchor and on the beach by Lysander, whose fleet made quick work of the helpless Athenians, destroying some 170 triremes. With Athenian lifelines to the Black Sea now severed and the fleet destroyed, all Aegean cities submitted to Spartan sea power, and Lysander commenced a land-sea siege of Athens itself. In April 404 Athens surrendered.

As long as Athens had followed Themistocles and Pericles in their maritime strategy aimed at commanding only the sea, she had prospered, but Athenian commitments on the mainland and abroad in Sicily had dangerously overextended her resources and irreparably undermined the thalassocracy. With the demise of Athens, maritime stability collapsed in the Aegean, and the victor states hastened to improve their fortunes.

## ALEXANDER THE GREAT

The events of the fifth century B.C. had so seriously weakened the Persian Empire, Athens and Sparta that a renewal of the fighting left any one or any combination of them impotent to provide stability in the Eastern Mediterranean. The Peloponnesian wars persisted well into the fourth century, until the Greek world succumbed to the military prowess of first Thebes and then Macedon. Dynastic struggles within Persia, along with fresh revolts of Egypt and the Phoenician cities, left that vast empire equally crippled. Into the growing chaos stepped Alexander the Great, conquering the entire known world east of the Adriatic and Libya during the 320s. But the brief stability of the Alexandrian Empire passed with his death, leaving his successors to war among themselves for yet another century. Through it all, the art of naval warfare did not change, although boarding tactics tended to replace the ramming tactics as practiced by the skilled Athenian navy. And though Athens lost her political and naval thalassocratic superiority, her culture during the ensuing years conquered everywhere it went. Henceforth, the Western—and briefly much of the Eastern—world was Hellenized.

The Persian support of the Spartan victory in 404 ended when, four years later, Sparta rallied to the support of the Ionian colonies which had been returned to Persia and now again revolted. The Spartan navy controlled the Aegean, and Spartan armies pressed into Asia Minor in 396. But Persia had, in addition to its 300 Phoenician triremes, the Athenian admiral Conon and his 8 surviving galleys, which alone had escaped from the disaster at Aegospotami by seeking asylum with King Evagoras in Cyprus. In addition, in 395 Athens, Corinth, Thebes and other Greek cities formed a new anti-Spartan league, forcing the Spartan army to abandon its offensive into Persia. Taking command of the Persian fleet, Conon in 394 used 90 galleys to sink 50 of 85 Spartan vessels at the naval battle of Cnidus near Rhodes. Drawing upon Persian financial aid, Athens exploited the destruction of Spartan sea power to restore the city walls and shipyards of Piraeus, build a new fleet under Conon's command, and seize several islands surrounding the Peloponnesus. Evagoras now revolted against Persia and, with a large fleet, at the end of the decade attacked Phoenicia, with Tyre and the other cities accepting his rule. The Athenian-Cypriot coalition led Persia in the 380s to shift its support to Sparta and to attack Cyprus. A general stalemate resulted, though Persia regained Ionia and Cyprus and held the balance of power in Greece between a shaken Sparta and a reviving Athens. But both states were so exhausted by the continuous fighting that they could not field sufficient armies and navies; many of Athens' 400 new triremes simply languished for lack of crews. Still, Persia and Syracuse supplied aid, playing the two powers off against one another. In the mid-370s Athenian squadrons defeated Spartan naval forces off Naxos and Acarnania and relieved a siege of Corcyra, while Thebes defeated the Spartan army at the battle of Leuctra in 371.

The resurgence of Athenian supremacy at sea led to retaliation by Persia, Thebes and Macedon and revolts by new Athenian allies over the next three decades. Though Persia now allied with Thebes, Persian influence in the Aegean waned, for revolts in Egypt and Phoenicia required that full attention be given to internal stability; Sidon even had to be burned to the ground in the 340s. Thebes, while further reducing Spartan arms on the mainland, constructed 100 triremes which in the summer of 363 attacked Athenian grain transports in the Bosporus, encouraging revolts among Athens' confederate cities, notably Byzantium and then Caria in Asia Minor. Theban military power suddenly succumbed to the army of Philip of Macedon in the 350s, and in 357 Chios, Rhodes and Cos joined the revolt against Athens and defeated an Athenian fleet off Chios, going on to blockade Samos and raid several Athenian possessions. Then 300 Persian triremes assisted the rebels to discourage the 120 triremes of Athens from seeking a decision at sea.

A brief maritime revival in Athens under Eubulus could not offset Macedonian conquests in the north, and Athens sued for peace in 346. But Philip then began to overrun the entire Balkan region from Epirus to the Danube River, Thrace and the Black Sea. With 300 triremes, Athens in 343 launched an ineffective attack on Macedonian shipping. Philip retaliated against rebellious Byzantium and Perinthus in 340, hoping to cut Athenian supply lanes, but Athens reinforced these strategically placed cities. Whereupon Philip mounted an overland offensive through Boeotia toward Athens. Destroying an allied Theban-Athenian army at Chaeronea in 338, Philip united the entire Greek world—except for isolated Sparta—under Macedonian rule. He called the new confederation the Hellenic League of Corinth, with which he planned to invade Persia, before he was assassinated in 336.

Under his son Alexander, Philip's plans to conquer the faltering Persian Empire reached fruition. Swiftly putting down revolts in Greece occasioned by his father's death, Alexander and his army crossed the Hellespont on Greek triremes in 334 and immediately defeated local Persian forces at the battle of the Granicus River. Alexander then adopted a continental naval strategy, deciding to neutralize Persian sea power by moving down the Asia Minor and Phoenician coasts taking all the imperial seaports. Politically, this wise policy meant that he did not have to draw on the 200-trireme fleet of subject Athens which thus remained inactive, and he would act as liberator by granting home rule to Ionians, Cypriots, Phoenicians and Egyptians—all of whom despised Persian rule anyway, but provided the 400 ships of its navy. This shrewd strategic policy thus undermined the political and military solidarity of King Darius III. Alexander pressed down the Ionian coast liberating cities and using the Athenian fleet only once—to discourage Persian fleet interference during the siege of Miletus.

Marching across Asia Minor and Cilicia into Syria, Alexander met Darius at the battle of Issus in 333 and through unsurpassed generalship routed the Persian army. Cyprus and the Phoenician cities of Sidon, Byblos and Aradus accepted him, and he in turn accepted the use of their warships. Only Tyre with its 80 triremes resisted. So Alexander besieged it by land and sea, using 120 galleys from Cyprus, 86 from Sidon, 10 from Rhodes, 10 from Lycia, 3 from Cilicia and only one (a penteconter at that!) from Macedonia—230 vessels in all. While the bloody siege raged during the first seven months of 332, Sparta declared war on Macedon, and the Persian admiral Memnon began an island-hopping campaign across the Aegean to attempt to incite a general Greek revolt. His small squadron took Chios, Lesbos (where he was killed) and Tenedos before being destroyed by a Macedonian naval force off Euboea. Then Antipater, Alexander's regent in Greece, conquered Sparta by land to end the threat at home. With galleys, fire ships, a long mole and numerous ruses Alexander took Tyre, pressed into Gaza and accepted the submission of Egypt without bloodshed. With his 200 triremes, Alexander sailed up the Nile to Memphis and founded a new great seaport on the delta, Alexandria.

The Persian Empire thus collapsed to Alexander's brilliant campaign, whereupon he set about consolidating his conquests into a systematic economic, political and social union. At sea, he joined the Phoenician ports and Alexandria in a maritime defensive network linked to the island of Cos, to which Antipater moved 60 triremes. Of the remaining 340 triremes available to him, 110 were employed convoying the wealth of Persia to Macedon. Militarily, Alexander turned north to annihilate Darius' last army at the battle of Arbela in 331 and then eastward toward the Indus River to subdue the most distant provinces. Politically, his benevolent rule and policy of self-determination enhanced his reputation as a great liberator and ruler. Crossing the Indus on a pontoon bridge in the spring of 326, Alexander and his army defeated local native forces at the battle of the Hydaspes, after which the homesick Macedonian troops refused to go any farther. So, for passage down the Hydaspes and Indus, Alexander put his shipwrights to work building a river armada of 800 vessels (of which 80 were thirty-oared), crewed by Phoenicians, Ionian Greeks, Cypriots, Carians and Egyptians, and commanded by Nearchus. Mutually supporting, army and navy moved down the Indus river system in November, overcoming all opposition and founding a naval base at Pattala at the start of the delta in July of 325. Then fleet and army turned westward along the coast to the Persian Gulf, logistically a difficult expedition for them and which included an attack by Nearchus' fleet against a school of whales, the sight of which Mediterranean eyes had never before beheld! But both reached the Gulf, the Eulaeus River and finally the river port of Susa early the next year.

Alexander then set about linking together his vast empire by a mammoth merchant and war fleet that would embrace the entire Mediterranean and create a veritable *Pax Alexandriana.* He authorized the development of Alexandria and Babylon into major port cities and the construction of 1000 war galleys in Phoenicia, Cilicia and Cyprus. From Babylon, Nearchus' enlarged Asian fleet would strengthen trade connections with India and to Egypt via the Arabian and Red seas and possibly a reopened Suez canal. The great fleet could then mass at Alexandria for the combined assault on the Carthaginian Empire in the West. Unfortunately for Alexander, as these preparations went into motion, during June 323 he contracted a disease and died. The brief unity of a Hellenized world then crumbled with the passage of its creator, whose subordinate governors attempted to divide up the empire between them.

The Wars of the Successors *(diadochi),* which lasted for a century and a quarter, began in the Aegean and spread across the Empire as a multi-sided struggle between Antipater and his son Cassander of Macedon and Greece; Antigonus and his son Demetrius of Asia Minor; Lysimachus of Thrace; Seleucus of Syria and Mesopotamia; and Ptolemy of Egypt, and their descendants. Sea power played an even larger role in these wars than it had during Alexander's original campaigns. Technically, the war galleys reached their greatest size of the ancient period under the naval arms race of the Antigonids and Ptolemies, in which fours and fives from the West were adopted and larger polyremes built, and lead began to be used as sheathing around the outer hull of many vessels as protection against shipworms. Tactically, the skill required for ramming as practiced by Athens passed with Athenian naval power, and although ramming survived, boarding tactics predominated along with large shipboard catapults, which earned Demetrius I the title *Poliorcetes,* the Besieger of Cities.

Strategically, the maritime sea lanes of the Aegean and the Phoenician coast remained key areas of dispute in the Mediterranean. The Successors so weakened themselves in the Aegean that in time Rhodes became the dominant maritime force there, developing the trireme-like *triemiolia* and lighter craft to chase pirates and the first systematic code of international law on the high seas. Like the Greek city-states, the

Phoenician cities never recovered their pre-Alexandrian greatness, although Sidon and Tyre periodically regained a modicum of autonomy. Only Egypt enjoyed lasting maritime greatness, the benefit of relative geographic isolation and the policies of the Ptolemies. The Seleucids controlled ancient Persia as far as the Gulf, but preferred overland traffic to India to that by sea, gave up rule over the Indus valley to the new Mauryan Empire and surrendered maritime control of the Gulf to the city of Gerrha—which carried the India trade as far as Seleucia on the Tigris, successor to the Euphrates port of Babylon.

Athens moved first to take advantage of Alexander's death and brought on the Lamian War. During the summer of 323 Athens formed a new Hellenic league and created a fleet of over 400 triremes, but a dearth of crews enabled her to man only 240 of them against Macedon. With only the 110 treasure galleys of Alexander's fleet available to him, Antipater was outnumbered; he retreated into the city of Lamia near Thessaly to await Macedonian reinforcements from Asia, whereupon he was blockaded by the Greeks. The Athenians sent 170 of their triremes under Euetion to the Hellespont to thwart those reinforcements, but were met and defeated off Abydos by 240 Macedonian triremes under Cleitus in March 322. Cleitus relieved Antipater by destroying the Athenian blockading squadron near the Lichinades Islands, then used his combined fleet to annihilate the main Athenian fleet of Euetion in battle off Amorgos in June. Macedonian troops crossed the Hellespont and forced Athens' unconditional surrender. The Athenian navy forever eliminated, Antipater placed a Macedonian garrison to watch over Piraeus and consolidated maritime control over the Aegean. When revolts followed in Syria, Antipater and Antigonus put them down, but Antipater's death in 319 ended the last real vestiges of Hellenistic imperial unity. Against Macedonian dynastic opposition, his son Cassander claimed the Aegean; Antigonus did the same over Syria and Asia, and Ptolemy over Egypt.

The first round of fighting between the Antigonids and Ptolemies focused on possession of first the strategically key Hellespont and then the Phoenician coast. In 318 Antigonus I and Cassander used Athenian ships to crush the Macedonian fleet under Cleitus in two actions at the Bosporus, Cassander then assuming the rule over Macedonia, and Antigonus driving overland to conquer Babylon in 316 and ally with maritime Cyprus and Rhodes. Ptolemy I ("Soter") aimed at checking Antigonus by conquering all of Phoenicia and allying with Cassander and with Lysimachus of Thrace. Antigonus sought to disrupt the maritime connections between the three allies by taking Syria and Phoenicia by overland attack in 315. When Ptolemy's Phoenician ships kept Tyre supplied in a successful defense, Antigonus and Demetrius in 314–313 built 330 war galleys in their Phoenician ports, Cilicia and at Rhodes and created the League of the Islanders in the formerly Athenian-controlled Cyclades Islands, which they garrisoned. Antigonus finally took Tyre after a fifteen-month siege, but Ptolemy conquered Cyprus, leading to a virtual stalemate at sea. Shifting to land operations, Antigonus attacked Seleucus in Asia Minor and successfully resisted Ptolemy's attempt to regain Phoenicia before suing for peace out of sheer exhaustion in 311. Antigonus and Demetrius had successfully used their new navy to command Ionian and Phoenician waters and keep Ptolemy separated from his allies.

In the renewal of the fighting from 309, Antigonus and Demetrius used 250 galleys to capture Athens from Cassander, assisted briefly by Ptolemy in the Gulf of Corinth, after which the former alliances were reestablished: the Antigonids against Ptolemy (Egypt), Seleucus (Asia Minor and Syria), Cassander (Macedonia) and Lysimachus (Thrace). To gain command of the sea, the Antigonids attacked Cyprus, Egypt and Rhodes in three separate operations. In 306 Demetrius with 118 ships blockaded 60 Egyptian vessels at Salamis harbor in Cyprus and used his missiles, rams and seaborne infantry to destroy the approaching main relief fleet of Ptolemy in a savage naval battle. Sinking or seriously damaging 80 enemy galleys, Demetrius captured 40 more plus 100 loaded army transports and the whole island of Cyprus. Turning against the delta of the Nile itself during the stormy autumn season of 306, Demetrius suffered a repulse by the winds and the Egyptian army. He then besieged Rhodes throughout 305–304, but Rhodes used its galleys to attack Demetrius' supply ships, keeping itself supplied by vessels from Thrace, Macedon and Egypt. By the time Demetrius quit Rhodes, Cassander had liberated Athens and its environs, requiring Demetrius to rewin them during 303. Two years later the four allies annihilated the Antigonid army and killed Antigonus at the battle of Ipsus in Asia Minor. Demetrius escaped westward to attempt to restore his control over the Aegean. With Cassander's death in 300 a relative calm returned —but only temporarily, since each Successor sought to establish his own dynasty as the heir of Alexander.

Though Demetrius was able to reestablish Antigonid hegemony over the periphery of the Eastern Mediterranean from the Aegean to Phoenicia, the early third century B.C. belonged to the Ptolemies. Ptolemy I and Ptolemy II ("Philadelphus") extended Hellenistic culture in Egypt and Syria, increased their war fleet and overseas trade from Alexandria, founded Arginoë (modern Suez) to protect Red Sea shipping, reopened the Suez canal, and constructed the great lighthouse on the island of Pharos in the harbor of Alexandria—one of the so-called Seven Wonders of the ancient world (another was the Colossus of Rhodes, a statue

built to overlook the harbor of Rhodes during the 280s). During the
first two decades of the century, the Ptolemies gradually reconquered
the Phoenician coast and Cyprus, battled the Seleucids on the frontier
of Syria and drove into the Aegean against Demetrius.

Demetrius, having seized the throne of Macedon and enlarged his
fleet to 500 warships, soon found himself surrounded by enemies on
land and sea. His fleet repelled the Ptolemaic naval expedition against
Athens, but Lysimachus of Thrace and King Pyrrhus of western Greece
drove him from Macedon in 287, followed by the revolt of Athens.
Demetrius in 286 crossed into Asia Minor, only to be cut off from the
sea by the army of Seleucus, which destroyed his army and took him
prisoner for the rest of his days. The Ptolemies filled the political vacuum
in the Aegean left by the demise of Demetrius, uniting the Eastern Mediterranean economically and militarily with Egyptian naval bases at
Samos and Thera. Sharing anti-pirate policing duties with independent
Rhodes, the Ptolemies shifted the centers of maritime trade away from
Corinth and Athens to Alexandria, Rhodes, Tyre, Antioch and Seleucia
on the Tigris.

Yet, tranquillity did not come to the former Alexandrian Empire, for
the continuous wars weakened the Ptolemaic navy and maritime order
throughout the remainder of the century. During the 270s a Celtic invasion of the Aegean lands, Asia Minor and Syria undermined the
Seleucid Empire and prompted retaliation by Ptolemy II and Demetrius'
son Antigonus II ("Gonatas"). The Antigonids restored their authority
over Macedon, but their fleet was defeated by Ptolemy's when it attempted to expand into the southern Aegean. Both rulers now engaged
in a frantic naval arms race, building many large polyremes to decide
which would command the Aegean Sea, simultaneously fighting disastrous internal and frontier land wars against many enemies. The Greeks
allied with Ptolemy against Antigonus, but failed to withstand his blockade of Athens, which fell in 262, or his subsequent thrust into the
Cyclades which defeated the Ptolemaic fleet at the battle of Cos and
took Samos and most of the other islands during the 250s. Rhodes then
joined the Antigonids, besieged the Ptolemaic base at Ephesus and defeated the Egyptian fleet when it tried to relieve the place. The Ptolemies,
suing for peace in 255, accepted Antigonid hegemony in the Aegean,
but kept Samos and Thera.

Nevertheless, the three-way wars soon resumed between Antigonids,
Ptolemies and Seleucids that weakened all three seriously. Antigonus III
("Doson") broke Ptolemaic naval power at the battle of Andros, over-
ran the Carian coast and reaffirmed Antigonid control over the Aegean
during the third quarter of the century. The Seleucids revived under
Antiochus III ("the Great") during the last quarter, reconquered most

of Asia Minor, Syria and Mesopotamia, and mounted an amphibious expedition into the Persian Gulf which brought about Gerrha's submission. But all three dynasties had by then lost any ability to bring about stability because of their incessant and costly arms races and wars.

The dream of Eastern Mediterranean unity exemplified by Alexander the Great passed during the last decade of the third century. The Antigonids under Philip V of Macedon allied with the Seleucids of Antiochus III in an attempt to conquer the Aegean basin. But Ptolemaic Egypt was too weak to stop them, leaving only small and independent Rhodes and coastal Pergamum in Asia Minor to resist. When, in the summer of 201, Philip's army swept into Ionia, these two states had but one recourse left for restoring any balance of maritime power in the Eastern Mediterranean. They applied to the only outside power capable of such a task—Rome. Already becoming masters of the West, the Romans heeded the call and began an intervention that would have ominous implications for the ancient middle sea.

# 2

## Pax Romana,
## 400 B.C.–A.D. 600

*They [the Romans] are masters of the sea; whatever lands they come to, they at once subdue.*

—LIVY

### THE PUNIC WARS

Unlike Phoenician Carthage and Greek Syracuse—cultural copies of their mother states, Tyre and Corinth—and other maritime states in the Western Mediterranean, the Roman Republic consisted of indigenous peoples with little or no interest in the sea. Indeed, surrounded by Punic, Greek, Etruscan and lesser Italiot seafaring communities, Rome spent most of the fourth century B.C. enveloping its continental frontiers through the victories of its superb legions and only came into direct conflict with these maritime states by conquering Etruria and encountering Greeks in southern Italy and Carthaginians in Sicily. In these waters, Carthage resisted the expansion of the Greek colonies but especially the rise of a dynamic empire from Syracuse in continuous wars throughout the century. The struggles focused on the island of Sicily, the strategic buffer of Carthage against all rivals in the Western Mediterranean. With the demise of Etruscan and Syracusan power there by the early third century, Carthage faced an expansive Rome across the Strait of Messina. What then began as a contest for control of Sicily between maritime Carthage and continental Rome at mid-century grew into a general conflict for hegemony over the entire Western Mediterranean. Out of necessity to fight and win the first two Punic wars, Rome—ever so painfully—had to develop a first-class navy, which would eventually extend maritime stability over the rest of the middle sea during the remainder of the first millennium B.C.

The emergence of Syracuse stemmed directly from the victory over the Athenian expedition of 413 and soon brought Syracuse into conflict with the Phoenician cities which shared Sicily with her. A Carthaginian fleet in 409 landed an expeditionary force at its Sicilian base of Motya which captured the coastal cities of Selinus and Himera in support of allied Segesta. Carthage had apparently built upon the larger Phoenician trireme to fashion the quadrireme (four) to allow superior force in boarding actions at sea. The Syracusan dictator Dionysius I reacted to the Punic attack in 406 by taking the south coast port city of Acragas, from which 50 of his triremes sallied forth against a Punic squadron off nearby Gela, only to be defeated. Suing for peace in 404, Dionysius set about pacifying local pirates, fortifying the island of Ortygia at the entrance of the city harbor, and building 200 new warships, including catapult-armed quadriremes, evidently copied from the Carthaginians, but he stepped ahead of them by inventing the quinquereme (five) in 398.

Dionysius renewed the war by besieging the Punic base at Motya in western Sicily, which he took during 398–397, also repelling one Carthaginian relief force and later damaging another en route to Panormus in the north. Though Dionysius razed and abandoned Motya, Carthage preferred to erect a new base a few miles south of it at Lilybaeum. From there Carthage mounted a cross-island attack on Syracuse via Greek Messana (Messina), which its army destroyed en route. The Punic fleet of 200 triremes and 300 transports, moving to a rendezvous north of Syracuse, instead encountered the enemy fleet of 180 light and heavy galleys under Leptines off Catana which it attacked, sending 100 Syracusan vessels to the bottom. The Carthaginians then besieged Syracuse by land and sea during 396, but a plague and land-sea counterattack by Dionysius and Leptines nearly destroyed their entire fleet. Dionysius then concluded peace, planted colonies in southern Italy, dominated trade in the Adriatic, supported Sparta in the Aegean, established a base on Corsica, checked Tyrrhenian and Etruscan piracy, and used mercenaries to gain more control over Sicily in three more wars with Carthage in 392, 385–375 and 368–367. In the latter struggle, a Punic fleet caught and burned 130 Syracusan galleys on the beach at Drepana, which along with the death of Dionysius ended the fighting. By then, however, Syracuse had replaced Etruria as the major maritime rival of Carthage.

Following the Dionysian example, Dionysius II and later Agathocles continued despotic rule over the Syracusan Empire, which meant a resumption of war with Carthage. Dionysius II so enraged his subjects that in 345 they obtained assistance from the mother city of Corinth in the form of Timoleon and only ten galleys to overthrow him. Carthage went to war in 344, but the next year Timoleon ran the Carthaginian blockade to besiege and take the dictator and exile him to Corinth. Then he rallied Syracuse against Carthage and defeated its armies by 338. Timoleon restored peace to Syracuse, which like Carthage then waited and watched in awe as Alexander the Great conquered the Greek and Phoenician homelands and threatened to head westward.

Upon Alexander's death in 323, however, Carthage resumed its expansion into Sicily, and soon faced a new Hellenistic alliance between Syracuse and Ptolemaic Egypt, which was expanding across North Africa. The Syracusan dictator Agathocles began another war in 311 by attacking Punic Acragas in southern Sicily. Carthage and most Sicilian cities counterattacked, relieved Acragas and drove Agathocles back into his city the next year. Agathocles thereupon ran the Carthaginian naval blockade with an army of 14,000 men aboard 60 galleys, which carried the war to North Africa. Shifting back and forth between Carthaginian and Syracusan home waters in the years 310 to 306, Agathocles failed to take Carthage but lifted its siege against Syracuse. In the meantime, the wars of Alexander's Successors kept the Ptolemies preoccupied in the East, whereas Roman overland expansion into southern Italy had led to the creation in 311 of two 10-ship Roman naval squadrons—Rome's first navy—to fight Tyrrhenian pirates. By the end of the century no one navy controlled the waters of the Western Mediterranean, though Rome and Carthage in 306 had renewed older treaties recognizing their respective spheres of influence.

The political upheavals of the post-Alexandrian Eastern Mediterranean directly affected the West, leading to a series of attempts by several powers to dominate Western waters during the first thirty years of the third century B.C. Agathocles of Syracuse invaded southern Italy with 200 galleys in the 290s, succeeded upon his death in 289 by the city of Tarentum. After sinking 4 and taking one of 10 Roman ships in 242, Tarentum solicited help against Rome from Pyrrhus, the son-in-law of Agathocles from Greek Epirus who was soon to conquer Antigonid Macedonia. In 281 Epirus invaded southern Italy with polyremes, a large army and elephants, which defeated Roman arms over the ensuing two years but with crippling casualties. When in 278–277 Carthage allied with Rome against Syracuse and Pyrrhus, the fighting shifted to Sicily, most of which Pyrrhus quickly overran—except for the Carthaginian base at Lilybaeum. Pyrrhus wanted to cross over to North Africa, but Syracuse refused, whereupon Pyrrhus in 275 embarked his army to carry the war back into Italy. En route, a Punic fleet attacked his convoy and sank all but 40 of its 110 vessels. The next year the Roman army drove Pyrrhus back to Epirus, from which he reconquered Macedonia before meeting his death before Argos in 272.

Rome filled the vacuum left by Pyrrhus' departure and conquered all

Italy. Only Syracuse and Messana, overrun by Campanian pirates, stood between Rome and Carthage, both of which needed Messana to defend their strategic frontiers. To crush the pirates holding Messana, Syracuse besieged the place in 265. The defenders called upon both Rome and Carthage for help. Carthage responded in 264, whereupon Rome and Syracuse allied against her. The major struggle for the Western Mediterranean had begun, just as the Antigonids were slowly driving the Ptolemies from the Aegean in the East.

The long First Punic War (264–241) pitted a maritime power against a continental one in the classic manner. In control of Western Mediterranean waters, Punic (meaning Phoenician) Carthage protected its naval frontiers with bases in Spain, Corsica, Sardinia, Sicily and across North Africa. Sicily as ever formed the northern apex of Carthaginian empire. Continental Rome with its victorious legions kept the cities of Italy allied but subject; it had no maritime tradition, though its coastal allies or colonies did. Roman security in the south focused on Messana and its strategic strait, so that Sicily became the objective for both sides, and with it the weakened Syracuse. The Roman legions could control the interior of Sicily, but Carthaginian command of the sea offered mobility between the coastal cities of (from south to north) Acragas, Heraclea Minoa, Lilybaeum, Drepana and Panormus. As a result, the Romans initially adopted the continental stratagem of neutralizing Punic sea power by attacking the ports from the land side. Thus the Roman attack on and sack of Acragas in 262 ended in the face of a naval relief force, all of which precipitated the alliance of many Sicilian cities with Carthage.

Such a strategic stalemate, plus Punic naval raids from Corsica on the Italian coast, convinced Rome in 261–260 to construct a large navy. To compensate for inexperience at sea, the Romans apparently copied a shipwrecked Carthaginian quinquereme to build eventually 120 of them, plus another 80 quadriremes and triremes, soon equipping the heavier galleys with the *corvus* ("crow"), a new Syracusan invention for grappling for the infantry-battle-at-sea. A boarding bridge which dropped over the prow from a pole to clamp on the enemy ship, the *corvus* made the Roman galley heavier and more dangerously topheavy than its Punic counterpart. But it enabled up to 120 marines and legionnaires to battle the inferior African troops. Also, with eventually 200 vessels always in commission, Rome hoped to keep a slight numerical edge over the navy of Carthage, although by the year 260 the number was probably only 160 against 130.

Rome's first war at sea proved difficult, frustrating and expensive, but also very instructive. During the summer of 260, after losing a skirmish near Lipara west of the Messana strait, 143 new Roman galleys under

Caius Duilius employed their *corvi* for the first time to surprise and defeat a slightly smaller Punic force of Mylae, Sicily. While the Roman legions then overran the interior of Sicily, Rome increased its galley strength to 230 for a seaborne invasion of North Africa. As the consuls Marcus Attilius Regulus and Lucius Manlius Vulso moved their 100 army transports and escorting armada from Messana to the debarkation port of Sicilian Gela early in 256, a large Punic fleet under one Hamilcar sortied from Heraclea Minoa to intercept them. Attempting a double envelopment of the triangular Roman formation off Mount Ecnomus, Hamilcar tried to avoid the dreaded *corvi* and succumbed to a determined Roman counterattack. The Romans sank 30 enemy vessels, captured 64 more, lost 24 of their own and gained command of Sicilian waters, proceeding thence to Cap Bon in Africa. When the Roman Senate prematurely recalled Vulso and most of the fleet the next year, Carthage attacked and captured Regulus, pinning his army against the sea at Clupea. Rome hastily dispatched a relief force of 210 galleys which annihilated an undertrained Punic fleet off Cap Bon, capturing or driving aground no fewer than 114 galleys. The victorious Romans then recovered their army from Clupea and sailed for home in a convoy of over 350 ships, only to have it struck by a storm off Camarina, Sicily. Most of the topheavy *corvus*-laden galleys capsized or broke up on the rocks, costing Rome nearly 100,000 soldiers and sailors—making this disaster undoubtedly the worst in naval history!

Racing to construct an entire new navy, Rome in 254 blockaded and took Panormus in Sicily, while Carthage held Lilybaeum against the Roman offensive. A new Roman expedition of 150 ships descended on North Africa, only to be utterly destroyed by another Mediterranean gale. Rome then preferred to rest its fortunes on land operations until 249 when it built another 120 quinqueremes, substituting simple grappling irons and boarding ladders for the cumbersome *corvi*. But this fleet perished off Lilybaeum at the hands of a Carthaginian naval force and yet another storm. Disgusted, Rome in 248 laid up its remaining vessels, but so did Carthage—a shortsighted measure in light of superior Roman arms on land. The war stalemated in Sicily until 242 at which time Rome built a fleet of 200 improved quinqueremes which besieged and blockaded Drepana. When Carthage hastened a navy of 170 quinqueremes into commission, with untrained crews, it was met and defeated by the Romans off the Aegates Islands in March 241. Without sea power, Carthage lost Lilybaeum and Drepana—and the war.

The Roman victory in the First Punic War, though at the heavy cost of four separate fleets and countless numbers of men, gave Rome command of Western Mediterranean waters, which the Republic exploited so fully that a renewal of the fighting became only a matter of time.

At least the source of the original rivalry, Sicily, was removed by being surrendered to Rome in the peace treaty—save for independent Syracuse. Rome also emerged from the war with some 220 quinqueremes, which deterred any Punic naval rejuvenation from its surviving fleet of 50 quinqueremes, 2 quadriremes and 5 triremes. Roman sea power policed Western waters against pirates, specifically against Illyria in the eastern Adriatic in 229–228 and again in 219, and fostered friendly relations in the East with the Ptolemies of Egypt during their decline.

Having acquired most of Sicily, however, Rome began its overseas imperialism by seizing Corsica and Sardinia in 238–237 and extending its imperial control along the Greek European coast as far as Spain; only Massilia (Marseilles) in southern France retained some independence, especially because its small navy of 40 galleys battled the Ligurian pirates. Alarmed by this further Roman expansion, Carthage in 237 began the creation of a new empire by ferrying an army across the Strait of Gibraltar into Spain and extending Punic political authority up the Spanish Mediterranean coast as far as the Ebro River. The ruling Barca family established new port cities at Lucentum and Cartagena (New Carthage) and exploited the Iberian peninsula for its silver, tin, timber and mercenaries. The Punic-Roman strategic frontier at the Ebro could never be stable, for Rome guaranteed its protection of the Greek coastal city of Saguntum, which lay south of the Ebro, and the Barcas under Hannibal (from 221) harbored vengeance against Rome for the lost war. So when Hannibal besieged, captured and razed Saguntum in 219–218, a new war ensued.

The Second Punic War (219–202) seemed strategically to be almost the reverse of the First, for Rome commanded the sea throughout it, and early Carthaginian victories on land led to Punic superiority in that quarter. Rome planned to contain Hannibal in Spain by ferrying troops thence from Ostia, seaport of the city of Rome, via allied Massilia, and to invade Carthaginian North Africa from Sicily. But Hannibal moved too quickly for Rome to implement such a maritime offensive. Keeping well inland from Roman naval power, he led an army of light infantry, cavalry and elephants through Gaul, across the Alps and into northern Italy during 218, forcing Rome to shift to a continental defensive strategy. After gathering at Lilybaeum and taking the island of Malta in preparation for the overseas invasion, the 160 Roman quinqueremes were now redeployed—50 at Lilybaeum and 110 at Ostia, the remaining warships and transports joining the Massiliots to operate in Hannibal's rear in Spain.

During 218–217, Hannibal crushed five of six Roman consular armies sent against him in Italy, but without siege engines he could not take Rome itself, confining his very limited goals to forcing the Romans to

negotiate a settlement. But Rome had no such intention. By keeping the
mother city supplied by sea and hammering away at Carthage-in-Spain,
the Romans preferred to await the growth and maturation of a new
generation of Roman youth to fill the legions and decide the issue on
land. Operating from the interior position, Rome concentrated the main
fleet of 135 galleys at Ostia-Rome, the 50 at Lilybaeum in Sicily and
another 35 at Tarraco in Spain. In this way Roman forces could be
supplied by sea (while Hannibal ravaged Italian farmlands), Punic
communications could not be established over water between Carthage
and Hannibal, and Roman naval forces could be shifted to any threatened point throughout the Mediterranean. This latter need assumed great
importance when Carthage was able to conclude an alliance with the
Antigonid King Philip V of Macedon, who by virtue of his victories in
the Aegean could pressure Rome in the Adriatic.

Roman command of the Western Mediterranean could best be assured
by an aggressive attitude in Spain, the economic base of the Carthaginian
Empire. There the Punic army of Hasdrubal (Hannibal's brother) and
the 40 quinqueremes of Himilco had been raiding the Roman base at
Tarraco and Roman shipping, so that Gnaeus Scipio took the offensive
at sea during the spring of 217. Sailing southward from Tarraco with 15
Roman and 20 Massiliot light galleys, Scipio surprised and routed the
Punic squadron encamped at the Ebro, destroying 4 and capturing 25
quinqueremes. With absolute control over local Spanish waters, the
Romans now focused several years of fighting on the mainland. That
summer, however, Carthage managed to send 70 quinqueremes to Sardinia and then off Pisa either to communicate with Hannibal or fight
the Roman fleet. They captured a Roman supply convoy en route to
Spain but fled before the approach of the main Roman fleet from Ostia.
The latter went on to its first of many raids of the war against the North
African coast. Rome transferred several vessels from Ostia to Lilybaeum
to deter further Punic naval sorties and began to replace its older ships
with new construction. Although Punic seaborne raiding continued in
the West throughout the war, Roman sea power kept Spain generally
isolated thereafter from Hannibal and the other theaters of war.

Security in the East would also insure the sea routes supplying beleaguered Rome, so that Rome assumed a limited offensive in this First
Macedonian War in order to tie down Philip V of Macedon and prevent
his joint operations with allied Carthage. When in 216–215 Philip built
100 light *hemioliae* to fight Rome and called upon his ally to provide
transports, Rome established a base at Brundisium (modern Brindisi)
and a squadron of eventually 50 galleys drawn from the main fleet to
control the Adriatic. Entertaining a desire to conquer piratic Illyria before facing Rome, Philip used his fleet in 214 to ferry an army thence

to take Oricum and move up the Aous River to besiege Apollonia. The Roman Brundisium squadron under Valerius Laevinus recaptured Oricum, bottled up Philip in the river and used a landing party to attack him at night. Thus cut off from the sea, Philip burned his ships and escaped overland with his army to Macedonia. The Romans then established a forward base at Oricum, and two years later the Brundisium squadron captured several Adriatic islands before wintering at Corcyra. A Roman alliance with the Aetolian League of central Greece that year led to Roman naval intervention in the Aegean for the first time in 210 to assist the League in capturing the city of Aegina. A feeble and ineffective Carthaginian naval sortie into the Adriatic and the alliance of Pergamum with Rome in 209–208 led both Philip and Rome to quit Greek waters, followed by Carthage in 207. Thus did Rome protect its Eastern flank and frustrate the Punic attempt to exploit the Macedonian alliance.

The war always focused on Hannibal and the attempt of Carthage to reinforce him by sea, so that Sicily grew into a major theater of war over the years 216 to 210. In 216 Hannibal unsuccessfully moved on Naples for an outlet to the sea, but Carthage did manage to send in the only reinforcing convoy of the war at Locri in southern Italy while the Roman Lilybaeum squadron was away routing a Punic squadron. Leaving but 25 galleys at Ostia, Rome now distributed its warships somewhat evenly between Naples, Brundisium and Spain, with the remaining largest contingent of 75 at Lilybaeum in Sicily. Then, in 214, Syracuse revolted against Rome, threatening the strategic pivot of Rome's maritime defenses.

Rome concentrated 130 galleys, many brand new, and army forces under Marcus Claudius Marcellus at a new base, Thapsus, six miles north of Syracuse, which they besieged. Carthage responded by instituting a major naval construction program and giving maximum support to Syracuse. While the Syracusan missile engines of Archimedes wreaked havoc among Roman blockading vessels, in 213 Himilco landed an army at Heraclea Minoa, captured Agrigentum (formerly Acragas) and marched overland to Syracuse, and a 55-ship fleet under Bomilcar ran the blockade and out again. Rome rushed 30 quinqueremes and another legion to Sicily but could not prevent Bomilcar from running in and out of Syracuse harbor three more times with his ever-growing fleet. Hannibal himself took advantage of Laevinus' absence with the Brundisium squadron in Illyria to attack and capture the fortified seaport of Tarentum in 212, but he could not dislodge the Roman garrison in the citadel which controlled the harbor entrance. Himilco's army was defeated by Marcellus before Syracuse and obliterated thereafter by a plague. As Hannibal campaigned throughout southern Italy, Bomilcar returned to Heraclea Minoa and Cape Pachynum with 700 transports and 185 quinqueremes to face Marcellus' fleet of 130 vessels. But when the latter offered battle, Bomilcar panicked, sent the still-loaded transports back to Carthage and took the battle fleet to Tarentum; frustrated from entering by the Roman citadel, Bomilcar ingloriously returned to Carthage, having accomplished nothing. The Roman Lilybaeum squaddon of 80 galleys then raided Utica in North Africa and seized 130 grain transports. Marcellus captured Syracuse, and the Punic effort in Sicily degenerated into desultory fighting.

The events before Syracuse ended Carthage's threat at sea and insured ultimate Roman victory. Carthage could ill afford the vast expense of both a large army and navy and from 210 allowed its poorly led navy to fall into disrepair. By contrast, Rome kept 215 galleys in commission and elected its two victorious commanders to the governing consulships in 211, Marcellus and Laevinus, commander of the Brundisium squadron since 215. Converting Syracuse into a subject state and naval base, Laevinus with 100 galleys pacified all Sicily in 210. Following Roman reverses in Spain in 211, an expedition of 30 quinqueremes and an army under Publius Cornelius Scipio (later Scipio Africanus) counterattacked, took Cartagena and its 18 warships in 209 and over the next three years killed Hasdrubal and conquered all Spain. Roman forces in Italy meanwhile retook Tarentum but lost Marcellus in battle with Hannibal. In 208 Laevinus took his 100-ship Sicilian fleet on a successful plundering expedition of the North African coast and defeated 83 Punic vessels in battle off Clupea. When Bomilcar's squadron, absent in Greece, returned in 207, the Roman fleet attacked and defeated the 70 Punic ships in battle in their home waters. The reduced navy of Carthage made one final attempt to retake Cartagena and the Balearic Islands in 206, only to be repulsed, with the Romans capturing the last Punic base in Spain, Cadiz. With 285 war galleys at its disposal Rome now left but 30 in Sicily and smaller units to patrol the coasts of Illyria, Sardinia and Spain and concentrated the rest at Ostia. It had regained undisputed command of the sea.

For the final grand campaign against Carthage, Rome in 205 elected Scipio consul for Sicily and made peace with Macedonia. Scipio captured Hannibal's seacoast base of Locri and assembled but 60 galleys for an overseas invasion of Carthage. He sent 30 of them under Laelius to plunder the North African coast and collected 400 transports for his 30,000 men and supplies for forty-five days in Sicily for the campaign —one of the most massive overseas expeditions of antiquity. Carthage tried to create diversions by sending three small convoys to reinforce Hannibal in Italy. Two of them, escorted by 55 warships under Mago Barca (another brother of Hannibal), took advantage of lax Roman coastal defenses to land ground forces at Genoa in the north, only to be contained there by a Roman army. The third, unescorted, was blown off course to Sardinia, where the Roman squadron there destroyed it. His communications and rear intact, Scipio crossed from Lilybaeum to Cap Bon in the spring of 204, escorted by only 40 warships. His siege of Utica failed, however, until the next spring when Scipio strengthened his bridgehead in Africa. Carthage recalled Hannibal from Italy, although he had to build his own transports to make the passage during the autumn of 203. The Romans frustrated Punic naval raids on their position and hastened more warships and transports to Scipio. In October 202 Scipio defeated Hannibal's army at the battle of Zama, thereafter sailing to the seaward side of Carthage with 120 warships to demonstrate Roman naval power. Duly impressed, Carthage sued for peace early in 201.

The First and Second Punic wars finished Carthage as a power and Phoenician maritime influence altogether and established Rome as master of the Western and Central Mediterranean. Rome stripped Carthage of all its possessions outside Africa and its war-making ability, including its navy. Scipio gathered and burned all 500 vessels—among them maybe 100 quinqueremes—in Punic waters, leaving Carthage but 10 triremes to protect its coast from pirates. A reluctant sea power, Rome had nevertheless achieved and maintained command of the sea in both wars. Between these wars, Carthage had shifted the basis of its economic and military power and strategy from the maritime to the continental, relegating its navy to a supporting role to the army. When that army lost, Carthage lost everything. But Rome's legions could never have been victorious without the security and mobility provided by the navy. Carthage followed the course of other victims of Roman might and became a vassal state. The Roman Republic had thereby become an overseas empire.

## THE IMPERIAL AND CIVIL WARS

By the end of the third century B.C. Rome had adopted an imperial strategy designed to maintain political stability not only in Italy and the waters west of it but throughout the entire Mediterranean. The virtual collapse of Ptolemaic Egypt before the onslaught of the Antigonids of Macedonia and the Seleucids of Asia had upset the delicate equilibrium in the Aegean and Eastern Mediterranean, leaving only tiny Rhodes and Pergamum to police Eastern waters against aggressors and pirates alike. Thus when Rome rallied at the invitation of these small states to intervene in their behalf in 201, the extension of the *Pax Romana* over the entire Mediterranean world became only a matter of time. In sheer economic terms, the Roman Republic now depended largely upon maritime trade, which made stability upon the seas absolutely essential. Culturally, the capture of Hellenic Syracuse in 211 had awakened the Romans to the glories of Greek learning and a desire to protect the Greeks against aggression. But politically, Roman republicanism would be increasingly weakened by the enlarged military and naval responsibilities of overseas conquest and pacification. Internal political crises thus led to civil warring within Rome and its imperial possessions, culminating in the triumphs of Julius Caesar and Octavian. During the last two centuries before Christ, therefore, the Roman fleet and its allied squadrons acted as the spokes of the strategic wheel tying together the Mediterranean littoral to the imperial city. All roads —land and sea—led to Rome.

The Second Macedonian War (200–196) eliminated the threat posed by Philip V. The latter, allied to Antiochus III ("the Great") of Seleucid Asia and the pirates of Crete, in 202 had set a new pattern for navies by creating a mixed fleet of 40 heavy and several light galleys with which to dominate the Aegean. In the summer of 201 Philip lost half this fleet in a naval battle with the combined Rhodian-Pergamine fleet off Chios. Rome then intervened, joining 50 galleys of its great reserve fleet of 280 to the 24 of Pergamum and 20 of Rhodes to besiege Philip's navy in Caria for the winter. Though Philip ran this blockade back to Macedonia, Rome moved to isolate Philip from his allies in Greece by transporting an army across the Adriatic and establishing squadrons at Corcyra and Piraeus. Rhodes assisted by bringing the Cretan towns over to the side of the alliance and creating its own league of the islanders within the Cyclades. With but 20 heavy galleys and many smaller *lembi,* Philip could never begin to dispute this allied control of the Aegean and Adriatic seas, and his navy ceased to be a factor in the war. Supported by sea, the Roman army crushed Philip's army at Cynoscephalae in 197 and achieved victory the next year. Stripped of all but 5 heavy galleys plus *lembi,* Philip concluded an alliance with Rome against Antiochus which also pacified piratic Sparta in 195. Rome guaranteed its protection of all Greeks and the next year withdrew, ignoring the warnings of Scipio Africanus that a political vacuum— and trouble—would result.

The Syrian War (192–188) between Rome and Antiochus indeed ensued, as Antiochus III strove to reestablish the old Seleucid Empire. He recovered the Phoenician coast in 200, built the first Seleucid fleet of 300 vessels there during 198–197, overran Cilicia and Asia Minor, crossing the Hellespont into Thrace and welcoming Hannibal as a political emigré into his service. But ignoring Hannibal's sage advice that Rome would fight to the last for Greece, Antiochus accepted the invitation of the Aetolian League to invade Greece. Rome and Pergamum declared war on Antiochus, and although Rome recommissioned 120 of its reserve galleys and authorized 100 new ones, she preferred to rely upon the navies of her allies—a practice generally followed during the imperial wars. Antiochus had 100 heavy galleys and many lighter vessels and a major base at Ephesus but lost the friendship of Rhodes, which declared war in 191. Driven that year from Greece by the Roman army, Antiochus now heeded Hannibal's prediction that Rome would carry the war into Asia, concentrated his army at the Hellespont, and ordered his admiral Polyxenidas, an exiled Rhodian, to prepare the fleet at Ephesus.

Satisfied that no invasion threat existed to Italy, Rome dispatched a fleet under Caius Salinator Livius to the Aegean during the summer of 191 which with the Pergamines defeated Polyxenidas at Cissus off the Asia Minor coast in September. Roman strategy then shifted to a land campaign directed by Scipio Africanus and his brother Lucius Cornelius Scipio, and the navy under new and sluggish admirals was relegated to a supporting role. For instance, in the spring of 190 the fleet seized part of the Hellespont coastline, months before the army was due to arrive there. Thus divided, the allied fleets lay open to piecemeal destruction, as Polyxenidas now surprised and destroyed most of the Rhodian squadron at Panormus near Ephesus. The 84 Roman ships now rushed southward to base at Samos and blockade Polyxenidas' 89 at Ephesus, leaving the Rhodian fleet of 38 to prevent Hannibal's approach from Phoenicia with 47 ships. Using the ram, the fleet of Rhodes under Eudamus defeated Hannibal off Side in the Asia Minor Gulf of Adalia and then rejoined the Romans. Polyxenidas attempted to surprise this allied fleet off Cape Myonnesus near Teos in September, only to lose half his galleys to Rhodian rams and fire-baskets and boarding Roman legionnaires. With absolute command of the sea, the army of the Scipios crossed the Hellespont and crushed the Seleucid army in 189. In the peace the next year, Antiochus lost all but 10 of his galleys, he himself being killed in 187.

Rome had restored the balance of power in the Eastern Mediterranean, but very soon assumed absolute supremacy over the region. Seleucid Syria had been reduced to an enfeebled minor status alongside Ptolemaic Egypt. Antigonid Macedon under Philip V had cooperated with Rome in the Syrian War but under Perseus waged the Third Macedonian War (171–168) against Rome and Pergamum. During this war Syria conquered Egypt, but Rome crushed Macedon, turned it and Greece into virtual protectorates and forced the Seleucids to quit Egypt. Allied Pergamum, while joining the Romans in policing the Aegean against pirates, extended its control over most of Asia

Minor by defeating such rival states as Black Sea Pontus (183–179) and Bithynia in 186. In the latter struggle, Hannibal made his last appearance against Rome in the role of a Bithynian naval captain who won a skirmish at sea by hurling pots filled with poisonous snakes (!) against the Pergamine ships. Three years later, tired of running from the Romans, Hannibal committed suicide. Suspicious of Pergamine power, Rome took advantage of its destruction of Macedonian power in 168 to assume a protectorate over most of Asia Minor, reducing Pergamum to a minor status. Allied Rhodes had chosen to remain aloof from the Third Macedonian War, angering Rome sufficiently to cause the Romans to shift their Eastern trade from Rhodes to the Roman-Athenian free port of Delos, which crippled Rhodian economic power. Throughout the century, the Syrian successors of Antiochus continued to war sporadically with Egypt, which became subservient to Rome in order to preserve its independence. One by one, the warring nations of the East thereby surrendered their autonomy to the growing might of Rome.

Such wars of expansion converted Rome into an overseas empire intolerant of outlawry and opposition. A new merchant class preferred slaves to tenant farmers, the latter making their way into the legionary armies of overseas proconsuls. As Roman power and wealth increased, public and private morality decreased, the Republican constitution succumbed to military strongmen, and Roman imperialism became ruthless and uncompromising. When Carthage became active again, Rome needed only 50 ancient quinqueremes and 100 light galleys with which to help the army annihilate that state in the Third Punic War (149–146). The restive Greeks felt Roman impatience when the Romans sacked Corinth and annexed the entire Balkan peninsula including Macedon in 146, and in 133 the last Pergamine king simply willed his weakened state to Rome, though a four-year war was required for final pacification. Professional proconsular armies evolved to keep the entire periphery of the Mediterranean under control through endless revolts, so that Roman ships provided the crucial mobility between these frontiers. Thus did fighting continue in Sicily, Gaul, Spain and North Africa during the second half of the century and even within Italy itself early in the first century.

With no naval power left to challenge Roman supremacy at sea, the Roman navy deteriorated and piracy increased. In the West, Massilia helped Rome contain the piratic peoples of the Tyrrhenian Sea, with Rome occupying the Balearic Islands in 123. In the Adriatic, the Istrians, Illyrians, Dalmatians and Liburnians continued to defy Roman authority upon the sea, while in the Aegean the pirates of Crete and and Cilicia seriously undermined the maritime stability of the East.

Indeed, Rome even encouraged the Cilician pirates by trading with them for slaves at Delos. Without a navy to police the seas, Rome— never a thalassocracy anyway—gradually surrendered the *Pax Romana* to pirates. And this deterioration proved serious when King Mithridates of Pontus on the Black Sea rallied the pirates against Rome.

The Mithridatic wars (89–65 B.C.) provided Rome with its last formidable enemies, Pontus and the pirates of Cilicia in concert. Marcus Antonius pacified Cilicia temporarily in 102, and Rome terminated the slave trade at Delos. The pirates, with a navy of some 1000 light *hemioliae* and *myoparones,* now began to help Pontus build, equip, train and organize a fleet of 400 galleys with which to confront Rome. The navies of Mithridates and the Cilician privates eventually became so similar with their admirals, squadrons, ships and tactics as to be indistinguishable. In 89 Mithridates seized the Hellespont, drove into Greece, liberated Athens, sacked Delos and took several Aegean islands until the Roman consul Sulla drove the Pontic army back to the coast and the succor of its fleet. Sulla and Lucius Lucullus then raised a fleet of Italiot allies and drove Mithridates from the Aegean by 84, repeating the feat during a second war in 83–81. Becoming military dictator of Rome, Sulla established a pacification policy of patrolling the Cilician coast and sending expeditions into the interior.

After Sulla's death in 78, his proconsular successors continued this policy. Servilius took the Cilician base of Phaselis in a major naval campaign and engagement, 77–75, and Marcus Antonius (son of his namesake) in 74 received supreme authority (*maius imperium infinitum*) to clear the Mediterranean of pirates. This was delayed, however, by several crises. Sulla's protégé Gnaeus Pompeius (later Pompey the Great) had to pacify a rebellious Spain (77–71); a slave uprising had to be repressed in Italy (72–71); and Lucullus used the navy and army to crush Mithridates and conquer Asia Minor in a third long war (75–65). These preoccupations enabled the Cilician and Cretan pirates to range throughout the middle sea, crippling Roman commerce, raiding the Italian coast with impunity, and even destroying a Roman consular fleet in the home harbor of Ostia itself. They even began to replace some of their light galleys with larger biremes and triremes. When Antonius invaded Crete in 72, the pirates overwhelmed his force and three years later overran Aegina and destroyed Delos as a major entrepôt. That year, however, another Roman force took and pacified Crete. The blockaded citizenry and merchant class of Rome now demanded action, and got it in the person of Pompey.

Conferred with the supreme Mediterranean *imperium,* Pompey in 67 initiated a systematic, three-month campaign to end the Cilician pirate menace. He raised twenty legions (120,000 men) and placed 270

Roman and a nearly equal number of allied warships into service, dividing them into thirteen separate commands from Gibraltar to the Black Sea. Two strong squadrons guarded the Italian coasts against Tyrrhenian and Illyrian pirates, and a third blockaded the Cicilian coast, while Pompey personally took a special task force of 60 galleys to Gibraltar. At a prearranged moment, all the local commanders attacked the pirate lairs in their region and Pompey departed Gibraltar in a swift, forty-day voyage eastward. The speed and suddenness of this general offensive caught the pirates off guard and unable to support one another. Demoralized, they submitted even more readily when they learned of Pompey's lenient policy toward prisoners—a realistic measure, for Pompey appreciated the fact that many men had been driven into piracy in desperation caused by the economic dislocations since the Punic wars. Pompey touched at Sardinia, North Africa and Sicily as the pirates surrendered or fled eastward, passed along coastal Gaul and Etruria, thence to Rome and Brundisium and eastward to Athens and Rhodes, where reinforcements awaited him. Then he launched a massive assault on the pirates' coastal strongholds of Cilicia, defeated their last stand at sea in battle off Coracesium, and shortly received their general surrender. The campaign resulted in the sinking of maybe 1300 pirate vessels and the ultimate capture of nearly 400 more. The power of Cilician piracy was shattered.

But the *Pax Romana* had yet to be fully restored, because of civil turmoil within Rome and the continued lack of a permanent maritime policy. In 60 B.C. three prominent military leaders created a triumvirate to govern Rome: Pompey, Gaius Julius Caesar and Marcus Licinius Crassus. Pompey's enormous prestige led him to dominate the government, while the other two attempted to enhance their own reputations through expansionist campaigns. In the East, Rome annexed Bithynia-Pontus, Cilicia, Syria and Cyprus, and Crassus made war against Parthia, only to be killed there in 53. Caesar spent the decade subduing Gaul in Western Europe, reaching the Brittany coast of France where he encountered the seafaring Gallic Veneti tribe. The latter employed all (animal-skin) sail vessels of solid oaken timbers that made ramming them ineffective, with high sides that discouraged boarding. So Caesar and his admiral Decimus Brutus constructed a fleet of galleys with long sharp poles to rip down the masts of the Veneti ships. Caesar brought the 220 Veneti war craft to battle in 56 near the Loire River and used his poles to defeat them in a six-hour battle. In August 55 Caesar crossed the English Channel to the mysterious British Isles, landing two legions near Deal under cover of catapult and other missile fire in heavy weather and difficult tides and against the fanatical defense of the barbarian Britons. He wisely reembarked and returned the next summer.

With 600 transports escorted by 28 galleys he landed five legions unopposed and subdued southern England. Caesar's light galleys compared
with the light craft used against the sporadic pirate outbreaks of the
Cilicians and Liburnians. The two-banked vessels of the latter pirates
in the Adriatic proved so effective and swift that Rome copied them
as the new standard Roman warship and called them liburnians, leaving
only Ptolemaic Egypt with the larger quinqueremes. Caesar's successes
in Britain and Gaul caused Pompey to be jealous and thus to seize
power in Rome late in the decade, precipitating a civil war between the
factions led by both men.

The Roman Civil War (50–44 B.C.) found strategically continental
Caesar opposing maritime Pompey. Caesar's legions in 49 pressed
from Gaul into Italy, coercing Pompey into evacuating Rome and all
Italy. Supported by his Eastern littoral possessions and their veteran
warships, however, Pompey had command of the sea and easily passed
from Brundisium into the Balkans. Caesar, however, promptly adopted
the tried Roman strategy of occupying these very same coasts from the
land side. Marching overland toward Spain, where Pompey had much
support, in May Caesar encountered a delay at the seaport stronghold
of Massilia. Opposed by the small Massiliot navy, Caesar had twelve
triremes built and employed under Decimus Brutus, who led them and
some captured vessels in two victorious skirmishes over Massiliot and
Pompeian galleys. The city surrendered from land and sea attack, the
last Western Greek city to submit to Roman control, and Caesar—his
communications secure—proceeded on to Spain, which his armies soon
conquered.

Caesar then shifted back to Italy, basing at Brundisium for crossing
the Adriatic and a direct confrontation with Pompey. Pompey placed
the large confederate fleet that he had assembled from Eastern Mediterranean supporters under the command of Marcus Bibulus along the
Illyrian coast to block Caesar's passage. But Caesar nevertheless crossed
with seven legions in the dead of winter, January of 48, to the deserted
anchorage of Oricum on the coast of Epirus where he established his
bridgehead. Pompey quickly dispatched Bibulus to isolate Caesar from
reinforcement, taking and destroying 30 of Caesar's transports, crews
and all. Thus blockaded, Caesar could not get the rest of his army
across from Brundisium. Conversely, Caesar's occupation of Oricum
and then Apollonia to the north meant that Bibulus could not land shore
parties from the blockading fleet to get water and provisions. Pompey's
main base lay at Dyrrachium (Durazzo) in Illyria, requiring that supplies for his army and navy be brought all the way from the island of
Corcyra in the south. In this duel of blockade and counterblockade,
Caesar had the advantage, for seaborne blockades were extremely dif-

ficult to maintain with open galleys. In addition to the logistical night-mare, the winter weather exposed the crew to rigorous living conditions on board. In his effort to keep station, Bibulus himself succumbed to these conditions and died.

Success for Caesar depended on breaking the blockade and bringing over the rest of his army under the command of Mark Antony, son and grandson of his namesakes who had fought the Cilician pirates. Pompey tried to strengthen the blockade by sending a squadron to occupy a tiny barren island off Brundisium. Antony, however, also kept shore parties from reaching water on the mainland, forcing the Pompeians to abandon their blockade here. Antony then embarked with the army and used a favorable wind to cross to Lissus, north of Dyrrachium. Caesar and Antony, south and north of Pompey's base, now moved to link up. They joined a few miles south of Dyrrachium and even succeeded in drawing Pompey away from the port itself. As long as Caesar kept Pompey blockaded from returning to those port facilities, Pompey's army might starve. But Pompey commanded the sea, and his son Gnaeus Pompeius used the Egyptian fleet contingent to destroy Caesar's transports both at Oricum and Lissus. So Caesar and Pompey again blockaded each other, this time in the siege confrontation below Dyrrachium.

Caesar realized that his lack of a navy (though he had vessels build-ing and gathering at Sicily and Gaul and in Italy) could be fatal, so when Pompey managed to break out of the siege Caesar determined to draw his enemy away from the sea. He fell back on Apollonia through Epirus and into Thessaly, gaining much popular support as he went. Pompey followed and met Caesar in the decisive battle of Phar-salus, where Caesar's legions defeated, trapped and received the sur-render of Pompey's army in August of 48, though Pompey himself managed to escape. At the news of this battle, Pompey's naval squad-rons, which had been plundering Caesar's new squadrons at Brundisium and Messina, withdrew. Pompey reached Cilicia, but Caesar's hot pur-suit struck fear in any potential allies for supporting Pompey, who went on to Egypt via Cyprus. The Egyptians, fearing that Pompey would attempt a military takeover of the country, murdered him.

The Civil War continued as Pompey's sons, Gnaeus Pompeius and the younger Sextus Pompeius, tried to defeat Caesar. Caesar had pur-sued their father to Egypt, then became embroiled in the civil strife engulfing the capital. In the brief Alexandrian War (48–47), Caesar's few warships fought two skirmishes after which Caesar burned the Egyptian war vessels and placed Cleopatra on the throne of Egypt in his service. Caesar, now served by 200 warships plus transports, has-tened to Asia Minor to repulse an invasion by Pontus, and in 46 returned to North Africa where he defeated the army of Sextus Pompeius at the battle of Thapsus. Sextus fled to Spain where he and his brother Gnaeus were defeated—and Gnaeus killed—by Caesar in battle in 45. The war thus came to an end, and Caesar was proclaimed dictator of Rome for life.

Rome and the Mediterranean world thus achieved unity under one ruler, only to have the new stability shattered in 44 by Caesar's assassination. In the renewed and quick civil war, Roman government followed a second triumvirate which brought the war to a close in 42 by destroying the rebel army at Philippi in Macedonia. The new triumvirate consisted of Antony, Marcus Aemilius Lepidus, and Gaius Julius Caesar Octavianus, Caesar's grandnephew, better known as Octavian. The new government soon had much to do in the maritime sphere, for Sextus Pompeius had mobilized the pirates against Rome. As a sop toward unity, the triumvirate in 43 had given this Pompeian command of the entire Roman navy, much of which he had succeeded in utilizing for piracy. He captured Corsica, Sardinia, Sicily and the Peloponnese and after the battle of Philippi carried on such a successful war of raiding at sea that the Italian coastal peoples were soon reduced to a state of near-starvation.

Sextus Pompeius followed his father's genius for naval warfare so successfully that Rome yielded to public pressure by concluding peace with him in 38, giving Sextus his conquered territories and other concessions. Sextus' political maneuvering, however, soon led to renewed fighting, with the government endeavoring to build a suitable new navy of its own. Several sharp naval battles ensued, all to the advantage of Sextus, whose 100 vessels defeated 90 of his enemy off Cumae; then with 130 he defeated Octavian near the Strait of Messina. After these typical land-battles-at-sea which left Sextus in command of Italian waters, Octavian borrowed 130 fresh galleys from Antony and appointed his military adviser Marcus Vipsanius Agrippa to command them. Agrippa spent most of the year 37 increasing his fleet to 370 ships, equipping many with a new catapulted grappling device known as the harpago (or harpax), and training his crews at the new base of Portus Julius on an inland lake connected by a canal to the bay of Naples. Sextus, instead of making sound countermaneuvers against these preparations, remained ever the pirate and spent the entire year plundering Roman commerce. In addition, independent pirates had reappeared along the Illyrian coast to compound Roman maritime difficulties.

To finish Sextus, the triumvirate moved in July of 36 with its huge new fleet, which included not only liburnians but quinqueremes and even sixes, and was divided into three separate forces. The triumvir Lepidus departed Africa to land in Sicily and conduct operations designed to retake Lilybaeum. Octavian moved on Sicily from his base at Tarentum, while Agrippa with the largest force moved south from the Naples area to engage Sextus. Driven back to Italy by heavy weather which destroyed dozens of warships, these two government fleets recouped their losses and sailed again in August. After taking the Lipari Islands, Agrippa with 100 of his heavy galleys encountered 100 of the lighter enemy ships off Mylae and gave them a severe beating. But the younger Pompey broke off and hastened through the Strait of Messina to repel Octavian's landing at Tauromenium in eastern Sicily. Sextus engaged Octavian's fleet off the beachhead, defeated it and sank or captured 60 galleys. In the meantime, however, the government's superior strength provided the telling strategic blow, for Agrippa now landed new legions on the north coast of Sicily unopposed and effected a union with the forces of Lepidus.

Sextus hastened back from Tauromenium to Naulochus to contest Agrippa's fleet. Agrippa obliged him, with each fleet numbering over 300 heavy galleys. On September 3, 36, the Pompeian vessels charged forward for the ram, but Agrippa played out his harpagones to enable his legionnaires to board. The massive battle of Naulochus favored Agrippa from the outset, continuing until Agrippa captured or grounded 250 galleys and sank 28 more, while Sextus managed to escape with only 17 ships. Agrippa suffered 3 vessels sunk. The pirate Sextus—a worthy admiral indeed!—was broken, and though he escaped to Armenia he was overtaken by the Romans and executed later in the year. The government could now use its new navy to clear the Illyrian coast of independent pirates and to pacify the interior, which it did promptly.

But still the civil strife did not end, for Octavian and Antony deposed Lepidus, divided up the Mediterranean between West and East respectively, and then turned against each other. Antony allied with Cleopatra in Egypt and set about building a great Egyptian-Roman fleet of large galleys all equipped with missile-throwing devices and ranging from quadriremes to tens. Finally, in 32, Rome—led by Octavian—declared war on Egypt, and Agrippa moved to cut the trade routes to Egypt. Antony hastened to Greece, establishing his forward base at Actium near the entrance to the Gulf of Corinth. To counter this fleet of nearly 500 galleys, Octavian massed his fleet of some 400 triremes, liburnians and a few quadriremes, quinqueremes and sixes at Brundisium and Tarentum under Agrippa and seized Corcyra as his forward base. There the fleets—with troops encamped nearby ready for embarkation— waited and watched. The last great naval battle of antiquity was shaping up, the last appearance of heavy galleys in ancient naval operations and the last action of an Egyptian navy, whose units were personally commanded by Cleopatra. Both fleets had their catapults on board, both had added armor belts of ironclad timbers to their hulls to ward off enemy rams, but only the Romans had the deadly harpago, and their crews were now well-disciplined, while Antony's were under-strength. The battle for Rome would again be at sea.

Octavian in the spring of 31 moved south from Corcyra to blockade Antony at Actium, thus making battle inevitable. To strengthen the crews of his best ships, Antony burned 200 of his lesser galleys. Then, preparing for battle in the late summer, he ordered furled sails taken on board his galleys—an unusual precaution since it could only mean that he intended flight. Indeed, Agrippa's arrangement of Octavian's warships around Actium dictated Antony's objective to be a breakout toward Egypt, unless Antony and Cleopatra could somehow destroy most of the force under Octavian and Agrippa. The Battle of Actium, fought on September 2 in the year 31 B.C., thus proved to be anticlimactic. The two lines of ships closed for action, and almost became stalemated since only missiles could be used between the huge galleys of Antony and the small liburnians of Agrippa, ramming and boarding being impos-sible. The government vessels thus swarmed around Antony's floating fortresses. At the height of the battle, Cleopatra's squadron—with mer-chant vessels, held back from the action—took advantage of a fresh breeze to charge through the center, placing it in an excellent position to turn the Roman flank in either direction. Instead, since she and Antony were so outnumbered by Octavian's fleet, she kept right on going toward Egypt, joined by Antony with 40 of his own ships. The re-mainder of his fleet soon came under a barrage of flaming arrows and catapulted fire pots to be consumed in flames, while others backed water to the shore where they were boarded and taken.

The Republic finally perished at the Battle of Actium. Antony and Cleopatra reached Egypt, but both committed suicide in 30, with Octavian annexing Egypt into the empire. Octavian then consolidated his position in Rome, where in 29–27 he officially inaugurated the Roman Empire by receiving the exalted titles of Caesar Augustus and *Imperator,* which made him commander-in-chief over all Roman armies and warships with the powers of infinite imperium. In other words, he became Em-peror, his authority based on the allegiance of the twenty-five standing legions and the Praetorian Guard which he established. But if the Re-public finally reached the climax of its long demise since the Punic wars, the prospect of the long-sought-after *Pax Romana* lay in the offing. All depended on the political genius of Caesar Augustus—a promise he ably fulfilled.

## THE EMPIRE

The Roman Empire became official under Caesar Augustus in 29 B.C. and brought maritime order to the Mediterranean world for the first lengthy period in history, subsequently weakening under various strains but retaining its essential strategic character through the Emperor Justinian in the sixth century A.D. Indeed, its strengths which established the Golden Age of Rome in the first and second centuries A.D. also provided the ultimate sources of weakness and collapse. Politically and thus strategically, the power of the Caesar or Emperor rested on the army, which retained the task of policing the extensive frontiers from barbarian intrusion; in time, the importance of the frontier armies would enable them to subvert and eventually overthrow the central government. Socially and economically, the good life became a major goal of Roman society so that long trade routes developed over land and sea to and from Rome, replacing Italian agriculture altogether; in time, attacks on the trade lanes would thus cripple Rome. Culturally, the Hellenism and republican heritage of Rome led the Empire to continue former practices of free republicanism so that citizen soldiers and allied freedmen continued to man the oars on warships; in time, the heavy demands for troops and rowers would thus lead to serious manpower shortages. Spiritually, absolute Roman domination over the middle sea enabled the government to safely extend the glories of Caesar and the imperial city to all the peoples of the Mediterranean littoral; but in time such mobility also enabled the disciples of Jesus Christ—born about 6 B.C. (the dating error came centuries later)—to spread His teachings in absolute security until they conquered the Empire itself. Finally, Roman command of the sea enabled the navy to replace the polyremes entirely with lighter triremes and liburnians for purely anti-pirate work; in time, however, Rome would find itself unprepared to meet fresh concerted efforts upon the sea by barbarian peoples. Still, in all, the *Pax Romana* brought a peace of remarkable durability—and Augustus deserves the credit as its principal architect.

Augustus by his imperial strategy distinguished himself as the most thalassocratic of Roman leaders. Of middle-class origins, he did not suffer from the anti-mercantile biases of the former ruling landed aristocracy. Instead he meant to take advantage of the new peacetime to promote overseas commerce and to use Greek geographers and sailors to explore for new markets and sources of goods beyond the Mediterranean. Entertaining, for instance, the desire to conquer the Arabian trade routes, he sent a fleet into the Red Sea and replaced the Arabs at Aden to dominate the vast Oriental trade of the Indian Ocean. A sagacious administrator, like Alexander before him, Augustus dispatched an army into the Germanies to stabilize that vital frontier, made peace with Parthia in the East and established a permanent standing navy to police imperial waters but patterned after the excellent Roman army organization from naval districts down to ships' crews.

Headquartered at Cape Misenum near Naples, the main Roman fleet of fifty triremes patrolled and ferried 10,000 legionnaires throughout the Tyrrhenian Sea and waters between Sicily and Egypt. Its commander, Prefect of the Misene Fleet, was a major officer in the Roman government. The second but smaller major fleet was based at Ravenna with 5000 troops to patrol the turbulent Adriatic region as far south as Crete and Cyprus. Detachments of these fleets helped the slowly emerging local provincial squadrons at several key strategic outposts: at Caesaria for Mauretania and the Western Mediterranean; at Seleucia for Syria and the Parthian frontier; and at Alexandria for Egypt and the Red Sea. The main fleets, manned and often commanded by freed professional Greek, Phoenician, Egyptian and Syrian sailors, drilled daily, their ships' hulls, sails and ropes camouflaged sea-green for surprise attacks. Two-banked liburnians comprised new river squadrons on the Danube and Rhine rivers and the coastal forces in the Black Sea and English Channel. Such superior organization made innovation unnecessary, and Augustus upon his death in A.D. 14 left the Roman Empire with a superior maritime order.

Though Rome entered upon a Golden Age triggered by this peaceful commerce and maritime-based cosmopolitanism, its cultural vitality— like its seafaring—remained largely derivative from the Greeks and centered on Hellenistic Alexandria, the geographical crossroad between the Mediterranean and Oriental worlds. Indeed, Egypt (and neighboring Cyrene) became the corn granary of the Empire, its interconnecting delta irrigation canals being restored by Augustus, especially the Suez canal connecting with Arsinoë on the Red Sea and another such channel completed a century later under the Emperor Trajan. Via the Red Sea came goods (especially spices) and ideas from India, China, Southeast Asia and East Africa—although alternate routes from thence to Alexandria, Antioch, Petra and Byzantium were overland roads and caravan routes, the Persian Gulf and the rivers Nile and Euphrates. Not only did Greek sailors discover the uses of the monsoons to trade directly with India, but from the opposite direction Indonesian outriggers voyaged to Madagascar, their wares finding indirect access to Alexandria and Rome. To such goods were added the raw materials of the Western Mediterranean and Atlantic and the manufactures of the Middle East, which spread westward.

Such a vast economic network, virtually uninterrupted until the early third century A.D., encouraged new learning as represented by the philosopher Seneca, the historians Strabo, Tacitus, and Arrian, the rhetorician Quintilian, the physician Galen and the scientific compiler Pliny the Elder. Other active minds took advantage of maritime security to travel widely, to learn and teach, among them St. Paul and the philosopher Plutarch. Alexandria, however, thanks to its central location and cosmopolitan population of Greeks, Egyptians and Jews, remained the focus of Roman intellectual vitality, especially in religion, philosophy and cosmology; witness the work of St. Mark, Philo, Plotinus, Clement, Origen and Claudius Ptolemy. Still, being a despotism, the Roman Empire could never boast the free intellectual vitality of a true thalassocracy. Its emperors could never permit that, as Jews, Christians and secular philosophers learned at their peril.

During the first century A.D. the successors of Augustus pushed the borders of the Empire to their greatest extent, several of them showing a particular appreciation for maritime and naval matters. Tiberius (ruled 14–37 A.D.) had the Ravennate Fleet suppress a Cilician pirate outbreak in 36 but found the military Praetorian Guard a threat to his authority. As a result of the latter problem, Claudius I (41–54) built up the navy as a counterbalance against the Guard; he expanded the port facilities of Ostia, put down the last Cilician pirates in 52, pushed farther along the Arabian coast, conquered Britain and established a squadron at Gesoriacum (modern Boulogne) to protect English Channel trade. Nero (54–68) continued Claudius' naval politics against the army and the improvement of Ostia and other ports, fighting Parthia and extending imperial rule over the Black Sea, where he established a fleet of forty galleys. Vespasian (69–79) cut back on public works but finally suppressed the last Jewish opposition by taking Jerusalem in 70 and extending the Empire into the Caucasus. Trajan (98–117) completed Roman imperial expansion by conquering Mesopotamia, Assyria and Armenia and as part of his benevolent rule systematized sailing schedules, extended trade to India, and carried out a great program of harbor construction, enlarging Ostia and building new ports at Centumcellae (modern Civitavecchia) north of Rome and at Ancona on the east coast. The second-century emperors then took the defensive, merely trying to preserve the dominions and trade routes. Hadrian (117–138) used a Roman squadron on the Red Sea to control pirates and usher in an entire century of even greater trade with the East, with Greek captains sailing directly to India, Ceylon and even the Malay peninsula. The long reign of Antonius Pius (138–161) was exceptionally peaceful, but then under Marcus Aurelius (161–180) the warring on the frontiers increased.

The decline of the Roman Empire and the *pax* it enforced began during the third century A.D. due to interrelated internal and external factors. Political leadership in Rome deteriorated so badly that the Praetorian Guard and later the men of the thirty-three legions and ten naval squadrons appointed the Emperor. Brutal and tyrannical, several emperors for years had amused themselves with gladiatorial contests that included mock naval battles to the death on artificial lakes, not to mention their persecutions of Christians (the latter obtained their religious freedom in 313 and finally victory as the new state religion). Extravagant living, corrupt rule and expensive defensive requirements combined to weaken the economy, legions and naval squadrons alike as barbarians and pirates burst out and the new Sassanid Empire of Persia emerged about 226. Scythians, Goths and Borani operated on the Black Sea, and at mid-century several Gothic expeditions forced the Bosporus. One group with no fewer than 500 ships plundered Macedonia and Greece, captured Athens, Sparta and Corinth and penetrated the Adriatic before being repulsed by a Roman fleet. And while Cilicians and other sea rovers raided as far south as Crete, Cyprus and Rhodes, a band of marauding Franks departed Thrace and passed the entire length of the middle sea through the Strait of Gibraltar and home to France via the Atlantic. The Roman merchant marine declined everywhere, but especially trade with the East; there the new East African state of Ethiopia closed off the exits from the Red Sea, and the Sassanids began operating from Persian Gulf ports. Rome thus missed contacting the dynamic third-century Chinese kingdom of Wu centered at Nanking, which utilized the new floating compass to help develop a sophisticated maritime policy; contemporary with Wu was the fourth- and fifth-century Indian Gupta dynasty which built upon an overseas imperial strategy to explore, settle and trade with the lands around the Indian Ocean littoral. Instead of meeting these peoples, Rome withdrew inside the Mediterranean to halt the onslaughts of the barbarians.

By concentrating upon the major threats on the European and Persian land masses, the emperors of the fourth century delayed but could not halt the collapse of the *Pax Romana*. Diocletian (284–305) reorganized the Empire into two separate divisions, East and West, streamlined the legions and reshuffled the navy into smaller squadrons. Wars of succession followed Diocletian, notably the struggles between Constantine ("the Great") and Licinius. In 323 both mustered new fleets of the trireme variety to settle the issue near the Hellespont. Constantine's army drove Licinius' back from Adrianople to Byzantium in July. With his army aboard 2000 transports and escorted by 200 Greek triremes under his son Crispus, Constantine besieged Licinius at Byzantium. The latter's fleet of 350 triremes from Egypt, Phoenicia and Asia Minor engaged Crispus in the Hellespont for two days during July, only to be scattered by a strong wind which dashed 130 of its vessels against the shore. Licinius evacuated Byzantium, after which Constantine's army landed and crushed him. Constantine reunited the Empire under his singular rule, by 330 built a new capital city near the site of Byzantium which he named—appropriately—Constantinople, accepted Christianity and maintained his navy around the light trireme. The exposed city of

Rome declined in importance before the barbarian attacks, and the Empire's activities shifted eastward. In 363 the Emperor Julian invaded Sassanid Persia by moving down the east bank of the Euphrates supported by 50 war galleys and 1100 supply boats, burning them up, however, in favor of an overland campaign that accomplished little. The legendary Roman legion finally came to an end in 378 when the Gothic cavalry obliterated the army from Constantinople at Adrianople in 378. With Roman naval power and also maritime trade virtually liquidated, the Empire was formally divided into two parts in 395, the Eastern Empire centered at Constantinople and the Western at the fortified naval base of Ravenna on the Adriatic. The city of Rome remained only a symbol of authority until 410, when the Visigoths sacked it.

The barbarian tribes overran and replaced the Western Roman Empire during the fifth century A.D. The Vandals in Spain under King Gaiseric crossed into North Africa on ships provided by the dissident local Roman governor in 428, then marched overland to drive the last Romans from North Africa by taking Carthage in 439 and making it their capital. Building a fleet of pirate ships, Gaiseric and the Vandals conquered Sardinia, Corsica and the Balearics, landed in Sicily, raided as far east as Illyria and the Peloponnese, and in 455 sailed up the Tiber River to sack Rome. The Romans rallied the next year to drive the Vandals from Corsica and Sicily, only to lose a large force of vessels gathering in Spain for an expedition against Gaiseric in 460. The Eastern Empire then rallied to the side of the West for a massive overseas invasion of Carthage, but Gaiseric attacked and destroyed this combined fleet with fire ships and rams when only a few miles from its destination in 468. But Vandal depredations on the seas ceased after Gaiseric's death in 477. Meanwhile, the Visigoths occupied the Mediterranean coasts of Spain and France, and in 476 another tribe destroyed the Western Empire in Italy altogether. It was superseded by an Ostrogothic kingdom centered at the former Roman capital of Ravenna.

The Eastern Roman, or Byzantine, Empire profited from its Vandalic experience to create a new navy in the early sixth century, just in time to face multiple threats from the Visigoths, Slavs and Sassanid Persia. The Emperor Anastasius I (491–518) established naval yards at Constantinople, Alexandria and Tyre and began constructing a large fleet of over 200 single-banked dromons, each probably powered by some fifty oars and a single mast with the quadrilateral and triangular lateen sails, an invention already centuries old but henceforth widely used. While confronting the Persians on land, Anastasius in 508 sent a 200-galley force to raid the Ostrogothic Italian coast and eight years later added an inflammable precursor of Greek fire to his fleet which used it to repel a Slavic fleet of 200 vessels in the Black Sea. The small dromon and light transports of 120 to 200 tons' burden reflected the relative unavailability of manpower to the Eastern Romans, so that the ram was emphasized and only light troops employed on board chiefly for missile fire; for the same reason the armies rarely exceeded 16,000 men. The rival Vandals similarly had a small navy of only 120 galleys; the Persians confined their naval activities to anti-pirate operations in the Indian Ocean; and the Ostrogoths maintained only small warships.

⌐Into this precarious balance of power stepped the Byzantine Emperor Justinian (527–565) who set for his goal the monumental task of reuniting the Eastern and Western empires to revive the *Pax Romana*. Combining a strong Christian faith and secular learning with maritime strategic wisdom, Justinian indeed accomplished his task, with no small help from such brilliant generals as Belisarius and Narses. Luring the Vandalic fleet to Sardinia to suppress an uprising, Justinian in 533 sent Belisarius with an army of 15,000 men aboard 500 transports and escorted by 92 dromons to crush the Vandals in North Africa. To avoid a pitched naval battle with the dreaded Vandal fleet, Belisarius landed 150 miles south of Carthage, marched overland with the fleet on his right flank and took the city in September. When the superior Vandalic fleet returned in December, Belisarius defeated it and accepted the Vandalic capitulation in 534. To regain Italy, the next year Belisarius landed at Catana in Sicily, blockaded and captured Palermo (formerly Panormus), then the entire island from the Ostrogoths. Crossing the Strait of Messina, Belisarius and later Narses used their mobility at sea to capture Ravenna and supply their army for the long war in Italy against the Goths and allied Franks. Simultaneously the Empire frustrated a Persian attempt to dominate the Black Sea. Building a fleet of over 400 small boats, however, the Goths in 549–550 retook Tarentum, all of Sicily (except Messina), Sardinia and Corsica, and drove the Eastern Roman forces back into Ravenna, Ancona and two other coastal enclaves. During the summer of 551, the Romans rendezvoused a fleet of 50 dromons at Sena Gallica, seventeen miles northwest of Ancona, where the 47 Ostrogothic vessels which had been blockading Ancona attacked them. The well-handled Roman rams and missiles destroyed the Gothic squadron, lifted the blockade and reasserted command of the sea. Narses with 20,000 men advanced overland from Asia Minor, sealifted his army around the Gothic-Frankish military concentration in the Po Valley, and crossed Italy to take Rome in 552. Over the next two years he defeated the barbarians, while imperial forces retook Sicily, Sardinia and Corsica and established a foothold in southeastern Spain. The wars with the Goths and Persia dragged on till 562, when Justinian's forces conquered all Italy and made peace with Persia.

The reestablished *Pax Romana* of Justinian bore striking resemblances to the imperial order of Augustinian Rome but could never last against the full force of its many enemies. Justinian advanced the Christian faith with a massive church-building program, patronized literature and the arts, but most significantly codified Roman civil law. The rising merchant class of independent shipowners also required a maritime code, for which Justinian and his successors drew upon the precedent of ancient Rhodes to establish the Rhodian Sea-Law (or *Nomos Nautikos*). One of his laws forbade, on penalty of death, the giving of the knowledge of shipbuilding to the unskilled barbarians. With too small an army, Justinian could not penetrate far into interior regions except on the Persian frontier, so that the revived Empire was purely maritime—a system of coastal enclaves from Gibraltar to Alexandria to the Crimea linked by Byzantine Roman sea power. Local militias manned frontier fortifications and could be reinforced by seaborne regular army units. The Empire and a main fleet of some seventy dromons survived Justinian's death and attacks at sea by Slavs and Lombards late in the century. But by the beginning of the seventh century renewed attacks on virtually all fronts would bring an end to the last Roman Empire of the Mediterranean Sea.

For nearly 900 years, from the Roman naval mobilization of the First Punic War to the end of Justinian's naval supremacy, the *Pax Romana* had exerted its influence over the middle sea and even beyond. Non-thalassocratic and ultimately despotic, the Romans had depended upon their army to control the coastlines and fight infantry battles at sea and upon subject Italiots, Greeks and others to man their vast merchant and war fleets. Their feat—that of a non-maritime people capable of commanding the seas for nearly a millennium—must stand as a testimony of what a continental nation can do upon the seas, given simultaneously favorable historical variables of geography, organization and disunited competitors. In the aftermath of Roman maritime order ensued chaos upon the seas.

# 3
# Maritime Empires in the Middle Ages, A.D. 600–1415

*The profits from maritime commerce are very great. If properly managed they can amount to millions. Is it not better than taxing the people?*

—EMPEROR KAO-TSUNG (*c.* 1145)
Founder of the Chinese navy

## THE BYZANTINE AND ARAB EMPIRES

From the early seventh till the mid-eleventh centuries the Byzantine Empire of Eastern Christendom maintained a tenuous maritime supremacy against several rivals: declining Persia, the former barbarians now evolving into the Roman Catholic city-states of Latin Italy, the restless peoples of the Russias and the far north, but especially the dynamic Arab followers of Mohammed (believers known variously as Islam, Mohammedans, Saracens, Muslims, Moslems, Moors and Moros). The Byzantine navy developed three types of war galleys, the large three-masted dromon with marines for boarding actions at sea, and two-masted *pamphyloi* and *ousia* for ramming. About 670 Byzantium developed the napalm-like inflammable weapon known as "Greek fire," spewed forth from shipboard containers as a devastating missile weapon. The initially landlubbing Arabs preferred to decide naval engagements by the traditional land-battle-at-sea and thus carried more troops in hulls shaped like the body of a whale. Larger Arab crews stemmed from their adoption of the lateen fore-and-aft rig, which for zigzagging in spite of wind direction offered greater maneuverability, but required more handlers than the square sail. In time, the Mediterranean Christian peoples also adopted this sail-rig arrangement. Whereas Byzantium had enjoyed naval-maritime superiority for the *Pax Romana,*

Islam created its own rival empire thãt turned the Mediterranean into a battleground over this half-millennium.

Byzantine Emperor Heraclius (610–641) began his reign with a virtual naval monopoly over a relatively quiet middle sea but soon became engaged in continental struggles with Persia and northern barbarians and finally in a maritime confrontation with the Moslems. The Persians took Rhodes, besieged Constantinople and attempted to join up with the northern Avars in the 610s and early 620s, only to be repulsed and finally defeated by the Byzantines during a combined Persian-Avar descent on Constantinople in June 626. Persia made peace two years later, but almost immediately thereafter the followers of Mohammed (who died in 632) began to expand out of their Arabian homeland with raids against Byzantine and Persian outposts. Within fifteen years they conquered the Persian Empire, Byzantine Egypt, most of the Middle East and central North Africa. When they took Alexandria in 641, the Greek naval commanders escaped to continue their leadership over the Byzantine navy, although most Christian-Coptic Greeks remained in Egypt to be drafted into Moslem employ at sea. Damascus in Syria became the Arab capital after being taken from Byzantium in 636, and Arab control of the Persian Gulf exposed the Moslems to trade opportunities with the Far East. The first overseas raids by Arabs took place in the 630s from the Gulf against the Indus and India coasts, but against the explicit orders of the ruling caliph. Arab seafaring had been all but eliminated by the Greco-Roman and Ethiopian seafarers long before Mohammed, and an anti-maritime bias had ensued in the Arab world. But the new strategic and economic needs and opportunities quickly overcame all such apprehensions.

The first maritime confrontation between Byzantines and Moslem Arabs followed from the naval building programs of Emperor Constans II and the Omayyad Caliph Muawiya in the mid-seventh century. The Arabs responded to a brief Byzantine naval reoccupation of Alexandria in 645 by undertaking a naval construction program and raids by Muawiya, then governor of Syria, against Sicily, Rhodes and Cyprus in the early 650s. In 655, 200 Arab vessels from Egypt defeated over 700 Byzantine vessels off the Lycian coast near Phoenix in the "battle of the masts"; the Arabs won by joining their ships with a long chain to ward off attacks and using long hooks to tear down enemy riggings. Six years later Muawiya as caliph initiated new construction in Syria and bases at Damietta and Rosetta in the Nile delta, Alexandria beginning to lose its former importance. Constans II, after relieving a Slavic attack on Salonika in 658, streamlined his naval organization into districts and fleets known as *themes:* the largest of Cibyrrhaeots off southern Asia Minor (Anatolia), with others in the Aegean, at Syracuse and at Ravenna, with the imperial fleet at Constantinople. From Syracuse, his naval forces pacified much of the central Mediterranean before moving against Muawiya in 666. Constans died two years later, but his successor, Constantine IV, repulsed two Moslem attacks on the imperial city, on land in 669 and by sea after a five-year naval blockade which ended in 677 when the Byzantines introduced Greek fire to drive off the Moslem navy. The Byzantine pursuit and a severe storm finished the fleet of Muawiya, who made peace in 679, then died the next year.

Moslem maritime expansion under the Omayyad caliphate progressed almost unabated into the Far East and Western Mediterranean but could not stand against Byzantine naval power in the Eastern Mediterranean. Having reopened Trajan's Suez canal, the Arabs extended their maritime trade eastward to China where the stable T'ang dynasty (618–907) welcomed their ships. Increasing their piratic operations in the West, the Omayyads finally overcame Byzantine naval expeditions and local Berber tribesmen to capture Carthage in 698, establish Tunis and a new shipyard nearby from which they advanced into Spain. The Byzantine government meanwhile checked Slavic and Bulgar pressures on the frontier and in 698 defeated a revolt of the Cibyrrhaeot themal fleet. In 716 the Arabs launched a massive overland assault on Constantinople via Asia Minor supported by a huge fleet of perhaps 1800 vessels. Already Byzantine grain routes to Egypt had been lost and those to the Adriatic weakened, so that the Arabs blockaded the northern approaches to Constantinople from its Black Sea supply lanes. Then, after a difficult winter in the Sea of Marmara, in the spring and summer of 718 the Arabs were driven back by Emperor Leo III's flamethrowing dromons and a newly allied Bulgarian army. A plague and two storms left the Arabs with but 5 ships (!), causing their withdrawal. This reverse, plus the repulse by the Franks of the Moslem army in France at the battle of Tours in 732, blunted the Moslem offensive and undermined Omayyad authority. The two empires continued to raid one another at sea and to fight over the large islands of the Mediterranean, but the Byzantines won final command of the sea when their dromons destroyed an Arab fleet of 1000 vessels off the coast of Cyprus in 747. In 750 the Omayyads fell from power, and in 752 the naval skirmishing ended.

Curiously, the Byzantine Empire and new Abbasid caliphate now retreated from naval concerns. The Christian state had become so dependent on its army and mercenaries for continental defense that it allowed the navy to deteriorate and the merchant marine to be taken over by Italians, Armenians and even Arabs. But to strengthen its own foreign trade, Byzantium severed overseas trade between the Arab world and the western Franks and Lombards, causing trade routes to shift to Constantinople and Trebizond on the Black Sea via the inland waterways of the Volga, Tigris and Euphrates rivers. The fleet remained strong enough to enforce this mercantilistic policy, finally defeating a last Arab naval effort in the Sicilian Bay of Attalia about 790. The Abbasids had shifted the Arab capital from Damascus to Baghdad between the Tigris and Euphrates, Baghdad becoming a major commercial center between Constantinople, East Africa and the Far East. To protect merchant craft passing through the Persian Gulf and Indian Ocean, Arab naval expeditions from Basra and merchantmen armed with Greek fire battled the pirates of Bahrain, Qatar, Socotra and the Indian coasts. Relatively safe after passing Ceylon, Arab seafarers penetrated the Malacca Strait to the Gulf of Tonkin and the great entrepôts of Luqin (Hanoi) and Khanfu (Canton). The shift of Moslem wealth from the West to East also resulted from a new power struggle in Western Europe. Omayyad Spain held out against the Abbasids, the Franks led by Charlemagne sought to consolidate all Italy under his control, and several Italian city-states had taken to the seas in support of the Western Pope in Rome. All these events meant that by the end of the eighth century, when the Pope proclaimed Charlemagne as Holy Roman Emperor, Byzantines and Arabs alike had allowed their navies to diminish to nearly nothing.

The ninth century thus witnessed a three-cornered power struggle between Eastern and Western Christendom and a disintegrating Moslem world. With the aid of the navy of Venice, in 787 Charlemagne had conquered the Lombards in Italy and then turned against Omayyad Spain. To secure control of the Adriatic, however, in 802 Charlemagne began to construct 1000 vessels and with them attacked Venice. In 807–809 Byzantium rallied to the aid of Venice with fresh dromons, causing Charlemagne in 812 to recognize Byzantine control over the Eastern Mediterranean, buffered by Venetian command of the Adriatic. Meanwhile, new Moslem vessels had resumed raiding Christian commerce in 805, only to be checked in 813 when Charlemagne's galleys defeated the Spanish naval squadrons in a great battle off Majorca in the Balearics. General peace followed for another generation, but not internally: the Italian city-states of Venice, Naples, Amalfi and the papal domains retained their independence; Byzantium in the 820s had to crush a revolt of the themal fleets; and the Arab Moslem world separated into the emirates of Spain, Algeria, Tunisia-Libya and Egypt-Mesopotamia, which warred between each other.

But the Arabs agreed upon a general attack on Christian shipping, using their own form of Greek fire and defensive hide covers soaked in vinegar against such fire. Between 827, when Egyptian Moslems took Crete, and 858, when a Moslem fleet destroyed 100 of 300 Byzantine dromons off Syracuse, the Arab offensive went unchecked. From conquests in Sicily, southern Italy, Malta and Pantellaria, Moslem pirates plundered Christian sea lanes in the Tyrrhenian, Adriatic, Aegean and Eastern Mediterranean seas. Emperor Basil I of Byzantium; Venice and other Italians; and Charlemagne's successors counterattacked on land and sea against not only Arabs but other sea rovers, notably Slavs in the Adriatic and Vikings from far-away Scandinavia. Basil's growing imperial fleet resisted a siege of Constantinople by Kievan Russians in the Black Sea in 860 and spent the remainder of the century regaining control over the waters of the Aegean and southern Italy.

These expensive wars drained the power of Christians and Moslems alike, but did not discourage their religious warlike zeal. Arab commercial connections with the East declined after a rebel Chinese army sacked and closed Canton in 878, beginning the collapse of the T'ang dynasty and causing Arab merchants to shift to Indonesia. A concurrent slave rebellion in Mesopotamia fatally weakened the Abbasid state, but its maritime trade in the Mediterranean continued without serious interruption until late in the tenth century when the Fatimids of Egypt took power. The Spanish Omayyad Abd-ar-Rahman III fashioned a sophisticated maritime domain and navy over the same area encompassed by third-century B.C. Carthage, but even he could not arrest the disintegration of Arab power in the West.

Byzantium, in the midst of its naval warring with the Arabs, rallied behind its Emperor Romanus Lecapenus, a former admiral who rejuvenated the themal fleets and in 941 led his imperial fleet in the destruction of a 1000-vessel Kievan Rus fleet besieging Constantinople. His successors utilized their interior position to jockey fleets between the Aegean and Black seas to counter Moslems, Arabs, Russians, Vikings and Slavs. With 2000 dromons and 1300 horse and supply transports, Nicephorus Phocas in the 960s conquered Crete and Cilicia, but was checked at the Battle of the Straits by a Fatimid fleet in 965. John Zimisces during the next decade repelled an overland Russian attack on Constantinople, blockading and defeating it at the mouth of the Danube before shifting south to conquer Syria and reach Jerusalem by the time of his death in 976. Emperor Basil II, over a long reign of 967 to 1025, neglected the fleet in order to pursue army operations in Syria, the Balkans and southern Italy. But the Moslems, though they defeated the Byzantine fleet off Tyre in the 990s, similarly disdained the sea, in particular further piracy.

Byzantine-Arab maritime rivalry ended in stalemate during the eleventh century as both neglected their navies in favor of the armies and found themselves too weak to withstand new enemies. As the army of Byzantium relied ever more exclusively on mercenaries like Vikings (Varangians), so too did the Empire turn to alliances to protect its maritime activities. With warships from Adriatic Ragusa, the Byzantines defeated a Moslem fleet in that sea in 1032, and with the Viking ships of Harald Hardraade they drove back Moslem pirates everywhere during the decade. Greek fire from Byzantine imperial dromons repelled the last Kievan Russian attack on Constantinople in 1043, while themal forces briefly regained parts of Sicily and Italy. At mid-century, however, the Seljuk Turks burst out of Asia to overrun the Middle East as far as the Red Sea and the Bosporus, crushing the Byzantine army at Manzikert in 1071. Meanwhile, the Italian maritime cities of Venice, Pisa and Genoa between 1016 and 1077 drove the Arabs from Corsica, Sardinia and Sicily, and in 1087 destroyed the last vestiges of Arab sea power in Tunisia. The fortunes of Islam on land and sea now lay with the Turks as they converted to the faith. As for Christianity, exhausted Byzantium could no longer wage religious war alone but must depend on the full assistance of the West—the Italian city-states at sea and Crusading Europeans on land.

## VIKINGS AND OTHER NORTHMEN

The disintegration of Roman imperial authority over the English Channel early in the fifth century combined with new aggressive barbarian migrations in Northern Europe to create a maritime era dominated from the ninth till the mid-eleventh centuries by the Viking (or Varangian) "Northmen" (Norsemen, to Normandy as Normans). As in the Bronze Age Aegean (third millennium B.C.), the rowed vessel emerged as the only Northern water craft, with planking being added in the late Bronze Age (early first millennium B.C.). The Romans of Julius Caesar and Caesar Augustus (first centuries B.C. and A.D.) introduced the Mediterranean galley with its auxiliary sail, exploring as far north as the Jutland peninsula in the year 5 A.D. But the peoples of the North and Baltic seas did not adopt the sail until long after the Roman period because their chief interest lay in coasting rather than open sea voyages and because their light hulls—with flat bottoms rather than true keels—could not support mast and sail. Saxon pirates near Boulogne in the early fifth century helped overland barbarians force the Roman Channel squadron to fall back to the Somme River, then out of the Atlantic altogether, the Visigoths briefly manning a fleet on the Garonne River.

Relative peace and occasional commercial intercourse followed among the North Atlantic peoples, save for occasional Saxon and Scandinavian pirate raids, and in the seventh century the sail began to appear. With stronger-keeled, clinker-built, double-ended single-mast vessels steered by a stern oar and built to withstand the heavy Northern seas, the

Scandinavian peoples in the mid-eighth century began to develop primarily short, squat sail-powered merchant ships and longer, single-decked, single-sail rowed warships of at least twelve oars to a side. The latter evolved into the large, swift, maneuverable thirty- to sixty-oared dragon-headed longship (drekkar), the standard Viking warship by the year 1000, though techniques of ship construction had by then been borrowed and shared between Norwegians, Danes and English. All fighting at sea was thus centered on boarding tactics.

By the time the new sail-powered vessels began to appear in any numbers, Western and Northern Europeans had begun to coalesce into general distinctive political-economic units. Long and bloody internal tribal struggles in the North culminated early in the eighth century when the Danish-Swedish alliance dominated by the Dane Harald Wartooth ended at the great naval battle of Bravellir in the narrow Baltic waters between Zealand and Skane when Harald was killed. Then came the oceangoing dragon ships, and in 787 the Vikings raided the south coast of Anglo-Saxon England and later the adjacent French coast.

The continent of Western Europe simultaneously came under the unified Christian rule of the Frank Charlemagne. Already occupied on his borders with Omayyad Spain, Charlemagne looked to the east and north to check rival Bulgars, Avars and Saxons from the Adriatic to the Elbe. In the 790s, he inflicted a bloody defeat on the Saxons which gave him control over the Frisian coast, the base of the Jutland peninsula, and a foothold on the Baltic shore. Alarmed by this threat to North Sea maritime commerce and especially to his key commercial center at Hedeby, King Godfred of Denmark early in the ninth century concentrated his enlarged fleet at Sliesthorp, began construction of a massive wall (the Danevirke) across the base of the Jutland peninsula, and used his fleet to raid the Frisian coast. Charlemagne for his part revived the old Roman strategy of controlling the Strait of Dover and erecting coastal defenses. Simultaneous with his naval program in the Mediterranean, he built a fleet at Ghent at the mouth of the Scheldt which he stationed at Boulogne, and with ships and fortifications defended the entrances to the rivers Rhine, Scheldt, Meuse, Loire and Garonne. He kept his Northern fleet on the defensive during his Jutland campaigns, except in 806 when it operated in support of the army. The two kings thus fought to a stalemate until both died, Godfred in 810, Charlemagne four years later.

The successors to the Frankish and Danish thrones fought on, but could not break the general deadlock at the Jutland frontier. Louis the Pious, the son of Charlemagne who had mobilized the naval defenses of the Loire and Garonne regions, was checked in his advance into Jutland by the presence of the Danish fleet under Godfred's sons. But

Viking raids along the French coast were stopped in 820 by Louis' fleet. Shifting toward the British Isles, the Viking adventurers in the 830s invaded England, Scotland and Ireland to begin two centuries of erratic struggles in these areas. Their raids along the coast of the continent also resumed, particularly as Louis the Pious had allowed his fleet to decay, and attacks on Antwerp in 836 and Walcheren in 837 were climaxed by the death of Louis in 840, after which dynastic struggles seriously weakened the Empire.

The major Viking assault began in the 840s and lasted into the next century, with great fleets being employed, such as the 350 dragon-headed ships that eventually landed troops to sack London. Not only did the Vikings raid the coasts and invade the interiors of Britain, Ireland and France, but they even reached as far as the Mediterranean to participate in the wars between Moslems and Byzantines. Like the Arabs, the Vikings were not unified and often attacked each other, but the consequences of such engagements were trivial compared with those of their campaigns against common enemies.

In 845 the Dane Ragnar Ladbrok penetrated the Seine River with 120 ships to defeat a Frank army and exact tribute, the first of many such incursions. In order to invade the interiors with their sizable armies, advance bases were necessary, notably the Isle of Wight in the Channel. Such a basic military requirement also led to Vikings settling coastal areas such as Dublin in eastern Ireland and Normandy in northern France, settlements that became permanent with intermarriage and successful commercial activities. In addition to overseas operations, the Danes, Norse and Swedes sailed on inland waterways such as the Gulf of Finland and the rivers Dvina and Volga to affect Russian life, as well as pressing on to the Black Sea and the employ of Byzantium as mercenaries. By the end of the century, Viking warriors had conquered Frisia (most of modern Holland), ravaged France especially in the long riverborne siege of Paris in 885–886 which ended through the Franks paying tribute, and established a continental Russian empire around Novgorod and Kiev. Unopposed at sea, the Vikings built better ships, navigated skillfully on the open ocean (possibly with the aid of the magnetic compass), explored and settled overseas regions from Iceland to North America from 850 to 1000 and after.

Viking triumphs proved less painless in the British Isles, where they encountered the only navy to oppose them in their offensive. Of the several independent kingdoms in Britain, by the ninth century the strongest was Wessex along the Channel coast. Starting in 875 King Alfred ("the Great"), realizing the Vikings could best be checked at sea, began building large sixty-oared warships for this purpose. Ten years later his fleet defeated a Viking force, only to be similarly bested in the erratic struggles which engulfed these islands. After Alfred's death in 899, his son Edward improved the navy, consolidated his reign in England, and repelled the last Danish invasion of southern England. Edward and his son Athelstan created three permanent squadrons: the North Sea (based at Sandwich, where a large Danish raiding force was defeated in 939), the English Channel, and in the West. In addition, they conquered all Danish holdings in northern England and unified all Britain under one ruler by absorbing Scotland. England's successful defensive fleet also protected maritime commerce, as the newly unified state became the major overseas trading power in the North Sea of the tenth century.

Internally, the aggressive Viking peoples also warred for supremacy in Scandinavian waters. Norway, normally subject to Danish suzerainty, was virtually unified by a long and bloody war during the late ninth century by Harald Fairhair, who showed a keen awareness of naval strategy. He culminated a series of victories at sea against his rivals at the massive battle of Hafrsfjord about 885, then mobilized the coastal peoples of Norway to provide ships and crews for their own defense. Harald's enemies fled to the islands off Britain in the North Sea—the Orkneys, Shetlands and Hebrides—from which they could operate as pirates. Instead of waiting for their return to his coasts, Harald took the offensive with his fleet to ravage and occupy these places. By 911, at the peak of Harald's fifty-year reign, the Viking kingdoms of Norway, Denmark and Sweden had been stabilized, each enjoying its own sphere of influence, with Norway becoming the closest approximation to a maritime empire with its systematic naval defenses and forces. This being the case, Viking piracy fell off, and the general offensive stopped. Like the balances of power of the Mediterranean, however, internal rivalries and aggressive policies continued to fragment political relationships on the continent, in the British Isles and in Scandinavia. And, as in the middle sea, Northern struggles involved the spread of Christianity over the pagan Vikings.

Viking infighting focused on the new autonomy of Norway, which both Denmark and Sweden opposed. A new strongman in Denmark, Harald Bluetooth, learned the value of formal navies from the English and in the 960s attempted the conquest of Norway. His victory there was only temporary, and later, in 974, his naval power was reduced at the naval battle of Hjorunegvar, south of Nidaros (modern Trondheim). Harald resumed his raids on England in the 980s, which were later stepped up by his kinsman Olaf Tryggvason who also conquered and became king of Norway in 995. Harald's son and successor, Swein Forkbeard, however, contested Olaf's throne by allying with Sweden against Norway. Olaf in his large 200-man, 34-oared flagship, *Long Serpent,* sailed down the west coast of Norway in the summer of 1000, gathering a fleet of sixty warships and other auxiliary vessels to repel the allied Danish-Swedish fleet under Swein. The fleets engaged at Oresund Sound near Rügen, and when the battle turned against him, Olaf jumped overboard and drowned rather than face capture. The Danes and Swedes divided up Norway between them. Three years later Swein and his son Canute invaded England in a war that took ten years to complete; then their successors took many more years of internal squabbling with the English to consolidate their gains. Danish invasions of Ireland and Scotland failed, but both areas remained in turmoil. Similarly, France was weakened by overland German incursions; the Viking menace there had passed with the assimilation of the invaders into the Brittany dukedom of Normandy.

The rise of Viking Denmark under Swein continued under his successors, especially Canute II who ruled from 1018 to 1035. Norwegian pirate raids on Denmark persisted, while the Norwegians drove out the Swedes from their occupied territories. Norway and Sweden combined against Canute, however, in 1026, and felt the full force of his naval power. That year Canute's fleet defeated the Swedes at the battle of Stangeberg, and two years later repeated the feat at the battle of Helgeaa over an allied Swedish-Norwegian fleet. For the remainder of his reign, Canute conquered Norway and strengthened his control over England. With Sweden neutralized, Denmark now had complete command of the North and Baltic seas. Swein Forkbeard and Canute II had carefully fashioned a maritime empire under Danish control, whose trade lanes not only covered Northern waters, but reached westward to far-flung colonies in Iceland, Greenland and Newfoundland and southward to the Mediterranean, where Norseman Harald Hardraade led a Viking fleet in Byzantine service against the Arab pirates. The possibilities of the eventual evolution of this empire into a stable thalassocracy were, however, shattered soon after Canute's death in 1035.

The disintegration of the Danish Empire came quickly. Dynastic quarrels throughout the Northern areas weakened the fabric of the Empire, leaving strong leaders only in Duke William (later "the Conqueror") of Normandy, Harold of Wessex and then king of all England, and Harald Hardraade, who returned from the Mediterranean to reassert Norwegian independence. Renewed internal fighting within the Kingdom of Norway and Denmark featured a great naval battle off the east coast of Jutland late in 1044. This battle left the kingdom intact, but three years later Harald Hardraade seized the Norwegian throne and immediately attempted to conquer Denmark. The Danes so successfully held that

Harald gave up the attempt three years later. He then turned against England, which now became the focus of the three strongmen of the North.

England, whose House of Alfred had initiated the first national navy in the North, would belong to the power with the strongest navy. The English fleet—manned by the descendants of the Angles and Saxons—guarded the coast at Sandwich throughout the 1040s against not only a resurgent Norway but also against the newly arising peoples of Flanders on the continent opposite the vital Strait of Dover. When no threat materialized, the English government unwisely disbanded its expensive collection of longships at the end of the decade. Harald Hardraade, fully occupied at home, resumed his war to conquer Denmark and nearly succeeded by his crushing victory over the Danish fleet at the naval battle of Nisaa just north of Copenhagen in 1062. After taking over a small section of Sweden, Harald stepped up his raids on England, and then decided to take advantage of dynastic troubles there to conquer the island. But the Norman William had similar ideas, and both men prepared great fleets for their respective invasions. Early in 1066 the Anglo-Saxon Harold occupied the English throne and levied an emergency fleet which he had great difficulty maintaining at the Isle of Wight; England was about to pay the full price for neglecting her regular defensive fleets.

The fate of England was decided during the summer of 1066. Harold mobilized several armies, but his navy then dispersed, with only part of it going to London. Harald Hardraade thus had a clear path for his landing on northern English shores in September. Harold hastened north from London and defeated the invader at the battle of Stamford Bridge on September 25 in which his army killed Harald Hardraade. With the English forces, however, preoccupied, William of Normandy three days later utilized favorable winds to ferry his army across the English Channel unopposed, and he occupied the southern port of Hastings. Harold hurried south to face William, only to be defeated and killed at the Battle of Hastings on October 14. In less than one month, the political balance in Northern waters had been settled by the deaths of Harold and Harald Hardraade and the Norman conquest of England. The Normans thus occupied both sides of the English Channel and controlled the adjacent sea lanes, while their adventurers under Robert Guiscard had penetrated the Mediterranean to attempt the conquest of Sicily.

The success of William the Conqueror and the death of Harald Hardraade brought an abrupt end to the Viking expansion. The great dragon longships of sixty oars and up to 500 fighting men virtually disappeared; the colonies in America slowly withered away; Viking adventurers to the Mediterranean degenerated into mercenary soldiers of fortune; and the kingdoms of Denmark, Norway and Sweden withdrew into preoccupation with the affairs of the Baltic region. The Viking society had never been sufficiently stable to enjoy long-term imperial endurance, yet the Viking attack had generated monumental historical changes. Its dynamic peoples by their assimilation into foreign societies contributed importantly to the rise of Western Europe; the Norman and Kievan kingdoms provide but two outstanding examples. As part of this metamorphosis, Viking piracy evolved into peaceful trading practices, while the Viking threat had forced the potential victims to congregate for mutual defense. This dual need in turn led to two important consequences. First, the rise of commercial towns with their merchant guilds in northern Europe from about 1000 would prove essential in the evolution of the European economic community. Second, the Viking wars had led to the raising of national organized fleets, not only in Denmark, Norway and Sweden but also in the enemy England. Though difficult to sustain such levels, the system nevertheless initiated a development and tradition that would reach maturity under the nation-state system. Finally, the Christianizing of the individualistic Vikings drained their wild energies and helped them to be absorbed into the general European Crusade effort at the end of the century. Danish raids on England in 1074 and those by Norway for the ten years beginning in 1093 were but a sorry anticlimax to the dynamic Viking era.

## THE RELIGIOUS WARS

The assault of Islamic Mongols and Turks upon Europe and the Middle East accelerated the pace of the religious conflict between Christianity and Islam, gave cause for the Crusades, and thus indirectly affected power balances along the Atlantic seaboard. These struggles from the late eleventh to the early fifteenth centuries (*c.* 1071–1415) raged on land and sea and brought the Atlantic and Mediterranean worlds into ever closer contact. At sea, these contacts fostered a cross-fertilization of ideas and techniques in naval architecture, navigation, tactics and maritime law. Merchant ships continued to be "round" sailers in both seas, though Northern influences predominated after 1200 with the carvel-built "cog" and later "hulk," the latter multi-masted using the lateen rig, both with a "castle" at either end for defensive purposes; the Italians developed the "great galley" for cargo and passenger service under sail and/or oars. The major change for merchant ship and warship came in the adoption of the stern rudder, possibly introduced during the 1200s, and then promoted late in the century by the Venetian adventurer Marco Polo after he had seen it used on junks in China. "Long" war galleys grew larger and stronger in the Mediterranean, North and Baltic seas alike, all using lateen rigs and reverting to single banks of oars, up to five men to the oar, with some adding a second mast and "fore" and "after" castles.

Improved ship types were accompanied by other maritime innovations. Navigation improved after 1250 with the magnetized marine compass which enabled sailing directions to be recorded and charted in special books known as portulans. Simultaneously, rediscovered Greek mathematics and geometry enabled mariners to measure their mileage at sea, the sand-glass to calculate intervals of time, both thus enhancing the accuracy of the new charts. Tactically, the Italian city-states led. Their fleets engaged enemy vessels in straight lines-abreast or in crescent-shaped lines with wings forward or back to entrap a foe or spearhead an attack. Catapults and arrows thrust Greek fire, stones, quicklime, boiling oil in pots, liquid pitch and soap to make decks slippery, while rams aimed to disable enemy oars rather than pierce hulls. Boarding then followed.

Though the wars of these centuries had strong religious motives, growing national awareness, economic mercantilism and rediscovered Greco-Roman knowledge (the early Renaissance) combined to stimulate impressive systematization of maritime operations, particularly among the Italians. For example, the Italians streamlined their naval administration with the formal titles of admiral and captain—introduced by Genoa and Venice to represent squadron commanders, the admiral briefly being considered as chief of staff to the captain, who, however, by 1400 came to represent the commander of one ship. More importantly, international maritime law was codified simultaneously late in the eleventh century in Italy and the Atlantic, based upon the precedent of the Justinian Rhodian Sea-Law and actual needs for adjudicating maritime claims. Known formally as the Judgments of Oléron, for an admiralty court on this English island off the west coast of France, these legal codes accompanied Atlantic mariners to the Mediterranean and Baltic seas. In the Mediterranean, from 1075, these laws, improved upon in the Amalfitan Tables, were embraced by the Italian city-states, the Crusaders and Byzantium throughout the twelfth and thirteenth centuries. During the latter century, the Judgments of Oléron reached the North Sea coast of Germany and influenced the formulation of the Sea Laws of Wisby, the chief Swedish Baltic seaport on Gotland Island. England officially incorporated the Judgments of Oléron in 1403 and practiced them throughout the North Sea in its contacts with other trading peoples. Thus was maritime legal order eventually reasserted after centuries of chaos upon the seas following the demise of the *Pax Romana*.

Beginning in the late eleventh century, however, the westward advance of the Mongols and Seljuk Turks from the steppes of Asia hastened political fragmentation in Europe, most notably the decline of Byzantine authority and the emergence of the Italian city-states as the bulwark of Christendom on the seas. The Viking-Norman menace also played its part as Robert Guiscard and others—supported by the Roman Pope as champions of Western Christianity—from 1060 began driving the Byzantines from Sicily, Italy and the Adriatic with a 150-ship fleet, culminating in 1081 with open war on the Byzantine Empire. Simultaneously, the Seljuk Turks had advanced across Asia Minor to the Aegean and in 1080 began to construct warships. Hard-pressed from both sides, the Empire in 1082 turned to Venice for assistance in return for which Byzantium gave Venice extraordinary trade concessions, such as exemptions from tolls. This one act recognized Italian supremacy at sea and admitted to Byzantium's utter dependence on outside help thenceforth. The Venetian fleet, however, over the next three years defeated Robert's fleet off Durazzo (formerly Dyrrachium) and—reinforced by Emperor Alexius Comnenus' new fleet of larger dromons— retook Norman Corfu (formerly Corcyra) and engaged the Norman warships repeatedly until Robert's death in 1085 ended the war. Other Normans took Syracuse and Malta in 1090, while Norman Kings William I and II used a coastal fleet to preserve their rule over England from the last Scandinavian threat. Meanwhile, Emperor Alexius used his enlarged fleet in 1091 to drive the Turks back from their new Aegean coastline. But Byzantium needed more help than just Venice could provide, and Alexius appealed to Western Christendom for volunteers to augment his mercenaries. The chivalric knights and common folk of Europe thereupon rallied to the cross in the First Crusade (1095–1102).

As the religious and strategic goals of the Empire and Crusaders became the recovery of the Holy Land, Jerusalem and the adjacent Phoenician coast from the infidel Moslem Turk, the Christians had to gain control of the Eastern Mediterranean for the transportation and supply of their armies there. Since Alexius' navy had regained the Aegean Turkish coast, the only Moslem threat came from the land, and Pisan, Genoese and Venetian ships easily landed the Crusaders in Phoenicia, which they captured along with Jerusalem. But always maritime opportunists, the Italian city-states—including Norman Taranto (formerly Tarentum) under Bohemund along with Norman Amalfi—soon warred with each other to gain trade advantages with the new Crusader states in Phoenicia and Palestine. For example, Genoa helped Bohemund take Antioch in 1098 and then received the trade concession there, while Pisa the next year did the same at Jaffa, its squadrons plundering several Byzantine Ionian islands en route. Venice, jealous of Pisa's expansion, used a fleet of 200 galleys to destroy 50 Pisan ships at Rhodes and force Pisa to quit Jaffa and the Eastern

Mediterranean entirely. Bohemund and the Crusaders overlooked their religious motives by making war on the Byzantine Empire itself. In 1107, however, Byzantine dromons blockaded Bohemund in the Adriatic and forced him to terms, although the Empire did not recover Antioch until 1144. For the next two centuries, Christian Italy maintained the maritime communications of the Crusaders, since no real Turkish naval threat existed, but their constant warring with each other and Byzantium fatally weakened the latter and diverted Christian energies.

In the twelfth century the religious struggles continued and accentuated divisiveness not only in the Christian but the Moslem world. In Northern Europe, the Viking states withdrew to meet the overland and riverborne advance of the barbarian Wends (Slavs). From 1157 Denmark expanded by capturing the major Wend pirate base at Rügen, gaining control over the German and Polish coasts, and crushing a Pomeranian fleet at the Baltic naval battle of Strala (or Stralsund) in 1184. Farther south, the new Plantagenet dynasty extended English control over much of western France, using ships primarily as transports. Moslem Berber pirates operated around Gibraltar and their native western North Africa, still controlled by an Arab caliphate. The Turks conquered Egypt and eastern North Africa by land, all the way battling the Christians. And the Moslem world fragmented even more so.

The wealthy but divided Italians and their Norman neighbors also fought on. In 1135 the Pisan fleet sacked Norman Amalfi, while the new Sicilian kingdom of the Norman Roger from 1129 conquered Arab Tunisia and Christian Corfu in the Adriatic before being repulsed by a Venetian-Byzantine fleet in 1147–49 and by the Arabs thereafter. Growing Venetian power convinced Byzantium to take countermeasures in 1155 by extending its special trade privileges to Genoa and others, leading Venice to ally with the south Italian and Sicilian Normans against Byzantium in an indecisive war during the 1170s. These Normans in 1185 renewed the struggle by again taking the offensive against Byzantine outposts in the Adriatic. A Byzantine fleet defeated a Norman fleet at the battle of Demetritsa in Greek waters that very year but took six more years to regain its Adriatic frontier. But by then Byzantium had reached near-exhaustion, compounded by Bulgar pressures from the north and the capture of Cyprus and Acre in the south by Crusader forces in 1190–91. Whatever imperial pretenses Byzantium still entertained lay completely vulnerable to any concerted enemy effort, and that came from Venice.

In the course of transporting the Fourth Crusade to reconquer Jerusalem, which had fallen to the Turkish sultanate, and also to liberate Egypt, Venice did nothing less than capture Constantinople itself! All the French Crusaders could not meet the scheduled sailing date in June of 1202, so the ruling ninety-five-year-old doge (duke) of Venice, Enrico Dandolo, induced those on hand to help his fleet subdue the rebellious Dalmatian coastal city of Zara—accomplished in November. With 50 galleys and the troops in 300 transports, this force sailed eastward the following spring to try to take advantage of a palace uprising by putting a Venetian candidate on the Byzantine throne. With no imperial fleet left to oppose him, Dandolo in July 1203 led his Venetians into the Golden Horn waterway on the north side of the imperial city for a successful assault on the seawall. When the Byzantine government vacillated, and the landward attack by the Crusaders failed, Venice besieged Constantinople in March 1204 and a month later assaulted and took the city under a hail of incendiary missiles which caused a severe fire. The victors sacked the city, reduced its commercial rank behind that of Genoa and Pisa, put their own man on the throne and created a new Latin Empire which encompassed the Aegean coasts from Greece to Pergamum. Venice acquired the key western islands of the Aegean, including Negroponte (ancient Euboea), Crete and the Cyclades, and control over the major seaports along the western coast. Venice now enjoyed a commercial monopoly over the Byzantine Empire and Aegean throughout the early thirteenth century.

But on land the migrations and invasions by Turks and Mongols, most of whom eventually converted to Islam, threatened Western civilization throughout the thirteenth and fourteenth centuries. In the North a Slavic German attack ended Danish supremacy in the Baltic in 1227, just as the Crusading Teutonic Knights advanced into Russia from Riga and the Mongols (or Tartars) of the Golden Horde under Genghis Khan swept in from Asia. Sweden joined the Knights in an attempt to capture the leading Russian commercial city of Novgorod, only to be repulsed in two epic land battles on the Neva River and Lake Peipus in 1240–42 by Alexander ("Nevski") of that city. Alexander prudently accepted vassalage to the conquering Mongols, while the Knights turned away to overrun Prussia. The Mongols also pressed in upon the Black Sea and Turkish Empire, defeating its main army in 1243 and thus weakening Turkish authority in Anatolia (Asia Minor), for which the Christians of the Aegean could be grateful. Nevertheless, the Turks recovered under the Mamelukes in Egypt and Syria and the Ottomans in Bulgaria and Anatolia, from which coast they began to operate piratic corsairs against Christian shipping. Thus while Mongols and Turks consolidated Asia and the Middle East under their control, the maritime peoples held the seas, carrying on their own naval wars in three general arenas: the Eastern Mediterranean, the English Channel and the North-Baltic seas.

In the Mediterranean, Venetian and Genoese command of the seas hindered but could not check Turkish expansion, especially as the inter-city wars drained their energies. The Mamelukes of Egypt drove the Crusaders from the Holy Land, Acre being the last stronghold to fall—in 1291. The Ottomans of Anatolia managed to bypass Constantinople to conquer much of the Balkan region, while such skilled privateers as Umur Bey operating from the environs of Smyrna gained valuable ex-perience for the Turks at sea during the early fourteenth century. And, the Timurid Turks under Tamerlane conquered Persia and Mesopotamia later in the century—but beyond the reach of the sea. Throughout these years of Moslem unrest and land wars, Arab vessels monopolized the India trade, while Chinese junks did all the trading between the Far East and India. As long as the Italians controlled the middle sea, how-ever, the Turks could not expand beyond the Balkan interior.

In the Eastern Mediterranean, the Venetian monopoly broke under a concerted attack by Genoa in four maritime wars that commenced in 1253, with erratic participation by Pisa and several emerging new rivals—Milan, Florence, Padua and the Norman Anjou dynasty of Hungary, Naples and Sicily. In 1261 Genoa restored the Byzantine Emperor and trade with the imperial city, establishing a maritime em-pire over the eastern Aegean from Chios to the Black Sea. Venice recovered her trading position in naval victories over Genoese fleets in 1263 and 1266 but then had to share with Genoa and Pisa the Aegean trade. The Venetian-Genoese war of 1294–99 settled little, despite a great naval victory by 78 Genoese galleys over 98 Venetian ones—of which 84 were destroyed—at Curzola off the Dalmatian coast in Sep-tember 1298. The Genoese navy again won the final battle in the strug-gle of 1352–54; Hungary took Venetian Ragusa (modern Dubrovnik) four years later; and in 1378 Genoa—aided by inland Padua—challenged Venice for control of both the Aegean and Adriatic. Both sides traded naval victories in the Aegean, after which Admiral Pietro Doria used the Genoese fleet to capture Chiogga, fifteen miles south of Venice, in August 1379. Venice enlarged its navy under its victorious Admirals Vettor Pisani and Carlo Zeno, besieged Chiogga, destroyed a Genoese squadron off Cyprus and by June of 1380 had retaken Chiogga, destroyed the main Genoese fleet and killed Pietro Doria. Genoa recognized Vene-tian supremacy at sea in the peace of 1381, and Venice spent the next forty years consolidating her control over the maritime cities of the western Aegean and eastern Adriatic, including the Gulf of Corinth in 1407. Venice checked the overland ambitions of Milan, but such pre-occupations led Venice to pay tribute to Ottoman Turkey in 1411 in the western Aegean, an intolerable expediency for the restless mercan-tile Christians.

In the Western Mediterranean, the rise of Christian France, Spanish

Aragon and the Angevins of Naples and Sicily did much to weaken the western Italian city-states of Genoa and Pisa. In 1229 Aragon began to expand by conquering the Balearic Islands and going on to establish a naval base at Barcelona, a merchant fleet far superior to that of Angevin Naples and a navy under a superb admiral, Ruggiero di Lauria. When France sent one hundred galleys (manned by Pisans) to support Naples in an overland invasion of Italy, Lauria in the years 1283–85 defeated the Franco-Neapolitan fleets off Malta, in the Bay of Naples and in the night boarding battle of Las Hormigas near Barcelona. These victories plus a revolt in Sicily gave Aragon control of that island and the Tyrrhenian Sea and frustrated Franco-Angevin-Venetian designs to conquer Constantinople. The war dragged on, but dynastic quarrels led France to turn against Sicily, and Admiral Lauria to change sides. In July 1299 Lauria led the French fleet in the destruction of the Sicilian fleet in the battle of Cape Orlando near Messina. The erratic war ended in 1302, however, when Anjou recognized Sicilian independence. Genoa, enjoying a respite from its wars with Venice, in 1323 seized Corsica to restore a general balance of power in the West with Aragon, France, Sicily, Naples, Pisa and a growing Florence. For a short time, galley squadrons even operated on Lake Geneva in Switzerland. The balance shifted in the first decade of the fifteenth century when Florence conquered Pisa, and Aragon conquered Naples. The Spanish thus began to intervene actively in Italy, becoming ever more sensitive to the emerging strength of France.

In the English Channel, France had more immediate concerns with the continental ambitions of Norman England. The English, with their overseas trade in wheat, wine, wool and early manufactured goods to the Mediterranean and Baltic growing, also began to develop a sophisticated naval administrative and operational system. During the twelfth century, they sharpened these through expeditions to the Crusades and to assist the Portuguese in capturing Lisbon from the Moslems. And with the feudalistic struggles of the thirteenth century, the English sought to maintain control over the western regions of France and to protect communications in the Channel with armed private merchantmen, royal galleys built at Portsmouth and elsewhere, and ships provided by the independent but loyal Cinque Ports—Dover, Hastings, Hythe, Romney and Sandwich. In addition to withstanding a Norwegian naval thrust at Scotland in 1263, the English spent much of the century waging civil wars and beginning the centuries-long struggles to subdue Scotland and Ireland. However, the major antagonist became France, which sought to promote internal strife in England and thus to weaken the English holdings on the continent. Until the thirteenth century, English ships had sailed the Channel with relative impunity, but now France took to the sea, and the English kings had to look for naval defenses, emanating from the central key port of London. Throughout this century, therefore, while the French unimaginatively employed their vessels as transports and piratic cruisers in support of their army, the English began to appreciate the importance of commanding the sea by developing—ever so slowly—a rudimentary naval strategy and tactics. The Channel thus became an Anglo-French battleground and focus of a rivalry that lasted for seven centuries (1200–1900).

The maritime rivalry during the thirteenth and early fourteenth centuries resembled the erratic feudal struggles on land, drawing heavily upon allies, subject peoples and mercenaries as well as indigenous people, but settling very little in the long run. King Philip II Augustus of France drove the English back to the Channel and in 1213 used his fleet to transport an invasion army across the Channel. But King John appointed the Earl of Salisbury to command an English fleet that in June caught and destroyed the French armada—maybe 400 vessels of varying size—beached or anchored at Damme near Bruges. Civil war then broke out against John—as corrupt a ruler as the legend of Robin Hood and the Magna Carta of 1215 attest—but the people rallied behind John when Philip invaded and overran southern England in 1215–16. The French fleet, under the Flemish mercenary Eustace the Monk (formerly a pirate in English service), assisted reluctantly by the rebellious Cinque Ports, raided the English coast and shipping and blockaded the ports of Winchelsea and Dover.

After John died late in 1216, English baronial forces defeated the French the following May while an English sixteen-ship squadron under Hubert de Burgh sortied from Dover in August to intercept a larger French convoy bound for Louis' army from Calais under Eustace with reinforcements. Off Dover, the English maneuvered upwind of Eustace to rain arrows and blinding quicklime powder on the French before grappling and boarding. They killed Eustace, dispersed the convoy and caused Louis to make peace. In 1242–43 the French fleet checked the piratic activities of Cinque Ports ships, while English King Henry III carried out a strenuous blockade of La Rochelle from the offshore islands of Ré and Oléron, but storms prevented any decisive fleet action. In 1264–66 the English navy proved inadequate to quell maritime opponents during another civil struggle. But in 1293 a skillful seventy-four-ship English fleet defeated the French off Point St. Matthew and thwarted a French attempt to use a mercenary fleet to enforce a "continental blockade" of closing continental ports to English trade. The French failure was partly caused by the Dutch, who continued to trade with England, so that France occupied Flanders in 1300, and four years later a French fleet defeated the Dutch at the battle of Zierikzee. Desultory fighting followed between the Anglo-Dutch and French ships for the next three decades.

The so-called Hundred Years War (1338–1453) ensued over the English desire to maintain their continental territories and even conquer France. King Edward III built upon the naval foundations of his two namesake predecessors to employ three separate fleets in the Channel, North Sea and western England. King Philip VI transferred his galleys from the Mediterranean and added contingents from Genoa and Spanish Castile, arming many of his allied vessels with the first crude (but ineffective) artillery pieces to be employed at sea. But when the latter fleet tried to intercept Edward's fleet off Sluys, near Bruges, Edward slugged it out all day and night on June 24, 1340, in a classic infantry-battle-at-sea to win command of the Channel. With this command, Edward's army in 1346–47 landed at Normandy, crushed Philip's army at Crécy and blockaded, took and made a base of Calais. An alarmed Spanish Castile now dispatched a fleet to the aid of the French, only to have twenty-four of its vessels boarded and captured by the English fleet—led personally by Edward—at the Battle of Winchelsea on August 29, 1349.

Such overwhelming supremacy at sea caused the English to neglect their navy, and between the erratic warring and occasional truces on the continent France and Spain gradually restored their own navies. A Franco-Spanish fleet used sailing ships, galleys and fireboats to defeat the English in June 1372 off La Rochelle, which it then occupied. Old King Edward died in 1377, the year that Jean de Vienne—the French high admiral—initiated a naval offensive that burned several English coastal towns and six years later threatened to invade England. A general peace followed, during which the French fought the Moslems in the south and lost de Vienne in battle. Early in the new century, the war resumed, and in 1415–16 Henry V defeated the French army at Agincourt and drove a Franco-Genoese galley fleet from the Channel. The fighting continued for years thereafter, the French reviving under Joan of Arc and finally driving the English from all their continental territories except Calais. The settlement of 1453 was enforced after four more years of French naval raids against England's Channel coast.

The North and Baltic sea peoples increased their trading connections with England and France during these same centuries, all the while forming their general balance of maritime power around the Hanseatic League. This loose economic confederation embraced several maritime cities that combined during the fourteenth century to regulate Northern trade and defense against pirates, rival Denmark and the several continental powers that pushed to the seaboard of Northern Europe. Originally, the Hanseatic port towns included English London; Germanic

Lübeck, Brunswick, Cologne and Danzig; Flemish Bruges; Norwegian Bergen and Russian Novgorod. Eventually, however, over the next two centuries, some 150 cities joined the Hanse and together based their maritime code on the Sea Laws of Wisby, the Hanseatic capital.

Though constantly anxious about the inland and coastal expansionism of the continental Teutonic Knights, Poles, Lithuanians, Germans and Tartar-ruled Russians, the Hanseatic League concentrated its naval efforts against maritime Denmark. King Waldemar IV of Denmark took the offensive in the 1340s to enhance Danish wealth, check the growth of German power in the Baltic and humble Sweden. His long campaign culminated in 1361 with the seizure of the Hanse capital of Wisby and control over the strategic Sound, the vital straits through which all maritime trade must pass between the Baltic and North seas and now had to pay a toll. The Hanse retaliated by capturing the Danish capital of Copenhagen, only to be defeated in 1362 by Waldemar's fleet at the battle of Helsingborg. Five years later the League resumed the fight by retaking Copenhagen, Helsingborg and Skane and in 1370 dictated terms to Waldemar: free passage of Hanseatic shipping through the Sound and the Baltic in general. Now centered on Lübeck, the League flourished, but Denmark did not suffer, for in 1399 it absorbed Norway and Sweden into one great union under a new Danish queen. Nevertheless, the several maritime powers continued to skirmish throughout the next century.

By the early fifteenth century, therefore, the Christian maritime peoples had managed to withstand their own wars between each other but especially against the Mongol and Turkish hordes, while their less fortunate continental brethren gradually built up strength not only to stop but to push back the forces of Islam. The Turkish conquests had severed Western connections with the Orient, and the Mongols spread across Asia to bring it into the Mongol Empire. As in Europe, however, their expansion halted at the seacoast. Only by successful Chinese and Japanese resistance would the Far East be able to survive and then open its markets again to the West.

## THE FAR EAST

Maritime enterprise in the Orient developed erratically from region to region but never into any grand thalassocracy, nor did formal navies begin to appear as other than army transport forces until very late in the Middle Ages. Nevertheless, coastal-insular-riverine peoples from India to Japan took to the sea as readily as other primitive littoral peoples, with China making the greatest strides forward in Eastern nautical technology, especially from the second century A.D. Unlike the peoples of the West and Middle East, the Chinese depended on bamboo rather than wood and used it in their vessels to construct transverse bulkheads with the resultant watertight compartmentation, possibly for counter-flooding—some sixteen centuries ahead of Europe! This solid hull construction enabled the placing of multiple masts with their fore-and-aft sails, especially the lug- and sprit-sails derived probably from ancient Egypt and the Indonesians. The keelless flat-bottomed ancestors of the Chinese junk and sampan also utilized both the median rudder and crude compass from the second century, a full millennium ahead of Europe, and later put copper sheathing on their hulls. Such advanced sailing techniques mitigated against the appearance of the multi-oared galley in China (though crude rowing craft were used). By the time of the maritime-oriented Chinese kingdom of Wu in the fourth century the Chinese had firmed up the basic sailing characteristics of their ships, adding soon afterward (fifth century?) the treadmill-propelled paddle-wheel boat and finally navigation tables with the magnetic compass at sea (eleventh century). Such innovations obviously affected less advanced seafaring peoples contiguous to China and began to influence European naval architecture from the twelfth century as East-West contacts began —ever so haltingly—to be renewed. In naval tactics, using several types of warships, the Chinese preferred missilry over boarding or ramming and in the twelfth century placed trebuchet artillery on large multiple paddle-wheelers, armoring their hulls and exposed upper works with iron plates against enemy missiles.

China thus stands out among ancient and "medieval" Oriental peoples in its maritime expertise, though none of these peoples could be regarded as truly oceanic. During the first millennium B.C. Chinese warlords employed paddled inshore boats with deck-castles for archers in their erratic struggles against each other and also Korea, and early in the next milliennium Chinese seafarers began to reach and trade with Indochina and Malaya. But the Chinese, who might even have participated in several Asian transpacific voyages to the Americas over these centuries, remained basically content as a continental people, protecting their frontiers and coasts, meeting and perhaps borrowing from new peoples, but not pressing westward to contact "barbaric" Europeans and their inferior culture. The Japanese in dugout rowed boats conquered their islands by sea late in the millennium before Christ, pacified the aborigines there, and during the first half of the new millennium carried out several overseas expeditions to conquer parts of the Korean peninsula. Japan developed seagoing rowed-sailing craft and a local seafaring tradition, but confined its waterborne naval operations to internal control and struggles, like the 180 ships that crushed an aboriginal uprising on Honshu in the late 650s. The Japanese also contested the independence of Korea, as in the 660s when a Chinese-Korean force repelled a Japanese invasion fleet at the naval battle of Hakuson-ko and then unified Korea under Chinese suzerainty for nearly a millennium. Southeast Asia remained subject to such piratic peoples as the Chams of central Vietnam, until Chinese warships began to escort their merchant vessels thence. Also, several maritime kingdoms emerged around the South China Sea to protect shipping, notably Srivijaya on Malaya and Sumatra, the Khmers of Cambodia and the Mekong delta, Java and the Malays. The peoples of Ceylon and southern India (after the maritime Gupta dynasty of the fourth century) utilized the sea, but only as an adjunct to their continental kingdoms.

Then, between the tenth and thirteenth centuries, these several Oriental peoples prosecuted various wars upon the sea because of internal tensions, frontier difficulties and the advance of the Mongols. In Japan the long-standing rivalry between the feudalistic Minamoto and Taira warrior clans reached its climax in 1185 at the missilry-boarding naval battle of Dannoura at the western end of the Inland Sea where 100 Minamoto oar-driven junks destroyed the 500-boat Taira fleet. In Southeast Asia, the Champa kingdom of Vietnam built a fleet of small single-banked galleys with rams of ivory and copper-reinforced wood in the 1170s to sail up the Mekong River into the great Cambodian lake of Tonlé Sap to loot the capital city of the Khmer kingdom. The Khmers retaliated by constructing their own fleet along Champa lines, using it to ram and defeat the Cham fleet on the lake, and then driving down the Mekong to conquer and absorb Vietnam into their empire. The trade routes between China and India were dominated by the kingdom of Srivijaya, which conquered coastal Malaya in the sixth century to control the strategic Malacca Strait, expanded significantly from the late seventh century, and late in the tenth century conquered rival Java with the support of China. Strongly influenced by Indian culture from its maritime trade, Srivijaya also accepted Chinese, Arab and Jewish merchants to develop into a very cosmopolitan maritime state, or even thalassocracy, centered on the Sumatran port city of Palembang. The empire generally controlled shipping routes from a fairly decentralized system of fortified harbors, warding off pirate attacks and even occasional overseas plundering expeditions, as by the continental Indian Chola state throughout the eleventh century. The Cholas, incidentally, though not maritime, did develop a merchant guild of overseas traders and managed to occupy northern Ceylon during much of the latter century. But all of these peoples, especially China, felt the effect—directly or indirectly—of the Mongol migration.

Only China, under the Sung dynasty from 960, could hope to save East and Southeast Asia from the Mongols, and responded to overland pressures from Manchuria and Mongolia by withdrawing the army, river and coastal vessels back behind the Yangtze River and the coast as a new "great wall of China" and removing the capital from inland K'aifeng to coastal Hangchow in 1127. This splitting of China into a northern Mongol half and the "Southern Sung" caused Chinese population shifts southward and the replacement of now-closed overland trade routes with maritime activity. In 1131 the Sung created the first Chinese admiralty and regular navy, eleven inshore squadrons deployed along the Huai and Yangtze rivers to naval headquarters in the Chusan Islands at the mouth of the Yangtze where they helped the army check Mongol advances during that decade. From the largest naval base at Hangchow, the Sung also attacked Vietnamese Annam and Champa to strengthen the southern frontier. Relatively secure on all fronts, the Sung then turned to the sea, borrowing many navigational techniques from the Arabs, and built large sailing junks so roomy, solid and luxurious that they quickly outclassed their Arab competitors in the Indian Ocean. Warship construction during the twelfth century stressed innovation: the marine compass, cloth instead of bamboo mat sails, paddle-wheelers (stern and side), some iron-plating, gunpowder fragmentation bombs thrown by trebuchets, experimental galleys and rams, rockets, flaming arrows and flamethrowers. When the next Mongol attack came in 1161 the navy, reinforced by armed merchant junks for a fleet total of 338 ships, repulsed them on the Yangtze—probably the first use of explosives in battle—and off the coast near Shantung. Needless to say, this new preoccupation with the sea had an electric effect on the traditionally isolated Chinese society and helped insure peaceful commercial intercourse for nearly a century.

Then, early in the thirteenth century, the fresh Mongol hordes under first Genghis Khan and then Kublai Khan drove across China to the seacoast, hell-bent on nothing less than world conquest. In 1237, two years after the attack on the Chinese Sung, the latter added nine more squadrons to make twenty in all and managed to fight a long and dogged but fruitless defense for forty years. Surprisingly, the Mongols acted in China quite differently than they had in Russia and Europe by taking to the waters. In 1270 Kublai Khan began to impress captured Sung warships and officers and to absorb the entire Korean merchant fleet into his new navy. In 1274, 900 of these craft sealifted a Mongol invasion army to Japan, taking Iki and Tsushima islands before landing on Kyushu, southernmost of the Japanese home islands. The Japanese navy had declined to impotence under Minamoto leadership, but a violent storm intervened to destroy almost half of the Mongol fleet and persuade the rest to return to Korea. Shifting against the Sung, Kublai Khan's navy destroyed the Sung fleet and dynasty at the battle of Yai-shan off

Canton in 1279. He established a new Chinese dynasty, the Yuan, absorbed the defeated remnants of the Sung fleet, and ordered the immediate construction of 1500 ships.

Then, with a huge armada of over 3500 craft, Kublai Khan launched another amphibious invasion of Japan in 1281. When a makeshift collection of Japanese boats manned by fanatical crews delayed the Mongol assault, the Mongols lashed their ships together and used catapulted rocks and darts to eliminate this opposition. But the Japanese defenders on land frustrated several landing attempts, more raiders resumed their hit-and-run tactics at sea, and then a typhoon-force wind (*kamikaze,* "divine wind") obliterated all but 300 of the Mongol ships. These devastating losses to the Khan saved Japan, yet did not prevent him from authorizing more vessels for new overseas thrusts into Vietnam and Java between 1282 and 1293. But guerrilla opposition and the tropical heat discouraged the Mongols, who quit both regions after obtaining nominal suzerainty.

The Mongol Yuan dynasty of China barely survived the passing of the great Khan in 1306, for with him ended all pretensions of world conquest. All Southeast Asian kingdoms owed at least nominal allegiance to the Yuan government centered in North China, which maintained a prosperous coastal grain traffic until the 1330s. During that decade, isolated Japan erupted in an internal dynastic war that lasted over half a century and contributed to the rise of piracy as an honored profession within Japan. Attacks by well-organized Japanese fleets of between 50 and 200 vessels on the coasts of Korea, China, the Philippine Islands and Southeast Asia led the Chinese Yuan to divert much of its waterborne commerce to a renovated inland canal network. Neither could the Yuan control the restless southern province of Fukien which began to break away from the Mongol overlordship when in 1348 the salt merchant Fang Kuo-chen launched a naval campaign in the South to destroy Yuan sea power. Successful, he helped contribute to the overthrow of the Yuan by the Ming dynasty in 1368. The Ming then crushed Fang and consolidated its power over China during the remainder of the century, while the Chams sacked Vietnamese Hanoi in 1371 and tried to throw off Chinese domination of Indochina.

During the early fifteenth century the Chinese Ming—destined to rule for three centuries—built upon Sung and Yuan foundations to create the closest approximation to a maritime empire that China has ever known. Emperor Yung Lo, architect of this program, developed Nanking in the South as the Ming capital, with the main fleet of 400 warships based nearby and another 2500 lighter warships and patrol craft deployed at coastal and island stations to frustrate Japanese and Southeast Asian pirates. The merchant fleet of 3000 vessels, 400 grain freighters and 250 large treasure ships could support the regular navy, but found usual employment in an expanded trade into the littoral regions of the South China Sea. Yung Lo conquered Vietnam (as far south as Da Nang) in 1407 and continued to exact tribute from the several kingdoms from Champa to Malacca, the latter a pirate state founded in 1402 by a Javanese political refugee named Paramesvara.

In order to impress such distant lands with Chinese supremacy, Yung Lo in 1405 launched the first of seven overseas expeditions thence under the Moslem eunuch admiral Cheng Ho. The sixty-two especially constructed long-range junks of the first expedition each displaced possibly 500 tons, had four decks and watertight compartments, made six knots in good winds, and mounted batteries of four large cannon, twenty smaller guns, twenty rockets and ten bombs. During the first three voyages between 1405 and 1411 Cheng Ho used the port of Malacca, received the loyal tribute of Paramesvara and conquered uncooperative Palembang on Sumatra, whose maritime power had only recently been subverted by Chinese pirates. The fleet also rode the monsoon winds across the Indian Ocean to Calicut in India, subdued an unfriendly Ceylon, suppressed pirates and generally created imperial order throughout the sea lanes. Taking on the additional character of scientific explorations, subsequent voyages between 1413 and 1422 also visited (but not for tribute) the Maldive Islands, the Persian sultanate of Ormuz, Aden and several Arab coastal settlements in East Africa. The final expedition of 1431–33 returned there, cruising also up the Persian Gulf and the Red Sea as far as Mecca.

But the Chinese maritime effort could not last. Although the scientific and cultural contacts had enhanced Chinese learning and literature, and the trade had greatly benefited Chinese wealth, internal and continental priorities brought an abrupt end to the Chinese overseas enterprise. Politically, the Chinese continental landowning scholar-aristocracy both frowned upon the Emperor's debasing himself in matters of trade and feared his reliance upon eunuchs like Cheng Ho, so that immediately after Emperor Yung Lo's death in 1425 they moved to dismantle the imperial merchant and war fleets. Private traders continued to flourish with the help of the eunuchs, but without the imperial security provided by a navy their ships fell victim to pirates and finally court disfavor. The growth of Islam in the navy as in Southeast Asia—including Malaccan Paramesvara's conversion in 1404—contested Chinese Buddhism, and after the Chinese withdrawal the Moslem faith spread throughout Southeast Asia as far as the "Moros" in the Philippines.

Strategically, Ming concerns had to deal with the continental northern frontier, so that even Yung Lo had moved the capital north from

Nanking to Peking to face first Tamerlane and then the resurgent Mongols, for which army appropriations required full support. No threat existed from the South, and after the successful Vietnamese revolt in 1427 the emperors were content to accept the former's tribute as token loyalty to their supremacy there; independent Vietnam even conquered neighboring Champa later in the century without arousing Chinese concern. Japanese piracy still hurt, but in 1430 the Ming simply reduced trade with Japan to virtually nothing. This measure barely affected the Chinese economy, for in 1411 the all-weather Grand Canal had been completed, leading to the outright cancellation of the maritime coastal grain-transport service four years later. So no new construction followed, the skilled seamen found jobs ashore, and the navy fell into utter disrepair. And by the end of the century, the Ming government actually forbade the construction of large seagoing vessels.

Ironically, just as the only major Oriental attempt to take to the seas dissipated, Western Europe was beginning its oceanic age that would bring it into the very waters only recently commanded by the Ming junks of Cheng Ho. Chinese contributions to the art of navigation and naval architecture had been considerable, but henceforth would be of no import in halting the determined overseas thrusts of the Portuguese, Dutch, Spanish, English and French.

# BOOK THREE

## The Oceanic Age

*Whosoever commands the sea commands the trade; whosoever commands the trade of the world commands the riches of the world, and consequently the world itself.*

—SIR WALTER RALEIGH

The Iberian peninsula forms the apex of the rough triangle that is the larger European peninsula, by the late fifteenth century at the crossroads of the world. Whichever people could dominate the strategic Strait of Gibraltar stood to manipulate the gradually converging commerce of the several distant maritime peoples. Northward from the Strait to the English Channel, Portugal and Spain flourished, then a power center emerged in and about the Channel shared by the French, Dutch and English, and beyond lay the more remote Scandinavians, Russians and Hanseatic towns of the North and Baltic seas. Eastward from the Strait as far as Sicily, Spain extended its power over rival France and the western Italian towns; the Republic of Venice prevailed over the Adriatic and Aegean seas; while Ottoman Turkey stabilized the maritime frontiers around the Middle East from the Black to the Red seas. Southward from Gibraltar lay the coast of West Africa and beyond the long-isolated Indian Ocean and Far East, revealed to modern Western eyes by the Portuguese explorer Vasco da Gama who sailed around Africa to India in 1498. Jutting westward out into the Atlantic, Iberia also acted as the natural jumping-off place for an apparent direct shortcut to the Orient, but which in fact led in 1492 to the rediscovery of the Western Hemisphere by the Spanish-Genoese explorer Christopher Columbus. Each of these several maritime power centers remained areas of conflict from the early fifteenth to the early eighteenth centuries, but simultaneously the major maritime peoples extended their rivalries ever farther abroad in a flourishing oceanic age. The ultimate spoils were not merely local superiority, but command of the major sea lanes of the entire world.

The strategic forces that shaped the Oceanic Age between roughly 1415 and 1730 combined traditional with genuinely new factors to establish unprecedentedly powerful thalassocracies and maritime-active continental states. The lure of quick money, whether from general European commercial intercourse, Asian spices or American precious metals, remained a central motive as throughout history. But economic gain could not alone explain the dynamic character of the era, for other catalysts of change stimulated progress. The Renaissance, or rediscovery of the ancient Greek knowledge, was one, enlarged by the related impetus for new learning through long-distance overseas exploration. Religious zeal from the Middle Ages continued apace between Christians and Moslems, but also in the Christian destruction of "pagan" societies in the "New World" and the Western exploitation of Oriental Hindus and Buddhists. The religious struggles grew within the Christian world from 1517 when Martin Luther initiated the Protestant Reformation against the Roman Catholic Church. Yet the religious motive gradually declined in the face of the new nation-state governed by a king who claimed his authority from God; the nation converted the Western rivalries into secular political conflicts from the early seventeenth century. This mix of economic, religious, political and intellectual forces led to new empires governed by the same constant strategic factors as always. Venice, the Netherlands and England became successive full-fledged thalassocracies, imperial nations which enforced maritime order through their command of the sea and which were challenged principally by the continental empires of Ottoman Turkey, Spain and France and the smaller but powerful land-sea states of Portugal, Denmark and Sweden.

## SHIPS AND SEAFARING

This age of overseas exploration, conquest, colonization and economic exploitation became possible through major improvements in navigation and shipbuilding, initially from the academic studies centered at Sagres in Portugal under Prince Henry "the Navigator" from about 1418, also thereafter from mariners of several nations borrowing from each other and the Arabs to improve the art and science of seafaring. Navigation progressed rapidly in the late fifteenth and early sixteenth centuries with improved instruments such as the magnetic compass, the seaman's astrolabe, the sea-quadrant and the cross-staff to measure star altitudes and thus latitude at sea. The discoveries of the sixteenth century in mathematics—notably geometry and trigonometry—promoted sophisticated chart projections like Mercator's, star and sun position tables which found their way into nautical almanacs from the late seventeenth century, and ever more precise instruments such as the reflecting sextant and octant in the 1730s. But the problem of longitude could not be solved during this period, and crude dead reckoning had to suffice. Weather forecasting became possible with the invention of the barometer during the seventeenth century, but it did not go to sea until the early nineteenth century. As knowledge of the sea evolved from an art into a real science, maritime academies not unlike Henry's at Sagres gradually began to appear in the several seafaring countries to offer instruction in navigation.

The art of shipbuilding also became more scientific, particularly as Atlantic and Mediterranean modes of naval architecture mutually influenced one another. The galley continued to flourish in the calmer middle sea, with Venice rejecting the technological advances in the sailing ships of the Atlantic powers to cling to the short-range and gradually outclassed rowing craft. The Italian three-masted lateen-rigged great galley of the fifteenth and the galleass of the sixteenth century culminated the long centuries of evolving galley merchant and naval ships. The galleass was a large quinquereme of twenty-five oars to a single bank, five men to the oar, designed for ramming and boarding as always in the past, although the raised fore- and after-castles carried firearms. After the disappearance of Greek fire (for reasons unknown), primitive hand guns were used, and the introduction of improved cannon enabled their placement in the galleass. One heavy and four or more light cannon in the forecastle could lay down a crude barrage before ramming, while light broadside and stern guns fulfilled a defensive role. These large and several smaller galleys such as the galliot and felucca dominated Mediterranean naval warfare down to the end of the Oceanic Age. The English also experimented with similar sail-rowed great galleys (and smaller pinnaces and rowbarges) in the sixteenth century, notably one called the *Great Galley,* four masts, eight sails, 800 tons, up to 160 rowers on 120 oars and perhaps 207 guns, and the next century developed a sail-oar hybrid they designated frigate. Then, as the galley lost favor in England toward the end of the 1600s, a revival of galleys and hybrid rowed sailing ships took place in the Baltic. The galley's longevity can be attributed to its long success and peculiar advantages for maneuverability in relatively calm

waters. Also, continental powers could still utilize their superior manpower in infantry-battles-at-sea, so that galley fleets perpetuated line-
abreast and crescent-shaped tactical cruising formations to achieve that
type of battle. But when the powerful, well-gunned Atlantic sailing
battleships entered the Mediterranean and Baltic seas, the galleys
proved no match for them.

The coming of gunpowder and improved cannon had the most revolutionary effect on Atlantic warships. The naval gun could, however,
only begin to have a decisive impact on warfare at sea when adequate
amounts of bronze (copper and tin) and iron were available and when
sailing ship design provided a stable gun platform. The rounded sailing merchant ship evolved from the cog, hulk and nef of Northern
waters into the fifteenth-century carrack and more streamlined caravel:
three masts and square sails with lateen fore-and-after rigs borrowed
from the Mediterranean, capable of long-distance voyages of trade and
exploration. These latter could be armed, but were not suitable for
fleet actions, whereupon specialized warship construction developed
from the caravel model, but centered upon the new naval gun. The
Portuguese pioneered in the development of this all-sail "galleon"—
three- or four-masted but incorporating the castles and the long, low
prows and hulls of the galley. Though sluggish in heavy seas, the
sturdy galleon acted as a floating fortress mounting fifty to eighty very
heavy cannon first in the castles and then—after the Portuguese found
that guns in their low caravels could skim cannonballs across the
water—in broadsides. Finally, in 1501, a Frenchman cut portholes
in the hull along the main deck for the broadside guns. Atlantic warship construction then followed two general courses. The Portuguese
and Spanish relied on the ornately decorated large galleon with heavy
broadside batteries but tactically oriented to the 500 to 800 troops on
board for closing and boarding à la Mediterranean. The Dutch and
English diverged by developing a lower, sleeker and swifter galleon,
less ornate and with few troops on board, designed to make an average
speed of five knots and to engage enemy galleons at long range with
guns known as culverins and thus to prevent closing and boarding.
Though the Iberian peoples remained committed to strong Mediterranean
influences, the English, Dutch and French by the end of the seventeenth
century had been adopting and standardizing their own capital ships to
meet the needs of worldwide naval operations.

The success of such heavily armed sailing ships in battle depended
on their tactical deployment. Initially, this proved difficult, for fifteenth-
and sixteenth-century cannon were notoriously poor in range and accuracy and had to be anchored down with ropes to the deck for absorbing the six-foot recoil; a loose one- or two-ton gun on a pitching
deck could be literal murder for the fourteen-man gun crew. But by

the time these guns, fired once every three to ten minutes, could achieve a range of 3500 yards, in the seventeenth century, the firepower of a single broadside salvo became devastating. And with heavier guns came heavier ships, a distinct disadvantage for the Dutch, whose ships required shallow drafts in their inshore shoal waters. Since the guns could not be individually aimed, the captain of the ship had to use the winds to maneuver his great gun platform into position for an accurate volley. By the same token, an admiral had to align his several ships in column in order to bring their broadsides into play, so that the line-ahead became the standard sailing tactical formation, and the capital ship became known as the ship of the line. The difficulties of achieving any near-perfect alignment in a naval engagement caused naval tactics to be very conservative in this period, and thus the battles were decided largely by the volume of their fire rather than by any tactical ingenuity. But at least the ship of the line drove the armed merchantman from the battle line during the seventeenth century and called forth professional naval officers to lead in battle.

The officers and crews of the Oceanic Age initially reflected the feudalistic Middle Ages, thus cementing a separation that continued throughout and beyond these centuries. Wartime naval officers were by no means professionals, instead being landed nobility and/or army officers, merchant mariners and private adventurers. Nobility sent its first sons into the clergy or the army, even in maritime countries such as England, with second sons being spirited off to sea four or five years (age of thirteen) before their formal educations were completed. Officers at sea stood lower on the social scale, were laid off on half-pay or none at all during peacetime, and could reap riches only from prizes they captured in war. Small wonder, then, that they preferred the merchant service, life as pirates, or private voyages of exploration and the hoped-for riches of the New World or the East. Though such sources of the officer corps did not change, professionalism began to develop and with it formal naval education and the ranks of admiral, commodore, captain, lieutenant and ensign, the pioneers being the Venetians, Dutch and English, but always borrowing from the ancients, each other and other peoples. The dichotomy between officer and rating became especially feudal in the mid-fifteenth-century Mediterranean when first France and then the Italian city-states, facing skilled manpower shortages for their oars, turned to impressment of criminals and other dregs of society to work their galleys. These virtual slaves manned the galleys until the latter's demise in the eighteenth century. And yet, the social standard of the sailing crewman of the Atlantic ships could be regarded as little better, impressment eventually becoming necessary there also.

Manpower shortages followed the worsening condition of the lot of the average seaman, whose wretched life was the result of cramped and filthy living quarters, harsh discipline, disease, poor food, serious maiming from accidents or death in battle. A sailor in the first place could feel no loyalty to a ship whose officers had kidnapped (politely "impressed"; later: "shanghaied") him. Then, to insure fighting efficiency, discipline had to be maintained by the officers, the surest means being flogging with the cat-o'-nine-tails. To protect the captain and officers from the crew, soldiers known as marines were kept on board. Disease mounted with the appearance of the sailing warship for several reasons. Epidemic and endemic diseases in Europe reached the ships through careless recruitment. Lack of ventilation, except through the gunports, and crowded living spaces led to all manner of sickness, compounded by the dampness of the seas and of the ship's timbers which "sweated." Vermin such as rats and cockroaches infested the ships, and the few pleasures of occasional liquor and visiting women in port only fostered drunkenness and venereal diseases. In addition, the long voyages without fresh vegetables and fruits that furnished vitamin C led to severe cases of scurvy. Then, in the tropics, malaria and yellow fever ravaged the defenseless bodies of the Europeans. And in battle, since cannon shot could rarely penetrate the solid 24" oaken timbers of the hull, gunners aimed at rigging and personnel. Wounds from this carnage and injuries from so many accidents on board ship could not be treated, for doctors and surgeons simply did not go to sea.

Yet, through it all, the Europeans conquered the oceans of the world—but *only* the oceans—during the Oceanic Age. On land, progress was not as impressive. Building upon Swiss techniques of infantry tactics and the replacement of the longbow and the crossbow with the hand gun, the French army invaded Italy in 1494 to initiate over two centuries of continental strife that kept Europe in turmoil. Thus embroiled, the Western powers could not begin to defeat the Moslem Turks, whose domains were extended impressively, until they undertook the second siege of Vienna in 1683. And in the Far East, the maritime powers sought only to establish trading posts, being unwilling and unable to attempt overland conquest of the Indian, Chinese, Japanese and Southeast Asian land and population masses. Only in the Americas did conquest become a simple matter, after which this hemisphere became but another theater of the European wars. Despite the turmoil, however, the thalassocracies hammered out international law upon the sea, and the combined overseas thrust of all the maritime peoples acted as a major force in the advance of Western civilization into the modern era.

# 4
# Supremacy of the Spanish Empire, 1415–1600

*The first thing that is seen to disappear in a state which is disintegrating is the navy.*

—DAVELUY

## VENICE AND THE OTTOMAN EMPIRE

The Italian Renaissance of the fifteenth and early sixteenth centuries coincided and interacted with the emergence of the Venetian and Ottoman empires in the Mediterranean littoral. Strategically, Venice grew into a true thalassocracy, a commercial maritime empire whose republican government was controlled by a doge (duke) and a wholly mercantilistic patrician class. Landowners counted for little, unlike inland Florence which had to depend on naval mercenaries for its maritime activities. But both city-states formed the cultural focus for the high art and culture of Italy's Renaissance: the painters Bellini (father and two sons), Giorgione, Tintoretto, Titian and the visiting German Albrecht Dürer; the architect-sculptors Lamberti, Donatello, Sansovino, Ghiberti and especially Michelangelo; the mathematician Tartaglia, the political philosopher Machiavelli; and the greatest universal mind of them all, Leonardo da Vinci. Wealthy, arrogant and proud, thalassocratic Venice challenged Christian and Moslem competitors alike in establishing its *Pax Veneta* across much of the Eastern Mediterranean during the fifteenth century. Leaving the fate of the Western Mediterranean to Genoa and the Spanish, Venice extended its control over the Adriatic and around Greece into the Aegean, where it confronted Ottoman Turkey. Traditionally continental, the Turks simultaneously took to the sea in order to conquer the coastal waters of the Black, Red and Eastern Mediterranean seas, thereby checking Christian territorial expansion into the

**111**

East but also enhancing their own trade relations with the Christian West.

The Venetian Empire consciously tried to imitate ancient Rome, hired soldier mercenaries (*condottieri*) to extend its territorial holdings inland and policed the Adriatic against the pirate galleys of Turkey, Spain, Ragusa, Ancona, Segna, Fiume and Trieste. Beyond these measures, the imitation can only be regarded as superficial, for Venetian imperial policy was never systematized into any formal long-range plan. Religious scruples were minimized to the immediate advantages of profit, so that throughout the fifteenth century Venice conquered most of the mainland Po Valley in wars with Florence, Milan, Hungary and other Christian peoples, undermined Byzantine and Genoese power and promoted trade with the Moslems, even while fighting them. Beginning about 1380, Venice used diplomatic and military means to absorb many east coast lands and towns along the Adriatic and stationed a fleet at Corfu commanding the entrance to this sea via the Strait of Otranto. Additional expansion into the Morea (Peloponnese) brought Athens under Venetian protection by 1402, Lepanto and thus the Gulf of Corinth five years later, and Navarino in 1417. Simultaneously, the Venetians took over such key Aegean islands as Mykonos and Tinos and later (1451) Aegina and (1494) Naxos. But the Venetian Empire remained essentially commercial, absolutely commanding only the Adriatic Sea while constantly battling Ottoman Turkey for the Balkans and Aegean and finally arousing an overwhelming, continental and hostile Franco-Spanish coalition against it at the turn of the next century.

Meanwhile, the Ottoman Empire sought to consolidate its continental frontiers primarily with its armies, but also by utilizing a coastal defensive naval policy to check Venetian expansion as well as to eliminate the nuisance of Constantinople and to unify the Moslem world under its direct control. For the first half of the fifteenth century, the Turks generally avoided the sea as their armies overran Anatolia and pushed into the Balkans. They began to develop Gallipoli (taken in 1357) into a naval base at the entrance to the Dardanelles and added Smyrna in southwest Anatolia in 1402, also pressing overland to capture Valona on the Adriatic coast in 1414. But their coasts lay open to Christian galleys and seaborne expeditions, as when the Venetian fleet defeated the Turks off Gallipoli in 1416 and took Thessalonika in Macedonia in 1423. Turkish armies could take that port city by land attack seven years later, but the Christian naval command of the vital straits dividing Europe and Asia kept the main Ottoman armies separated and almost upset the Turkish repulse of the Christian armies during 1444. The only way for the Turks to control the Bosporus and Dardanelles was obviously to capture the ancient Byzantine imperial city of Constantinople, now completely dependent upon Italian maritime supply and defense for its survival. Therefore Sultan Mehmet "the Conqueror" built a large fleet of at least eighteen large galleys and several hundred smaller craft to join in the landward siege of Constantinople in 1453. The Turks took the city by assault on May 29 to end the last remnant of the Byzantine Empire, but most importantly giving them undisputed control of the Black Sea and a Greek community of seafarers that they wisely incorporated into the Ottoman imperial system. Mehmet made Constantinople his own imperial city, though the Empire remained fundamentally agricultural and continental, and created a regular Ottoman navy that could protect the Moslem coasts and even capture important coastal ports such as Piraeus in 1455.

Though neither Venice nor Turkey had desired or attempted the ultimate destruction of one another's political and commercial systems, their confrontation at sea led to a growing rivalry during the latter half of the fifteenth century. To be sure, merchants from both plied between their respective ports in East-West trade, and Venice often preferred to pay tribute to the Turks in certain areas in order to concentrate on other rivals, such as the Genoese in the eastern Aegean. But Mehmet looked to world conquest and needed first to dislodge the Italians from their coastal strongholds in the Black and Aegean seas. In 1460 the Ottomans conquered most of the Morea, in 1461 the Grand Vizier Mahmud Pasha led the fleet in the conquest of the Black Sea ports, and in 1462 he drove the Genoese from their Aegean possessions, culminating in a naval victory at Mytilene. Venice, though rejoicing in the demise of Genoa's maritime power, could not tolerate Ottoman expansion by land and sea at the expense of Venetian imperial security and thus declared war in 1463. Impressed by Venetian naval power, the Turks avoided a direct engagement and kept their fleet of 100 to 300 galleys in raiding operations or in direct support of army operations as when a land-sea blockade and assault led by Mahmud took Negroponte in 1470. For its part, Venice could not muster sufficient Christian forces on the ground to halt the Turkish overland advance to the Adriatic before peace was finally secured in 1479. But a cold war immediately followed. In 1480–82 Venice took the island of Zante and held on to Crete and Cyprus and coastal Modon and Koron in the Morea; the Turks seized several Ionian islands, a base near Cattaro and Otranto in the Adriatic, only to be repulsed by the Crusader Knights of St. John on Rhodes and lose their foothold at Otranto after Mehmet's death. Venice finally absorbed Cyprus in 1489, and the two empires settled into a precarious strategic stalemate in the Eastern Mediterranean.

Indeed, both Venice and Turkey had more immediate continental concerns that took priority over future conflict at sea. The Venetians had strengthened their overland expansion by allying with Florence in 1425, the war galleys of both working in unison during the continuing struggles against Milan. In 1439 Venice even transported a squadron overland and by river to contest and finally take inland Lake Garda from the Milanese squadron there. But Venetian expansion alarmed even her allies, and in 1452–54 Florence made war on her. And by the 1480s Venice was becoming involved in the affairs of the Western Mediterranean, where Genoa had begun to dominate the carrying trade of Spain (Columbus was Genoese) and where Spanish Aragon continued to rule Italian Naples. And Venice took the dangerous step of encouraging France to intervene in Italy against Spain just as the Turks were being repelled. When this maritime city-state promoted large continental participation in the affairs of Italy, it invited its own destruction. As for the Ottoman Empire, the Sultan Bayazid II during the 1480s and early 1490s stimulated Turkish naval expansion in order to make Holy War on all Christians throughout the Mediterranean and to overcome the rival Mameluk Moslems of Syria, Egypt and Arabia. He enlarged the galley fleet, recruited famous Aegean corsair captains like Burak Reis and Piri Reis into the navy, and encouraged privateering from Moslem North African ports. Finally, in the years 1499–1503, Venice and Turkey renewed their official warring, but it had far broader implications than ever before.

Henceforth, the Republic of Venice and the Ottoman Empire would trade and war with each other in the Eastern Mediterranean but only as one aspect of the larger political changes of the global Oceanic Age. For in 1494–95 France intervened in Italy as part of the general European power realignment and concurrent crusade against Islam, and in 1497–98 Portugal circumnavigated Africa to threaten the Mamelukes in the Indian Ocean and cause an upheaval within the Moslem world.

## MEDITERRANEAN STALEMATE

The emergence of Spain as prime defender of Christianity in the Western Mediterranean during the mid-fifteenth century served to weaken Italian intercourse with the Moslem Middle East and to divide the middle sea into two distinct and stalemated strategic and economic spheres by 1580. Initially, Spanish expansion emanated from the Catalans of Aragon whose merchant ships and pirates based at the great ports of Barcelona and later Valencia to establish maritime colonies in Sicily, Sardinia and the Balearics during the thirteenth and fourteenth centuries and then to conquer the Kingdom of Naples in 1455. The maritime and cosmopolitan Aragonese dominated the Western Mediterranean with their maritime law, the *Llibre del Consolat,* to frustrate the Moslems in North Africa and to encourage Italian trade through the Strait of Gibraltar with the North Atlantic peoples. But suddenly the continental and more medieval kingdom of Castile with its splendidly armored and armed infantry extended its authority over most of the Iberian peninsula, replacing the Aragonese in Sicily and Naples and in 1492 driving out the last Moors and pursuing them into North Africa. Not being maritime, Castile depended on Genoa to control much of its commerce and shipping and to utilize its excellent Atlantic ports of Seville and Cádiz. Spain unified formally with the marriage of Ferdinand and Isabella in 1469, the latter becoming queen of Castile in 1474, the former king of Aragon five years later. Both could support the Genoese Columbus and his successors on their transatlantic voyages, just as Portugal spent the fifteenth century pushing down the west coast of Africa, but both countries were too Catholic and medieval to allow the discovery of "new" worlds and peoples to stimulate any intellectual Renaissance in Iberia. Like the shipping, Renaissance thought belonged to the thalassocratic Italians. Spain focused its major energies in the Mediterranean against Islam and any European rivals which thwarted this effort. Conversely, Ottoman Turkey pushed its defensive perimeters as far into the central Mediterranean and Arabian seas as possible to strengthen its own continental empire and to stand off Spain and Portugal.

Within the Christian world, however, the common crusade against the infidel became obfuscated by the rivalries of the new nation-states of Western Europe and the maritime city-states of Italy. In particular, King Charles VIII of France's Valois dynasty aimed at thwarting the expansionism of the Habsburgs of Spain and Austria, who through dynastic marriages and diplomacy between 1496 and 1519 joined each other, Germany and the Netherlands into the loose political alliance of the Holy Roman Empire. So Charles initiated a half-century of nearly continuous warfare between Valois and Habsburg by invading Italy in 1494. Ostensibly, the French planned to conquer Naples as a prelude to an ultimate assault on Moslem Constantinople and the occupied Holy Land. Needing naval forces, however, France overrode a Spanish edict of 1489 against privateering in the Tyrrhenian Sea by collecting a fleet of privateers (including Spanish adventurers) at Toulon for the attack on Naples. The fleet of almost one hundred French galleys brushed aside Italian vessels off Rapallo in September 1494 and supported the relatively easy overland conquest of Naples the following February. Venice and Spain quickly rallied against this French incursion, with Spain asserting its command of the Tyrrhenian Sea by transporting an army to Italy under its brilliant general Hernandez Gonzalo de Cordoba. Cordoba and his Italian allies took three years to drive the French from

Naples, and in 1498 Charles died, ending the French "crusade." Not content with this situation, however, the several powers of Venice, France and even Ottoman Turkey sought to take advantage of apparent weaknesses of several Italian city-states with new coalitions and wars.

In 1499 France and Venice declared war on the strange coalition of Moslem Turkey and Christian Milan, Florence and Naples in an erratic struggle that lasted four years. Swift French success over the enemy Italian armies alarmed France's Venetian ally for its future security and led Venice to extend its own imperial rule farther inland. At sea, Admiral Antonio Grimani's fifty galleys met defeat at the hands of a Turkish fleet under Burak Reis at Porto Longo on August 12, 1499, after which the Turks retired to Navarino in Greece. The French and Venetians reinforced Grimani till his fleet numbered about 175 vessels, while the Turks enlarged their force to over 250. When Grimani failed to support the French ships during the ensuing naval battle of Modon (or Lepanto) on August 25 and retreated ignominiously, France quit the alliance. Spain then rallied to the side of Venice, and in 1500 their combined fleet captured the island of Cephalonia in western Greece and defeated Turkish squadrons in three separate skirmishes. But the Ottoman navy of Bayazid II succeeded in taking the Venetian coastal bases of Navarino, Durazzo, Lepanto, Modon and Koron and several Ionian islands over the next three years. Despite these losses, Venice's empire remained relatively intact, and she extended her overland holdings in Italy. France and Spain initially agreed to divide up Naples, but in 1502–03 the Spanish fleet occupied Taranto and ferried Cordoba's army to another successful conquest of Naples. These European interventions in Italy in the war of 1499–1503 had ended the political and commercial importance of Florence and Milan, leaving only Genoa and Venice powerful. Genoa had become intimately interdependent with Spain, but Venice continued her independent imperial expansion.

The European powers therefore created the massive League of Cambrai to reduce Venetian land power: Spain, France, the Holy Roman Empire of Austria and Germany and the Papal States. When Venice in 1508 refused passage of the Holy Roman Emperor to Rome to be crowned, and followed up with successful naval assaults on Trieste and Fiume, the League declared war on Venice. The advance of the allied armies in 1509 took several Venetian towns and forced the Venetians to scuttle their three galleys on Lake Garda. But the Valois and Habsburgs were strange bedfellows, and shrewd Venetian diplomacy soon divided them and undermined the coalition altogether. By 1516, when the war finally ended, Venice had lost Ravenna and several recent conquests such as Trieste and Fiume, but the great powers generally restored most of her Italian territories. Venice still controlled the Adriatic as a buffer against the Ottomans and used galleys to patrol the Po River and hinterland against possible future continental threats. And Venetian commerce continued throughout the Mediterranean. But Venetian imperialism had been forever checked, and as the Atlantic maritime powers opened up the New World and Indian Ocean with their sailing ships, Venetian galley-borne commerce began to decline in importance. And as Spanish power grew, Venice became merely a Christian buffer against the Islamic world.

But any stalemate between Christian and Moslem worlds would not be complete without a settlement along the North African coast, to which Spain and Portugal gave attention early in the sixteenth century. Moslem Arabs had controlled the Berber coasts of Morocco, Algeria and Tunisia for centuries, being blocked from their outlet into the Atlantic by the Portuguese descent on Ceuta, Morocco, in 1415 and down the African west coast thereafter. The Italian wars of the 1490s led Ferdinand to authorize the use of privateers in 1498, and these lost no time in operating singly or in squadrons against the Moslem Barbary coast as well as against European enemies. "Unofficial" Spanish and Portuguese expeditions captured Moslem pirate strongholds at Cazaza and Mers-el-Kebir in 1505 and Oran, Bougie, Algiers and Tripoli in 1509. The Iberians' success can be attributed largely to their superiority in firearms, especially since the Spanish commander in 1509 was Pedro Navarro, a pioneer in the early use of explosives. But there the Iberian assault ended, for in 1510–11 the Moslems repulsed an attack on the island of Djerba, south of Tunis, and then launched a seaborne counterattack. Its leaders were two Greek Moslem natives of Lesbos, the brothers Barbarossa ("red beard"), Aruj and Khizr, who had accumulated a small fleet and fortune as Tunisian pirates. Aruj Barbarossa failed to retake Bougie in 1514 and 1515, but led the Arabs in the reconquest of Algiers in 1516 and repulsed a Spanish relief expedition to its island fortress of Penon in the harbor the following year. He also took Tlemcen, west of Oran, but in 1518 was driven out and killed by the Spanish. Meanwhile, his pirate ships had been raiding Christian ports, and Captain Andrea Doria of Genoa had led a successful amphibious raid against Tunis. Spain elected to concentrate its efforts in Europe, Italy and America, and henceforth allowed the North African front to degenerate into a piratic cold war, strategically stalemated.

Moslem maritime assertiveness at both ends of the Mediterranean coincided with new responsibilities in the Black and Red Seas occasioned by European Christian pressures from the North and the Indian Ocean. To unify the Moslem world threatened from all sides, therefore, the Ottomans under Selim I ("the Grim") sought to unify the world of Islam into a coordinated defensive system, which meant absorbing the Algerian

Berbers and the Syrian Mamelukes into the general Ottoman Empire. The Mamelukes, having no sizable navy, could not check the Portuguese incursion from 1500 into the Indian trade routes and their threat to the Moslem Holy Cities of Mecca, Medina and Jerusalem and the Red Sea port of Jedda. Following Portuguese maritime successes over the Mamelukes in 1506–09, the Mamelukes turned increasingly to their Ottoman rivals for naval assistance. This help, plus the Turkish victory over Persia in 1514, encouraged the Ottomans to extend their authority over the Mameluke regions. So in 1516–17 the Turks sent a fleet down the Red Sea to absorb South Arabia, and their armies conquered Mameluke Syria and Egypt. Selim thus assumed direction over Moslem defenses against the Portuguese in the South, and in 1519 he did the same in the Western Mediterranean by accepting the proffered services of Khizr Barbarossa—now Khair ed-Din—to make Algeria into the Western Moslem buffer against the Christians. As governor-general of Ottoman Algeria and general of the sea in the West, Barbarossa strengthened the Western Moslem naval position, aided greatly by a storm which in 1519 wrecked a Christian punitive expedition to Algiers. By the time of Selim's death in 1520, the Ottoman Empire had reached the limits of its maritime expansion.

Under the new dynamic sultan, Suleiman the Magnificent, who ruled from 1520 to 1566, the Ottoman Empire concentrated its strategic endeavors on continental objectives in Europe, utilizing its substantial galley navy to preserve internal stability and the maritime frontiers. For instance, after a Syrian revolt in 1520–21 and the simultaneous decision to invade Eastern Europe, Suleiman decided upon the seizure of Rhodes from the Crusader Knights of St. John both to eliminate its presence so close to the rebellious Syrians and to protect Moslem lines of communication to Europe. The costly campaign of Rhodes in 1522–23 ended with the negotiated withdrawal of the Knights, who were subsequently relocated by the Holy Roman Emperor at Malta and Tripoli. Meanwhile, the Turks conquered Belgrade and pressed into Austria, leading to a strategic debate over priorities—in continental Europe or in the maritime East against Portugal. After quelling a revolt in Egypt in 1523–24, Grand Vizier Ibrahim Pasha joined Admirals Piri Reis and Salman Reis in arguing the maritime case. But Suleiman in 1525 decided against them, ruling that the tactically defensive Moslem fleets in the East be reduced in size and used only to protect the Moslem sea frontiers in the Red Sea and Persian Gulf. In this way, Mediterranean-oriented galleys could continue to operate comfortably and effectively within these inshore waters, and the Ottomans had no need to adopt the new sailing ships of Europe which plied the blue waters of the Indian Ocean. By the same token, Barbarossa pacified and consolidated Algiers and its borders and carried on galley corsair operations in the Western Mediterranean to secure the Western Moslem sea frontier against the Christians. And the Black Sea became an Ottoman lake. Suleiman could then concentrate his efforts on continental Europe, resumed in 1526 with his invasion of Hungary.

The Christian West had thus to face continuous Moslem dangers while it divided over the Valois-Habsburg dispute. In 1519 the Pope crowned the new Spanish king as Charles V, Holy Roman Emperor, which relocated the center of Habsburg power from Austria to Spain where it remained until Charles's death in 1556. To check the growing power of the Empire under Charles V, King Francis I of France resumed the wars in 1521, only to have his army crushed by the Spanish army at the battle of Pavia four years later. Genoese Admiral Andrea Doria ably served France until going over to Charles in 1528, for whom he occupied and then governed Genoa. Anxious to relieve the combined pressures of France and Turkey on the Empire, Charles decided to attack the Ottoman Empire, and in 1530—following Barbarossa's capture of the Spanish Penon fort in the harbor of Algiers—Charles sent Doria on a two-year campaign that captured Tunis and other North African coastal cities and Patras in the Greek Morea.

Suleiman responded in 1533 by appointing Barbarossa High Admiral of the Ottoman navy with orders to create a new fleet of galleys and galliots for a naval offensive against the Habsburgs. Supported by Valois France, in 1534 Barbarossa sortied from Constantinople for a devastating raid against the west coast of Italy and then wintered at Toulon in the vain hope of active French naval cooperation, while the Turkish Jewish pirate Sinan retook Tunis for the Ottoman Empire. Barbarossa's threat to Spanish Sicily induced Charles V to send an imperial fleet of some 500 Italian, Maltese (Knights of St. John) and Spanish galleys under Andrea Doria to capture Tunis in 1535. Whereupon Barbarossa bypassed Doria at Tunis to attack and utterly destroy the Spanish port city of Mahon on Minorca in the Balearics. Suleiman then allied formally with France and declared war on Venice in 1537, sending Barbarossa and the fleet into the Adriatic and Aegean. The Turks failed to take vital Corfu by land-sea siege, but did capture all minor Venetian islands in the Aegean and raided Crete before confronting Doria's fleet at the battle of Preveza near Actium in September 1538. Unwilling to engage decisively except under the most favorable conditions, Barbarossa and Doria only maneuvered and skirmished in an indecisive draw. Venice made peace in 1540, retaining only Cyprus and Crete in the Eastern Mediterranean.

The strategic stalemate in the middle sea continued as the Christians and Moslems consolidated their respective spheres of influence. The

Ottomans extended their western maritime frontier across North Africa under the naval command of another Greek Moslem, Torghoud (or Dragut), who succeeded Barbarossa upon the latter's death in 1546. Malta withstood an attack by the Turkish fleet under Torghoud and Sinan in 1541, but the Knights of St. John lost Tripoli. The Turks again supported France and the Pope against Spain—Sinan's 100 galleys actually anchored for supplies at Ostia in 1552—by raiding the coasts of southern Italy, Sicily and Corsica, and in 1559 Algerian corsairs even passed into the Atlantic to raid the Spanish and Portuguese coasts. The Ottomans retook Bougie and Djerba, losing the latter to Doria in 1560, then retaking it again. Their inshore squadrons continued to command the Black and Red Seas, with occasional forays from the Persian Gulf against the Portuguese in India; the trade routes north, however, were shut off by a Russian advance down the Volga River. The Christians in 1559 ended their Valois-Habsburg wars—which had spread into northwestern Europe—with the succession of Philip II to the throne of Spain but not of the Holy Roman Empire, that title returning to the Austrian branch of the Habsburgs. France dismantled its fleet in the middle sea, weakening its ties with the Ottomans and introverting for religious turmoils of its own.

Spain thus controlled the Western Mediterranean, save for North Africa, from 1560, but with ever less reliance on the Genoese. Admiral Doria died that year—five days shy of his ninety-second birthday!—and Genoa was turning much of its carrying trade over to foreign owners, while Adriatic Ragusa gradually took over the trade of the Tyrrhenian Sea and distant waters such as the Ottoman Black Sea. By then, Portuguese and other Atlantic shippers had quit the Mediterranean altogether after nearly a half-century of flourishing trade there, partly due to a world economic recession, and though Ragusans and Venetians replaced them, the middle sea had become divided into two distinctive cultural and strategic spheres—Christian Spanish and Islamic Turkish.

But the fighting resumed in the 1560s because of mutual religious hatred, especially Philip II's toward Islam. Anxious to eliminate the last Christian bastions in Moslem waters, the Turks unsuccessfully blockaded Spanish Oran (Algeria) and raided the Adriatic in 1563, losing Moorish Vélez Gomera the next year. This loss prompted them to attempt the capture of Malta from the Knights of St. John in 1565. In May they landed 30,000 troops from 140 galleys and other transports to besiege the harbor of Malta by land and sea, only to be persuaded to withdraw by the severe losses inflicted on them by the Knights. And during their retirement in September, the Turks received an additional battering from a Spanish relief squadron. Nevertheless, they finally recaptured Tunis in 1569. Shifting to the Aegean, the Turks took Chios without resistance in

1566 and four years later moved against Cyprus. This decision thus ended the thirty-year relative calm between Turkey and Venice, and it gave the Spanish cause to undermine Venice's power by intervening on her behalf. Following the Turkish landing on Cyprus in 1570, the new Spanish Captain-General of the Mediterranean, Don John of Austria, began to mobilize a fleet of some 180 galleys from Venice, the Pope and the Spanish cities of Italy. The several commanders' quarrels caused delays, though they did carry out several raids against Turkish ports in the Balkans. They avoided the nearly 250 Ottoman galleys, even as the Turks occupied Candia and the north coast of Crete during the spring of 1571. Raids and counterraids culminated in September as the reinforced Christian fleet of some 210 galleys rendezvoused at Messina, moving thence to Venetian Corfu, while the Ottoman fleet put in to Lepanto at the entrance to the Gulf of Corinth. As these two great fleets converged for what would be the last major naval battle between galleys in history, the Christians learned that the island of Cyprus had fallen to the Turks.

The Battle of Lepanto took place on October 7, 1571, over control of the Adriatic and Central Mediterranean waters. The two fleets bumped into each other almost by accident at the entrance of the Gulf of Patras. The Turks, about 225 galleys and 55 of the smaller galliots under Admiral Ali Pasha Monizindade, faced out of the Gulf in three connected divisions in line-abreast, although they had originally approached in crescent formation, wings forward. Don John's Christian fleet of 210 galleys was similarly aligned facing in on the Gulf, plus having a small reserve behind the center. The Christian left and Turkish right hugged the north shore to avoid being flanked; the centers remained tied to this main action, while the southern divisions maneuvered away seeking a flanking attack. The action around the shore and centers was a typical galley battle of missilry and boarding, but the Christians soon carried the day by judiciously committing their reserve. A particularly fierce descent by the Turkish left on the Christian center was checked by Don John's flagship and a counterthrust by the Italians on the right. When the battered Turks retired, they left behind all but 40 vessels of their force plus 30,000 (of 80,000) dead. The Christians lost but 12 galleys and some 9000 men (of 84,000).

Despite the great losses at Lepanto, the Ottoman Empire recovered quickly and spent the remainder of the decade rounding out its defensive maritime perimeter in the West. The lateness of the season prevented the Christians from following up their victory of 1571, and over the winter the Turks constructed a new fleet. No general battle resulted from much maneuvering in 1572, and Venice concluded a separate peace with Turkey the next year, giving up Cyprus but keeping Crete. That year Don John retook Tunis, then lost it and the fortress of La Goleta again in 1574. Spain still held Melilla, Oran and Mers-el-Kebir along the northwest African coast, while Ottoman imperial trade routes and territories east of Algiers remained intact. And there the stalemate rested. For the Spanish faced new enemies in the Atlantic, and the Ottomans resumed a costly war with Persia in 1577. So Spain and Turkey concluded a truce that year, although naval raids by Italian, Maltese and Moslem galleys continued. Ragusan and Venetian trade had begun to suffer as English merchantmen now returned to the middle sea and concluded a commercial agreement with the Turks in 1580. The Ottomans then closed out Ragusan shipping from the Black Sea and opened their ports first to English and then Dutch shippers. And with the demise of Genoese capitalism, Spain had no seafaring population with which to counter these new and bold businessmen from the North. With them came piratic adventurers, but still none more devastating than the Algerians, whose galleys had been the only ones among the Moslems to distinguish themselves at Lepanto. Algeria now resumed its semi-independent frontier status enjoyed in the early days of the Barbarossas, with Morocco as the buffer zone between Christian Spain and the Islamic Ottoman Empire.

The strategic stalemate of 1580 in the Mediterranean thus ended the era of religious rivalry of the Spanish and Italians against the Turks and reduced the middle sea to but one more theater of competition in the great struggles now engulfing Europe and the global waters being plied by its wide-ranging sailing ships.

## THE SPANISH AND PORTUGUESE
## OVERSEAS EMPIRES

Though the Iberian powers assigned their strategic priorities to Europe and the Mediterranean, the arrival of Columbus aboard the carrack *Santa Maria* in the Caribbean Sea in 1492 and of da Gama in the caravel *San Gabriel* at Calicut, southwest India, in 1498 committed Spain and Portugal inextricably to overseas imperial ventures. Spain had earlier begun to probe out into the Atlantic, but Portugal had pioneered Iberian oceanic expansion. Through the efforts of Prince Henry the Navigator, the internally united and Catholic Portuguese between 1419 and 1460— the year Henry died—explored along the West African coast to discover and settle Madeira, the Azores and the Cape Verde Islands, though the nearer Canaries remained disputed with Spain. With papal blessing, these early seafarers conquered the west coast of the dark continent, enslaving the "heathen" natives, placing slave trade to Europe on a permanent basis in 1441, and exploiting the land for gold. In the 1480s more explorers rounded Africa's Cape of Good Hope in search of Eastern spices and of the legendary Ethiopian Christian kingdom of Prester John, paving the way for da Gama's epic voyage. Though Portugal was by no means the military or political equal of Spain, the seafarers who carried the cross and trading purse from Lisbon and other Portuguese ports created so much maritime prestige that in 1492–94 the Pope saw fit to declare the unexplored regions of the world as divided equitably between Spain and Portugal.

Had no enemies existed elsewhere, the Iberians would have been able to exploit the riches of the New World and Orient with impunity. For the primitive Carib Indians and high American civilizations of the Aztecs in Mexico, Mayans of Guatemala and Incas of Peru could not stand up against the firepower of Spanish hand guns, while the Eastern Moslems and Indians could only protect certain coastal positions but not challenge well-gunned Portuguese galleons in the blue waters of the Indian Ocean. Indeed, the relative ease by which Spanish adventurers conquered their American lands convinced the crown to let these private entrepreneurs provide their own defenses with a minimum of governmental interference—or assistance. The Portuguese took a different course, with the crown closely directing its seafarers, but because of manpower shortages Portugal tried to minimize its defensive needs by creating coastal enclaves and not conquering inland.

Both imperial defensive philosophies generally worked against indigenous natives, but proved increasingly inadequate against new European privateering corsairs. The Protestant revolt of the early sixteenth century combined with growing European nationalism and jealousy of Iberian achievements, with the result that first the French and English, then the Dutch, preyed on Spanish and Portuguese colonial shipping and settlements. The Habsburg-Valois wars stimulated French animosity, but especially as the Protestant faith spread across the maritime provinces of western France and encouraged the Protestant Huguenot admirals to attack Spanish shipping from the late 1540s. Huguenot corsairs became particularly active during the French religious civil wars of the 1560s, the same decade that English corsairs mounted several major attacks against Spanish America. Finally, Dutch shippers at that time began to replace Genoese bottoms in the Spanish carrying trade at Seville, even as the Dutch revolted against Spanish political rule over the Netherlands from 1566. Portugal suffered less from European rivals, but quarrels with neighboring Spain led to the outright Spanish conquest of Portugal in 1580. By that year, Spain had reached its Mediterranean stalemate, just in time to face the Protestant onslaught throughout the world.

The Spanish overseas empire established its basic form and size within one generation. The first actual fleet to follow Columbus' voyages comprised thirty vessels which arrived in the West Indies in 1502, to be followed over the next twenty years by merchant ships which haphazardly carved out the empire. The Amerindian peoples succumbed swiftly to Spanish firepower, and, just as slavery had received papal justification for raids on pagan shores in Africa, so too did these unfortunates find their way into this wretched institution of the conquistadors. The remarkable thing about the origins of the Spanish maritime empire was that it was founded by a landlubbing, agricultural band of medieval aristocrats. From Seville, and secondarily Cádiz, they chartered merchant ships to reach the new base at Santo Domingo on Hispaniola, going thence to Jamaica in 1509, Cuba in 1511, and the Isthmus of Panama in 1513, seeing the Pacific Ocean for the first time and founding the city of Darien as a major competitor to Santo Domingo. In Panama, they built ships and coasted down the west coast of South America to Peru, where they arrived in 1527 to begin exploiting the gold and silver treasures and mines from the helpless Incas. The greatest feat of navigation during this initial period of discovery was the voyage of the Portuguese sailor Ferdinand Magellan, who in Spanish service left Spain with five ships in 1519, rounded South America and sailed west to the Philippines, where he was killed by natives. When his last surviving vessel, the *Victoria,* reached Spain via the Cape of Good Hope in 1522, it had circumnavigated the globe, the first ship to accomplish the feat.

The conquest of Mexico proved less easy. Natives drove off the first attempt in 1509, but Hernando Cortez tried again ten years later and needed naval power to accomplish it. With a dozen older vessels, probably small two-masted, thirty-oared brigantines, and carrying shipwrights and soldiers, Cortez landed near present-day Vera Cruz early in the spring of 1519 and discarded his vessels, though salvaging important parts. Penetrating inland, in November the expedition received the open welcome of the Aztecs under King Montezuma on their island city of Tenochtitlan in Lake Texcoco, connected to the mainland by causeways. Along with the insular nature of the city and its defenses, the Mexicans drew on hundreds upon hundreds of war canoes. Feeling trapped, Cortez then had four brigantines constructed by his shipwrights, each vessel mounting one bronze cannon. When he returned to the coast to absorb another expedition into his force, however, the natives burned the craft. Soon after Cortez' return to Tenochtitlan in June 1520, the Mexicans turned upon their leader, Montezuma, killing him, and drove the Spanish from the city. The night retreat was bloody and costly for Cortez' army of 1200 men plus native allies, which moved along the exposed causeway while being relentlessly assailed by missiles from the myriads of native war canoes.

Cortez now undertook the construction of thirteen brigantines and recouped his losses in preparation for the conquest of the Mexican Indian capital. Early in 1521 the army again moved inland, fighting as it went, while timbers were cut in a convenient forest and the various parts of the brigantines fashioned prior to transport overland for the rendezvous near the shores of Lake Texcoco. Launched there at the end of April 1521, this first inland fleet in America included about 900 men armed with crossbows, muskets, swords, pikes, three heavy iron and fifteen light bronze cannon; most were infantry, but horses were carried for 86 cavalrymen. A balanced galley force, it was designed for amphibious assault and combined land-sea siege operations. Since no European navy faced this fleet, the ships' captains could be soldiers like Cortez; as in the battles of Europe this force would operate in support of the army along the causeways and during the siege. This army would include some 600 troops from the ships plus a huge allied Indian force of at least 25,000 troops who had been subject peoples of the hated Aztecs.

The campaign began on May 31, 1521, and lasted until August 13. Augmented by a large number of allied Indian canoes, the brigantines that first day drove out under full sail and easily destroyed by fire and ramming (or more correctly, running down) the Aztec canoe fleet sent to oppose them. From then on, army and navy battled the Aztecs along the shore toward Tenochtitlan. By the end of the first week, the city was under naval blockade and siege. The Indian allies of Cortez, eager to destroy their former masters, soon brought their own canoe strength up to 16,000, creating probably the largest naval force of individual units in history. Slowly but ever so surely, the siege strangled the defenders into starvation, while smallpox ravaged the battered city. The final assault by land and sea on August 13 met the sally of fifty large enemy war canoes, easily overwhelmed by the brigantines. Capture of the Aztec commander quickly led to the surrender of Tenochtitlan. The Aztec resistance was broken, but Cortez needed several more years to pacify the countryside—keeping his brigantines to defend the new Mexico City—and organize the province of New Spain as part of the Spanish Empire.

The Spanish Empire of the Western Hemisphere, though beset by Indian revolts and civil strife among the conquistadors, especially those with Francisco Pizarro in Peru, filled the coffers of the Spanish-led Holy Roman Empire of Europe. Individual ships from Peru to Panama, Panama and Vera Cruz to Santo Domingo, and Santo Domingo to Seville carried the gold and silver to Iberia, making Spain indisputably the most powerful nation in the world by 1550—despite the frontier wars with the French and Turks. The borders of New Spain expanded to the Pacific coast and Central America, while Spanish adventurers extended south into Chile. Other explorers temporarily crossed the Rio Grande River, and still others drove French colonists from their one settlement in Florida. Spanish men flocked to the New World to seek their fortunes; women were initially excluded, so that intermarriage with native women soon created hybrid races. Missionaries carried the cross, but the government of Charles V endorsed the institution of slavery in order to have a work force to mine the riches and to build a few local ships.

The increase of European corsair attacks on the Spanish West Indies and Main (north coast of South America) from the 1520s required improved defensive measures, but especially from the 1540s when American shipping peaked during the richest discoveries of silver in Peru. These attacks, in peacetime and war, transcended international law just as the religious struggles of the Mediterranean did, especially as Spain in the late 1530s forbade foreign entry into American waters. The Spanish crown thus had to accept, reluctantly, the realization that local militias, inadequate fortifications and private armed patrols in the Caribbean were no substitute for regular, systematic transatlantic convoys, escorted by regular navy galleons and protected at the points of departure and arrival by permanent coastal patrols of galleys and small sailing warships. Such a system took several decades to evolve and in the face of perhaps 100 enemy corsairs operating yearly—70 off Spain and 30 in the Caribbean. Between 1535 and 1546, most of the attacks occurred off the Atlantic coast of Spain, and the colonists in America generally had to fend for themselves. But the arrival of many corsairs on plundering as well as smuggling ventures in the Caribbean during the 1550s caused the crown to experiment with countermeasures that became permanent after 1560. These came in the form of direct government regulation of Spanish America's maritime defenses, embodied in an annual escorted convoy sporadically from 1553 and permanently from the 1560s. The major tool became the escort for this convoy: the *Armada Real,* two to twelve galleons, created in 1568 and commanded by Pedro Menéndez de Avilés. Two plate (silver) convoys sailed annually, the spring voyage to the Antilles and Vera Cruz, the late summer expedition to Cartagena on the Spanish Main and Nombre de Dios at the Isthmus of Panama. Both wintered in the Caribbean, then rendezvoused at Havana the following March for the return voyage to Seville.

Expensive though the *Armada Real* was, it achieved for Philip II the desired effect of acting as a deterrent to corsair attacks on the plate fleets. To be sure, the *Real* could not stop corsair depredations of coastal settlements, especially as they intensified along the Spanish Main from the late 1560s. French, English and Dutch even began to cooperate in common cause against the Spanish imperial monopoly, sometimes in small squadrons of twelve ships or more off the Spanish coast and in the Caribbean. Such dangers could only be thwarted by largely ineffective galley patrols in both places, or by more successful Spanish and (from 1552) Portuguese galleons between the Iberian coast and the forward island base in the Azores. The Ottoman naval offensive of the 1560s also brought Turkish and Barbary corsairs in squadrons of six galliots or more into the Atlantic to join in the assault. Indeed, a Turkish corsair squadron entered the anchorage of Cádiz during the late summer of 1568 and burned three of Menéndez de Avilés' original twelve galleons preparing for the first sortie of the *Armada Real*. But the Moslem danger diminished as the Ottomans pulled back to their Central Mediterranean defense perimeter during the 1570s, and the *Armada Real* assumed its permanent escort role. Even following Menéndez' departure to lead an expedition against Holland in 1574 (when he died), the system continued with unqualified success for over two centuries. Stragglers from the convoy occasionally fell prey to corsairs, but the *Armada Real* was rarely intercepted by any formidable enemy force over the ensuing decades, the first time not coming until 1628.

Concurrent with the founding of Spain's empire in America, Portugal followed up da Gama's original voyage to India with a powerful naval and maritime enterprise that within one generation created an equally impressive empire. By sailing south and east, the Portuguese absorbed the lands and coastal waters bordering the South Atlantic and Indian oceans. Unlike the Spanish system which was generally developed by landlubbing private entrepreneurs under loose royal control, the Portuguese effort was entirely maritime and strictly directed by the government of King Manuel I, who ruled from 1495 to 1521. The royal government and overseas administrators of this small peninsular country established set trade routes from Lisbon to the Far East and bases at key coastal points and naval squadrons at crucial strategic waterways to protect shipping. And at the very outset, in 1500, the India-bound squadron of Pedro Alvares Cabral was blown off course to the coast of Brazil, which Cabral immediately claimed for Portugal. Similarly, the Portuguese extended their claims down the west coast of Africa at such places as Luanda in Angola and around the Cape to Mozambique on the east coast. Sea-based in every respect, the Portuguese Empire monopolized and commanded the seas to the Orient.

Portugal reached the height of its political and commercial power at the same time as Spain, though it never had any continental aspirations in Europe as did the Spanish. Short of manpower, Portugal had no interest in conquering large land masses around the world, preferring fortified coastal points that could dominate trade. What army Portugal had was needed at home, because of the ever-present threat of its aggressive and powerful Spanish neighbor; any outside help could come to Portugal only by sea, so that it nurtured a policy of friendship and alliance with

England, initiated by treaty as long before as 1385. Not desirous of antagonizing Spain, the Portuguese had followed the papal treaty of 1494 which divided the unexplored world between them, with Brazil actually inside the area assigned Portugal even though it meant competing somewhat with Spain in the New World. Jealous of Portugal, Spain sent Magellan to the East by sailing west in 1519, thus beginning a serious rivalry over the spice trade between the two powers in Southeast Asia. In the Indian Ocean, Portugal had to contend with divided native kingdoms in India and Indonesia, including the Malaccan kingdom, and fought the Mamelukes and then the Ottoman Turks of the Red Sea region. Unlike the primitive American natives, these peoples employed firearms, though less advanced ones than the Europeans.

The Portuguese penetration into the Indian Ocean met minimal opposition, because of the disorganized and relatively defenseless Arab seafaring monopoly. After da Gama, Cabral destroyed Arab shipping at Calicut and severely cannonaded the town itself in 1500, followed by a second destructive attack by da Gama in 1502. Responding to the latter event two Arab fleets of some 170 sailing dhows of varying sizes from the Red Sea and Indian Malabar coast challenged the Portuguese off Calicut. Da Gama had eighteen ships with longer-range artillery which, in the battle of Malabar, easily defeated the Moslem force. Portuguese arms thus demoralized the Asiatic peoples from formal resistance, and King Manuel then dispatched Alfonso de Albuquerque to organize the Indian Ocean trade.

With a keen strategic eye, Albuquerque quickly perceived that three strategic waterways held the key to the commerce of South Asia: the Strait of Bab el Mandeb commanding the outlet from the Red Sea at the Gulf of Aden; the Strait of Ormuz which dominated Persian Gulf traffic at the Muscat coast; and the Strait of Malacca, which connected all Western shipping routes with those of the South China Sea. By gaining control of the first two, Albuquerque realized he would eliminate Arab competition and dominate the coastal shipping of the region. By holding the third, he would effect the same result over Indonesian and Malayan traders. In both areas, Arabia and Malaysia, rival warships could be used against him only by concentrating at the narrow passages or as individual raiders. Since the strong monsoon winds often limited the time for sailing across the Indian Ocean and because Albuquerque had no large fleet to protect all these places equally, he decided to center the Portuguese Empire along the western Malabar coast of India which offered the ports (north to south) of Diu, Bombay, Goa, Calicut and Cochin. In strategic terms, this placed Portugal in the interior position, able to dispatch warships from the India ports east or west to blockade or attack enemy forces at any of the three key straits, where fortified bases would be established. With this grand strategic plan in mind, Albuquerque returned to Lisbon to recommend its implementation to the king.

At that moment, Francisco de Almeida arrived at Cochin as Viceroy of India and immediately set about realizing some of the goals Albuquerque had already outlined. Returning with orders to assume eventual authority in the East as Captain-General, Albuquerque in 1507 attacked, took and fortified Socotra Island at the Strait of Bab el Mandeb. With his six ships, he then proceeded to the port of Muscat with the object of mounting a similar attack on Ormuz. Ignored by Moslem authorities at Muscat, Albuquerque opened fire on the place and quickly forced its surrender. He fortified Muscat as a Portuguese base and in 1508 went on with his six vessels to Ormuz, where an Arab fleet of over 250 vessels awaited his approach. Audaciously, the Portuguese commander sailed straight into the harbor and demanded the surrender of Ormuz. Ignored again, he lowered away boats to board the three largest Arab craft. The daring of these intruders completely astonished and demoralized the Arabs, who abandoned their entire fleet and fled. Uncontrolled plunder and pillage by the invader ensued, followed by the surrender of Ormuz. A large Moslem fleet in the Persian Gulf never dared challenge him, but Albuquerque had insufficient strength to hold the place against them, so he sailed back to Socotra, promising to return to Ormuz.

Meanwhile, Almeida and his son Lorenzo consolidated the Portuguese strategic position in India by establishing bases on Ceylon and at Kilwa and Mombasa in East Africa and concluding a commercial treaty with Malacca in Southeast Asia. Almeida created a permanent naval squadron off the Malabar Indian coast, which Lorenzo led in destroying Arab trade in these waters. This rapid consolidation of Portuguese power in the Indian Ocean alarmed all local Moslem rulers sufficiently to combine against Portugal, and the Mameluke Sultan of Egypt constructed a modern galley fleet at Suez which he dispatched in the summer of 1508 to Diu, where it allied with the local fleet of Indian Gujarat for offensive operations. In the autumn, this combined fleet trapped Lorenzo and an eight-ship squadron at the entrance to the Chaul River south of Diu. But Lorenzo, typical of overseas Iberian adventurers, fought so ferociously that he held the Moslems at bay for three days, at the end of which Lorenzo went down with his flagship while two vessels of his force managed to escape. But his defense had been so impressive that the Moslems retired to Diu, gave up their campaign and never again challenged Western rule in the Indian Ocean with a major fleet.

At the moment, however, Almeida could not know the extent of his late son's achievement, and he bent all his energies to avenging his loss and to neutralizing the Moslem fleet at Diu. When Albuquerque arrived at Cochin in December 1508 to relieve Almeida, the latter threw him in jail and early in the new year took nineteen ships to engage the Moslem fleet. In February Almeida sailed directly into Diu, ignored the forts, boarded and took the undermanned warships there, burning all but four. The forts did nothing, and the King of Gujarat granted trade rights to Portugal at Diu. Almeida returned to Cochin, where a new squadron had arrived and forced him to hand over his command to Albuquerque. En route back to Portugal, Almeida died on board ship. But he had accomplished much in realizing the Portuguese strategy in South Asia.

Albuquerque quickly completed the imperial consolidation. After a rather needless and costly attack on restive Calicut, early in 1510 Albuquerque took the seaport of Goa, but then was trapped in the harbor by a native counterattack. He frustrated enemy attempts at bombardment and used fire ships and his ships' boats to raid the forts and galley sheds of the enemy. His force finally escaped in August, but the initial Portuguese prestige was slipping. So in November Albuquerque returned to Goa with twenty-three galleys, carracks and caravels, assaulted and captured the city. He made Goa the capital of Portuguese Asia, fortified it, and blockaded every other harbor in southwestern India with small naval patrols, so that all incoming Arab and Indonesian-Malaysian trade had to go to Goa. He further halted all seaborne trade to Egypt and the Red Sea, thus crippling Mameluke and Arab coastal trade. The Indian rulers quickly accepted the Portuguese commercial monopoly and allowed forts to be built at their harbors. The center of the Empire intact, more Portuguese trading fleets hastened to the East, and Albuquerque looked to his frontiers.

The potential threat of the Mameluke Red Sea fleet, now being strengthened under Ottoman direction, and the hostile treatment of Portuguese traders at Malacca required that Albuquerque strengthen his naval defenses on both flanks. In 1511 he took eighteen ships to Malaysia, seized and burned much Asian shipping at Sumatra and Malacca, then besieged the latter port, which fell after a devastating ten-day bombardment. He fortified Malacca, sent exploratory expeditions further into the East Indies, and left a naval force of ten ships permanently based at the Malacca Strait. But Albuquerque had less success in the Red Sea. Having abandoned his base at Socotra as unfavorable, in 1513 Albuquerque with twenty ships besieged, but failed to take, Aden. He sailed into the Red Sea to capture Kamaran Island and thus threatened the key Moslem port of Jedda, then withdrew, having choked off trade in this region by his long-range commercial blockade. In 1514–15 Albuquerque returned to Ormuz to complete the fortifications there, his squadron at Malacca defeated a Javanese fleet, and he died at the end of 1515 while returning to Portugal. Albuquerque had completed Portuguese imperial defenses and the commercial monopoly in South Asia, a system that lasted unchallenged by major European powers for another century.

But Albuquerque's successors, in holding these imperial positions and extending their trade for pepper and cloves farther eastward, had to contend with the southward extension of Ottoman maritime power by establishing a strategic frontier in the Arabian Sea. As the vanguard of the Ottoman conquest of the Mameluke domains of Egypt, Syria and Mesopotamia, the Ottoman captain Salman Reis pushed down the Red Sea at the head of the Mameluke fleet to occupy the coast of Yemen and unsuccessfully attack the Portuguese at Aden in 1516. Retiring to Jedda, Salman Reis the next year arranged his galleys inshore with supporting artillery on land to discourage an approaching Portuguese sailing squadron from giving battle against such a strong defensive position. Lacking the manpower of the Moslems, the Portuguese could not fight infantry battles on land or sea and so employed a shrewd diplomatic policy of aligning Ethiopia, Persia and south India against further Ottoman expansion. The Ottomans did conquer Egypt in 1517, however, and set about solidifying their frontier against Portugal by strengthening Zabid in Yemen inside Bab el Mandeb as the Portuguese did the same at nearby Aden outside the Strait. Salman Reis argued for an expanded Red Sea galley fleet to fight Portugal in the early 1520s, but Suleiman the Magnificent preferred to divert Ottoman energies northward into Europe and assigned a mere twenty-five vessels to base at Jedda and hold the Red Sea. Thus, as in the Mediterranean, the Turks and Portuguese established a strategic stalemate in the Arabian Sea.

The Portuguese trading monopoly to India and Southeast Asia remained generally intact throughout the sixteenth century, suffering only from occasional forays against their western frontier by Moslems and Indians. In 1538 the Turks captured Aden, but the Portuguese consolidated their control over the East African coast and the Malabar coast of India by occupying Diu in 1528 and Bombay six years later, repulsing a Turkish attack on Diu in 1538 and occupying adjacent Daman in 1559. The Indian and Ottoman Moslems allied against Portugal in the 1540s, but when the Turks built a fleet on the Persian Gulf and sent it against Muscat in 1546, the Portuguese repulsed it with severe losses. The great Ottoman admiral Piri Reis in 1551–52 used twenty-three galleys to sack Muscat, only to receive another bloody repulse, this time before Ormuz. The Indians mounted an overland attack on Goa and Chaul in 1571, but the Portuguese held. Though these frontier struggles taxed Portugal's defensive purse, they never seriously threatened the Iberian imperial monopoly in the western Indian Ocean.

In the Far East, the Portuguese spread their spice trade into the East Indies and up the Asian coast as far as Japan. They established their trade monopoly over Southeast Asia by occupying Amboina, Ternate and Tidore in the Molucca Islands, and for a time they ran afoul of Spanish competitors. But so preoccupied was Spain in Europe, the Mediterranean and America that in 1529 it renounced its earlier claim to the Moluccas, shifting instead to the Philippines as an extension of its American empire. Not until 1564 did Spain finally conquer the Philippines, operating from Cebu and after 1571 from Manila in opening trade routes eastward from China to New Spain and in trying to suppress the tireless Moslem Moro pirates of Mindanao. Malacca remained the strategic base of the Portuguese as they traded eastward, but they had to repel Indonesian naval attacks with fleet actions in 1518, 1538 and four times between 1572 and 1575. Strategic Portuguese difficulties lay in shifting their few busy warships between East and West, so that they lost Ternate to the local sultan in 1575 and five years later suffered their last attack from the Ottoman Turks who plundered Muscat. All that remained was strengthening the ports of Colombo and Trincomalee on Ceylon against local uprisings in the 1580s. On the whole, however, Albuquerque's imperial maritime strategic policy succeeded in protecting the Portuguese commercial monopoly.

## THE FAR EAST

The appearance in the Far East of Portuguese and Spanish armed traders awakened China and Japan to the new European forces of exploration, exploitation and religious conversion. China, not long removed from her own maritime period, sent her barely surviving coastal fleets into action after the initial Portuguese contact of 1517 and drove them away in 1521–22. The declining Ming dynasty, however, could no more prevent the coastal communities of Kwangtung and Fukien from smuggling with the Portuguese than it could check the seacoast raids by Mongol tribes during the 1540s and by Japanese pirates, who were strong enough to besiege Nanking in 1555. Portugal finally established a trading base on the Chinese coast by capturing the island of Macao in 1557. In addition, since the Ming forbade its countrymen to trade directly with Japan, Portugal soon monopolized the carrying trade between the two—Chinese silk and gold for Japanese silver. Portuguese trade to Japan was eventually limited to an annual carrack from Goa to Nagasaki (after 1570 via Macao). In 1572, Spanish Manila began its profitable role as intermediate base between bartered Chinese and Spanish goods from New Spain and Peru. After an attack by a large Chinese junk fleet on Manila in 1574, the Spanish created a defense fleet of 200 galleys manned by Chinese rowers. During the last decade of the sixteenth century, Portuguese and Spanish trade and profits with the Orient reached their peak.

Simultaneously, the Eastern balance of power underwent major strains. The Ming dynasty of China, weakened by the internal pressures of the rising Manchus, became the target of conquest by a newly unified Japan of the dictator Toyotomi Hideyoshi, who came to power through civil wars using mostly land forces. The Sino-Japanese battleground, as before and since, became Korea, the various provinces of which had developed considerable naval defenses against Japanese pirates because of the failure of the Ming to protect them. Hideyoshi, who outlawed Japanese piracy in 1587–88, two years before ordered the construction of 2000 ships—none with guns but many embodying European features—and failed to obtain the services of two well-armed Portuguese ships. In May 1592 Hideyoshi sealifted his army of 200,000 across the Straits of Tsushima to Pusan in 700 vessels, then advanced north to Seoul and Pyongyang where it was to receive supplies and reinforcements from Japan by sea and river. Hideyoshi had a large fleet, but he had failed to train its sailors for warfare at sea, believing the navy to be only a transport force. Meanwhile, the Koreans had been at work under the leadership of a brilliant admiral, Yi Sunsin, building a genuine secret weapon: the "tortoise ship," a galley with a small broadside battery, reinforced ram and (possibly iron-plated) turtle back deck covered with sharp spikes for discouraging the traditional tactic of boarding. With two of these craft and conventional wooden vessels of the Korean fleet—which enjoyed supremacy over the army—Yi in June and July sailed south through the Yellow Sea and using line-ahead tactics with rams and flaming arrows swept the poorly led Japanese fleet before him in several engagements. He proceeded to annihilate the Pyongyang-bound convoy with its twenty-five escorts and, lingering off the southwest coast of Korea, on August 14 he lured a Japanese fleet of several hundred transports and escorts into a trap in Hansan Strait in which he sank a great many and routed the rest. Having lost command of the sea and cut off from much-needed support, the Japanese army now reeled under a counterattack by the Chinese army and fell back toward Pusan. In October Yi attacked the Japanese anchorage there and inflicted heavy damage on the Japanese fleet, but failed to destroy it.

A stalemate and negotiations followed the Japanese evacuation of Korea in 1593 while Hideyoshi—back in Japan throughout these campaigns—prepared a second offensive. In Korea, the political opponents of Yi secured his replacement, and the Chinese army withdrew. The Korean navy fell into disrepair and was easily defeated twice by the new Japanese invasion armada in the summer of 1597. But the Chinese had begun pouring troops back into Korea so that they checked the Japanese advance deep into southern Korea. Moreover, Yi Sunsin returned to command the shattered Korean fleet, which had lost its tortoise ships (probably by shipwreck), and late in the year he defeated a Japanese squadron near Chindo Island. The Japanese again fell back to their defensive perimeter around Pusan. The main Japanese fleet was held in support of the army, though vastly superior to that of the Koreans, which, however, was now reinforced by a revitalized Chinese fleet. The new stalemate ended early in 1598 with Hideyoshi's death and his successor's decision to quit Korea. Admiral Yi determined to disrupt the withdrawal, and in December he led his fleet against the 400 vessels of Japan for the last time. The hard-fought Battle of Chinhae Bay cost Yi Sunsin his life and many ships on both sides, hurting Japan severely and bringing an end to its first invasion of Asia, which had never even reached the real objective, China. Japan and China now returned to domestic concerns, not the least of which was profiting from trade with the West.

Though China and Japan (and Korea) had relearned the efficacy of naval power, they remained generally continental states concerned with defensive postures and relying upon their armies. They subordinated their navies therefore to the generals and sought to minimize exploitation by the Western traders. Both Portugal and Spain enjoyed tenuous economic contacts with these great Oriental powers, but their future dealings would be largely affected by the intrusion of European rivals, notably the Dutch, into the Eastern trade lanes. Thus, aside from the general growing isolation of China and Japan from European exploitation, the Far East became but another maritime battleground of the European Oceanic Age.

## THE PROTESTANT CHALLENGE: THE ARMADA

Just as the Iberian powers reawakened the Christian cause in the Mediterranean, opened up the New World and renewed relations with the Far East, so too did the Renaissance—stimulated by Italy—spread northward into the generally localized countries of the North and Baltic seas regions. Internal and small wars continued to plague Scandinavia throughout the fifteenth and sixteenth centuries, but the spread of the Protestant Reformation quickly embroiled the peoples around the English Channel in the great wars of Europe. The economic motive was ever-present, but not only from coastal trade and the fisheries; Europe in general had begun to feel the impact of the arrival of hard money siphoned off from Spain, which lacked a manufacturing base and which then spent its new treasures to purchase goods from the North. At the funnel of European trade, the Strait of Dover, stood the Dutch and English whose full maritime energies, like those of Scandinavia, remained to exert their decisive impact on the Oceanic Age.

The general North Sea balance of power between Denmark, Sweden and the Hanseatic League began to disintegrate during the fifteenth century because of the constant warring between them. The League continued to fight Denmark, and although it sometimes suffered in naval actions its pressure enabled Sweden to break away from the union and keep the Scandinavians disrupted. Wars on the continent included a victory of the Poles over the Teutonic Knights, with Poland receiving the Pomeranian coast in 1466 and becoming a major Baltic power. Another new force arrived in the North in the form of shipping from the Dutch cities of Antwerp and Amsterdam. The important Hanse port of Bruges silted up during the 1430s, with the concurrent refusal of the Dutch to submit to Hanseatic trade stipulations in the Baltic. The Hanseatic fleet therefore sank a Dutch grain fleet in 1437, leading to a four-year war from which Antwerp gained the right of free trade in the Baltic. By the end of the century, Dutch shipping outnumbered that of the Hanse in that enclosed waterway, while Danish and Swedish naval power began to grow. Simultaneously, the Russians of Muscovy began to throw off Mongol rule; Tsar Ivan III ("the Great") in 1474 sent a mission to Venice to study its commercial and military techniques, then determined to reach the Baltic, which he did in 1492, two years later expelling the Hanseatic traders from Novgorod and ending their trade routes into Russia.

By the same token, the ancient rivalry between England and France continued both between them and as a result of internal strife. England's Cinque Ports lost importance during the fifteenth century as their harbors silted up, to be replaced by such rival entrepôts as London, Bristol, Plymouth and Falmouth. The Hundred Years War between medieval England and France finally stopped in 1453, ending the English presence on the continent save for Calais and leading to fresh civil wars in the British Isles. After the rule of the dynastic houses of Normandy (1066–1154) and Plantagenet (1154–1399), the rival houses of Lancaster and York fought for control of England. Each put sovereigns on the throne, but fought the Wars of the Roses from 1455 to 1485, during which (1475) the fighting briefly spilled over into France. In 1485, the exiled Henry Tudor of Richmond invaded England by landing at Milford Haven with French mercenaries to gain English support, seize the throne as King Henry VII and end the wars. His House of Tudor would govern England for over a century, during which time the center of Renaissance Europe would shift northward and help to undermine the supremacy of Spain. Valois France became one key agent of this gradual change, but Tudor England and the rebellious Dutch were equal partners.

Henry VII marks a major change in English history, not only for ending the wars over the succesion, but for consciously making the crown an instrument of English maritime expansion. Theretofore, the Cinque Ports and then individual seaport towns had dictated maritime policy, often as part of the continental-centered Hanseatic League, and as independent shippers had had to provide what amounted to private navies to protect their vessels from rivals, pirates and the emerging navies of France and Spain. The kings of England had had to depend upon the baronial aristocracy which owned these merchant-naval fleets and thus were subject to their policies. Henry VII changed all this. He inherited some private vessels from his predecessors, to which he added five more which could be employed as warships. He encouraged shipbuilding, which he helped subsidize with special bounties. He initiated Navigation Acts in 1486 and 1489, creating tariffs and other rules that he enforced. All of these things strengthened his authority (for he still had challengers to the throne whom he eliminated in the 1480s and 1490s), provided an additional challenge to the rapidly declining Hanseatic League, and further separated England from the continent, making her indeed an island nation.

France remained a serious rival to England in all respects, and Henry VII could not resist one last attempt to test French strength. But France had other concerns that demanded her full attention to continental matters. Political, civil and religious forces on her German and Spanish frontiers required that France maintain the superior professional army that had expelled the English from the continent in the 1450s. Under Kings Louis XI and Charles VIII, France ended her feudal period, consolidated into a strong Catholic monarchy, and engaged in a number of wars that included isolated naval engagements with single ships or small squadrons of the Dutch, English, Spanish, Venetians and Genoese, thus making her a strong Mediterranean as well as Atlantic power. When a revolt broke out in French Brittany in 1487, Henry VII decided to support the rebels, even though they were decisively defeated on land the next year. A treaty in 1491 supposedly ended the fighting, whereupon Henry crossed the Channel the next year and was about to invest Boulogne when the peace of 1492 ended the intrusion. Henceforth, England ceased its continental aspirations and looked to the sea.

English maritime expansion under Henry VII had not begun to challenge Spain and Portugal either in merchant shipping or naval power, tasks to which the new king, Henry VIII, addressed himself immediately after his father's death in 1509. Three years later, England joined Spain and Venice in the war against Valois France, leading Scotland also to renew formal hostilities against England. The naval aspects of the northern theater of fighting resumed their traditional medieval character: a brief English blockade of Brest, naval skirmishes between the rival fleets using boarding tactics, and cross-Channel hit-and-run raids. By the end of this indecisive war in 1514, however, Henry VIII had raised his father's Navy Royal from five to twenty-nine warships through construction and purchase. Partly lacking galleys and a clear doctrine, Henry became discontented staying with medieval concepts.

The continued naval program of Henry VIII earned him the subsequent distinction of being the "father of the British navy." Over the next three decades Henry molded the first real composite fleet of modern history, designed to command the waters around the British Isles and to perform diverse functions. For battle at sea he relied on what the twentieth century has known as "capital ships": great battleships to face the largest vessels of any enemy fleet—heavy galleys and galleasses, supplemented and eventually replaced by the all-sail galleons of which *The Great Harry* of 1515 was the first. To support these men-of-war in any fleet action, to scout and operate inshore, Henry created a "flotilla" of smaller escorts and auxiliaries: small frigates, brigantines, pinnaces, rowbarges and small sailing vessels. He constructed shipyards, iron foundries for cannon, and castles and other fortifications along the English coast. For Henry VIII, the Navy Royal became the first line of defense. In fact, it was almost purely defensive, with his army still fairly medieval, based on militia for home and border service and on amateur volunteers for occasional overseas expeditions such as in the inconclusive wars against France in 1512–14 and again in 1522–23.

With a superior navy, Henry VIII brought England into the strategic arena of international maritime conflict, while his tactical achievement proved to be equally considerable: he initiated serious developments in the use of broadside batteries and issued the first systematic tactical instructions governing sailing men-of-war. Fighting instructions were not necessarily new—individual commanders in Renaissance Venice had issued them for galley warfare—but only in the age of emerging naval thought did they become systematized in the same spirit as Henry the Navigator's navigational instructions. In Spain about 1530 Alonso de Chaves summarized naval tactics by advocating a regular formation to achieve order for a line-abreast approach prior to boarding. Henry VIII, kept informed of such Spanish thought, issued his own instructions in 1530, also dealing with boarding but now taking into equal account the crucial factors of wind and artillery. He instructed his fleet to gain the "weather gauge"—tacking to a position upwind of the enemy, thus having the advantage of maneuver over an enemy to leeward. Cannon fire could then have the advantage of better range and cover from the smoke. Finally, individual vessels could square off for boarding. From this cardinal rule of obtaining the weather gauge followed all subsequent British naval tactics in the age of sail.

Henry broke with the Pope and Catholicism and took over the church in England in the 1530s, leading to renewed hostilities with France in 1544. The next year he issued his navy a new set of fighting instructions in preparation for a fleet engagement, calling for a line-abreast approach in three ranks of eight, twelve and nineteen sailing ships, each supported by rowed galleys and galleasses on the wings. The French also had three squadrons, but arranged in broad files. But so crude were naval tactics in this curious admixture of different ship types that bringing on a true fleet action became exceedingly difficult. From Portsmouth and Calais the English raided the French coast, and from Le Havre the French replied in kind against the Channel coast of England. In July 1545 the galley-led fleet of over 200 French vessels under Claude d'Annebaut, Admiral of France, attacked the 63 ships of Lord Lisle, Lord Admiral of England, off Portsmouth. Maneuvering about in line-abreast, the French and English galleys and rowbarges engaged, but the crude English broadside guns could not be brought to bear in this formation. Henry afterward reinforced and reorganized his fleet and ordered his van to break through and come up to the lee of the French so that his guns could perform. The two fleets of Lisle and d'Annebaut met again off Shoreham in the open Channel on August 15 and though Henry's tactics could not be realized, Lisle did manage to get off the first naval broadside in history. The battle ended inconclusively, like the war which ended the next year, but the tactical lesson was clear: ships had to be lengthened for better gun platforms and sailing directions revised to line-ahead so that the broadside could be utilized. This evolution took nearly a century to perfect, but Henry—who died in 1547—had started it all.

During the 1550s England finally became embroiled with the Spanish Empire. Charles V, realizing that his son Philip II would not succeed to the throne of the Holy Roman Empire, in 1554 married Philip to the new Catholic queen, Mary Tudor of England. Between England and the Netherlands, Spain would thus have a new maritime imperial focus to make up for the loss of the continental Habsburg domains and to help contain Valois France. Philip succeeded to the Spanish crown in 1556, but two years later both Charles and Mary died and with them the dream

of the new united Catholic empire. For into Mary's place stepped the
Protestant queen, Elizabeth I, and the Protestant faith grew concurrently
in England and Holland. But Philip had other problems, for in 1557
the strained financial structure of Spain—despite the riches from America—resulted in the first of several national bankruptcies. Philip managed to end the Valois-Habsburg hostilities with France in 1559, but
strengthened the Counter-Reformation and Inquisition against infidel
Jews, Protestants and Moslems alike by pressing the struggle in the Mediterranean against the Turks, capturing Calais from the English in 1558,
and enforcing the state Catholic faith over uncooperative Dutch Protestants. As a result, the Mediterranean wars further strained the Spanish
economy, and in the 1560s Protestants ran wild in the Spanish Netherlands, even as Dutch financiers and merchants from Antwerp were wresting control of the lucrative trade of Seville from the Genoese.

Philip's several religious commitments and mercantile needs thus led
to an overextended strategy of warfare on three fronts from the late
1560s as he endeavored to meet both the Moslem threat and the Protestant challenge led by England. Philip weakened his Italian garrisons
facing the Turks to send an army overland to Holland which temporarily
succeeded in pacifying the rebellious Netherlanders led by William of
Orange. But fresh threats came from the sea, when in 1568–69 warring
French Protestants cut Spanish seaborne communications to Flanders
with naval raids along the Biscay coast of Spain. At the same time,
William of Orange commissioned Dutch privateers—known as Sea
Beggars—to raid Spanish coastal positions in the Netherlands. Largely
a pirate force, the Beggars evolved from 1568 to 1572 into a war fleet
under Lumey van der Marck that based in England to land in the
Netherlands in 1572 and help spread the revolt. Simultaneously, French
and English corsairs in the Caribbean reached dangerous proportions
when in 1568 John Hawkins of England ravaged Spanish possessions
with five vessels, only to lose three of them late in the year in an engagement with the escorted annual plate fleet at San Juan de Ulua (near
Vera Cruz). The surviving two vessels captained by Hawkins and Francis Drake limped back to England; Spain instituted the *Armada Real;*
and the era of intense Anglo-Spanish rivalry at sea commenced.

During the 1570s Spain maintained its stalemate in the Mediterranean
but faced intensified attacks on its worldwide shipping and possessions.
Raids by French and English privateering corsairs in the Spanish and
Portuguese South Atlantic and Caribbean continued and spread to the
Far East, especially by Englishmen John Oxenham, Martin Frobisher
and again Drake, whose circumnavigation of the globe in 1577–80 was
sustained by his raids on Iberian imperial wealth. No less active, the
Dutch Sea Beggars helped to frustrate the Spanish pacification program

in the Netherlands by defeating Spanish squadrons in naval actions at Zuyder Zee in October 1573 and off Walcheren early in 1574. Spanish expenditures hastened another national bankruptcy in 1575, leading to a bloody riot of unpaid Spanish troops in Antwerp the next year. Philip appointed his half-brother Don John, the victor of Lepanto, to command in Holland, and this ardent Catholic schemed to precipitate an open war with Elizabeth's England. Philip would not endorse John's invasion schemes, even after England began to encourage the Dutch openly in 1578, but Philip did send reinforcements to Holland from Italy under Alexander Farnese, who succeeded John when he died later in the year and who eight years later inherited the title Duke of Parma. The continued Spanish attempt to pacify Holland had so aroused the Netherlanders that in 1579 the northern provinces united under William to declare their independence from Catholic Spain.

Strategically, the crisis of the Spanish Empire fast approached. A land power, Spain was clearly failing to exert a *Pax Hispanica* over the continent, while her defensive measures overseas appeared to be dangerously inadequate. The Turks had recovered from Lepanto to dominate the Eastern Mediterranean and even to open regular trade with England. France was embroiled in religious civil wars that still took their toll of Spanish shipping. England fought an undeclared naval war with Spain, and the northern Dutch remained unpacified. The only bright spots in Spanish fortunes lay in the southern Netherlands (modern Belgium), which Farnese-Parma gradually reconquered, culminating in the capture of Antwerp in 1585, and in Portugal. As financially weak as Spain, imperial Portugal undertook a disastrous crusade into Morocco in 1578, which led to the death of the Portuguese king. Philip claimed the throne of Portugal and achieved it in 1580 after the fleet of 87 galleys and 30 ships under his Captain-General Don Álvaro de Bazán, Marquis of Santa Cruz, supported the army in capturing the Algarve and sealifted a second army to take Lisbon from the west. The Spanish fleet protected the new union by defeating Franco-Portuguese attempts to regain the country in two naval battles off Terceira in the Azores in 1582–83. Spain operated a combined merchant fleet of almost 300,000 tons (average vessel 100 tons), opposed to 232,000 of the Dutch and only 42,000 of England, and now had general control over the Portuguese Empire. But Dutch merchants manipulated the trade emanating from Seville, and the new English Levant Company from 1581 began to garner the trade of the Mediterranean. English pirates ravaged rival vessels in the middle sea, just as Dutch Sea Beggars plundered the Spanish in the North. And England, traditional ally of Portugal, had been antagonized by the Spanish annexation of that country.

The Marquis of Santa Cruz, the most distinguished naval officer in

Spanish service, now perceived a grand design whereby the decline of
Spanish and Catholic fortunes might be arrested at one masterful stroke.
Having played a leading role in the victory at Lepanto and the deciding
role in the conquest of Portugal, Santa Cruz in 1583 recommended to
King Philip that the spreading English menace be eliminated directly by
an invasion of England. Don John had wanted it, and a detailed study
of such a project had been made early in the decade. Philip, however,
was not ready to accept such a drastic—and expensive—plan. But the
longer he waited, the more powerful would be the Protestant defense.
In 1584, William of Orange was assassinated and succeeded as Stadtholder of the northern Netherlands by the young Maurice of Nassau,
destined to become the most brilliant military commander of his day.
The next year, the English settled their immediate differences with the
Scots and sent military aid to the Dutch. Simultaneously, English colonists sailed for Nova Scotia and Virginia in North America, and Hawkins,
new treasurer of the navy, overcame conservative opponents to begin the
modernization of the high-castled warships into longer, sleek, well-
gunned galleons.

Formal war finally broke out in 1585 when Philip, alarmed by his
vigorous competitors, declared an embargo on Dutch and English ships
(those present he seized) in Spanish and Portuguese harbors. Queen
Elizabeth retaliated by helping Drake to outfit a "joint-stock company"
for a massive raid against the Spanish Caribbean with twenty-nine ships,
two of them from the navy. Drake as Admiral and General and Frobisher
as Vice Admiral led the squadron out of Plymouth in September 1585.
It raided Vigo on the coast of Spain, the Canary and Cape Verde islands,
crossed the Atlantic and early in 1586 assaulted and took Santo Domingo
on Hispaniola and Cartagena on the Spanish Main. Nombre de Dios
and Panama were spared only because disease had weakened Drake's
force. But even before the military helplessness of the Empire had been
revealed, Philip had seen in the raid on Vigo the apparent exposure of
his homeland to enemy depredations. In January he ordered Santa Cruz
to prepare for the invasion of England.

From the beginning, Philip regarded the "Invincible Armada" as a
great amphibious crusade. Santa Cruz wanted the fleet to sealift an invasion army of 60,000 men directly from Spain to England. With the
approach of this liberating instrument of the Counter-Reformation, English Catholics would rise up in revolt behind Mary, Queen of Scots,
the Catholic pretender to Elizabeth's crown. This crusading goal was
never abandoned. But the role of the fleet itself was. With too few troops
available in Spain for such a vast undertaking, and the fact that supplying them would be such a logistical nightmare, Philip decreed that Farnese-Parma's army in Holland, fresh from its capture of Antwerp, would

be the invasion force. Parma would have to build his own ships and flatboats for towing the army across the Channel to the English beaches. Santa Cruz would rendezvous with these invasion craft in the Channel and escort them across. The plan seemed sound, assuming all operations were coordinated and all plans carefully understood by the widely separated participants.

But Spanish administrative inefficiency (the navy was separated from the army only in 1586) and lack of naval experience combined with untimely events and bad luck to jeopardize the project. Sufficient shipping, seaborne troops and artillery had to be brought to Iberia from Italy, consuming so much time that the campaign could not be started in 1586 or 1587. Support from Catholic Englishmen waned as rumors of attempts on Elizabeth's life rallied the country behind her, and she had Mary executed in 1587. The same year Thomas Cavendish entered the Eastern Pacific to capture the first of twenty Spanish galleons with their wares, and Drake descended on Cádiz where he destroyed one division of the Armada and all the barrel hoops and drying staves so crucial for preserving the food and water for the Armada's planned cruise. This daring seafarer then raided Spanish shipping off Cape St. Vincent, demonstrated before the main Armada base at Lisbon, and concluded his foray by taking a rich Portuguese East Indiaman at the Azores. In Holland, the Dutch Sea Beggars maintained such an active blockade that Parma could not complete and thus not rendezvous his shipping and landing barges. To complete Spanish woes, early in 1588 Santa Cruz died.

Nevertheless, Philip pressed forward with the project and Elizabeth rallied England for the defense. The new Spanish commander was Don Alonso Pérez de Guzmán, Duke of Medina Sidonia, a veteran of the Portuguese conquest, able administrator and crown adviser on maritime affairs who had been involved with Armada planning, but who had absolutely no sea experience. His fleet was modernized with long-range guns aboard mostly heavy sailing galleons but also a few galleys, 130 ships in all. But Spain, in the midst of her naval transition, still clung to the doctrines learned in the Mediterranean and with the Atlantic convoys and proved at Lepanto and in the Azores in 1582: the Armada would sail in crescent formation carrying 19,000 soldiers to only 8,000 sailors for grappling and boarding. Once this fleet cleared the Channel of the enemy fleet, Medina Sidonia would land some of the troops for service with Parma, and then escort the lot to England. But Elizabeth's navy had no such Mediterranean tradition, and Lord Howard of Effingham, Lord High Admiral of England, organized a fleet of some 120 warships plus auxiliaries manned mostly by skilled seamen and gunners for a broadside artillery duel at sea.

Howard concentrated his four squadrons at Plymouth under himself, Hawkins, Drake and Frobisher, while an eastern force remained at the Downs, ready to intercept Parma. These energetic gentlemen urged their queen to allow another attack on the Iberian coast, but in vain. Still Philip, like Elizabeth, had to mobilize an army for coast defense.

The Spanish Armada sailed from Lisbon to Corunna in May 1588 and from thence on into the Bay of Biscay in July, its mission to rendezvous with Parma at Calais. Thus when it arrived off Lizard Head in mid-July it had the weather gauge and could have sailed straight into Plymouth to destroy the leeward-bound English navy, though its narrow entrance and coastal guns discouraged the Spanish. More importantly, the Catholic strategy called for the invasion rendezvous, so that Medina Sidonia sailed on by. The wind changed, and Howard's squadrons sailed out, tacking skillfully until windward of the Spanish. Thus holding the weather gauge, the English pursued the Armada up the Channel in a running fight that lasted ten days, frustrating the duke's hope to anchor at the Isle of Wight. Tactically, the English were superior, for they would outmaneuver the heavy Spanish galleons in hit-and-run snipes at the edges of the crescent formation. In ordnance, the English also excelled, their guns longer-ranged than those of the Spanish, but equally inaccurate; skillfully maneuvered, however, English broadside guns could harass effectively yet stay out of boarding range. And logistically, the English held the decided advantage: with the interior position, they ran back and forth to nearby ports to reprovision, while the Spanish had to ration their ammunition and supplies until they could establish a new supply base at the rather poor anchorage of Calais.

Medina Sidonia achieved the first aim of Spanish strategy when he reached Calais on July 26. But there the Spanish crusade died. Parma could not break out of the Dutch blockade at Bruges with his few warships and troop barges, so no cross-Channel attack could take place. Furthermore, Parma had not collected provisions and ammunition for the Armada, the fault of poor administration, and since leaving Lisbon and Corunna the contents of Medina Sidonia's rationed supply caskets had been leaking and turning the fresh food and water into green slime; Drake's Cádiz raid had forced him to use green, bacteria-ridden wood for his barrels. Worse, no amphibious operation could take place without command of the sea, and the Spanish had not even come to grips with Howard's squadrons, which were now all concentrated in the Strait of Dover. The Armada could not retrace its track down the Channel due to the wind and the reinforced, replenished English fleet. The vigorous English gave Medina Sidonia no chance to weigh the alternatives; in the predawn darkness of July 28th they

sent fire ships into the Calais anchorage, causing the Spaniards to cut
their anchor cables and panic in flight into the open sea. At daylight
the English pressed home their attack off Gravelines, inflicting heavy
casualties and taking a few vessels. Unfavorable winds over the next
two days kept the Armada from reaching any Dutch port, and Medina
Sidonia decided to quit the region altogether.

The English commanded their own waters, with no small help from
the Dutch, and as the Armada stood out into the North Sea on August
1, the Spanish Empire had passed its high-water mark. Medina
Sidonia had no choice but to return to Spain via the turbulent route
of the North Sea over the top of Scotland and Ireland. Low on ammunition, the English let them go. Throughout August and September,
Spanish warships struggled north, then west and south, some being
dashed against the hostile coasts of the British Isles. Perhaps more
than half of the fleet reached Spain, but with the crews too sick and
starved even to furl their sails. Medina Sidonia had battled nearly
impossible odds to execute an intricate and unprecedentedly bold plan;
his failure could be attributed largely to the different skills of naval
warfare between the oceanic English and continent-oriented Spanish.

The wars between Catholics and Protestants went on unabated, but
the stunning results of the Armada's expedition alerted the Western
world to new political realities. Internally, Spain reeled from the psychological depression of a major defeat. The Empire could now expect
attacks on an increasing scale. England felt the pride of national
achievement, and though the Englishmen were not ready to mount
a counteroffensive against the Spanish colossus, they felt emboldened
enough to seek new gains abroad. The Dutch, however, now knew
their independence was assured. More significant, they lost no time
in launching a policy aimed at nothing less than the destruction of
the Spanish maritime monopoly.

# 5

# The Dutch Seaborne Empire, 1600–1675

*Your Honours [directors, Dutch East India Company] should know by experience that trade in Asia must be driven and maintained under the protection and favour of Your Honours' own weapons, and that the weapons must be paid for by the profits from the trade; so that we cannot carry on trade without war nor war without trade.*

—JAN PIETERSZOON COEN, 1614

## HOLLAND UPON THE SEA

The Protestant Netherlands stood poised to conquer the carrying trade of Europe and of the world at the turn of the seventeenth century. Spain and the Spanish vassal Portugal were in marked decline, leaving a virtual worldwide vacuum in maritime efficiency and economic stability. Not a large country, or even a truly united one, the Netherlands prospered and expanded largely because England was not yet ready to assume such a role. To be sure, Elizabethan England was a dynamic people, just getting its "sea legs" in maritime ventures and awakening to the nationalistic and cultural forces of its own Renaissance; witness the brilliant works of its writer-thinkers William Shakespeare, Christopher Marlowe, Francis Bacon, Edmund Spenser and Walter Raleigh. But Elizabeth's passing in 1603 was followed by a new dynasty, the Stuarts, less interested in naval-maritime enterprise, very idealistic, and destined for decades of domestic unrest. The Dutch had no such inhibitions, and thus in a very real sense the focus of Western civilization rested on the Netherlands throughout much of the seventeenth century.

The Northern Netherlands which dominated world trade for the seventy-five years beginning about 1600 were a confederation of seven maritime and inland provinces in successful rebellion against Spanish rule. Of these seven, two dominated their maritime affairs, facing directly onto the North Sea and the funnel of all northern European oceanic traffic: Holland, which included the major cities of The Hague, Amsterdam and Rotterdam; and Zeeland, the many islands and the coast closest to England and bordering the province of Flanders, the one maritime province of those in the Southern Netherlands remaining loyal to Catholic Spain—including the port city of Antwerp—and which would evolve into the modern state of Belgium. For convenience, the Protestant peoples of the United Provinces are referred to interchangeably as the Dutch, residents of the Netherlands or Holland. These seven United Provinces still remained distinctive, though the interests of the aggressive maritime peoples often conflicted with the landlubbing instincts of their brethren of the interior. These differences, however, never interfered enough to affect the singular economic front presented by the Dutch abroad.

Dutch national, economic and cultural characteristics combined to create a thalassocracy very much like those of ancient Athens and early Renaissance Venice. Overseas exploration and foreign contacts, religious independence and toleration, the predominance of the profit motive and a strong merchant class all did their part to advance individualism and democratic institutions, attracting English and French intellectuals as visitors or residents. Instead of a king, the Dutch preferred an elected stadtholder or later even a republican government without one head. These dynamics of Dutch life made the seventeenth century the golden age of Dutch culture, reflected in the art of Rembrandt van Rijn, Frans Hals, Jan Vermeer and Willem Van de Velde, the philosophy of Baruch Spinoza, Desiderius Erasmus and the French immigrant René Descartes, the science of Anton van Leeuwenhoek, Simon Stevin and Christian Huygens (including the invention of the telescope), the medicine of Hermannus Boerhaave and the legal writings of Hugo Grotius (Huig de Groot), known to history as the father of international law. The work of the latter individual was particularly timely, as Dutch national fervor burst its short geographic boundaries to spread overseas and create the Dutch Empire.

The homogeneous character of the Dutch challenge to Spanish supremacy perhaps accounts for the fact that the Netherlands became the first genuine nation-state of modern Europe; it was certainly the first government to systematize its maritime and naval policy into one integrated whole, embracing political goals, economic gain, maritime law, strategy, naval architecture, cartography, logistics and tactics. And the guiding concept was embraced in the idea of mercantilism. Mercantilism simply meant the devotion of a nation to maritime trade, the exchange of goods by sea, but usually monopolistically. Spain had stumbled into such a policy, but never systematically enough to make it really work. The Dutch knew exactly what they wanted and how to achieve it. In order to gain political power, they sought economic wealth and thus a large merchant marine, overseas colonies and a navy to protect both. The tool the Dutch utilized was the chartered company, borrowed from the English, whose joint-stock companies had harassed the Spanish and culminated in the founding of the English East India Company in 1600; the Dutch East India Company was created two years later. Merchant seamen and ships of these companies became the nucleus of the war fleet, which had to protect the companies. The competitive merchants thus controlled state policy. And the merchants, warships and overseas colonies thus became interdependent.

To legalize such a policy of breaking the monopoly of a competitor, the Dutch went beyond the simple preferential navigation acts introduced by Henry VII of England. Holland, through the genius of Grotius, fashioned an entire new legal philosophy based on the principle of freedom of the seas. Grotius' ideas emerged in 1604 with his defense of the Dutch East India Company's seizure of a Portuguese galleon near Malacca and were expanded in two important treatises, *Mare Liberum (The Free Sea)* in 1609 and *De Jure Belli ac Pacis (On the Rights of War and Peace)* in 1625. Though pro-Dutch, Grotius maintained that all men enjoyed free navigation on the high seas and thus the right to trade thereon. He accused Spain and Portugal of greed and avarice with their policy of maritime monopoly, and said that any man or nation had the right to trade freely at sea, a right to be enforced by arms. Turning against England, Grotius also denied the right of that country to exert exclusive dominion over the rich fisheries of the North Sea. Speaking in broad, general and flexible terms, Grotius enunciated legal precedents that formed the basis for international maritime law in the modern world.

Grotius' reasoning had even broader implications that easily reduced his critics to making inferior arguments. The weakened Spanish and Portuguese could not repulse the might of Dutch naval arms that enforced Grotius' laws; neither did their Catholicism discourage Protestant intruders throughout their overseas domains. England produced a major refutation in the writings of the jurist John Selden, who argued from 1617 until the publication of his book *Mare Clausum (The Private Sea)* in 1635 that dominion over the waters—particularly the North Sea fishing grounds—was fitting and proper. He further advocated that dominion over the sea included the right of excluding competitors and of levying tolls. Selden's preoccupation with national interests, however, made his stand appear less convincing alongside that of Grotius, who called for freedom of the seas for the benefit of all mankind. Indeed, Grotius went much further. By seeking internationally recognized laws, based on human reason, he aimed at regulating competition, which he knew led to warfare. By regulating competition he hoped warfare would be limited and restricted. Echoed by contemporary philosophers, Grotius sought a civil code of universal conduct that would initiate a trend in Western Europe toward reason and order. Following Grotius and others, religious law thus yielded to the laws of men and the new nation-states.

To be sure, Grotius' concepts could be bent to meet the needs of Dutch policy, and they left several questions unanswered, but on the whole they introduced the legal basis for mercantilistic and imperial ventures in the modern world. The unwritten implication behind both Grotius and Selden was simply that to be effective, such legal pronouncements had to be enforceable. The sea could be closed or kept open only by a navy powerful enough to command that sea. And so Holland undertook shipbuilding of vast proportions, founded special academies to train professional naval officers—the first country in history to do so—and molded a navy adequate to carry out its bold national policies.

The Dutch navy, controlled by the elected States General, became the first professional navy of modern times. Though it relied heavily on armed merchantmen for overseas ventures, it also maintained a nucleus fighting force of sleek galleons for defense of home waters and of inbound and outbound convoys. Netherlanders had deep maritime roots because of their geographical proximity to the sea, but the first formal naval force—eighteen warships of Sea Beggars—had not put to sea until the autumn of 1569 to harass Catholic vessels. Joining English and French ships, this privateering force within two years had grown five-fold. It was these Sea Beggars that grew into the formidable Dutch navy which had successfully supported the insurrection and dashed Parma's hopes of rendezvousing with his escort for the invasion of England. If Holland was to survive as a maritime competitor, this navy had to be enlarged, with vital stores and equipment always being available. Thus Dutch national strategic policy always had to take into account the needs of the navy.

The evolution of imperial maritime policy by the Netherlands involved several steps and operations in various parts of the world. First and most immediate was the need to overcome the Spanish attack at home and to consolidate the new independent nation; this meant relying heavily upon the English alliance as in 1588. Next, in order to secure adequate shipbuilding supplies such as timber and the naval stores of pitch, tar, resin, turpentine and pine oil, as well as cannon and grain, the Dutch had to secure their vital lifelines to the Baltic. Commercial expansion could occur simultaneously to the Baltic, the Far East, the Mediterranean and the Americas. Such aggressiveness would naturally mean conflict with Spain and Portugal and, when the Dutch monopoly extended over the coastal trade of the continent, confrontations with neighboring England and France. So developed the general pattern of Dutch strategic policy.

Fortunately for the Dutch, the repulse of the Armada of 1588 did not discourage Spanish involvement in the struggles of Northern Europe. On the contrary, Spain set about building another grand fleet and in 1589 sent Parma into France to intervene in the religious civil wars there on the side of the Catholics. These moves only compounded Spain's material and psychological losses of the Armada campaign. Mounting Spanish debts, epidemic diseases and deaths among overseas colonial laborers, the end of an earlier economic boom, an internal revolt in Aragon and continued fighting on land and sea led Philip II again to declare bankruptcy in 1595. The Dutch in 1588 had appointed the brilliant commander Maurice of Nassau as Captain and Admiral of the United Provinces, and the next year he took advantage of Parma's absence in France to mount an offensive. The Dutch fleet easily commanded the approaches to the coast, while an English squadron landed a patriot group in Portugal that had to withdraw after it failed to generate a popular uprising against the Spanish overlords. Spain lashed back at Protestantism, lost Parma to mortal wounds in France in 1592 and vainly sought to establish a forward base in the Channel by taking Calais and Brest at mid-decade. But stiff Anglo-French resistance and a mutiny in the army convinced Philip to quit his Brittany venture. Meanwhile, Maurice consolidated Dutch military control over the homeland. Grossly overextended, Philip thus watched his continental aspirations crumble, culminating with an ignominious peace with France in 1598, though he fought on against the English and Dutch.

Overseas, the Spanish Empire fared little better against the Anglo-Dutch attack. Economically, the colonies were now overstocked with certain European goods, and without manufactured products being available from agricultural Spain, the colonists had little choice but to turn to smuggled products from English and Dutch corsair traders. Militarily, however, the Spanish faced a greater danger abroad from a bold idea of their English nemesis, Sir John Hawkins. Hawkins formulated the first genuine "blue-water" strategy of modern times by proposing the defeat of Spain through the use of a naval blockade. To cut off Spain's vital Baltic trade for timber and naval stores, Hawkins wanted the English to maintain command of their Channel with a permanent fleet of twelve warships and six pinnaces. To cut off Spain's crucial lines of communications to the Americas, he advocated a permanent squadron of queen's ships (including rotating relief vessels) off the Azores; its major objective would be the capture of the annual plate fleet. This sound strategy proved premature and simply too difficult for the England of 1589 to implement, however, and both the plate fleets and Baltic convoys managed to reach Spain.

The battle for command of Iberian waters raged on, as the new Spanish fleet—modernized along English lines—mobilized under the command of Admiral Don Alonso de Bazán, brother of the late Santa Cruz. In 1591 Bazán's force of twenty galleons engaged the blockading English squadron of six ships off the Spanish coast, and succeeded in covering the plate fleet's passage, though the English galleon *Revenge* alone sank four Spanish vessels. The queen of England then abandoned her expensive blockading attempts and preferred instead to launch small cross-Channel landings to assist the French Protestants. English privateers continued to operate off the Azores, but did not seriously endanger Spain's command of its own waters. The war dragged on, but the Dutch continued to extend their control over Spanish merchant shipping. Poor grain harvests in Spanish Italy during the late 1580s prompted Dutch and Hanseatic shippers to penetrate the Mediterranean along with the English. The Hansarders did not remain beyond the 1590s though, while Dutch and English merchantmen and pirates swarmed over the middle sea, trading with Venetians and Turks alike and attacking competitors. And the Protestant Netherlands, by their proximity to the Spanish Netherlands, stood to dominate Seville completely as soon as the formal hostilities ended.

The Empire in America held the key to Spanish survival, and the Spanish knew it. Survival of shipping between Cádiz and the Caribbean was difficult enough because of natural conditions: late summer and autumn hurricanes ranged throughout the Caribbean, sudden and violent "northers" ravaged the coast of New Spain, and unpredictable winds and uncharted reefs surprised the few reliable pilots to take their toll. In 1563 alone, for instance, no fewer than twenty-seven ships were lost to these various causes. Free-lance pirates and commissioned privateers made the Florida Straits a hazardous passage. For these reasons, the Spanish from the 1560s had begun reorganizing their port system, and by the 1590s—when their American trade peaked—they were strengthening their imperial defenses. Santo Domingo on Hispaniola had the best harbor in the Caribbean, but declined in importance to Havana in Cuba, better placed to protect the outbound plate fleets. Santiago de Cuba and San Juan del Puerto Rico became secondary bases. Vera Cruz was moved fifteen miles down the coast to a point opposite the island of San

Juan de Ulua for better protection against the weather. Nombre de Dios was the main Panamanian port for the Peruvian trade until superseded by Porto Belo. Cartagena remained the center of the Spanish Main, and Acapulco served the Manila trade. Along with Menéndez de Avilés' *Armada Real,* the Spanish strengthened their West Indian defenses with galley patrols. In 1582 the first two galleys arrived from Spain for service out of Santo Domingo and Cartagena against pirates. Rowed craft were excellent for such work, but the difficulty of finding rowers plus the turbulent winds caused constant shortages in keeping the galleys afloat and on regular service. Still, they were successful enough to chase down a large number of pirate ships. And in the 1590s Spain erected new fortifications until Cartagena and Havana became virtually impregnable. Fast dispatch boats then made the Spanish Caribbean into a rather sophisticated interlocking defensive network.

Against these preparations, the English renewed their attack on the Caribbean in 1595. Hawkins and Drake commanded the expedition, but just as they arrived off Puerto Rico Hawkins became ill and died. The Spanish repulsed the attack on the island, and Drake suspended his designs on Cartagena in favor of Panama. In January 1596 Drake attacked and sacked Nombre de Dios so thoroughly that the Spanish abandoned it altogether, but Drake also perished aboard his flagship from a tropical disease. The force then headed for the Florida Strait and home, the local Spanish flotilla in close pursuit. Spain hastened a relief force from Cádiz to the Caribbean, but all this did was to leave Cádiz open for an Anglo-Dutch naval raid in July in which eighty-two vessels turned Spanish naval and commercial shipping at Cádiz into a conflagration. France's brief entry into the Protestant alliance forced Spain to cease her convoys to the New World, and her communications across the Atlantic remained cut for two years, while Dutch smugglers and privateers quickly outnumbered those of the English in the crossing to the Caribbean.

Philip II, his health declining, still saw the one hope for survival in a successful invasion of Elizabeth's England. He quickly mobilized an armada of one hundred sail that departed for the Channel in the autumn of 1596, only to be dispersed by a storm off Cape Finisterre. He tried again the next year, and this armada got as far as the Brittany coast when it too met a similar fate. "Protestant winds" and inferior Spanish seamanship had saved England three times. In 1598 Philip died, France quit the enemy alliance, and Spain determined again on another invasion attempt. But Spain's long involvement in France had enabled the Dutch to build up a formidable military presence. A Dutch fleet threatened the Azores and the reestablished plate convoy, the defense of which took precedence over any invasion scheme. And in 1600 Maurice invaded

Spanish Flanders, so that Spanish arms had to concentrate there, laying siege to Ostend. Supplying the garrison by sea, the Dutch managed to hold the port from 1601 to 1604. The Dutch navy controlled its own waters, thus frustrating Spanish efforts.

In the final years of the long war Spain assumed the defensive. A Spanish force invaded Ireland in 1601, hoping to enable a general invasion to take place the next year, but in 1602 an English squadron eliminated these hopes by defeating a Spanish fleet in its home waters. Early in 1603 Queen Elizabeth died, and her successor, James I, made peace the following year. But the Dutch fought on. Already, reacting to a second Spanish embargo on Dutch shipping in 1595, the Dutch had outfitted merchant convoys to tap the Portuguese East Indies, formalizing their East India Company in 1602. Challenged by the Iberians there, the Dutch enlarged their insurrection to break the Catholic overseas monopoly. Learning that a Spanish fleet was outfitting at Gibraltar to deal with them in the Far East, the States General early in 1607 dispatched a fleet of twenty-six armed merchantmen to Gibraltar under Admiral Jacob van Heemskerck. Late in April this force attacked the ten Spanish galleons at anchor in Gibraltar roads, two Dutchmen doubling on each Spaniard. Both van Heemskerck and the Spanish admiral were killed in the gunnery duel, but the Dutch destroyed all ten galleons. Spain, exhausted, arranged an armistice and declared her national bankruptcy for the third time. Two years later, Spain and the Netherlands concluded a formal truce, virtually recognizing Dutch independence.

The long wars between Catholic Spain and Protestant England and Holland, with occasional participation by Protestant French forces, broke the Spanish overseas trade monopoly and hold on the balance of power in Europe. Spain depended on her treasure convoys from the Americas and Portuguese spice convoys from the East. By sheer inertia, and because the seventeenth century became a period of endless bloodshed on the continent, Spain was yet able to maintain her hold on most of Latin America, though helpless to stop the new flood of Northern European colonists and competitors to North America. So preoccupied, Spain left vassal Portugal to maintain its own possessions in the Orient and even granted an *asiento* (special trade privilege contract) to Portugal for supplying African slaves to the Caribbean. Spanish imperial ports remained closed to foreign shippers, but Spain had to concede to the English in 1604 and to the Dutch in 1609 that she had no authority over unoccupied territory—hence another reason for the new migrations. The truce of 1609, supposed to last twelve years, left the imperial sea routes intact, so that King Philip III allowed the Spanish navy to deteriorate.

During the same period, King James I demobilized the English war fleet, leaving his shores open to depredations by pirates from French Dunkirk, the distant Moslem Barbary coast and even England itself. With Spain and England thus preoccupied and weakened, the Dutch moved abroad, but especially into the Baltic, threatening Spain's vital supply line to the timber and naval stores of that region. By the same token, England and France came to depend upon the Dutch merchant marine for supplying them with these vital Baltic goods.

## BALTIC BATTLEGROUND

Just as the Mediterranean area balance of power had been fashioned by the Turkish-Christian wars and that of Western Europe by the Spanish-Protestant conflict, so too had the sixteenth-century Baltic undergone power struggles between various rivals of which the Dutch were only the latest. As in the former two regions, with their fragmented Iberian kingdoms, Italian cities and Dutch provinces, the Baltic remained a collection of loosely joined Hanseatic cities and Scandinavian kingdoms. But as the forces of nationalism, commerce and religion checked the Turk and caused new political unions in the rest of Europe, also did they repel the Mongol (Tartar) and create leading powers in Sweden, Denmark and Russia. Naval operations played their part in these conflicts, but never on the scale of the Mediterranean or Atlantic wars. Squadrons or fleets of ten or twenty warships, galley and/or sailing, were common. Strategically, these navies almost always worked in support of army operations on the shores surrounding this inland sea.

In the twenty-five years after 1500, while Spain and Portugal were exploring abroad, the Baltic power balance consisted of dying political arrangements. The Union of Kalmar between the kingdoms of Denmark, Sweden and Norway had never been strong, and in these years it finally collapsed as Sweden broke away from Denmark-Norway, and the latter was convulsed in civil strife. The Swedish War of Liberation, 1521–23, followed the leadership of Gustavus Vasa, an advocate of naval power but almost helpless against the Danish navy under Admiral Sören Norby. Soliciting the aid of Lübeck, which still directed declining Hanseatic influence over the Baltic, Gustavus' allied fleet raided the Danish coast and retook Stockholm from the Danes in 1522–23. The victory resulted in an independent Sweden under King Gustavus, though he required three more years to halt Norby from his semi-piratic activities. On the east coast of the Baltic, the Muscovite Russians who had reached the coast in 1492 bogged down driving back their Mongol overlords, while the Teutonic Knights, Lithuanians, Poles, Prussians, Germans and various Hanseatic cities led by Lübeck all competed as in the past, unaware that fresh activities at sea would create a new power relationship.

The Baltic battleground was determined by the leading trading centers, their fortifications and the sea routes leading to them. The strategic key to the Baltic remained as always the Sound, the narrow waterway through which all European shipping had to pass to get in and out of the Baltic. Denmark occupied the Jutland and Scandinavian peninsulas (mainly Norway) which border on the North Sea, Skagerrak and Kattegat leading to the Sound. The actual lands facing on the Sound are mainland Scania on the east from Helsingborg down to Malmo and Trelleborg and the larger island of Zealand on the west from Elsinore to Copenhagen, the Danish capital. Though possible alternate passage around Zealand through the Belts existed, this lay in Danish waters and was more difficult, so maritime traffic funneled through the Sound, where the Danes had levied tolls since the early fifteenth century. Up the east side of the Scandinavian peninsula lay Sweden and the offshore islands of Bornholm, Oland and Gotland with the city of Wisby, leading to mainland Stockholm. On the continent side stood the leading cities of Lübeck, Rostock, Stralsund and Stettin in Germany; Danzig in Poland; Königsberg in Prussia; Teutonic Riga; Viborg at the base of the Finland peninsula; and the Lake Ladoga-river routes to Russian Novgorod. Control of the Baltic meant a rich trading monopoly for any superior power.

Denmark (which usually included Norway) and Sweden (which usually included Finland) emerged as the major maritime powers competing for control of the Baltic. But first they had to destroy the last major vestiges of Hanseatic power, and did so by allying against Lübeck in 1533. Gustavus began to build a navy, which included purchases of ships from the Dutch and later the French, all under Admiral Mans Svensson Some, but the major part of the allied fleet was provided by Denmark under its brilliant admiral, Peter Skram. After some skirmishing and naval maneuvering, in June 1535 Skram's twenty ships defeated nine of the enemy's off Bornholm Island. He then pressed on to the Sound, where he joined the allied army in joint land-sea sieges of Copenhagen and Malmö, both in rebellion against Denmark and allied with the Hanse. At this point the Holy Roman Emperor Charles V ordered the Dutch to prepare a fleet to relieve Copenhagen, but as the Dutch were competitors of Lübeck they delayed until it was too late. The coalition took the rebellious city and ended the war in 1536. Now that Lübeck and her allies were checked, both Sweden and Denmark kept naval squadrons active in the Baltic over the next three decades. The power of the Hanseatic League thus declined to political impotence by the end of the century.

Lübeck's land position was equally threatened by rising continental powers. The Teutonic Knights succumbed in 1526, their territories grabbed up by Sweden, Denmark, Russia and Poland. The conflict for this territory, called Livonia, lasted sporadically for decades, especially as continental Poland expanded and sought to halt Russian designs on the Baltic and European interior. In Russia in 1547 came the rule of Ivan the Terrible who advanced Russian claims on Livonia. Meanwhile, with the decline of the Hanse, Dutch traders were gradually taking over Baltic trade, and in 1554 Ivan welcomed the new Dutch Muscovy Company, which improved on its commercial near-monopoly over Novgorod. England also sought Northern markets, and in 1555 Ivan signed a commercial treaty with England. By this time, however, Ivan's depredations aroused the Swedes to retaliate, and in the summer of 1555 Gustavus sent a fleet under Admiral Jacob Bagge and an army to the Gulf of Finland to attack the Russians. Operating from Helsingfors (modern Helsinki), the Swedes moved up the River Neva, but were repulsed. Neither could Ivan dislodge Gustavus from Helsingfors, and the war ended in stalemate in 1556. Two years later Ivan reached Narva, where he hired four privateers, and then took the ice-free port of Riga. His ruthless rule gained him few supporters and hastened the coming of a general war for possession of these territories.

The Scandinavian Seven Years War (1563–1570) began with the Swedes under their new king, Eric XIV, fighting the Danes under their new king, Frederick II, and Lübeck for mastery of the Baltic. Both kings, very naval-minded, enjoyed the services of skillful veteran admirals leading their small fleets, the Swedish Bagge and the Danish Skram. Unfortunately, the two aged men failed to fight any decisive action in the first year of campaigning; Bagge was censured by his king and Skram replaced by his king with the younger Herloffe Trolle. The fleets finally engaged in a two-day battle late in May 1564 off Öland Island; the allies got the better of it and even succeeded in capturing Bagge. Command of the Swedish navy was then vested in a tried army commander, Klas Kristersson Horn. Both powers hastened construction of new warships, with the Danes turning to Dutch shipwrights to direct their work.

The naval campaigns of 1565–66 pitted the Swedes and Danes in decisive actions. Horn began with successful attacks against Danish naval shipping using a large fleet of forty-eight ships and over 1600 cannon. Trolle put to sea with thirty-two allied warships and engaged Horn in June 1565 off Bukow in Lübeck waters. The action favored the Swedes, for Trolle received wounds which were mortal. In July Horn defeated the allied fleet in the bloodiest naval battle of the war, fought midway between Bornholm and Rügen. More Swedish maneuvers succeeded, especially with an enlarged fleet in 1566. The allies suddenly suffered a serious reverse in July when a storm caught their fleet at anchor off Wisby and destroyed eleven large Danish warships and three Lübeckers. Natural disaster also hurt Sweden, for the plague then sweeping Europe claimed the life of Horn in September. From then on, the war degenerated into internal quarrels, desultory maneuvering and a general stalemate at sea. The treaty in 1570 realized little gain for either side.

The last third of the sixteenth century was turbulent for the Baltic region, although Sweden and Denmark remained at peace with one another. The Russians under Ivan stepped up their attacks on eastern Swedish territory, thus prolonging the Livonian wars until 1583, when Ivan admitted defeat and ceded Estonia and Narva to Sweden. Internal problems over the Swedish succession led to war with Poland and Russia during the 1590s. During these border struggles, the Swedish navy maintained its army's communications from the homeland to forward bases in the Gulf of Finland, blockading Russian outlets with a force of twelve to twenty vessels. Penetrating up the Neva, the Swedes built galleys along Venetian lines for smooth-water operations against a similar Russian force on lakes Ladoga and Peipus. The Russians, torn by internal troubles, made peace in 1595, but intermittent fighting between Sweden and Poland continued into the new century. Throughout these years, Swedish relations with the Netherlands grew importantly, first because of a large migration of Dutch to pro-Protestant Sweden, then because of Dutch investments in new Swedish mining and cannon founding, and finally because of the great amount of Dutch shipping to the Baltic. The presence of the Dutch in Sweden helped in the expansion of the Swedish navy to 151 warships of various sizes by 1611. Dutchmen also sold their services along with Frenchmen and Scots to Denmark which enlarged its own navy to some sixty large and formidable men-of-war.

As the religious difficulties of continental Europe heightened following the Spanish-Dutch truce of 1609, Swedish-Dutch relations also cemented. The Danes, by their traditional supremacy in the Baltic and their monopoly over the Sound bottleneck, could force the Dutch to conform to their own policies. The Dutch, however, who by their naval supremacy in the North Sea commanded these trade routes as far as the Sound, now took over all French trade to the Baltic, and were in position to cut off Spain from the Baltic altogether. The Netherlands therefore improved relations with Sweden, then Denmark's only serious Baltic rival. The short and inconclusive War of Kalmar (1611–13) between Denmark and Sweden brought the young and aggressive Gustavus Adolphus to the Swedish throne and served to aggravate Danish relations with Holland, for the Danish king refused even to recognize the sovereignty of the United Provinces as independent of Spain. The

Dutch were therefore eager to accept a defensive alliance with Sweden in 1614. When Gustavus renewed Sweden's border wars with Russia, the Dutch mediated the peace in 1617, in which Russia surrendered the entire Gulf of Finland and Livonian coast to Sweden. Russia thus ceased to be a Baltic power, while Holland controlled the maritime traffic of the region and held the fulcrum in a delicate balance of power between Denmark and Sweden.

## NETHERLANDS EAST AND WEST INDIES

The Baltic, though crucial to Dutch trade throughout the seventeenth century, acted as only one area of Dutch maritime supremacy on the eve of the disastrous Thirty Years War which began to engulf Europe in 1618. Netherlanders pressed into the Portuguese East Indies, Spanish West Indies and Turkish Eastern Mediterranean, maintained good trade relations with England and France, and even built up a lucrative trade with isolated Russia. While continental Europe became preoccupied with massive warfare, the Dutch merchant marine and navy set out to conquer the sea lanes of the world. Whether at peace or formal war with other powers, the Dutch continued to trade with friend and foe alike, even with their own enemies. Grotius' legal policy of *Mare Liberum* supported this practice when Holland was neutral; free ships should be able to trade at will. Strategically, just as the narrow Strait of Dover (and friendship with England) and the Sound (and friendship with whoever controlled it, Denmark or Sweden) held the key to supremacy over adjacent waters, so too did the Dutch look to the control of vital waterways—terminal points for maritime and naval operations—across the world. And as Dutch wealth grew, so too did the Dutch navy: such was the strategic cycle of mercantilism and the Dutch seaborne empire.

The Dutch assault aimed at destroying the Portuguese monopoly over the Far East and, to a lesser extent, at breaking the Spanish monopoly over the Caribbean. The vehicle was the commercial trading company, the East India Company founded in 1602 and the West India Company in 1621, the year that the twelve-year truce with Spain ended. These companies received full commercial and political power from the States General to make war, to gain economic concessions and bases from native peoples, and to colonize, so that they inevitably became the embodiment of the imperial power of the state. Their initial offensive against the weakened Iberian powers was imitated by the English and the French, who in the early 1600s renewed their colonization attempts—which had earlier failed—in North America. The English, whose major colonization effort had theretofore been into nearby Ireland, in 1607 settled Virginia, in 1620 Massachusetts, and in the 1620s St. Kitts and

Barbados islands and parts of South American Guiana. The French settled Maine in 1604, Nova Scotia in 1605, Quebec in 1608 and Caribbean Martinique and parts of Guiana in 1635. From the beginning, the English and French fought over Maine and Nova Scotia, wars, however, which had very little effect on the general Anglo-Dutch-French attack on the Spanish American monopoly.

The Dutch excursion into the New World aimed at crippling Spanish commercial power and at establishing bases for the attack on Portuguese sea routes to the East. The Dutch thrust therefore fell on North America, the West Indies and Guiana-Brazil ("the Wild Coast"). Like the English and French, the Dutch in the 1620s sought new American bases and thus established New Amsterdam on Manhattan Island as well as settlements on the Caribbean islands of Saba, St. Martin and St. Eustatius. From these, Dutch traders could compete with French and English traders and colonists, and Dutch naval units could harass Spanish shipping in the Caribbean. Admiral Piet Heyn (Pieter Pieterszoon Heyn) realized the latter goal most dramatically in 1628 when, in command of thirty-one ships, he captured the Spanish plate fleet off Matanzas harbor, Cuba. This blow crippled Spain's economy, and the loot enabled the Dutch to finance a major attack on South America. The uneven Dutch penetration into Guiana and Brazil had begun in 1610, as the Dutch attempted to steal away the slave trade from Portugal. In the 1620s they tried in vain to settle Surinam, Curaçao and Bahia, Brazil, and were repulsed in an attack on Spanish Puerto Rico. But with the captured Spanish treasure, the Dutch could launch an all-out invasion of Portuguese Brazil, via Pernambuco (Recife), in the 1630s, and take Curaçao on the Spanish Main. Conquering Pernambuco in northeast Brazil and renaming it New Holland, the Dutch fought a long and exhausting war to maintain their position. At first, they were successful, even repulsing a Portuguese naval attack on Pernambuco in 1640. But they soon wearied of the costly struggle, and by 1654 they had abandoned Brazil altogether.

Dutch sea routes into the South Atlantic, however, were not severed by the failure to secure Brazil. Conquests along the Guinea coast of West Africa in the 1630s were climaxed by the Dutch occupation of the Cape of Good Hope at the tip of South Africa in 1652. This strategic if turbulent and dangerous harbor linked Dutch trade routes with Europe, America, Guinea and the Far East, and it outflanked the similarly strategically located Portuguese way station of Mozambique, which the Dutch had failed to take by assault in 1607–08. Dutch activities in the Atlantic, along with the Thirty Years War, hastened the demise of Spanish overseas trade and contributed to the successful revolt of Portugal against Spain in 1640. The recovery of Brazil meant little to Portugal, however, until the 1690s, when gold was discovered there and turned it into a flourishing colony. The Dutch, concentrating on the Far East, fortified their African coastal bases against competitors as they battled to create a colonial system of their own.

The major Dutch thrust into the East developed more successfully, just as had that of the Portuguese a hundred years before, but was confronted with an entirely different collection of competitors and enemies. From Mozambique to Malabar in India, Portugal held tenuous command of the sea, though the Ottoman Turks still held the Arabian coast. Portugal also controlled the eastern half of the Indian Ocean from the Coromandel coast of India to the Malacca Strait. The Dutch penetration into this ocean in 1601 thus confronted the Portuguese, but also after 1608 English traders (English East India Company founded, 1600) and especially after 1666 the French (French East India Company founded, 1604). In the East Indies, where the Moslem faith continued to spread, the Dutch faced several local kingdoms and sultanates —especially Mataram—with which the Portuguese had had to battle for trade concessions. Spain occupied the Spice Islands of Molucca as well as several places in the Philippines. In these areas, native pirates like the Moros also presented a constant menace. In China, Formosa and Korea—with which both Portugal and Spain traded—civil war raged as the Chinese Manchus drove back the Ming. And in Japan, internal wars between Hideyoshi's successors and the Tokugawa clan threatened the European commerical position there.

Formidable as were the tasks facing the Dutch in exploiting the Far East, success lay in overwhelming the Portuguese, and to this end the Dutch devised a masterful strategy. Though the first regular Dutch voyages to the Indian Ocean in 1601–03 followed da Gama's first route to Calicut and thus broke the Portuguese trade monopoly in India, the Dutch adopted an alternate route of attack to destroy the Portuguese trade position altogether. Dutch plans were based on the extensive navigational and geographical findings of the late sixteenth century, especially those of the English Hakluyts and the Dutchman Jan Huyghen van Linschoten. The armed Dutch East Indiamen bypassed India by sailing directly to the East Indies, thus flanking the Portuguese sea routes from the Persian Gulf to the Malacca Strait and entering the Java Sea via the alternate entrance of the Sunda Strait. The first expedition reached the Moluccas in 1598–99, and in 1605 another seized Tidore and Amboina from the Portuguese; the Spanish, however, drove them out of several captured places the next year. Also in 1607 the Portuguese repulsed a Dutch attack on Malacca in two severe naval battles. Undaunted, the Dutch abandoned this goal, fostered relations with anti-Portuguese Indonesians, and searched for a base in the Indies.

Commodore Jan Pieterszoon Coen achieved the strategically key base when he led the Dutch seizure of Jakarta from the Javanese kingdom, renaming it Batavia, in 1618–19. Building upon this centrally located port, the Dutch could extend their commercial control over the Indies, giving them an interior position for attacks westward against the Portuguese in the Indian Ocean and northeastward against the Spanish in the Moluccas and the Philippines. Because of the distance of Chinese and Japanese waters, the Dutch focused their efforts against the rich Portuguese Empire. In fact, the Spanish resistance proved very stubborn. Not only did the Spanish hold on to their Spice Islands, but they repulsed Dutch attacks on the Philippines in 1610, 1617 and again in 1647–48.

The Netherlanders had better luck in Japan, where Hideyoshi's successors so feared the Portuguese that they opened their initially closed ports to Dutch and English traders in 1611. The English withdrew three years later, but the Dutch—remaining strictly traders—stayed and played on Japanese distrust of Portuguese missionaries and troops. Finally, in 1638 after forbidding all Japanese oceangoing trade, Japan expelled all Europeans in a new policy of seclusion, but two years later Japan granted to the Dutch trading rights at one port, Nagasaki. Civil strife in China also eventually benefited the Dutch, who in the 1620s had begun to settle the island of Formosa on agreement with its Japanese residents. As the Manchus drove the Ming back at mid-century, many refugees went to Formosa, causing conflict there. Finally, in 1661, the last Ming defender, Coxinga (Chêng Ch'eng-kung), using a formidable navy drove out the Dutch. But this event did not affect Dutch trade to Japan, and it posed such a threat to the Philippines that the Spanish evacuated the Molucca Spice Islands in order to reinforce Manila. The Dutch then occupied these places and renewed trade relations with China, ruled completely by the Manchus, who overthrew Coxinga's successors on Formosa in 1683. China then completely repudiated naval operations. By the end of the century, the Dutch had become the preferred European traders in the East, enjoying a monopoly with Japan and bartering with the Chinese, especially at the port city of Canton. The Chinese also traded with the West through Portuguese Macao and Spanish Manila. This general relationship between the East Asians and Europe remained in effect for the next two centuries.

The Protestant assault on the Portuguese Indian Ocean monopoly was led by the Dutch, but the English also played a prominent role in breaking the Portuguese hold on the Persian Gulf area. The Moslem Persians, already undermining the Portuguese, retook Bahrain in the Gulf in 1602, and pressed overland to confront the European bases from the land side. The English arrived in the area six years later when their East India Company tried to lease the use of Surat on the Gujarat coast from the local Indian ruler. The Portuguese interceded until 1612, when an English fleet defeated a bigger Portuguese force of four large galleons and numerous galleys in the area. As the English established their base at Surat, the Portuguese again attacked them there in 1614 with nine galleons, only to be driven off. The English then opened trade relations with Persia, twice defeated Portuguese squadrons off Jask in the Arabian Sea in 1618, and the next year joined the Dutch in a four-year alliance against the Moslems in Indonesia. In the North, however, in 1621 the English allied with the Mogul Empire of India and cooperated with the Persians to drive the Portuguese from Ormuz back to Muscat. For the remainder of the decade, the English and Dutch combined to stop a Portuguese counterattack, especially against Ormuz in 1630. Having in fact achieved Grotius' ideal of a *Mare Liberum* by breaking the Portuguese monopoly, the English expanded their Indian Ocean trade and established bases at Madras on the Coromandel coast of India in 1640 and at Hoogly on the Bengal coast in 1651. These adventures inevitably brought them into close competition with the Dutch.

Ironically, as the English followed the Dutchman Grotius to create a "free sea," the Dutch policy evolved away from Grotius to embody the Englishman Selden's concept of *Mare Clausum;* as the Portuguese retreated, Holland filled the vacuum to create its own imperial hegemony. In many ways this eventuality, like the takeover of the slave trade from Portuguese Guinea, was unpremeditated. But as Dutch fortunes improved, the enthusiasm of the aggressive Dutchmen led them to compromise their legal and moral ethics and to exploit their competitors' weaknesses for profit.

Commodore Coen, a self-styled empire builder, began this extension of Dutch empire after his founding of Batavia in 1619 by driving out English competitors and conquering the Banda Islands throughout the 1620s; when the natives resisted, Coen had them annihilated. Coen's similar actions against English settlers, though rarely that severe, hurt Anglo-Dutch relations at home, where the Thirty Years War had broken out, but he persisted in his company's monopolistic policies by forcing the English to abandon their trading posts at Dutch Batavia and Amboina. The Indonesian people also resisted, but in vain. The Javanese kingdom of Mataram besieged Batavia in 1628–29, and though Coen died during the siege, it failed. The Dutch successors of Albuquerque and Coen, especially Antonio van Diemen, then extended these gains over the Indian Ocean by adopting a purely maritime strategy and sending such distinguished explorers as Abel Tasman into the Pacific.

Feeling incapable of assaulting the strongly fortified Portuguese cities of Goa and Malacca, in 1630 the Dutch began a distant naval blockade of both places, forcing local trade to divert to Dutch Batavia. Malacca received the first pressure in this new strategy; then in 1636 the arrival of van Diemen as Governor-General of the Indies with reinforcements led to an equally strong naval isolation of Goa. Both blockades, which affected the midway Portuguese bases in Ceylon, spelled the doom of the Portuguese Empire in the East.

The Dutch naval blockades which reduced Portuguese Goa, Malacca and Ceylon to commercial impotence reached their climax with direct naval assaults in the years 1638 to 1645. In 1638, the first of eight annual blockading expeditions descended on Goa under van Diemen, who the next year bombarded Portuguese positions on Ceylon, especially the excellent harbor at Trincomalee. During the ensuing years, the blockade destroyed Goa commercially, and the Dutch extended their control over much of the Ceylonese coast. In 1641, the year after Portugal revolted from Spain, the Dutch attacked and captured Malacca, giving them absolute control over the East Indies. The next year the Netherlands and Portugal agreed on a ten-year truce, but it did not prevent the Dutch East India Company from consolidating its Eastern monopoly. By 1648, when the war in Europe ended (and Portugal was granted the return of several of its Eastern ports), Dutch power had reached its peak. But like Spain and Portugal before it, the monopoly now enjoyed by the Dutch Empire incurred the ill will of the newly emergent maritime nations.

Whatever happened in Europe, of course, would decide the fate of Dutch power, but the Dutch overseas offensive by 1652—the year they occupied the Cape of Good Hope—had established navigational patterns in the Far East for the next two centuries. India was effectively bypassed, with European commercial traffic to the East going directly round the Cape of Batavia, which controlled all spice trade in the Indies, much of the commerce to China and all of it with Japan. Three annual convoys passed between Amsterdam and Batavia, giving the Dutch absolute supremacy over Eastern sea lanes for the rest of the seventeenth century. England slowly advanced into the trade of India, as did France, but the Aden-Ormuz axis passed to local Moslem control, which fostered slave trade and local intercourse that bore little on the affairs of the West. So the Dutch monopolized the pepper and spices, but Indian textiles and cottons and Chinese silks after 1650 attracted European competitors. New products such as Japanese precious metals and Eastern tea and coffee made the East ever more important. These goods remained under Dutch control, however, but only as long as the Netherlands survived the maritime and continental wars of Europe.

## THIRTY YEARS WAR

Although the centers of maritime traffic and international finance shifted away from Seville, Genoa and Venice to London and Amsterdam, and the Cape route began the eclipse of Mediterranean trade, the middle sea remained the major naval arena of the Moslem-Christian conflict and became a secondary theater in the Thirty Years War (1618–48). For the first three decades of the seventeenth century, the Mediterranean continued to wane in importance—not only because of the incursions of Dutchmen and Englishmen but due to several Italian city-states continuing to fight one another, and Venice persisted against Spain in a vain effort to maintain its earlier political grandeur. Much naval maneuvering and some sharp skirmishing occupied these Mediterranean states, but squadrons rarely numbered over a dozen vessels each. In 1619–20, Spain and Venice settled their differences in the Adriatic, while the Netherlands signed a defensive alliance with Venice just as they had done with Sweden in the Baltic. The Christian-Moslem stalemate persisted in the Mediterranean, though the Ottoman Empire continued its wars in Eastern Europe and Persia. From 1580, the Ottoman imperial Barbary states of Algiers, Tunis and Tripoli assumed a virtually independent status from Constantinople to employ privateer corsairs against Christian shipping. The Knights of Malta responded by outfitting their own fleet of corsairs, organized and directed from 1605 by its own legal licensing court, the *Tribunale degli Armamenti*. These last representatives of the Christian Crusades dedicated their purpose to attacking Moslem shipping and the Ottoman and Barbary coasts.

The corsair wars between Berbers and Maltese in the Mediterranean implicated the European maritime powers, assumed much of the normal ferocity of religious struggles, and continued throughout the seventeenth and much of the eighteenth centuries. Though it was actually licensed piracy and robbery, the corsair activity of both sides assumed the status of a major business enterprise in general booty, captured ships and slaves (needed especially to man the galleys of the middle sea powers). Strongest in the early seventeenth century, the Barbary States relied on galleys, then on sailing warships captained by renegade Christian Europeans, Turks and occasionally North African Moors, crewed by similar persons of lower station and Christian slaves, and defended by a complement of up to 200 regular Turkish janissaries who carried out the principal tactic of boarding. The largest Barbary fleet, that of Algiers, in the 1620s included some six galleys, sixty large sailing ships of up to thirty guns each and forty smaller sailers. The Maltese corsair navy, which reached its peak strength after 1650, resembled its adversary in ship and crew characteristics, except for being heavier and slower because its emphasis lay in superior gunnery in both quantity and quality.

As in the previous century, the Christian Mediterranean powers licensed corsairs to prey indiscriminately on Moslem shipping, while the French privately financed the Maltese, and outright pirates from the Atlantic states plundered far and wide. But officially, Holland, England and France preferred not to antagonize the Ottomans because of their new trade connections in the Levant. So, after several punitive expeditions against the Barbary ports during the second half of the seventeenth century, the three major Atlantic maritime powers negotiated treaties with the three Barbary States, agreeing to pay tribute to them in return for guarantees that the Barbary corsairs would not attack their merchantmen. Though often broken, these treaties seriously reduced Barbary operations against weaker European states such as those from the Baltic, Spain and Malta.

So the Barbary maritime wars received much attention throughout the seventeenth century. Berber and independent Moroccan corsairs operated out into the Atlantic, while Ottoman Turkish corsairs cruised the Adriatic, contributing ultimately to renewed war between Turkey and Venice. The Ottomans provided the manpower to their nominal Barbary subjects, but timber, naval stores and guns came by purchase and later tribute from such Northern Europeans as the Dutch and Swedes. The Moslems showed remarkable forbearance over European violations of several treaty stipulations, for the Christians regarded and treated these enemies as pirates and infidels. Brutality was practiced by both sides, however, toward their prisoners. Still, in all, strict legality prevailed more often than not, with the Berbers boarding and inspecting foreign merchantmen to ascertain nationality before plundering cargoes of vessels not protected by treaty. In time, Christian corsairs seem to have succeeded more than the Moslems; punitive expeditions against Barbary ports began to take a toll later in the century; and toward its end England and France made treaties ending the Berbers' right of search of their flag vessels. Gradually, however, the corsairs of Malta found themselves ever more restricted by the French, who in the 1660s assumed much of the carrying trade of Ottoman Turkey and in 1673 ended the Maltese right of search of French vessels. The Maltese then turned against the Ottoman Greeks—Christian or not—and privateering became so complicated that a new prize court had to be established on Malta in 1697, the *Consolato di Mare*. Such legal restrictions and the growing maritime strength of the Atlantic powers combined to weaken the scope of corsair activities by Christians and Moslems alike.

Religious motives also began to be eclipsed by political factors during the Thirty Years War which engulfed continental Europe and spilled over into its waters between 1618 and 1648. First a religious battle between the Catholic Habsburgs and Protestant Germans, this struggle had the chief effect on the maritime powers of enhancing their wealth by being isolated from the widespread devastation. The Holy Roman Empire, centered on Austria and parts of German lands and loosely including Habsburg Spain, warred against the Reformed peoples of Northern Europe and also France. The religious strife inside France had resulted, in 1610, in the reestablishment of an absolute monarchy under the Catholic Bourbon dynasty, headed by King Louis XIII and his political lieutenant, Cardinal Richelieu. But Catholicism ceased to be the basis of French foreign policy, so that the French alliance with Protestant powers set the model for the new despotic nation states of Europe. A strong, right-wing Anglican church persisted under the English Stuart kings, James I and Charles I, but civil war in 1649 overthrew this government, thus reducing any vestige of religious determinism in England. Only Habsburg Spain, medieval and increasingly irrelevant, dreamed of restoring its Catholic Empire by overcoming the Dutch and English. And Sweden under Gustavus Adolphus sought to expand its rule inland from the Baltic coast. All Europe, except for Russia, was brought into some aspect of the fighting.

The economic devastation caused by the outbreak of this war brought collapse for Spain, the Spanish Netherlands (Belgium) and most of Central Europe, and provided the impetus to the growing wealth of the Netherlands, England and Sweden, while France and the Italian states suffered only minimally. The Dutch, in addition to their imperial holdings, controlled the key European river traffic to the sea, focused on the Rhine, and increased their investments in Sweden for the mutual benefit of both nations. The financial empire of Dutchman Louis de Geer represented the interdependence of Swedish iron and copper (hence cannon) with Dutch shipbuilding. Thus stimulated, the Swedes took to the seas with warships and colonial ventures to North America alongside Holland. The Dutch had also introduced a new swift, lightly manned merchant ship, the *fluyt,* so commercially successful that the English soon imitated it. England, unlike Sweden and Holland isolated from the battlefields of Europe, turned to trade, shipbuilding and crude industry even at the expense of its navy. The pacifistic James I nearly lost England's prosperity by laying up the Navy Royal and discontinuing the privateer-licensing Letters of Marque, which almost succeeded in finishing off English corsairs, but exposed English shipping and coastal towns to Algerine and Dunkirker pirates, whose raids on English soil were scandalous. On the whole, however, England profited along with Holland and Sweden from the continental struggle. As a result, the sea powers of the North and Baltic coasts evolved, along with France, to positions of predominance over Western Europe—and the world. In this sense also then, the age was Oceanic.

The maritime powers did not become involved in the fighting until 1621, when the Netherlands allied with the Protestant Germans against Austria and resumed hostilities against Spain at the end of their twelve-year truce. The heavy fighting on the continent reached Holland the next year, when an attacking Spanish army was driven out by the Protestant allies. Finally, in 1624, the German and Dutch Protestants were joined in the war against the Catholic Habsburgs by France, England, Sweden, Denmark, Venice and Italian Savoy. The Mediterranean members of this coalition, France, Venice and Savoy, attacked Spanish communications in the South, while the others supported the United Provinces against attacks from the Spanish Netherlands. In August 1624 a Spanish army laid siege to the Dutch fortress of Breda, which commanded the approaches to Utrecht and Amsterdam. The defenders held out until the following June, when they were allowed to surrender on the most magnanimous of terms—a sure sign of declining religious hatred and the growing humanity in the midst of an otherwise devastating war. Simultaneously, the Habsburgs employed the mercenary Count Albrecht von Wallenstein to command their armies along with the incumbent general, Johan Tserclaes, Count Tilly.

In 1625, the war shifted to the Baltic and assumed more maritime proportions. Gustavus Adolphus of Sweden had captured Riga in 1621 in his running border war against continental Poland, but now the Germans elected Christian IV, king of Denmark, to direct their operations against the Habsburgs, thus turning the Baltic into a battleground for two separate wars. The Danes invaded Germany in 1625, but in two years of fighting were driven back by the armies of Wallenstein and Tilly. Simultaneously, an unsuccessful French Protestant revolt around La Rochelle brought English intervention in 1625, leading to a five-year undeclared naval war pitting France and Spain against England and Holland. The French fleet under the admiral Duke Henry of Montmorency defeated a Protestant force off La Rochelle in September 1625, joined in a land-sea siege against the rebels there, and drove off the English fleet twice in 1628. Meanwhile, the Swedes of Gustavus and his able minister Axel Oxenstierna had been reinforcing their navy under the administrative genius of Klas Fleming and the command of Karl Karlsson Gyllenhjelm. From 1626 to 1628 this fleet blockaded Danzig and supported army operations against Polish Prussia; for the first time in its history, Poland raised a navy, a squadron of ten ships which defeated the Swedish fleet off Danzig in November 1627. But Poland suffered from internal problems that led her to welcome peace negotiations.

Inevitably, as the Habsburg armies approached the Baltic coast, Sweden was drawn into the main war. Early in 1628, Wallenstein besieged Stralsund, one of the Hanse ports allied to Denmark which, if it fell, would give the Habsburgs access to the Baltic. Aware of this, the Austrian Holy Roman Emperor appointed Wallenstein to be Admiral of the Baltic and Ocean Sea, Austria's first experience with a navy, a small collection of coastal vessels hardly worthy of the name. Wallenstein enlisted the aid of Spain with a view toward taking key ports and thus winning command of the Baltic. Thoroughly alarmed, Sweden immediately came to the aid of Denmark, drove back the Austrian squadron threatening Wismar, kept open Stralsund's communications by sea, and generally became hostile to the Catholics. Though checked on land, the Danes kept their navy so active that Lübeck and the other Hanseatic cities decided to join the fight against Wallenstein. The Danes blockaded the German coast and sent naval units into the North Sea to cooperate with Dutch and English ships against the Catholics. With the maritime powers—Holland, Denmark, Sweden and England—in full command of Northern waters, Wallenstein quit the siege of Stralsund and abandoned his grand designs on the Baltic. In the next year, 1629, Denmark withdrew from the war, and France managed to arrange a truce between Sweden and Poland, thus releasing Sweden for full participation in the war against the Habsburgs.

The brief hiatus of the winter of 1629–30 allowed Gustavus to consider his strategy as the new champion of the Protestant cause in which he soon enjoyed the support of the maritime powers and of France. The alliance with the Netherlands continued when the Dutch-Swedish munitions entrepreneur Louis de Geer supplied both Sweden and Holland with enough cannon to fight both the Austrian and Spanish armies. Denmark, now out of the fighting, did not interfere with Sweden's operations, and kept busy by controlling the Sound, which involved a long though undeclared naval war with Hanseatic Hamburg from 1630 to 1643. England in 1631 began to shift her support from Denmark to Sweden, but played no active part in the war. France, however, under the shrewd statesmanship of Cardinal Richelieu, in 1631 allied with Sweden and sent her money in return for Swedish cannon and warships. Gustavus had collected a fleet of twenty-seven warships and thirteen merchant vessels and in the summer of 1630 used it to transport his army for the capture of Usedom Island, his springboard for the invasion of Germany.

Gustavus quickly proved his genius as strategist and field commander. Capturing the port of Stettin, he advanced up the Oder River, building fortified magazines to protect his ever-lengthening lines of communications. The Swedish navy controlled his rear and in 1631 absorbed fourteen small vessels of the fledgling Austrian navy. The same year

Gustavus overcame logistical difficulties by capturing Frankfurt and Leipzig and decisively defeating Tilly at the battle of Breitenfeld. The next year Gustavus continued his successes, killed Tilly in battle on the river Lech, and in November defeated Wallenstein at the battle of Lützen, in which, however, Gustavus himself was killed. Chancellor Oxenstierna succeeded to the Swedish leadership as regent for the new minor queen, while Wallenstein attempted a *coup d'état* in Bohemia which led to his own assassination in 1634. That year Swedish arms were severely defeated, leading the French to come to the open aid of the Protestants. The Swedish navy kept open communications to the continent and that year was elevated to the position of a major administrative department within the government.

The French entry into the war in 1635, marked by formal alliances with Holland and Sweden and a declaration of war against Spain, considerably changed the nature of the struggle. Religion assumed a secondary role as France for the first time introduced the notion of maintaining a modern political balance of power between the emerging nation-states of Europe. From 1635 till the end of the Thirty Years War in 1648 France matured as the first large united nation-state of Western Europe based on political rather than religious motives. Political goals and actions merged with diplomatic and military factors in the emerging art of modern statecraft. Louis XIII was the titular head of this state, Richelieu the architect. The army became the major tool of French policy under the administrative leadership of Michel Le Tellier and the command of Henri de Turenne. Cooperating with the Swedish army in the North, and with the Dutch and the German Protestant princes on the frontiers, French arms waged successful war against the Habsburgs of Austria and Spain. The death of Richelieu late in 1642 had no effect on French arms, which crushed the Spanish army at Rocroi the next year; Richelieu's successor, Cardinal Giulio Mazarin, proved to be an even more powerful figure.

At sea, the Dutch predominated, as they whittled away at Spanish imperial communications and enjoyed at least a tenuous peace with England. The new English king, Charles I, though Anglican and anti-Dutch, had internal difficulties, not the least of which resulted from lack of a decent navy. Pirate attacks forced him to tax his people in 1634–35 to pay for his new "Ship-Money Fleet," a measure that decreased his popularity among the English people and their Parliament. The Dutch had had to carry on the fight against the Dunkirker pirates virtually alone, a war which cost Holland the life of its brilliant admiral Piet Heyn in a naval skirmish in 1629. But the lack of a formal enemy battle fleet led the Dutch States General to neglect the fleet, and such veteran ship captains as Martin Tromp and Witt Corneliszoon de With retired. The battles in Brazilian and East Indian waters continued, however, and Spanish and Dunkirker successes at sea forced the Dutch to reinforce their home squadrons. In 1637, to command the fleet, the States General appointed calm, calculating Tromp as Lieutenant Admiral and the fiery de With as Vice Admiral. Both men quickly reorganized and disciplined the fleet, and none too soon, for Spain in 1639 launched another armada, this time to invade the Netherlands.

The naval battle of the Downs settled the independence of the Protestant Dutch nation. In the midst of Tromp's operations against pirate Dunkirk, in September 1639 Admiral Don Antonio Oquendo arrived in the English Channel with the Spanish-Portuguese armada of 77 galleons and 24,000 men. On the 18th Tromp and de With charged their 31 ships into the sprawling armada formation in mid-Channel. The swifter Dutch craft, manned by the first professional admirals in history, outmaneuvered and outfought the Iberians until a fog ended the fighting. Oquendo ran on to Dover, anchoring in the Downs, where he expected help from the English fleet based there. But the English did nothing in this ticklish diplomatic situation, and Tromp promptly sealed up the Spaniards with a blockade. New ships and other reinforcements hastened from Holland, so that within a month Tromp had 105 galleons and armed merchantmen and 12 fire ships. On October 18 Tromp attacked Oquendo with such fury that his Dutchmen sank, burned or forced ashore no fewer than 70 Spanish and Portuguese galleons; only 7, including Oquendo's flagship, escaped to Dunkirk. The battle of the Downs had finished Spanish naval power.

The Dutch triumph had lasting implications. By crippling the navy of Spain, Holland insured its independence from the Catholic Empire; Spain never again tried to conquer the Netherlands. In addition, Dutch prestige was considerably heightened throughout Europe and the disputed lands abroad. By the same token, Spain appeared enfeebled. In the Western Mediterranean, France had obtained command of the sea by dispatching ships from its Atlantic ports to support the army attacking Barcelona and to keep Spanish squadrons at bay through continuous though usually indecisive maneuvering. Then, in 1640, Portugal threw off Spanish rule, and the French navy spent the next few years checking Spanish naval activities on the east side of Gibraltar. Dutch command of the English Channel enabled Tromp to battle the Dunkirkers and to join the French army in besieging Dunkirk by land and sea in the autumn of 1646. But by commanding the Channel and even violating the waters of Dover, the Dutch had offended England, whose king had been humiliated by failing to use his expensive Ship-Money Fleet to enforce English neutrality. Charles's grip on Parliament was further weakened, leading to civil war in 1642. And Dutch supremacy at sea began to run afoul of the steadily growing English merchant fleet. Relations between these two basically Protestant nations deteriorated.

Dutch naval power expanded even further as a result of the continuing rivalry between Sweden and Denmark in the Baltic. Both Holland and Sweden resented the Sound dues of the Danes, backed up by a declining Danish navy, so the Swedes briefly diverted their army from Germany to launch an attack on Denmark without warning late in 1643. Swedish troops easily overran Jutland and Scania, but were kept from the Danish islands by the presence of the defending fleet. Louis de Geer therefore journeyed to Amsterdam where he outfitted two separate fleets of 33 and 21 warships for Sweden under the command of veteran Dutch Sea Beggar Maarten Thijsen, who was commissioned an admiral in the Swedish navy. The first contingent engaged the smaller but more powerful Danish fleet personally commanded by King Christian IV off List Deep and was defeated in mid-May 1644. The Dutch force then left the Baltic, but in June Admiral Klas Fleming with about 40 warships operated in Danish waters. On July 1 Fleming engaged Christian's similarly-sized navy in battle off Kolberger Heath near Femern in which the heavy gunnery duel failed to sink any ships or bring about a decision. The two fleets, including Thijsen's, returning from Holland with de Geer's second fleet, skirmished over the ensuing weeks, including one incident which led to the mortal wounding of Fleming. The success of Denmark's naval king made Dutch intervention mandatory if Sweden was to win the war.

In July 1644 the Dutch made deliberate moves into the Baltic. Vice Admiral de With with 32 warships escorted over 900 merchant ships in convoy through the Sound, forcing Christian to negotiate. Then early in August Admiral Thijsen engaged Christian's fleet near Copenhagen before joining up with the Swedish fleet. The Swedes, endeavoring to seize command of the sea, united their fleet and Thijsen's under the command of the general Count Karl Gustaf von Wrangel. On October 13, near the scene of the earlier action off Femern, Wrangel with 37 ships met and defeated Christian's force of 17 ships. The Danes lost 14 vessels and four of their commanding officers. The battle was a serious blow from which Denmark never fully recovered, and the next year de With convoyed 300 merchantmen with 48 warships through the Sound without bothering to pay the tolls. Denmark no longer commanded the Baltic or even the respect of her adversaries, who forced her to terms in 1645, notably, preferential reduced tolls through the Sound. Thus Holland and Sweden gained control over the Baltic, much to the pique of England, which still had to pay the higher duties. In the Mediterranean, Spain managed to check the French fleet besieging Orbitello in 1646 and frustrated a French attempt to support an abortive revolt of Naples against Spanish rule in 1647–48.

When the peace was signed in 1648 ending the Thirty Years War on the continent, the Netherlands boasted the strongest navy in the world and an army equal in prestige to those of Sweden and France. Spain, torn by internal revolts and committed to continuing the war against France, by the terms of the peace treaty with the Netherlands formally recognized Dutch independence and further agreed to close the Scheldt to international traffic, thus eliminating Antwerp and the Spanish Netherlands as competitors of Amsterdam. Sweden extended her control over much of the Baltic coast, and remained allied with Holland. Denmark, however, realistically accepted the supremacy of the Dutch and in 1649 signed a defensive alliance with them—which further served to antagonize the English. International relations in North America also reflected Dutch hegemony; from 1647 to 1655 the Dutch colonists from the Hudson Valley region drove the Swedish settlers from the Delaware area and then only faced the English. Dutch trade traveled almost unmolested throughout the world, fighting successfully to expel the Portuguese from Indonesia but unsuccessfully to do the same in Brazil. The only area where Dutch naval arms played no major role was in the Cretan War which had broken out between Venice and Ottoman Turkey in 1645. True to their business-oriented policy, the Dutch traded with all belligerents.

By the middle of the seventeenth century, the Netherlands ruled the major sea lanes of the world. As Dutch trade grew, the Spanish and Portuguese powers declined, while war-torn Central Europe sank into deeper economic chaos. The period of major explorations was over, and the Dutch reaped the profits of their own stability as a maritime empire. Even at home, they threw off the conservative rule by abolishing the central stadtholder in 1650 and further embracing republican institutions. Dutch resources had enabled them to defend their homeland against all enemies and to project their power overseas. But, importantly, they had not the resources to go beyond these frontiers in war. Such was the threat posed by the rise of England and France after 1650, and though Dutch civilization continued to flourish and its great naval wars were yet to be fought, the Dutch seaborne empire would survive only at the sufferance of these two growing political giants.

# 6

# England and France, 1650–1730

*. . . he that commands the sea is at great liberty, and may take as much and as little of the war as he will; whereas those that be strongest by land are many times, nevertheless, in great straits; and the wealth of both Indies seems, in great part, but an accessory to the command of the seas.*

—FRANCIS BACON

## THE BALANCE OF POWER

The carnage of the Thirty Years War, the end of the major explorations and the triumph of the Dutch maritime trade by 1650 all combined to usher in a new era of rivalry based not on total religious struggles but on political maneuvering to maintain certain balances of power between the established nation-states. Emulating the Dutch, the other powers now turned toward industry and commerce, especially at sea. In the years roughly 1650 to 1730, therefore, the goals of warfare shifted to economic motives, and the techniques of fighting became more limited. Instead of religiously-charged marauding armies aimed at widespread destruction, the powers turned to warships that could compete for control of vital sea lanes and colonies with more subtle but equally decisive effect. In the true Dutch fashion, business and war became ever more interdependent. England and France, though hampered initially by internal disorders, took the lead, but most of Europe followed suit. Naval warfare—and the substitute for it, tariff barriers and preferential import duties—did their part to tone down violence and to increase the cause of reason and humanism. Only in Eastern Europe did the old bloodshed persist, in the wars of the Ottoman Empire and Persia and of the continental domains of Austria, Poland, Russia and briefly Sweden, France and Spain.

As the Western powers mobilized their finances and commerce to construct and maintain expensive navies, merchant marines and maritime empires, centralized government became paramount. Whereas private companies had carried trade—and sea war—to the West and East Indies and to the Levant and Baltic, so now the national effort required national control. Trading "factories" had to be concentrated near the major ports, great shipyards erected for maritime and naval construction, and authority wielded to fill the crews of the enlarged men-of-war. Whether a king or stadtholder headed these governments and played a direct role in the mobilization, such as Cromwell of England or Peter of Russia, strong professional administrators became indispensable to devise and execute sound maritime policy: Colbert in France, Pepys in England, Jan de Witt in Holland and Oxenstierna in Sweden. Such men raised the industrialist and merchant to greater status in traditionally maritime countries and—more gradually—to new respectability in the rigid aristocracies. In so doing, they helped to mold the modern nation-state. Yet, as long as the great powers warred, production and trade suffered, so that the late seventeenth and early eighteenth centuries served both as the embattled end of the Oceanic Age and as the transition to the tenuous equilibrium of the next era.

Warship construction became standardized under governmental controls, and armed merchantmen gradually passed out of general service. The galleons were enlarged, and timber and naval stores abroad were more precious to the maritime powers (though at first France could tap her own largely virgin forests). Hence the English and Dutch considered trade with the Baltic as a cornerstone of their national policies. The art of naval construction advanced, particularly through the French, though a major dispute arose over the use of superfluous embellishments. The Spanish, for instance, had made their galleons into magnificent works of art with carvings and gilt on the hulls and with attractive designs on the cannons. Carried to the extreme, however, the decorations proved more important than the functional aspects of the design, as in 1628 when the 1400-ton, 64-gun Swedish flagship *Vasa* turned turtle on her maiden voyage inside Stockholm harbor (raised in 1961 and now on display there). The model for such instruments of fighting beauty became the English *Sovereign of the Seas,* launched in 1637, over 1100 tons with 100 guns on three gun decks, but which had to be modified before she could see action. By 1650, English warships were classified into one of six rates, eventually judged by the number of men required to work each gun. The issue over ornamentation was finally climaxed in France in 1670, but utility did not entirely win out, so that even as late as the last wooden warships of the 1850s did they retain the superfluous figurehead.

For the nations whose very life and trade depended upon the sea, Holland and England, functionalism and economy of labor dominated warship construction from about 1650 onwards, due to the harsh lessons of battle. Tactics simply decreed that opposing lines or squadrons of vessels lay themselves alongside the enemy for point-blank artillery broadsides. So frightful was the resulting bloodshed that gun decks were painted crimson, a pragmatic effort to reduce psychological casualties. As ship designs became standardized, so too did those of the cannon. Modern science produced lead and then copper sheathing over hulls to combat hungry marine organisms, while the range of cannon gradually increased. Also, new forms of naval weaponry emerged from earlier theory into the experimental stage: the crude submarine; bomb ketches with small mortars (such as the Dutch coehorn) to lob improved exploding bombs; "stink-pot" poisonous grenades; and muskets. Well-armed galleons drove more lightly armed warships from the battle line, while frigates, armed merchantmen and sloops took on auxiliary tasks, and galleys and fire ships approached outright obsolescence. Ships of the line came to be known roughly by their numbers of guns: by 1675 the average English first rate mounted 100 guns, the second rate 74, the third rate 60, the fourth 50. These floating fortresses were likened to the great forts then in vogue on the continent, but with one crucial difference: mobility!

By the mid-seventeenth century, the balance of maritime power in Europe and the world revolved around six imperial powers: the Netherlands, Spain, Portugal, Sweden, England and France. The great continental powers of the Germanies, Austria (Holy Roman Empire), Poland, Russia and the Ottoman Turks had either become too exhausted to affect this balance, had internal troubles, or continued to fight along their unstable frontiers.

Holland, by any measure the most prosperous nation in the world, with Amsterdam at the center, had monopolized most of the European overseas carrying trade in Dutch bottoms. Dutch trade lanes to the North gave them control over the Baltic, including the mutual shipbuilding and cannon trade with both Sweden and Denmark, in addition to a gun foundry in Moscow. To the West, the Dutch had colonies between New England and Virginia, islands in the Caribbean, a foothold in Guiana and a temporary hold on the coast of Brazil. But Holland's real empire centered on the East Indies, and the Dutch occupation of the Cape of Good Hope sealed their control over all maritime communications to the Far East. In the 1650s Dutch colonial leaders accelerated their attempts to secure bases in West Africa and to subdue all hostile native kingdoms in Indonesia and the Ceylonese coast. The Dutch also continued to fight Portugal, driving its colonials from the

Malabar coast of India, conquering the intermediate kingdom of Macassar, and playing a small role in the native wars of Vietnam. These activities gave the Dutch control over native shipping, and following the conquest of Javanese Mataram in 1677, Dutchmen extended their control over Java, monopolized and began active colonization of the East Indies, traded with the kingdom of Siam, carried much of China's trade, and continued to monopolize Europe's contact with Japan. Considering the wars at home during these years, these achievements by the United Provinces seem all the more remarkable.

Spain survived as a European and world power only at the sufferance of maritime Holland and neighboring France. The war with France, begun in 1635, continued throughout the 1650s until Spain yielded her primacy among continental powers to France. This struggle so drained the Spanish economy that the Dutch both absorbed much of Spain's foreign commerce and sheltered French and English colonists in the Caribbean against the weak Spanish naval patrols. This latter policy severely damaged the security of the Spanish Main, since mercenary corsairs and buccaneers smuggled with and raided Spanish outposts throughout the century. Spain tenaciously clung to her American *Mare Clausum,* refusing not only to allow foreign trade with her colonies but also barring independent trade between the separate Spanish colonies. But since the home government could not provide enough of the necessities for life abroad, Spanish colonial administrators cooperated unofficially with foreign smugglers and buccaneers. Militia and lancer detachments were ineffective anyway, though fortifications were improved, a ten-frigate squadron added, Spanish colonial privateering encouraged, and the *Armada Real* continued in escort of the vital treasure convoys. The feeble administration of King Philip IV could only turn to the *asiento,* contracts to foreign powers for specific commercial awards (as Portugal had enjoyed over the Spanish slave trade up to the Portuguese revolt in 1640), but this had the long-range effect of undermining the Spanish imperial monopoly. Only in the Pacific Ocean, or rather the thin trade routes from Manila to Acapulco, Panama and Peru, did the Spanish navy remain supreme—possible only because the rival powers were preoccupied elsewhere and took no interest in the Pacific. Spain kept naval forces at both ends to discourage foreign penetration into the Pacific: at the River Plate (Argentina), the Falkland Islands (off Argentina), Juan Fernandez Island (off Chile), the Galápagos Islands (off Ecuador), Panama, the Ladrone (Marianas) Islands and Manila. Dutch supremacy in Indonesia, however, isolated the Spanish Philippines and made them a mere distant appendage of Latin America.

Spain's original preserve, the Mediterranean, already in eclipse, became a commercial backwater when the Dutch shifted the major trade routes via the Cape in 1652. Spain remained a major power with its possessions in Italy, but all Western nations bordering on the Mediterranean declined due both to the alternate Cape route and to the competition by Dutch and English trading companies whose commercial goods became essential to the Ottoman Turks. All Mediterranean traders continued to suffer in varying degrees from the corsairs. Malta built a squadron of ships of the line after 1700, but these never operated out of the Western Mediterranean after 1716, while the Barbary corsairs declined to but a shadow of their former might due to their many treaties and resulting lack of enemies to prey upon and prosper thereby. Venice, in the Cretan War of 1645 to 1670, battled the Ottoman Empire, but gradually such galley actions again in the middle sea acted as minor adjuncts to the general Christian-Moslem struggle in Eastern Europe. A series of major naval battles near the Dardanelles between 1649 and 1657 led to a Turkish naval revival and offensive into the Aegean, culminating, finally, in the capture of Candia, Crete, in 1669. After the Turks fought Russia in a short war, 1678–81, and were repulsed before Vienna by Austria and Poland in 1683, Venice launched an offensive .in 1685–88 which succeeded in regaining the Morea and Athens. These wars exhausted all the belligerents and reduced Venice, Genoa and even Spain to the rank of minor Mediterranean powers; Savoy and Austria grew in importance, and the Turks turned to face the growing power of Russia. Through it all, the Atlantic traders profited from increased commerce with Mediterranean Christians and Moslems alike.

Portugal declined as a maritime empire even more rapidly than did Spain, thanks not only to the Dutch offensive but also to Spanish overlordship of the country from 1580 to 1640 and the continued attempt of Spain to recover Portugal which lasted until 1668. The fact that Portugal regained its independence was due largely to English friendship out of mutual fear of the Dutch, and Portugal even ceded Moroccan Tangier (occupied since 1471) to England in 1661. Since the two powers did not often work in concert, however, Portugal fought the Netherlands alone from 1657 to 1661 and in the East Indies until 1684 when the Dutch finally gained an absolute monopoly over the Indies. Dutch bases there and in Ceylon and India practically destroyed Portugal's trade from Goa to Macao. The Portuguese maintained this thin commercial thread from their old empire, and in fact fought the Moslems in Oman over it for the century after 1650. The once-sprawling Portuguese Empire during these years thus contracted back to the African littoral from Mozambique around to Angola and thence across the Atlantic to Brazil, which the Dutch quit, but which by 1700 yielded important new gold deposits. By then, however, Portugal was finished as a great power.

Sweden at mid-century controlled the Baltic, but her destiny as a great power depended on the power balance in Western Europe. At sea, Sweden required Dutch naval support, but as weakened Denmark moved into league with Holland, Sweden began to court the favor of newly emergent France. Sweden consequently became embroiled in the maritime struggles of the North Sea. More importantly, Sweden sought to extend its territorial holdings along the east coast of the Baltic south from Livonian Riga and thus participated in the continental wars between Poland and Russia. The first Northern War of 1655–60 began with Sweden invading Poland, then having to defend Riga against Russia, then invading and taking most of Denmark, and finally being repulsed from a naval blockade of Copenhagen by intervening English and Dutch fleets. The war extended Sweden's territory over Scania to the shores of the Sound but led to renewed fighting with Denmark in the 1670s, entanglement in the wars of Western Europe, and eventual confrontation with Russia. The timber and naval stores of the Baltic were so important to Holland, England and France that the Baltic, like the Mediterranean, after 1650 became a secondary theater of war in the maritime struggles of Europe.

France came out of the Thirty Years War as the military equal of neighboring Holland but with the roots of an imperial desire realized in the late seventeenth century under King Louis XIV. Being continental, France depended on her army and a new system of defensive fortresses to prosecute the successful war against Spain until 1659. Then Louis XIV ascended the throne to build an ever greater France, assisted by Jean Baptiste Colbert, his powerful finance minister who looked with envy upon the Dutch maritime empire and navy. Building upon the foundations of a modern navy begun by Richelieu, then dormant under Mazarin, Colbert meticulously fashioned a fleet of modern, sleek galleons and merchant ships and sent them throughout the world to seek colonies. Between 1659 and his death in 1683, Colbert had great naval arsenals built at Brest at the western end of the Channel, at Rochefort near Oléron on the Biscay coast, and at Toulon in the Mediterranean. In addition, he established naval academies at Rochefort, Dieppe and St. Malo. In 1666 French ships entered the Indian Ocean in strength, in 1670–71 established bases in India near the Ganges River and on the Coromandel coast, and in 1686 claimed Madagascar. The French strengthened their colonies in Canada and at Martinique, Guadeloupe and Guiana in the Caribbean, placed them under the administrative control of the navy, and in the 1660s waged naval war against the Barbary pirates and the Ottoman Turks. To enhance French prestige in the middle sea, the Galley Corps was established in 1665, officered by Maltese Knights with the religious motive enhanced by the presence of Catholic chaplains, and manned by con-

scripts, criminals, debtors and Moslem slaves. France identified with
Sweden in the Baltic, in 1667 began penetrating into Western Africa,
and in the next decade became involved with Siam. To lend legal order
to this vast enterprise, Colbert in 1681 established France's own maritime code, the *Ordonnance de la Marine,* including a royal admiralty
court which became the model for other European powers.

As if Colbert was bent on creating a thalassocratic culture from a
non-maritime-centered people, he founded French academies in art, science and architecture that played no small part in the classical grandeur
of Bourbon France symbolized by the great palace at Versailles—hence
the plays of Molière and Racine, the volumes of La Rochefoucauld,
the science and philosophy of Descartes and Pascal and later Montesquieu, Voltaire and Rousseau. Inevitably, however, France's new national vitality interfered and led to conflict with the other powers, especially maritime England.

England's rise as a major sea power after the Armada campaign had
been delayed by the pacifistic neglect of the Navy Royal of King James I
and the internal troubles which mounted under Charles I, culminating
in the English civil war of the 1640s. Charles's "Ship-Money Fleet"
bore no loyalty to its king since pay and living conditions had become
so poor. The fleet therefore supported Parliament against Charles in
the fighting of 1642–45, isolating the Royalists from any outside help,
particularly from France, and enabling Oliver Cromwell to fashion the
parliamentary forces into the New Model Army which finally defeated
the king. In 1648, however, the year of peace on the continent, civil
war flared up again, as Cromwell and the army broke with Parliament
and most of the navy and within three years had executed the king,
defeated Parliament, put down uprisings in Scotland and Ireland, and
created the Commonwealth. These events stunted the growth of English
mercantilism, as did the free run of Barbary and Dunkirker corsairs
against the British Isles.

England by 1650 had established some colonies in North America—
Virginia, Massachusetts, Rhode Island, Connecticut and Maryland, and
in the West Indies—St. Kitts, Barbados and Antigua. Bermuda was
occupied in 1609, and to the Indian settlements of Surat and Madras
was added a post in Bengal in 1651. But because of the troubles at
home, these colonies had to fend for themselves and therefore, unique
among European colonies, they were allowed to develop their own institutions of self-government. Gradually, English trade increased to the
Baltic, Mediterranean, Americas and Far East. Spain and Portugal were
declining competitors, and France began an undeclared naval war with
England in 1649. But everywhere the English went, they confronted the

vigorous Dutch. The oceans of the world seemed increasingly unable to accommodate the needs of both these maritime peoples.

The Commonwealth of Oliver Cromwell therefore decided to challenge Dutch maritime wealth directly, and in October of 1651 Parliament passed the fateful Navigation Act. This legislation forbade goods from entering English ports unless aboard English bottoms or those of the country of origin. Since the Dutch trade supremacy was founded not on Dutch goods, which were few except for imported spices, but on the Dutch carrying monopoly over European seaborne trade, the Act served as a patent challenge to the Netherlands. Cromwell, however, was in a position of strength and not blind to the possibilities of a foreign war reunifying his divided country. The new Commonwealth Navy since 1649 had been battling the now-dispersed Royalist naval forces under Prince Rupert and their supporters, the Catholic Bourbon royal fleet of France. Three excellent colonels from the undefeated New Model Army had been commissioned as "Generals at Sea," and the whole naval administration had been drastically reformed to a high state of efficiency. The fleet's strength doubled in the shipyards at Chatham, Deptford, Portsmouth and Woolwich between 1649 and 1651 with forty-one new warships. The Convoy Act of 1650 led to the government's official entrance into the field of commerce protection, thus following the example of the Dutch. Escorted convoys by General at Sea Robert Blake and other officers in 1650–51 had kept open English commercial communications to the Levant against French and Moslem privateers. Cromwell preferred not to fight his fellow Protestants, but the Navigation Act set in motion a rapid sequence of events that could only end in war.

Early in 1652, the Dutch reacted by authorizing 150 more ships of war, a larger fleet than England's but in many ways inferior as the latter navy built only large galleons for war, whereas the Dutch still utilized dual-purpose armed merchantmen. The English responded immediately by ordering General Blake to concentrate the Commonwealth fleet at the Downs, which would be near the strategic center—the Strait of Dover, the "bottleneck of Europe," through which all North European maritime traffic must pass. In May Lieutenant Admiral Martin Harpertzoon Tromp put to sea with a strong Dutch force, and Blake did likewise; both men with their officers and crews were in ugly moods over the mutual hostility. They came together off the Downs, opened fire and fought a brisk gunnery duel in which two small Dutch ships were lost. The Dutch spared no time in declaring war and concluding a new pact with Denmark which closed the Sound and the vital Baltic trade to England for the duration.

## ANGLO-DUTCH WARS

The three Anglo-Dutch wars which began in the summer of 1652 are the most dramatic naval conflicts in history, since both England and the Netherlands as primary naval powers aimed at commanding the seas. To be sure, both had fine armies—Maurice's veterans and Cromwell's New Model Army, which even supplied admirals to the fleet. But the national destinies of these peoples lay inextricably with the sea— the carrying trade and fishing grounds of Europe, the markets of the Baltic and the Mediterranean, and the colonies and sea routes of North America and the Indian Ocean. In battle, both fleets fought to the bitter end; the final victor would have absolute command of the oceans of the world.

The Dutch entered the first war at a disadvantage. The dissolution of the stadtholdership in 1650 undermined the principle of unity of command at just the wrong time: the five boards of the Admiralty of the United Provinces, especially Holland and Zeeland, quarreled. Republicans supporting the States General and Orangemen favoring the infant William III to become stadtholder split the people and the navy. The emergence of Jan de Witt as Grand Pensionary of the Netherlands at least restored central leadership, but conflicting admiralty orders would often impair fleet operations. Dutch wealth depended upon the security of the Baltic, Mediterranean and Eastern merchant convoys, but these forces of from 100 to 400 vessels lumbering along at two knots required the protection of the home fleet when near the English coast. So the Dutch admirals early faced the nearly impossible dual responsibilities of protecting commerce and warding off—or better, engaging and defeating—the English fleet. The decentralization of authority, internal quarrels, lack of discipline and use of armed merchantmen all compromised the superb leaders, galleons and judiciously used fire ships. With their larger stakes, the Netherlands assumed the defensive—just as had the Portuguese they had attacked two generations before.

England went to war to strangle that trade; witness the Navigation Act. Strategically, England could assume the offensive, for her agricultural economy was still self-supporting. Only the coastal coal traffic and occasional shipping had to be defended. Otherwise, Cromwell's admirals could command the Channel trade and concentrate on attacking the Dutch convoys; they took *1500* Dutch prizes, over twice England's merchant marine, in this war! After indecisive skirmishing and maneuvering during that first summer, however, the English realized that the quickest way to destroy Dutch commerce lay in seeking out and destroying the Dutch fighting fleet. Such a major engagement ensued on September 28, 1652, at Kentish Knock, north of the Strait of Dover. Admirals Witt de With and Michiel Adriaenszoon de Ruyter with seventy-two ships met Blake and Sir William Penn with sixty-eight stronger vessels and in a general scramble were soundly defeated.

The issue was drawn: the English had to remain concentrated near the strategic center—the Strait of Dover—either by keeping a fleet there or by being able to call in distant squadrons to rendezvous in the Channel, while the Dutch had to break that concentrated English naval power. This policy remained fundamental to English naval strategy down to the twentieth century. The surest means to allow flexibility of movement was to destroy the enemy fleet in battle, in this case the Dutch. Absolute English control of the Channel would mean the blockade of Amsterdam and other Dutch ports and the freezing of all imports and exports with the Empire. To keep this from happening, Tromp put to sea with de Ruyter, Jan Evertsen and seventy-three ships, and soundly defeated Blake's force of half that size inside the Strait of Dungeness on November 30, and thus protected an outbound 300-ship convoy.

Whatever the merchants of London and Amsterdam may have felt about strategic priorities, their naval leaders now determined that fleet actions were primary. Destroy the enemy navy and command the sea, thus protecting trade. With only limited success, Tromp and de Ruyter pressed their shortsighted government to adopt this policy. But Cromwell had no doubts: he ordered Blake to make the Dutch war fleet his prime target, reformed the navy around definite articles of war, eliminated merchant vessels from the battle force, and bestowed the title of admiral upon his generals at sea, especially Blake, Penn and George Monk. In February 1653 this strengthened Commonwealth fleet sallied forth to strike a homeward-bound Dutch convoy in the Channel and engage the escort under Tromp in a running battle up-Channel—the Three Days' Battle—which cost the Dutch seventeen warships and over fifty-five merchantmen. This action gave England control of the Channel, forced the Dutch convoys to go over Scotland, and enabled Tromp to convince the States General to keep merchant ships in port until he could fight and win the battle.

English naval arms were now improved by tactical changes. Heretofore, fighting instructions had been issued to govern maneuvers in battle, and these maneuvers had been aimed at bringing the broadsides of the three squadrons—named White, Blue and Red—to bear on the enemy. Ever so slowly but perceptively both English and Dutch forces had fallen into crude lines of battle. Now, in March 1653, Cromwell's Parliament (for Cromwell now became virtual dictator of England as Lord

Protector) ordered that the line-ahead formation be formally adopted. So ordered, each galleon or "ship of the line" could deliver broadside volleys upon its opposite number. Such a tactical innovation in the middle of a war took time to perfect, but the official Fighting Instructions of 1653 became the basis of all subsequent British naval tactics well into the twentieth century.

English naval superiority in strategy, tactics, discipline and ordnance now weighed heavily against the Dutch. On June 23, 1653, Admirals Monk, Blake and Richard Deane with some 100 ships against a like number of inferior vessels under Tromp with de With, de Ruyter and Evertsen stunned the Dutch fleet at the Gabbard Bank (or the North Foreland) north of Dover. Using the new line-ahead, the English claimed 19 enemy ships and drove Tromp back to Holland which they then proceeded to blockade. As the merchants of Amsterdam faced ruin, Tromp at the end of July finally managed to break the blockade and clear the Texel for action. It came the next day, July 31, off Scheveningen. Both fleets—Monk's and Tromp's—used identical tactics: maneuvering for line-ahead with the weather gauge. Tromp got the wind first, but was killed early in the cannonading. For twelve hours the slaughter continued, with the English finally gaining the wind and winning this first true line-ahead action in history. The Dutch lost Tromp, over 1500 other men and 14 ships, and—in fact—the war.

The price of total destruction of the enemy fleet—the objective inherited from the fanatical nationalism of Cromwell's New Model Army —was considerable. The English retired from the Battle of Scheveningen so badly battered that they had to lift the blockade for repairs, and a great Dutch convoy of 400 vessels soon entered the Texel. Closure of the Baltic had also hurt the English, but gradually timber and naval stores were obtained from neutral powers and especially from New England, giving these North American colonies a new strategic importance. Dutch naval units had also punished the English at the naval battle of Leghorn in the Mediterranean—England's first real naval campaign in that sea (save for 1621)—so that Oliver Cromwell not only wanted to end the war, but to reunite both countries in common cause against Catholic Spain. The difficulty was that Cromwell saw England as the senior partner, an effrontery intolerable to the proud Dutch. But peace was paramount to Holland. It came in April 1654 and as a considerable blow to the Dutch: they acknowledged the Navigation Act, agreed to pay for the privilege of fishing in English waters, compensated for outrages against English traders in the East Indies and submitted to the demand to salute the English flag in the Channel, thus acknowledging English command of these waters.

Suddenly, England stood as a power equal to Holland, and Cromwell lost no time in improving England's strategic position abroad at the expense of Spain and the Barbary States, trying in vain to encourage the friendship of the Dutch. With undisguised arrogance, the English extended their naval influence beyond the Channel and North Sea. Late in 1654, Admiral Blake—taking advantage of a new treaty with Portugal, still fighting for independence from Spain—cruised to Gibraltar, lingering there long enough to interrupt French naval operations against Spain. In 1655 he descended with twenty-four warships on the Tunisian harbor of Porto Farina, which he reduced, and burned the corsair warships there. The same year an amphibious expedition against Spanish Hispaniola in the Caribbean was repulsed with severe loss, but the force moved on to occupy Jamaica, giving England a base in the very midst of this Spanish lake. The next year Blake began an intensive blockade of Spain itself by basing at Portuguese Lisbon. His fleet in September 1656 took part of the Spanish plate fleet off Cádiz and the following April destroyed an entire treasure convoy—six transports and ten escorts —at Tenerife in the Canaries. In 1657 England formally allied with France against Spain, and in May and June of 1658 an English fleet and army joined the French army under Marshal Turenne to capture Dunkirk in the Spanish Netherlands. Dunkirk was ceded to England, which sold it to France four years later. Hard-pressed on all sides, Spain, finally yielded, and in 1659 ended her various wars. France reigned supreme on land, Holland and England at sea. Religion became ever more private, and the slowly decaying Spanish Empire became the spoils in the new wars based on the European balance of power over political and commercial strength.

Despite England's rapid rise under Cromwell's Commonwealth and Protectorate, however, the expense had been almost too great to be borne by a mercantile system as yet underdeveloped. The sheer cost of the navy alone had been monumental; to offset continual struggles in the Baltic, where the Danes had closed the Sound to her ships during the war, England had to wield her weight there for keeping open her naval supply sources, while long sea routes to New Hampshire and Maine in North America were now maintained for tall mast timber. The economy sagged under the weight of these wars, and internal dissatisfaction with the government grew. The dynamic Blake—ranked by British naval historians as second in naval stature only to Nelson —died at sea in 1657, followed in death the next year by Cromwell himself. Political chaos then wracked the country, culminating in the seizure of power in 1660 by Monk, who restored the Stuart family to the throne.

Charles II became king of England, with a strengthened Parliament to serve him. Strongly pro-navy, Charles proclaimed the fleet as the

Royal Navy, with his brother Prince James, Duke of York, as Lord High Admiral and Monk, now Duke of Albemarle, as Captain General. The detested army, symbol of Cromwell's rule, received no such honor. The navy and merchant service were strengthened and streamlined, reforms being instituted under the firm and able administrative leadership of Samuel Pepys and a naval board. Charles II reaffirmed English mercantile and colonial policy throughout the world, sent naval forces against the Barbary pirates, and ordered attacks on Dutch outposts in African Guinea. By marrying into Portuguese royalty in 1662, Charles continued the ancient friendship between the two countries. In return for English assistance against the final Spanish thrust into Portugal in 1661–63, Portugal ceded African Tangier and Indian Bombay to England in 1661. This somewhat minor event had major implications for English military and strategic policy, for it meant that the army now had a new mission to garrison overseas posts against enemy pressure. The first long-distance troopships in English history took 3000 troops to Tangier that year to fight off Moslem attacks, and used an experimental galley squadron to protect English shipping during the 1670s. In addition, sea-based infantry seemed to be necessary for such overseas expeditions as well as for augmenting the navy at sea. Thus in 1664 the king created just such a regiment, following earlier examples by the Spanish and French. These troops became a regular feature of the Royal Navy and evolved into the Marine Corps (renamed Royal Marines in 1802). Anglo-Portuguese friendship and English imperial designs in the Mediterranean and India now alarmed the French of Louis XIV and the Dutch, but England proved equal to such competitors.

The Netherlands emerged from their first war with England weakened but by no means crippled as a great commercial power. Tromp was dead, but the Republic under Jan de Witt continued to flourish. Jacob von Wassenaer, Lord of Obdam, became Lieutenant Admiral, and with de With and Evertsen assisted Denmark against Sweden in the Northern War of 1656–60, though their successful relief of Copenhagen cost de With his life. The Dutch quit Brazil in 1654, but attempted in vain for the last time to regain their hold there in 1657–61. The center of Dutch colonial power remained the East Indies, where their consolidation proceeded without serious interruption. De Ruyter, who became Lieutenant Admiral in 1659, punished the Swedes once more and then proceeded to the Mediterranean, where he subdued the Barbary corsairs, first with his own fleet and then with joint English help in 1664. Dutch naval power proved to be as strong as ever.

But Anglo-Dutch friendship was tenuous at best, and commercial competition continued with such intensity that resumption of open warfare seemed inevitable. England wanted a larger share of the European carrying trade still monopolized by Holland, and in 1660 Parliament passed another Navigation Act, extending the English monopoly over England's own carrying trade to her colonies. The Dutch sought allies and in 1662 concluded a treaty with the rising French power of Louis XIV and Colbert. England and Holland skirmished in West Africa in 1663–64, culminating in a naval attack by Sir Robert Holmes and a counterstroke by de Ruyter in which several Gold Coast posts changed hands. The most far-reaching act of unofficial war came in 1664 when an English squadron assisted English-American settlers in the capture of New Amsterdam, which, in honor of the king's brother, the Duke of York, was then renamed New York. After another English squadron attacked the homeward-bound Dutch Levant convoy in the Strait of Gibraltar and the king ordered all Dutch shipping in English ports seized, in January 1665 the Netherlands declared war.

The second Anglo-Dutch War developed into an almost exact duplicate of the first. The issues, strategy, tactics, ships and many of the men were the same. Again, the battles focused on the strategic center of the Dover Strait and the adjacent Channel and North Sea. And again, the English sought command of these seas by forcing the Dutch fleet to action by threatening Dutch merchant convoys, the lifeblood of the United Provinces. Neither side was disappointed in its desire for decision by battle, for on June 3, 1665, the Dutch fleet of 103 men-of-war with nearly 5000 guns and 11 fire ships under Lord Obdam met the English of 109 of the line with 4200 guns and 28 fire ships under the Duke of York, Sir William Penn, Prince Rupert and the Earl of Sandwich. The two forces passed in close-hauled line ahead on opposite tacks off Lowestoft, pounding away with their murderous cannonading. From predawn till noon, the two lines passed back and forth in this manner, then bore up into a general scramble at close quarters. The Dutch flagship blew up, taking Obdam with it, and 31 other vessels succumbed to the deadly English fire. Jan Evertsen covered the retreat. This first conscious line-ahead engagement by both sides gave the English command of the sea early in the war, though Dutch trade still managed to reach Amsterdam, while Dutch squadrons hurt English trade, as did the plague of that year.

Unlike the first war, which had been generally confined to local waters and the trade routes, this conflict spread quickly. In August, the Earl of Sandwich pursued a Dutch East India convoy into Norwegian Bergen, where he was repulsed by Dutch ships and Danish shore batteries; deteriorating relations led to formal war between England and Denmark a year later. More serious was the French intervention on the side of ally Holland in January 1666. Colbert's young navy had been operating against Barbary Algiers, and new concentrations of French naval units along the Atlantic seaboard now alarmed the English, who could not discount the possibility of a French invasion attempt. Consequently, the main English fleet under Monk, now Duke of Albemarle, concentrated at the Downs to watch the Dutch, while Rupert moved down-Channel with twenty-four ships to counter French preparations. Under the circumstances, this strategic decision seemed prudent, as the French navy was a relatively unknown factor. In reality, however, the move proved a blunder, for the Dutch bases lay so close to the strategic center that de Ruyter could sally forth to strike the weakened Albemarle before full concentration could be effected by the recall of Rupert. Which is exactly what happened.

The so-called Four Days' Battle earned the distinction of being one of the bloodiest naval actions in history, due largely to the determination of the Cromwellian Duke of Albemarle not to yield. The two fleets clashed on June 1, 1666, at mid-Strait between the Downs and Dunkirk, with line-ahead maneuvering, broadside exchanges, boarding and grappling fire ships. Albemarle, though outnumbered, boldly attacked the Dutch van under Vice Admiral Cornelis Tromp, son of the late Martin. But de Ruyter came up to rescue Tromp, a sequence of events repeated on the second day. Badly battered, Albemarle fell back fighting and continued in this mode on the third day, at the end of which Rupert's squadron appeared, inducing the Dutch to break off the action. June 4 the slaughter resumed, and after five separate close actions both fleets withdrew. The Four Days' Battle ended in a draw, though 5000 Englishmen were dead, 3000 prisoners, eight English ships sunk and nine captured; the Dutch fared only slightly better—four admirals, 2000 other men and eight ships lost. Strategically, Holland had the better of it; de Ruyter blockaded the Thames estuary, where the English fleet anchored for repairs.

All pretense of commerce warfare paled into insignificance as the belligerents determined to settle the contest by achieving victory at sea through fleet action. On July 25 the restored English fleet of 81 sail and 18 fire ships under Albemarle and Rupert attacked the 88 men-of-war, 10 yachts and 20 fire ships of the Dutch under de Ruyter, Evertsen and Cornelis Tromp. This so-called St. James Fight which took place off the North Foreland reflected the high state of English naval administration; the repairs directed by Pepys and James, Duke of York, combined with the skill of English crews and the leadership of the two brilliant admirals to give England superiority in battle. Well-spaced in a line extending some six miles, the English opened fire on the disjointed Dutch line which was bowed into a half-moon shape. The disciplined English firepower battered the Dutch, killed Evertsen, sank 20 ships and drove off the rest at the cost of but one man-of-war. Now the English blockaded the Dutch coast and fleet, and in August Sir Robert Holmes entered the Vlie with a squadron which destroyed 150 Dutch merchant ships and the warehouses ashore. "Holmes's bonfire" had struck a blow at the heart of the Dutch Empire, and the failure of the French to join up with their own fleet forced Holland squarely onto the defensive.

All parties desired peace, but this took another year to realize. Plague and a great fire swept London, so that the king entered into negotiations with the Dutch and then—of all things—laid up his expensive fleet in the Medway. The Dutch maintained a loose blockade while watching their land defenses with alarm as their allies, the French, made inroads into the bordering Spanish Netherlands. As the talks dragged on into the late spring of 1667, the Dutch made a bold move. De Ruyter sailed up the Medway on June 17, broke the boom across the river, burned three men-of-war and towed off the veteran English flagship, the *Royal Charles,* to become his own flagship. Though aroused, the English now concluded a peace slightly favorable to Holland, in that the Navigation Acts were modified and Dutch supremacy in Indonesia recognized. But the Dutch left New York to England, which now controlled the American seaboard from the Bay of Fundy to the borders of Spanish Florida.

The end of the second Anglo-Dutch War and the French attack on the Spanish Netherlands in 1667 together created new strategic relationships in Europe. Louis XIV with his leading minister Colbert and Marshals Turenne, Condé and Vauban suddenly appeared in the role of aggressor on the continent, abroad and in the Baltic, so that early in 1668 England, Holland and Sweden formed a Triple Alliance against France. Their fears were justified. Interested in extending France's "natural frontiers" to the Rhine and Mediterranean coast, Louis had his great engineer Vauban build fortifications along France's borders from which French armies could move. Hoping to weaken, isolate and perhaps overcome the Austrian and Spanish Habsburgs and Holland, Louis claimed the Spanish throne by right of succession, but was frustrated by the diplomatic pressure of the Triple Alliance. In May 1668 France made peace with Spain, but by then had gained valuable footholds in Belgium and Flanders. Three months earlier Charles II of England had mediated peace between the new Spanish king of the same name and Portugal, in which Spain finally accepted Portuguese independence after a struggle of twenty-eight years. French animosity and Anglo-Portuguese ties further reduced Spain's influence on the continent, while abroad French and English pirates and buccaneers assailed Spanish imperial trade lanes and bases. From 1668 to 1671 Henry Morgan operated out of Port Royal in English Jamaica to sack Porto Belo, Maracaibo, Panama and other Spanish Main ports, torturing or killing his prisoners, and finally retiring to become lieutenant governor of Jamaica. In the latter year, pirates also began entering the Pacific to attack the shipping between Peru and Panama. Thus did France join in the general assault on the declining Spanish Empire.

Against Holland and Northern Europe, Louis XIV now turned his major attention. Aiming to undermine the Dutch maritime monopoly, Colbert formed a trading company for the Baltic and sent expeditions to India. Neither provided a serious enough threat to alarm either the Dutch or the English. But Louis' secret diplomacy achieved decided results. In 1670 he destroyed the Triple Alliance by signing a secret alliance with Charles II of England. By its terms, France would attack Holland by land while England struck its islands by sea. Such a combination would surely overcome the Dutch, thus giving Louis absolute supremacy over the Channel and North Sea coasts, a fact the English realized too late. Two years later, Louis signed a new alliance with Sweden, aimed at reducing Dutch trade in the Baltic. The Swedish Empire had effectively engulfed most of the shores of the Baltic, reducing Denmark's authority importantly, but new powers were emerging. Russia, excluded from a water outlet, was growing in strength in its wars against Poland and the Turks. Brandenburg-Prussia, united under the dictatorial powers of Frederick William, the Great Elector, in 1660, rested upon a formidable army to check Sweden (and eventually France). The Elector in the 1660s built a canal between the Oder and Elbe river systems, diverting traffic from Swedish Stettin to Prussian Berlin, and in the 1670s added a small ten-ship naval squadron to guard Prussian Baltic trade. France's Europe-wide endeavors thus involved a major challenge to existing power relationships on land and sea.

The Dutch response to these mounting pressures was to avoid war, but when this appeared impossible the States General made ready for the third major struggle in less than a quarter-century. In February 1672 it ordered 75 ships of the line into commission, but in March the English under Holmes attacked the Dutch Levant convoy from Smyrna off the Isle of Wight, followed closely by English and French declarations of war on the Netherlands. The new allies immediately concluded that destruction of the Dutch battle fleet had to be prerequisite to victory, so the untried French fleet rendezvoused with the English under the Duke of York at Solebay on the southeast coast of England. Their strategy was to station the combined fleet at Dogger Bank in the North Sea athwart Dutch shipping lanes and thus to force the Dutch war fleet to sea and battle. But Admirals de Ruyter and Adrian van Trappen Bankert caught the allies still at Solebay on June 7, and taking advantage of allied disorganization and the French inexperience, the Dutch used their broadsides and fire ships to maul the allied force. The Dutch East

Indies convoy got through, but these were false signs of the tide of the war.

The French invasion of the Dutch homeland in May sealed the fate of Holland, though the Dutch made France pay dearly for its eventual victory. Shifting men from de Ruyter's ships to the hard-pressed army and finally opening dikes to save Amsterdam, by July the Dutch had stopped Turenne and Condé. This strategic necessity struck long-range blows to the Dutch government and economy. Enraged by the invasion and devastation, in August the Netherlanders revolted and assassinated the Grand Pensionary de Witt, rejecting republican rule in favor of the centralized authority of a new stadtholder, Prince William of Orange. Needing an army and navy to hold the frontier and bring in the convoys, William battled the starvation and plague then ravaging his tiny country. Suddenly, however, the Dutch found themselves no longer alone, for Louis XIV's aggression had aroused the fears of other European powers, and in the late summer of 1672 the Austrian Empire, Spain and Brandenburg-Prussia formed a coalition against France. Even in England, public opinion in and out of Parliament mounted against the war of their Anglican king against Protestant Holland. For example, the veteran Duke of York had converted to Catholicism and because of it was now relieved as Lord High Admiral by Parliament. But the English fleet, in union with the French, maintained its pressure on Holland.

The Dutch did not relish being placed on the defensive, protecting convoys, holding off invasion by land, and trying to prevent the allied fleet from supporting that invasion. So in 1673 de Ruyter almost succeeded in plugging up the Thames with sunken hulks, while a Dutch squadron crossed the Atlantic to sink much English shipping in the Caribbean, in the James River of Virginia, and off New York and to capture St. Eustatius Island and New York itself. And when Rupert brought up the Anglo-French fleet to land an expeditionary force on the Dutch coast, de Ruyter seized the initiative and sallied forth from his anchorage at Schooneveldt. In late May and early June the two forces skirmished and maneuvered, with de Ruyter getting the best of it again, forcing the allies to withdraw. Relentlessly, the English under Pepys and Rupert recouped their losses and again attempted to invade the Netherlands by sea. Again de Ruyter came out, and in the naval battle of the Texel on August 21, 1673, de Ruyter, Tromp and Bankert with 60 ships easily pushed aside the 30 French vessels and slugged mercilessly with Rupert's 58 until the English withdrew. Another Dutch convoy passed into Amsterdam, and the Dutch remained in command of their coastal waters.

De Ruyter had saved Holland, for now all Europe rallied against

France. Nine days after the action off the Texel, the Spanish-Austrian-Prussian coalition formally allied with Holland. Unable to expect help by a seaward landing, Louis XIV pulled his armies out of Holland and placed them on his frontiers against the new alliance. The English, disgruntled over the poor performance of the French navy in the battles against de Ruyter, further opposed the war. Parliament could now soberly view a French-dominated Holland as a pistol pointed at England and realistically assessed friendship with Holland as preferable to a fickle alliance with the despot Louis XIV. England therefore opened negotiations with the Dutch and concluded peace in February 1674. By the terms of the treaty, New York was restored to England, and the Dutch agreed to pay an indemnity. But, more importantly, in the continuing legal debate over maritime rights, the English yielded to the Dutch demand that neutral shipping—upon which the Dutch had leaned heavily in wartime—would be immune from attack by the belligerents. Free ships, claimed the Dutch, meant free goods, a policy England would later challenge. Freed from watching England with the end of the third Anglo-Dutch War, the Netherlands could now look to checking France on land.

## THE FRENCH SEABORNE CHALLENGE

Despite the phenomenal naval building program of Colbert which increased the French navy from 20 to 270 warships between 1661 and 1677, Louis XIV viewed France as a continental power, with the fleet in support of the army. In 1674–75 Louis' armies and fortresses battled on the borders against the Habsburg Austrian Holy Roman Empire and its German subjects, against Habsburg Spain as well as Holland, and inside the Germanies, where Turenne fell in mid-1675. At this moment, allied Sweden under its King Charles XI entered the war on the side of France, which brought in Denmark also on the side of Holland, creating a separate conflict in the Baltic known as the Scanian War. For the latter half of the decade, therefore, France with Sweden fought the coalition of Holland, Austria, Brandenburg-Prussia, Spain and Denmark. The fighting focused on the continental frontiers of France, though naval forces battled on the periphery—in the Baltic and the Mediterranean. French arms generally triumphed on land, but at terrible expense to the state, while the naval actions only really affected the local regions involved.

France, which had unsuccessfully assisted Venice against the Turks in 1669, in 1674 took advantage of the Italian city-state Messina's revolt against Spanish rule to divert allied attention to the Mediterranean by occupying the city. Hard-pressed Spain appealed to equally exhausted Holland for naval help, and late in 1675 de Ruyter himself was sent. His nineteen ships and four fire ships met a French force of similar size under Admiral Abraham Duquesne at the battle of Stromboli near the Strait of Messina on January 8, 1676, and fought a spirited draw, notable because of the excellent tactics and maneuvers of the French navy. Now a Spanish force of ten warships arrived, and its commander Don Francisco de la Cerda took over supreme command, making the veteran de Ruyter subordinate. The joint fleet blockaded Toulon. The French force under Duquesne was doubled to thirty-three warships and seven fire ships, and on April 22 the two fleets engaged off Augusta, Sicily. The Spanish fell back to fire at long range and failed to support the van under de Ruyter, which engaged in the usual Dutch manner at close range. As a result, the French carried the day, and the valiant de Ruyter was mortally wounded, dying a week later at Syracuse. On June 2 the French struck the allied force at Palermo and sank nine of its large ships, and thereby obtained general command of the Western Mediterranean. These actions by the French had done much to further weaken the Dutch, whose navy was reduced to near impotence by the financial demands of the war on land.

The Scanian War in the Baltic also taxed the resources of the Dutch, who nevertheless rallied to the side of the Danes and Brandenburger-Prussians against France's ally Sweden. As in the Mediterranean, small squadrons carried on the struggle, maneuvering about the Baltic and skirmishing until the first major fleet action in mid-1676 when Cornelis van Tromp of Holland was made General-Admiral of the Danish Navy, supported by the native Dane Admiral Niels Juel. Juel with 20 Danish and Dutch men-of-war, the largest mounting 76 guns, and 7 frigates fought an indecisive duel with the Swedish fleet of Admiral Lorens Creutz, 27 men-of-war—126 guns on the flagship *Krona*—and 11 frigates, between Bornholm and Rügen on May 25. Tromp then joined up with 6 more heavy ships and engaged Creutz off Öland on June 1. Early in the action the great *Krona* blew up from a fire in her magazine, taking the admiral and 800 men with her. Tromp attacked, claimed the next two largest Swedish vessels, and carried the day. The battle of Öland gave the allies command of the sea, and troops were immediately ferried from Copenhagen to Scania. Tromp returned home for the winter, and before he could come back next spring the Danes under Juel renewed the attack. On May 31–June 1, 1677, a Danish squadron under Juel defeated a Swedish force near Warnemünde, and on July 1 Juel used the main Danish fleet of 25 large warships to engage the larger Swedish navy of 31 men-of-war at the battle of Kjöge Bay. The Danes fought masterfully, capturing 7 large Swedish vessels and burning another; had he not failed to pursue, Juel might have taken the lot. Nevertheless, the victory insured allied naval supremacy in the Baltic. Tromp's return achieved little, and he retraced his track to Holland in the autumn to succeed the fallen de Ruyter as Lieutenant Admiral of the United Provinces. The Danish and smaller Brandenburger navies continued to support the armies along the Baltic seaboard, but the Swedish and French ground forces were so successful that Denmark and Brandenburg had to negotiate peace in August 1679.

Though French victories on land favored Louis XIV, they also aroused the fears of the English, who increasingly threatened to enter the struggle. In January 1678 England allied with the Netherlands and reinforced its fleet. Louis evacuated Sicily and attempted to avoid conflict with England, but he pressed his attacks on the Spanish Netherlands. Finally, in August 1678, France made peace with Holland, in September with Spain, and the following February with the Austrian Emperor. The final settlements in the North took place during the summer of 1679. France emerged from these wars triumphant on the continent, with an improved merchant marine and navy and an embryonic overseas empire. England also profited from her four-year neutrality during which the carrying trade of Europe shifted from the hard-pressed and overextended Dutch to the English. Holland survived the wars without the loss of any territory at home or abroad except for a few African stations; her own empire based on the East Indies remained intact. But she had forever lost the monopoly over European seaborne trade, and her navy henceforth depended on the friendship of England. The only obvious loser was Spain, rapidly deteriorating under a decadent Habsburg rule. A precarious balance of power existed in the Baltic, to which England now turned for the same reason Holland had—preservation of trade in timber and naval stores.

By 1680 France had reached the pinnacle of its success, while England—though formidable—was torn anew by internal political and religious strife. The new decade witnessed the crystallization of both nations into power blocs which would remain basically antagonistic into the early nineteenth century. Colbert's maritime policies heightened France's open competition with England and the other powers. In the Baltic, Holland allied with Sweden again in 1681 to offset French designs, whereupon Louis allied with Denmark the next year. In 1683 a Franco-Danish fleet under Admiral Juel nearly brought on war by searching for a Dutch fleet in the Baltic, and again in 1684 the Danes nearly precipitated war again with Sweden. The region remained a potential source of trouble. In the Mediterranean, the Barbary Moors bothered the Europeans so much that England simply evacuated Tangier in 1683–84 at the same time the French fleet under Duquesne was bombarding Algiers with the newly invented bomb ketches using mortars. As the English and Spanish retreated from the middle sea, France took over, bombarding pro-Spanish Genoa in 1684 and warring actively against Barbary Algiers in the West for most of the decade, while Venice battled the Turks in the East. France thus offered a major threat to all the powers in the waters of Europe—and abroad.

Overseas, France proved equally troublesome in the 1680s. In the Caribbean, buccaneers such as Morgan's former gang had terrorized Spanish possessions and were supplied by the French. Spain had therefore agreed with England in 1670 and with Holland in 1673 to recognize the English and Dutch American possessions if these countries would help put down the buccaneers. Their depredations against Spain mounted after the European war ended in 1678, culminating in the sack of the theoretically invulnerable San Juan de Ulua, New Spain, in 1683. In the latter year, however, Spain and France signed a truce, leading the French to turn against the buccaneers. So bothersome had these renegades become that the European governments steadily turned against them. In 1685 when a buccaneer force burned Campeche in Yucatan, the English sent a special squadron to Jamaica to deal with them.

In the Pacific and Indian oceans, both French and English pirates, some with letters of marque from the home government (legally making them privateers), plagued the Spanish. In 1683 an Anglo-French pirate force of seven ships intercepted, but failed to take, the Panama-bound Spanish silver fleet from Peru, and three years later the English pirate William Dampier sailed west to raid the Spanish Philippines, but with equal lack of success. The Dutch monopoly over Indonesia was finalized in 1684, but in the next years the French and English opened trade with nearby Siam. In India, these two powers faced conflict with each other. Throughout the latter half of the century, the dominant Moguls of southern India came under attack by the rising Marathas. The French at Chandernagore and Pondicherry and English at Hoogly and Bombay therefore had to fortify their posts in the 1680s. To combat the Moguls the English in 1686 built forts on the modern site of Calcutta. Also in these years the French and English began to push the Dutch out of West Africa, with the French claiming Madagascar in 1686 to further isolate the Portuguese in East Africa. Slowly, but gaining momentum, France and England infiltrated the imperial waters of the Spanish, Portuguese and Dutch.

Yet, with all these overseas adventures, France did not rely upon them for her wealth as did England, Holland, Spain and Portugal. So she was not vulnerable as were the others when attacked at sea. In this respect, Colbert's thalassocratic achievements increasingly became a luxury, and after his death in 1683 his son, the Marquis de Seignelay, the naval and colonial minister, found it increasingly difficult to administer and meet the logistical demands of Colbert's navalism. On the continent of Europe France remained vulnerable, so that Louis increasingly used his finances to support the army reforms of his war ministers Le Tellier and Louvois and the fortifications of his brilliant engineer Vauban. In 1682 he became involved in war with the Turks over Hungary, a struggle which lasted until the end of the century. The Moslem Turks indirectly decided French strategy, for following their repulse by the Austrians before Vienna in 1683 the Habsburg Emperor could turn his attention to offsetting France's gains, a desire shared by the rest of France's neighbors.

To compound France's problems, the English and Dutch became antagonistic. In 1685, King Charles II of England died and was succeeded by his brother, the Duke of York of naval fame, who became King James II. The new king was not only a friend and admirer of Louis but a Catholic, and the same year Louis forced the emigration of Protestants from France. This move provided an excuse for William III of Orange to mobilize Louis' enemies against him. In July 1686 the League of Augsburg formed between the Austrian Emperor, Holland, Spain, Sweden, Brandenburg-Prussia and several other German states. William now conspired to overthrow James and put himself on the English throne, and Louis helped inadvertently when in November 1687 he revoked trade concessions he had given the Dutch at the end of the war nine years before. English and Dutch opinion quickly mounted against the Catholic kings, Louis XIV and James II.

France and England converged toward war through the actions primarily of Louis and William III, who was married to James II's Protestant daughter Mary. In September 1688, seeing the Turks in retreat before the Austrian Empire, Louis invaded Germany, hoping to rally the Turks. Instead he caused the German princes to ally with Austria against him. In England, the pro-navy James with the able Pepys as his administrator had strengthened the fleet, but the prospect of its possible use on the side of Catholic France further alienated Parliament and the people against their king. Several leading statesmen invited William and Mary to come to England as co-sovereigns. They accepted and in the summer and fall mobilized a fleet of 70 men-of-war and 400 troop-laden transports in Holland. Unfavorable winds kept this armada in port until November, when the crossing was made under the command of Admiral Arthur Herbert of the English navy and two Dutch admirals. Louis stupidly—but with diplomatic and logistical rationales—made no attempt to take advantage of his fine navy to try to prevent the crossing—though he now declared war on Holland, while James's own fleet stayed inactive because of its divided loyalties and indecisive leaders. Before the end of the year, William had rallied most of England behind him and his wife, and the following February they were proclaimed king and queen of England, with William remaining as stadtholder of the Netherlands. Louis then completed the union of Europe against him by declaring war on Spain in April and on England in May, the same month that Austria and Holland formed the Grand Alliance against him. The other belligerents, already members of the League of Augsburg, quickly joined.

The War of the League of Augsburg (or the War of the Grand Alliance, or in America, King William's War) lasted from 1689 to 1697 and served as a major watershed in the history of naval warfare. It marked the end of the great naval battles in which both fleets endeavored to destroy each other and obtain absolute supremacy at sea, an era begun with the English and Dutch fleet engagement off Kentish Knock in 1652. Louis XIV entered this war with some 200 ships of the line and over 80 privateers based along the Dunkirk coast, but the combined Anglo-Dutch fleet was superior. In this war, strategic thought crystallized into two schools, the continental and the maritime. The continentalists, symbolized by France, came to prefer victory on land with the navy in support by convoying troops and supplies and attacking enemy commercial traffic, a strategy the French called *guerre de course*. The maritimists, symbolized by England, sought command of the sea whereby the enemy's homeland would be blockaded, his shipping destroyed, and his colonies captured. For England, from this time forward, the occupation of the Low Countries—Antwerp, Amsterdam, the Rhine delta and the mouth of the Scheldt—by a great continental power became intolerable and a pretext for war, which France would discover repeatedly, as Germany would later. The threat to English possessions abroad later became a similar pretext. The War of the League of Augsburg therefore acted as the dramatic climax of the Oceanic Age, the last clash between equally strong (or nearly so) naval powers and the first during which theoretical strategic and tactical principles were formulated as alternatives to decision by a direct gunnery slugging match at sea.

English strategy represented several viewpoints in this war and those of the next two and a half centuries. First and foremost, the British Isles—England, Scotland, Wales and Ireland—had to be defended against invasion by sea, which meant concentrating the fleet in the Channel or thereabouts whenever invasion threatened. Secondly, the trade lanes between the Isles, the colonies and neutral countries had to be kept open, for now the Anglo-Dutch king determined to make England the supreme shipper. The nice problem lay in reconciling these goals, *i.e.,* protecting inbound and outbound convoys beyond the Isles without uncovering the strategic center—the Channel coast—to invasion. To improve the chances for flexibility in this strategy, the English in the 1690s developed a new major base at Plymouth at the western end of the Channel. Offensively, the English divided into the continental and maritime school. The Whigs preferred to send troops to the continent of Europe to aid their allies, with the navy in a supporting role. The Tories preferred to decide the issue at sea, though giving material and financial aid to continental allies.

French strategy also reached some conclusions in this war. Defensively, Louis XIV wanted to secure his frontier, which he felt fronted the Rhine River; therefore, his first object in this war became the occupation of the Spanish Netherlands, a move which forced him to face the armies of the Grand Alliance. His other goal, the restoration of James II to the throne of England, would take England out of the war and probably doom Holland. His navy, retrenching under Seignelay to deal with Spanish Italy and the Barbary States during the mid 1680s, now faced huge tasks. It ferried James and an army to Ireland in March 1689 and therefore had to keep open communications with the main naval base at Brest. France had an additional problem of defending two coastlines, so that the Toulon and Brest fleets remained divided, and between them lay Spanish Cádiz, which had superseded Seville in commercial importance and was now available to the English. To strike a decisive blow against the great Anglo-Dutch fleet, Louis therefore had to unite his two fleets, not an easy task. Also, urged on by such men as Vauban, he preferred to use warships and privateers for *guerre de course,* while Seignelay's understrength navy could do little else. Seignelay with great administrative energy enlarged the fleet, but no longer had Colbert the elder to press him on to achieve command of the blue water. Neither had he a parliament to debate various strategies. Louis therefore never succeeded in using his fleet to control English waters and place James back on the throne, though an invasion of England remained in his long-range plans.

As the armies mobilized along the French frontier and in Ireland, the French navy—in no condition to seize the initiative—did achieve much at the outset. It sustained James in Ireland, drove off Admiral Herbert's squadron in a skirmish at Bantry Bay, Ireland, in May 1689, and avoided an English squadron to unite the Toulon squadron with the main force at Brest in July. Thus superior in numbers to the English—the Dutch had not yet arrived—Seignelay determined to destroy the main enemy fleet in battle and ordered his protégé, Admiral the Count Anne Hilarion de Tourville, to use the French fleet to defeat Herbert (now Earl of Torrington) and carry James and a French army to England. Torrington shrewdly adopted the policy of a "fleet-in-being": being inferior, he would actively harass the enemy with his divided squadrons, protect William's communications to Londonderry in northern Ireland, and judiciously avoid a general action until he could concentrate with the Dutch in the Channel against Tourville. This strategy—and French inaction—enabled an English squadron to relieve besieged Londonderry and keep alive the fight against James and other units by preserving the trade lanes. Tourville put to sea finally with 75 ships of the line and 18 fire ships in June 1690, frightening the English government into ordering Torrington to abandon his fleet-in-being stratagem and to engage the enemy. This was unfortunate, since the English fleet was not yet concentrated, though Admiral Cornelis Evertsen had joined with 22 Dutch men-of-war to Torrington's 35, plus 20 fire ships. So ordered, Torrington on June 30 brought his allied line down on the French fleet in the Channel off Beachy Head. Needless to say, the allies fought well, but the superior French fleet drove them back to the Thames, taking a dozen ships and losing nine of their own. Tourville had insured French command of the sea, but he did nothing to exploit it and soon returned to Brest. The French army was too overcommitted to provide troops for an invasion of England, and French strategy had not been formulated sufficiently to take advantage of a victory upon the sea.

Though defeated, the English navy was by no means finished. Torrington's original fleet-in-being concept had saved England from invasion, and now French strategic and logistical shortcomings caused a delay which enabled outlying English squadrons to concentrate again in the Channel. Seignelay died in France shortly after the battle, and in England an uncomprehending government relieved Torrington from command; it might have replaced him with the dynamic Lieutenant Admiral of Holland, Cornelis Tromp, had not Tromp died in May 1691. The command instead passed to Admiral Edward Russell, who put to sea with 74 of the line, the result of a rapid construction program. Tourville had but 69 and found the situation reversed as he harassed the English, but avoided battle with their slightly superior fleet throughout the summer of 1691. Command of the sea thus passed to the allies. French privateers, led by such skilled commanders as Jean Bart, achieved much success, and French arms mounted victories on the continent, but the battle in Ireland went to William, whose victory there in 1691 insured his crown. All these efforts cost the French dearly, so that when Louis determined to invade England in 1692 his fleet was understrength. He ordered Tourville to give up waiting for the delayed Brest fleet and to win command of the Channel for the invasion transports. He had but 44 men-of-war and 38 fire ships. Russell, with an improved manual of fighting instructions and tactical signals issued the year before, had a force of 63 English and 36 Dutch ships of the line and 38 fire ships.

The Battle of Cape La Hogue (or Barfleur), fought in the Channel May 29, 1692, decided the future of the French navy. Tourville tried to compensate for his inferior strength by massing on the rear of Russell's line. By masterful maneuvering, he thus avoided the allied van comprised of the Dutch and exchanged broadsides with the English in the center and rear. But the English broke through the French center and doubled back on several vessels. The French retreated in the late afternoon, and Russell gave chase which lasted over the next five days. In it, the English destroyed twelve ships of the line that had taken refuge near La Hogue. The French fleet recouped its losses almost immediately and no doubt would have carried on the fight in the Channel in the do-or-die manner of the English and Dutch had not Louis XIV decided otherwise. His expensive commitments on the continent meant that naval losses could no longer be replaced, so that the navy now shifted totally to a strategy of *guerre de course*. Like Torrington in 1690, Tourville now had to use his inferior fleet to avoid a direct confrontation. But the theory of the fleet-in-being supported the offensive use of the fleet, looking as it did to eventual superiority in numbers so that a fleet action would be possible. *Guerre de course* meant always avoiding a major battle by using the fleet along with the privateers to defend or attack shipping, while the war was decided on land. Colbert's dream of blue-water superiority thus died at La Hogue; in that sense, all Anglo-French naval battles after 1692 were anticlimactic.

Tactically, the massed firepower of the large line of battle had required order, rather than the idea of initiative by individual squadron commanders for independent maneuver. Thus the tactical fighting instructions had evolved from the Duke of York in 1673 to those of Torrington and Russell in 1689–91 into a rigid, formal line-ahead formation in which each ship squared off with its opposite number. So many ships, up to ninety, comprised the line that this practice now became the cardinal rule of English tactics and lasted virtually unchanged for the next century. For purposes of historical nomenclature, this tactical doctrine is known as formalism. It remained largely unchanged after 1692 for the simple reason that the French thereafter rarely offered battle which might have necessitated changes. Tactical thought thus stagnated, and the naval wars for the remainder of the age of sail (till the 1830s) were decided more by superior strategic dispositions.

Thus freed from fear of invasion, England after 1692 looked to protecting its trade and colonies. With the Dutch, the Royal Navy controlled the funnel of European trade at the Strait of Dover—the strategic center—so that the major fighting took place between escorted convoys and squadrons, isolated warships and privateers, and colonists against colonists using native allies. The theaters of active naval combat therefore shifted from the Channel to the Mediterranean, the Baltic (after this war), America and India. For England, this shift raised the important strategic question of bases, made all the more pressing by Tourville's successful attack on an Anglo-Dutch convoy bound for Smyrna late in June 1693; off Lagos, near Cape St. Vincent, Portugal (west of Cádiz), he scattered the escort and sank 100 of a 400-ship convoy. The English retaliated with shore bombardments of Dieppe and St. Malo, but the major event was the wintering of Admiral Russell's fleet at Cádiz, Spain, during 1693–94, the first time an English fleet had remained abroad after the sailing season. It thus kept the French trade lanes split and gave England a key base—as long as Spain remained allied. The event also meant that warships remained in commission year round, with officers, sailors and shipboard marines in continual pay, so that the professional—rather than seasonal—naval seaman was gradually being established within the Royal Navy. This evolution, embodied in continual and painful administrative reforms, was realistic, for England had increasing demands placed upon its navy throughout the world.

The War of the League of Augsburg was not a global conflict, since the decisive fighting was done around the borders of France, but enough action took place abroad to suggest that thenceforth the balance of European power in the future would include colonial and trading relationships on a global scale. The French used their navy and privateers, especially those Dunkirkers under Bart, to support their army and colonists, and the English used their fleet to counter such actions. In America, while colonists with Indian allies raided each other, mostly in New York, Maine and the Hudson Bay area, small naval forces were employed. Of particular notice were an abortive seaborne assault and bombardment of French Quebec by thirty-four New England ships with troops aboard in 1690 and the arrival of a fifteen-ship French squadron at Newfoundland in 1697 that never realized its plans to burn Boston. That year in the Caribbean, however, the French used buccaneers, as they had throughout the war against the allies' colonies, but now for the last time, to assist in the capture of Spanish Cartagena. In the Indian Ocean, the powers fought less against each other than the Moslem and Maratha pirates, though the Dutch still wielded local mastery over these seas and with twenty-three ships took Pondicherry, French India, in 1693. In the Baltic, William III carefully nurtured neutrality, so that England and Holland could profit by trade there, but to cut off Swedish cannon and naval stores exports to France, he used privateers to raid Scandinavia. The Baltic powers thus entered into an armed neutrality in 1691–93, but in 1696 Denmark allied with England and Holland. The Swedes counterattacked at hostile privateers while seeking to mediate peace. In the Mediterranean, Tourville's fleet supported Louis' siege at

Barcelona until Russell's fleet lifted it in 1694. Two years later, fearing a French invasion scheme, the English concentrated in the Channel and even carried out an abortive amphibious raid near Brest, whereupon the French ships returned to the Mediterranean and took Barcelona in 1697. None of these efforts radically changed the international situation as it had existed in 1692, so in October 1697 Louis XIV, William III and the Austrian Emperor negotiated peace.

## ENGLISH VICTORY AND RUSSIA

The treaty of 1697 proved to be only an armistice, agreed upon by the aggressive Louis XIV so that he could replenish his losses and seek a more fruitful theater to attack; the hiatus also gave the other powers the chance to take stock of the changing balance of power in Europe and the world. England had surpassed the Dutch in the carrying trade and now cast covetous eyes on the Spanish Caribbean. The Royal Navy had become very professional, with many career sailors replacing mere aristocratically appointed admirals. Allied to England, the Netherlands prospered as in prewar days, but early in the new century became embroiled in the native wars of the Javanese succession. The Dutch navy could no longer be superior, as the army had to be kept at peak strength on the frontiers to watch France. The French had forsaken a large blue-water navy in favor of commerce warfare, but nevertheless the navy chaplain Paul Hoste published an excellent treatise on battle tactics in 1697. In 1700 the decadent Habsburg king of Spain, Charles II, died, whereupon Louis XIV placed his own Bourbon grandson, Philip V, on the Spanish throne. This succession created an alliance that provided easy grounds for the renewal of the conflict. Before that happened, however, dramatic events in Eastern Europe were having important consequences on its peripheral salt-water lakes, the Mediterranean and the Baltic, especially with the rise of Russia as a maritime contender.

The Mediterranean, a battleground between Christians and Moslems throughout the Oceanic Age, took on new importance as Russia emerged under Peter the Great in the fight against the Ottoman Turks. On land, Austria and Poland had saved Vienna in 1683 and were joined by Russia in preventing further Ottoman expansion. At sea, Venice still warred in the Aegean against the Turks. Peter, assuming virtual dictatorship over Russia in 1689 and beginning systematically to convert his people from an Oriental into a Western culture, hired a Dutch shipwright to build warships and educated himself in the ways of the sea. In 1695, Russia declared war on Turkey, and Peter, following Savoy which used a flotilla in the Danube, brought warships down the Volga and Don rivers to besiege and finally—with the army—capture Turkish

Azov in the Black Sea during the spring and summer of 1696. Peter erected a naval base at Taganrog, returned to Western Europe where he hired English and Dutch seamen, and continued the war on Turkey till 1700. Russia's contribution had been slight, but had helped to force the Turkish retreat from Eastern Europe, begun about 1697. Venice held Crete against a Turkish siege and in the general peace settlement in 1699 was awarded the Peloponnesian and Dalmatian coasts. The real victors, however, were Austria and Savoy, the latter embracing Sardinia to begin domination over the Western Mediterranean. Thrust on the defensive, the Ottomans had now to face Austria, Savoy, Venice, Genoa and Russia. The Turks thus promoted peace and to strengthen their economy they now allowed Western merchants to penetrate beyond Smyrna and the Levantine coast to trade in the interior of their Empire.

Peter's navalism had a more decisive impact in the Baltic where Sweden remained supreme under its new, young and aggressive king, Charles XII, who ascended the throne in 1697. Over the next two years, Peter allied with Poland and Denmark in order to challenge Swedish supremacy. The maritime powers did not favor any conflict there which might endanger their own supply zones, so in January 1700 England and Holland allied with Sweden, an alliance which equally anxious France supported. Three months later, the Danes invaded the continental territory of a Swedish ally, thus inaugurating twenty-one years of Baltic strife that came to be known as the Great Northern War. An Anglo-Dutch fleet under Admiral Sir George Rooke hurried to the Sound, where it bombarded Copenhagen, while the Swedes crossed the Sound and attacked the Danes by land; Denmark sued for peace in August. The English and Dutch now withdrew their aid to Sweden, whereupon Charles XII decided to cut off their supply lanes in the north, beginning with the destruction of the key Russian seaport of Archangel. In the autumn of 1700 he crossed to Livonia and drove the allied Russian-Polish-Saxon forces before him, but his naval attack on Archangel in June 1701 was repulsed. Charles then invaded Poland, dangerously ignoring Peter and the Russians, and began the long ground war which the Great Northern War became. Peter immediately built small fleets of galleys and brigantines on lakes Ladoga and Peipus and the River Neva; in 1702 two naval skirmishes on Ladoga went to the new Russian navy. The English and Dutch, thoroughly alarmed at the Russo-Swedish conflict in the Baltic, could do nothing, for the war with France now resumed.

The War of the Spanish Succession began in March 1701 when Louis XIV and the Austrian Emperor Leopold I both claimed the Spanish throne for the Bourbons and Habsburgs respectively. The continental war involved a renewed French attack on the Spanish Netherlands, which alarmed William III, king of England and stadtholder of Holland, sufficiently to prepare for entry into the war. In September 1701 the Grand Alliance re-formed against France: Austria, England, Holland, Prussia and most of the Germanies. Later Sweden and Portugal joined the alliance. In May 1702 England formally declared war on France, hoping not only to isolate Louis XIV and keep him from dominating Spain but also to extend English imperial influence into Spanish America. The war was thus crucial to English supremacy at sea, but it also proved decisive for the internal evolution of English government. Queen Mary had died in 1694 and was followed by her husband, William III, in March 1702. The succession passed to Mary's sister Anne, the last Stuart ruler, but after her death (which came in 1714) it was to go to the Germanic Hanover line and to be forever Protestant. Furthermore, in 1707 England finally created a formal union with Scotland—as Great Britain. And henceforth the British would be obliged to repulse the attempts of the French to place a Catholic pretender—descendants of the late James II—on the throne. As for the Dutch, they did not replace William with another stadtholder for two generations but reverted again to strict republican government. The British and Dutch might be allies, but never again were they united under one ruler. In the largest sense, however, the War of the Spanish Succession (1702–14) was fought for the creation of the British Empire.

More immediately, the war focused on commerce, and France never attempted to command the seas. Colbert's dream for a blue-water fleet was now rejected by Louis XIV in favor of trade war using the policy of *guerre de course*. The main fighting revolved about Louis' fine army, so that Britain endorsed a generally continental strategy by sending John Churchill, Earl of Marlborough, to the continent in supreme command of an Anglo-Dutch army. Other theaters of war were secondary and focused on England's chief aim, trade. In North America, the struggle was known as Queen Anne's War. In the Baltic, the Great Northern War continued. And elsewhere—the Mediterranean, Caribbean, Indian Ocean and even the Pacific—the allies battled the French and their Spanish confederates.

The naval theater most directly influential on the fighting on the continent was the Mediterranean, because of the seacoasts of Spain and France on the one side and those of Savoy and Austria, at Trieste, on the other. Marlborough wanted the allies to take Toulon for pressure on the enemy from the South while he and Prince Eugene of Savoy overran the Spanish Netherlands. To apply such pressure, Britain needed a convenient base of operations in the Mediterranean. The English had abandoned Tangier in 1684 and now Cádiz in the late summer of 1702, but did seize the Spanish plate fleet and destroy its heavy Franco-

Spanish escort at Vigo Bay, northwest Spain, in October. The next year Portugal joined the allies, giving them Lisbon, where Admiral Rooke based in 1704. Attempts to take Toulon and Barcelona failed, but in July 1704 an Anglo-Dutch fleet bombarded Gibraltar and took it with a force of 1800 marines. As the French and Spanish could not accept this strategic loss, Louis XIV immediately dispatched his son, Admiral the Count of Toulouse, with a Franco-Spanish fleet to regain it. This fleet engaged that of Rooke, which included a Dutch squadron, at the naval battle of Malaga on August 13. The gunnery duel was fought with rigid and conservative long-range, line-ahead tactics that led to no clear decision; indeed, no ships were lost on either side, even though the French even used galleys to augment their line. But it was a British strategic victory, for it secured Gibraltar from the sea side, and the garrison resisted a siege by land over the next seven months. Malaga thus contributed to allied fortunes, for on the very same day of the battle, the armies of Marlborough and Eugene utterly crushed the Franco-Bavarian army at the Battle of Blenheim. The image of French military superiority was thus shattered, and the allies pressed on into the continent and on the Mediterranean front.

From Gibraltar, the allies brought their warships and troops against Spanish Catalonia and the south of France. In March 1705 Admiral Sir John Leake's squadron destroyed a French naval unit at Marbella near Gibraltar, and three months later an English expeditionary force landed in Catalonia, finally investing Barcelona in October. Leake's supporting ships helped this force repel a Catholic counterattack and in the summer of 1706 captured Cartagena, Alicante and two Balearic islands. Marlborough again defeated the French army at Ramillies in May 1706, after which his navy supported an invasion of western Spain via Portugal, which, however, was repulsed. The allies invaded Spain again in the summer of 1707 from Savoy and nearly captured Toulon, whereupon the French scuttled their fifty men-of-war there. This act gave the allies absolute command of the Mediterranean and although the fighting reached a stalemate on land, Admiral Leake's ships and marines took the key islands of Sardinia and Minorca, with its excellent harbor at Port Mahon, in August and September of 1708. Eugene defeated the French army at Turin in September 1706 and he joined Marlborough to win at Oudenarde in July 1708, but French arms rallied sufficiently to keep the issue in doubt on the continent. The allies were eventually driven from Spain, with the French recapturing Barcelona in September 1714.

With the war to be decided on land, the British used their command of the sea to isolate France from her colonies and overseas trade—the embodiment of a strategy of concentration. While holding down Franco-

Spanish reinforcements from the sea, Britain supplied an army and financial aid to allied armies to wield a decisive victory on the continent. In 1708 Parliament passed the Convoys and Cruisers Act, requiring the Royal Navy to protect all shipping and authorizing privateers to be awarded prize money for any captures of enemy ships. Britain thus clamped an economic blockade around France and Spain which lasted from 1709 to 1713 and brought Louis XIV to near-bankruptcy. British raiding parties harassed the French Channel coast, while French cruisers attacked British shipping. In the Western Hemisphere, colonists combined with the natives to war upon each other. Strategically, the powers depended upon their bases, and to these they dispatched their warships. In the Caribbean, the Spanish operated from their Spanish Main ports and St. Augustine and Pensacola in Florida. The French used Mobile to protect Spanish shipping and their own (having the slave *asiento* since 1702) and to take British Nevis and St. Kitts in 1706; but they no longer used buccaneers, who had degenerated into rank outlaws. French naval forces also raided Portuguese Brazil and took Rio de Janeiro in 1711 under the superb leadership of Admiral DuGuay-Trouin. The English used their colonial ports from Maine to the Carolinas and in the West Indies to attack Catholic trade. Repeated assaults on French Nova Scotia finally led to its capture by British naval and ground forces in 1710; a similar attempt on Quebec the next year was frustrated by weather and navigational difficulties. English privateer William Dampier unsuccessfully harassed Franco-Spanish Pacific shipping from Acapulco to Peru, though Woodes Rogers had better fortune, including the rescue of Alexander Selkirk, the now-legendary Robinson Crusoe, from Juan Fernandez Island in 1709. In these ways, Great Britain strained Franco-Spanish resources and helped force Louis XIV to terms.

The War of the Spanish Succession dragged to a close in a series of treaties in 1713–1715, giving Britain absolute imperial supremacy throughout the world. Louis XIV recognized Protestant rule in Britain, going to the Hanoverian King George I following Queen Anne's death in 1714. The allies recognized the Bourbon King Philip V of Spain, with guarantees that the crown would never be united with that of Louis XIV, who died in 1715 and was succeeded by Louis XV. Britain had gone to war to break the imperial monopoly of Spain in the New World, and it virtually succeeded. The French renounced their protectorate over the Spanish Main and transferred their slave trade *asiento* to England; in addition, the British Empire gained control over Hudson Bay, Nova Scotia and Newfoundland in Canada, and Nevis and St. Kitts in the Caribbean. In the Mediterranean, Britain retained Gibraltar and Minorca, while Austria got Naples, Sardinia and Milan. These events settled the balance of power in Europe for years to come, for Spanish power was forever broken. Spain ceded her own Netherlands (Belgium) to Austria and retained only a tenuous hold over Latin America and the trade route to the distant Philippines. Portugal remained her unfriendly neighbor, supported by England. But the fighting also finished the Netherlands as a major power, for the Dutch economy had been weakened to the point where the Dutch had to depend on the English carrying trade. In her place on the continent emerged the growing strength of the Prussian state. So France had been checked on the continent, and England had emerged as the supreme oceanic power. The future of this balance depended largely on international relations in the Baltic, to which Britain now gave first attention.

The Great Northern War had continued as an independent struggle, with Charles XII of Sweden and Peter the Great of Russia being the major antagonists. At the outset, Sweden had the advantage of a well-honed army which overran Poland with relative ease between 1701 and 1706. Charles XII also had inherited from his father a fleet of forty-seven sailing men-of-war concentrated at Stockholm and the new base at Karlskrona, along with the commander of continuing Swedish naval construction, the veteran General Admiral Hans Wachtmeister. With this heavily gunned navy versed in line-ahead tactics, the Swedes commanded the Baltic and were able to support their army on the shores of the Gulf of Finland. By contrast, Peter had only his small lake craft to support his own army, but in early 1702 he took the Swedish fortress at the mouth of the Neva, giving him an outpost on the Baltic coast and thus changing the strategic situation importantly. For at that spot, in May 1703, he began to erect the new capital of St. Petersburg and the following winter began to fortify the island of Kronstadt, both of them withstanding Swedish land- and sea-borne attacks in 1704–05. Till this time, Peter had used only small craft such as barges, rafts and twenty-men *lodki* in the Baltic, but in 1704, building upon his limited naval experiences in the Black Sea, he created the Galley (or Rowing) Fleet, augmented the next year by a Sea Regiment much like similar units in the English and Swedish navies. Peter hired foreign shipwrights and naval officers to create and lead this fleet, with aristocratic troops to man the galleys. The elite Galley Fleet was then strengthened in 1708 by the creation of an amphibious command. Because Charles was occupied in Poland and Saxony during these years, Peter fashioned his young navy without serious interference. Then, in January 1708, the Swedish army invaded Russia.

The Great Northern War took on a new direction when Peter's army and a fierce Russian winter combined finally to crush Charles' army at the battle of Poltava in June 1709. Charles barely escaped to Ottoman Turkey, leaving Peter free to reoccupy Poland. In October Denmark, having strengthened its fleet after the truce of 1700, declared war on Sweden and crossed the Sound to invade Scania. Peter laid siege in 1710 to Swedish Viborg and Riga, which fell during the summer despite the presence of Swedish warships. Seeing the need for a covering force of his own, Peter now created the Ship Fleet. The next year, the first seven men-of-war put to sea; manned by foreign officers and Russian troops as well as sailors, this force had the exclusive mission of supporting the Galley Fleet and therefore army actions on land. It was not supposed to fight fleet actions in line-ahead. That, the allied Danes could do, and between 1710 and 1713 the Danish fleet under General Admiral Lieutenant Count Gyldenløve skirmished with the Swedish squadrons of Wachtmeister. The new Russian galleys and men-of-war were also active against the Swedes, but Peter was tied down elsewhere in a war with Turkey, brought on by Charles against him in 1710. The Turks defeated Peter in battle the next year and exacted a truce which forced Peter to return Azov to them. The formal peace between Russia and Turkey came in 1713, the same year that England and France came to terms, but the Baltic war continued as usual.

The end of the War of the Spanish Succession had important strategic implications for the Baltic region, for now Britain determined to keep any one power from dominating Baltic waters. To offset the aggressive Charles XII of Sweden, Great Britain (as well as Holland and Denmark) had been building and selling warships to Russia. From 1713 on, the British fleet also played an increasingly active role in the Baltic. But Peter's Ship Fleet, aided by the Danes, was improving steadily. Peter completed his conquest of the eastern Baltic coast by overrunning Swedish Finland, and in the summer of 1714, as rear admiral of the galleys, he accompanied his General Admiral Feodor Matveievitch Apraxin—the first Russian admiral—in their destruction of a new Swedish force at the battle of Hango Head (or Gangoot). Charles XII now returned from Turkey and attempted to blockade the Baltic coast. Not only did he refuse mediation by Britain and Holland, but he sent out privateers against their ships. His obstinacy in trying to destroy Russia thus brought on the wrath of the maritime powers, who now created escorted convoys for the Baltic, bypassing Stockholm in favor of St. Petersburg. Admiral Sir John Norris arrived with an Anglo-Dutch fleet of thirty men-of-war in the summer of 1715, sending half his force to aid the Danes at Copenhagen and the rest to support Peter at Reval. Britain did not formally enter the war against Sweden, but Prussia and Hanover did, and the Hanoverian George I was now king of England. The Danes and Swedes continued to skirmish at sea, and in March 1716 Charles XII invaded Danish Norway. His irritated enemies now concentrated a massive Anglo-Dutch-Danish-Russian fleet of sixty-two men-of-war mounting over 3600 guns at Copenhagen under Admirals Norris and Gyldenløve. The alliance suffered from internal quarrels, however, and all the fleet did was protect allied convoys and help to frustrate Charles's campaign in Norway. Various assaults on his forward bases led Charles to abandon the effort, and soon after he invaded Norway again late in 1718, he was killed in battle.

By now, the changing alliance structure in Europe had brought Britain into the active role of offsetting aggression throughout Western Europe and trying to maintain balances between lesser powers in both the Baltic and the Mediterranean. While bringing her naval weight to bear on Sweden, Britain was also confronted by a sudden revival—of all things— of Spanish naval power in the Mediterranean. Though practically bankrupt, the new Bourbon Spanish king Philip V decided, upon the death of Louis XIV in 1715, that he would like to join Spain and France under his own crown and also restore Spain's supremacy on the Italian peninsula. Britain and Holland opposed the union as vigorously as they had when Louis XIV had tried it, but this time France did as well. A new maritime power also now figured in the new balance. Continental Austria had been awarded Naples, Milan and Sardinia in 1713, and the Austrian Emperor Charles VI then built a road across the Alps connecting Vienna with Trieste on the Adriatic. He then, in 1719, declared Trieste and nearby Fiume free ports, thus initiating Austrian interest in maritime trade. None of these powers wanted Spanish hegemony in Italy to be restored, so in 1717 England, France and Holland allied to frustrate Philip's designs. Austria, tied down in the East with a war against Turkey, did not join immediately. So Spain, having started a naval revival ostensibly to strengthen the West Indies against smugglers, occupied Austrian Sardinia in November 1717 and the following July took Savoyan Sicily. With the balance of power in the Mediterranean thus threatened, England acted. In August 1718 she led the creation of the Quadruple Alliance with France, Austria and Holland (a silent partner) against Spain. When Philip refused to evacuate Sicily, war followed.

The War of the Quadruple Alliance lasted two years and was largely shaped by British command of the sea. Taking advantage of internal disputes regarding the recent successions in England and France and the Austrian preoccupation with Turkey, Spain used her new French-model ships to attempt to retrieve control over the Central Mediterranean as well as drive off interlopers in the West Indies. But the alliance against her proved to be simply too strong. A British fleet of twenty-one men-of-war under Admiral Byng landed an Austrian force near Messina and on August 11, 1718, overwhelmed a weaker Spanish fleet at the battle of Cape Passaro off Syracuse, taking sixteen galleons and four frigates. Formal declarations of war followed in December, and the Austrian army, supported by Byng, besieged Messina, taking it finally in October 1719. The same month British landing parties took Vigo and Pontevedra on the coast of Spain, while a French invasion army operated in the country. Frustrated everywhere, Philip V made peace early in 1720. Among other agreements, Austria traded Sardinia to Savoy in return for Sicily. Britain had thus salvaged the balance of power in the Mediterranean, though strategically her retention of Gibraltar provided a potential source of renewed conflict with Spain. Spain was perhaps fortunate to settle the conflict so amicably, for Britain had begun to penetrate the Pacific with a "South Seas" joint stock company and a privateer company of "The Gentlemen Adventurers." The latter with two warships failed to intercept the Manila galleon to Acapulco in 1719, and the next year the South Seas financial "bubble" collapsed. But the Spanish Pacific and Caribbean monopolies continued at best only precariously.

Meanwhile, the nearly restored balance in the Baltic upon the death of Charles XII and the neutralization of the Swedish fleet was suddenly upset by the direct assertion of absolute supremacy of Tsar and Vice Admiral Peter of Russia. In 1718 Peter began organizing the Russian government around the needs of the Great Northern War, and over the next two years he and Admiral Apraxin carried out devastating naval raids against the Swedish coast. Accordingly, British Admiral Norris returned to the Baltic in the spring of 1720 with twenty of the line and united with forty-nine Swedish vessels to contest the new Russian supremacy at sea. Due largely to differences between the British and Swedish naval commanders and to the South Sea crisis, no naval action took place. Also, peace negotiations had begun to end the Great Northern War. In the years 1719–21 they ended the hostilities and led to a new system of alliances. Russia now commanded the Baltic, with St. Petersburg as a major seaport and with control over the former Swedish coast from Viborg to Riga. The Swedish Empire was ended, and Sweden entered into alliances with Denmark, Prussia, Hanover and Great Britain. To keep this new balance intact Britain also allied with Prussia, which had abandoned all maritime aspirations, and a British fleet remained in the Baltic. This presence led Sweden and Russia to sign a defensive pact in 1724, but in general Great Britain henceforth became the champion of the Scandinavian nations against Russia. As in the Mediterranean, then, Britain used her sea power to create a shaky political stability in the Baltic region.

The Oceanic Age came to an end in the 1720s in the strategic if not the exploratory and colonial senses. The long struggles for imperial hegemony culminated with the ascendancy of maritime Britain to unquestioned supremacy. Spain still had Latin America; Holland ruled the East Indies; Portugal held Brazil; and France retained scattered possessions throughout the world; but Great Britain monopolized the bulk of the carrying trade of Europe and commanded the major sea lanes of the world. For this mercantilistic system to work, Britain needed peace, or—more properly—a balance of the powers in major geographic areas.

To maintain such a strategic equilibrium, Britain actively discouraged the growth of any new maritime nations. Russia had emerged as a threat in the Baltic, and by the time of Peter's death in 1725 the fleet included 58 ships of the line, 30 frigates, nearly 300 galleys of various sizes and 150 brigs. Peter had not only stimulated the growth of a navy in Russia, but had backed it with naval and engineering academies, an improved canal system between the rivers Neva and Volga, and a generally Westernized society. But Russia had continental worries relative to Poland and Turkey, so that Britain could combine with Sweden and Denmark to offset any Russian power play in the Baltic. The British could no longer regard Russia as a mere local concern, as they had, say, with Denmark in the past, for Russia was growing into a major European power beyond the Baltic. She had a small squadron on the Caspian Sea and had lost a base on the Black Sea in the prolonged wars with the Turks. Russia even looked abroad, along with Sweden, to a possible protectorate over the buccaneer-pirate refuge at Madagascar, but these designs collapsed in 1724. Finally, however, Russia figured in the future of the Mediterranean, joining Spain there against England in 1726, leading to the dispatch of a British force to the Baltic that year and the next. Baltic policy was therefore inextricably interwoven with that of the Mediterranean, or, more correctly, with the European balance of power at large.

The other new maritime nation, Austria, Britain countered even more vigorously when Emperor Charles VI—determined to enjoy the mercantilistic fruits of the Oceanic Age—sided with resurgent Spain. In 1722 the Austrians created their own Ostend Company to commence maritime commercial activity out of Ostend, Trieste and Fiume. They even established two bases in India, from which they were soon expelled by the monopolistic English and Dutch. Hiring English, Italian and Spanish officers, Austria fashioned a small Adriatic fleet of three ships of the line, one frigate and some large galleys. Spain, meanwhile, angered by Britain's refusal to restore Gibraltar and Minorca to Spanish control, in 1725 allied with Austria to support the Spanish claim for Gibraltar, Spain to advance the interests of the Ostend Company. And Russia supported this alliance. But England, France, Holland and Denmark soon formed a coalition against this potentially serious Austro-Spanish threat. A British squadron went to the Caribbean to stop the sailing of the annual plate convoy; other warships cruised the Spanish coast; and Gibraltar was reinforced by sea. Austria and Spain were thus rendered helpless against the Royal Navy, and the Spanish landward blockade of Gibraltar of 1727–28 accomplished nothing. In the diplomatic maneuvering of the latter two years, England ended the brief conflict and signed an alliance with France, Holland and Spain to restore the maritime equilibrium. To further isolate Russia in the Baltic, the British also made defensive pacts with Denmark and Sweden. Having halted Spanish protests in the Mediterranean by a few minor concessions —but not Gibraltar—Britain joined Holland in 1731 to force the Austrian Ostend Company out of business. The Austrian fleet soon melted away, and general peace reigned in European waters—under the British flag.

Thus did Britain, in three quarters of a century, overcome the Dutch maritime supremacy, stop the French challenge at sea, restore equilibrium in the Baltic by checking first Swedish then Russian aggressiveness, undermine the Spanish monopoly in the West Indies, check Spanish naval resurgence in the Mediterranean, and destroy Austria's bid for sea power at the outset. By 1730, the mercantilistic wars of Europe were over, and the creation of the British Empire begun. Britain had now but to maintain command of the sea to enforce the balance of power throughout the world and to reap the full profits of her monumental efforts.

# BOOK FOUR

## British Empire and the World Wars

*Command of the seas, as Admiral Mahan so often remarked, was an exclusive thing; it could not be shared, and was applicable to one nation at a time.*

—GERALD S. GRAHAM

The eighteenth century belonged to Great Britain, whose geographic insularity—as before—enabled her to survive the tumultuous upheavals of the continent and to initiate the industrial revolution that would characterize the Western world in the nineteenth century. More important, however, was the imperial thalassocracy that Britain had become by the time of the accession of the peaceful Sir Robert Walpole as prime minister and virtual ruler during the 1720s. Building upon the firm intellectual foundations of the age of William Shakespeare and Francis Bacon and inheriting the mantle of thalassocratic vitality from war-weary Holland, Great Britain entered her golden age of fine arts and philosophy in the late seventeenth century, an age that lasted for a century. Not only were these great minds English, but several were born or lived in Scotland, Ireland or the American colonies, while continental thinkers ventured to Britain or America to partake in the free intellectual atmosphere of the British nation. From this environment, and similar but more isolated contributions in France and the Germanies, sprang the Age of the Enlightenment, celebrating the search for reason through nature and the rights of the individual.

211

So intellectually vigorous did Britain's thalassocracy become that a brief mention of its leading minds will suffice as evidence. In scientific thought the Royal Society was founded in 1662 and flourished through the works of such men as William Harvey and Robert Boyle, while John Milton and John Dryden suggested the trend of English literature, and John Locke wrote on political philosophy. Then the new century was dazzled by a profusion of British intellect: in science Isaac Newton, Benjamin Franklin and Joseph Priestley; in philosophy David Hume was most prominent, while the leading mind of the age, the Frenchman Voltaire, following the example of Descartes who lived in Holland one hundred years before, spent the late 1720s in England; in literature and poetry Alexander Pope, Daniel Defoe, Jonathan Swift, Samuel Johnson, Robert Burns, William Blake and Horace Walpole, the prime minister's son; in painting William Hogarth, Thomas Gainsborough, George Romney, John Constable and Joshua Reynolds, who founded the Royal Academy of Arts in 1768; in law William Blackstone; in history Edward Gibbon; and in political theory the Irishman Edmund Burke, the American Thomas Jefferson and the Englishman Thomas Paine, whose political ventures later led him to nationalistic activities in America and France. Britain by no means monopolized the Enlightenment, but her political and imperial hegemony throughout the world played a major role in setting the tenor of the age.

The British, victors in the mercantilistic struggles of the Oceanic Age, found their prosperity emulated by other states whose leading minds were no less active. France especially began to flourish economically again in the 1720s and 1730s, directly imitating much of British life. And whereas British political stability represented the acme of enlightened order, the century became a period of strong continental monarchs aimed at achieving similar order through the nation-state; King Louis XV in France from 1723, King Frederick II the Great of Prussia from 1740, Archduchess Maria Theresa in Austria also from 1740, and Tsarina Catherine the Great of Russia from 1762. Much of what these monarchs did was clearly despotic, but their techniques were representative of the mood for order and reason. Mercantilism demanded rules of economic conduct, competition was regulated and violence reduced, warfare became ever more limited, tactics rigid and formal, and a new respect for law was a growing theme of the times.

International and maritime law had evolved over the centuries to the point where Grotius and Selden had debated, but in the eighteenth century Burke and Blackstone proclaimed law to be "natural" and thus binding to all nations, a view shared across the Channel by Voltaire and Montesquieu. Absolute sovereignty over the seas by any one state was rejected by the new legal attitude, the chief spokesman being the erudite

Dutch lawyer Cornelius van Bynkershoek who outlined his views in his treatise *De Dominio Maris (The Sovereignty of the Sea)* in 1703. Rejecting Selden's notion of the closed sea, Bynkershoek echoed the spirit of the Enlightenment when he declared the sea lanes open to all nations, except those offshore waters within the three-mile range of a piece of coast artillery ("the three-mile limit"). He assumed like Voltaire and others that the new rationality put an end to war over economic wealth as typified in the Oceanic Age, thereby making command of the sea a moot question. However, since several nations pressed to preserve local maritime monopolies, especially a mildly prosperous Spain, limited wars persisted and legal discussion shifted to the rights of neutral vessels carrying goods to belligerents in time of such wars. Traditionally, the rule followed in the Spanish *Consolato del Mare* of 1494 allowed such "free ships" to trade openly but be deprived of any cargo destined for a belligerent as "contraband of war." After the confiscation, however, the neutral vessel must be allowed to go its way. In 1697, however, the Dutch had insisted that "free ships" meant "free goods," thus neutral vessels passed almost unhindered by the belligerents in the War of the Spanish Succession. But Bynkershoek, writing in 1737, rejected this notion of "free ships, free goods" in favor of the old *Consolato* rule, an opinion upheld by most contemporary writers on maritime jurisprudence. Great Britain, supreme at sea throughout most of the eighteenth century, supported Bynkershoek's views on the seizure of contraband at sea, its implications for enforcing a blockade and his rule that "effective occupation" of the shore meant control of adjacent waters. Britain therefore monopolized its colonial waters in peacetime and closed enemy ports to neutral shipping in time of war. Its enemies, conversely, thus argued for freedom of the seas via the principle of "free ships, free goods." The discussion remained academic, however, for by maintaining active command of the sea Britain enforced her own interpretation of international law.

The British Empire during the eighteenth century matured from a loose system of chartered companies, colonies and sea lanes into an ordered mercantilistic network, held together by the ships of the Royal Navy. Like the Spanish in Latin America and the Dutch in the Far East, the British economic system was closed, based on the Navigation Act of 1660 with modifications thus restricting trade not only with Britain itself but with the overseas colonies, the chief of which were in North America and the Caribbean. For the first three quarters of the century, colonial wealth in the form of rum came from the British West Indies (Jamaica, Barbados, St. Kitts) as well as slaving from the *asiento* with Spain. Secondarily, the American colonies from New Hampshire to the Carolinas provided various goods, the most important being timber and naval stores and much tobacco production; these colonies numbered thirteen after North and South Carolina split in 1712 and Georgia was settled in 1733. To prevent smuggling into the British Isles and to these colonies, the Royal Navy in 1696 became an agency of enforcement of the Navigation acts. To protect and promote overseas imperial trade, and to weaken the Spanish and French holdings in the Americas, the fleet was also the chief agent of the government. It helped the chartered companies to ease the Portuguese and Dutch out of India and to compete with the French there. The navy helped to offset Russian designs and to enforce the peace in the Baltic and the Mediterranean, where the Barbary corsairs were as troublesome as ever. The merchant traders of the Empire thus depended upon naval protection, but so too did the navy depend upon trained seamen from the merchant marine in time of war. So the Empire, ever-expanding, was the culmination of the mercantilistic urges of the Oceanic Age and a seemingly natural expression of the ordered Enlightenment of the Western world.

But these appearances were deceiving, for the eighteenth century enlightened more than the landed gentry, aristocrats and kings. Just as the application of new knowledge in science and medicine took many decades, so too were the ideals of the philosophers who preached about the rights of man delayed. And the monopoly of mercantilism became but one of the targets of popular agitation. In the name of empire and kings, the powers engaged in worldwide wars. Too late did they recognize the protestations of their exploited peoples. For Spain, the forbidding of intercolonial trade (such as Peru to New Spain) was not modified until 1774, but this did not appease the inhabitants of a long-decadent colonial system. For France, the excesses of the Bourbon nobility could not be excused by a belated recognition of the ideals of the French *philosophes*. For Britain, the protests of the American colonists against revenue laws and the economic theories of Adam Smith calling for free trade and an end to mercantilistic monopoly were equally recognized too late. And for all the powers, the bloody stains of Negro slavery—originally promoted by the Portuguese and Dutch—were not erased soon enough. So, beginning in 1775, the century erupted in revolution, creating conflicts of intensity and geographic range unlike any the world had ever witnessed. But through it all, Britain and her navy labored mightily to control the seas—and succeeded.

## SHIPS AND SEAFARING

The world wars of the eighteenth century provided one impetus for major advances in the art and science of seafaring, but so did a second wave of overseas exploration and mathematical developments in navigation. The ability of mariners to navigate without determining accurate longitude had led to severe handicaps and even some disasters at sea, so that the British Parliament in 1714 had offered a reward for the solution of the problem. Instruments were the first difficulty, but the development of a marine sextant by 1730 (for accurate measurement of latitude), an octant the next year, and a crude chronometer in 1735 helped to solve the problem. The octant was used to plot the position of a vessel relative to the moon, sun or a star, but this was not generally successful until the publication of the first accurate nautical lunar ephemeris after 1752. This technique was used to determine longitude throughout most of the century until replaced entirely by a superior marine chronometer based on a model adopted by the Royal Navy in 1765 which used time as the measurement of longitudinal position. From these important innovations the art of modern navigation progressed, the first important textbook being published by the American mathematician Nathaniel Bowditch in 1802.

In the midst of these developments, a new series of explorers ventured to unknown waters and lands, most of which were in the Pacific and American regions, till then largely Spanish preserves. The movement began with the voyages of the Dane Vitus Bering, in Russian employ, into the sea which now bears his name in the 1720s to 1740s. Russian traders then penetrated from Siberia to North America and French and British explorers moved westward across the continent, so that Spain launched her last colonization effort overland by settling Texas in the 1720s and California half a century later as extensions of Mexican New Spain. Spain established potentially major seaports along the Pacific coast in rapid succession: San Diego in 1769, Monterey and San Francisco in 1776, and Los Angeles in 1781. The search for a Northwest Passage to the Pacific was continued by many explorers unsuccessfully, and a large number of British, French and Russian marine explorers were active throughout the Pacific at the end of the century and the beginning of the next. The greatest and most successful of them all was the British captain James Cook, who, using the new marine chronometer, made three Pacific voyages beginning in 1768 to Tahiti, New Zealand, Australia, Antarctic waters, Alaska and Hawaii, where he was killed by natives in 1779. All these exploratory efforts had strategic consequences in that they undermined Spanish hegemony and changed the Pacific into a potential region of imperial conflict.

Navigational instruments were not the only innovation in the eighteenth century which improved the ability of maritime nations, particularly Britain, to operate navies, merchant marines and exploratory expeditions successfully. Living conditions on board ship were also revolutionized, though not as thoroughly as the Enlightened knowledge of the age might have achieved if it had been systematically applied. The old difficulty of discipline was not solved by any changes, especially as criminal-types and unskilled labor were recruited or impressed to fill up depleted crews. Flogging therefore continued and was abused so flagrantly that even the more reliable enlisted men—trained in the merchant service—rebelled; the British naval mutinies of 1797 were one result. Pay remained a small compensation for the men, with prize money from captures at sea going mainly to the officers. And the food remained miserable especially in tropical climes where the preservation of it was most difficult. The diet of the crews was therefore shaped by the limits set by preserving the food. This state of affairs existed from pre-Armada days to the introduction of refrigeration in the late nineteenth century.

The British navy's victuals were typical of the abominable food and drink available at sea in these times. The main staple, biscuit of mixed wheat and pea-flour (and sometimes bone dust), became hard and sour and so unattractive that it had to be eaten in the dark of night; it also tended to breed weevils and in the tropics maggots. Cheese hardly kept at all at sea, smelled, tasted awful and soon bred long thin red worms. The prescribed weekly issue of four pounds of beef and two of pork per man, after maybe years in salt as the preservative, was as hard as mahogany and was often used for the same purpose in carving figurines. The oatmeal was nauseating, until sweetened early in the nineteenth century with molasses and butter. What was edible and tolerable was the hot pea soup, plum duff (ground-up flour baked with sugar and currants), Scotch coffee (boiled burned biscuit) with sugar, occasional fresh fruits and many forms of alcoholic beverages. Fresh fruits played havoc with Northern digestive systems accustomed to salt and meat diets, while the lack of vitamin C continued to foster scurvy. The distilled spirits led to widespread alcoholism. In port or on short voyages, London river water could be supplemented by beer, rum and brandy, and Spanish white wines enjoyed popularity too. After the supply of these drinks was exhausted on the high seas, grog was issued—an eighteenth-century innovation of the British navy. Twice each day, the sailor was issued a pint of grog, made of one quarter 100-proof rum and three quarters brackish water, plus a dash of lemon acid and sugar in the midday ration. The amount was sufficient to warm a sailor in wet clothes high in the rigging, but it also left his mind fogged, so that accidents such as fatal falls were commonplace. The grog helped the men forget the food, and the sailors combated the everpresent taste of salt by also chewing tobacco, rigging grease or anything—which also might lead to disease and death. The liquor also combined with the "women-on-board" practice while in port (not abandoned until 1880) to provide some pleasure, but also to promote venereal diseases.

The eighteenth century marked the first major steps to alleviating such distresses of the common seaman, and not surprisingly the British led the way, though the innovations came slowly. The first British naval asylum for aged and disabled seamen opened in 1704 and expanded over the years. The first of several Royal Navy hospitals admitted its first patients exactly fifty years later. The checking of sea diseases was due mostly to the findings and recommendations of a prominent British naval physician, James Lind. He attacked the problem of scurvy with great zeal, writing his first treatise in 1754 and others which recommended the issuing of antiscorbutics in the form of lime and lemon juices. Captain Cook tried it in his circumnavigation of the globe in 1772 and lost not one man from scurvy or dysentery, though not until 1796 did the Admiralty order a lemon juice ration for all hands. (It was lime juice, however, that earned the British sailor his fond sobriquet of "Limey.") Fresh food and water became standard through Lind's advice, proved through Admiral Sir Edward Hawke's provisioning during the long and successful siege of Brest in 1759. Lind was the first to realize that the nondescript and dirty clothing of the men fostered disease (though the agent of transmission, lice, was not discovered till 1909), so he initiated means of cleansing the ship and individual crewmen. Ships and sleeping hammocks were scrubbed and aired out, and in 1781 new recruits were washed thoroughly and issued new clothing, thus reducing typhus. Actual uniforms were not yet contemplated for the men, though noncommissioned ratings got them in 1787. Surgeon Lind also distinguished between two tropical "fevers"—malaria and yellow fever (or the black vomit)—and joined others in recommending the distillation of fresh water from sea water. Lind's lead provided a catalyst for hygienic reforms in the world's navies. The British followed French and Spanish practices of isolating the sick from the rest of the crew, and a Russian draft of beer and brandy was adopted to combat the chills. Some vaccination against smallpox in the Royal Navy began in 1798, each man was issued two hammocks as part of several health reform measures in 1804–06, and in 1810 soap became standard issue for all sailors and marines. The reduction of British naval sick from over 32,000 in 1780 (of 85,000 enrolled) to some 8,000 (of 120,000) in 1805 speaks to the effectiveness of such reforms which spread to all navies.

Officers naturally profited from these general improvements in health, though their general isolation from the men—by armed marines and separate living quarters and battle stations—minimized the possibility of contracting disease or injury from sick or disgruntled crewmen. The social separation in all navies was symbolized by the British navy's adoption of a standard officer's uniform dress in 1746. Aristocratic standing was even more rigid than in armies, where commissions could be purchased. Political favoritism therefore remained strong, and landed gentry often sent sons to particular ships as midshipmen either to curry favor or cancel debts to the captain. Formal training schools had existed since Henry the Navigator's day, but the Dutch pioneered with advanced ones in the seventeenth century and were imitated by the French under Colbert; the national French Marine Academy was founded in 1752 and became a state institution seventeen years later. The British did not found a naval academy until 1733 at Portsmouth-Gosport, expanded in 1806 into the Royal Naval College. But this was only a two-year school to augment the tried-and-true method of instruction at sea. The first-class volunteer who attended Gosport required private means, but after graduation he was subjected to the same regimen on board ship as less privileged midshipmen. After six years at sea, two as passed midshipman (ensign), such a nineteen-year-old could be examined for promotion to lieutenant. Elevation to ship command then came either rapidly or not at all. Horatio Nelson was a lieutenant at nineteen, but then became a captain two years later in 1779, languished at half-pay in peacetime, and reached the rank of rear admiral at the age of thirty-eight in 1797. The true measure of a naval officer was thus not his social station or his theoretical knowledge—though these things helped—but his ability to command a ship of the line.

The standard warship by the eighteenth century reached its technological ceiling, meaning no real changes could be made to it. The galley had survived, but only barely. The galley last saw battle in the Mediterranean in 1717, and the states of this region quickly discarded it: Naples in 1734 and France in 1748, while a few Italian galleys and half-galleys stayed in service as late as 1798. The Mediterranean-type galley—twenty to thirty oars and two or three lateen sails—was employed in the Baltic, however, in Denmark from 1664, Russia from 1704 and Sweden from 1712 but was modified with square sails during the course of the eighteenth century. Similarly, the fire ships so popular with the Dutch passed out of favor, though sixth-rate warships could be adapted for the purpose. The modified galleon had evolved into the standard ship of the line, and its basic form, speed (average five knots) and armament did not change markedly during the course of the eighteenth century. The hull decorations were reduced to a minimum, copper sheathing covered all hulls soon after 1783 to ward off the teredo (shipworm), and simultaneously the short-range carronade was invented to smash into hulls and produce fragmented splinters to wound personnel.

Because of heavier cannon, only the size of these vessels increased, from about 1500 to 3000 tons for first-rate ships of 100 guns. The British standardized their warships up until 1750, making them somewhat inferior to the more individualized, scientifically designed French and Spanish vessels of similar qualities. In general, however, the designations of sailing men-of-war applied in all Western navies, with Britain as the model.

Properly speaking, a "ship" was designated by three masts, all ships of the line were rated by the number of guns and gunners, and lesser vessels according to rigging, size, armament and mission. The first three rates were two- or three-deckers mounting 70 to 120 guns and meant solely for fleet action. Britain only built six First Rates between 1750 and 1790, of which the *Victory* (launched in 1765 and preserved today at Portsmouth) is an excellent example; these usually wore the flag of a fleet commander. The obsession of the British to cram guns aboard their battle-line ships, making them less maneuverable and efficient than those of the French, yielded later in the century to following the French preference for 74-gun two-deck Third Rates, a type which came to dominate the battle lines by 1800. The 50-gun Fourth Rate acted as the standard convoy escort, while the more lightly armed two-deck Fifth Rate proved less successful in a similar role. Instead, the French again initiated the trend toward large single-deck frigates, mounting 36 to 50 guns; one of the best examples is the American frigate *Constitution* (launched in 1797 at Boston, where she is still preserved). Lesser vessels of various armament and rigging carried out commerce raiding, coastal patrols, revenue service, scouting and miscellaneous duties: the Sixth Rate, sloop of war (or corvette in France), barque (bark), barkentine, brigantine and snow (both merging to become the man-of-war brig), schooner, cutter, horse transport, gunboat, lugger, mortar-armed bomb ketch and well-armed merchant vessels like the East Indiaman. The collective success of such varieties of eighteenth-century men-of-war was due to their great range—worldwide—and tremendous staying power, in blockade and battle.

## NAVAL TACTICS

As in previous centuries, the successful use of these great vessels depended largely on the tactical enterprise of the commanding admirals. Unfortunately, however, the events of the Anglo-Dutch-French wars between 1652 and 1714 had led to the stagnation of British naval tactics. To be sure, the British navy had evolved its battle line from the squadron system, and even divided its fleet into three theoretical parts, the Red, Blue and White, by which its senior admirals were ranked. But the

regimentation of the Fighting Instructions in 1703, like the standardiza-
tion in ship types and cannon, was affirmed by the final success of the
British in these wars. Commanding admirals could and did issue their
own sets of Additional Instructions to improve the opportunity for tactical success, but rarely did they exploit them to real advantage.

The tactical lesson missed by the Admiralty, however, was that victory
had been due largely to strategic, not tactical, superiority. So senior admirals used only the strict tactical "formalism" of the tightly controlled
"conterminous" battle line for exchanging broadsides. British captains
were to approach from windward (the weather gauge) in line-ahead,
engage their opposite number, and fire on the down-roll of the ship to
sink or disable their adversary. The trouble with this, as events would
prove, was the difficulty of achieving a perfect battle line simultaneously
engaged, along with the shortcomings of the primitive signal system
available to the commanding admiral. Neither did such formalistic tactics
allow the exploitation of sudden opportunities by the personal initiative
of subordinate admirals and captains. Conversely, this possibility was
embodied in the "melee" school of tactical thought, where the fleet "concentrated" or "massed" on part of the enemy line, thus defeating it piecemeal. Melee tactics required that one portion of the enemy force be held
out of action by the wind, a feint or other circumstances while the remaining portion was defeated. The most effective means of achieving
mass was to "break" or "double"—either passing over the head or
through the midst of the enemy line to deliver fire from both sides. The
English had used doubling with some success against the Dutch at
Solebay in 1672 and against the French at Beachy Head in 1690 and
Barfleur in 1692. But lack of decisive battles thereafter and the retirement at half-pay of the more innovative junior officers after 1714 left
formalist tactics entrenched in the Royal Navy. In fact, eighteenth-
century admirals were aware of the advantage of achieving tactical concentration, but they preferred to let their opponent create an opportunity
for it.

The smaller size and different strategies of the French and lesser
navies allowed for greater tactical flexibility, since no other power aimed
at winning command of the seas in the eighteenth century like the British.
Small squadrons or single ships had no need for rigidity and thus depended on the initiative of their senior officers. Hence local squadrons
made their own rules—the Spanish in the Caribbean, the Dutch in the
East Indies, the Danes, Swedes and Russians in the Baltic, and the
French, British and later Americans in far-flung waters. The French
navy, when mobilized for war, remained the most serious contender to
Britain. But the French locked in on their own tactical conservatism—
because of old, unretired veteran admirals, the need to preserve and thus

not risk losing valuable warships, the commitment to *guerre de course* over fleet action, and the overriding importance of subordinating all naval operations to support of the army. Whenever a French squadron met a like force of British warships, the French elected to fight on the leeward gauge, which enabled the British to seize the initiative and to blind the French with the smoke from their cannon, upwind. But the French fired on the up-roll, hoping to shoot away the rigging and immobilize the foe, then use their superior, faster vessels to break off the action and escape to fight another day. French tactics thus aimed at preserving the fleet's strategic support of the army. This also required fewer men, for the French would only have to man the broadside guns to windward; if doubled by the foe, they would be in trouble, but they were supposed to retire before any such thing could happen.

With such rigidity on both sides, the British and French fought very few decisive battles in the years 1692 to 1782. By the time the British admiral formed his ideal conterminous line, the French would break and run. For the British to pursue would mean violating the formal line of battle. But there was one allowance for initiative in the Permanent Fighting Instructions. If the British admiral was convinced he had beaten the French fleet, he could violate his line and let his ships pursue at will to overcome stragglers. The catch, of course, was to be certain the enemy was really defeated and fleeing in panic. If the enemy turned to engage his pursuers, he might reverse the situation. So risk was involved in ordering the chase, and risk meant melee tactics. In these ninety years, the British and French fought fifteen major naval battles using the conterminous line. Not one ship was sunk on either side in these battles, and only six of the engagements were decisive British victories; in each of these six general chase was used. Only then, in 1782, with such overwhelming evidence against them did the Royal Navy abandon its penchant for formalist tactics. By that time, also, a new generation of naval officers had appeared to develop fresh tactical doctrine. Despite the long-term tactical sterility, however, the British navy maintained its general command of the sea because of its superior strategic dispositions.

# 7
# Seven Years War, 1730–1763

*Command of the sea . . . means nothing but the control of maritime communications, whether for commercial or military purposes. The object of naval warfare is the control of communications, and not, as in land warfare, the conquest of territory.*

—Corbett

## RUSSIA AND THE BALANCE OF POWER

For Great Britain, prosperity depended upon enforcing a balance of power in the waters and on the continent of Europe—especially with regard to Russia—and upon expanding markets and colonies abroad. The quarrels over trading privileges meant constant cold war in the West Indies with Spain and France and fresh clashes with the French in India, since the French trading company under Joseph François Dupleix intervened in the Indian civil wars in 1749. When the British followed in like manner, India became a European battleground on a par with North America. The other Eastern area of potential commercial rivalry, the waters of China and Japan, did not erupt because of the policies of these peoples. Japan remained in self-imposed isolation, save for the Dutch mission at Nagasaki. China enjoyed a great cultural era under the Manchu dynasty, but only minimal relations with the West. When, however, the Emperor declared Canton as the only open entrepôt for European trade in 1757, the British trading mission there (since 1699) expanded to the point where it surpassed in importance the leased Portuguese trading center of Macao. As Britain thus expanded her commercial profits, the lure of overseas wealth through commerce spread to France and other monarchies, so that carefully preserved order became essential to promote this intercourse. The sea wars fought between the

1730s and 1775, especially the global Seven Years War, thus focused—as before—on the balance of trade and on mercantilistic empire.

The rivalry between Britain and France continued therefore in the tradition of the struggles of the two preceding centuries, but in Eastern and Central Europe new forces were at work to add a new dimension to world affairs. From the Baltic to the Mediterranean, the rise of Russia and Prussia combined to challenge the older powers of Poland, Austria and the Ottoman Empire. While Prussian interests remained concentrated in the North, Russia emerged in the eighteenth century as a major force in Europe, becoming conspicuous in the Seven Years War. In contrast to the fragmented states of Scandinavia, the Austrian Holy Roman Empire, and the Italian kingdoms, Russia under Peter the Great had centralized into a great monolith that, properly mobilized, bore sufficient strength to dominate the Baltic, cripple Poland, threaten Austria and push back the Turks. Fully Westernized, the Russian state, army and navy could become major elements in the European balance of power. The cultural transition was slow, however, but under Catherine the Great Russia's power grew to substantial proportions so that by 1775 the Russian state dominated Eastern Europe.

In the Baltic region, from 1721 Russia's navy was supreme, aimed at placating Sweden and weakening Poland while simultaneously fighting the Turks in the South. In 1722 the Swedes began to build seventy galleys to face the Russians, and rather than unnecessarily antagonize the Swedes Russia allowed her Ship and Galley fleets to deteriorate until they were at parity with Sweden. Then Russia turned against the new Polish king in 1733 to begin the War of the Polish Succession; Russian and Austrian armies invaded Poland, whereupon France and Spain moved against Austria, achieving some successes in Italy. The French sent a naval squadron to Poland to relieve the siege of Danzig, but the fifteen-vessel Russian Kronstadt fleet under the Scotsman Admiral Thomas Gordon successfully blockaded and shelled the port, which capitulated in July 1734. The peace of 1735 changed nothing. Six years later, the Baltic stalemate was interrupted when the Swedes took advantage of the larger War of the Austrian Succession to attack Russia in an effort to regain possession of Viborg. Russian arms triumphed on land, the few Russian line-of-battle ships covered the amphibious galleys, and no real naval battles were fought in the struggle which lasted from 1741 to 1743. Meanwhile, Denmark had maintained a respectable fleet which threatened Sweden in 1744, but Russia supported her late enemies and nothing happened. By 1746 Russia had nineteen battle-line ships at Kronstadt and five at Revel, commanding the Baltic, and in 1755 England concluded an alliance with Russia in which the latter agreed to protect Hanover, homeland of Britain's King George II. The normal peacetime deterioration of the Russian fleet took place, but many British officers had entered Russian service to give it a solid professional core.

In the Mediterranean and adjacent Black and Adriatic seas, Britain and France worked at keeping the *status quo* by halting Russian as well as Austrian designs there. The British occupation of Gibraltar and pressure on Austria to abandon maritime adventures worked toward this end in the West, but the older antagonisms of the East were harder to control.

The incessant naval-commercial war between Moslem Algeria and Christian Malta grew into a major struggle when the Ottoman Turks, with their Algerine vassals, declared war on Venice and the Knights of Malta late in 1714. The Turk fleet outnumbered the Venetians who also had a few vessels of the papal fleet, and during the summer of 1715 Turkish forces overran all of the Morea, the Aegean islands and Venetian territory on Crete. Correctly anticipating that the Turks would next move up the Adriatic to Corfu and Dalmatia, Austria early in 1716 declared war on the Ottoman Empire, while Spain and Portugal dispatched reinforcements to the new allied Christian fleet. When the Turkish battle force of some fifty sailing warships reached Corfu in July the Venetians of half that strength delayed them in a broadside duel, then used allied galleys to support the garrison at Corfu. Hard fighting and an overland Austrian invasion of Hungary led to the capture of Belgrade and the Turkish retirement from the Adriatic. The next spring the twenty-six-ship Venetian fleet advanced into the Aegean and on to the Dardanelles where it fought several small engagements with the larger Ottoman fleet. When reinforcements arrived from Portugal, Tuscany, Malta and the Pope, the Venetians had 33 heavy battle-line ships and 24 galleys under Captain Extraordinary M. A. Diedo. The Turks under Ibrahim Pasha had 44 and 4 respectively. The two forces fought a scrambled battle off Cape Matapan, southern Greece, on July 19, 1717. The Turks retired first after much damage but no ship losses to either fleet in this last galley battle in Mediterranean history. More inconclusive encounters took place in these waters the next summer, after which peace was concluded. Austria, more interested in confronting Spain in Italy, had liberated Hungary; the Turks kept the Morea; and Venice got several coastal points in Albania and Dalmatia. The stalemated peace resumed in the Eastern Mediterranean, thus fulfilling the desires of Britain and France.

Russia became the chief benefactor of the new quiet in the Mediterranean. Venice was reduced to the status of a very minor power, the Western and Central European powers were occupied elsewhere, and the Ottoman Turks fought a long land war with Persia, 1730–36. The British navy convoyed its merchant ships, the French navy and Knights of Malta battled the Barbary corsairs, while Spain in 1733 occupied

Naples and Sicily to create the pro-Spanish Kingdom of the Two Sicilies. Russia therefore determined to resume its expansion southward at the expense of Persia and Turkey. Russian needs included control of the Caspian Sea, where several western coastal towns were taken from Persia temporarily in the 1720s; control of the Black Sea, an Ottoman lake; and access to the Mediterranean through the Dardanelles—a year-round warm-water outlet. If this was accomplished, the Russians nurtured dreams of an Eastern Orthodox Empire centered on the Aegean, which meant the revolt of the Christian Ottoman subjects of Greece and the Morea. Then Russia would have to contend with British sea power, which had forced Austria from its brief naval aspirations. Meanwhile, both Austria on the Danube and Russia on the Don and Dnieper rivers had had to be content with occasional gunboat forces. But with the end of the Polish succession and Turko-Persian wars in 1735–36, Russia launched a general attack on Ottoman Turkey.

Strategically, the war of 1736–39 involved Russia's attempting to seize Azov, as Peter the Great had done in 1696, and thereby have its outlet into the Black Sea. In the summer of 1735 Vice Admiral Peter Bredal, a Norwegian with twenty-one years in Russian service, hastened the completion of 15 bombardment "prams," some of 44 guns, with 64 galleys and smaller "kaiks" at Voronezh on the Don and cruised down the Don in the spring of 1736 to join the army in the encirclement of Azov. The place surrendered at the end of June, enabling the boats to enter the Sea of Azov, whereupon the Russians set about building 500 two-gun boats at Voronezh and 400 two-gun double sloops on the Dnieper in order to support the army. The task before the Russian army commanders, the Irish-born Marshal Count Peter Lacy and the German-born Marshal Count Burkhardt von Munnich, was an amphibious one. The Turkish defenses in the Black Sea centered on the Crimean peninsula, behind the six-mile-long fortifications of the Perekop Isthmus, which connects the Crimea to the Ukraine mainland. Marshals Lacy and Munnich intended to use Admiral Bredal's boats to ferry and support their troops in attacking the Crimea and the Ukrainian port city of Ochakov farther to the west at the estuary of the Bug River. In January 1737 Austria entered the war against Turkey, though without coordinating its efforts with the Russians. In addition, France urged the Turks to fight on against the aggressive Russians. The fighting thus involved much campaigning in the Balkans and Ukraine, away from the sea.

While the Austrians traded blows with the Turks on land and Munnich's army battled serious disease, Lacy and Bredal opened their amphibious campaign. In June 1737 Munnich crossed the Bug and moved down the west bank of the Dnieper, his supplies and siege guns aboard 350 boats, to besiege Ochakov. Simultaneously, Bredal with an equal number of vessels moved from Azov two hundred miles westward and threw up a floating bridge of 217 boats across which Lacy's troops moved into the Crimea on the eastern shore, thus outflanking the Perekop defenses. Turkish naval reinforcements failed to reach Ochakov where the detonation of the city's magazine led to its surrender in July. A Turkish flotilla, however, did shell Lacy's beachhead the same month and then engaged Bredal's 47 gunboats, sole survivors of a gale that had sunk 170 craft the day before. Lacy marched across the Crimea, then returned to the east coast in August where a new pontoon bridge of Bredal's reinforced squadron took off his army. Harassed by the Turkish flotilla and more heavy weather, Bredal withdrew to Azov. In 1738 the continental fighting seesawed; Turkish men-of-war, galleys and half-galleys skirmished with Bredal in the Sea of Azov; and Lacy captured and destroyed the Perekop fortifications. The Austrians meanwhile were succumbing to the Ottoman counterattack, so Munnich threw a pontoon bridge across the Dniester River in July 1739, soundly defeated the Turkish army, and prepared to advance down the Black Sea coast on Constantinople. Russia now stood on the verge of overrunning the entire north and west shore, when Austria quit the war.

The Western powers, especially France, and even Austria, could not bear the prospect of Russian victory in the Black Sea, and therefore they sought to restore the balance of power in that region. Austria made an ignominious peace in September, surrendering Belgrade and other possessions to Turkey and thereby losing its position as a major power in the area. Faced with a full Turkish attack, Russia ended the war in October, surrendering all its gains except Azov, whose fortifications were dismantled and gunboats broken up. Worse, Russia agreed to give up its aspirations for a navy or merchant marine on the Black Sea, so the war ended in defeat for her. The entire Black Sea and Eastern Mediterranean regions now enjoyed a long period of peace, except for the obnoxious Barbary corsairs and pirates, for Russia had to fight Sweden in the war of 1741–43, and the accession of Maria Theresa to power in Austria in 1740 led to the War of the Austrian Succession. Both Russia and Austria thus looked westward and even concluded a defensive pact in 1745–46. The decline in the political fortunes of the Ottoman Empire was thus arrested, and the final reckoning with Russia postponed. Like the Baltic, the Mediterranean in the 1740s became a secondary theater to the larger power struggles of Europe.

## MARITIME WARS OF THE 1740s

For Great Britain, the border and succession squabbles of the continent appeared insignificant compared with the Franco-Spanish challenge to English shipping in the Caribbean—the only major obstacle to British maritime hegemony throughout the world. The Portuguese Empire was all but destroyed by the 1730s, save for Brazil. Outflanked and neutralized by the Dutch in the Indian Ocean, Portugal was repulsed in an attack on Mombasa by the Moslems of Oman in 1728–30 and thereafter abandoned East Africa north of Mozambique to the Sultan of Oman, whose power grew with his slave trade. Similarly, Portugal's influence in West Africa declined, and she warred with the Spanish in Latin America in the late 1730s. The Dutch decline was less pronounced but nevertheless certain. The little shipbuilding done in the Netherlands was superintended by English shipwrights, and Britain so controlled the carrying trade of Europe that Dutch merchants invested in English commercial enterprises. The Dutch East Indies flourished, but the colonial government was bogged down in the Javanese native civil wars throughout the first half of the century, after which weakened Dutch power and influence reduced the country to a minor status. The French Empire of North America threatened Britain's colonies there, while France's control of the Spanish trade *asiento* made her a major commercial rival. Spain still claimed an absolute trade monopoly over the Pacific Ocean and her own extensive possessions in Latin America. But her plate convoys had declined ever since the War of the Spanish Succession, and those to Vera Cruz ceased altogether in 1736, those to Panama in 1740. The major reason was British and Dutch smuggling between their Caribbean possessions and Spain's, along with the difficulty of policing Caribbean sea routes. Henceforth, Spanish shipping circled South America to reach Peru, thus finishing the importance of both Vera Cruz and Panama. Yet, somehow, Spain had to protect her Caribbean hegemony.

Because the sea lanes between British North America and the British Caribbean islands passed through the Florida Strait, commanded by Spanish Cuba, the Spanish stopped, searched and sometimes confiscated ships or goods they believed were being smuggled to the Spanish colonies. Atrocities were committed by Spanish coastal patrols, such as their punishment of the smuggler Captain Robert Jenkins by cutting off one of his ears in 1731. The British retaliated with similar acts, but were louder in their denunciations of Spain than the reverse, compounded by accelerated Spanish seizures by 1737. The next year the British public learned of Captain Jenkins' treatment, and anti-Spanish feeling became so intense that Prime Minister Walpole had to dispatch naval squadrons to the Caribbean and Mediterranean. Spain did not moderate her attitude, and in October 1739 Britain declared war on Spain.

The so-called War of Jenkins' Ear began as a purely colonial quarrel between Britain and Spain, but was soon drawn into the struggle known as the War of the Austrian Succession (1740–48). Spain had declined to a power rank nearly as low as Holland, but still dictated maritime matters in the Western Mediterranean and Latin America. Furthermore, by the *asiento* with France and because of France's possessions in the Caribbean, Spain involved France in her stand against Britain. The France of Louis XV had again become the major European power on the continent, playing Turkey against Russia and anxious to contain Austria at her northeastern frontier, from the Austrian Netherlands (Belgium) to the Swiss border. When Maria Theresa became Archduchess of Austria in 1740, tension over her succession to the throne grew until late in the year when the new Prussian king, Frederick the Great, invaded Austrian Silesia. Soon most of Western Europe was involved in the complex issues of this war, some unofficially at first, then formally. France and her southern neighbor Sardinia-Savoy declared war against Austria; England and Holland supported Maria Theresa. And pro-French, pro-Prussian Sweden exploited the turmoil to fight Russia in the war of 1741–43, thus bringing eventual Russian support to Austria. The war was largely a continental one in which the bloodshed resulted in virtually no change in the map of Europe except for the Prussian annexation of Silesia. For Britain, however, Austria had to be preserved against the aggression of France and Prussia, and with her the United Provinces and the Austrian Netherlands with their strategic location on the North Sea coast. Abroad, the British determined to break the Spanish monopoly in the Caribbean and Pacific during the War of Jenkins' Ear and, after the formal French declaration of war in 1744, to cripple French trade to the West Indies and the French hold in India. The war therefore almost reached major global proportions.

Britain's initial campaign against the Spanish Empire was twofold, into the Caribbean and into the Pacific. The latter attack, reduced from two fleets to one in the planning, aimed at exposing Spanish weaknesses between New Spain and the Philippines and was carried out by Commodore George Anson. The eight-vessel expedition was beset by scurvy, foul weather and sorry crews but in 1740–41 managed to negotiate Cape Horn, replenish at Juan Fernandez Island and take several Spanish prizes along the Pacific coast. In 1742 Anson's reduced force sailed westward to the Ladrones (Marianas), thence on to Macao for refit. The next year it cruised in Philippine waters where it engaged and captured the silver-laden Manila galleon bound for Acapulco. Keeping the treasure and selling his prize at Macao, Anson and his flagship—the only vessel that survived the rigors of the expedition—set out via the Indian Ocean for England. Luckily avoiding a French force, he completed his difficult circumnavigation of the globe in 1744. He had proved his point that the Pacific Ocean was a hollow defensive shell of Spain's empire.

The expedition to the Caribbean was more difficult, but the British achieved adequate results. Vice Admiral Edward Vernon with four men-of-war and a small landing party captured and demolished the Spanish Panamanian base of Porto Belo in December 1739 and in early 1740 bombarded, but failed to take, Cartagena. The latter expedition, which lasted some three months, was plagued by difficult climate and inter-service rivalries, not to mention the stout Spanish defense, and put a damper on subsequent British enthusiasm for amphibious operations. Similar attempts on Cuba—Santiago and Guantánamo Bay—in late 1741 and on the Caracas coast in 1743 also failed because of the Spanish defenses. The British had other concerns, however, for in 1740 France dispatched a squadron to the Caribbean, thus giving the Franco-Spanish naval forces slight superiority. These forces remained on the defensive, however, for Spain sought to protect its base at Havana and its treasure ships convoyed between there and Vera Cruz, and the French were content to apply their doctrine of *guerre de course* against British shipping. The British, however, basing at Jamaica and in the Leeward Islands, successfully preserved the integrity of their own convoys. In 1744, when France became a formal enemy, the British navy clamped a very effective blockade on French Martinique and Dominica and thereafter tore apart several large French West Indian convoys. Still, French and Spanish convoys got through, and privateers on both sides went unchecked, for the center of the war shifted to Europe and smaller escort vessels could not be spared for the Caribbean. And Britain had to protect its own trade routes to the North American colonies.

In North America, where the conflict eventually came to be known as King George's War, the British and their colonists had to deal with their enemies in Spanish Florida and French Canada. A force of colonists joined in the Cartagena expedition (one of their officers named his Virginia plantation after the commander—Mount Vernon), while others failed in a combined land-sea attempt to take St. Augustine in June 1740. Two years later a Spanish amphibious attack on the coast of British Georgia was repulsed, then answered by an equally unsuccessful British attack on St. Augustine again in 1743. The attention of the American colonists then shifted north in 1744, when the war with France became formal. As in the previous Anglo-French clash in North America, the fighting took place between colonists and Indians in the maritime settlements and northern New England, both supported by regular naval units. Two French expeditions failed to dislodge the British in Nova Scotia in 1744 and 1746, but in 1745 New England forces besieged and captured the new French fortress and naval base at Louisbourg on Cape Breton Island commanding the mouth of the St. Lawrence River. The war in the colonies, however, remained a sideshow to the fighting in Europe, degenerating into Indian raids, privateer attacks and one small

Spanish naval raid on North Carolina. Though France wanted desperately to retake Louisbourg, as well as to secure her trade with the West Indies, British naval operations around Europe eventually made this impossible.

Britain's strategy shifted to continental proportions because of King George II's family roots in Hanover and because of Britain's determination to offset Spanish ambitions in the Mediterranean, especially in Italy. Growing British involvement in the European war led to Walpole's resignation early in 1742, the loan of funds to Austria, the subsidizing of Hanoverian and Hessian troops and the landing of a British army in Holland in 1743 under the personal command of the king. There in June a French army attacked the force, but George managed to repulse this still-unofficial enemy. In September Britain formally allied with Austria and Savoy and reinforced its Mediterranean fleet which now had the use of the Savoyan port of Villefranche in addition to Gibraltar and Minorca. Simultaneously, France and Spain joined forces to gain the Austrian Netherlands for the former and regain Gibraltar and Minorca for the latter. In addition, the French planned to invade Britain and place "Bonnie Prince Charlie"—heir of the late deposed Catholic Stuart king, James II—on the throne of England. What had started as intervention in a European war now became a war of survival for Britain.

The French aimed at the element of surprise to invade England, since they had not the fleet to win absolute command of the Channel before crossing. Morale in the Royal Navy was low, with eighty-four-year-old Admiral Sir John Norris in command, and only one quarter of the fleet was in home waters. Furthermore, France would launch its invasion prior to declaring war and in the midst of winter, when least expected. With great secrecy, the French moved 10,000 troops in Flanders to Dunkirk where they were placed under the command of the brilliant Marshal Maurice de Saxe. The transports collected quietly at other ports, as if assembling for an expedition to the West Indies. The plan was for the Brest fleet under the Marquis de Roquefeuil to sortie and blockade or battle the British fleet at Portsmouth. Simultaneously, one squadron and the transports would rendezvous off Dunkirk, embark the army, and cross for a landing in the very entrance to the Thames River. The expedition, set for mid-January 1744, was postponed until February, giving the British the chance to collect reinforcements. Despite his age, Admiral Norris had a keen sense of strategy and when he learned of French ships moving to Dunkirk he moved his force from Portsmouth to the Downs, concentrating with the Nore division at the strategic center to prevent an invasion. With his thirty-five of the line, late in February he blockaded Dunkirk. Marshal Saxe became nervous and refused to move until Roquefeuil used his full force of fifteen men-of-war to escort him across. When Roquefeuil thus approached, Norris realized his own superiority and that he could attack the Brest fleet without uncovering his blockade by using fire ships and bomb vessels against Dunkirk. So he ordered general chase, but a sudden calm enabled Roquefeuil to escape without battle. Then a gale came up which destroyed several French transports. French dreams of invasion thus vanished without the ability to command the sea.

British strategic and tactical boldness in the Channel did not typify their operations in the Mediterranean, where sixty-eight-year-old Admiral Thomas Matthews maintained a loose blockade of the Franco-Spanish ships at Toulon in order to hamper Spanish operations in Italy. When, in mid-February, the allied force sortied from Toulon, Matthews pursued for three days before closing for battle. His rear squadron too far off, its commander probably deliberately uncooperative, Matthews signaled for line-ahead battle as required by the Fighting Instructions, then violated his own order by engaging the enemy center and rear. The hard but confused six-hour naval battle of Toulon ensued, but with inconclusive results. Looking perhaps for a scapegoat, the British Admiralty court-martialed and convicted Matthews and seven of his captains. In any case, the British naval presence was enough to convince France to shift out of the Mediterranean to the Atlantic even before the formal declaration of war. Britain held Gibraltar and Minorca and thus blockaded Cádiz and Cartagena, but Franco-Spanish-Italian arms overran the disputed coasts, including Villefranche, turning the Mediterranean into a general stalemate for the rest of the war.

France finally declared war on England in March 1744, and British military fortunes soon waned. Saxe's armies did not invade England, but they overran Flanders and defeated the allied army in this spring. To make matters worse, a single French frigate landed Prince Charles, the Young Pretender, in Scotland in August, and Charles's Jacobite army spent the autumn conquering Scotland and invading England from the north. A new army of invasion gathered at Dunkirk to cross the Channel, and gloom engulfed England. But the irascible Admiral Edward Vernon, having relieved the aged Norris, followed the latter's example of exploiting the interior position to thwart French invasion schemes and upset French communications to Scotland. He created a Western Squadron to patrol with the main warships off Plymouth and thus prevent a French fleet sortie from Brest to Dunkirk or English shores. With his own small force, he remained at the Downs and then sent privateers from Dover to patrol the Channel and other squadrons to frustrate French attempts to supply Charles in Scotland. By this system, he protected his country from invasion, escorted inbound and outbound convoys and isolated the Young Pretender. The ultra-conservative Admiralty supported Vernon's program, but was sufficiently irritated by his abrasive manner to force his resignation a week before the year ended. But France again abandoned its schemes for invasion, the Jacobite rebellion was crushed in 1746 and Vernon's strategy of concentration was preserved by his successors.

Britain could now shift to the offensive and devise her strategy accordingly. King George remained committed to a continental presence and thus continued to battle unsuccessfully against the great Saxe as his armies invaded the Austrian and Protestant Netherlands in 1746–47, but the promise of Russian help kept Anglo-Hanoverian fortunes alive in the Low Countries. At sea, however, the French had maintained their policy of *guerre de course,* even when contemplating invasion, and made no real attempt to coordinate their activities with the Spanish navy. The naval war thus remained one of trade, and the surest means of waging offensive commerce warfare for Britain was by blockade. The Admiralty decided to give great freedom of movement to its key fleet commander and sought a younger and more vigorous officer to command the Western Squadron. After the eighty-four-year-old Norris, sixty-eight-year-old Matthews and sixty-one-year-old Vernon, the forty-nine-year-old Admiral George Anson came as a welcome relief, and already a proven officer from his famous voyage into the Spanish Pacific. Taking command of the reinforced Western Squadron (twenty-three men-of-war and four frigates) in August 1746, Anson could both defend the Western Approaches to the Channel for friendly convoys and cruise in the Bay of Biscay to intercept French trade. He thus had wide strategic discretion to use the fleet offensively and defensively, while never violating the principle of concentration.

Anson's strategic dispositions brought important results in 1747, for the fleet was being reinforced by new construction. The prevailing southwesterly winds became severe enough to keep French sailing ships harbor-bound in their few Atlantic ports, and now the British fleet virtually closed these ports, especially Brest. The only way that the French could hope to get vital convoys or overseas expeditions in or out was by fighting through Anson and his patrols. In April 1747 Anson trained his ships in line-ahead maneuvers and with fourteen ships of the line cruised far south to Cape Finisterre to intercept a French convoy bound for India. Early in May he bore up in line to engage the nine sail of the line escorting the convoy. The French broke off and tried to escape before closing, whereupon Anson ordered general chase to cripple and take as many prizes as possible. His well-gunned ships and disciplined crews thus overhauled and took six warships and several Indiamen. This victory at the first battle of Finisterre was repeated by a second—the following October in which Rear Admiral Edward Hawke used general chase with fourteen of the line to reduce and capture six of eight battle-line vessels. True to French strategy, the outgunned French escort sacrificed itself in order to cover the passage out of its West Indies convoy. But Hawke dispatched a fast sloop to the Indies to alert the British squadron there which easily intercepted and took most of the convoy. In addition to the lost French warships, Britain now instituted two permanent blockade squadrons to patrol the Bay of Biscay and off Cádiz. Franco-Spanish trade came to a standstill with the Royal Navy in command of their seas.

By 1748 the War of the Austrian Succession had reached a stalemate and was thus concluded by extensive negotiations that lasted over several months. French arms had been victorious on the continent, overrunning Antwerp and the Austrian Netherlands. The economic devastation wrought by Bourbon arms against Holland was so great that Dutch power was now permanently reduced. But the British blockade had also threatened the very economic lifeblood of France at home and abroad. In the North American King George's War, the capture of Louisbourg challenged the future of France in Canada. In the First Carnatic War in India, however, the French had had more success. The French ground forces under Governor-General Dupleix had combined with a French fleet of armed merchantmen based at the island of Mauritius under Admiral Count Mahé de la Bourdonnais to besiege British Madras. La Bourdonnais brushed aside a British naval squadron in the naval battle of Negapatam off southeastern India in July 1746 and joined Dupleix before Madras, which surrendered in September. In 1747 Dupleix tried to take Fort St. George by siege, but it was supplied by sea. Simultaneously, the British fleet blockaded Pondicherry, which was not reinforced thanks to Anson's victory at first Finisterre. The stalemate in India existed at the time of the peace, and the settlement solved nothing. France evacuated the Austrian Netherlands and gave back Madras in return for Canadian Louisbourg (to the disgust of American colonists who had taken it). Maria Theresa's succession in Austria was recognized, but so was Prussia's conquest of Silesia. So the balance of power in Europe was restored, and the sources of the conflict abroad left unsettled.

In fact, the peace of 1748 was no more than a truce. On the continent, France remained the focus of the still-discontented Prussia and Austria, with Russia balancing off formidable Swedish and Danish fleets in the Baltic, and Spain anxious to retrieve British friendship and trade in the Mediterranean and hopefully possession of Gibraltar and Minorca. Holland ceased to be a major power, but was a source of trouble to the British imperial system, its traders smuggling into England in violation of the Navigation acts. Abroad, where the struggles of the 1740s had erupted, the conflict actually continued with little interruption. In India, the Second Carnatic War began in 1749 as part of the Indian wars which involved the declining Moguls, growing Marathas, invading Afghans, French and British East India companies. French control over much of southern India began to slip under the attack of the British Company forces led by Robert Clive from 1751, and three years later the British government dispatched its first regular regiment of infantry to India. In America, the Spanish ended their annual convoy to New Spain in 1748, but two years later signed a commercial treaty with Britain, revoking the slave *asiento*. Britain had already forced her way into Caribbean trade, however, and in 1754 Spain resumed some transatlantic convoys on an irregular basis. The real imperial dispute in America was between Britain and France, whose colonial clashes over the Ohio Valley led to the posting of regular troops there by both powers early in 1755. Both countries mobilized rapidly, and the cold war abroad intensified.

Britain's new strategical device, the blockade, would obviously be employed, but not without equally new legal overtones. Since 1713 several nations had agreed in various treaties that neutral shipping could trade noncontraband (non-war materials) goods at belligerent ports not effectively blockaded. By 1756, most maritime nations agreed that to be legal a blockade had to be effective, for which each blockaded port had to be patrolled by an armed naval force of at least two enemy warships or the approaches commanded by shore batteries with intersecting arcs of fire. Though not enforced or universally recognized during the Seven Years War, the notion came to be recognized that a blockade merely proclaimed but not enforced was unjust. In terms of naval strategy, this emerging statute of international law meant that Britain—which declared France under blockade in August 1756—would have to command the waters of enemy ports actively for a direct, enforceable naval blockade. Or, of course, Britain—like less powerful naval nations—could ignore the new legal rules of war. In this age of emerging legalism, the concept of the enforced naval blockade remained disputed till after the end of the century.

## THE SYSTEM OF PITT

The so-called Seven Years War, dated 1756 to 1763, was in fact a continuation of the fighting started over Jenkins' ear in 1739 with mostly the same powers involved, but in different roles. The conflict became global, centered so much on the American colonies—with the continental and Indian theaters as secondary—that this struggle can be considered the first real world war. After England and France intensified their colonial rivalry in 1755–56, France convinced Austria and Russia to join her in challenging the growing might of Prussia and Frederick the Great. Frederick attacked first, however, solicited an alliance with Britain, and between 1756 and 1762 waged brilliant campaigns against the coalition, which from 1757 also included Sweden. By his strategic and tactical skills, Frederick thus preserved the prewar Prussian state and did much to tie down French arms in Europe while Britain carried on the war abroad.

At first, Britain stumbled somewhat aimlessly into the formal war under the inept direction of the Duke of Newcastle's administration. British naval policy still aimed at commanding the sea, and the Royal Navy enjoyed several aggressive admirals in First Lord of the Admiralty Lord Anson, Edward Hawke and Edward Boscawen. French naval policy still embraced *guerre de course,* which sufficiently terrified Newcastle into acting indecisively abroad and accepting the bluff of an invasion threat at home. French expeditions not only evaded British squadrons on both sides of the Atlantic, but French troops with Indian allies lost no time in defeating British and colonial forces, winning control of the Great Lakes, and generally jeopardizing the British possessions in North America in 1755–56. Admiral Hawke controlled the Western Approaches so thoroughly that no invasion would have been feasible, and Hawke was soon taking French merchant prizes as he began to reapply the techniques of his wartime blockade. Suddenly, in the spring of 1756, the British realized that the French navy was preparing an expedition at Toulon to take Minorca. In April Rear Admiral John Byng left England with a small squadron for the Mediterranean, but did not arrive before Admiral de la Gallissonière with 12 ships of the line and 150 transports landed 15,000 troops from Toulon on Minorca. As the French army besieged Port Mahon, on May 21 Byng came up with 13 of the line and engaged Gallissonière's 12 off the island. In the cannonade, Byng's line was fouled so thoroughly by the French fire that the French fleet sailed away and Byng returned to Gibraltar. Minorca eventually surrendered, and war was finally declared May 17.

The Newcastle government could hardly stand under the misfortunes of 1756–57, blame for much of which fell upon the navy. Lord Anson had not distributed his ships evenly, so that French reinforcements had reached Canada and others had taken Minorca. The rage of the British people over the Minorca fiasco was only heightened by later news of the Indian massacre of British subjects in the infamous "black hole of Calcutta." British naval tactical sterility had been partly to blame for Byng's bumbling in the naval battle. Anson replaced him with Hawke and then, answering to public and government clamor, had Byng court-martialed and executed! King George II, fearful for the safety of his native Hanover, had allied with Frederick's Prussia, which invaded Saxony in August, thus committing Britain to the broader continental struggle. Strategically confused, the Newcastle government was replaced in the late autumn of 1756 by one virtually run by a new secretary of state and head of the House of Commons, William Pitt. But the king disliked Pitt so much, and palace intrigue so nurtured this dislike, that he relieved him in April 1757, and British military fortunes everywhere flagged—except in India, where Robert Clive drove back the French and their native allies.

Frederick the Great lost little time in appreciating the advantages of the new alliance and found himself in close agreement with the astute Pitt. Frederick had an amazing grasp of the strategic uses of sea power for his continental nation and army. He wanted subsidies from the British treasury to finance certain German forces; British intervention in the Baltic where the Swedo-Danish "Armed Neutrality" was antagonistic to the alliance; British amphibious attacks or diversionary raids against the Channel coast of France, Corsica, North America, India and Africa; and the active intervention of Turkey and Sardinia (Savoy) in the Mediterranean. Pitt shared many of these ideas, though he considered any attack on the French colonies overseas as a primary task in Britain's war aims. He earnestly desired to keep peace with the neutrals in the Mediterranean, especially Spain, Naples and Sardinia, and generally did so. The Baltic was different. Russia declared war on the alliance early in 1757, and Sweden was decidedly unfriendly. Pitt could do little to formulate a strategy because of his dismissal in April 1757, but then Britain seemed incapable of any decisiveness without him either. So, late in June, the king formed a new cabinet with Pitt as Secretary of State for the Southern Department and virtual head and Newcastle as titular prime minister. The office gave Pitt official control over British foreign affairs with France, Southern Europe, the Levant, Africa, India, the Americas, the Far East and all British colonies. The Secretary of State for the Northern Department dealt with the Baltic and North Sea states, the Germanies and Austria. But Pitt predominated and quickly asserted supremacy as the war minister of England.

Pitt could now apply his strategic genius which not only fashioned British victory in the Seven Years War but systematized the British overseas colonial holdings into a well-built empire. His personal initiative in combination with his strategic principles—drawn from past British experiences—came to be known as Pitt's "system." Pitt's aim was to destroy the overseas French Empire and to frustrate Franco-

Habsburg designs for hegemony on the continent of Europe. To achieve this, he adopted a strategy of concentration, holding down French land and naval forces while the Prussian army and British fleet hammered away at French territory at home and in America. Money thus went to Frederick's army, and other money went to the construction of more men-of-war for Lord Anson's navy. To hold down the French army and navy, Pitt reinstituted the blockade of the principal French naval bases of Dunkirk, Cherbourg, St. Malo and Brest on the Channel, Belle Isle and Rochefort in the Bay of Biscay, and Toulon and Minorca in the Mediterranean. The Atlantic blockade could be maintained by squadrons operating from the English ports of Chatham, Portsmouth and Plymouth, the distant Mediterranean blockade by the British hold on Gibraltar. If French naval forces collected for a major sortie or another invasion attempt, the British fleet could concentrate in the Western Approaches off Ushant and destroy its adversary. Pitt also followed Frederick's suggestion to carry out diversionary raids on the French coast, thus hoping to draw French troops away from the main Prussian front. Finally, Pitt's system utilized the "Rule of War, 1756," an Act of Parliament authorizing the navy to stop and search neutral ships trading with France. This measure, never before successful, thus extended the naval blockade into a broader economic blockade. Immobilized at home, France would suffer economic and military reverses and be unable to defend her colonies abroad. Britain would triumph everywhere by utilizing general command of the sea, and France would be in no position to bargain as in 1748.

This essentially maritime strategy needed successful naval tactics, both in the battle line and in amphibious operations, and the fact that both left something to be desired speaks to the compensating genius of Pitt's strategy and the skill of his commanders. Formalism was so entrenched that it had led to the execution of Admiral Byng, an act so tragically ludicrous that the Permament Fighting Instructions began to fall into disrepute and the loophole of "general chase" for a melee battle gradually gained popularity. In combined army-navy amphibious operations, tactical doctrine had been even more discredited and vague due to the failures of Vernon in the Caribbean in the 1740s. Naval landings had been little more than makeshift operations in which warships carried army forces to a beach, then ships' crews rowed them ashore in longboats. Coordination between the senior admiral and general was rarely cordial, and such activities were unpopular with all forces involved. Nevertheless, the overseas nature of the Seven Years War led to important developments in amphibious tactics. After initial failures, Pitt began to *order* his generals and admirals to cooperate, which they soon did and with remarkable results, developing

long-range tactical planning, special signals, precise command responsibilities and sophisticated techniques of ship-to-shore movement. In
addition, Commodore Richard Howe, commanding a raiding squadron
off the coast of France, did much toward the design and construction
of special landing craft for men and horses. Shallow-draft flatboats of
sixteen to twenty-four oars, they carried up to sixty men and were
especially suited for assaulting beaches. The major ingredient for
tactical success was experience, of which the British got plenty in this
first world war.

Pitt's political objective, to wrest control of French North America
for the British Empire, meant capturing the French settlements in
Canada, along the shores of the Great Lakes and in the Ohio and
Mississippi valleys—a region from Louisbourg to New Orleans. His
secondary objective was to assist Frederick in Europe, not only with
money but with British troops. His continental policy was very different from that of Marlborough two generations before: the continent
remained ancillary within his maritime strategy, and the British expeditionary force would be assigned only to a theater of operations close
to the sea, where its logistics and possible escape route would be in
touch with the navy. Thus the first task of the Channel fleet was to
defend the home islands against invasion and to keep open the lines
of communication to the continent, tasks performed by the Western
Squadron at Plymouth and Torbay and the Eastern (or North Sea)
Squadron at the Downs. The English Channel therefore remained—
as before—the strategic center of Britain's defenses.

The Seven Years War became a conflict over maritime trade, so
that the Western and Eastern squadrons could be used—as in the
previous war—both to defend incoming and outgoing British trade
and to attack that of the French. The range of the Western Squadron,
sometimes augmented by a cruiser force based at Cork in Ireland, thus
stretched across the Bay of Biscay, while that of the Eastern Squadron
extended to the entrances of the Baltic Sea. Auxiliary cruiser divisions
of frigates and lesser craft operated along the English coast, especially
in the Channel. The geographic keys to Pitt's war of seaborne communications were the terminal points through which all trade had to
pass. The Channel was the prime example, then the Skagerrak covered
by the Eastern Squadron and the Strait of Gibraltar commanded by
the Mediterranean Squadron. As outlying global regions such as the
Indian Ocean came under British naval control, the terminal points
formerly key to the Portuguese and Dutch would figure in this strategic system. Save for the two main battle squadrons of the heavy men-
of-war, the terminal points and connecting sea lanes were patrolled by
cruiser forces and occasional heavy ships. Conversely, the battle forces

had to protect these cruisers by neutralizing or destroying enemy battle units. Then British convoy escorts could actively counter French cruisers which attempted to carry out their naval policy of *guerre de course*. The object of Pitt's maritime strategy therefore was the control of seaborne communications.

Pitt and Anson clearly understood that command of the sea lanes held the key to success, and they therefore properly allocated a sufficient number of frigates to control the terminal points and to blockade French ports. This sometimes meant weakening the main battle squadrons by reassigning their escorting cruisers elsewhere, but British naval superiority was great enough to allow such risks during the Seven Years War. Britain also floated enough warships eventually to institute a close, as opposed to an open, blockade. The open blockade first used in this war was the easiest, keeping the Western Squadron in home waters with the hope of luring French battle units to sea, where they could be brought to battle and destroyed. The close blockade, aimed at absolutely stifling any maritime traffic (and the subject of legal discussion), had great psychological effect on the blockaded peoples. It required large reserve forces to rotate ships on station— so rigorous was such duty—but improvements in naval medicines and diets alleviated much of the rigor in this war. A proper, effective blockade of France meant that Britain could attack French possessions in North America without fear of interference from the home country.

Pitt's "system" (or "plan") was therefore a closely knit maritime strategy in which all parts cooperated to defend Britain and her trade, support her continental ally of Prussia and expeditionary force there, cripple French trade and conquer French North America. By commanding the North Atlantic, Britain could achieve her mercantilistic aims and set a strategic example for ensuing generations. For more remote regions, Pitt had less interest though he made British actions in the Mediterranean, Baltic and Indian Ocean support his system. In the Mediterranean, the British sought only to keep the French Toulon fleet from reaching the Atlantic. The Mediterranean Squadron therefore blockaded Toulon as well as occupied Minorca and Corsica (used by France by agreement with the government of Genoa). Battling French and Barbary cruisers, by 1759 the British had effectively neutralized the French naval presence in the Mediterranean. In the Baltic, late in 1757 Sweden joined Russia in the war against Prussia, but their considerable galley forces were never united for joint amphibious operations, though the Russian Ship Fleet took part in the successful siege of Memel that year. The Swedes and Russians continually anticipated a British naval appearance, and neutral Denmark was well-armed for any contingency, but little happened through 1759. In India, the English and French East India companies continued to fight and often with some governmental reinforcements. A British squadron engaged a French naval force indecisively in the Bay of Bengal in April 1758 and then victoriously off Negapatam in August. A third naval engagement off Pondicherry in September 1759 ended in the French naval withdrawal from the region. The same year, the neutral Dutch sent a fruitless naval expedition to British India only to be driven out of India altogether. And in Africa the British captured French Senegal in 1757. These theaters of war were important but never primary to Pitt's strategy.

Initially, Pitt had difficulty implementing his plan. Lack of sufficient shipping explains part of the reason, also inferior leadership especially in the army, and lack of enthusiasm within both services for combined amphibious operations. The year of 1757 was therefore fraught with frustration as Pitt endeavored to achieve command of the sea and implement his strategic system. The British blockading squadrons off Brest and Toulon were too thin, and the weather too unfavorable, to prevent French naval units from escaping to reinforce French forces in America and India. Thus Pitt's hopes of an attack on Canadian Louisbourg were frustrated when his naval force found itself inferior to the French squadron there in September. Combined with French and Indian successes in the interior, Pitt's colonial offensive achieved nothing. Other aspects of the blockade met with uneven results. The Rule of War, 1756 was increasingly employed to halt neutral shipping to France which particularly hurt the neutral Netherlands, while late in the year a strong British naval concentration at Gibraltar forced an outbound Toulon force to seek refuge at neutral Spanish Cartagena. And the one amphibious raid of the year against Rochefort in September was abandoned after mutual agreement of the reluctant commanders, but tactical mistakes there led to substantial improvements in amphibious doctrine. About the only great success of the year was allied; Frederick brilliantly defeated the French army at Rossbach and the Austrians at Leuthen. But by removing less competent commanders and building more warships Pitt would yet have his way.

The campaigns of 1758 gradually turned the tide of the war to Britain's favor. The blockade was tightened with more ships and more vigorous leadership at sea. Successively commanding the Western Approaches, Admirals Anson, Hawke and Charles Saunders nearly closed Brest, though some ships broke out, while Admiral Sir Henry Osborne virtually closed the Mediterranean to French shipping after one skirmish off Cartagena and careful vigilance at Gibraltar. The British conducted more amphibious raids along the French coast but with such inconclusive results that they were discontinued. Designed

to relieve the pressure on Frederick, these raids became almost superfluous, for Frederick seemed quite able to do without, crushing now
the Russian army at Zorndorf. With British fortunes improving, Pitt
could mobilize his major attack in America. He dispatched no fewer
than twenty-three ships of the line from the home squadron under
Admiral Boscawen escorting an army on transports under General
Jeffrey Amherst to take Louisbourg. This force easily sealed up the
five French warships there, landed the troops in early June, besieged
and invested the place after seven weeks. From the other end of the
St. Lawrence, Fort Frontenac, a British colonial force drove out the
French, burned their flotilla there and seized control of Lake Ontario.
With their link between the Ohio and Mississippi valleys in jeopardy,
the French managed only to resist attacks against Fort Ticonderoga on
Lake Champlain near the northern end of Lake George.

## YEARS OF BRITISH VICTORY

As soon as the blockade of France was sealed shut early in 1759,
Pitt's system could be enforced. This done, 1759 would come to be
known as the "Year of Victories." To begin with, Admiral Hawke
decided to reinterpret his blockading orders of Brest from the distant,
open patrol from Torbay—which had allowed French ships to sneak
out—to that of a close blockade. Britain now had sufficient warships
for the relays involved, so that the French were unable to reinforce
their forces in America at all, and then Pitt could mount his final
offensive there. But British successes had their effect on the enemy
system, notably the appointment of a new minister of war by Louis
XV late in 1758. Duke Étienne François Choiseul resurrected the old
scheme of invading southern England and hoped to arouse such alienated neutral powers as the Netherlands and Denmark and allied Russia
and Sweden to join in the attempt; Dutch and Danish warships would
be welcome additions to the inferior French fleet. Pitt's careful diplomacy, however—despite the Rule of 1756—kept these countries at
peace with Britain. But the threat of invasion led Hawke to tighten his
blockade even more.

In the spring, as Admiral Boscawen took command in the Mediterranean to prevent the passage of the French Toulon fleet to Brest,
the British expeditionary force for America began its campaign to
take Quebec and the St. Lawrence and thereby all French Canada.
Admiral Saunders in late June ferried 9000 troops under General
James Wolfe to an island below Quebec, but the French position was
so well placed on high ground that the British bogged down for several weeks looking for a place from which to assault the town. Mean-

while, however, in July General Amherst captured Fort Ticonderoga and Crown Point in New York, while a small force of troops crossed over Lake Ontario by boat to take Fort Niagara. Finally, Saunders and Wolfe discovered a footpath on the heights upriver and devised an excellent amphibious plan to land and attack the city. Utilizing the elements of tactical mobility and surprise to the full, the warships had been demonstrating up and down the river, thus keeping the French troops and their Indian allies on the move. Now, on the night of September 12–13, 1759, Saunders delivered a diversionary bombardment of Quebec while marines entered the boats to feint a landing there, and Wolfe's troops landed upriver and ascended the footpath to the Plains of Abraham. There, in daylight, the British attacked and defeated the poorly organized French. Though Wolfe was killed in the battle, Quebec surrendered five days later.

With the waning of French fortunes abroad and the tightening of the blockade, French Foreign Minister Choiseul hastened preparation for the one decisive blow at the strategic center of the British war effort, thus to win the war and recover his losses. The successful invasion of England depended upon the concentration of the French Mediterranean, Atlantic and West Indies fleets off Brest. Admiral the Marquis Hubert de Conflans assumed command of the Atlantic fleet to carry out Choiseul's plan of concentrating the warships at Brest and escorting amphibious flatboats from Le Havre and the south Brittany coast near Quiberon Bay cross-Channel, while a diversionary raid was made from a force at Dunkirk. News of this buildup caused much alarm throughout Britain during the spring and summer, but Pitt did not deviate from his system. Frederick was in trouble on the continent and needed his British troops, and the important American expedition was just getting under way. Pitt called out the militia and raised a mobile defensive force at the Nore which could be ferried to any place on the coast under threat of invasion. But his first line of defense remained the battle navy, and Pitt gave command of the Channel fleet again to Hawke and of the Mediterranean squadron to Boscawen.

From the beginning of the campaigning season of 1759, the vigilant and close British blockade of both Brest and Toulon doomed Choiseul's hopes for a fleet concentration. Hawke and Boscawen, both aggressive fighters and tireless blockaders, gave constant attention to the health and provisioning of their crews, the clarification of battle tactics through "Additional Instructions" to their captains, and the refitting and hull-cleaning of their ships. Without Minorca, Boscawen's watch over Toulon and Marseilles was exceedingly difficult, so that when he retired for a much-needed refit at Gibraltar the French Mediterranean squadron broke out. On August 17 Admiral de la Clue passed through the Strait of Gibraltar with twelve of the line and three frigates. Boscawen immediately put to sea with fourteen of the line in pursuit. Five of the French men-of-war pressed on to Cádiz according to plan while de la Clue waited for his stragglers. Instead, he sighted Boscawen coming up on the morning of the 18th and attempted to escape. Boscawen ordered general chase and came into gun range of de la Clue's rear ships early in the afternoon. He engaged and took one ship in a furious daylight duel, allowed two to escape, and chased the rest into the neutral Portuguese Lagos Bay. There, on the forenoon of the 19th, Boscawen burned two and captured two French ships of the line. De la Clue died from wounds and his surviving ships were blockaded inside Cádiz harbor. The battle of Lagos Bay had finished the French Mediterranean fleet.

France was still determined to invade Britain, but with diversionary attacks on Scotland or Ireland and only with the cover of the Brest and West Indies naval forces. But the naval dispositions of Pitt, Anson and Hawke—plus the British land victory over the French at Minden—made this impossible. A British naval bombardment of Le Havre in July destroyed the invasion flotilla there, Boscawen's victory in August allowed him to reinforce Hawke, and British cruisers patrolled from Dunkirk to Biscay. All that the French could count on was the approaching storm season, which would force Hawke to retire the Western Squadron to Plymouth and Torbay for safety. When this occurred in October and November, the French transports rendezvoused in the Morbihan inlet of Quiberon Bay and the West Indies squadron beat into Brest, its ships too worn for further service. But Admiral Conflans transferred their veteran crews to his own and put to sea, twenty of the line and three frigates, to drive off the British cruisers before Quiberon and escort the transports to Ireland. At the moment Conflans set his sails in the good weather, so did Hawke from Torbay with twenty-seven of the line and six frigates. Learning of the French sortie, Hawke pursued, hoping to engage and destroy the French fleet and any further danger of invasion.

The battle of Quiberon Bay completed Pitt's system by eliminating the French battle fleet as a major threat to British campaigns in Europe or abroad. Hawke's fleet came upon Conflans on the morning of November 20 off Belle Isle, just south of Quiberon. Conflans, in the act of driving off a British cruiser force, now formed his line and made for Quiberon Bay, hoping for a good defensive position within its rocky surf and waters. Like Boscawen at Lagos, Hawke ignored the dangers— and the rigid Fighting Instructions—and ordered general chase. The running battle began in the early afternoon and lasted into the night. Rain squalls and heavy autumn gales frustrated the fleets, but the finely

honed British crews pressed on to frustrate Conflans' attempt to form
his line into the bay. Several French ships were severely mauled, and
Conflans could not return to open water. When night descended, both
fleets anchored in angry seas among the rocks. The dawn revealed two
British vessels aground. Five French warships were destroyed, four others rode high water upriver and were trapped. Other French warships
escaped but were scattered, thus ending the French Brest fleet. Only the
Dunkirk flotilla placed a small invasion force in Ireland, after which its
ships were quickly destroyed by units of the Royal Navy. Quiberon
Bay gave Britain absolute command of the sea.

The virtual achievement of Pitt's system in 1759, including the capture of Guadeloupe in the Caribbean, made operations in 1760 a mere
tightening of the system. Hawke and Boscawen alternated in command
of the Channel fleet and so thoroughly blockaded the Atlantic coast of
France that they anchored in Quiberon Bay and used its tiny islets to
grow fresh vegetables for the fleet. Saunders took command in the Mediterranean and closed the French coast there in addition to checking the
activities of the Barbary corsairs. The blockade secure, Pitt turned to
protecting British commerce against French privateers, mopping up the
conquests of Canada and India, and continuing subsidies to Frederick,
who defeated the Austrian army again, this time at Torgau. In North
America, the French besieged the British garrison at Quebec until a
British naval force arrived. Then the British launched a three-pronged
overland attack on the last French stronghold at Montreal, which surrendered in September. In India, British troops besieged French Pondicherry in August, and when reinforcements never came from the
blockaded homeland, the place surrendered, January 1761. France was
sealed off, her overseas empire, merchant marine and navy facing extinction.

The rank conquest of French possessions and absolute domination of
the seas by Britain led, however, to important repercussions in Spain.
Spain was Pitt's greatest concern, since a new and pro-French king
ascended the throne in 1759, and King George II died a year later, only
to be replaced by George III who advocated peace. The Spanish economy revived under the new king who also resolved to halt English
privateers in the Caribbean and to aid the French in Europe. To counter
this new threat, in 1761 Pitt launched an all-out offensive to capture
the French West Indies which succeeded in taking Dominica that summer. Simultaneously, in June Pitt sent an amphibious force to take Belle
Isle at the approaches to Quiberon Bay. By this time, combined British
army-navy operations had been perfected after many expeditions, and
the place was easily captured. This event gave Britain a forward blockading base on the Biscay coast athwart the Franco-Spanish trade route

between Brest and Cádiz. This event further antagonized Spain, which now opened discussions with France. Pitt, fearing a new Bourbon coalition, ordered a force of sixty sail to lie off Cape Finisterre to intercept the Spanish plate fleet. The other British ministers did not share Pitt's fears of Spanish hostilities and when they did not support his measures, he resigned in October 1761. But Pitt had been correct, for Choiseul hoped to utilize both Spain and Portugal to renew French fortunes and possibly invade Britain after all.

Spain declared war on Great Britain early in 1762 but quickly regretted it. Though Pitt was out of office, his successors carried on his strategic system. Anson reinforced Hawke in the Channel and Saunders at Gibraltar, so that France's new gift of Minorca to Spain achieved nothing; Spain was as tightly blockaded as France. To force a reluctant Portugal into the alliance, Spain invaded her, but the British quickly brought in army reinforcements to Portugal to repel the invasion and carry the land war back into Spain. Anson himself died in June, as Boscawen had the year before, but younger flag officers of equal merit maintained the Pitt-designed system. Admiral George B. Rodney commanded the successful assault on the chief French sugar island of Martinique and then seized Grenada, St. Vincent and St. Lucia, all in the French West Indies. Admiral Sir George Pocock, having achieved command over the Indian Ocean, then took a fleet to join Rodney for an assault on the supposedly impregnable Spanish fortress of Havana, Cuba. The fleet bottled up twelve Spanish ships of the line at Havana and in a seven-week siege took ships, port and the valuable merchandise therein. As if the British could do nothing wrong, another expeditionary force took Manila and the Spanish Philippines in October. The capture included the rich Acapulco-bound Manila galleon, just as Saunders' cruisers captured an incoming Peru silver ship. The Spanish Empire joined France in defeat.

Whereas British command of the sea brought France and Spain to the negotiating table, Frederick of Prussia was less successful, for Austria and Russia were as strong as ever, and Pitt's resignation had deprived Prussia of much support. Despite Frederick's dramatic victories on land, Prussia's war debt was mounting; he was less able to repel invading armies; and enemy pressure on his Baltic coast continued. The small Prussian flotilla of thirteen galleys had been captured by the Swedish galley force before Stettin in September 1759, thus closing that port to blockade. The next two years the sizable Russian Ship Fleet of twenty-seven men-of-war each mounting up to 100 guns and attended by a Swedish squadron bombarded Kolberg unsuccessfully, though it eventually fell to land attack. Denmark became increasingly friendly to this alliance, with loose guarantees that she would close the passage of British warships through the Sound. Prussia was now exhausted and on the verge of defeat when, early in 1762, a change in the Russian succession brought to the throne Catherine the Great, who took Russia out of the war. Frederick now rallied, and Austria agreed to negotiate the peace, which changed little on the continent.

The signing of the peace ending the Seven Years War in February 1763 created the British Empire and reflected the fruits of Pitt's maritime strategy. The objective, acquisition of North America, had been gained. In 1762 France had ceded to Spain by treaty New Orleans and all the Louisiana territory from the Mississippi River to the Rocky Mountains. Now France gave up to Britain all her claims to North America east of the Mississippi, and Spain similarly surrendered her territory of Florida to the British. In the Caribbean, Britain retained Dominica, St. Vincent, Tobago and Grenada, but returned Martinique, Guadeloupe and St. Lucia to France, and Havana to Spain. In the Mediterranean, Britain retrieved Minorca, and in West Africa Senegal. In the East, India all but passed into British hands completely. The British East India Company, thanks largely to Clive, now dominated Bengal, while the French were allowed to retain Pondicherry and several Coromandel posts, but agreed to strip them of military defenses. Outside the peace settlement, Spain got back Manila and the Philippines, but had to combat the Moro pirates as always, and the Dutch remained in control of the East Indies where they were plagued by the native pirates of Malaya.

The Seven Years War thus ended with a systematic and formidable British Empire controlling the sea lanes and most of the prime colonial regions of the world, especially North America. So thorough was the British victory and so great the colonial expense, however, that Britain had in fact created intolerable political situations, and the peace of 1763 could only be transitory. Though Colbert's overseas French empire had been virtually annihilated, Choiseul determined to regain much of it at a later time, so that France could yet be reckoned as the major power in Western Europe. Also, Baltic Russia had emerged as a major force in this war, so that Catherine the Great posed a potential threat on land and each of the inner seas—Baltic, Black and Eastern Mediterranean— alike. To these great powers the others would react—the security-conscious Prussians and Austrians and the lesser maritime states of Spain, Sweden, Denmark and the Netherlands which had been offended by Britain's maritime arrogance during the war. And, to add to Britain's new imperial responsibilities, disgruntled American colonists demanded special treatment that would violate the precepts of British monopolistic mercantilism. If and when these volatile forces again erupted, Pitt's strategic precedent would be severely tested.

# 8

# War of the American Revolution, 1763–1783

*In any operation, and under all circumstances, a decisive naval superiority is to be considered as a fundamental principle, and the basis upon which every hope of success must ultimately depend.*

—GEORGE WASHINGTON

## RUSSIA AND THE MEDITERRANEAN

Before the proverbial ink was dry on the treaty of 1763, the new and mighty British Empire faced opposition from every quarter. Philosophically, the closed system of mercantilism began to be challenged by increasing numbers of even British thinkers, notably Adam Smith, whose *Wealth of Nations* in 1776 advanced the idea of replacing the monopolistic chartered companies and Navigation acts with principles of free trade. Arguing that productive capacity rather than gold produced economic wealth, Smith supported Britain's increased competition. Such arguments found little favor in the government, but were voiced abroad in the American colonies and in the jealous rivals on the continent in the phrase "freedom of the seas." To preserve the imperial system, Britain therefore utilized—as usual—its command of the sea to enforce the law in colonial waters, especially the vital Baltic. This political objective of enforcing the *status quo* had the cumulative effect of fostering revolt in America and finally the renewal of hostilities with France in the second great global conflict, which came to be known as the War of the American Revolution.

If Britain controlled trade through the funnel of Europe, Russia was the power that emerged on the enclosed Baltic and Black seas to offer a formidable maritime presence. Tsarina Catherine II upon her accession in 1762 determined to enforce Russian domination over the Baltic, which required a fleet. Catherine could count generally upon the friendship of Britain which depended increasingly upon Russia for sailcloth, masts and hemp. But Sweden and Denmark bore careful watching as their navies were shifting from the old galleys to new and impressive rowing gunboats and half-square sail, half-oared men-of-war. Catherine accordingly initiated a naval expansion program that was to last thirty years. In addition to major construction of 40 men-of-war and 150 galleys, she sent officers to England and Venice for training and continued the practice of hiring foreign officers. The British government was only too willing to cooperate, providing such excellent officers as John Elphinstone and Samuel Greig. The British also allowed the Russians to use their ports from Portsmouth to Minorca whenever the need arose. As Russian ship and amphibious fleet strength in the Baltic grew, Denmark became alarmed, but an alliance between the two nations in 1773 insured a peaceful stability in the region.

Russia's major concern remained, as always, continental; hence she had entered the Seven Years War. In 1763, the border of Russia faced Poland, from Livonia on the Baltic coast to the Turkish frontier on the Bug River near the Black Sea. As in the past, Russia, joined by Frederick's Prussia, intervened in the affairs of Poland, resulting in a Polish civil war in 1768. When Catherine dispatched Russian troops into the troubled kingdom, they carried the fighting over into Turkish territory. The Ottomans promptly declared war on Russia in October, and the eternal Russo-Turkish struggle over the Black Sea was resumed. As Russia thus energetically fought the Turks, other powers sought to help the Poles. The French sent some help, but not enough to offset Russian arms in Poland, and when Austria threatened to intervene on the side of the Poles against Russia, Frederick of Prussia acted. In 1772, he promoted the partition of several Polish lands to the three interested parties: Galicia went to Austria, the Danzig corridor to Prussia, and a large section of the Dnieper River basin to Russia. Poland's reactions were crushed, and Russia could concentrate its full energies on the war against Turkey.

The Russo-Turkish War of 1768–74 demonstrated the full military maturity and potential of the sprawling Russian Empire and the equal weakness of the declining Ottoman Empire. Turkish subjugation of the ancient lands of Egypt and Greece had long been resented by their peoples, who now rose in revolt. These events played perfectly into Catherine's strategy. Without a fleet on the Black Sea, she stood at a disadvantage if she tried to mount an offensive through Azov again. So she and her advisers determined to utilize elements of the fine Ship Fleet in the Baltic to strike the Turks in the rear by liberating the Balkans, supporting the Egyptians and attacking Turkey by way of the Aegean.

The Russian naval offensive began with the creation of the Mediterranean Fleet under Vice Admiral Gregory Spiridov from Baltic Fleet units in the spring of 1769; initially, it included one 80-gun and six 66-gun ships of the line plus auxiliary craft. Sailing in early autumn from the rendezvous at Copenhagen, these vessels utilized the British bases at Portsmouth, Gibraltar and Minorca, but suffered heavily from rough weather and seas. A second squadron under Rear Admiral Elphinstone had such difficulty that it did not straggle into the Mediterranean until the following spring. Picking up the commander-in-chief, Count Alexei Orlov, at Leghorn, Italy, the fleet pressed on toward Greece. The novelty of a Russian fleet in these waters alarmed many nations, but especially Venice, which determined to deny the Russians any access to the Adriatic. Orlov arrived off Greece in March and proclaimed Greek independence from Ottoman Turkey, then pushed on to Navarino, which the fleet invested on April 10, 1770. With Greece and Egypt in revolt and a Russian army under Count Peter Rumiantsev pushing the Turks back from the banks of the Dniester to those of the Danube, Orlov thought the Turks were overcommitted. He underestimated the Turkish army, however, which quickly rushed into Greece to crush the insurrection. With too few men to aid the Greeks, the Russians reembarked their troops from several coastal toeholds and resolved to settle the issue at sea.

The naval forces of the Eastern Mediterranean thus arranged themselves for deciding command of the sea. The defenders, as in bygone days, depended upon the leadership of an Algerian corsair, Hassan Pasha, whose fleet had a mixture of old and new, about a dozen line-of-battle ships each with up to 100 guns, frigates, galleys and galliots. The invaders, generally inexperienced in sea battles, depended heavily upon their British officers. The non-sailor Orlov held supreme command, but leaned upon Commodore Greig for advice. Spiridov and Elphinstone each commanded a squadron, but the latter enjoyed greater prestige during these operations. When Elphinstone arrived off Greece with reinforcements late in May, he skirmished with Turkish fleet units before seeking to join Orlov at Navarino. But the Turkish pacification of the Morea was so swift that Orlov had to evacuate Navarino early in June, and after the entire fleet rendezvoused at sea he anchored at the island of Paros. Meanwhile Hassan Pasha concentrated the Ottoman fleet between the island of Chios and the harbor at Chesme on the Turkish mainland. Orlov sailed north in search of this force early in July.

The Battle of Chesme was fought on July 5–7, 1770. The Russian fleet of 9 of the line, 3 frigates and a bomb vessel bore in toward the shore above Chesme where the 21 Turkish heavy vessels were anchored in two staggered lines supported by 45 galleys and galliots. The parallel lines began the general action about noon of the 5th and it was about two hours before the two flagships in the course of their duel caught fire and exploded. Spiridov and Hassan survived with their officers, but most other hands were lost. The Turks now cut their cables and drifted downwind into the confined waters of Chesme harbor and presumed safety. There the Russians blockaded them on the 6th, and the British officers Elphinstone and Greig planned a fire ship attack—a tactic as archaic as the galleys in the Ottoman fleet facing them. Just before midnight of the 6th, part of the Russian fleet moved forward for the attack. In the early minutes of July 7, the Russian guns opened up and soon started fires among several Turkish vessels, at which time—2:00 A.M.—Greig launched his 4 fire ships which soon made the fire general. By mid-morning, the entire Ottoman fleet was destroyed: 11 of the line, 6 frigates, 6 twenty-to-thirty-gun shebecks, 8 galleys and all 32 galliots lost, plus one battle-line ship and 5 galleys captured intact. This victory by the world's youngest battle fleet over the world's oldest at Chesme is one of the most decisive engagements in naval history.

With absolute command of the sea, the Russians had the Ottoman Empire at their mercy. Admiral Elphinstone urged Orlov to let him attack Constantinople at once, but the landlubbing general had less faith in his fleet. Instead, Elphinstone was allowed to use his squadron to bombard Turkish positions at Chios and the Dardanelles before laying down a blockade of the straits. The rest of the fleet under Orlov and Spiridov landed a force on Lemnos and besieged Pelari. As these prolonged naval operations settled into a stalemate, broken only by occasional skirmishing with light vessels under Hassan Pasha, the Russians lost the opportunity to exploit their great victory. On land, Russian fortunes were equally impressive: in August, Rumiantsev repulsed a Turkish offensive at the battle of Kagul, then swept down the Danube and Pruth rivers, taking all Turkish fortifications. By the end of the year, the Russians had established the Danube flotilla to watch Turks and Poles alike. Reinforcements from the Baltic were dispatched to the Mediterranean, where Hassan, however, raised the siege of Lemnos in October. The fleet wintered at Paros and suffered from political troubles with Britain that led to the recall and resignation of most British officers, among them Elphinstone, who resumed command of a British third-rate man-of-war.

Perhaps the absence of British-loaned officers led to the Russian inability to bring about a decision against Turkey in 1771–72. The Mediterranean Russian forces remained on station but never pressed the blockade of the Dardanelles with any vigor. A number of the ships were in various stages of upkeep and repair, some lent support to the revolt in Egypt, and the only notable achievement was Orlov's amphibious raid which destroyed the Ottoman shipyard at Mitylene on Lesbos in November 1771. The same year, however, Russian naval forces in the Black Sea supported an overland attack on the Perekop peninsula which a Russian army overran before proceeding on to conquer the Crimea. The Turks now agreed to negotiations, and a truce was observed throughout the summer of 1772. The Russians utilized the opportunity to raise the first privateer force in their history for raids on the rebellious coasts of Egypt and Syria, but these few vessels achieved little. And when Catherine demanded the ceding of the Crimea the Turks called off the truce. Before the fighting resumed, France, fearful of growing Russian power in the Mediterranean, began sending aid to Turkey.

Russia now tightened its command of the sea on both sides of Constantinople, but could do nothing to prevent the Turks from crushing the Egyptian revolt in 1773. Early in November 1772 a force under Rear Admiral Greig bombarded Chesme and another destroyed nine Turkish frigates and six shebecks in several days of fighting off Patras. The next year the Russians operated with impunity between the Dardanelles and Beirut in Syria which they bombarded and captured in October. Simultaneously, a new Russian Black Sea Fleet successfully drove back Turkish naval units in a series of skirmishes between light vessels. Russian arms continued to triumph on land, though a peasant revolt in Russia demanded attention. A strong Turkish naval presence on the Black Sea in 1774 did not affect the outcome of the war, for both sides agreed to end the struggle in July.

The success of the Russian Ship Fleet in the war of 1768–74 was impressive and bore upon both the peace settlement and future power balances throughout Europe. Most importantly, Russian warships and merchant ships were allowed untrammelled passage through the Bosporus and Dardanelles, thus assuring Russia's future role in the affairs of the Mediterranean powers. The Russians returned their Danube basin conquests, but retained such key Black Sea coastal points as the mouth of the Dnieper River, the Kerch peninsula of the Crimea, the ports of Azov and Kinburn, Taganrog and adjacent lands, and a protectorate over the Crimea, now declared independent. Turkish naval supremacy in the Black Sea was thus broken, though the Russian fleet in the Aegean was ordered to return to the Baltic in the summer of 1775. This was partly due to the lack of any Russian merchant activity in the area. But now Russian agents in Greece began to allow these Turkish subjects to trade under the Russian flag, so that before long Greek merchants soon dominated all overseas trade between Azov and Alexandria. Such economic autonomy weakened the Ottoman hold on the Balkans and brought the Greeks into closer contact with the West. The emergence of Russia as a maritime power now had ominous overtones for the balance of power in the Baltic, whose trade Britain's fleet depended upon. Russia thus could unite with the other disgruntled European maritime nations in time of war, meaning that Britain must encourage cordial Anglo-Russian relations.

In the Western Mediterranean, Britain had similar concerns as the anti-mercantilistic feeling spread across the waters from Spain to the Levant. The Moslem corsairs of Morocco, Algiers, Tripoli and Tunis— though weakened and ever more piratic—remained constant problems, and British warships from Gibraltar and Minorca were assisted by other nations in checking their illegal activities: Venice had to use warships to preserve her North African treaties of 1763–65; French ships bombarded two Moroccan ports in 1765; and in July 1770 a Danish squadron began a two-year presence in the Mediterranean by bombarding Algiers. The greatest threat to British hegemony, however, came from the Bourbon dynasties which ruled France and Spain, the latter still dominating much of Italy, save for the free port of Leghorn used extensively by Britain. Genoa, friendly to France, sold Corsica to her in 1768, thus shielding the approaches to Toulon. Finally, in 1770, Marie Antoinette of Austria married the heir to the French throne, thus drawing together in alliance most of the states of the Western Mediterranean. Austria made one more abortive attempt to create an East India trading company based at Trieste in 1770s, while British trade in the Mediterranean also declined. The chief rivals to Britain became a rejuvenated Spain and France, both of whose interests were still worldwide.

Despite Spain's slow but steady political and economic decline since the end of the sixteenth century, repeated bursts of imperial prosperity and naval growth kept the old kingdom prominent in world affairs. After the Seven Years War, the Spanish Empire grew by the occupation of parts of the vast Louisiana, Texas and California territories. It was also modernized by an increasing questioning of strict mercantilistic policies: after 1763 all Spanish ports, rather than just Cádiz, were allowed to trade with the West Indies, while Peru and the newly created colonies of New Granada (1739; modern Colombia and Venezuela) and Rio de la Plata (1776; modern Argentina, Paraguay, Uruguay and Bolivia) were allowed to trade directly with New Spain and West Indies ports. The government monopoly thus passed to joint-stock companies, nearly two centuries later than those first used against Spain by England, and these served to exploit and antagonize the native Latin American-born Creoles. To enforce the new arrangement and to offset British and Portuguese rivals, Spain practically replaced church authority in Hispanic America with that of the army, a measure which further aggravated the Spanish American colonists. Defensively, the peacetime convoys were replaced altogether by permanent fortifications and troops, especially in

Puerto Rico and Cuba, and naval bases between New Orleans and Buenos Aires were connected by a new permanent force of ships of the line. The major obstacle to this revised imperial system was Britain, which used the Mississippi River to trade with Indians in Spanish North America, continued to smuggle goods into the Spanish West Indies, and in 1771 forced Spain to give up the Falkland Islands—thus threatening Spanish shipping at Buenos Aires and the River Plate as well as Spanish communications to the Pacific. Britain was also the traditional friend of the Portuguese, who were starting to press southward from Brazil against the new Spanish settlement of Montevideo on the north side of the Plate. Anglo-Spanish relations thus worsened, especially as France strengthened her ties with Spain.

## CHALLENGES TO BRITISH EMPIRE

For France and Choiseul, the peace of 1763 provided breathing space for the country to recoup its losses and eventually to renew hostilities. Already, in 1761, Choiseul had been appointed minister of war and of the navy, and had to combat the reluctance of Louis XV to rebuild the fleet. But by appealing directly to the local French governments, Choiseul in 1763 began to obtain subscriptions from the people to build warships, the greatest example of the popularity of the navy in French history. Fashioning his program of modernization on the achievements of Colbert, Choiseul issued the Ordinance of 1765, promoting the officers on merit, issuing them uniforms, and improving the engineer corps so that new warships would be superior to new British construction. The Ordinance continued defensive tactics, but strengthened the battle line so it could not be broken in battle, and two excellent treatises on tactics were published by Captain S. F. Bigot Vicomte de Morogues in 1763 and Captain Bourde de Villehuet in 1765. To train his officers, Choiseul created "squadrons of evolution," and in 1769 he established a formal marine corps like that of the British. Choiseul compared closely with his predecessor, Colbert, for by the time of his retirement late in 1770 he had brought into commission sixty-four men-of-war and fifty frigates. But France still had no maritime empire for the navy to serve; the French East India Company collapsed in 1768, and the West Indies colonies of Martinique and Dominica fit into the Spanish defensive system. So the navy remained in home waters and the newly strengthened ports of Brest, Rochefort, Lorient, Toulon and Marseilles.

Reformers like Choiseul, however, could not overcome the continental and hence anti-maritime bias of French aristocratic tradition. Louis XV appointed one such unsympathetic minister who offended the navy in 1772 by unifying it into the army hierarchy and requiring the red-

and-blue-uniformed marines to wear the white of the infantry. Morale in the fleet thus plummeted and was salvaged only by the death of the king in 1774. The new king, Louis XVI, had more interest in the navy and appointed Gabriel de Sartine to be Secretary of State for the Navy. The non-aristocratic Sartine initiated an administrative upheaval which offended the aristocracy and undermined its support of the navy and hence the leadership at sea. Naval conscription and shipboard life frustrated and angered the lower deck, also a sign of the general deterioration of the French social system ashore. Naval education and shipbuilding continued to suffer, but Sartine kept the squadron of evolution and managed to place the fleet on a war footing, raising ship strength to 79 of the line, 86 frigates and 171 smaller vessels by the end of his administration in 1780. This navy, the largest in France since Colbert, could if allied with Spain's outnumber that of Britain.

Like France and Spain, Great Britain had to look both to new overseas defensive requirements and to new patterns of thought dangerous to her political and economic order, especially the growing notions of colonial self-government and free trade. And like the others, Britain preferred generally to maintain the *status quo* but with the least expense possible. The Navigation acts insured monopoly within the British imperial system and thus the British merchant marine remained supreme and provided an important manpower reserve for the navy. In time of war, the government could license merchantmen as privateers and issue letters of marque to armed cargo-carrying merchant ships to take any enemy prize they encountered. But this system of profit also had its drawbacks. The Royal Navy had to be kept strong to deter growing Bourbon naval strength, but instead was allowed to fall into disrepair. No major improvements were made to the sterile Fighting Instructions, though gunnery was improved. When the retired Pitt, now Earl of Chatham, in 1770 called for a two-ocean navy to police the Atlantic and Mediterranean, he was ignored by George III and Parliament. Smuggling to England and from the American colonies to the French West Indies had also to be stopped, the former by the army at home, the latter by the navy, so charged in 1763 when it was made part of the customs service. In addition, the government decided that the American colonies should start to help finance their own defense—and again the navy would help police the taxation. Overgrown with vast maritime and colonial commitments, the British Empire which emerged from the Seven Years War thus sowed the seeds of its own destruction.

Considering the great wealth of the British mercantilistic system centered on America, it is not surprising that in 1763 Britain made the North American Station its largest fleet outside the Channel, a fact that in due course failed to impress those disgruntled colonists of New En-

gland and the Middle Atlantic region. Headquarters were established at
Halifax, Nova Scotia, linked administratively with the West Indies
squadron at Jamaica. In 1763, the fleet began a three-year campaign
against American smugglers from especially New York and Philadelphia
that was so successful that the practice practically ceased. In 1764,
Parliament passed a Revenue Act on sugar that the American colonists
paid without much protest. But almost immediately, a harsher tax from
stamps followed, along with the navy's attempt to carry the already-
unpopular practice of impressment to the colonies. The merchants of
North America found these measures unduly repressive and began to
oppose them. Some of the revenue laws were repealed soon, but not
without the navy feeling obliged to land troops at Boston in 1768.
Without a potential foe any longer on the Canadian frontier, the colonists could see little need to help pay for Britain's defenses, and the
tension mounted. The Royal Navy established a permanent base at Boston in 1770 to protect the king's authority, while the king himself ignored
the warnings of Pitt to acknowledge the colonists' grievances before it
was too late. More revenue acts ensued, leading to such resistance as
the Boston "tea party" of 1773 and the forming of the First Continental
Congress the next year. Open rebellion began in Massachusetts in 1775
and quickly spread.

The American colonists by their actions boldly challenged not only
British rule but the presumed natural order of European mercantilism.
From April 1775 to April and July of the next year, when American economic and political independence respectively were declared,
the revolutionaries upgraded their dispute from localized rebellion to
a national effort. The new United States (which common grammatical
usage has since evolved into the singular) created a government army,
navy and marine corps to drive the British from Philadelphia and appointed General George Washington to command the Continental Army.
And Washington lost little time in creating, through Congress, a tiny
Continental Navy under his own command to harass British supply lanes
to Boston and thus support the army on land. Strategically, Washington
and the Americans had the benefit of the interior position and could
operate overland to threatened points along the coast. But Britain had
the mobility to utilize the sea in order to paralyze American shipping
between Halifax and Jamaica and thus cut off these united "states" from
the outside world by blockading Cape Cod, Long Island Sound and
the Chesapeake Bay. Help from abroad became the key to any possibility of American success.

Needless to say, the other maritime nations looked with favor on the
crisis facing Britain. French rearmament could gain more time as Britain
rushed warships and troops to America, and Spain could rest in its

Caribbean monopoly. In 1776, with Britain preoccupied in North America, Spain launched an attack on the Portuguese in South America. A combined land-sea expedition drove the Portuguese from their forts near Montevideo, and the next year Spain made Buenos Aires into a separate political capital. Britain could do nothing, as she cared not to hurt her good relations with Spain in the Mediterranean. Also, the Baltic assumed a new importance. New England timber had provided masts for British men-of-war; in fact, one third of Britain's merchant vessels had even been built in America. With this supply cut off, the Royal Navy now came to depend wholly upon the timber and naval stores of Russia and the Scandinavian countries. Also, as British regulars were hastened to America, militia units in England could do little to stop the increased smuggling by the Dutch and Danes. And British naval operations against such interlopers would hardly improve British foreign relations. The sooner Britain could settle the disturbance in America, the less likely it was that these nations would take advantage of it to reopen the war of the 1760s. But time favored the Americans, who soon began to receive clandestine aid from France and allowance for free use of the Mississippi River from Spain.

Unfortunately for Britain, the government was no longer controlled by the aging Pitt but by George III himself and a collection of mediocre, indecisive ministers—Lords North (the prime minister), Dartmouth, George Germain and the Earl of Sandwich. Political favoritism so permeated the highest offices of the nation that a number of the better admirals not among the king's intimates resigned or refused to serve out of fear of lack of support. This sorry situation was compounded in 1775 by conflicting attitudes toward the rebellious colonists, and the government's turning over the prosecution of pacifying the colonies to the incompetent and unsympathetic Colonial Secretary, Germain. The First Lord of the Admiralty, the Earl of Sandwich, however, had his own ideas. He wanted to wage total war to crush the rebellion and mobilized the navy to achieve that end. To compound such diversity of attitude, early in 1776 one man was appointed to serve both as peace negotiator to the rebels and as their main antagonist as Commander-in-Chief, North American Station. This was Vice Admiral Lord Howe, personally hated by Sandwich.

The strategic problem was thus confused by conflicting interpretations of British war aims. To Sandwich, the navy should seize the major harbors of North America, destroy colonial shipping and generally blockade the insurgents. These were the orders he gave Admiral Howe, and he dispatched an army of British army regulars and Hessian mercenaries to put down the Americans: 10,000 to hold Canada and 35,000 to base at New York under General Sir William Howe, the Admiral's brother. Had the Howes followed their orders strictly, the issue might have been settled quickly. But Admiral Howe, eager to save the British Empire by not antagonizing the rebels, later called in to port all but six of his seventy-five blockading vessels. To keep the war limited, he decided to confine the fighting to maritime New England and to parley with General Washington. But by the time Howe instituted this policy in the spring of 1776, it was too late. The naval base of Boston was under siege by American ground forces which had punished the British army at the Battle of Bunker Hill in June 1775. American forces had meanwhile taken the forts of Ticonderoga and Crown Point near the south end of Lake Champlain, and driven into Canada to capture Montreal and besiege Quebec, from which they were driven by British seaborne reinforcements in the spring and early summer of 1776. At sea, merchantmen were being armed as privateers to raid British shipping, Washington's schooners operated off Boston, and an eight-vessel squadron, the largest ship mounting twenty-four guns, cruised from Philadelphia to take several prizes and capture Nassau in the Bahamas early in 1776. Conciliation was furthest from Washington's mind.

In fact, the American strategic defense admirably frustrated Admiral Howe's limited war measures, while at the same time Howe taught Washington and his officers the value of sea power. British command of the sea had saved Canada, and in March 1776 this same fact enabled the British to abandon besieged Boston and return to Halifax. Exploiting the interior position, Washington shifted his army overland to New York, while General Benedict Arnold built a fleet of gunboats on Lake Champlain. Then, in the summer of 1776, the British launched a three-pronged offensive to quell the rebellion. The Howes landed on Long Island in July and in a series of battles on land drove Washington's army into New Jersey by December, but in the ten days after Christmas Washington's brilliant tactics won the battles of Trenton and Princeton. The British navy in New York, pursuing its light blockade, felt the brunt of "Yankee know-how" when the first real submarine in history—invented by David Bushnell—unsuccessfully attacked a British 64. The American coast defense of Charleston, South Carolina, was most successful, as the defenders drove off the second prong of the offensive, a British amphibious attack, in June. The third thrust was decided by the naval battle of Valcour Island. General Sir Guy Carleton built a squadron of 20 row-and-sail gunboats plus other light warships at the north end of Lake Champlain and sortied toward Crown Point where the lake narrowed fifteen miles north of Fort Ticonderoga. On October 11 Arnold met him with a mixed force of 16 craft, mostly rowbarges and 3-gun gondolas, off Valcour Island halfway down the lake. Superior British firepower carried the day, but Arnold escaped south to Split Rock, where two days later he was forced to scuttle his surviving vessels. However, the British, who lost a 12-gun schooner and a gunboat, were so sufficiently delayed that, after a short occupation of Crown Point, they were obliged to return to Canada to winter. By mid-January 1777 the defenses of the rebel nation were intact, save for New York.

Now, two years late, Admiral Howe decided to prosecute the war as vigorously as originally ordered by Germain. He tightened the blockade, thus neutralizing the thirteen frigates then under construction in American yards by order of the Continental Congress. But privateers were already harassing the British merchant marine, and in May and June 1777 an American squadron of two brigs and one cutter operated out of French ports to successfully raid British shipping. Germain now prepared a grand pincers plan that would again focus on the North, but unfortunately for Britain, the government failed to coordinate it properly—with devastating results. The original architect of the plan, General John Burgoyne, was to retrace Carleton's path down the line of Lake Champlain and the Hudson River, driving American forces before him. General Howe was to push up the Hudson from New York to meet with Burgoyne at Albany, where a third force would also rendezvous by way of the St. Lawrence River and Lake Ontario. The trouble was that while Germain and Burgoyne understood the plan, Howe's orders left him free to operate fairly independently, and the Howe brothers preferred to end the war by capturing the rebel capital, Philadelphia.

Again, British waterborne mobility enabled them to move freely, but again Washington utilized his interior position to parry the uncoordinated thrusts by Burgoyne and Howe. Burgoyne had little difficulty passing down Lake Champlain with some 7200 troops and capturing Fort Ticonderoga in July 1777. In August, he pressed on, but learned also that the Howes had left New York with 18,000 men bound for Philadelphia instead of Albany. Furthermore, Washington dispatched troops northward which that month repulsed the thrust from Lake Ontario and contested Burgoyne's offensive across Lake George. In September Burgoyne, deciding to drive on without Howe's participation, crossed the Hudson River near Saratoga, where he was engaged by the American troops. The next month, following a feeble diversionary feint by General Henry Clinton at New York, Burgoyne was defeated before Saratoga. Surrounded, he surrendered his entire force. General Howe was more successful in his operations. Sailing up the Chesapeake Bay aboard his brother's fleet, Howe landed before Philadelphia and drove Washington's army before him, occupying the rebel capital late in September. The Continental Congress fled the city, but Washington's forces controlled the surrounding countryside. General Howe therefore had to keep open his communications to the sea by the Delaware River, which, however, was still blocked by American shore batteries and light naval forces. Throughout October and November, therefore, Admiral Howe painfully worked upriver removing these obstructions, but it cost him a 64-gun ship of the line. Washington therefore lost Philadelphia and its approaches, but as his depleted Continental Army settled into its dreary winter quarters at Valley Forge, the inventor David Bushnell early in January gave Howe's fleet some anxious moments by launching—unsuccessfully—a barrage of floating mines.

Britain's failure to settle the American revolt, especially with the loss of a small army at Saratoga, changed the entire character of the war. In the winter of 1777–78, France decided to ally with the United States, thus recognizing her independence and preparing for eventual war with Britain. American agents in France signed the necessary treaties in February 1778 and French military aid became open—not the least of which was supporting the operations of an American sloop-of-war out of Brest that spring under the command of the Scotsman John Paul Jones. In America, Britain held only Philadelphia and New York, plus part of Rhode Island, while the rebel forces still controlled the interior and the rest of the coast. General Howe resigned his command in order to defend his actions to the Lord North government; disgusted with the policies of that government, Admiral Howe retired from the naval service. But to the disappointment of that government's critics, their greatest champion, Pitt of Chatham, died in May. The next month France made general war on England.

## THE GLOBAL STRUGGLE

The War immediately took on global proportions, which greatly enhanced the cause of the Americans. Henceforth, American fortunes would depend upon the successes or failures of the French fleet. This fact General Washington soon appreciated when in July 1778 the approach of the French Mediterranean fleet of twelve heavy ships of the line caused the British fleet and army to evacuate Philadelphia and make haste for New York. As far as Washington and the Americans were concerned, a combined Franco-American land-sea attack against the main British army in America would settle the issue. But the heavier-draft ships of Vice Admiral Count Jean Baptiste C. H. H. d'Estaing could not pass over the bar off Sandy Hook to decide that issue at New York, while a storm broke up such an attempt on the British forces at Newport, Rhode Island, in August. The French fleet then based at Boston, the British at New York, while the Americans awaited with impatience the pleasure of the French to join them in the long-awaited joint effort.

But France had greater strategic commitments—namely, the destruction of the British Empire. Victory for the new United States would accomplish this in North America, but more important was the taking of the British sugar islands in the West Indies. So major naval operations shifted away from New England for the rest of the war to the South— which included the American ports of Charleston and Savannah, virtual islands because of their geographic isolation from Virginia and the Northeastern seaboard. For these operations in the Western Hemisphere the French had but one fleet, the very same that was home-based at Toulon. But their Mediterranean interests could be guarded by a friendly Spain. The main fleet remained at Brest, an excellent force of thirty-two ships under Vice Admiral Count d'Orvilliers, the deployment of which was debated within the French government. Most notably, Count Maurice de Broglie, a diplomat, recommended that all overseas expeditions and convoys be rejected in favor of one decisive blow at the British Channel fleet; France could thus seize command of the sea at the outset and end the war quickly. But Louis XVI and his ministers were unsympathetic and preferred the old defensive subordination of the navy to the army while waging *guerre de course* against the enemy. In this strategic stance, France counted on the help of the Americans, whose shipbuilding talents were exemplified by the 74 which they built and presented to France in 1782 and by their privateer and regular cruiser captains, most notable of whom was Paul Jones whose depredations in British waters in 1779–80 created a great psychological effect within England. Between them, the French and the Americans thus planned to destroy the British mercantilistic empire.

For the British Admiralty, the successful strategy of Pitt in the Seven Years War would be the most desirable course to pursue, but the situation was different and the means did not exist. The war was strictly a maritime affair, so that England could not count upon an ally to attack France on the continent. Indeed, the aging Frederick of Prussia had lost his bellicosity, while Russia had become a maritime power in her own right and was unfriendly to British rule at sea. Neither had the Royal Navy ships enough to sufficiently blockade France in Europe, command the Caribbean and suppress the rebellion in America. Rather, Britain sacrificed command of the sea in order to keep open her own lines of communications and to protect her prized possessions from Gibraltar to Jamaica to India. As a result, the blockades of the continent and America were difficult to enforce, leading Dutch and Danish smugglers to run illegal goods into England with increasing impunity and French warships to easily transport an army to America. Accepting France's challenge, Britain fought the war for the very survival of her Empire.

That the North government was wholly unprepared became immediately apparent. Unlike Anson's practice of keeping sufficient frigates throughout imperial sea routes and bringing the enemy fleet to action before it could threaten those communications, the North administration could only feebly imitate this precedent. While the fleet in North America was being reinforced, the Channel fleet put to sea under Admiral Augustus Keppel, who encountered the French Brest fleet under d'Orvilliers off Ushant in July 1778. The French, with 32 of the line and 13 frigates, closed with Keppel but maintained their defensive tactics by shooting into the enemy's rigging. Keppel, in the new 100-gun *Victory* with 29 others of the line and 6 frigates, held to the formal conterminous line until it was obvious he could not secure a decision. But his order to his second squadron to violate the Fighting Instructions was not executed, and the French escaped with no ships lost on either side. The failure resembled Byng's 1756 action off Toulon, and now Keppel, who had sat on the late Byng's court-martial, was also tried. But unlike Byng, he was acquitted, the Permanent Fighting Instructions being so discredited that the way now lay open for admirals commanding to exercise their own tactical judgment. But change still came slowly, for now more of the better admirals refused to serve under the inept George III-North-Sandwich regime; Keppel joined Howe in retirement. And inferior commanders would be less willing to experiment with their tactics.

With public and official upheaval over the war in Britain, and the state of the Royal Navy in serious question, Spain decided the time had come to throw its new navy in common cause with France to help destroy the British Empire. Already, with the end of the May-to-October hurricane season, the focus of the American war had shifted southward —with Spain covetous of regaining Florida and of weakening the British presence in the Caribbean. In September 1778 the French seized Dominica Island, but in November the British took St. Lucia and in December Savannah, Georgia, to begin a long campaign in that region. More importantly, the Spanish wanted back Gibraltar and Minorca and considered war with Britain as the perfect opportunity. During the spring of 1779, therefore, Spain made plans with France to combine fleets and invade England. As Britain began to prepare a defense, Spain in June declared war on Great Britain and immediately laid siege to Gibraltar. The Spanish did not recognize American independence, but the governor of New Orleans did encourage the Americans to create a three-vessel squadron on the Mississippi which took a number of prizes.

Suddenly outnumbered, the British organized their naval defenses around the "fleet-in-being" concept. Admiral Sir Charles Hardy, Norris' second in command thirty-five years before (!), was given command of the Home Fleet, but his chief of staff, the younger and brilliant Captain Richard Kempenfelt, initiated much of the leadership. When the French transports gathered at the secondary Channel ports of Cherbourg and

Havre, the British placed cruiser squadrons at the Downs and the Channel Islands to prevent them from concentrating. Lack of a close blockade of Brest enabled the Spanish fleet to join the French off Cape Finisterre, but Spanish delays enabled the British to develop their strategy. On Kempenfelt's advice, Hardy stationed the fleet west of the Scilly Islands in August, both to cover incoming convoys and to challenge the allied crossing of the Channel. The twenty-five British ships of the line, all with coppered bottoms and thus able to keep the sea longer, would thus face sixty-six of the Franco-Spanish line. But Kempenfelt doubted his enemy's ability to coordinate in such a campaign, and if the allies reached the transports, the men-of-war would be so encumbered with escorting duties and cruising formations that they could never cross without facing the homogeneous British fleet-in-being. He was correct. In mid-August d'Orvilliers entered the Channel hoping to bring Hardy to battle before having to break the cruiser blockade and make the unwieldy crossing. The British, however, avoided battle, so that the allies exhausted their disease-ridden crews on maneuvers and inadequate supplies and then abandoned the campaign altogether in September.

The Channel thus became the defensive theater and the West Indies the offensive. Kempenfelt, soon promoted to rear admiral, reasoned that a flying squadron of cruisers would keep the French concentrated at Brest guarding the coast and convoys and not breaking up into squadrons to interrupt British communications. Simultaneously, these two-deck men-of-war played havoc on French trade. The concentration at the Western Approaches by this fleet-in-being continued for the duration by Kempenfelt whose policies were accepted by three aged commanders. The Home (or Grand) Fleet gradually grew, slowly adopted the new anti-personnel cannon, the carronade, and made tactical improvements as Kempenfelt introduced a better signal system—prerequisite to replacing formalism with any new melee tactics. Kempenfelt also rejected Hawke's precedent of close blockade year-round in favor of the looser open blockade in the sailing season, which proved sufficient to discourage the French and Spanish from carrying through their repeated invasion designs. It also enabled British warships to seize neutral vessels trading with Britain's enemies—an enforcement of the Rule of 1756 which quickly led to naval expansion by neutral Denmark, Holland, Russia, Sweden and Portugal.

The war was prosecuted most vigorously overseas, especially in the West Indies. The British virtually drove the French from India, while the French retook Senegal in Africa, and the Spanish still besieged Gibraltar. The allies rarely coordinated their efforts, so that they lost any opportunity to obtain command of the sea. Particularly in the West Indies were the allies favorably placed, their bases at Martinique and

Havana being windward of the lee-bound main British base at Jamaica. But the French operated virtually independently of their unpredictable Spanish allies. In June and July 1779 Admiral d'Estaing captured St. Vincent and Grenada in the British Windward Islands before finally being intercepted by the British West Indies fleet under Vice Admiral John Byron at the latter place on July 6. With 21 of the line Byron sighted d'Estaing's 25 clearing the harbor at Grenada in apparent disorder, so he prematurely signaled general chase. The French, however, formed up, shot away the British rigging (with no small help from shore batteries), and then broke off the action before claiming a greater victory. But d'Estaing followed French policy of avoiding decisive engagements and rested his laurels on the capture of Grenada. Byron retired to the lesser British base at St. Kitts and into history—best known for his famous poet grandson.

The other major naval events of 1779 concerned amphibious operations. The British had so perfected their "combined" army-navy operations that they had converted a merchantman into a warship solely for shore bombardment, mounting sixteen 24-pounder guns. With their amphibious mobility they had taken several West Indies islands, the port of Savannah and in June 1779 the shore commanding Penobscot Bay in Maine as a base for operations against New Hampshire and Massachusetts. The British had fortified their new conquests in order to withstand counterattacks by the French and Americans. The Americans launched their largest naval effort of the war from Boston with 7 warships (the largest a 32-gun frigate), 12 privateers and 22 transports with embarked troops aimed at dislodging the British from Penobscot Bay. Late in July this force attacked the British foothold there, but failed to press the attack and reverted to siege operations. In mid-August the British fleet at New York relieved the garrison with a 7-ship squadron led by a 64 that chased the American ships up the Penobscot River, where 38 of them were scuttled and the other 3 captured. In the South, during September and October, Admiral d'Estaing used his fleet and French and American ground forces in an attempt to retake Savannah, but he failed, then sailed home.

The British had their own difficulties with keeping Gibraltar supplied and assigned this mission as the first task of their new West Indies fleet commander, Rear Admiral Sir George B. Rodney. He left England in December 1779 and early in the new year overtook a Spanish convoy off Cape Finisterre; along with the merchant vessels (which he sent on to Gibraltar) he captured a Spanish 64 and six frigates. Rodney, like Kempenfelt a student of the new tactics now evolving, learned of a Spanish squadron off Cape St. Vincent, Portugal, and went after it. On January 16, 1780, he with twenty-two of the line encountered the Spanish force and ordered general chase. This so-called Moonlight Battle ended with Rodney taking six of the line, or half the enemy force. He then proceeded to the offensive in the West Indies.

The shift of Channel Fleet units to the waters of the West Indian colonies seriously weakened Britain's position in Europe. The greatest danger at the beginning of 1780 was the neutral coalition known as the Armed Neutrality, formed in February by Russia, Sweden and Denmark to protect the free use of the sea—or neutral trade with France and Spain. Eventually, the Netherlands, Prussia, Austria, Portugal and the Two Sicilies (Naples) also joined. Allied naval strength was so great in the summer of 1780 that the British lost control of the Channel. The French and Spanish failed to exploit this advantage, but the British Admiralty had some tense weeks as the Russian, Swedish and Danish fleets sortied into the North Sea to protect their merchant shipping. Most active were the Russians, who operated as far south as Lisbon and Leghorn in 1780 and 1781 and who maintained their Ship Fleet in 1782 when Sweden and Denmark reduced their active forces. Actually, however, the Russians needed the British, both to help command their fleet and for the long Russian voyages made via Dover and Portsmouth. Of the armed neutrals, Holland most irritated Britain because of the smuggling into England and the trade between the Dutch West Indies and the rebels in America. With the Dutch fleet of 46 of the line and 38 frigates seriously undermanned, Britain declared war on the Netherlands in December 1780. Dutch smuggling to England stopped, and the armed Dutch convoys reminiscent of the previous century resumed.

The goal of Britain's sacrifices at home—supremacy in America—was pursued vigorously. Admiral Rodney arrived in the West Indies late in March 1780 and immediately sought battle with the French fleet now under Vice Admiral Luc-Urbain du Bouexic, Count de Guichen. The two engaged off Martinique on April 17. Rodney with 20 of the line abandoned the old formalist line in order to mass on the French rear, but his captains so abided by the Fighting Instructions that only confusion resulted. De Guichen, with 23 of the line, fired at the rigging, then broke off the indecisive action and retired. Trying to break tradition and promote melee tactics, Rodney censured his captains and drilled them thoroughly with his own signals and maneuvers. Seeking out de Guichen again, Rodney spent much of May within sight of the French fleet. De Guichen and Rodney adroitly maneuvered near Martinique for many days, each trying to assume a favorable position for battle. It never came, although twice in mid-May the fleets exchanged cannon fire and to the French advantage. Their crews exhausted by these activities, Rodney put in to Barbados, de Guichen to Martinique. At the latter place, a Spanish squadron of 10 of the line arrived in June, but as in the Channel the allies were unable to cooperate in the Indies, and in August de Guichen sailed for Europe, escorting a convoy of 95 merchantmen.

French failure to support the new United States with naval forces enabled the British to improve their fortunes in the Southern colonies. In February 1780 the new commanders in America, Admiral Marriot Arbuthnot and General Henry Clinton, left New York to besiege Charleston, South Carolina, which finally fell in May. British regulars and a few American loyalist troops under General Lord Cornwallis then spent the summer pacifying the Carolinas against rebel guerrilla forces. The Americans rallied, however, in the autumn and engaged in a rigorous campaign against Cornwallis throughout the winter. In the meantime, a French expeditionary force had landed at Newport from a convoy escorted by seven of the line, only to be blockaded there by the British fleet. Rodney arrived at New York in September, thus frustrating General Washington's plans to attack that place, but Rodney had left half his force in the Indies where it was decimated by a hurricane and earthquake, costing the fleet two of the line, six frigates and five lesser vessels. The year 1780 ended in virtual stalemate, with Rodney hastening back to Barbados to fill the vacuum left by the disaster.

Although the French were troubled by lack of Spanish cooperation, they could pride themselves in the navy fashioned since Choiseul's administration. Choiseul, though aged and without power, was part of Louis XVI's court, and in 1780 a new and very talented individual assumed the post of Secretary of State for the Navy, Charles Eugène Gabriel de la Croix, Marquis de Castries. In addition to enlightened civilian leadership, the French navy could boast increasingly able admirals. D'Orvilliers, d'Estaing and de Guichen had all been worthy antagonists of their British counterparts, who, however, had left something to be desired. For a new and important offensive in 1781, two fresh names appeared in command of French naval expeditions: François Joseph Paul de Grasse-Tilly and Pierre André de Suffren. De Grasse would take the fleet to America, while Suffren would lead a squadron to South Africa and India, where the war had been progressing only as part of the larger Indian native struggles. In addition, a Franco-Spanish expedition would attack Minorca in the Mediterranean, while Spain continued the siege of Gibraltar. So threatened, British naval requirements would be severely stretched.

The British, however, were enjoying a smaller offensive of their own in the winter of 1780–81 as well as the fruits of improved leadership. Under the Earl of Sandwich, Sir Charles Middleton (later Lord Barham) was directing fleet operations and paying attention to the tactical and signal changes being introduced into the Home and West

Indies fleets by Kempenfelt and Rodney. The offensive was against the Dutch Empire: in February 1781 Rodney took the Dutch West Indies islands St. Eustatius and St. Martin before returning to England, while another force moved to the Cape Verde Islands in preparation for a descent on the Dutch station at the Cape of Good Hope. The British also made war on Dutch shipping, and on one occasion—in August 1781—a British convoy escorted by 7 of the line engaged an equal Dutch force at Dogger Bank in a typical old-fashioned slugging match, the Dutch being forced back into port. The British blockade of New England also continued as Arbuthnot engaged the French Newport squadron off Delaware in mid-March, keeping it from supporting Franco-American forces in Virginia. Where the British were weakest was at home, their Channel fleet greatly inferior to the French at Brest and the Spanish at Cádiz. But the allies again failed to act in concert when, in March, that Channel fleet of 28 of the line escorted 100 supply ships to relieve Gibraltar. Before the fleet returned to England in May, de Grasse and Suffren had broken out of Brest.

The French fleet sortie was most timely, as events soon proved. De Grasse and Suffren separated near the Azores and proceeded to their separate destinations. Suffren with 5 of the line (4 of them with coppered bottoms newly introduced into the French fleet) in April attacked the smaller British force at the Cape Verde Islands then preparing for an attack on the Cape of Good Hope. Suffren was beaten off, but his attack caused the British to abandon their enterprise. Franco-Dutch communications to the East were thus preserved. Suffren landed troops at the Cape and proceeded on to the island of Mauritius, where he assumed command over French naval operations in the Indian Ocean. De Grasse with 26 of the line escorted a large convoy to Martinique, then turned south to capture the British island of Tobago. With Rodney returning home, de Grasse was occupied only with the smaller force of Rear Admiral Sir Samuel Hood. In the meantime, a Franco-Spanish expeditionary force landed on British Minorca in the Mediterranean in July and laid siege to Port Mahon. Overextended, the British could not relieve their garrison, which surrendered the following February. Hard-pressed in the Mediterranean, America, West Indian and South Asian waters, the British Empire had reached the crisis stage.

The British struggle in America presented a new and extremely perilous strategic situation. They still held New York as their primary advanced base, with General Clinton in command of the army and Rear Admiral Thomas Graves relieving Arbuthnot in command of the navy. General Washington and the Continental Army and Lieutenant General J. B. Donatien de Vimeur, Count de Rochambeau, with the French expeditionary force, held the territory inland and northward to Boston, with a French naval squadron under Rear Admiral de Barras at Newport. During the spring of 1781 General Cornwallis shifted his operations from the Carolinas to Virginia where he was harassed by American forces under the young French Marquis de Lafayette. Cornwallis realized his position in Virginia depended entirely upon keeping open his sea communications with Clinton in New York, so in August he concentrated near Yorktown on the Virginia "peninsula," formed by the York and James rivers from Hampton Roads to Richmond. Meanwhile the French and Americans realized that the division of the British army should be exploited by a combined land-sea operation. Washington preferred to strike at New York, but eventually decided to move on Cornwallis at Yorktown. Yet everything depended upon de Grasse, coming north from the Indies to join the attack in August.

Uncertain of the allied design, the British decided to concentrate their naval forces at New York. Admiral Rodney prior to his return to England had ordered Rear Admiral Hood to place 15 of the line in the Indies at the disposal of Graves at New York. Hood therefore hastened north from the Caribbean and joined Graves on August 30. By this time, however, Washington and Rochambeau were marching south with 6000 troops to reinforce Lafayette's 8000 before Yorktown, wherein lay Cornwallis and his 8000 men. Vital to the siege were special heavy siege guns, so these were put aboard Admiral de Barras' 8 ships of the line, which sortied from Newport late in August bound for the Chesapeake. The key to the entire operation, however, was Admiral de Grasse and his 28 of the line, needed to cut Cornwallis' seaborne communications and to provide 2500 additional troops. The allied strategy, a masterful one, called for strategic concentration against half the British army in America. De Grasse arrived off Cape Henry at the mouth of the Chesapeake on August 30 and established contact with Lafayette. Washington was nearing Philadelphia, from which he would march down the Delaware shore and be ferried down the Bay by de Grasse's ships.

Strategic success also depended on surprise, for the British believed the main threat to be in the New York-to-Newport area. When de Grasse did not arrive at Newport, and de Barras departed, Graves put to sea from New York on August 31 with 19 of the line (plus 7 frigates), Hood commanding the van squadron of 6. Assuming correctly that de Barras was bound for the Chesapeake, Graves hastened thence with his swifter copper-sheathed warships hoping to prevent de Barras from entering the Bay. In this attempt, Graves succeeded. But arriving off the entrance to the Bay on the morning of September

5, he was surprised to see de Grasse's fleet anchored inside Cape Henry. De Grasse also was surprised by the appearance of Graves and Hood rather than de Barras. Four of his 28 ships were moving up the Bay to blockade the York and James Rivers, many of his crewmen were ashore establishing contact with Lafayette, and a contrary wind and tide made beating out difficult. But de Grasse, superior to Graves 24 to 19, waited till noon before slipping anchors and riding the ebb tide out to sea.

The Battle of the Virginia Capes (or the Chesapeake Bay), September 5, 1781, was fought on the same strategic and tactical traditions as always. The French gave battle in order to support the army, drawing Graves away from the Chesapeake and thus protecting the approach of de Barras from Newport. Assuming the lee tack, de Grasse's undermanned ships formed a line as they emerged from their anchorage and began their usual cannonade on the upward roll. Though superior, de Grasse's strategic mission was not to seek a decision but to draw Graves to seaward. Graves on the other hand gave no thought to general chase as the French straggled out, but formed an orderly conterminous line as he approached the Bay. Then, at 2:15 P.M., Graves had his fleet turn together, each ship coming about to face eastward and then close with the parallel French in an old-fashioned formalist battle. As usual, the vans closed first in a murderous fire that began about 4:00 and gradually spread to the center vessels. But Hood, now in the rear squadron, deliberately delayed closing up for various questionable excuses and never really got into the action. Both fleets exhausted themselves and ceased firing by 6:00. The cannonade, though indecisive, hurt the British more than the French, one British vessel having to be scuttled and Graves having to avoid action when de Grasse tried to renew it on succeeding days. Tactically, the battle provided the final discredit to formalism, and the Permanent Fighting Instructions were never again issued. Strategically, it was a clear allied victory, for de Barras passed in behind the two fleets and anchored safely in the Chesapeake on the 10th with Washington's valuable siege guns. De Grasse did as well, and the arrival of Washington completed the encirclement of Cornwallis at Yorktown.

The brief French command of the sea in Virginia waters sealed the fate of the British Empire in America. Graves and Hood had no choice but to return to New York and seek repairs from the inadequate facilities there. Finally, on October 19, Graves sortied again with 23 of the line embarking 6000 troops under Clinton. But de Grasse with his 36 of the line had combined with the equally superior Franco-American army to starve out and reduce Cornwallis' defenders. Cornwallis thus surrendered his army on that same day, the 19th, so that

Graves and Clinton could do nothing when they arrived but return to New York. Washington followed overland, to increase Continental pressure on the British, and sent other forces back into the Carolinas. De Grasse sailed for the West Indies, seeking to operate against the British naval bases at Jamaica, Barbados and St. Kitts, and Hood was obliged to follow. In the meantime, Suffren was entering the Indian Ocean to challenge British naval supremacy there. With the Empire in such peril and the extension of the war in North America promising to drag on for years, Parliament early in 1782 moved to give America its independence, and the North regime collapsed. Throughout 1782 therefore both British and French forces evacuated the new United States.

Though America was lost, and the rest of the Empire in jeopardy, British fortunes began to improve almost from the moment Cornwallis surrendered at Yorktown. In December Admiral Kempenfelt with 12 of the line defeated a fleet of similar size under Admiral de Guichen off Ushant and took 15 merchantmen of the convoy it had been escorting. The next month Admiral Sir Edward Hughes supported amphibious forces which took Dutch Trincomalee, Ceylon, and Admiral Hood with 22 of the line severely punished de Grasse's 25 in a cannonade in the harbor of St. Kitts. The island fell to the French, but in February Rodney returned, giving the British 36 to the French reinforced 32 of the line. Though Rodney shared much of the blame for the outcome of the Yorktown campaign, he was an innovative tactician as were his two key subordinates, Rear Admiral Hood and Fleet Captain Sir Charles Douglas. Hughes, a superior officer, commanded in the East, while a number of other excellent officers returned to service with the fall of the North government. Sandwich was replaced as First Lord of the Admiralty by Admiral Keppel, and Admiral Lord Howe returned to duty as commander of the fleet, ably assisted by Kempenfelt.

Britain needed such commanders for the campaign of 1782, which would be focused on a grand strategic design by the allies on both sides of the Atlantic and in Indian waters. De Grasse would launch an offensive in the West Indies and Suffren in the East, a Franco-Spanish fleet would operate in the Channel, and a Dutch force would move into the North Sea. The objective of the allies was to so threaten British home waters and imperial communications that the Royal Navy could not adequately defend its key bases at Jamaica and Gibraltar. Allied captures of these places would give the Bourbons control of the Western Mediterranean and Caribbean, thus reversing the losses of earlier wars. To meet these serious threats, the British adopted an ingenious strategy of flexible concentration utilizing the tried-and-true fleet-in-being idea. Hughes was left on his own to deal with Suffren, while Rodney was given a powerful fleet to carry out offensive operations in the West Indies against de Grasse. Howe, commanding in the Channel with perhaps thirty of the line, would frustrate allied plans by sending out squadrons south to Ushant and north to the Texel to harass enemy trade and leave the impression that his fleet was strong enough to enforce an open blockade not only of Brest, but of Amsterdam and Cádiz as well. Operating from the interior position with his strategic reserve at Spithead and the Downs, Howe could concentrate or shift his forces at will, thus keeping the enemy off balance.

Before the sailing season began in Europe, and just as it was ending in the Caribbean, in April 1782, de Grasse opened his offensive to take Jamaica—only to be stopped by Rodney at the Battle of the Saints. Learning that de Grasse had sortied from Martinique on April 8 with 35 of the line convoying 150 transports and merchantmen, the latter bound for France, Rodney left St. Lucia with 36 ships to bring about an engagement. De Grasse skirmished with Hood's squadron on the morning of the 9th, but the general action did not ensue until the morning of the 12th off the islets of the Saints, between Dominica and Guadeloupe. De Grasse's escort duties and several collisions at sea left him with 30 of the line all spread out in ragged battle formation heading south toward the lee side of Dominica. Rodney turned on a converging course in excellent order. When the two fleets intersected about 8:00 A.M., the cannonade began and told immediately in favor of the British, who had increased their rate of fire through new techniques and by now fully employing the new carronade "smasher." The firing and wind changes ruined any order among the French and, almost by accident, Rodney broke through the French line simultaneously in three places. The battle then broke into parts, with de Grasse endeavoring to escape. Instead, however, de Grasse himself and 5 of his ships were taken, his attempt on Jamaica destroyed. Rodney lost the opportunity to take many more prizes by failing to pursue. But in not following formalist doctrine and by allowing a melee battle to develop, he had saved the British West Indies. The French and Spanish, as usual, could not combine to continue against their adversary, while the active Hood took 2 more French ships a week after the action, some compensation for 5 damaged British ships of the line which soon foundered in a great storm near Newfoundland.

The strategic situation in India was different, for the French admiral there, Suffren, had a very un-French concept of naval warfare. A passionate student and admirer of the Dutch fighter de Ruyter, Suffren believed command of the sea to be essential for victory, and that such command could be obtained only by attacking and destroying the enemy fleet. He also advocated melee tactics by massing on the enemy fleet, but his ship captains were too schooled in defensive tactics to provide the daring and initiative that Suffren required. Departing Mauritius late in 1781, Suffren had no real commitment to support French ground forces as had de Grasse; the British held the key Indian and Ceylonese ports, although they were hard-pressed on land by the Mysore Indians, allies of France. By the same token, however, Suffren had no advance base from which to operate, refit and replenish, whereas his British adversary Admiral Hughes had the excellent roadstead of Trincomalee. Suffren therefore captured British merchantmen to supply him and operated without a base. This kind of daring and aggressive leadership especially endangered the British Empire, for with the loss of the American colonies, India had to be held.

Admiral Suffren lost no time in attacking his enemy, a rare policy for a French fleet. Arriving off British Madras in February 1782, Suffren maneuvered his 12 ships into position to engage Hughes's 9. Hughes, fearful that Suffren would seek to recapture Trincomalee for an advanced base, also sought a decisive victory, so that the battles of these two men closely resembled the slugging matches of the English and Dutch a century before. On February 17, south of Madras, Suffren attacked and doubled on the rear and center of Hughes's line —brilliant melee tactics. The reluctance of some of his captains and the coming of night ended Suffren's chance for a decisive blow, and the fleets parted. Hughes retired to Trincomalee and Suffren to Pondicherry, where he landed French troops. Hughes went on to Madras to receive two fresh 74s; upon his return voyage he was intercepted north of Trincomalee by Suffren on April 12, the same day that his countryman Rodney was attacking de Grasse. Suffren changed his tactics for a general line-ahead action with his extra ship massing on the British rear, but the vagaries of battle suddenly brought a massing on the British center which badly punished Hughes's force. After the battle, shortness of supplies prevented Suffren from taking the offensive until a convoy arrived in May, and he was assisted by Dutch authorities on Ceylon. Then, on July 6, off Cuddalore, the two forces, each 11 of the line, fought a standard line-ahead action, because Hughes had the wind and did the attacking. The battle was a draw and like the other actions, no ships were lost by either side. But Suffren's uncanny ability to recover his losses soon placed him in the position of the strategic initiative.

Reinforced, Suffren now moved with 14 of the line to control the Indian Ocean. His objective was Trincomalee. On August 26, while

Hughes was refitting at Madras, Suffren landed an army to besiege Trincomalee and then provided fire support. The port surrendered on the 31st, just two days before Hughes reappeared with 12 of the line. Maneuvering offshore, Suffren attacked Hughes on September 3, but his own fiery haste combined with cautious and inferior commanders to thoroughly confuse his line and lead to another draw. In contrast, Hughes kept his line in excellent order and came out with lighter casualties and damage. With the approach of the monsoon season, however, Hughes with no forward base had to retire from the east coast to Bombay, where reinforcements had arrived. The French had equal difficulties, however, for two of three convoys dispatched from France for India had been intercepted; the British were negotiating peace with their various Indian enemies; and the lack of supplies and healthy conditions at Trincomalee forced Suffren to winter his squadron at Achem in Dutch Sumatra, to which port he repaired in October. When the convoy and reinforcements hastening thence via the Cape of Good Hope reached him, Suffren could support French army operations in India. At bottom, however, French hopes depended upon the course of the war at the strategic center—the English Channel.

Admiral Lord Howe—known as "Black Dick" to the fleet—carefully maintained his strategy of concentration with his fleet-in-being. In April 1782 he had Vice Admiral Samuel Barrington avoid any general battle off Brest unless under the most favorable conditions, and Barrington responded by capturing one of the three great French East India convoys bound to supply Suffren. In May the sailing season opened in the North Sea, so Howe and Barrington moved thence to blockade the Texel, leaving Kempenfelt to watch Brest. The British cabinet urged Howe to conduct offensive operations against Dutch shipping, but Howe only wanted to cover incoming British Baltic convoys and not violate his concentration at Spithead. Leaving 9 of the line to watch the Dutch coast and fleet of 16, Howe then shifted back to Kempenfelt off Brest. But sickness drove the lot into port, making them helpless to intercept a Franco-Spanish fleet sortie from Cádiz to Brest. In July, the British West Indies convoy from Jamaica approached, so Howe got to sea with but 22 of the line to cover it, while the allies with 36 hunted him for battle. The French and Spanish, as before, refused to enter the Channel until the British Channel fleet was defeated, but Howe avoided battle until the convoy arrived safely. These maneuvers consumed an entire month, which so exhausted the allies that they had to return to port to replenish. Howe could now concentrate at Spithead, reinforce his fleet and prepare for fresh operations against the continent.

Though still taxed by its far-flung commitments, Britain had made the defense of Gibraltar a top strategic priority in its war aims. Accordingly, Howe made ready to sail there with the Home Fleet while strengthening the North Sea squadron to blockade the Texel and protect incoming Baltic convoys. But he lost the services of his most brilliant lieutenant, Kempenfelt, whose flagship, rotten clear through from prewar lack of upkeep, sank at her moorings at Spithead with nearly all hands in August. Before Howe could move, however, the Spanish had recalled their ships from Brest to join in a major assault on Gibraltar. On September 8–13 some 50 battle-line ships, plus frigates, gunboats, bomb vessels and 10 floating batteries joined in a massive land-sea bombardment of "the Rock," but in vain. The garrison held, the defenders using red-hot cannonballs to sink 9 of the floating batteries. The allies gave up the attack, though the Spanish fleet remained in blockade off Algeciras. Nevertheless, Howe departed Spithead on the 11th and proceeded unmolested past Brest and Cádiz with 34 of the line and 12 frigates escorting 137 transports and supply ships plus an East India convoy bound for Hughes. The latter went on its way, but Howe ran past the 49 Spanish ships of the line to relieve Gibraltar in October. His work done, he passed outward again, drawing absolutely no response from the Spaniards.

By this time, the autumn of 1782, the allied French, Spanish and Dutch were exhausted, while Britain had lost her American colonies and like them sought an end to the fighting. American independence having been granted, the French having failed to destroy Britain's hold in the West Indies, and the Spanish resigned to the permanent loss of Gibraltar, negotiations proceeded quickly, and on January 20, 1783, the war between France and Spain and Britain was ended. The Dutch fought on, while word of the peace did not reach India for many months. Suffren continued to bother the British, who had besieged by land and sea French ground forces at Cuddalore. With 15 of the line Suffren appeared there, so that Hughes departed with his 18 to anchor nearby, and Suffren embarked army cannoneers to help man his guns. In the late afternoon of April 20, 1783, Suffren bore down in perfect line-ahead to engage the superior force of Hughes. In the savage cannonade of this last battle of the war, Hughes's ships took the greater punishment and had to abandon the siege. Only the arrival of the news of peace nine days later saved the British from their predicament. Suffren, by his five battles against Hughes, emerges not only as the most successful tactical commander of the war at sea, but also the greatest sailor in French history. A meleeist and skilled leader, he is ranked above Tourville and Duquesne, both products of the one period in French naval history when France had actively sought command of the sea. But with only a squadron, Suffren could not defeat the British in India, and Hughes's obstinacy played no small part in that defense.

In fact, the British hold on India eventually made up for the loss of the thirteen American colonies and provided the basis for a new, Indian Ocean-oriented Empire. In the Western Hemisphere, only Tobago and St. Lucia were ceded to France, though also the Floridas went to Spain and all territory east of the Mississippi to the United States. But Britain kept Canada and her original West Indian islands. In the Mediterranean, she gave up Minorca to Spain, but retained Gibraltar. The French posts in African Senegal were also returned, and the Dutch retained Ceylon. Britain held most of the Indian coast, however, and in 1788 founded her first colony (of convicts) in Australia at Sydney, thus creating the need for imperial routes across the Indian Ocean. This new strategic axis took some time to appreciate, however, for, aside from American independence, very little changed in the great power relationships of Europe. Only the Netherlands suffered a near-fatal blow; her economy was nearly ruined by the British blockade, with hostilities not ending until 1784. The Dutch East India Company collapsed the next year, and continued Dutch flirtations with France worked against Holland's restoration within the British economic sphere. For Great Britain still ruled the seas.

The War of the American Revolution had been a global conflict for command of the seas that ended the American-based empire of Britain but still left her—again—as the only formidable naval power in the world. Britain's chief difficulty had been the neglect of her navy after the Seven Years War and the resultant lethargy that had created both strategic and tactical sterility in the government, Admiralty and fleet. In strategy, Britain lacked a Pitt to enlist continental allies and promote a blockade of the continent itself, as well as to deal reasonably with the American revolutionaries. In strategy as well as tactics only junior or anti-North admirals excelled, particularly Howe and Kempenfelt, and to a lesser extent Rodney, while the example set by Suffren was not lost. The strategy and tactics of concentration employed by these men under extremely adverse conditions saved Britain from naval ruin and educated an entire generation of subordinate officers. But whereas concentration would be the great strategic and tactical lesson of the war, so too would the example set by the American patriots provide the catalyst for revolution throughout the world for the next two centuries. And Britain would have to fight more worldwide wars over these many years.

# 9

# The Nelson Era, 1783–1815

*If any one wishes to know the history of this war, I will tell them it is our maritime superiority [which] gives me the power of maintaining my army while the enemy are unable to do so.*

—Duke of Wellington

## THE NEW BRITISH EMPIRE

Though European culture and economic mercantilism continued to appear harmonious, the events of the 1770s and 1780s in fact undermined both. The alignment of all the maritime powers as enemies or armed neutrals against Great Britain had led to the destruction of Britain's economic self-sufficiency, had advanced the cause of freedom of the seas (*Mare Liberum*), and had left the balance of power in Europe and the world still unsettled. Of special concern to Britain was the growth of Catherine's Russia, whose wars with Sweden and Turkey continued and which carved up Poland between 1772 and the death of Catherine in 1796. France, Spain, Sweden, Denmark, Holland and even Austria had so accepted the British example that they with Russia took to the sea to threaten the peace of 1783. In France, Navy Minister Castries had all ships' bottoms coppered, carronades employed, more warships built, personnel reforms instituted, Cherbourg strengthened and Marseilles abandoned as naval bases, and a commercial treaty signed with England in 1786. But the treaty was unpopular in France, and two years later Admiral Suffren took command of the fleet at Brest as war appeared imminent. The other powers were implicated because of the wartime British blockade of Holland, which had forced the new Austrian emperor to reopen trade through the long-closed Belgian port of Ostend. Postwar quarrels over Ostend led to a Franco-Dutch alliance along with the possibility of Russia and Austria combining also against Britain.

276

Danish vessels increased their smuggling of goods from Spain to England, and Sweden rearmed in the Baltic. The Anglo-French crisis (during which the great Suffren died) passed, however, as the powers soon faced more pressing concerns.

Western political, economic and social assumptions had been shaken to the core by the success of the American revolutionaries, thus providing the stimulus for an even greater upheaval, the French Revolution of 1789 and subsequent years. This crisis soon threatened the very survival of the European class structure upon which the mercantilistic system rested. For the British Empire, the loss of the American colonies and, temporarily, that of the carrying trade of Europe seriously weakened the source of manpower for the merchant marine and hence for the navy. Impressment and discipline over British and foreign sailors became ever harsher, leading to several diplomatic crises and the fleet mutinies of 1797. Only by relaxing her monopolistic Navigation acts to allow trade with the new United States, however, could the British hope to feed Canada and the British West Indies, a principle rejected by most Englishmen before 1800. The Spanish Empire also suffered from the American Revolution. Defensively, it had been so weakened that in 1789 the peacetime plate fleets were discontinued altogether, the same year that Spain almost went to war with Britain over the Pacific trading station at Nootka Island—which, however, Spain gave over to the British. Worse for Spain was her wartime aid to the North American rebels against European colonial authority at the same time several bloody Indian and Creole revolts wracked the Spanish colonies of Peru and New Granada (Colombia). In the 1790s exiled Spanish Americans organized in Europe, looking to the day when they might return to the Spanish Main to lead a South American revolution on the model of the one in the North.

The success or failure of the new American republic would also bear on how well subsequent revolutionary movements fared, and the Americans shrewdly utilized diplomacy to quiet the fears of their British neighbors to the north and the Spaniards in Florida and west of the Mississippi River. Carefully avoiding any involvement in balance of power arrangements with the European nations, and finally creating a constitutional democracy under President George Washington, the Americans sought only to protect their frontiers, a need made more difficult by the disbanding of the wartime army, navy and marine corps. The British refused to evacuate their water-connected forts from Lake Champlain to Lake Superior because of their defenses of Canada and of their Indian allies, so that Anglo-American relations remained strained into the 1790s. Similarly, Spain tried to dispute American authority west of the Appalachians by assisting the Indians and by closing the Mississippi to American commerce in 1784. Four years later that trade was again allowed but with duties paid to the Spanish Louisiana government. In addition, Spain established a squadron of eight light galleys on the Mississippi River which from 1788 patrolled and convoyed river boats against Indian and white pirates between New Orleans, Natchez, New Madrid and St. Louis. After the Spanish built a fort on Chickasaw Bluffs on the American side of the river in 1795, a Spanish-American treaty settled their differences, though the fort was not evacuated till 1797 and the galleys continued their patrols between St. Louis and New Orleans. Lacking river and lake forces, the United States could not dislodge the British and Spanish patrols. And at sea, Yankee merchantmen no longer had the protection of the Royal Navy against the Barbary corsairs. Without a navy, the American shippers sought commercial protection by their former masters. On the whole, however, the American experiment seemed to be working.

Despite the far-reaching effects of the American Revolution, new forces were at work that began to give Great Britain even greater power abroad, enabling her to survive the tumultuous quarter century from 1790 not only as victor but as the greatest power in the world. Britain's eternal geographic isolation preserved her from invasion and the social upheaval then spreading across Europe. The United States also enjoyed such insularity, save for the British and Spanish frontiers in the wilderness. But for Britain, this physical separation enabled her to proceed with the Industrial Revolution which from the mid-1780s gave her a generation's head start over the embattled French and other continentals. Such a new economic monopoly not only made the former mercantilistic barriers seem irrelevant but helped to undermine them. For the new class of manufacturers which appeared was dedicated to the principle of increased competition and therefore free trade. These new British capitalists sought to eliminate competition with lower prices and surplus capital, making navigation acts and naval revenue patrols unnecessary. As these trends developed, Britain's friendship with her lost colonies became essential—for the Canadian Maritime Provinces needed supplies from New England, and British industry needed the American consumer. Despite their quarrels over the frontiers then, British statesmen welcomed the Americans back into the imperial economic system. The difficulty of the growing industrialism, however, was that the principle of free trade was not accepted by the government for many years, and industrial wealth was first incorporated into the mercantilism of the pre-industrial system.

New life in the British economy was attended by the creation of a virtual new Empire powerful enough to arrest the aspirations of Revolutionary France and to overshadow and then check the dramatic continental gains of imperial Russia. The new Empire centered on India, where the British East India Company built upon the political ruins of the Moslem Maratha-Mogul-Afghan-Gurkha-Iranian native wars to become the supreme power in that subcontinent. The Moslems could never unite against the Company's troops and "sepoy" native mercenaries which continued to intervene in Indian political affairs. The Company's power rested on the East Indiamen, great merchant ships which carried supplies and soldiers between Liverpool and the ports of India. In time of war these same merchantmen plus some converted frigates acted as troopships to the Orient on contract with the government. The Company also enjoyed sole trading rights with a dynamic Manchu China through the port of Canton. From the expulsion of the French and new offensives of General Cornwallis in the 1780s until 1818 the British brought all India under Company rule and strengthened imperial trade routes thence in the world wars of these years. The success of private companies in the East (and in British North America) made them less willing to surrender their skilled manpower to the navy in wartime, thus providing a stimulus for professional naval schools and for alternatives to impressment. These new realities—industrialism, the urge to free trade, company independence and power abroad, and the new Empire centered on the India trade—were difficult to appreciate and might have overwhelmed the British government had not superior leaders risen to give new and vital direction.

For Britain, the Empire and the navy, no greater person could have been appointed prime minister than the son of the late Pitt of Chatham. William Pitt (the Younger), twenty-four years old, assumed the post in December 1783 and provided dynamic leadership over the trying years ahead, generally without the interference of King George III. As an imperial leader, Pitt exhibited much practical wisdom. In 1784, he established controls over the British East India Company which guided it for over half a century. By this time, also, Britain controlled the slave trade (except for the Moslem activities around the Red Sea), and in 1787 added Sierre Leone to its African possessions. Western social attitudes were beginning to harden against slavery, however, and Pitt supported a bill to abolish slave trade. Success did not come until 1811, five years after his death, and when it did the navy assumed new duties to enforce the law. As a strategist, Pitt inherited some of the erudition of his late father, then making up by experience what he lacked in strategic theory. Realizing that lack of continental allies in the American Revolution had been a major source of Britain's weakness, Pitt in 1787–88 concluded treaties of alliance with Prussia and the Netherlands. The other weakness had been the fleet at the outbreak of war, so that Pitt kept up warship construction and maintenance levels in the 1780s as a powerful deterrent to war. That he was able to do so was due not only to a sympathetic government but to a superior group of naval officers and administrators.

The Royal Navy in the late 1780s and 1790s represented the culmination of over a century of evolving organization and tactics. Pitt himself played no small part in the affairs of the navy, supporting the dockyard reforms of the excellent Comptroller, Sir Charles Middleton, who later became Lord Barham. The senior administrator, First Lord of the Admiralty, was Admiral Lord Howe from 1783 to 1788 and afterwards Pitt's own brother, another Lord Chatham. The Board of Admiralty executed policy. Within the fleet came the greatest changes of all. The melee battle at the Saints in 1782 had ended the ninety years of tactical formalism begun at Cape La Hogue in 1692. Oddly, it was a few French officers from Tourville to Suffren and writers from Hoste to Morogues who had kept alive the aggressive melee spirit of the Dutchman de Ruyter. The perpetual tactical sterility of the British navy over these years had been due to strategic superiority and a lack of battles. The many indecisive naval actions of the American Revolution acted as catalysts for change among British officers and naval writers alike—from formalism to melee tactics. For concentrating upon part of the enemy's line by the maneuver of massing, breaking and/or doubling, superior signals were prerequisite. In these matters, the late Kempenfelt had been the foremost authority, passing his thoughts on to Howe, who made them into doctrine during his tenure as First Lord and upon again taking command of the Channel fleet in 1790. The Scottish naval writer Clerk of Eldin in 1782 and the Frenchman Vicomte de Grenier in 1787 agreed with him. Howe's new signal books gave the commanding admiral the opportunity to issue detailed tactical orders for the melee and formed the basis for the navy's first official Signal Book in 1799 and a year later Admiral Sir Home Popham's improved vocabulary signal book. The Kempenfelt-Howe tactical reforms had only to be practiced by officers of like mind for Britain's command of the sea to be assured.

The Nelson era was the result of these tactical innovations, embodied in the incredible resourcefulness of one man, Horatio Nelson. To be sure, more senior men practiced the resurrected melee tactics under the guidance of Howe, among them Hood, Sir John Jervis and Adam Duncan. But it was Nelson who exalted the personal initiative that turned the simple melee tactic of concentration into the total rout and destruction of the enemy fleet. For these attributes, displayed in his battles of 1797 to 1805, Nelson would earn the designation by naval historians as the greatest naval commander in history. A midshipman in 1770 at the age of twelve, he had displayed such unusual talents that within nine years he had risen to post captain. After wartime service in the West Indies, he returned there to enforce the Navigation acts in 1784–87, and then went into semi-retirement on half-pay because of peacetime surpluses of captains. In the 1790s he commanded a small 64 and then, as commodore, a squadron in the Mediterranean. Before and after his routine promotion to rear admiral in 1797 Nelson constantly discussed his tactics with his officers so that they too could be expected to utilize his brand of personal initiative in battle. As a result, Nelson's so-called "band of brothers" evolved to help him win his glorious victories and to spread the same gospel throughout the fleet. The name of Nelson dominates the naval wars between Britain and France from 1793 to 1815.

## RUSSIAN NAVAL WARS

Before the British naval tactical, imperial, economic and industrial revolutions, and even the French Revolution could begin to transform Western civilization, Russia continued to expand along the familiar strategic lines of border accessions on the Ottoman and Polish frontiers and by naval domination of the Baltic. And, as before the world war of 1778–83, Britain stood in a position to restore the balance of power in Europe, according to the policy of Pitt and his ministers. Pitt wished to assert British authority in the Mediterranean, but the surrender of Minorca to Spain had diminished British influence and interest in the region. Instead, when the Tunisian corsairs became active again not Britain but Venice—with its reduced navy of some half-dozen first-rates and heavy frigates plus lesser craft—warred on Tunis over 1782–92 by repeatedly bombarding the Tunisian coast. And when Russia (soon joined by Austria) provoked war with Turkey in 1787, Pitt could not convince his ministers to use the fleet to discourage the Russians. The war helped to hasten the Anglo-Prussian alliance, however, and when Sweden decided to attack Russia in the North in mid-1788 England and Prussia gave encouragement to the Swedes. The Baltic with its timber and naval stores remained vital to the British Empire, whereas the Eastern Mediterranean did not. Both regions, however, were of equal importance to Catherine's Russia, which now had to fight two wars simultaneously.

The Russian navy, at its peak in the late eighteenth century, enjoyed a strong enough Ship Fleet to flirt with the idea of a blue-water policy. Catherine in the 1780s had built 8 massive deep-draft three-deckers suitable for operations in the open ocean. In various stages of upkeep, Russia's fleet in 1787 had 54 ships of the line—48 in the Baltic facing 26 of the Swedes, 6 in the Black Sea against 22 of the Turks. The Rowing Fleet was strong enough to match the galleys of Sweden, while the Danube Flotilla augmented the galley force in the Black Sea. Catherine strengthened her naval presence in the South by instituting a naval patrol on the Caspian Sea in 1781 and constructing Black Sea naval bases at Kherson from 1778, Sevastopol from 1785 and Nikolayev from 1789. The tsarina also continued to rely heavily upon foreign officers such as the Scotsman Admiral Greig, the American veteran John Paul Jones, and the German mercenary Prince Charles Henride of Nassau-Siegen. A blue-water fleet, however, must be able to transfer part of its Baltic contingent to the Mediterranean as in the previous war with Turkey, but this was frustrated when neutral Britain and allied Holland refused to allow their merchants to supply the Russian logistics for the expedition. Furthermore, the Swedish attack tied down the Baltic fleet in the North, and each war had to be fought separately.

Left without naval reinforcements from the Baltic, the Russian forces in the Black Sea depended largely on the army and considerable genius of General Alexander Vasiliyevich Suvorov. Operations centered around the Crimea and its base of Sevastopol, to the east the Strait of Kerch into the Sea of Azov and the ports of Azov and Taganrog at the mouth of the Don River, and westward to the Liman, the lagoons at the mouths of the Dnieper (near Kherson) and the Bug (near Turkish Ochakov and Russian Kinburn and Nikolayev). Strengthening Ochakov, the Turkish fleet entered the Liman late in September 1787 and finally managed to land an amphibious force of 5000 men before Kinburn in October. Suvorov counterattacked and, ably supported by one very aggressive galley under Sub-Lieutenant Juliano Lombard, practically annihilated the expedition. The few Russian vessels at Kherson then bombarded Ochakov, while the line ships at Sevastopol sortied into an autumn gale that inflicted great damage among them. The Turks retired to Constantinople for the winter, both sides preparing to renew operations in the Liman in the spring. The Turkish commander was Kapudan Pasha, the admiral afloat, Hassan el Ghazi. The Russian commander-in-chief was the bumbling Prince Grigori Alexandrovich Potemkin, with the army under Suvorov, the Ship Fleet under Rear Admiral John Paul Jones, the Rowing Fleet under Rear Admiral Nassau-Siegen, and the naval forces at Sevastopol under Rear Admiral Count Voinovich. The actions of this war would produce several brilliant Russian commanders.

The campaign of 1788 aimed at the Russian capture of Ochakov, with the allied Austrian army holding the Danube line so that the Turks could reinforce Ochakov by sea only. On May 31 a mixed force of some 45 Turkish warships under Hassan arrived off Ochakov, confronted by a smaller but well-armed Russian fleet supporting Suvorov's drive down the Liman coast early in June. The ships skirmished sporadically until the 18th when a Turkish attack on Nassau-Siegen's galleys was met and repulsed west of the mouth of the Bug. After more inaction, the decisive action in the Liman took place June 27–29 during which the uncoordinated squadrons of Jones and Nassau-Siegen and shore batteries at Kinburn severely damaged Hassan's fleet and drove most of it from the Liman. Voinovich now sortied with 12 heavy ships from Sevastopol so that Hassan abandoned Ochakov to engage this new force. Nassau-Siegen and Jones now closed the blockade around Ochakov and on July 12 burned the last 14 galleys trapped there. Two days later Voinovich's 12 ships met Hassan's 17 of the line and 8 frigates nearby at the battle of Fidonisi. A standard line-ahead action was upset when the commander of the Russian van, Captain-Brigadier Fedor Fedorovich Ushakov, aggressively broke up the Turkish van and caused Hassan to break off the action. Voinovich and Ushakov tried to renew the action for two more days, but Hassan shied away, thus abandoning Ochakov to its fate. As the vise on Ochakov tightened, Voinovich sent out raiding squadrons which plundered the coast of Anatolia at such key ports as Sinope and Samsun; particularly successful was a foray under Captain-Lieutenant Dmitri Seniavin. Meanwhile, quarrels between Nassau-Siegen and Jones led to the dismissal of the latter and the transfer of the former to the Baltic to command the galleys there. Neither man was indispensable to the siege of Ochakov, which the Russian army finally assaulted and took in December.

In 1789, while one of the last diplomatic maneuvers of the French monarchy included the sale of heavy gunboats to Turkey, the Austro-Russian armies launched offensives westward from the Bug toward the Dniester and Danube river basins. The initial operations under Potemkin were generally unsuccessful, but in August Suvorov took charge and forced the Turks back across the Danube. The Russian left flank now fixed on the coast at Ochakov and could not move because reinforcements were not forthcoming from the Baltic to give them numerical superiority over the Turks. In addition, the forces of Vice Admiral Voinovich and Rear Admiral Ushakov were split up between Taganrog, Sevastopol and Kherson. Fortunately, the superior Turkish fleet of seventeen of the line now under Hussein Pasha contented itself with meaningless demonstrations out of the new forward base at Hadji Bey near the mouth of the Dniester. Without command of the sea, the Russians utilized classic continental techniques to harry the enemy. Privateers and raiding cruisers continued their work, and late in September Suvorov captured the Turkish base at Hadji Bey from the land side. This capture led immediately to the fall of the nearby Turkish port of Akkerman and, five years later, to the founding of Odessa on the site of Hadji Bey —giving the Russians an ice-free port in the winter. The Turkish retreat enabled Voinovich and Ushakov to concentrate the fleet in October but without taking any decisive action. Before Russia could undertake more vigorous operations in the Black Sea region, Catherine and her advisers had had to take into account shifting diplomatic relations throughout Europe.

The success of Russian arms against Turkey confirmed the fears of the maritime powers which had thrown their support behind Sweden when it began an undeclared war against Russia in June of 1788. Sweden had a formidable fleet of ships and galleys under the personal direction of King Gustavus III, who moved Admiralty headquarters from Karls-krona to the capital at Stockholm. In command afloat was the king's younger brother Karl, Duke of Södermanland. French subsidies had been mainly for the fleet, and the Ottoman government contributed to the same end. Prussia encouraged the Swedes for fear of Russian expansion, but the greatest force in preventing Russia's upsetting the balance of power in the North was Britain. Pitt encouraged the Swedes, thwarted Russia's attempts to move its fleet units out of the Baltic, and when Denmark took advantage of Sweden's preoccupation to the east to invade Sweden via Norway Pitt's ministers forced Denmark to desist. The possibility of active British naval intervention in the Baltic was very real, but short of it British officers such as Captain William Sydney Smith were detached to serve in the Swedish navy. That the Russians still had a number of British officers in their Baltic fleet was evident by their refusal to serve alongside the notorious American sailor, John Paul Jones, who had thus been originally assigned to the Black Sea. The superb Scotsman Admiral Samuel Greig retained command of the Baltic Ship Fleet, although Russia's admiralty was becoming less dependent on foreign officers.

The Russo-Swedish War of 1788–90 began with a Swedish thrust into Russian Finland, just as Admiral Greig was endeavoring to collect his force for passage to the Mediterranean. Advancing from Helsingfors into the Gulf of Finland toward St. Petersburg, Admiral Karl with 16 ships and 7 heavy frigates met Greig who had 17 ships on July 17, 1788. The two forces clashed in line-ahead at the battle of Hoglund, some 100 miles west of Kotlin Island, but stayed at long range with much maneuvering. Finally, after dark, Karl broke off the action and retired, leaving Greig in possession of the battle area but so damaged in ships and personnel that he could not pursue. Each side lost one ship. Though tactically indecisive, strategic honors belonged to Greig, who had stopped the Swedish offensive and then placed detachments off Hango Head and Porkkala to interrupt Swedish communications between Stockholm and Helsingfors. Though generally successful, in the midst of these operations in October, Greig became ill and died. In the meantime, the Danes had briefly entered the war and operated a squadron with a Russian force in the North Sea during the autumn but to no effect. Beset with a mutiny in his army and in Sweden along with the Danish attack, Gustavus ended his offensive into Finland for the winter.

No further operations could take place on land until the Swedes gained command of the sea, Gustavus' prime objective in 1789. To accomplish it, he had Karl's fleet of 25 of the line at Karlskrona and a large galley force of 150 vessels. But the Russians, though separated between Kronstadt, Revel and Copenhagen (where the Danish fleet guarded them), had 35 of the line under Admiral Vasili Chichagov and no less than 163 galleys under Vice Admiral Nassau-Siegen. In July, Chichagov left the Gulf of Finland with 20 ships and 6 frigates to unite with the force at Copenhagen, and was chased by Karl with 21 and 8 out of Karlskrona July 25–27. This running skirmish off Öland Island was but a futile attempt of Karl to bring Chichagov to action by doubling on his rear. Chichagov then united his fleet south of Karlskrona, forcing Karl into port and leaving Russia in command of the Baltic without a fight. Meanwhile, the Russians had resumed Greig's blockade at Porkkala which the Swedish galleys tried in vain to break. In mid-August, just as Chichagov was returning to the Gulf of Finland, Nassau-Siegen trapped the Swedish galleys under Count Karl Ehrensvärd at Svensksund (near Rochensalm) on the northeast coast of the Gulf. There on the 24th Nassau-Siegen with 86 rowing vessels of various types tried to outflank and destroy Ehrensvärd's 49. But he was much too sluggish and managed to destroy only 9 warships (14 transports were scuttled) and capture one gunboat and 2 hospital ships before allowing the rest of the Swedish force to break out and escape. The Russians lost 2 vessels. Still, the Swedish retirement enabled Nassau-Siegen to support Russian army operations in Finland in September. The year ended in the same stalemate.

For 1790, King Gustavus determined to dominate the seas, drive up the Gulf of Finland, liberate Finland and attack St. Petersburg by land and sea. He personally commanded a huge galley fleet of over 300 various rowing vessels, while Admiral Karl had 25 of the line and 20 frigates. His chances for success were promising, for Russia was still fighting Turkey, Austria was threatening to leave the war, and the Russian commanders had failed to use their numerical superiority decisively. Also, because of the cramped winter conditions in the iced-up harbors, the Russians had again divided up their Baltic fleets: 24 of the line at Kronstadt and 10 at Revel, 125 galleys between Kronstadt and St. Petersburg, 80 at Fredrikshamn (near Svensksund) and 42 at Viborg.

If Gustavus could remain concentrated and defeat these forces piece-meal, he could command the Gulf of Finland and thus execute his amphibious program.

Gustavus moved boldly into the Gulf in May 1790 in two separate columns. On the 13th Admiral Karl with 22 ships entered the bay at Revel to eliminate the 10 of the line there under Chichagov while Gustavus with 110 row-craft leapfrogged on to knock out the 60 Russian gunboats under Major General Peter Slisov at Fredrikshamn. A strong wind prevented Karl from massing on the individual ships of the anchored staggered line of Chichagov, so that the battle of Revel developed with the Russian gunners driving off the Swedish force as it passed down the line. Three Swedish ships were lost. But Gustavus then surprised Slisov at Frederikshamn two days later with a bombardment that claimed 26 Russian gunboats. Reinforced, Karl then bypassed his king with 23 of the line and 8 frigates to attempt the destruction of the main force of the Russian Ship Fleet at Kronstadt. The latter, 17 of the line under Vice Admiral Alexander Kruse, sortied on May 23 and eight days later was reinforced by 8 new 38-gun "rowing frigates." The two battle fleets maneuvered together off Cape Styrsudden (or Krasnala Gorka) not far from Kronstadt, joining battle June 3–4. Firing at long range with the conterminous lines reversing course, Karl and Kruse fought an indecisive duel. With the approach of Chichagov from Revel, Karl broke off the action and headed for Viborg under the cover of fog. On the 5th the Swedish ships and galleys united before Viborg, but closing the sea behind them were the ships of Kruse and Chichagov. Over the next two weeks Gustavus and Captain Sydney Smith (of the British navy) began to use the galleys to land troops before Viborg, but were alarmed by the union of the galleys of Slisov from Fredrikshamn and of Nassau-Siegen from Kronstadt with Chichagov and Kruse. The Swedish expedition now faced a crisis, and Gustavus began to lose his nerve.

Catherine the Great could now envision victory in the war, if not the annihilation of the Swedish fleet. With the blockade of his forces tightening before Viborg, King Gustavus III made a wild breakout the night of July 2–3 just as Nassau-Siegen began to attack far on the Russian right. The Swedes used fire ships to sink 2 Russian ships and managed to get half their heavy vessels free before the Russians reacted. In the flight, which lasted throughout the 3rd and 4th, the Swedes lost 11 of the line to mishap and the Russian pursuers. As Karl anchored in the roadstead at Helsingsfors, Chichagov threw a blockade around the port. The galleys under the king, however, generally survived and made their way to Svenskund, the scene of the battle the year before. Here on July 9 Nassau-Siegen attacked them, 30 light Russian sailing craft and over

100 row-craft against 150 Swedish gunboats and 40 other vessels. Stupidly ignoring the worsening weather, Nassau-Siegen pressed his attack, only to be badly routed and then struck by a counterattack the next morning. This last great galley battle in history, Second Svensksund (or Rochensalm), cost the Russians over 50 vessels and the Swedes only 4. But this event could not replace the loss of Sweden's battle strength, and Gustavus was ready to end the war. Without command of the sea, an invasion of Finland was impossible.

The stunning successes of Russia, coupled with the neutralization of France by her Revolution, led to much diplomatic maneuvering in Europe. Most bellicose was Prussia, which early in 1790 annexed parts of Poland, joined Britain and the Netherlands in support of Sweden and Turkey, and applied pressure to Austria to withdraw from its Russian alliance. Discontentment was spreading throughout the Austrian Empire, not the least an armed revolt in the Austrian Netherlands (Belgium) in the summer of 1789 which the Dutch now threatened to support. The Austrians therefore opened negotiations with Turkey and withdrew from the war late in July 1790. They then suppressed the Belgian revolt, but not without granting the insurrectionists' demands. Wary of openly antagonizing Prussia, Catherine of Russia concluded peace with Sweden in mid-August. Though dissatisfied with this settlement, return to the *status quo antebellum* with Russia in absolute naval control of the Baltic, Prussia ceased her war preparations. Russia, now without the Austrian army, restricted her objectives against Turkey and looked toward a conclusion of that war. A revolt against Turkey had broken out in Greece, hurting the Ottoman war effort, but in May the light Russian cruiser squadron in the Aegean was broken up by a Moslem force of seven vessels from Algiers. Catherine therefore made her final objective the city of Ismail, commanding the mouths of the Danube into the Black Sea, and waited until the autumn to act decisively so that the Prussian and Swedish questions could be settled.

Meanwhile, however, the Turks were not idle, trying to recover some of their losses to the Russians. Their new antagonist was Rear Admiral Ushakov, to Russian naval history what his contemporaries Suffren and Nelson were to French and British history. With a large cruiser force, Ushakov swept the coast of Anatolia, bombarding Sinope, Samsun and Anapa and destroying much Turkish shipping in May and June of 1790. The Turkish fleet of the Kapudin Pasha, 10 ships and 8 frigates plus smaller vessels, retaliated with a sortie toward the Strait of Kerch, threatening the approaches to Azov in July. Ushakov thus put to sea from Sevastopol with 16 ships, 13 privateers and several lesser craft and anchored in the strait. The Turks came up and both fleets formed lines for a long-range gunnery exchange on July 19. Through adroit maneuvering, Ushakov won the battle of Kerch Strait by stealing the weather gauge from the Turks and forcing them to flee. The Turks escaped, with Ushakov in pursuit, only because their coppered hulls gave them greater speed. The separate peaces of Austria and Sweden then took place, and the Russians launched their offensive against Ismail.

To invest Ismail, Prince Potemkin planned to isolate it by sea and take it with Suvorov's army by land. Ushakov was ordered to escort the galleys, now under Spanish-Neapolitan Brigadier Joseph de Ribas, from the Liman to the Danube, but upon arriving off the Liman Ushakov found Hussein Pasha blockading de Ribas with the Turkish fleet. Approaching in three columns on September 8, Ushakov and his captains brilliantly formed into line and opened the battle of Hadji Bey (or Tendra). Attempting to mass on the Turkish rear, the Russians outgunned and outmaneuvered their foe, who broke in confusion and again fled after a second day of battle. The Turks lost 3 of the line and over 1700 men to 25 Russian sailors killed. Late in October and November Ushakov covered the galley and amphibious operations of de Ribas against the Turkish forts and row-craft at the mouths of the Danube leading to Ismail. Pressing upstream, de Ribas' galleys and light craft destroyed over 150 Turkish vessels and closed the vise on Ismail. On December 22, Suvorov launched a combined land-river attack on Ismail using his army and 9000 men embarked on 145 vessels under de Ribas which provided covering fire. In a great slaughter, the Russians killed 26,000 Turks and captured only 9000 against less than 2000 Russian dead, many among the bombardment force. The stunning victory and capture of Ismail caused great repercussions throughout Europe in fear of the Russians, and Catherine transferred Suvorov to command the defenses of St. Petersburg.

To hasten the Ottomans to peace terms, the Russians pressed their attacks in the spring of 1791. Russian troops and galleys took several places on the Danube, destroying more light Turkish craft after which the army moved south from Ismail toward Varna. The still-intact Turkish battle fleet sortied from Constantinople to support the defense of Varna, while part of it cruised eastward to try to relieve Anapa, east of Kerch Strait, but arrived too late to prevent its capture by the Russians. Hussein Pasha anchored the main fleet just south of Cape Kaliakra, twenty-five miles northeast of Varna: 18 ships, 17 frigates and 43 other craft and covered by shore batteries. On August 11, 1791, Admiral Ushakov came up from Sevastopol with 18 ships in three columns, and seeing the Turks anchored close inshore boldly used the weather gauge to charge in between them and the shore. The Turks slipped their cables and both fleets formed into line; after Ushakov foiled a Turkish attempt to double on him, the battle of Cape Kaliakra became a formalist affair. But again it was the Turks who broke off the action at sunset and fled for Constantinople. Some skirmishes followed before the word of an armistice reached the fleets. The war was virtually over, with the Russians in command of the Black Sea.

By the end of 1791 the Russian navy was second in power only to that of the British. In the Baltic Sea, Russia had in commission 46 of the line, giving it absolute supremacy over the 16 left to the Swedish, while Denmark was little stronger than Sweden at sea. Catherine, seeing the collapse of the French subsidy to Sweden, replaced it with one of her own and in September 1791 signed a defensive alliance with Sweden. In March of that year, William Pitt tried to use the British fleet to force Catherine to abandon territorial claims on Turkey. But the British people did not support him, although Catherine demanded very little from the Turks, keeping only Ochakov and the territory between the Bug and Dniester rivers in the final treaty of January 1792. In the Black Sea, Russia, by virtue of its new shipyards and superb admirals, commanded the waters with 21 ships and heavy frigates over a slightly smaller and poorly led Ottoman navy. Her coastal frontiers secure, Catherine could now complete (with Prussia and Austria) the wanton partition and final dissolution of Poland. That she was able to do this without interference was due to the preoccupation of the other great powers with France, whose revolutionary movement began to spread beyond France in 1792.

## FRENCH REVOLUTIONARY WARS

The French Revolution created a frenzy that destroyed the old social order within France from 1789 to 1792 and thereafter threatened to do the same throughout all Europe. Initially, the French navy was isolated from and indifferent to the upheaval, but by 1790 the fervor had reached the coastal cities and was carried to the French West Indies by the incited crews. Mutinies and the collapse of discipline soon undermined and immobilized the navy, and the Republican French Assembly completed this trend in May 1791 by suppressing the officer corps. Naval officers by the hundreds emigrated abroad, most never to return and many to enter foreign navies—like the superb Marquis de Traverse, appointed to command the Russian Baltic Rowing Fleet in 1794. The Revolutionary regime turned to the merchant marine and junior officer cadres of the navy for its new commanders and during the reign of terror executed those senior officers of the old regime who had dared to remain in France—many of whom, such as Admiral d'Estaing, had sympathized with the Revolution. To compound all these difficulties, the new regime put political advisers on board each ship to insure loyalty and to practically dictate orders. The many years of professional expertise were thus lost, leaving the Brest fleet impotent and the Toulon fleet—where Royalist officers stubbornly retained control—neutralized. The Revolutionary army had less need of trained technicians (except in the artillery, which supported the new regime), and when in the spring of 1792 France declared war on Austria, Prussia and Savoy these troops swept into the enemy countries, driving those armies before them and spreading the revolutionary doctrine by conscious propaganda. In November the French conquered the Austrian Netherlands and declared Antwerp an open port, thus violating the time-honored British and Dutch agreements keeping the Scheldt closed. England's alarm was climaxed in the winter of 1793 with the execution of King Louis XVI and French declarations of war on Britain, Holland and Spain. All the allies now launched a series of offensives that drove back the French armies, the venerable Admiral Lord Howe moved into the Channel, and Admiral Sir Samuel Hood in August led an Anglo-Spanish fleet into the harbor of Toulon, where Royalist officers turned over the French Mediterranean squadron to them—30 of the line, or about half the French navy. But the Revolutionary leaders proved equal to the occasion. Beginning late in August, they instituted the *levée en masse*—national conscription—and drove back the allied invader everywhere. Republican forces even besieged Toulon from the land side and when their artillery gained the range of the harbor in December, the allied fleet departed, destroying or taking out but 15 of the 30 ships. The Revolution thus recovered, and world war again pitted France and Great Britain against one another.

The strategy adopted by the British drew upon the many lessons of previous wars, though Pitt the Younger and his principal ministers and admirals were not at first prepared to apply these lessons. Command of the sea became the first prerequisite to victory and suitable allies on the continent the second. Thus a strategy of concentration was adopted from the beginning: British fleets would isolate the French in Europe while a strong army invaded France proper. The difficulty arose, however, when the two schools of strategy divided over the emphasis in this policy. The maritimists preferred the blockade of France, the destruction of the French merchant marine and navy, and the capture of France's overseas colonies, while Austria and Prussia invaded France. The major effort would thus be spent on the fleet, with the British army defending the homeland and participating in combined amphibious operations. The continentalists, however, wanted a British expeditionary force ferried to the continent to join the allies and bring about a quick victory, although these hopes were dashed by the defeat of the Anglo-allied armies in Flanders during the autumn of 1793. As the British debated their strategy for victory, Admiral Howe had no doubts about the naval dispositions for defense. He immediately reinstituted his strategy of 1782—an open blockade of Brest so that the Channel fleet could attack French shipping and then concentrate in the Western Approaches (between Portsmouth and Ushant) if the Brest fleet should sortie for any reason, especially to invade England or to escort incoming shipping. As the war progressed, Pitt the Younger came to adopt the maritime strategic system of his late father, while his admirals generally followed the practice laid down by Howard, Monk, Anson, Kempenfelt and Howe of concentrating at the strategic center whenever danger of invasion arose. But awkward leadership, internal quarrels and lack of coordination with allies frustrated the fulfillment of this system for several years.

Working outward from this strategic center, Great Britain in 1794 was faced with the usual strategic problems in maintaining a blockade of the continent: frustrating neutral commerce to France and finding adequate bases. The Rule of 1756 was proclaimed, enabling Britain to use search for contraband to stop neutrals from trading with her enemy, although Howe's open blockade and a consistent lack of cruisers made the dictum difficult to enforce. In time, however, France would raise the cry of "freedom of the seas" and appeal to neutral shippers to arm against British arrogance as they had in 1780. Bases were a more immediate problem in 1794. In the North, Britain had signed a commercial treaty with Russia in 1793 and now all three Baltic maritime nations had squadrons at sea to protect their own convoys, with Russia promising to halt French trade in the Baltic and to provide on demand a squadron to aid Britain against France. With Holland allied, the British had few initial difficulties in the Baltic and North seas. In the South, Spain was allied, but Portugal too, both of which would deal with the Barbary corsairs. Lisbon and Gibraltar thus remained key bases. Within the Mediterranean, Sardinia was allied, and a British amphibious force took French Corsica in August. The rest of the middle sea was politically weak: northern Italy provided little defense against France, the Austrians had but two armed cutters at Trieste, Venice still managed to police the northern Adriatic, the Kingdom of the Two Sicilies (Naples) and the Knights of Malta were doubtful powers, and defeated and demoralized Ottoman Turkey loosely controlled the distant Eastern Mediterranean of Greece, Crete, Cyprus, Anatolia, Syria and Egypt. Allied Holland secured British sea lanes to India with its possessions at the Cape of Good Hope, Ceylon and the Dutch East Indies. The Dutch and Spanish West Indies were also allied, and early in the year Admiral Sir John Jervis took the French West Indian islands of Martinique, Guadeloupe and St. Lucia. However, yellow fever and a French native uprising soon forced the British to evacuate these conquests. British relations with the young United States were badly strained because of the border forts and the Rule of 1756. Sympathetic to Republican France, and also angered by Barbary piratic seizures at sea, the Americans in 1794 began building frigates and coastal fortifications. Late in the year, however, Britain signed a commercial treaty with the United States in order to avert an open break. How well Britain's policies with all these nations succeeded, of course, depended entirely upon the performance of her navy.

Tactically, the Royal Navy was primed to gain and maintain command of the sea over France. Upon taking command of the Grand Fleet in the Channel in 1793, Admiral Howe had issued new signal and tactical books advancing melee tactics. Putting to sea to wage war on French commerce, Howe was determined to utilize his new breaking maneuver on the French fleet. (His second-in-command, incidentally, was Admiral Thomas Graves, who had lost the action off the Virginia Capes.) The French, as always, preferred to avoid a general confrontation with the British fleet, but in the spring of 1794 logistic matters required a French fleet sortie from Brest. In April, a French convoy of some 130 merchantmen and 4 escorts left the United States; Howe sortied to intercept it; and the Brest fleet under Rear Admiral Louis Thomas Villaret-Joyeuse attempted to draw Howe away from the approaching convoy. The French succeeded, but paid dearly for their merchantmen. Anxious to use melee tactics, Howe closed with Villaret some 400 miles off Ushant, each fleet numbering about 26 of the line throughout the long battle. Heavy seas and French reluctance to engage on Howe's terms continually frustrated the British attempts to break the French line on May 28 and 29, though not without punishing several enemy vessels. Finally, on June 1, Howe got his chance. He brought his line down on Villaret's but encouraged as many of his captains as possible to break through the French line and engage from the lee side. Ten captains utilized the opportunity, passed through and discovered the lee gunports on the French ships still closed. The other 16 British vessels lay alongside to windward, so that Villaret was pounded from both sides. This battle of the "Glorious First of June" ended with Villaret extricating all but 7 of his ships and returning to Brest. The French convoy had meanwhile gotten through, but the French losses in warships could not be replaced, and the British now monopolized the Western Approaches. The sixty-eight-year-old Howe claimed a major victory for British tactical doctrine, but his age required that he end his exhausting sea duty by going ashore for his last three active years in the navy. He had more than compensated for his part in the loss of the American colonies.

British command of the sea spread throughout the months following the Glorious First of June, but not without difficulties. British squadrons operating from Halifax (Nova Scotia) and St. John's (Newfoundland) used American ports, especially in the Chesapeake Bay, for refuge, supply and refit, which was perfectly proper. However, these British warships then cruised out beyond the three-mile territorial limit of American waters to destroy French privateering operations north of Cape Hatteras by mid-1794. At that time, the French began outfitting privateers for operations against the Spanish Floridas and West Indies at Charleston, South Carolina, a clear French violation of American neutrality. But these operations also supported French-led Negro revolts in the British West Indies throughout 1795, causing the British squadrons at Jamaica and Antigua great difficulty. Several islands were lost and when a large amphibious expedition set out to regain them it was frustrated by contrary weather, disease and inexperienced leadership. Despite these reverses, the British blockade of France crippled the French merchant marine and navy. In June and July 1795 the British unsuccessfully attempted to land Royalists at Quiberon and skirmished with Villaret's fleet, but the latter was so inferior that it generally languished in port. The French fared little better in the Mediterranean, their smaller Toulon fleet in March and again in July indecisively engaging the larger British fleet in that region. Thus British command of the sea was generally being asserted, but without much effect on the continent, for the unaggressive commander in the Mediterranean failed to interrupt French coastal communications in Italy, while British ground forces were withdrawn from Europe.

In fact, whenever the allies won by supremacy at sea, they lost to French arms on the continent. In the summer of 1794 the French finally drove the Austrians from Belgium and occupied Antwerp, pushed up the Rhine, marched through Savoy to the Italian coast, and invaded Holland. In January 1795 the French army invested Amsterdam with its cavalry riding across the ice of the Texel to capture the entrapped Dutch fleet. Holland now went over to the French side, and in the spring of 1795 exhausted Prussia and several German principalities made separate peaces with France. While Austria stood virtually alone on the continent, Britain moved decisively to counteract the effect of the French inheritance of the Dutch Empire. Five vessels were detached from the Channel fleet to blockade the Texel, and the promised squadron from Russia was requested; twelve of the line and six frigates from Kronstadt reinforced the force of Vice Admiral Adam Duncan off the Texel in August. The next month a British expeditionary force occupied the Dutch Cape of Good Hope, while other units took Ceylon, Malacca and the Dutch West Indies. The British now extended their commerce warfare on the Dutch merchant marine, especially in the East Indies. The loss of this minor ally was not especially serious abroad, but against the reverses on the continent it contributed to the general decline of allied fortunes.

In 1796 the French ground offensives, especially that into Italy under General Napoleon Bonaparte, contributed to the restoration of the old Franco-Spanish alliance. Spain changed sides in the summer, thus forcing important strategic decisions by Britain. In America, French privateering from Charleston against Spain's possessions had already declined, so that now the French could use ports in Cuba and along the Spanish Main to attack British shipping. On the other hand, early in the year, British expeditions retook most of their lost West Indian possessions and reasserted general command over these waters, culminating in the capture of Spanish Trinidad in 1797. For Spain this would be ultimately disastrous, for the colonies were generally cut off from home rule for the duration, thus heightening colonial aspirations for independence. Spain had to open the Indies to neutral shipping, ending the 300-year-old policy of monopoly, and the chief benefactor was the United States. To offset British penetration from Canada into Spanish Louisiana, Spain's galley force on the Mississippi began operating from St. Louis as far north as Iowa country. In the Mediterranean, the Spanish declaration of war on Britain grievously hurt the allied cause. There the command had fallen to the aggressive Admiral Jervis, ably supported by Commodore Nelson, both men trying manfully to protect British shipping without an adequate base. Turkish neutrality had been violated when enemy ships often engaged in Ottoman waters, and in March 1796 a six-vessel British squadron sailed into Barbary Tunis and seized three French warships. But such audacity could not stop Napoleon's army, which conquered northern Italy and neutralized the Austrians in the Adriatic by taking the Italian port of Ancona. The French occupation of Leghorn cut off the British supply source for Corsica, where an anti-British revolt broke out, and helped convince the Two Sicilies to enforce its own neutrality by closing Naples and Palermo to British warships. In addition, Sardinia withdrew from the war. With the French and Spanish assembling warships and privateers at their numerous continental ports, Pitt and the British government decided to evacuate Corsica and quit the Mediterranean altogether. Jervis therefore retired to Lisbon in December, his ships battered and crews exhausted after long operations and damaging storms.

French naval policy after the battle of June 1, 1794, had reverted to *guerre de course* and coast defense, but the alliance of the maritime powers Holland and Spain created possibilities for bolder naval operations. The harsh lessons of inexperience at sea and the reaction to the reign of terror convinced the governing French Directory to reform the navy in the autumn of 1795. A new Republican officer corps was established and a reform-minded former Royalist lieutenant appointed Minister of Marine, Vice Admiral Jean François Truquet. As the navy revitalized, cruiser squadrons and privateers became ever more vigorous, harassing not only British shipping but neutral vessels as well. The British Channel fleet had increasing difficulty making Howe's open blockade of Brest work, especially when commanded by a lesser leader than Howe, namely Admiral Lord Bridport (formerly Alexander Hood, brother of Admiral Sir Samuel Hood, who had retired). So ineffective was this blockade that in December 1796 the French had no trouble putting to sea from Brest with an invasion force for Ireland. Only foul weather frustrated the attempt, which the French then resolved to repeat on a larger scale—with the aid of their new Spanish ally.

The attempted invasion of England in early 1797 was made under escort of the combined and superior French and Spanish fleets, while the Dutch prepared a fleet to cooperate from the north. Accordingly, the Channel fleet was strengthened with every available ship, and Jervis at Lisbon ordered to intercept the Spanish fleet sortie from Cartagena en route to Brest in February. Jervis with 15 of the line met the Spanish fleet of 27 under Vice Admiral Don José de Cordoba off Cape St. Vincent, Portugal, on February 14, while the Spanish were endeavoring to reach Cádiz with a convoy. Jervis caught Cordoba's fleet divided into two parts and raced into the gap to keep it so, concentrating his attack on the main group of 17 under Cordoba. Disorganized by this skillful and bold maneuver, the rear of the Spanish main line was then doubled by Jervis. In the midst of the furious cannonade, the Spanish flagship appeared to be trying to effect a union with its other division around the British rear, whereupon the commander of the rear, Commodore Nelson, cut off the Spanish maneuver with his own 74-gun flagship. This act was not only a violation of the strict rule of keeping station in the line but it placed him before 4 huge Spanish ships mounting 428 guns in all. But Jervis turned to support him, and in the wild melee Nelson personally led boarding parties to capture two of the Spanish men-of-war. As the Battle of Cape St. Vincent drew to a close, 2 other Spanish ships had struck their colors and surrendered, and 10 were badly damaged. Cordoba then ran into Cádiz, still with a superior force, where he was blockaded forthwith by Jervis. The union of the French and Spanish fleets was thus prevented, and no invasion could take place. Jervis became Earl of St. Vincent, Nelson was promoted, and melee tactics and personal command initiative ever more accepted.

But though Britain was asserting command of the Western Approaches, she had lost the Mediterranean altogether and in 1797 calamity struck in many places. On the continent, Napoleon's army swept deeper into Italy, conquering and ending the Venetian Republic forever, then invading Austria so successfully that the Austrians made peace in April. Without an ally left on the continent, a basic tenet of British strategy collapsed. Simultaneous with these events, disgruntled British sailors mutinied throughout the fleet, but this occurred especially among the Channel ships at Spithead and the Nore. Admiral Bridport was helpless, but Howe, St. Vincent and Duncan soon restored order by granting some reasonable concessions and by rigorous discipline. Luckily, neither the French fleet at Brest nor the Spanish at Cádiz sortied during this crisis. Neither did the Dutch, who could have greatly upset Duncan's thin blockade, as the Russian squadron remained virtually absent that year. But peace was out of the question for Britain, for in October France annexed Belgium and other conquered parts of Europe, turned over fallen Venice to Austria, and continued to plan for an invasion of England.

The so-called First Coalition against France thus collapsed, and Britain stood alone as invasion forces gathered abroad. Repelling invasions was a British specialty, however, and when the Dutch sortied from the Texel in October, the British responded with alacrity. Admiral Duncan was unaware, however, that the original plan for an actual invasion had been abandoned due to the inability of the French to mobilize the Brest fleet to join in. Duncan sighted the Dutch fleet under Admiral Jan Willem de Winter off the village of Camperdown on the Dutch coast on October 11. Both forces numbered 16 ships, but the British were larger and better armed. When de Winter sighted Duncan's approach, he tried to let his line of shallow-draft vessels fall off into shoal water. Duncan thereupon boldly ordered general chase, so that his vessels broke through the Dutch line (following Howe's tactics), came up on the lee side to halt the Dutch escape and then fought the typical Anglo-Dutch slugging match. Two separate melees ensued, ending with the capture of 9 of the Dutch line and 2 frigates by the British. Duncan kept the blockade over the Texel after the action off Camperdown, and though Napoleon amassed a large invasion army at Dunkirk he had no naval force to escort it cross-Channel. So 1797 ended with Britain in absolute command of the Atlantic, France in control of Western Europe, and Spain sharing with France the Western and Central Mediterranean. In the midst of this stalemate, of all countries the United States entered the war.

Young as she was, the United States had resumed her status as a major seaborne people which required adequate naval protection. Though politically independent of Britain, the new nation had returned to the commercial system of the British Empire. Britain was therefore careful not to seize neutral American vessels, although the search and delay procedures often frustrated Yankee skippers. Another flagrant British practice was the impressment of no fewer than 2400 American seamen into British service for the ten years from 1793. If these practices angered Americans, French effrontery enraged them, for France depended also on the American trade and resented American trade concessions to Britain. By 1797 French privateers had abandoned the use of United States ports in favor of those in the Spanish Caribbean and had begun to violate the neutrality of American shipping. Accordingly, in the spring of 1798, led by President John Adams, a keen student of British sea power, the American Congress created the Navy Department, the United States Navy and Marine Corps, and dispatched its first frigates to protect American shipping by attacking French privateers and frigates. For two years, this quasi-war between France and the United States centered on the West Indies, where American warships operated from British bases to deal a blow to French shipping. The most notable American frigate commander was Captain Thomas Truxtun, while Captain Edward Preble took a frigate to convoy merchantmen to and from the East Indies. Without a formal maritime ally in these years, Britain welcomed American cooperation.

Early in 1798 France, curiously, decided to conquer Ottoman Egypt, setting in train a succession of events that enabled Britain to create a Second Coalition on the continent. An expedition against Ottoman territory meant war with Turkey, in addition to which France in 1797 had occupied the former Venetian islands of Ionia and the western Balkan coast. Not only was Turkey aroused by this threat, but also Britain and Russia. Britain worried the French might endanger her position in India should they overcome the Ottomans, also that the absence of British warships in the Mediterranean allowed the French free and unfettered movement there. So Rear Admiral Nelson was ordered into the Mediterranean with a small force to investigate French intentions. He had great difficulty, due largely to foul weather, in even learning of the French sortie from Toulon in mid-May 1798: Vice Admiral François Paul Brueys d'Aigailliers with thirteen of the line, plus frigates and auxiliaries escorting an army of 50,000 under Bonaparte in transports from Toulon, Marseilles, Genoa, Corsica and Civitavecchia (the port of Rome). En route to Egypt, on the night of June 11–12, the force landed at and received the surrender of Malta, ending the long maritime power of that state and indirectly hastening active Russian entry into the war. Tsar Paul I was made Grand Master by several Knights of Malta in his service, and its capture by the French convinced him to launch a crusade against the French Egyptian expedition. Already, Russian naval units were operating with the British in the North Sea, so that now

Britain, Russia and Turkey allied—with open cooperation from the Two Sicilies—in the Second Coalition against Revolutionary France.

Before the new coalition could act decisively, however, Admiral Brueys landed Bonaparte in Egypt on July 1, successfully eluding Nelson, frantically searching for him. The French took Alexandria the next day, then Napoleon moved up the Nile to defeat the antiquated Mameluke Egyptian army and take Cairo on the 22nd. Brueys meanwhile anchored his fleet in a line close inshore to the shoal waters of Aboukir Bay east of Alexandria. Nelson had been reinforced to a strength of fourteen of the line which he organized into three subsquadrons in order to attack the convoy at sea—one to engage the transports, two the escort; the transports had to be destroyed as the prime target. Nelson had also begun to indoctrinate his "band of brothers" into what came to be known as the "Nelson touch." Holding councils of war with his subordinate admiral and captains, he inculcated into them his doctrine of personal initiative in order to achieve tactical concentration for a melee battle at sea. Nelson's greatest weakness was lack of frigates—his "eyes of the fleet" for locating Brueys. As always, however, these vital cruisers were needed in the protecting and attacking of commerce plus many other duties. So not until the end of July did Nelson learn of the arrival of the French in Egypt. Without delay, he steered course thence, arriving off Alexandria after noon of August 1.

The Battle of the Nile, fought that day and through the night, was one of the most stunning in the annals of naval history. Rounding Aboukir Island late in the day, Nelson ignored the waning daylight and bore down on the anchored French fleet of Brueys, planning to mass on the van and center. With the French close to the shoals, Nelson ordered his lead captain to drop anchor to seaward of the first French man-of-war, the next ship passing around his predecessor for covering fire and anchoring in front of him, with each ship to anchor thus in succession. However, the lead captain, Thomas Foley, noticed that the French had carelessly drifted away from the shoals, and he boldly steered course between the French line and the shoals—raking the lead Frenchman as he went. Four other British ships followed Foley's example, anchoring shoreward, and Nelson then led the rest of the line as originally planned—anchoring to seaward and thus doubling the French line. Superior British gunners, utilizing the carronade smasher, pounded the French vessels into submission throughout the night. Brueys himself was killed and his flagship, its magazine afire, blew up, while nine other ships, all badly damaged, surrendered. The three rear vessels managed to break out and were led back to Malta by Commodore Pierre Charles J. B. S. de Villeneuve. Nelson lost not one vessel.

Britain had at one stroke regained command of the Mediterranean, enabling the allies to immobilize the French forces at Alexandria, Malta, Corfu and Ancona. Though inferior, the French still maintained the Spanish alliance and were able to utilize some of the vessels they had captured from Venice and the Knights of Malta. But the allies had overwhelming power between Nelson's fleet, a Portuguese squadron of four ships that helped the British besiege Malta, and a large Russo-Turkish fleet under Vice Admiral Ushakov which entered the Eastern Mediterranean from Constantinople early in October. British, Russian and Turkish ships easily blockaded Bonaparte's force in Egypt, while British vessels besieged Malta, Nelson refusing to allow the Russians to join in liberating the place. Moving into the Adriatic, Ushakov with six Russian and four Turkish ships of the line in October and November captured by small landings all the Ionian Islands, save Corfu, which they besieged. Allied presence off Corfu thus interrupted French sea-borne communications between Ancona and Toulon, giving added reason for the Austrians to reenter the war against France. Also in November a British force took Minorca, thus splitting the Franco-Spanish sea track between Toulon and Cartagena. The only other offensive effort by the allies was an abortive attempt of the Neapolitans in November to attack the French in Italy via Leghorn, with Nelson in support. Instead, the French took Naples, and Nelson had to evacuate its government to Sicily.

The official coalition was formed on Christmas Eve of 1798 primarily between Britain and Russia, but including Austria, Portugal, Turkey, the Two Sicilies and the Vatican. Pitt the Younger thus again had his continental ally to concentrate against France on land while the Royal Navy ruled the seas. To check distant French enterprises, the British —with American help—policed the Caribbean and for the first time had to look to defending the European approaches to India. The East Indies Company in 1798 reorganized its "Bombay Marine" into a regular navy and joined the Royal Navy in patrolling the Red Sea-Persian Gulf region; in May 1799 a British expedition seized Perim Island in the strait of Bab el Mandeb at the entrance to the Red Sea. These measures not only countered Bonaparte's thrust into Egypt, but protected British shipping against Arab pirates and began British defenses against any Russian designs into that region. Bonaparte's whole enterprise had been wrecked, however, by Nelson, and to check a Turkish offensive against him, early in 1799 Napoleon marched up the coast into Syria, taking seaports as he went. He defeated Turkish arms everywhere, but could not overcome the Anglo-Turkish garrison at Acre, supplied by sea and supported by the guns from the squadron of Commodore Sir Sydney Smith. After a two-month siege, the French in June retreated back into Egypt. There at Aboukir on July 15 a large Turkish expedition from

Rhodes was landed under British naval escort. But in less than three weeks the French annihilated this beachhead. A second, smaller landing was made by the Turks in November, but with the same result. An earlier French naval concentration at Toulon had failed to proceed to Egypt, so that late in August Napoleon simply boarded a frigate which eluded the British fleet and returned him to France—where, curiously, he was welcomed as a victorious hero.

French fortunes in 1799 reeled before the new and powerful coalition. In the South, Austro-Russian armies under the brilliant Suvorov drove into Italy and defeated all the French forces sent against them. Admiral Ushakov's Russo-Turkish fleet finally took Corfu by amphibious operations in March, bombarded the French at Ancona and supported Suvorov's offensive into Italy. The Austrians with flotillas at Trieste and Venice also supported their army. The Adriatic was thus commanded by the allies, whose armies then overran the coast, taking Ancona finally in November. In the North, the Anglo-Russian naval blockade of Holland continued as the British determined to eliminate the Dutch fleet and place an Anglo-Russian expeditionary force on the continent. In August the force landed on the Helder peninsula, while British and Russian warships moved into the Texel and captured the eight Dutch ships of the line there. The combined army fought a spirited campaign in Holland throughout September and October but could not cooperate to get far beyond the beaches. So the force was withdrawn, a failure for the army, but a victory for the navy, for the Dutch fleet was now absorbed into the British navy and the blockade of the Texel became unnecessary. In Central Europe, Austrians, Russians, Swiss, French, Italians and Germans fought erratic campaigns that had two prime results: the dissolution of the allied coalition due to mistrust, and the appointment of Napoleon Bonaparte as First Consul and virtual dictator of France.

The withdrawal of Russia from the Second Coalition in the autumn of 1799 proved nearly fatal for Britain, for Napoleon was able to restore French fortunes and thus to eliminate allied gains on the continent. The Russians were especially irritated by the Helder fiasco and by the refusal of the British to allow them to help besiege Malta, which finally fell in September 1800. Ushakov withdrew to Sevastopol, the Turks to Constantinople, although the Ionian Islands were garrisoned by Russian troops under Ottoman sovereignty. The British still controlled the Mediterranean, and with the Austrian army succeeded in taking Genoa in June. But Napoleon had rallied France behind him, taking personal command of the army and the navy. The fleet, including the Spanish contingent, was concentrated at Brest under Vice Admiral Étienne Eustache Bruix. Along with its potential traditional threat to Britain, the French navy there was experimenting with a crude submarine invented by the American Robert Fulton; Napoleon favored the new weapon, but his admirals considered it uncivilized and fit only for pirates, so it was broken up. With the army, Napoleon crossed the Alps and crushed the Austrians at Marengo in June; further victories gave France most of Italy by the end of the year. Napoleon also succeeded in ending the quasi-war with the United States and in courting the Russians into forming an armed neutrality against Britain, made possible partly by repeated incidents when British warships tried to search those of Denmark, but mostly by the British refusal to turn over Malta to the Russians. In December the Armed Neutrality was formed between Russia, Denmark, Sweden and Prussia.

As these events unfolded, the British government made new strategic adjustments. In April 1800 the ineffective Lord Bridport was relieved as commander of the Channel fleet by the aggressive St. Vincent (formerly Jervis) who instituted a close and really effective blockade. Not only did this blockade totally immobilize Admiral Bruix's fleet, but it insured the security of British home waters and supply routes. A related matter was fresh troubles in Ireland, which led to the fall of the Pitt government in March 1801. As the continental coalition disintegrated and the threat to Britain's logistics in the Baltic grew, the British saw two opportunities to apply their superiority at sea decisively. One way was to destroy the French army stranded in Egypt, the other to coerce the Danes to abandon the coalition of the North. Vice Admiral Lord Nelson was no longer in the Mediterranean; certain open indiscretions with Lady Emma Hamilton, wife of the elderly ambassador to the Two Sicilies, had led to his recall. Command of the Egyptian expedition went to George Elphinstone, Admiral Lord Keith. Command of the Baltic foray went to Admiral Sir Hyde Parker with, however, Nelson as second-in-command. As Napoleon concluded peace with the Austrians and even obtained American Louisiana from Spain early in 1801, the two British overseas expeditions sailed.

The Egyptian affair developed into a classic amphibious operation. Admiral Keith and Lieutenant General Sir Ralph Abercromby, the two tactical commanders in the abortive Helder expedition, established their advance base at Rhodes, where the Turks supplied them with more transports and where landing rehearsals were conducted. Escorted by seven of the line and lighter bombardment vessels, the force departed Rhodes late in February 1801 and made the assault at Aboukir—the scene of Nelson's victory—on March 8. The first prerequisite, command of the sea, was assured by the absence of French warships. Then rapid ship-to-shore movement took place in three waves of flatboats and launches under the covering fire of supporting gunboats. By the end of the day, all 16,000 troops were ashore and had dislodged the light opposition. Abercromby pushed down the Aboukir peninsula, driving the French into Alexandria, although he himself was killed in the fighting. During the summer, Admiral Keith frustrated French naval attempts to reinforce their army in Egypt, which was isolated in Alexandria and Cairo. Early in the year, Britain had concluded an alliance with Persia, so that British reinforcements were brought from India up the Red Sea, marching overland to Cairo. Turkey also landed troops in April, while British and Turkish gunboats moved up the Nile to support the land operations. In July and August, the French forces in Egypt surrendered and were repatriated forthwith.

The Baltic expedition was not a landing force but a fighting fleet of 20 of the line plus lesser craft which prompted the Armed Coalition—Russia, Sweden and Denmark—to mobilize an allied fleet. Fortunately for the British, Parker and Nelson arrived off the Sound late in March before the mobilization could be completed. The Danes instead threw up an anchored line of 18 various ships in combination with the shore batteries before Copenhagen. At Nelson's request, Parker gave him 12 of the line plus frigates and bomb vessels to pass down the Danish force and reduce it. Making careful preparations, Nelson undertook this mission on April 2, 1801. No maneuvering could affect this battle, which became such a bloody cannonade that Parker ordered Nelson to break off the action. Nelson ignored the order, continued the pounding at severe cost to his own crews, and then boldly issued an ultimatum to the Danish government. The Danes, duly impressed, capitulated, having lost one ship and 12 captured. The ineffective Parker was replaced by Nelson, who then entered the Baltic in hopes of forcing an action with the Russian fleet. But the war was drawing to a close. Denmark quit the Armed Neutrality and Tsar Paul of Russia was assassinated, thus weakening Russian hostility. The Baltic powers sought peace, so that the British fleet left the Baltic late in July.

Hostilities ceased in October 1801, formally the following March. The peace was only a breathing spell as far as Napoleon was concerned, though the British stupidly disarmed, even returning Minorca to Spain and several conquests in the East Indies to the Dutch. France thus remained in control of Western Europe, Britain over the sea, and Russia in Eastern Europe. Virtually impotent by now were Austria, Spain and Ottoman Turkey; as imperial powers, Portugal and the Netherlands were finished; and Venice had ceased to exist. While Britain and France battled, however, two other powers were growing—Russia and the United States. Neither were blue-water sea powers, though Russia had enjoyed a period of considerable naval activity in Catherine's reign and the young United States had a flourishing maritime trade still within the general British economic system. The Imperial Russian Navy, directed by ministers of marine Admiral Chichagov from 1803 to 1811 and the Marquis de Traverse thereafter, relinquished its large ship navy, weakened its rowing fleet and naval infantry, and generally resumed its continental strategic stance. The United States Navy was even weaker, due to the demobilization and strategic policies of President Thomas Jefferson, beginning in 1801. Like Russia, the Americans—save for the New Englanders—were basically continental, so that Jefferson preferred the passive defenses of coastal fortifications and inshore gunboats plus frigates to protect commerce on the high seas.

In fact, Imperial Russia and the United States of America now accelerated their respective expansions that would one day bring them face-to-face in the Pacific. Despite the decline of Spain, she still dominated the Pacific and adjacent lands from California to the Philippines, but her influence was waning. The Manila trade declined; British, French and now Russian adventurers were mapping the Pacific; and her presence in North America was seriously weakened by her sale of the vast Louisiana Territory to the French in 1801. France in 1803 then resold it to the United States, which extended the borders of the United States to Spanish Texas and the Rocky Mountains, though the last two Spanish galliots on patrol did not leave the Upper Mississippi until 1804. American explorers now pressed on to the Pacific Northwest, while an American convoy had crossed the Pacific to Dutch Batavia in 1800. The Russians were no less active, with new continental expansion occurring at Persia's expense in a war which lasted from 1804 to 1811. Also a new Russian-American company tried unsuccessfully to open up trade with Japan in 1804–07. Both powers by these and similar activities had to deal with the British, since their continental and commercial expansion was global.

The British were generally sympathetic with both Russia and the United States, although they clashed in certain crucial areas. Britain needed Russian friendship for naval supplies in the Baltic and for a major continental ally if ever Napoleon was to be defeated. But Russian expansion into the Eastern Mediterranean and toward India did not please her at all. Anglo-American friendship grew from the unofficial alliance of 1798–1800 and the British only too happily supported a concerted American attack on the Barbary corsairs in 1801. Annoyed by having to pay tribute to the piratic states of Tripoli, Tunis and Algiers for the privilege of trading in the Mediterranean—a practice long accepted by Europe—the Americans sent a frigate squadron into the Mediterranean where it fought the Barbary States for four years. Finally successful, due largely to the leadership of Commodore Edward Preble, the American warships forced Tripoli and Tunis to terms in

1805. Commodore Stephen Decatur and a ten-vessel squadron then finished the job with an expedition against Algiers ten years later. In the meantime, the United States established a small permanent squadron in the middle sea. But American problems with Britain were very great: the British refused to evacuate the Upper Mississippi region; the practice of impressing American seamen continued; and, when the war with France resumed, the British blockade and search of American vessels bound for France led to several incidents and worsening relations. The strategic requirements to defeat France took precedence over all British policies with other nations.

## NAPOLEON

The resumption of the Anglo-French conflict in May 1803 taught Britain that Europe and the world would not rest until Napoleon was crushed. Total war must therefore be waged, and the British leadership and people—their patience with French perfidy spent—were equal to the challenge. Their hatred of Napoleonic France was equaled by their experience and skill in dealing with this final test of supremacy. And no new surprises accompanied the renewal of the conflict: the stakes, strategy, tactics, equipment and leaders were all the same—and anything unproven or unsuccessful was being expunged from the inventory of war. Aged and infirm King George III had ceased to influence the course of events; Pitt returned as Prime Minister in May of 1804, while St. Vincent as First Lord reformed the shipyards and was eventually replaced by the equally experienced Lord Barham. Lord Keith commanded in the Channel and Nelson in the Mediterranean, with a collection of St. Vincent-Nelsonian "brothers" commanding squadrons and ships. Britain stood alone in 1803–04 and even declared war on Spain late in 1804 after Spain allowed French ships to use Spanish ports. Searching for continental allies, the Pitt regime was not able to form a third coalition until 1805 when Russia, Austria and Sweden mobilized for war. French strategy remained basically continental, and at sea followed *guerre de course* as usual. And, true to the French habit, Napoleon planned to invade England. Equally predictable, the British utilized the same strategical and tactical tools to meet these threats. The sailing ships of the line remained the first line of defense, utilizing melee tactics in traditional fleet formations.

While waiting for continental allies to complete the strategy of concentration, the British used the fleet to protect communications, blockade those of the enemy, and try to force a decision at sea by luring the French fleet into battle. The essential requirement was keeping open the trade routes to the Empire and those of the neutral powers to Britain, especially as French privateers operated from Mauritius and Muscat in the Indian Ocean to the East and as American merchantmen attempted to trade with the French in the West. Cruiser-frigate squadrons thus operated in these vast and distant waters, while an open blockade was maintained around the Iberian peninsula. Nelson had to keep the French warships confined to Toulon and frustrate any French thrust into the Eastern Mediterranean or southern Italy. Closer to the strategic center, the Channel, however, a stringent close blockade was clamped onto Brest, Rochefort and Ferrol. This system, effective as never before, enabled all blockading squadrons—from the Mediterranean to the North Sea—to concentrate if necessary off Ushant. The only difficulty lay in keeping the blockade tight enough to strangle French and Spanish shipping and yet seemingly loose enough to tempt the combined Franco-Spanish battle fleet to put to sea. If and when this happened the British squadrons could concentrate and destroy it in one decisive battle.

Napoleon never understood this loose concentration, preferring to think in terms of land warfare that the enemy fleet was weaker because it was divided. His admirals could do nothing to dissuade him, so that he spent two years preparing for his cross-Channel invasion. The army gathered at Boulogne, while over 2000 landing barges were constructed along the French Channel coast. But British frigates kept harassing these craft so that they could not concentrate, and a fire ship attack by Sydney Smith against the vessels in the Rhine delta in October 1804 did considerable damage. By 1805, Napoleon had decided to attempt the invasion by a transatlantic scheme designed to force the British to uncover their strategic center: Vice Admiral Villeneuve would break out of Toulon, evade Nelson, picking up French and Spanish vessels at Cartagena, then pass through the Strait of Gibraltar and head westward to the Indies hoping to lure Nelson after him. With the British fleet thus divided, Villeneuve would double back to the Bay of Biscay, effecting a union with the Spanish ships at Ferrol and the main French force at Brest. The combined armada would then proceed toward Boulogne, brushing aside the separate British squadrons before Nelson could rejoin. The invasion could thus proceed, well escorted. Flying in the face of all previous lessons, Napoleon thus failed to appreciate British strategic concentration at sea, while his amphibious doctrine was virtually nil. Without absolute command of the sea—obtained by battle—an unencumbered and smooth major landing operation could never take place.

With the unfolding of the elaborate French strategic design, the British applied their strategic principles with cool certainty. In March 1805 Villeneuve took advantage of Nelson's open blockade of Toulon to break out and join up with the Spanish contingent at Cádiz before

heading west. The ships from Brest could not join him there as Lord
Barham called in his squadrons to concentrate off Ushant. Meanwhile
Nelson, after looking eastward to cover Sicily and the Levant, passed
by Gibraltar after Villeneuve in May. The Franco-Spanish fleet began
attacking the British West Indies as bait for Nelson, who was indeed
anxious about British commerce. Nelson followed, but vigorously,
knowing that the rest of the fleet was covering the Channel and blockading Brest. Though with fewer ships than Villeneuve's 23, Nelson pressed
so hard that he hoped to engage and disrupt the French operations. But
Villeneuve, sole flag survivor of the conflagration at the Nile, lost no
time in quitting the Caribbean when he learned Nelson was in hot
pursuit. In mid-July the allied force hastened eastward with Nelson
setting course for Cádiz in order to guard his Mediterranean station
and dispatching a fast brig to England with his report. The brig did
more than that; it paced Villeneuve until sure that the French were
bound not for Cádiz but some northern enterprise.

The British now tightened their strategic concentration to cover the
Channel. Barham ordered the Channel fleet under Vice Admiral Sir
William Cornwallis and the reinforced squadron off Finisterre under
Vice Admiral Sir Robert Calder to sortie in the most probable directions of Villeneuve's approach, but never really uncovering the Channel. Cornwallis relaxed his watch on Brest (an opportunity the French
forces there were not ready to exploit) to head westward, while Calder
hastened toward the Spanish port of Ferrol, where 16 allied vessels
were awaiting Villeneuve's arrival. With 14 of the line, Calder intercepted Villeneuve's 20 off Ferrol on July 22 and fought an indecisive
skirmish with them. Failing to renew the action next day, Calder thus
allowed Villeneuve to escape to nearby Vigo Bay. Calder then concentrated with Cornwallis off Ushant, where Nelson joined them after
touching at Gibraltar; the British fleet numbered 39 of the line. Napoleon's strategy had failed, and Villeneuve cruised away from the
Channel to Cádiz in August, where Calder soon blockaded him. Command of the British naval force then based at Lisbon went to Vice
Admiral Lord Nelson late in September, with Vice Admiral Cuthbert Collingwood second in command. England was saved. Without an escort,
Napoleon abandoned his plan to cross the Channel and began to redeploy
his army from Boulogne toward an invasion of Austria. He thereupon
ordered his fleet to leave Cádiz and return to the Mediterranean for
operations against Naples. Nelson at the same time encouraged such
a sortie by maintaining a loose blockade of Cádiz in the hope of luring
out Villeneuve for a decisive battle. In this, he eminently succeeded.

The epic Battle of Trafalgar finally realized Britain's ambitions. On
October 19 Villeneuve sortied from Cádiz, and Nelson let him get well

out to sea so there could be no escape. Then, two days later, Nelson closed near the entrance to the Strait of Gibraltar, off Cape Trafalgar. He formed his 27 of the line into two separate columns, under himself and Collingwood, and issued very loose melee orders saying that the order of sailing would be the order of battle and giving his captains wide discretion. In perhaps the most brilliant demonstration of melee tactics in history, Nelson planned and executed a perfect double massing and breaking of the 33-ship Franco-Spanish fleet. Advancing on parallel tracks, Nelson and Collingwood approached obliquely into the allied line. Collingwood broke through the line to sever the rear, upon which he then doubled. Nelson sailed on, threatening either to engage the van or to break through the center, so that Villeneuve in the van was helpless to initiate any action. Nelson in the *Victory* had the weather gauge and suddenly turned into the allied center, breaking the enemy line in the second place. The wind kept the French van out of action, while Nelson engulfed the center in a wild melee. In the general slaughter, Nelson received a mortal wound, but did not die before learning that Villeneuve's flagship had struck its colors along with 15 others. The French van was towed back into the battle by its own longboats, only to be repulsed with the capture of 2 of its number. Fifteen allied vessels managed to disengage and escape back to Cádiz. British command of the sea was undisputed.

Trafalgar settled the question of British naval supremacy on the oceans of the world, no matter how long the war on the continent might rage. Even should Napoleon raise another fleet, as indeed he did, the French defeat at Trafalgar had been psychologically as well as physically crushing. Nelson's relentless pursuit of Villeneuve throughout 1805 had unnerved the man, making his desperation at the final battle almost anticlimactic. Poor Villeneuve's ill-starred career was hastened to its close by Napoleon's wrath; upon being exchanged in 1806, he committed suicide. No admiral or combination of admirals and captains existed in Europe the equal of the late Nelson and his band of brothers, even if a new allied fleet could be mobilized. And Napoleon had no real sense of naval strategy for employing such a fleet. But he might yet prevail with victory on the continent; his armies crushed the Austrians at Ulm in October and the Austro-Russian army at Austerlitz two months later. Austria sued for peace, whereupon Prussia entered the war, only to be defeated by Napoleon's armies at Jena and Auerstadt in October 1806. Russia stood alone, only to meet a similar fate in 1807 at Friedland. In July 1807 the Third Coalition collapsed when Napoleon dictated peace terms in Europe, with Russia allying with France against Britain. Yet throughout these reverses on land, the Royal Navy dominated the seas.

But in 1806–07 Napoleon attempted a unique offensive upon British shipping: a paper economic blockade. Through various proclamations, the French Emperor (as he had become) created the Continental System, whereby all his subject continental allies were forbidden to trade with Britain. As a countermove, the British government (deprived of Pitt, who died early in 1806) began issuing Orders-in-Council freezing belligerent and neutral trade to France and its allies. The chief difference between the two blockades was that Britain's was enforceable, particularly with regard to countering the trade of the world's largest neutral carrier, the United States, with the continent. Similarly, French cruisers were to prevent American vessels from maritime intercourse with Britain. The chief loser in this application of legal coercion was France, for Napoleon could not supply his subject peoples with the necessary goods so that many of them turned with great zeal toward open smuggling with the British. The other loser from this new weapon was the United States; irritated and offended by the limitations placed on its profitable trade, the young republic passed self-embargo laws in 1807 and 1809 that nearly ruined its own economy. A byproduct of the economic blockades, however, was to stimulate the Industrial Revolution in the British Isles and to a lesser extent in America. Such manufactured goods Napoleon required, but he could not get at them until he broke the British blockade and negotiated an end to the American embargo. For this purpose he needed a navy.

After Trafalgar, Napoleon began to nurture plans to create a new and more powerful fleet than ever before to wrest command of the sea from Britain. This was no small undertaking, considering the shattering effect of Trafalgar and subsequent British naval dispositions on the French war effort. While Britain was still allied with Russia, her logistics to the Baltic were secure, and both navies complemented one another in the Mediterranean. Admiral Collingwood replaced the fallen Nelson in the middle sea, clamped a tight blockade on Cádiz and thus prevented the enemy naval concentration that the Battle of Trafalgar had once frustrated. In 1806 British forces occupied Messina to prevent a French descent into Sicily, while a Russian fleet under Admiral Seniavin besieged Ragusa and generally harassed the French in the Adriatic. Late in the year, war broke out between Russia and Turkey over traditional frontier issues and lasted five years. At first, the winter of 1807, the British and Russian navies attempted in vain to force the Turks to terms and renounce their friendship with France, with a British squadron before Constantinople being driven off by heavy artillery fire. Admiral Seniavin's force defeated the Turks in a naval skirmish off Mount Athos (Lemnos) in June, after which the peace settlement with France led to the recall of his fleet to the Baltic. The Russians thus abandoned the

Mediterranean, turning over the Ionian islands and Dalmatian coast to France, but continuing the desultory war with Turkey around the Danube River and adjacent Black Sea coast until the spring of 1812 when Turkey ceded more territory to Russia. Similar hostilities with Persia led to more Russian territorial acquisitions in 1813. The British retained command of the Mediterranean in 1806–07, although lacking enough cruisers to watch all enemy naval movements. The area was visited by only one far-ranging British expeditionary force that landed in Egypt in March 1807 in an abortive attempt to influence the internal politics of the apparently disintegrating Ottoman Empire.

If Napoleon's efforts in the Mediterranean in 1806–07 yielded limited gains for any new navy, he and his overseas empire suffered greatly from British naval operations. In the Western Hemisphere, a British squadron destroyed the French West Indies squadron in battle off Santo Domingo in February 1806, while the local British commanders decided to take advantage of Spanish naval impotence by forcing trade concessions in Spanish America. An expeditionary force thus occupied Buenos Aires in June 1807, only to be driven out by the colonial militia several weeks later. A similar attempt against Montevideo a year later met the same fate, leading the successful defenders to begin the first of many revolts against their ineffective Spanish rulers. In Ireland, General Sir Arthur Wellesley, later the Duke of Wellington and a veteran of several successful campaigns in India, raised an army for a projected overseas invasion of New Spain (Mexico). In the East, the British protected their trade lanes by reoccupying Dutch Capetown in January 1806 and by intensifying cruiser operations in the Indian Ocean against the French, who allied with Persia in 1807, causing a British naval squadron to enter the Persian Gulf early the next year. In fact, by this time, Napoleon was practically abandoning his overseas aspirations, instead looking to naval supremacy in European waters, where its realization was prerequisite to success abroad. Still, French privateers and cruisers carried on their *guerre de course* wherever they could elude British patrols.

After the Treaty of Tilsit in the summer of 1807 where Napoleon wrecked the Third Coalition against him, he laid secret plans for the assembling of a vast confederate fleet of his subject republics. He could draw upon the Russian Baltic fleet of 20 ships and hopefully the Danish force of 17 that seemed ready to join him. The Swedes, with 12 of the line, had briefly allied with Britain, but French victories in Prussia cost the Swedes some southern Baltic territory and made them prey to the French onslaught. At Brest, Rochefort, Cádiz, Cartagena and Toulon were remnants of the pre-Trafalgar Franco-Spanish fleets, upon which Napoleon could draw. And at Lisbon were 6 of the line belonging to neutral Portugal; arriving there also for refit in the fall were 10 of the Russian line under Seniavin en route from the Mediterranean to the Baltic. Napoleon thus resolved to unite all these vessels, over 100, to challenge British supremacy at sea. In order to bring in Portugal—and thus eliminate Britain's last official entrepôt on the continent—Napoleon planned to invade Portugal (with Spain's permission) in the autumn of 1807.

But the stubborn British leadership refused to allow such an enemy naval concentration. In August, an expedition of 25 of the line and many other lesser vessels under Admiral Lord Gambier entered the Sound in order to neutralize the Danish fleet. When diplomacy failed, a force of troops including General Wellesley was landed, and Copenhagen and the Danish fleet were isolated by land-sea blockade, then reduced into surrender by bombardment early in September. The chief strategic effect of this operation was the utter annihilation of Denmark's blue-water fleet and the siding of Sweden—though officially neutral—with Britain in countering Russia's Baltic fleet. Fifteen Danish battle-line ships were incorporated into the Royal Navy, but only four were fit enough for service; Denmark was so antagonized by this that she allied with France and began a massive construction program of rowing gunboats then in vogue among the three Baltic powers. Then, as Napoleon's troops trudged across Spain to invade Portugal, Rear Admiral Sir Sydney Smith's squadrons hastened to Lisbon in November, evacuated the Portuguese government and small fleet to its Brazilian colony, and then doubled back to blockade Admiral Seniavin's fleet which had just put in at Lisbon. Thus, although Napoleon controlled the continent, by the end of 1807 the British had neutralized all the ships destined to comprise Napoleon's projected new grand fleet. And all the while the continuous close blockade of Brest remained so effective that the French began to abandon its use as a major base. The proverbial whale and elephant had reached the same stalemate that had been so common in their previous wars.

But Napoleon was not to be deterred; on the advice of his naval minister, Admiral Denis Decrès, he decided to build a brand new navy for an offensive in the Mediterranean which eventually would spread to the Atlantic. In December 1807, therefore, Napoleon laid plans for building no fewer than 150 ships-of-the-line! Such overwhelming numbers of larger ships would compensate for inferiority of fleet commanders and crews, giving the French decided superior strength over the British fleet, which rarely numbered over 100 of the line. By focusing in the Mediterranean, Napoleon's new fleet would be secure from British naval concentrations off Ushant. Toulon remained the key base in the Mediterranean, while Pola was to be developed as the base for a new Adriatic squadron; construction took place at Genoa, Naples, Toulon and

Venice. Concurrent building of the big capital ships would take place at the Atlantic ports of Bordeaux, Rochefort, Lorient, Brest and Cherbourg, which was finally developed into a major base. The Dutch and Belgians would build at the Texel, Amsterdam, Rotterdam, Flushing and Antwerp, which was expanded to accommodate 90 ships in winter. With such a force coming off the ways over the ensuing three or four years, Napoleon believed he would be able to outmaneuver and finally defeat Britain at sea.

As Napoleon developed a new strategy in 1808, he was plagued by uncertainties about his new Russian ally. He managed to get his Rochefort squadron to Toulon where a 10-ship fleet was readied under Vice Admiral Comte Honoré Ganteaume for a descent on Sicily. But Napoleon's interest suddenly shifted to the Eastern Mediterranean and possible future offensives to offset the British in India and the Russians in the middle sea. When the Russians had left the Ionian Islands to France, Collingwood's ships and frigates had taken Corfu under siege. To protect his communications to the East, therefore, Napoleon diverted Ganteaume to relieve Corfu in February. But Collingwood quickly concentrated 15 of the line, forcing Ganteaume's hasty return to Toulon. Sicily remained under British control, but Napoleon encouraged his Russian ally to look northward and to attack Swedish Finland. Russia therefore attacked Sweden simultaneously with the Corfu cruise. The British hastened a fleet to the Baltic to support the Swedes, but the Russian army gradually overran Finland, supported by its Rowing Fleet which fought seven encounters with its Swedish counterpart near Abo. A Russian thrust into Sweden proper one year later brought on the Swedish capitulation, they ceding Finland to Russia. The Russians thus in 1809 found relative peace in the Baltic, but continued the incessant fighting with the Turks. With Russia an ever more unpredictable aggressive and untrustworthy ally, Napoleon increasingly looked to the Western Mediterranean as the basis for his offensive against Britain.

Napoleon therefore overran Portugal and in March 1808 swept into Spain, bent on bringing Cádiz, Ferrol and Lisbon into his firm strategic grasp and 28 Spanish ships of the line into his new grand navy —a major strategic blunder by the French Emperor. Instead of improving his interior communications, reducing Gibraltar from the land side and gaining naval reinforcements, Napoleon instead aroused the Spanish people to revolt. He placed his own brother on the throne, only to find one of his armies surrounded and butchered in July at Baylen. Admiral Collingwood assisted the Spanish rebel *junta*s in taking the Napoleonic ships at Cádiz and in protecting and thereby gaining use of the excellent port facilities of Minorca. The British immediately extended aid to the Spanish rebels, and the expedition in Ireland under Wellesley was diverted from its Spanish-American aims to a landing at the mouth of the Mondego River in Portugal early in August. By the end of the month this army and a popular uprising in Lisbon had brought about the capitulation of the main French army in Portugal. The terms of the surrender included the transport by the Royal Navy of the French prisoners on parole to France and the Russian naval officers with Admiral Seniavin to the Baltic, their ships interned in Britain. On the continent, therefore, the French supremacy was threatened enough for Napoleon to hasten to Spain to take personal command. And at sea, he had lost 4 French and 10 Russian ships of the line at Lisbon and the 25 Spanish ships scattered along the coast and now in British hands as an Anglo-Spanish army drove the French north back across the Ebro River nearly out of Iberia.

The Spanish uprising would eventually evolve into a fatal cancer in French imperial strategy, but the initial opportunity for the British was lost in the autumn of 1808. Napoleon had hoped to be able to feint eastward with 48 of the line and then enter the Atlantic to challenge Britain. The lost ships frustrated that plan, to be sure, but the French still had 11 of the line and 7 frigates at Toulon, while Collingwood had but 17 of the line to patrol from the Ionian Islands to Gibraltar. The British held general control of the Mediterranean, but failed to stop the fall of the isle of Capri off the Neapolitan coast in October. A British expeditionary force landed at Corunna on the Biscay coast, the fleet supporting, while Collingwood's ships and frigates supported Spanish army operations on the Mediterranean coast. But Napoleon's counter-attack in November forced the British evacuation by sea early in the new year and enabled the French to reconquer Spain. The naval blockade continued, loosely, while distant British naval command was exercised. A British expedition had journeyed to the Persian Gulf to frustrate French designs in the East, while British forces kept Western Hemisphere waters under continuous surveillance—much to the growing displeasure of the neutral Americans—and captured French Martinique and Santo Domingo in June 1809. Spain's imperial rule was irreparably undermined, as *juntas* in Spain would not cooperate with each other; neither could they control the Latin possessions where revolutionary *juntas* formed to contest colonial rule. Guerrilla warfare engulfed Spain and South America, all the direct result of Napoleon's Spanish policy.

Napoleon's preoccupation in Iberia encouraged fresh attacks on his empire in the North and South. Most importantly, Austria again declared war, invading Napoleonic Bavaria and Italy. But Napoleon rallied so thoroughly that he was able to crush the Austrians at Wagram in July 1808 and end this new threat. The settlement, however, included the cession of the Austrian Adriatic coast and vessels to France. While his army continued its successes, Napoleon's growing navy anticipated the ultimate concentration against Britain. When ten of the line escaped from Brest to Rochefort in February, the Admiralty ordered Admiral Gambier and Captain Thomas Cochrane to destroy them. Lord Cochrane led the attack—with fire ships—on these men-of-war at Aix Roads in April 1809, destroying three and damaging the rest. British naval units and amphibious forces attempted briefly to coordinate with the Austrian thrust into Italy on both coasts, but Wagram ended that. In October, however, Collingwood dispatched an expedition which painlessly occupied several Ionian islands and reduced French Corfu to impotence by blockade. The British also thrust northward hoping to eliminate Napoleon's vast naval program at Antwerp, but the expedition was frustrated by lack of decisive planning and command. The amphibious force landed on Walcheren Island in July and with naval fire support took Flushing the next month. Napoleon rushed troops to the defense, so that the British withdrew in the fall. Though a tactical blunder, the Walcheren expedition had strategic importance: the dockyards at Flushing were destroyed, and Napoleon now had to spend vast sums to fortify Antwerp, where he concentrated a huge army for fear that a large British expeditionary force would make another attempt. Instead, the year ended with the continent only blockaded, although Collingwood's vigil over Toulon led to the destruction of three French ships of the line and a convoy of eleven merchantmen off the Spanish coast in October. The rigorous blockade thus continued to cripple the French navy and economy; but it also claimed the health of many British blockaders, including that of Lord Collingwood, who died early in the new year.

The Iberian theater, Britain's only foothold on the continent, thus grew into becoming the area of its major offensive thrust. In the spring of 1809 General Wellesley again drove the French from Portugal and followed them into Spain. He had not the troops for a massive offensive, so he developed a brilliant strategy of limited warfare after the French again forced him back on the coast. Beginning in the winter of 1810, Wellesley based his operations on strong fortifications around Lisbon and Cádiz. The Spanish were besieged passively by the French at Cádiz, but Wellesley used Anglo-Portuguese forces throughout 1810 and 1811 to parry with the French army before him, he always falling back on his entrenchments in the Torres Vedras mountains. The British navy supplied the defenders of Lisbon and Cádiz while Spanish guerrillas whittled away at the French logistical bases and lines of communications. Furthermore, the withdrawal into the Torres Vedras lines had been accompanied by the burning of crops—a scorched earth policy that contributed mightily to the demoralization of the French army on the Iberian peninsula. This so-called Peninsular War, though initially limited, became so hard-fought that it began to undermine the French army as thousands of Frenchmen perished in the bloody battles and hostile environment. By August of 1812 when Wellesley, elevated to be the Duke of Wellington, took Madrid, Spain had become a major theater, and the French were losing—thanks to Wellington's strategic and tactical genius and to British command of the sea.

At sea, Napoleon still entertained grandiose schemes while the British carefully absorbed the remnants of the French overseas empire. In 1810 Napoleon planned for a descent on Sicily, but British fleet units stood in the way. He then decided instead to focus on naval construction, especially in the Mediterranean, planning to have a massive force of 104 ships of the line for a possible invasion of England via Scotland or Ireland in 1812. In the Baltic, he had allies in Russia and Denmark and in 1810 managed to place one of his own marshals on the throne of Sweden, thus bringing in the last of the Baltic powers on his side. However, the British, especially Vice Admiral Sir James Saumarez commanding in the Baltic, wisely refused to prosecute the war on Russia or Sweden, both countries being angered at Napoleon for his Continental System of blockade and anxious for British and neutral trade. So Saumarez kept the trade going while operating actively against only Denmark in order to keep open the Sound. As a result, Russia and Sweden incurred Napoleon's wrath and drifted away from his empire. In the East, the British ended the French naval presence altogether by capturing their Indian Ocean bases of Mauritius and Réunion in December 1810 and by launching a large amphibious expedition from India which overran the Dutch East Indies in the summer of 1811. British diplomacy with these belligerents was thus achieving much success, but that with the major neutral—the United States—was less successful. The stop-and-search Rule of 1756, impressment of American sailors and border incidents along the Canadian frontier led to outright though belated hostilities. Russian and American friendship with Britain might provide the final elements for a new offensive against the French despot.

But Napoleon appeared to be—and was—as formidable as ever in 1811 and 1812. His naval construction program for 150 ships of the line was progressing well, while British finances and manpower were so stretched that annual ship strength began to drop from the 1809 high of 113 and foreign and impressed (especially American) seamen provided the majority of the crews. In Napoleon's major area of buildup, the Mediterranean, French fleet preparations were impressive, especially at Toulon and Venice. The French hoped to clear the Adriatic of

British frigates by capturing the excellent port of Lissa on the Yugoslav coast, and in March 1811 a Franco-Italian fleet of six frigate-size vessels made the attempt, only to be intercepted and decisively defeated by a British squadron of three frigates and one lesser craft off Lissa. British attacks on enemy shipping in the Adriatic then increased, for the French naval threat continued to grow. Despite the apparent invincibility of the British fleet, anti-British elements in the United States could argue that Napoleon's new grand armada might soon tip the balance. Before this happened, and the French might return to North America, these people advocated a war to dislodge the British in Canada and right the injustices committed against American shipping. For these and other reasons, the United States declared war on Great Britain in June 1812. But Napoleon's patience with Russia had ended and he began raising a new army for war in Eastern Europe. He conscripted shipyard workers in Antwerp and other northern ports for service in his armies, thus curtailing naval construction there. Still, he hoped for a naval descent on England, and continued the construction in the Mediterranean. Then, only days after the opening of Anglo-American hostilities, Napoleon made his second strategic blunder (the first being his Spanish policy) by invading Russia.

Europe's opportunity to throw off the yoke of Napoleon was thus created, though everything depended on the Russian army. The British government therefore subordinated all else to supporting that force and creating a Fourth Coalition against France. Most immediate was securing the Baltic; pushing aside the small Danish navy, the British fleet there escorted the Russian fleet to England for the duration. In addition, the British kept Riga supplied by sea in the face of a French siege, and a large Anglo-Russian gunboat force attacked French logistics until the siege was lifted late in the summer. The only other major task for the Royal Navy during this crucial year in Europe was in protecting British Canada and the Atlantic commerce from the Americans. The British refrained from having to prosecute a vigorous war against their former colonies, so important had American trade become to the British economic system. A feeble American attack on their northern frontier was thus checked, but several heavily gunned American frigates defeated British vessels in single-ship duels, while American privateers preyed on British commerce. The decisive action of the year, however, was the masterly retreat of the Russian army before Napoleon, leaving a scorched earth and gutted Moscow for the hungry French and their subject allies to occupy in September. When Russia did not surrender, her army intact and unbeaten, and the winter approaching, Napoleon began his retreat from Moscow in October. The harassing Cossacks virtually escorted him from Russia, while the severe cold practically annihilated his starving army of over half a million men. Back in France by the end of the year, Napoleon was thrown upon the strategic defensive.

Britain now had the hitting element to complete her strategy of concentration against Napoleonic France. The Fourth Coalition grew around Britain and Russia to include, in 1813, Prussia, Sweden and Austria, whose armies, though initially checked by Napoleon's tactical genius and yet another army, were able to defeat him in the decisive Leipzig campaign which ended in October. Simultaneously, Wellington's Anglo-Spanish army drove the French from Spain and established their new base at Santander on the Bay of Biscay. In the Baltic, Swedish and British gunboats crushed those of Denmark, which sued for peace and ceded Norway to Sweden early in 1814. In the Mediterranean the British burden was greatly eased by the arrival from England of a Russian squadron of fifteen of the line and seven frigates. As a result, offensive operations were intensified against the Franco-Italian coast (in cooperation with the Austrian army) and many shipwrights could be released to go to Canada. The latter place being seriously threatened by the Americans, Britain now determined to prosecute an all-out war against the United States. The shipwrights began building a fleet at Kingston, Ontario, to operate on Lake Ontario, and the British squadrons at Halifax and Bermuda were ordered to blockade the American seaboard.

While the allies carried the war to the continent of Europe and France itself, the luckless Americans felt the full fury of British naval power in their own so-called War of 1812. The blockade reached from New England to New Orleans in 1813 and quickly brought a halt to most American overseas trade. A different sort of contest developed on the Great Lakes, however, a struggle which resembled that of the American Revolution there. In 1813, the British controlled the St. Lawrence River and set about building a fleet of ships of the line at Kingston to command Lake Ontario. The Americans did the same, these activities taking most of the year, although various raids were conducted over water by both sides. On Lake Erie, Captain Oliver Hazard Perry commanded a small American force of nine light vessels which defeated and captured a similar British lake force of six craft at the battle of Lake Erie in September. Perry then repaired damages and sealifted an American expeditionary force across the lake which forced the British garrison to evacuate Detroit and then surrender to its attackers after a vigorous pursuit and battle. As winter approached, the forces of the frontier were stalemated, with the Americans anxious for a final thrust to wrest Canada from the British Empire.

In 1814, however, the Napoleonic Empire collapsed and with it British fears for Canada. Wellington drove into France from the South, while the allied armies in the North finally managed to reach Paris after furious fighting; Napoleon abdicated early in April. The British now redeployed ships and veteran troops to North America. The blockade halted even the coastal shipping of the United States; a British landing force took and burned Washington, D.C., in August, but the supporting fleet was repulsed during a bombardment of Baltimore. On the lakes, however, the forces were more equal until British reinforcements from Europe settled the issue. An American army invaded Canada in July and was successful until British superiority forced its withdrawal. The Americans commanded Lake Erie, the British held Lake Ontario, and in August the British army left Montreal to invade the United States along the route of Lake Champlain, supported by a squadron of four sailing ships and twelve galleys at the Canadian end of the lake. Again, however, the Americans had improvised a lake fleet the same strength as the British force and commanded by Lieutenant Thomas Macdonough, who like most American naval officers was inspired by the Nelsonian spirit. When the British army took Plattsburg, New York, on the western shore Macdonough moved up in conjunction with a force on shore. The British squadron attacked him at anchor there on September 11, only to be defeated and captured in its entirety. The British army retired back into Canada, and the Americans remained on the defensive. The Canadian-American border was thus confirmed.

While the peace settlements settled the war in Europe and America, several anticlimactic events took place. American General Andrew Jackson, in his war against the southern Indian tribes allied to Britain, invaded Spanish Florida in November 1814 and captured Pensacola. He then went on to New Orleans, learning of a British expeditionary force forming at Jamaica. In December that force landed below New Orleans, only to be repulsed during a frontal attack on Jackson's position early in January. Several more cruiser actions took place, leading to the capture of Captain Stephen Decatur, while the tight blockade of the United States continued into 1815. These events were minuscule compared to Napoleon's return from exile to again attempt to conquer Europe. His buildup began in March and ended in June at the battle of Waterloo, where Wellington and the allies defeated him decisively. Sea power played no role in Napoleon's brief "hundred days," as events had moved too rapidly, but it did play a part in eliminating Napoleon from any future impact on Europe. British warships took him to exile at St. Helena Island in the South Atlantic and made certain he would never return. At long last, the Napoleonic wars were over.

Britain's command of the sea had finally been realized, though not without considerable worry over Napoleon's naval program. When hostilities ended in April 1814, the Royal Navy had 99 ships of the line in commission, while France had 80—24 at Toulon, 22 at Antwerp, 13 at Lorient and Rochefort, 4 at Venice, 17 scattered elsewhere and 35 under construction. The British blockade had kept them scattered, and with the elimination of this navy no power remained to challenge Britain at sea. In the Baltic Russia had 26 of the line, Sweden 13 and Denmark one; in the Mediterranean Spain's 25 had seriously deteriorated; and overseas the United States had none, although she was building 4. In frigates and privateers, however, France and the United States had excelled, causing the British considerable difficulty and heavy losses in merchant shipping. Convoys, however, had insured the integrity of sufficient British shipping to keep the British economic empire intact. Galleys, sailing gunboats and lake brigs and schooners had been decisive in such local waters as the Baltic and North American lakes, but not enough to affect British command of the blue waters. The capital ship of the line had determined command of the sea.

The Congress of Vienna in 1814–15 decided the political arrangements of continental Europe, especially through the efforts of the Austrian minister Prince Klemens von Metternich, but Britain's supremacy at sea also enabled foreign minister Viscount Castlereagh and the government of King George III to decide the fate of the surviving maritime empires. The overriding policy was to replace the revolutionary and Napoleonic regimes and to return the former monarchies. So the Bourbons returned to rule France, but the once vast overseas empire was reduced to a few insignificant islands or posts such as the French West Indies, African Senegal, Madagascar and Réunion. Spain's king was also restored, and troops were dispatched to South America to quell the revolutionaries there under Simón Bolívar, so that colonial rule was generally if temporarily reestablished by the winter of 1815–16. Insurrectionists, however, had taken Montevideo and the River Plate region, and the British refused to allow Spanish colonial intervention there, while guerrilla bands were active throughout Latin America. So the Spanish Empire was dying internally, while commercially the last Philippine-bound ship departed Acapulco in 1815, thus ending Manila's important imperial role. Portugal retained Brazil, where the exiled monarch remained, while the Netherlands, now united with Belgium, were given back the East Indies. In the Baltic, Russia reigned supreme, though Prussia got Pomerania from Sweden via Denmark. In the Mediterranean, Venice was ceded to Austria, along with five men-of-war, while the French defeat gained time for the declining Ottoman Empire. Other territorial concessions were made at the discretion of the four great powers—Britain, Russia, Prussia and Austria.

Only one naval power and empire emerged from these world wars intact and supreme, and this was Britain's. Despite the urging of the other powers, the British government refused to alter its interpretation of maritime law in wartime, keeping blockade and the Rule of 1756 (right of search) as indispensable weapons. Only the matter of impressment was conceded to the United States, which Britain hoped to reintegrate into her economic system. With its powerful navy, the British Empire was now linked together by new territorial concessions, notably Capetown, Malta and Mauritius, giving it enhanced control of the sea lanes between Europe, the Middle East and India. The only sprawling empires still growing were continental, those of Russia and the United States. To offset Russian expansion eastward and to check Arab piracy, British naval units patrolled the Persian Gulf. To check American ambitions into the Oregon country, occasional British warships had begun to call in the area of Vancouver Island. Neither of these nations desired command of the sea, however, and Britannia could rest confident in the knowledge that the nearly continuous sea wars of over half a century had finally ended—and decidedly in her favor.

# BOOK FIVE

## Pax Britannica

*. . . industrial civilization . . . [tended] to underrate the significance of military strength as the basic framework that alone enabled it to attain its present pre-eminence. [This] development . . . was furthered by the peculiar nature of the deterrent force that throughout the nineteenth century did most to maintain the peaceful atmosphere in which capitalism could flourish. This was the British Navy, whose influence was exerted not so much by the actual exercise of its power as by its mere existence. Growing up under the shield of the silent presence of sea power, . . . the new industrial culture was geared to peace, rather than to war, in a way that the older civilizations had never been.*

—HERBERT ROSINSKI

Just as the ordered world of the eighteenth century underwent monumental upheaval before the old order was restored, so too did the nineteenth century begin in the guise of tranquillity and peaceful intercourse between nations, only to be dramatically transformed by new historical forces already in motion by 1815. The Industrial Revolution, begun in Britain during the 1780s, spread to the continent and to North America to provide both the sources of unity and divisiveness that characterized that century. From about 1815 to 1860, free trade replaced the old mercantilism and fostered general acquiescence in Britain's lead in maritime and commercial matters. But concurrent forces of nationalism would combine with the new technological-industrial growth and lead—from the 1860s—to a return to the former pre-industrial urge to national economic self-sufficiency and concomitant trade barriers, arms races, colonial expansion and violent competition prerequisite to world war.

Despite these great changes wrought by applied science, even to weaponry, the British navy remained in undisputed command of the sea—by means of a superior number of ships, its judicious employment in support of free trade, and the staggering reputation gained from the long wars with France. The capital ships of the Royal Navy—from the sailing *Victory*s of 1815 through the steel *Dreadnought*s until 1914—commanded such respect that no nation or combination of nations dared challenge them. They were the prime, though subtle and usually invisible, deterrent to further world war. Their enormous prestige combined with other factors to sustain a new balance of power in Europe and throughout the world for one hundred years. To this era of outward stability and deceptive tranquillity historians have thus given the name *Pax Britannica*—the peace dominated by the British navy in the tradition of the navies of the fifth-century B.C. Athens, first-century A.D. Rome and fifteenth-century Venice. This peace, like all such "peaces," was actually the balancing of international tensions short of general war, though about midway during this century the balance began to deteriorate steadily.

During this transition century in which the wooden, then iron, then steel, warships of Great Britain policed the sea lanes of the world, the old political and human relationships succumbed to new forces unleashed by the industrial-technological revolution and by the American and French upheavals. The exclusiveness of oceanic peoples to monopolize wealth overseas—to explore, to trade, to colonize and to man navies—passed as the new technology enabled second-rate maritime nations to mechanize the elements of thalassocratic greatness where before skilled manpower had been the basic building block. From about mid-century, as each of these nations entered upon their industrial phases, the wealth enjoyed by the British Empire came to be shared, the British system envied, then coveted until eventually attacked. Thus as France, Germany, the United States, Russia and Japan adapted their technologies in order to imitate Britain's greatness, they came to face the same problems and responsibilities as their teacher. Indeed, though this phenomenon (particularly after 1870) sowed the seeds of general conflict, it more importantly bred a global cosmopolitanism that could only result in an at-first precarious unity of purpose among civilized peoples. If the Industrial Revolution bred competition among nations, it also continued the social trends begun in the Enlightenment—a wave of commercialism and humanitarianism that undermined the old monarchies which were based on control of land. Furthermore, all these nations so opened the non-Western world to these common problems and aspirations that no one nation or coalition would again be able to assert hegemony throughout the world.

Such a global cosmopolitanism was not anticipated, much less planned or even desired; it merely evolved from previous trends and historical accidents. Thus, the British Empire came to endorse the free trade formulas preached earlier by Adam Smith and used its naval might to insure that no other nation dared to erect trade barriers to inhibit this new formula for the accumulation of wealth and profit. Also, by this trend, Britain accepted the concept of "freedom of the seas" so long advocated by its maritime enemies into the mainstream of international law. This interpretation of international law met with such approval throughout the Western world that the era of *Pax Britannica* continued the legalism of the age of reason; nations not only endorsed Britain's new imposed maritime order, but expected it to eliminate the previous causes of war altogether. British customs upon the sea were universally accepted; the evolving admiralty courts codified maritime laws on the English model; and the system of marine insurance that had begun unobtrusively in London as Lloyd's Coffee House in 1688 came to monopolize world shipping in the nineteenth century as *Lloyd's Register of Shipping*. The legal reforms expressed an abhorrence of such activities upon the sea as piracy, the slave trade and smuggling, and even raised questions about the continuing efficacy of the legalized wartime practices of blockade and privateering. As a *Zeitgeist* of humanitarian reform developed against the excesses of industrial cities in England and the United States, so did it reach the ships that plied the sea. The lot of the seaman was slowly improved throughout the world and the activities of the slave traders curtailed progressively from the outlawing of that practice in 1807–14. Then when Britain outlawed slavery altogether in 1833—followed thirty years later by the United States—it was the policing warships of the Western world that had to enforce this new law.

The communications and transportation revolution, stimulated by the steamship at sea and the railroad on land, also helped to create a closer unity of spirit and cross-fertilization of ideas. Now nations with short coastlines and small fleets could afford to participate in the activities of and enjoy the benefits once monopolized by thalassocratic peoples. Britain remained the leader, of course, and her institutions—with those of the strategically insular United States—were still the most liberal, but the ideas once predominantly Anglo-American now came to be shared by other nations taking to the seas. The last unsailed waters were conquered, the barometer went to sea to give storm warnings, and the

secrets of the ocean currents themselves were revealed in the oceanographic discoveries of the Briton James Rennell, the German Alexander
von Humboldt and the American Matthew F. Maury. Early in the century the last remote regions of the Pacific were explored by such seamen
as Frenchmen Louis C. de S. de Freycinet and Dumont d'Urville and
the American Charles Wilkes, while even an Austrian frigate circumnavigated the globe on a scientific cruise in the 1850s. The Russians and
Scandinavians probed the Arctic regions, especially the Russian Ferdinand P. von Wrangel in the 1820s, and the quest for the Northeast
Passage from Atlantic to Pacific across the top of Russia was finally
achieved by the Swede Nils Nordenskiöld in 1879. The Northwest Passage across the top of North America from East to West was discovered by the Briton Robert J. L. McClure in the 1850s and first sailed
by the Norwegian Roald Amundsen in 1903–06. The voyages of particularly the British explorer James C. Ross in the 1840s opened Antarctica
to adventurers of several nations. The American Robert E. Peary
reached the North Pole in 1909 and Amundsen the South Pole in 1911.
These momentous events contributed only partly to the tremendous intellectual fervor of an age that came to be known for its intellectual
cosmopolitanism and unity even in the midst of recurrent and divisive
nationalism. Men from many lands thus helped to close the frontier of
the sea in this century—yet, still within the strategic global hegemony
governed by the *Pax Britannica*.

As the machines and ships of the West awakened the East and undeveloped regions of the world (including the tropical interiors, deserts
and mountains of South America, Africa and Asia), they were unwittingly unleashing a whole new set of historical forces that created
unprecedented problems. The colonial peoples, so exposed to Western
culture and values, notably liberal ideals, eventually came to desire a
share in the profits being gleaned in part from their own lands. The
Western nations, especially Great Britain, were unsuspectingly Western-
izing the rest of the world. As the nineteenth century ended, many of
these peoples clamored for independence from colonial rule. Such a trend
was incompatible with the neo-mercantilistic surge of this period, so
that the overseas colonial powers—again led by the British example—
had to exercise policing activities in the colonies. Naval patrols, in which
the gunboat was the capital vessel, combined with professional imperial
armies to control and keep pacified disgruntled subject natives. Closely
related to anti-pirate and anti-slaving activities, these peace-keeping
functions broadened the scope of the nineteenth-century *pax*. That the
efforts of the old Western powers did not ultimately succeed would be
borne out by the nationalistic "wars of liberation" in these regions during the mid-twentieth century.

## SHIPS AND SEAFARING

The inventions that made the industrial age revolutionary naturally revolutionized naval technology—the first major change since the sailing galleon had begun to supplant the war galley in the sixteenth century. The desire for speed and efficiency in warships had led to sleeker 74s over heavier-gunned line-of-battle ships, which saw no significant improvement in the early nineteenth century, although the swift Yankee clipper ship briefly sped up the American merchant sailers. The advent of steam and the growing abundance of coal, however, in these years led to the total abandonment of all-sail warships by the last third of the century. For efficiency and protection to augment steam propulsion, applied scientific developments in metallurgy led to the concurrent use of iron-plating for armor on wooden vessels and eventually iron hulls, then the complete steel-armored and steel-hulled battleship by 1900. Advanced technology gave these new vessels unprecedentedly powerful ordnance. Stronger metals led to such improved smoothbore muzzle-loaders as the "soda-bottle" gun of the American John A. Dahlgren in 1850 and the huge breech-loading rifled guns of the Americans Robert Parrott and J. T. Rodman and Briton Sir William Armstrong during the 1860s. The gunnery principles embodied in these weapons underlay all subsequent developments in naval gunnery. Similarly, the fundamental inventions in explosives were made in this era, from the largely unsuccessful rockets of Sir William Congreve between 1812 and 1885 to the explosive shells introduced by the Frenchman Henry J. Paixhans and the smokeless powders especially of the Swedish inventor Alfred Nobel late in the century. Evolving naval weaponry thus resulted in the all-big-gun floating fortress epitomized by HMS *Dreadnought* in 1905.

The perfection and adaptation of these weapons over an entire century bear partial witness to the reluctance of particularly the British navy in accepting new techniques which would threaten the superiority of its standing fleet. This was particularly true of devices that came to threaten warships from beneath and above the surface of the water. The naval mines or torpedoes, with the vessels for employing them, represented such a major departure from accepted modes of war at sea that the Western nations initially assumed them to be uncivilized—a naive attitude and luxury surviving from the Enlightenment that moral distinctions could be made between various devices of death and destruction. Since weapons of underwater warfare appeared to be cheap substitutes for blue-water fleets, continental naval powers such as Russia and Austria turned to their development initially. But it was the Americans, from Bushnell and Fulton to Hunley, who most advanced the submarine mine and submersible vessel, first employing them fully in their Civil War. Then, in the 1870s, the floating mine and spar torpedo were replaced by the propelled auto-motive torpedo of the Scotsman Robert Whitehead in Austrian service, while experiments went forward in several countries, notably France, leading to surface torpedo boats and genuine submarines by 1900. Scarcely less revolutionary, but slower in development, was naval weap-onry from the air. Again, several nations supported experiments in manned balloons and heavier-than-air craft, but again the Americans seemed to prevail. As early as 1862, a military observation balloon was borne aloft from a barge in Virginia waters, and after the American Wright brothers invented the airplane in 1903 all industrial nations ex-perimented in its military and naval uses. As much promise as such weapons held, however, their actual development as major elements of naval power belong to the years after 1914.

Surprisingly, with such sweeping changes in naval technology, naval tactics did not change significantly over this century. The battle line not only survived the Napoleonic wars, but the British Admiralty as early as 1816 began to return to its rigid formalism of pre-Nelson days—no doubt due largely to stagnation from a dearth of pitched battles. Lack of tactical innovation combined with the general conservatism toward new weapons in resisting change. This attitude hurt the advent of steam-driven iron warships mounting a few heavy guns up to 300-pounders which caused a serious rent in traditional fleet composition—until the line-ahead formation was abandoned altogether in the 1860s. For two brief decades, well-armored warships were designed with underwater rams for line-abreast formations, tactics dormant since the last Mediter-ranean galley battles. The rise of the all-big-gun battleship in the 1890s, however, brought about a return to the line-ahead and conservative formalism in the Royal Navy and most of its imitators. Without full-scale world wars, tactical innovations could never occur with respect to combined amphibious operations, and throughout the long anti-pirate, pacification and other limited wars of the century small units improvised their own tactics. So-called naval brigades were formed from one or more ships' companies of sailors and marines with artillery to land and fight ashore. But some of these missions became so extensive that elements of, for instance, the Russian Naval Infantry and United States Marine Corps were often merged with their respective armies, and in 1862 the British Royal Marines were divided into the Royal Marine Light Infantry and the Royal Marine Artillery, a division which lasted until 1923. Tactical doctrine for nineteenth-century navies thus lacked the innovation typical of wartime.

The revolutions in science, industry and humanitarianism did, how-ever, together stimulate sweeping naval reforms which improved the life of the seaman in these years. In the field of naval health and diet, as in strategy, Britain led the way, but in such traditional areas as naval education and custom, like tactics, the British were less innovative than younger navies. For instance the United States, Japan and Germany all established four-year naval academies before Britain followed suit with Dartmouth in 1905, the same being true of advanced naval war colleges. Similarly, the British custom of the grog ration introduced in the mid-eighteenth century despite the alcoholism it bred survived the temperance crusaders of many decades (although it was cut in half in 1850). Whereas the United States Navy, for instance, abolished grog in 1862 and all alcohol on board in 1914, the Royal Navy kept its rum concoction till as late as 1970. Most importantly, however, Britain pioneered in the improvement of living conditions at sea. Largely due to American insistence, in 1815 the British agreed to abandon impressment (officially in 1833), meaning that enlistment became wholly voluntary and then the harsh discipline used to cow impressed sailors could be relaxed, with sailors being allowed shore leave without fear of their desertion. The latter change helped raise morale and reduce the sickness caused by continual confinement on board damp wooden men-of-war. Uneducated, rugged, fun-loving swabs still had to be disciplined and kept from deserting, but the popular mood of this democratic age spelled the end of flogging. This occurred by Act of the American Congress in 1850, in practice in the British and most other navies by the 1880s, and by British law finally in 1939. Continental navies continued to have their usual manpower problems, because of demands made by their armies. For example, Frenchmen living on the coast continued to be conscripted into the French navy, while the continental navies generally tended to lag behind the Anglo-American examples in maritime reforms.

The health and diet of the British tar and thus other navies by imitation improved with the introduction of canned foods in 1814, water stored in iron tanks rather than foul wooden casks in 1815, fresh vegetables, beef and bread ten years later, along with chocolate, sugar and tea, and preserved potatoes in 1850. Salt beef and salt pork became less frequent until the former was phased out in 1906, the latter finally by 1926. The health of the sailor naturally improved, but especially after steam made voyages of shorter duration and iron replaced disease-prone wood. More of the crew served in the fresh air of the new single upper gun deck, thus recreating the healthful conditions of the open-air galleys of antiquity. Finally, the last tropical diseases of malaria and yellow fever were conquered by modern medicine between 1866 and 1900. These events, along with the appearance of contracts, pensions, popular naval journals and religious activities, all combined to raise the common seaman of most navies and merchant marines to the status of a normal human being.

But if Great Britain ruled the waves by example, she faced old and new rivals that led her statesmen in the age of Queen Victoria (who reigned from 1837 to 1901) to promote a balance of the great powers in Europe and abroad. The Concert of Europe first seemed to preclude any fears of a continental aggressor, but continental naval rivals arose first in France from the 1830s and then in the newly unified Germany from the 1890s. Abroad, however, persistent concerns were aroused from two rather new powers on other continents, Imperial Russia and the United States. Both nations were appendages of Western Europe, and the navies of both were outgrowths of the British fleet of the late eighteenth century. Russia under Catherine the Great had drawn upon her Baltic and Black sea populations to take to the blue waters, and the New England-centered American republic had created a merchant marine by 1815 second only to Britain's. But in the course of the nineteenth century the energies of both these nations turned toward overland expansion, Russia eastward across Asia and the United States westward across North America, where they posed threats to British imperial hegemony in the Middle East and India on the one hand and in Canada and the Caribbean on the other. Furthermore, by the 1860s both powers reached the Pacific and were moving steadily into the virgin markets of the untapped Orient. As Russia and the United States fought their respective frontier wars with native inhabitants and suppressed rebellions of Poles and Confederates respectively, their political and defensive orientations became largely continental. Their armies remained the senior services, which reflected pro-French attitudes from Peter the Great through Thomas Jefferson and deeply admired the achievements of Napoleon. In this sense, neither country was thalassocratic, nor did their respective cultures especially reflect a maritime-oriented vitality. To be sure, an obscure Russian naval officer named Nikolai Andreyevich Rimski-Korsakov could write the first important symphony of a Russian composer in the 1860s, and an equally unknown American ordinary seaman named Herman Melville could produce two highly acclaimed novels in the 1840s. But such men typified isolated elements of emerging societies that could hardly compare with the cultural greatness of Victorian Britain, a dynamic thalassocracy which produced such geniuses as the likes of Charles Dickens, John Stuart Mill and Charles Darwin.

Only toward the end of this period when the industrial and social revolutions and the imperial urge engulfed all Western civilization, including Russia and the United States, did the political power and intellectual greatness dominated by Britain come to be challenged, then shared, especially by Germany and France. When this happened, not perhaps coincidentally, *Pax Britannica* came to an end.

# 10
## Oceanic Policeman, 1815–1860

*The circumstance peculiar to us which determines all others is that for us not land, but sea, is the connecting link of the nation; it is for a most important part of the nation their home, and it is for all of us the great factor of our wealth, of our danger, of our advantage, and of our security.*

—MAJOR-GENERAL FREDERICK MAURICE,
British Army, 1897

## THE STRATEGY OF EMPIRE

The postwar urge to demobilize and return to the old order initially dominated Metternich's Concert of Europe, fashioned in 1815 by the victor powers Britain, Austria, Russia and Prussia. Even imperial Britain directed by Viscount Castlereagh, prime minister from 1812 to 1822, shunned the prospect of becoming policeman of the world's oceans. Just as the former monarchies were restored on the continent of Europe, so too did the British government and Admiralty reembrace the old system of economic monopoly. Castlereagh even went so far as to encourage the new Netherlands government (politically united with Belgium) to rebuild its Asia-centered empire on the basis of mercantilistic principles. But within two or three years Dutch enterprise in the Indian Ocean, Russian diplomacy in the Mediterranean and growing American maritime strength seemingly everywhere convinced the British government to take active measures to assert its commercial prestige. Internally, the rise of a new merchant-industrial class also led to rejection of the old values. A generation ahead of potential competitors on the continent, these entrepreneurs in coal, iron, cotton and steam-powered machinery wanted open competition so that they could be free to tap sources of cheap raw materials throughout the world and to undersell continental rivals. By the time of Castlereagh's passing, economic reform was inevitable.

British society embraced the principle of free trade in the early nineteenth century as readily as it had supported trade barriers one hundred years before, and with no appreciable change in its national institutions. Part of the reason was no doubt due to the vitality and flexibility of a thalassocratically influenced liberal tradition, but even this was made possible by the singular fact that Britain had remained geographically isolated and thus emerged largely unscathed by the murderous bloodshed of the world wars. Shielded by her navy, Britain had begun her industrial revolution in the 1780s which had barely paused in its phenomenal growth to take notice of Napoleon's demise. The only change was the brushing aside of the timeworn economic traditions as part of the evolving profit-system of the merchant class. Unlike the great changes on the continent, continuity prevailed in British society and culture into the new century. The same king, George III, head of state since 1760(!), even lingered on as titular leader till his death in 1820. By now, however, the crown had long since surrendered its active direction of national affairs, first to the ministries of both Pitts and then to the men who had helped defeat the French dictator before going on to direct British policy in the new age: Castlereagh, George Canning in the 1820s, and finally Viscount Palmerston, foreign secretary for most of the years 1830 to 1851 and usually prime minister from 1855 to 1865.

Economic reform then joined domestic and legal reforms to transform Britain's role but not her goal—which was, as always, prosperity. The old notion of *Mare Clausum* thus faded, to be replaced by new catchphrases: freedom of the seas (a greatly enlarged view of *Mare Liberum), laissez faire* (no governmental interference in trade practices), and free trade of imports and exports. Smuggling within the British Isles declined as these practices were adopted, although the new Coastguard's role to blockade smugglers in 1831 had great effect. Tariffs and obsolete customs acts were steadily repealed, the major one being the 410-year-old so-called Corn Laws regulating wheat, struck down in 1846. Three years later the trade barriers that had launched England into mercantilistic conflict in 1651, the Navigation acts, were abolished. And in 1854 foreign vessels were even allowed to participate in the coastal trade of Britain. Smuggling, save for such few taxed luxury items as whisky, tobacco and silk, practically disappeared, and Britain prospered. Her carrying trade dominated Europe and much of the world, although the United States crowded her for half a century. But Britain also interpreted her new free sea policy to include enforced orderly and legal commerce upon the global sea lanes, so that the Royal Navy had to insure that no second-rate naval power dared to create a *Mare Clausum* in any sea and that pirates and slave traders be utterly suppressed.

The navy, now in peacetime, was hardly up to these tasks due to the global requirements for many ships. Traditionally, Britain had policed the Atlantic and much of the Mediterranean, and its fleet was able to help maintain the European balance of power by its continued role in these waters. But beyond the periphery of Europe, heavy demands were made upon the Admiralty. The fear of power plays by the Dutch in Southeast Asia, the United States in Latin America, the Russians in the Middle East and even the French in North Africa meant that appearances of British naval supremacy in these waters had to be maintained. Worse, however, were the non-Western peoples of Asia, Africa and South America who had little use for the legalism of the West and to whom piracy (occasionally still disguised as privateering) and slave trading remained accepted ways of life.

From 1815 to about 1850 the British navy was able to police most troubled waters by means of its wooden sail navy. Steam engines were considered unreliable for large warships, while the paddle wheels were exposed to enemy fire, so the old triple-deckers remained the backbone of the fleet until the 1850s. Lesser vessels adopted steam, however, and after the Swede John Ericsson and the American Robert F. Stockton introduced the underwater screw propeller to replace the paddle wheel, in 1845 the British began converting and building capital ships to steam power. Similar reluctance attended the use of iron for warships, but the work of the Frenchman Stanislas C. H. L. Dupuy de Lôme in the 1840s became the harbinger for dramatic changes in the rise of iron in steam vessels late in the 1850s. Line-of-battle ships, however, best served the role of deterrence in the balance of the great powers. For the demanding work of policing distant and inshore waters, the British and other navies relied on lesser vessels. Frigates remained important workhorses, first as the large wooden sailers, then in the 1840s as paddle-wheel steam-frigates, and finally as screw-frigates thereafter. The development of sailing corvettes, sloops and hermaphrodite brigs (brigantines) and then steam-sloops followed the same general evolution. The same is true of the gunboats, although the Russians and Danes were still building excellent rowing-sail gunboats and gun sloops in the early 1850s when steam-powered gun-vessels appeared. The advent of the Paixhans explosive shell gun by 1839 raised major questions about the use of iron for armor, but iron plate was not introduced until the mid-1850s. It must be realized that when steam engines were first developed, they were for auxiliary power only. With coal difficult to obtain and store, not to mention its great expense, and often with the early engines unreliable, steam warships through the 1850s actually depended primarily upon sail power for cruising; the steam was for maneuverability in battle or in contrary tides and weather.

General peace prevailed in Europe and most of the world during the early *Pax Britannica* from 1815 to the early 1850s, so that the most convenient way of examining Britain's role as oceanic policeman is by tracing the presence of its navy in each major region of the globe and in this order: the Baltic, the North Sea, the Mediterranean and North Africa, the Middle East, the African sea route to India, the Orient and, considered separately, the Western Hemisphere.

The Baltic Sea had so thoroughly become a Russian lake that the Scandinavian nations (including an independent Norway, but until 1905 ruled with Sweden by the same king) were reduced to the status of minor naval powers. By the 1840s Russia had over two dozen line-of-battle ships, Sweden but ten and Denmark barely a half-dozen. The British navy was ready to intervene against any aggressive move by Russia, but Russian interests were more oriented toward the Middle East. Prussia, however, growing ever stronger in the nineteenth century, instigated a revolt of the Schleswig-Holstein duchies from Denmark in March of 1848, and Britain and Russia immediately threatened to intervene on the side of the Danes. A shaky truce was signed in August before any real naval operations took place, although the following April a large Danish ship of the line was so badly damaged by shellfire from a shore battery during a landing at Eckernförde near Kiel that it had to be scuttled upon capture—the first practical demonstration of the effectiveness of the Paixhans-type exploding shell. In 1850 a treaty restored the duchies to Denmark, whose only real source of maritime power—beyond her small fishing fleet, carrying trade and a few islands in the West Indies—was control of the vital Sound, for which she had so often fought over the centuries. But even that was compromised by the naval power of Britain and Russia, who could control the Sound with impunity. Finally, in 1855, the United States refused to pay the ancient Sound dues, whereupon an international agreement in 1857 simply had them abolished.

In the North Sea the continuing rise of Prussia and the relative decline of the Netherlands enabled Britain to control these crucial waters with little effort. Prussia had no navy worthy of the name though her army was growing importantly through the new general staff system, the writings of Karl von Clausewitz, and the new network of military railroads that would later bear on British sea power. The Dutch had always been formidable rivals upon the sea, and even without a battle fleet they still successfully competed with British trade in the Far East. Internally, the Netherlands were vulnerable, however, for in 1830 the fifteen-year-old union between Holland and Belgium was shattered by the latter's secession, a move condoned by a subsequent meeting of the great powers in London. As a result, the Protestant Dutch invaded Belgium in August 1831, attempting to coerce it back into the union. The British fleet sailed into the Scheldt to blockade the Dutch garrison at the fortress of Antwerp, while the British government declared an embargo of Dutch shipping throughout the world. A French army plus naval units also intervened in Belgium to repulse the Dutch attack. By the end of 1832 Anglo-French land and naval forces had taken Antwerp, leading to an armistice and the eventual (in 1839) Dutch recognition of Belgian independence. Throughout the century, however, Britain never had to worry seriously about the occupation of the Low Countries—the pistol aimed at England—by an aggressor.

## MEDITERRANEAN BATTLEGROUND

The traditional continental powers of Central and Southern Europe provided no threat to the peace of Metternich, although all suffered internally from the difficulties of the Restoration; liberals at home and in various colonies resisted the return of the despotic monarchs. Britain's prime concerns over these difficulties were insuring that neighboring nations did not intervene in such civil strife to upset the European balance of power and that the restored governments not be usurped. These goals were not easy to achieve, given the growing spirits of liberalism and nationalism exemplified by the Belgian struggle for independence. In the 1820s these forces erupted in wars within the three peninsulas of the Mediterranean—the Iberian, Italian and Greek. As this sea lane had become vital to European political stability and to the British land-sea route to India via the Suez Isthmus and the Red Sea, the British were obliged to intervene. In so doing, Britain aroused the monarchies of France, Austria and Russia, thus undermining the Quadruple Alliance that had been built upon the defeat of Napoleon. Small wars resulted, and the liberal spirit spread in revolt to several of the great powers, especially in 1848. The result was the growth of the liberal democratic influence in all the Western governments. Yet, Britain's role upon the seas did not diminish.

The westernmost Mediterranean peninsula of the three torn by strife in these years involved Spain and Portugal. Civil wars in both countries required the Quadruple Alliance to send the French army into Spain in 1823, while the British navy landed an expeditionary force in Portugal in 1827 to maintain political order. The latter force proved inadequate, for the pretender to the Portuguese throne, Miguel, raised a fleet against the ruling constitutional government and drove out Queen Maria in 1828.

The Portuguese crown had divided its political rule between the home-land and Brazil since the Restoration, however, so that it now drew on its South American resources as well as Anglo-French volunteers first to retake the Azores. When Miguel's fleet attempted to recover the islands, it was defeated in August at Praia Bay. As the Miguelite Wars dragged on, Britain sold a naval squadron to Maria, and in July 1831 the French seized Miguel's fleet in the Tagus. One year later the crown's expedition from England landed in Portugal. Its naval commander, Sir Charles Napier of the British navy, in July 1833 defeated a Miguelite naval force off Cape St. Vincent and moved on to take Lisbon. The Quadruple Alliance then isolated Miguel, bringing about his defeat and surrender the next spring. These civil wars, which continued to wrack Spain through the 1830s and the early 1840s, were all related to the final demise of her American-centered empire. Both Spain and Portugal had degenerated into minor naval nations.

Austria, by the terms of the 1815 agreements, dominated the Italian peninsula and occupied new territory which included the Adriatic Coast from Venice to Dalmatia. This vast coastline thus encouraged Austria again to entertain maritime aspirations. Trade was increased with the Levant from the 1820s, and the small Austrian navy checked Barbary attacks by bombarding the Atlantic coast of Morocco in 1829. The fleet, based at Venice and manned largely by Italians, grew in size and operated with the great powers in the Middle East until, by the end of the 1830s, it had become a major force in the Eastern Mediterranean. It reached its greatest peak under the command of its young but veteran commander, Archduke Frederick, from his appointment in 1844 till his untimely death three years later. Austria, however, was torn by revolts in Italy from 1820, culminating in the general European strike of 1848. In March of that year, Sardinia declared war on Austria, and Venice proclaimed its independence, both states joining their small naval forces to confront the Austrian vessels before Pola and Trieste. The tiny fleets avoided an engagement, however, and Austrian arms gradually tri-umphed on land, aided by a French intervention in 1849. Simultane-ously, the Hungarians revolted against Austria, only to be put down with the help of the Russian army. That year the strengthened Austrian navy was placed under the command of a ruthless Danish admiral who resigned after two years. In 1852 the fleet of fourteen ships now largely manned by Germans cruised the Mediterranean under the new twenty-year-old Archduke Ferdinand Max, an excellent admiral who became commander-in-chief in 1854. But Austrian dominance over the Italian states, and British support of this situation, could never last, thanks to the incessant nationalistic activities of such Italian patriots as Garibaldi and Cavour.

The peninsula of Greece, long a Turkish preserve, erupted in revolt in 1821 and gradually involved the powers. Britain and France at first avoided intervening, but the early successes of the Greeks made the war a democratic *cause célèbre* in Europe, and the fear of Russian intervention added larger strategic dimensions to the struggle. Russia, excluded by Napoleon from the Mediterranean, had allowed Greek vessels to register under the Russian flag, and the Russians were eager to weaken Ottoman Turkey and gain a warm-water outlet from the Black Sea. About the only great power to act early in the war was Austria, which based its fleet at Smyrna for the duration, but as a neutral.

The Greeks quickly drove Turkish forces from most of the Morea and raised a formidable collection of armed vessels; in so doing, they crippled the Turkish fleet, which had relied heavily on Greek seamen. But many of the so-called patriots outfitted their ships as privateers only to degenerate quickly into pirates. The indiscriminate attacks of such vessels upon Western merchantmen increased great power apprehension over the conflict, accounting for the Austrian naval presence at Smyrna. Nevertheless, the Greek revolutionary government established two regular war fleets in the summer of 1821 which skirmished indecisively with Turkish warships, often using the old technique of fire ship attack. In March 1822 the belligerent fleets fought a long indecisive gunnery duel off Missolonghi; in April a Turk landing force massacred much of the population of Chios; and in June a Greek fire ship attack off Chios destroyed the Turk flagship, killing its admiral. The leader of the latter exploit, Konstantin Kanaris, repeated his feat in November at Tenedos, destroying another flagship with its admiral. Sharp skirmishing at sea and coastal raids by both sides continued throughout 1823, and divisiveness within the Greek movement led to a stalemate.

The War of Greek Independence assumed new dimensions in 1824 when the Sultan of Turkey called upon his powerful vassal, Mohammed Ali of Egypt, to suppress the Greeks. This ruthless despot had modernized his army and navy to the point of superiority over the main Ottoman armed forces; his expansionist policies in North Africa had led the Sultan to award him Crete in return for help in the Morea. In June, 45 Egyptian sail and a landing force made a devastating hit-and-run raid on the Greek base at Kaxos near Crete, a Turkish force of 82 craft doing the same at the base of Psara near Chios in July. The Moslem fleets attacked other islands, but were often obliged to draw away upon the approach of the Greek fleet, largely because of their fear of Kanaris and his relentless fire ships, which sank a 54-gun Ottoman frigate in a skirmish off Samos in August. The Turko-Egyptian fleet of some 130 warships covered the crossing of Mohammed Ali's army in 150 transports and skirmished with the Greek fleet of 75 war vessels, but again never really closing out of respect for the fire ships. The latter thereby repeatedly frustrated Moslem attempts to cross the Aegean to the mainland of Greece. The Egyptian commander and son of Mohammed Ali, Ibrahim Pasha, embarked part of his army in warships and made the crossing while the Greek fleet had retired for the winter. More Egyptian troops from Crete landed in Greece early in 1825, and Ibrahim established a loose blockade, though at the sufferance of the intrepid Kanaris with his fire ships. The land-sea blockade of the Greeks at Missolonghi was lifted late in July when the fire ship-led Greek fleet drove off the Moslem ships. But the Egyptians under Ibrahim were overrunning the Morea, and though the Greek navy was keeping supplies running through the Ottoman blockade to Missolonghi, Ibrahim finally assaulted and took the fortress in April 1826. Now the Turkish fleet under Khosrev Pasha attempted to take Samos, but was attacked at its main base of Mitylene by the Greek fleet under Admiral Andreas Miaoulis, September 10–11. The hard-fought action was a draw, but by now the general situation of the Greeks was dire, while Ibrahim was generally triumphant. Against these reverses, public opinion in the Western world clamored for Greek independence.

The great powers decided to act. In 1826–27 Great Britain, Russia and France agreed to isolate Ibrahim in Greece, while British officers took command of the Greek forces, with Admiral Lord Cochrane leading the navy. The Austrians remained neutral, though their ships acted as mediators and chastised Greek pirates. Greek republican fortunes continued to wane, however, and Ibrahim sent another large expeditionary force under Tahir Pasha from Alexandria to Navarino late in the summer of 1827, hoping ultimately to capture the key Greek island naval base of Hydra. But now an Anglo-French fleet under Admirals Sir Edward Codrington and Henri G. de Rigny had arrived to blockade Tahir Pasha's fleet at Navarino, while Cochrane's reinforced Greek fleet moved into the area. Early in October the allies were also joined by a Russian squadron. Tensions mounted until finally, on October 20, the allied force of 20 men-of-war, each mounting 28 to 84 guns, sailed into the Bay of Navarino and were given battle by the similar-sized Ottoman force; many smaller vessels took part on both sides. The allied guns crushed their foe, who burned what damaged ships were not sunk in the fight. The shore batteries were also silenced. The Turkish fleet had been virtually destroyed in one stroke, the remnants being allowed to return to Constantinople and Alexandria, while the British and Russian vessels retired to Malta, the French to Smyrna. While the powers then pondered their next moves, the British and French wiped out a Greek pirate base on the west end of Crete early in 1828 and tightened a blockade around the Egyptian-held ports of Navarino and Modon.

The independence of Greece was now assured, despite the fact that Turkey lashed back by initiating open war with Russia in April 1828. In May Admiral Codrington declared a general blockade against all Moslem forces in Greece and initiated direct negotiations with Mohammed Ali for the evacuation of his forces, which occurred between August and October. The French landed an expeditionary force in Greece which overran several Ottoman positions in October, while the Russian squadron in these waters remained in a nonbelligerent status. Then the Greek navy joined in the seizure of Lepanto and Missolonghi in May 1829. Meanwhile, the Russo-Turkish War had focused on the Black Sea, where the Russian Rowing Fleet supported the army's advance across the Danube to take Varna in the west and the thrust eastward which captured Anapa during 1828. Later that year, a second Russian squadron arrived at British Malta from the Baltic, then moved up the Aegean to Tenedos to blockade Constantinople from the south. In 1829, the Russian army and navy pressed south from Varna, the fleet taking Sizeboli for raids on the north coast of Turkey. A makeshift Ottoman fleet failed to check these operations, and in August the Russian ships bombarded, assaulted and took Midia, only fifty miles from Constantinople, while the army took Adrianople. In September, the Turks sued for peace, giving up to Russia the delta of the Danube and the eastern shore of the Black Sea from Anapa southward, also granting Russian merchant ships passage through the Bosporus. The Ottoman Empire also lost Greece, which was declared an independent kingdom by treaty in 1832.

The events of the 1820s had reaffirmed the status of the Mediterranean as the prime area of strategic importance in Europe, a predominance dating from the post-Trafalgar warfare against Napoleon. The great powers, Britain, Russia, France and Austria, all had economic and thus political interests there and supported maritime stability in the face of incessant depredations of the Barbary corsairs of Morocco, Algeria and Tunis. Even the young United States continued its naval presence in the region after forcing Algeria to terms during a brief war in 1815. The American squadron began using Port Mahon in Spanish Minorca as a makeshift base that year, until Mahon became a permanent base facility supporting the seven-ship squadron in 1825. These ships paid annual visits to each Barbary port from 1816, with special pressure on Algiers again in 1822, protecting American commerce which pressed eastward into the middle sea until, in 1830, the United States signed a formal trade agreement with Ottoman Turkey. The American squadron continued its presence, save for its absence during the Mexican War, after which it based at Spezia in the Gulf of Genoa. The British, however, held the Mediterranean balance of power, and from their bases of Gibraltar, Malta and the Ionian Islands they policed the Mediterranean. In 1816 an Anglo-Dutch force bombarded Algiers, a British blockade and threat of bombardment again brought Algeria to terms in 1824, and a blockade of Tangier four years later achieved the same result from Tunis. The lesser powers of Spain, the Two Sicilies and Sardinia relied largely on British protection, but France with its own southern ports and the island of Corsica began to use its own initiative, blockading Algiers from 1827 to 1829.

The French naval recovery from the defeat of 1815 became evident gradually with the French naval actions in Holland and Greece, culminating in 1830 with a French overseas expedition which easily conquered Algeria. The French fleet had only slowly begun to be rebuilt by June and July when this event occurred, simultaneous with a revolution which placed Louis Philippe on the throne of France. For Europe, the French conquest of Algeria meant the end of the main source of Barbary piracy; the French heralded their military colonization of this North African state as the beginning of *la Paix Française*. For Britain, however, the event marked the beginning of a new French overseas empire which now stood athwart British communications to India. Furthermore, the pacification of Algeria with large troop reinforcements was accompanied by French pressure throughout the Mediterranean littoral, leading directly to Anglo-French antagonism.

The advent of steam in the English Channel eventually became the leading source of British fears regarding France, though the real geographic confrontation of these two powers occurred in the Mediterranean. The concentration of the new French fleet at Toulon and the annexation of Algiers in the 1830s disturbed Palmerston and the British because of what the French might ultimately do—which was to make a power play in the Moslem world. In fact, the French lost no time in supporting Mohammed Ali in his revolt against Ottoman Turkey; should he overthrow his master, France might then block British trade across Suez and the Red Sea to India or develop an alternate route overland to the East via the Euphrates River and the Persian Gulf. Britain intervened in 1840 to halt the Egyptian revolt, however, and the French enterprise in the Middle East did not materialize. In the Western Mediterranean, Britain suspected French designs on Spain and downright resented a French incursion into Morocco and naval bombardments of Tangier and Mogador in 1844 as part of the pacification of Algeria. The same year, the commander of French naval operations in Morocco and son of the king, Admiral the Prince of Joinville, wrote a pamphlet describing how easily the new steam vessels of the French navy could mount a cross-Channel invasion of England. This pamphlet, the Moroccan affair and the French annexation of Tahiti in the South Pacific created an invasion scare in England and brought the two countries to the brink of war during the late summer of 1844. However, the crisis passed, although Joinville led France's naval building program until he and his father were overthrown in the revolution of 1848—a year which witnessed a second naval scare in England. Anglo-French relations remained cordial until yet another invasion panic during the creation of the so-called Second Empire under Louis Napoleon throughout 1851–1853. Such fears proved unrealistic, however, for France's new imperial commitments required that its fleet not be concentrated on the Channel coast but in the Mediterranean.

The Russian naval menace to the British, like that of the French, was supposed to be in the Atlantic, particularly the Baltic, but was really focused in the Mediterranean. During the first half of the nineteenth century, in fact, Russia enjoyed a brief period of maritime activity; for instance, no fewer than thirty-six Russian voyages circumnavigated the globe by 1850. The Russian Baltic Fleet caused Britain anxiety through the 1830s, and the presence of the Russian squadron in Greek waters in the 1820s aroused British suspicions about Russian intentions in the Mediterranean. Simultaneously, 1825–1828, Russia fought a boundary war with Persia which was so successful that it gave Russia naval control over the Caspian Sea and crippled Persia permanently as a Middle Eastern power. The Russian victory over Turkey in 1829 so humbled the already weak Ottoman Empire that the powerful Mohammed Ali of Egypt rose in revolt and threatened to destroy the political power of the sultan. Russia began to strengthen Odessa and Sevastopol as naval arsenals in order to maintain the control she had already won over the Black Sea. Britain therefore feared for the integrity of the Ottoman Empire. Should it collapse, either under the weight of Russian pressure or by the advance of the French-supported forces of Mohammed Ali in Egypt, a rival power could cut British Middle Eastern communications to India. In addition, the Russians were expanding eastward, overland toward the Pacific, arousing British fears (though unsubstantiated) of a potential Russian descent on India itself. Thus the British, led by Palmerston, from the 1830s assumed the role of shoring up a Middle Eastern buffer zone against Russia that centered on the Persian Gulf and included, west to east, Turkey, Persia and Afghanistan.

The Middle East had degenerated apace with the Ottoman Empire, leading to constant warring among Turks, Persians and independent Arab tribes such as the Wahhabis who had established a livelihood from piracy in the Persian Gulf by 1810. The Egyptians of Mohammed Ali and Ibrahim destroyed the Wahhabis in Arabia in 1818, but their fleet of some 250 war dhows continued to create havoc with coastal trade between Basra in the Gulf and Bombay. In 1819–20 the Bombay Marine combined with British regulars and sepoy troops to occupy points along the north "Pirate Coast" of the Gulf, but the piracy continued. A six-vessel East India Company Gulf Squadron began to cruise the Gulf, operating mainly from Basidu, in 1821, but with uneven success, since continuous maritime wars with the various Arab principalities (as between superior Muscat and Bahrain 1829 to 1835) bred indiscriminate raiding. Both Persia and Turkey were powerless as sea powers to stabilize the area when, in 1831–32, Mohammed Ali's Egyptians overran Ottoman Syria and defeated the Ottoman army. The Turkish appeal to Britain was refused, simply because the Royal Navy was overcommitted elsewhere in the world, whereupon the Turks reluctantly signed, early in 1833, a defensive alliance with Russia. A Russian squadron then anchored off Constantinople, but Turkey sued for peace, ceding Syria to the Egyptians. In the 1830s Turkey hired American shipwrights who came to Constantinople to begin rebuilding the Ottoman navy up to rough parity—a dozen ships of the line plus frigates—with the Egyptian fleet and Russian Black Sea Fleet. But without British support this balance of power could only be temporary.

In April 1839 the Turks attacked the Egyptians in an effort to reassert their supremacy in Mesopotamia, but were so shattered in land battle in June that the great powers had to intervene in order to save the Ottoman Empire from utter ruin. In July the entire Ottoman fleet defected to the side of Mohammed Ali, while an Anglo-French fleet of nineteen of the line moved to Cyprus. By now, the British were thoroughly alarmed, for Russia might come to dominate Turkey and the Dardanelles; France might join Egypt to control the Middle East; and Mohammed Ali might occupy the vitally strategic coasts of the Red Sea and the Persian Gulf. To frustrate the latter design, British forces had occupied the strategic island of Kharak (modern Kharg) near Bushire on the northwest coast of the Gulf in the summer of 1838; the following January a Bombay landing force had occupied Aden at the entrance to the Red Sea; and in June 1839 the commander of the East Indies Squadron moved to defend Bahrain Island in the Gulf against Egyptian occupation. Concurrent British naval commitments in China, however, frustrated an attempted warship demonstration in the Gulf for later that year, and as 1840 began, the British feared an Egyptian descent on the Pirate Coast. The French became increasingly bellicose during that winter, contemplating even a bombardment of British Malta, so confident were they of their fleet's superiority. But the prospect of a French presence in the Middle East at the expense of Turkey was unacceptable to Russia, Austria and even Prussia, and all three joined Britain in July 1840 in declaring their intentions to uphold the Ottoman Empire—a stroke of strategic genius by the calculating Palmerston.

Allied naval strength now outnumbered that of the French and Egyptians, enabling the powers to expel Mohammed Ali from his conquered dominions. They moved none too soon, for in June a large naval expedition had left Alexandria to suppress an uprising in Syria. Anglo-Turko-Austrian naval forces under the supreme command of Admiral Sir Robert Stopford now concentrated off Alexandria and Beirut, cutting Mohammed Ali's sea communications to Syria, and in September they bombarded Haifa, Tyre and Sidon, followed by Beirut in October, and a large land-sea assault took Acre early in November. The next month Mohammed Ali ended the war by negotiating his immediate withdrawal from Syria with the local British commanders. Early in 1841 he and Ibrahim withdrew from Syria, Crete and Arabia, thus quieting all British fears of French power in the Middle East and of the possible loss of the Persian Gulf to one overall ruler. The British evacuated Kharak at Russian insistence, but made Aden into a permanent base commanding the Red Sea. The two Egyptian Moslem rulers died before the end of the decade, but not before establishing a dynasty that lasted until 1953. The teetering Ottoman Empire was thus shored up, and the powers agreed in July 1841 to close the vital straits of the Dardanelles and the Bosporus to all foreign warships in time of peace—a happy solution to all the powers (except Russia), a situation which has survived generally intact to the present, with some modifications.

The British also solved their apprehensions over the internal chaos of the Persian Gulf by establishing an ingenious arrangement known as the Trucial System. The six Arab maritime sheikdoms on the south coast of the Gulf had warred indiscriminately against each other for centuries, for piracy and pearling were their major incomes. The maritime power in the region had been the united kingdom of Muscat and Oman, since 1806 ruled by Seyyid Said, who, however, in 1828 established a base in Zanzibar and in 1840 shifted his capital there and his power into East Africa, away from the Gulf. The only other political units of consequence were the non-piratical sheikdoms of Bahrain and Kuwait within the Gulf. The virtual political vacuum was thus being filled, however inadequately, by the East India Company's cruisers (designated the Indian Navy in 1830). After a stunning blow by one of these cruisers over six pirate vessels in April of 1835, however, Captain Samuel Hennell secured a maritime truce among the six piratical sheikdoms. A neutral highway on the Gulf was closed to war dhows, and the tribes abstained from fighting at sea during the summer pearling season, though they still warred on land. The rival tribes so honored this maritime truce that it was made formal in 1843, followed by a "treaty of maritime peace in perpetuity" in 1853. This so-called Trucial System was administered by the East Indies Company, whose vessels, with occasional help from the Royal Navy, policed the Gulf. The System, administered by the Royal Navy after 1859, was so successful that it survived down to 1971. Company flotillas in the 1840s also patrolled the Red Sea and Tigris, Euphrates and Indus rivers and protected Bahrain's independence from Persia and in 1851 from Turkish encroachment.

Shielding the Persian Gulf from outside aggression by sea, Britain also needed to uphold Persian sovereignty as part of its buffer against Russian expansion—a considerable task, as Persia had a long continental frontier. This was similarly the case with the subcontinent of India, a virtual island sealed off from Asia by the Himalaya Mountains, and with the intermediate kingdom of Afghanistan. In addition, the British continued to be occupied with the final pacification of India itself. As the British began to penetrate into Afghanistan, Russia persuaded Persia to invade Afghanistan, an attack repulsed through British aid in the war of 1836–38. These events led to First Afghan War, 1839–42, in which the British East India Company army failed to occupy Afghanistan as a buffer against primarily Russia. The Russians, however, had little real interest in India or Afghanistan, but rather Persia, wresting more territory from that luckless country between 1849 and 1854. The Company fought two Sikh wars to subdue India finally in the 1840s, so that by the early 1850s Britain generally had achieved its strategic goal of creating the buffer zone against Russia from the Bosporus to the Khyber Pass on the northwest frontier of India—although the Russians still persevered in their eastward drive to reach the Pacific.

Behind this continental defense perimeter lay the vital British sea lanes to India. The route from Liverpool to Bombay via the Suez camel road was eventually improved by a rail line from Alexandria to Suez in 1858, but the major commercial and military track remained completely by sea around the Cape. Three major shipping companies operated British troopships gradually converting to steam in the late 1830s to speed up the transit which with the old sailing East Indiamen had taken over four months. By steam, England to India, the time was cut to six weeks via Suez (the steamers having insufficient coal storage capacity for the Cape route) by the 1850s. The speed would be increased even more when the canal, begun in 1859 by a French company, was completed across the isthmus of Suez.

Continued French interest in the Middle and Far East led to continued rivalry with Britain along the Indian Ocean trade route. Having lost the key island of Mauritius to Britain in the Napoleonic wars, France was left with only tiny Réunion Island. The former Portuguese island of Socotra appeared as a possible base for controlling the exit of the Red Sea, but both Britain in 1836 and France in 1845 abandoned it after only brief occupations, poor health conditions being a major reason. So the French focused on Madagascar, on which they had had sporadic settlements since the mid-seventeenth century. Both British and French warships bombarded points on the island in these years, disputing the native government, but in general the French failed to reestablish their former posts on the island. The major importance of Madagascar in the early nineteenth century, however, was as a center of Arab slave trading.

The Western crusade to stop the slave traffic (Britain's decision in 1807) and then the abolition of the institution of slavery altogether (Britain in 1833) corresponded in time with new British and French imperial conquests along the African coasts. This coincidence thus heightened the tension between the Christian settlers, the black chieftains who dealt in slaves, and the Arab merchants who transported such human cargo throughout the world of Islam, a faith which embraced slavery. West Africa provided slaves to the Barbary States, the Sudan to Egypt and Asia Minor, and Abyssinia and East Africa to Arabia and the Persian Gulf. In West Africa, the British drove the Ashanti tribe from the Gold Coast 1824–31; the French occupied the Ivory Coast 1842–43 in addition to their older post at Senegal; and the United States established the independent state of Liberia with freed American slaves between 1822 and 1847. In South Africa, the strategic Cape Colony remained unsettled by continual strife between the British, Dutch Boer farmers and various local tribes such as the Zulus and Kaffirs which erupted in open wars during the 1840s. The Boers protested British annexation of Natal in 1843, but found no interference when they created the neighboring South African Republic and Orange Free State. In East Africa, where the slave traffic was greatest, Seyyid Said of Muscat-Oman gradually extended his political control southward through Mombasa and Zanzibar to border the Portuguese colony of Mozambique across the channel from Madagascar.

With heavy strategic commitments across the globe, the suppression of the slave trade was an added burden on the Royal Navy. All Western maritime nations endorsed the suppression of slaving soon after Britain did so, but vested interests immediately compromised these decisions in every country but Britain. Slave-holding Portugal and the United States were particularly reluctant to enforce their anti-slaving laws. The American Congress outlawed the slave trade in 1808 and twelve years later equated slavery with piracy and made the trade punishable by death, but politicians from the slave-holding Southern states frustrated rigid enforcement and Southern naval commanders were purposely lax during anti-slave cruises. France simply refused to join Britain in any cooperative effort until 1845 when each country agreed to employ cruisers off the coast of West Africa, but France never contributed its full share of the responsibility. The new Latin American republics were also reluctant to accept the abolitionist sentiment of the northern nations, Brazil not closing its slave market till 1853. Two issues remained at the center of unsuccessful British efforts to get cooperation: the right to search was jealously guarded by each nation, so that as late as 1861 British, French and American vessels would never search suspected slaving ships flying one of the other's flags; and the equipment clause, gradually accepted by all after an Anglo-Dutch treaty of 1822, declared that even vessels without slaves but equipped for slaving could be seized. All prizes were dispensed by bilateral admiralty courts, while the British even awarded slave prize money to successful crews. Finally, Seyyid Said of Oman and Zanzibar was downright opposed to abolishing the chief income of his Arab subjects. Instead of being an easy problem to solve, the slave trade expanded to its greatest proportions after it had been declared illegal by most countries in the 1830s. And the Royal Navy, though occasionally assisted as well as hindered by foreign warships, had to be the chief agent of enforcement.

British naval strategists and diplomats thus virtually alone developed the techniques and means that eventually destroyed the illegal slave trade. Even the British were reluctant at first, so that separate attempts with but few warships were made from isolated captures at sea from 1807 (while the Napoleonic wars were far from over) to the first interventions at Mauritius and Mombasa in the 1820s. Then in the 1830s, with abolition as British law, the British launched a massive effort, sending anti-slaving cruisers to their various squadrons around Africa: 26 to North America and the West Indies, 23 in the Mediterranean, 16 off South America, 15 at Lisbon, 14 divided between the Cape and West Africa, and 10 in the East Indies. In the 1840s other nations began to cooperate more fully, with even Ottoman Turkey and Said at Zanzibar outlawing the external slave trade. By 1847 Atlantic anti-slave patrols included 30 British, 7 French, 7 Portuguese and 5 American cruisers usually operating separately to capture a total of 55 slaver vessels in that year alone. In addition, the Royal Navy began the practice of going ashore to make treaties of cooperation with African chiefs and destroying the coastal installations of slave shippers. Slaving was thus virtually stopped from Cuba and severely restricted from West Africa, while diplomacy remained the chief weapon in East Africa. In 1852 Persia agreed to allow the British to search its vessels and Said remained cooperative till his death in 1856, though the Trucial States kept the Arabian side of the Persian Gulf active in slaving. The Brazilian supply of slaves was cut off in the 1850s, but the aggressiveness of pro-slave Americans helped revive the Cuban trade. By 1860, the slave trade had been checked everywhere except in the Caribbean Sea and Indian Ocean, where all depended on internal conditions within the United States and the Arab sheikdoms.

## REOPENING THE ORIENT

The suppression of slavery and piracy also went hand in hand with the commercial rivalries and search for political stability in the waters east of India. And, equally typically, Great Britain dominated Western activities in the Far East through its East India Company. From Trincomalee on Ceylon to Calcutta and Chittagong, the Company commanded the Bay of Bengal, with small bases at Penang Island off the Malay coast and Bencoolen on Sumatra; in addition, it utilized the Andaman and Danish Nicobar islands. But when the Dutch began returning to the East Indies in 1816, they threatened to restore their old commercial monopoly, whereupon the East India Company in January 1819 occupied Singapore Island off the tip of Malaya. This brilliant strategic move gave Britain virtual possession of the Malacca Strait which commanded the trade route between the Indian Ocean and Canton, China. The Dutch had no choice but to acquiesce, and in 1824 they ceded their last Indian settlements as well as Malacca and their claims in Malaya to the British in return for Bencoolen. The Dutch, however, from their base at Riau opposite Singapore tried to undercut British trade to China, but were continually frustrated by Royal Navy units of the East Indies Squadron. Still, Dutch trade in the Far East flourished, and Holland continued to enjoy the trade monopoly to Japan, still shut off from the rest of the world. The Portuguese at Goa and the Spanish in the Philippines had long been reduced to impotence, though the latter were able to beat off a French attack on the Sulu Archipelago in 1845. France became only slowly involved in the Far East, its warships beginning to intervene in Vietnam from 1824 to protect Europeans there. But just to check Dutch and French alike, the British occupied coastal points in northern Australia near present-day Darwin between 1824 and 1849, but these enterprises failed.

The search for stability was the prime concern of all Western nations in the waters of the Far East, so that their navies were mostly employed against Asian natives resisting European overlordship on land or acting as pirates at sea. The European powers often cooperated to protect their shipping, while even the United States created an East India Station in 1835. In the colonies, anti-pirate activities were often part of the general pacification, and Indochinese frontier wars occasionally involved the British. The three Oriental areas of active naval combat in the early nineteenth century were the mainland of Southeast Asia (Burma, Siam, Vietnam), the offshore islands and waters (Malaya, East Indies, Philippines) and the Chinese coast.

On the mainland of Southeast Asia, the East India Company soon became involved in the continuing struggle of Burma to dominate the region, particularly at the expense of Siam, although Vietnam, Cambodia and Laos were constantly fighting among themselves. Burmese advances into Indian territory below Chittagong led to open war in March 1824. Basing in the Andamans, a British expeditionary force departed aboard Bombay Marine and Royal Navy vessels to drive up the Irrawaddy River. The fleet included much of the old and new: sailing frigates and brigs, a flotilla of twenty armed rowboats, the first British paddle-wheel steamer to see action, and an arsenal that included Congreve rockets. In opposition were a force of formidable 100-oar Burmese bireme-type praus. Rangoon took most of the remainder of 1824 to be invested, while the winter river drive was slowed by unenlightened army command and tropical disease. Nevertheless, throughout 1825, the British expedition pushed up the Irrawaddy almost to the Burmese capital of Ava destroying the Burmese army in the process. Early in 1826 Burma surrendered much of the coast below Chittagong to Britain, and later in the year Siam agreed to halt its designs on British Malaya. The British needed a buffer for eastern India as in the western part, but the Burmese were uncooperative. Renewed war threatened in 1838–39, then occurred early in 1852 when another Company amphibious force took Rangoon and then required another year to annex South Burma. As on the Afghanistan frontier, sea power proved inadequate, and imperial ground forces were needed to maintain the British defense perimeter on the Asian continent.

The waters of the South China Sea required extensive naval activities for policing. The Spanish fought a centuries-old war against the Moro pirates of the southern Philippines, while in 1816 the Dutch at Batavia created a special Colonial Marine which they soon integrated into the regular Netherlands navy for anti-pirate operations throughout the Indies. Heavily committed to pacification operations in Java and Bali, however, the Dutch required help from the Spanish and British against the pirates, particularly in Borneo. The main source of pirates were the Lanun and Balanini tribes of southern Mindanao and Sulu islets, far out of reach of Spanish authorities. These pirates annually sailed south and west in a fleet of 200 praus before breaking into squadrons of some twenty vessels for operations based on the northwest coast of Borneo. In addition, local Malay tribes plagued British colonial waters, so that regular patrols were instituted in the Malacca Strait in the early 1830s which also helped Siam put down various insurrections. By such cunning as using disguised merchant vessels as decoys, British commanders later in the decade began the effective suppression of the Malay pirates. By terms of the Anglo-Dutch treaty of 1824, the British could not operate off Borneo, but when in 1841 the local sultan made a British sailor-adventurer named James Brooke rajah of the Sarawak coast of Borneo the situation changed. The British East Indies Squadron destroyed a pirate stronghold at Marudu Bay in North Borneo in 1845, found coal at Sarawak, and helped Brooke establish a naval station at Labuan Island in mid-1846, simultaneous with the assault and capture of coastal Brunei. But it was Brooke of Sarawak, and not the British fleet, who thereafter waged successful anti-pirate operations henceforth in northern Borneo. The last major anti-pirate offensive was undertaken by the Spanish, who in 1848 assaulted and took after three attempts the main Balanini stronghold in the Sulus. By 1850, Western efforts had effectively checked major pirate operations in the waters of Southeast Asia.

Policing of Chinese waters was undertaken only after the British government ended the East India Company's trade monopoly to China in 1834, and then events quickly led to war. The Manchu dynasty had been so weakened internally that by 1800 many pirates easily ravaged Chinese coastal waters, one fleet numbering over 500 junks. Most of the Western powers let the pirates go unchecked, although the Chinese government in 1806 had wedded its rather ineffective water force to a small Portuguese squadron at Macao for some defense. Piracy tended to abate after 1810, but the English (and some American) smuggling of opium from India into China increased so much that Sino-British relations rapidly deteriorated in the 1830s. Finally, late in 1839, the First Opium War erupted. China's defenses were purely continental: coastal fortifications supported by the Manchu armies and a motley array of war junks. So the British decided to blockade the Chinese coast, neutralize the junk fleets, and take key cities in amphibious and river operations. After the first naval skirmish near Canton in November 1839 in which several British warships defeated a junk fleet, the British moved against North China. In the summer of 1840, a British expeditionary force landed on Chusan Island and blockaded the mouth of the Peiho River leading to the capital at Peking. When the Chinese agreed to negotiate, the fleet moved south to Canton; then the negotiations broke down. The British resumed hostilities in 1841 by taking Canton in May, Amoy in August, Chusan again and Ningpo in October, and despite stretched logistics and severe living conditions, held on to their gains, utilizing a new base they had occupied early in the year below Canton—Hong Kong. Taking Shanghai in June 1842, the British moved up the Yangtze River toward Nanking, forcing the Chinese to sue for peace. In addition to extensive economic and legal concessions, China formally ceded Hong Kong to Britain.

Suddenly, Britain assumed the role of policeman of the lawless Chinese waters, while the Chinese government reeled helplessly under the impact of Western culture. Another treaty with Britain was followed by similar agreements with France and the United States, 1843–44, while in the latter year the Taiping Rebellion began against the Manchus, growing until it had split all China with the capture of Nanking in 1853. Tradition-bound, the Manchus generally ignored reforming and modernizing their coastal-river navy, which, however, won important victories over the equally old-fashioned rebel vessels on the Yangtze and Poyang Lake in the mid-1850s. The Western powers made little impact on these events, but British Hong Kong and the East Indies Squadron were now faced with the monumental task of eliminating the Chinese pirate menace. The reluctance of the Chinese government—which depended largely on coastal convoys—to accept British naval aid made policing difficult, until 1848 when the regime finally acquiesced. The next year British warships took the offensive, joining the naval forces of Vietnam in destroying one great pirate fleet in three separate battles. But lesser squadrons of pirates persisted, requiring the British in 1854 to lead a joint expedition of Chinese, Portuguese and American warships to seek out and destroy a large number of pirate craft. Until the governments of these nations and that of France as well mounted a major effort, however, the British assumed the full responsibility for combating pirates in China. Hong Kong became a key advanced base, Trincomalee a backwater, and Singapore the pivot as the British extended their *Pax Britannica* into the Pacific.

As an extension of events around the Asia littoral, various Western nations began to penetrate farther eastward to establish formal colonial governments in Pacific islands where only adventurers, outlaws, missionaries and occasional traders had gone before, often at the expense of the natives. The Dutch annexed western New Guinea in 1828, the French the distant Tahiti and the Marquesas Islands in 1842–43, but again it was the British who dominated the white settlement of Oceania, most importantly asserting authority over the entire continent of Australia by 1829 and proclaiming official sovereignty over New Zealand in 1840. Generally, such colonization was loose and peaceful, but the British developed differences with the Maori natives of New Zealand that led to open war, 1843–48. Warships of the Australasian Squadron based at Sydney, Australia, operated along the New Zealand coast, using their guns, Congreve rockets and landing parties to help counter the very effective guerrilla tactics employed by the Maoris. Gradually, by this colonizing thrust eastward, the European maritime powers were filling the vacuum left by the collapse of the old Spanish Empire and would eventually link up with their trade routes in the Americas. But first, they had to settle some lingering differences in Europe.

## THE TURBULENT 1850s

The tottering Ottoman Empire suddenly became the object of French and Russian imperial designs in the early 1850s, though the ostensible issue was religious supremacy in the Holy Land. All Europe mobilized in defense of Turkey, but only Britain, France and Sardinia actually rallied armed forces to her side. Hostilities opened in the fall of 1853, with the Russian and Turkish armies clashing on land and their Black Sea naval squadrons concentrating for support and raids on rival seaports. After some indecisive bombardments and isolated skirmishes, on November 30 a Russian squadron of three 120- and 84-gun line-of-battle ships, two frigates and three steamers under Rear Admiral Pavel Stepanovich Nakhimov attacked a Turkish force of seven frigates, three corvettes and two steamers at Sinope on the north coast of Turkey. Using the new shell guns, the Russians in but one hour utterly annihilated the Turk squadron, allowing only one steamer to escape. This crushing victory proclaimed the obsolescence of wooden warships, and the French immediately began to introduce armor on board their warships. Strategically, Western Europe arose against this Russian aggression, and in January 1854 an Anglo-French fleet entered the Black Sea to protect the integrity of Turkey. Early in the spring Britain and France declared war on Russia, which reciprocated—the first war between major powers since the Congress of Vienna.

The Crimean War caught the British and French unprepared, a fact revealed in their makeshift and downright shoddy prosecution of the war. Former rivals, they now joined fleets in the Baltic and Black seas in hopes of destroying the Russian navy, while Austria and Prussia forced Russia to quit its advance into the Danube basin. In addition,

Anglo-French forces occupied Piraeus, frustrating Greek designs to join Russia and thus grab adjacent territory from Turkey. The much-vaunted Russian command of the Baltic proved empty, for the Russian fleet elected not to move against the combined Anglo-French fleet of Vice Admiral Sir Charles Napier. Still, the Russians utilized the latest weapons of the Industrial Revolution to defend their northern coasts: steam vessels easily violated the blockade, while submarine mines protected the Baltic Sea Fleet at Kronstadt and Sveaborg. Needing something to do, Napier's force took the Aland Islands after an eight-day bombardment and siege in August 1854. But, aside from a minor shelling of Sveaborg one year later and some raids, this was the extent of Baltic operations, and the Russians were totally unable to send reinforcements to the Black Sea via the Mediterranean.

Initial Black Sea operations, however, were little more impressive; in April 1854 the British and French landed troops at Varna to help force the Russians from the Black Sea and bombarded Odessa. Then they decided to destroy Russian naval power by taking the base at Sevastopol. The force at Varna was sealifted aboard 300 transports escorted by an Anglo-French fleet under Vice Admiral Sir James Dundas, and finally landed in the Crimea thirty miles up the coast from Sevastopol in September. Russian naval power was then liquidated when the crews and Naval Infantry went ashore to help man the defenses, and the ships, including Nakhimov's veteran vessels of Sinope, were scuttled to block the entrance to the harbor. But the Russian army stalemated the allied expeditionary force, which was then subjected to a harsh winter of siege. In mid-1855 the mismanaged campaign finally led to amphibious-land assaults which took Kerch in May, Sevastopol in September, and Kinburn in October. Ninety allied war steamers, including French ironclad floating batteries, made a dramatic impression at Kinburn, adding to the general Russian decision to end the war. After evacuating their defenses at Ochakov, Russia sued for peace early in 1856.

The settlement of the Crimean trouble did much to eliminate further causes of war and to resume the Concert of Europe and *Pax Britannica,* with Russia making the necessary sacrifices: no new Black Sea fleet for Russia or Turkey, and the neutralization of the Black Sea and Danube basin for the commerce of all nations, including the razing of the defenses and naval installations of Sevastopol. Though warships of all nations were now excluded from this great sea, the naval power of Britain remained available as usual to enforce the terms of the peace. The Russian influence over Ottoman Turkey was thus eliminated, the latter managing to survive politically for several more decades. The legalistic spirit which neutralized the Black Sea also led to the Declaration of Paris during the peace negotiations of 1856, issued by Britain, France, Austria, Russia, Prussia, Turkey and Sardinia. The Declaration abolished privateering, allowed neutral shipping of noncontraband materials to belligerents, and stated explicitly that for a blockade to be legal and binding it had to be effective; that is, blockaded ports had to be patrolled by warships of the blockading nation. But again, such a statement of international law depended upon the adherence of the maritime power which commanded the seas, namely, Great Britain. With such new rules of sea war the European powers turned to converting their navies to steam, armor plate, iron and shell guns.

Post-Crimean Europe was generally stable politically, with the seeds of future conflict in the growing forces of nationalism among subject peoples and the imperialistic and commercial enterprises in the non-Western world. One short war erupted in Europe, as the Italians renewed their attempt to unify and achieve their independence from Austria. Sardinia (Piedmont) concluded a secret treaty with France, gaining her support in the attempt, then mobilized early in 1859. In April war broke out, Sardinia and France against Austria. The very respectable French fleet laid a blockade on the Austrian coast, while the allied armies soundly defeated those of Austria. Peace followed quickly in July, Sardinia gaining new territory but allowing the Austrians to keep Venice. Displeased, the Italians led by Cavour and the king of Sardinia revolted in 1860, Garibaldi leading an army over water from Genoa to liberate Sicily in May, June and July. Obtaining British aid, Garibaldi crossed the Strait of Messina and took Naples in August and September. The French again intervened, stationing a squadron off the Neapolitan coast, and occupied Rome to protect the Pope. But the Italians launched a pincers movement, a Sardinian army advancing from Piedmont in the north into the Papal States and Garibaldi driving from the south against Gaeta in September and October. He besieged Gaeta in November, and after the withdrawal of the French squadron in January 1861 used the Sardinian navy to bombard Gaeta into submission. In March 1861 the united kingdom of Italy was proclaimed, save for French-occupied Rome. Thus a new unified power appeared in the Mediterranean to check the maritime thrust of Austria.

Britain, ever sensitive to its Middle Eastern defense perimeter against Russia, remained embroiled in fighting there in the late-1850s. Expecting a Russian victory in the Crimean War, Persia had broken diplomatic relations with Britain, leading to a British naval demonstration in the Persian Gulf early in 1854. The next year Persian troops occupied Afghan territory, leading the British to intervene. In November 1856 the Indian navy sealifted an expeditionary force into the Gulf from Bombay and other Indian ports. It took Kharak and Halilah Bay early in December, moving up the coast to invest Bushire in January 1857. While the British negotiated a peace settlement to preserve Persia's national integrity, Company steamers supported a drive up the delta of the Tigris River. By spring, the fighting was ended, Britain obtaining the same trade concession enjoyed by Russia with Persia; the border dispute with Afghanistan was not really settled. Peace was concluded none too soon, for in May 1857 the Great Indian Mutiny broke out. The bloody uprising lasted thirteen months before it was crushed, and in September 1858 the British government ended the rule of the East India Company in India. Regular forces would thereafter operate with sepoy troops under direct command of the crown. Britain became understandably anxious about her northwest frontier, for the Russians were moving down the Syr Daria River to conquer the last Mongol tribes, using steamboats in support of the army, while farther north Russia was pushing into Eastern Siberia toward the Pacific, intruding upon China.

The chaotic condition of China, rent by the growing Taiping Rebellion, made the country vulnerable to possible economic or even territorial designs by Great Britain, Russia and the United States. The inability of the enfeebled Manchu government to suppress either the Rebellion or piracy led to the assistance—however unwelcome—of the Western powers, particularly since many of the pirates themselves were Western adventurers. From 1853, United States warships began to work in active concert with those of the Royal Navy against pirates and hostile Chinese ashore. Then, in October 1856 the Chinese seizure of a British vessel at Canton led to a second war with Britain over larger issues centering on treaty revisions. In this, the Arrow War (named for the vessel seized) or Second Opium War, China was feebler than in the First, for the Taiping Rebellion undermined internal unity. Admiral Sir Michael Seymour's ships quickly reduced the forts below Canton, then shelled and briefly occupied the city itself. The next month, November, the Chinese brought on the wrath of the local American squadron when one of their forts fired on ships' boats being led away from Canton by Commander Andrew H. Foote. Foote then under the cover of his guns personally led an assaulting naval brigade that took all four barrier forts below Canton. Sino-American relations were not hampered, although the Americans agreed to assist the British whenever necessary to protect Western lives and property. Also, Chinese butchery of at least one French missionary brought in France as an active enemy. With Russia moving eastward along the Amur River, China faced a coalition of unfriendly Western nations.

Attacked from within and without, China during 1857 and 1858 resisted ineffectively and turned halfheartedly to diplomacy, for the inexorable advance of the Western powers threatened China on all sides.

To check the Russians, in May 1857 China ceded the left bank of the Amur to Russia, which included her Maritime Provinces. Below her southern frontier, in Vietnam, the murder of a Spanish missionary led to a joint Franco-Spanish naval bombardment and occupation of Tourane in August and September of 1858. The force, commanded by Vice Admiral de Genouilly, for logistical reasons transferred to Saigon in 1859, beginning the French conquest of Cochin China. Anglo-French operations against China focused on Canton, where Chinese fire rafts, mines and junks only delayed the ultimate attack which came in December 1857. Canton fell to a naval bombardment and amphibious assault led by Admiral Seymour, who then—the following May—directed a similar seizure of the Taku forts at the entrance to the Peiho River leading to Tientsin and Peking. Turning as a last resort again to diplomacy, China made peace in June 1858—granting additional trade concessions and opening more ports to all the Western powers. These losses were too much to bear, however, and China renewed hostilities.

The Arrow War resumed when, in June 1859, an Anglo-French naval force attempted to retake the Taku forts. These defenses had been strengthened, however, and the attackers were repulsed with heavy losses. The neutral American warships present assisted their withdrawal downriver, thence to Shanghai. The allies now resolved to settle the issue with a massive assault on the Taku forts, using the new Armstrong guns for the first time. Rendezvousing at Hong Kong, the new allied force under General Sir James Hope Grant occupied Chusan Island in March 1860 for a forward staging base, the British going on to Dairen, the French to Chefoo in the Yellow Sea. The combined landings in August were made on the coast above Taku, whose forts were then taken from the rear. Pressing up the Peiho to Tientsin, General Hope Grant divided his force for the advance on Peking—perhaps because of his disdain for the French performance. With the British and French gunboats and service craft in the river, the British army on the north bank, the French on the left, the allied force drove toward Peking which fell early in October. The Chinese had no choice but to submit to the terms of the treaty of 1858 and to cede Kowloon to Britain, leaving them powerless to halt the Russian penetration of the Maritime Provinces and to view with some apprehension the sudden reappearance of ancient Japan.

While Britain was so heavily occupied in China, Russia and the United States both sought to force open Japan, thus ending her centuries-old policy of seclusion and broadening the base of her commercial intercourse from the Dutch monopoly. A Russian naval force left the Baltic in October 1852 with this object in view, but did not arrive before an American naval squadron under Commodore Matthew C. Perry achieved the same feat, arriving at Tokyo Bay in July 1853. After a short visit,

Perry wintered at Macao, returning to Japan the next year to obtain the treaty. Granting the Americans trading rights at three ports, the Japanese were soon obliged to conclude similar agreements with Britain, Russia, France and the Netherlands, 1855–58. Thus committed, Japan soon opened other ports and lost little time in seeking to understand the West. In one respect, naval knowledge, Japan was most interested; the apparent power of Perry's four ships led the Tokugawa regime to seek Dutch advice late in 1854. The next year, the Dutch, losing their long trade monopoly, established a naval training detachment at Nagasaki, teaching the Japanese the art of steam engineering before being asked to leave early in 1859. Unlike wartorn and backward China, Japan was eager to improvise and modernize and began turning also to the British, Americans and French for assistance—although various feudal lords were more progressive than the government, which was criticized by its conservative traditionalists. Somehow, the Japanese seemed to realize the inability or undesirability of the Russians to assist them in naval matters, and aside from a brief association in 1855–56 Japan never again turned to Russia. A wise choice, for the aggressive Russians reached the Pacific coast opposite Japan in 1860.

Russia in the late 1850s had reached something of a strategic crisis. Defeat in the Crimean War had cast doubt on the traditional thrust into the Middle East. Indeed, loss of Black Sea bases necessitated a Russian base at Villefranche on the French-Italian border from 1858 to 1860. Now, however, a new school of strategic thought developed under Commodore Andrei A. Popov which advocated that the prime area of expansion be into the Far East. In the late summer of 1854 a Russian frigate and shore battery had repulsed a landing attempt by five allied vessels at Petropavlovsk on the Kamchatkan peninsula; otherwise, the British fleet in Asia had discouraged any Russian naval movements in the Pacific during the Crimean War. Now, the Russian fleet was being modernized with steam vessels under its new commander-in-chief, Grand Duke Constantine Nikolaevich, whose key administrator for shipbuilding was Popov. Popov wanted his nation to promote overland and maritime expansion and to use the Amur River as a base for a major Russian Pacific fleet for wartime attacks on British colonies and stations in the Orient. Believing the United States could act as a political balance between Britain and Russia in the Pacific, Popov advocated the use of California ports by Russian raiders. Jealous of the British presence in China, the Russians founded the town and port of Vladivostok in 1860–61 and in July 1861 occupied Tsushima Island between Japan and Korea, lest the British grab it. In addition, now Rear Admiral Popov was dispatched on a reconnaissance mission to study the suitability of a Pacific strategy. By now, however, a British squadron had reached

Yokohama, Japan, and threatened to visit Tsushima. Taking the hint, the Russian government ordered the island evacuated late in 1861. From this incident, Russian relations with Japan deteriorated, and Anglo-Japanese rapport grew.

*Pax Britannica* was a reality by the beginning of the 1860s. In Europe, even the Crimean War had failed to upset the balance of power, with Britain's traditional French antagonist allied. The revolution in steam had been expanded by the advent of armored sail-and-steam seagoing battleships, with Dupuy de Lôme's 5600-ton iron-plated *Gloire* being launched in 1859. Not surprisingly, this vessel and other innovations helped to create another British invasion scare in 1859–60, abated in the latter year by the 9000-ton British iron-built *Warrior*. Across the world, the British had acquired twenty-five bases and posts manned by 45,000 regular troops by the time of the Crimean War. Among the most important naval depots outside Britain were Lisbon, Gibraltar, Capetown, Malta, Aden, Bombay, Trincomalee, Calcutta, Singapore, Hong Kong and Sydney. Obtained during the last days of sail, this system of bases became a ready-made network of coaling stations for steamships, while Britain and her colonies provided sources of cheap coal—advantages the French could never emulate. The chief maritime competitor during the first half of the century, however, had been the United States. And though Britain often differed with its progeny, political stability in the Western Hemisphere required general Anglo-American cooperation. So, the base system was maintained at Halifax, Quebec and Jamaica and extended to British Honduras and the Falkland Islands. With such heavy global responsibilities, the British had good reason to beware of the growing influence of the embryonic American colossus, particularly in the least patrolled regions of the Western Hemisphere and the Eastern Pacific.

# 11

# The Western Hemisphere
# and American Empire,
# 1815–1860

*Our confederacy must be viewed as the nest from which all America,
North and South, is to be peopled. . . . My fear is that [Spain is] too
feeble to hold [her colonies] till our population can be sufficiently advanced to gain them piece by piece.*

—THOMAS JEFFERSON, 1795

## LATIN AMERICAN INDEPENDENCE

The extension of the *Pax Britannica* into the Western Hemisphere
became particularly necessary, for Britain relied heavily on the imports
from Latin America, required adequate defenses of Canada in North
America, and faced a potential power struggle in the Eastern Pacific,
the solution of which would decide the level of political stability in the
vast waters between the Americas and the Far East. Because of the wide
virgin continents beyond the influence of British sea power, the task
of policing the Americas was particularly difficult, except wherein
the Royal Navy could control seaborne communications between Spain
and Portugal and their American empires and also check the particular
designs of Russia and France to create new colonies in the Americas.
But the position of the United States was quite another matter. Strategically placed between Canada and the British West Indies with aggressive pioneers pushing across North America into territory claimed by
Britain, the American Republic also boasted a dynamic maritime community that exerted a great influence on the affairs of Latin America
and which came to compete successfully with the British merchant carriers everywhere else in the world. The United States thus provided
the key to the Western Hemisphere, and when that burgeoning nation

grew into a sprawling continental empire and was then wracked by a monumental civil war, Britain and the other powers had to treat their diplomatic policies vis-à-vis the United States with great care. The technological and strategic impact of the American Civil War upon Europe was profound and bore significantly upon the future of the *Pax Britannica* and great power relationships in general, not the least result being the emergence of the United States as a major industrial nation.

Anglo-American relations in the years after 1815 first involved the defensive frontiers of both countries. Sensitive to the recent British blockade and bombardments of its Eastern seaboard, the United States returned to a strategy of coast defense. Beginning in 1817, for the first time, the American government began to systematize its permanent fortifications from Maine to Louisiana, but relying upon the navy as the first line of defense. Line-of-battle ships and 44-gun frigates had been laid down during the War of 1812, and these plus new construction could now theoretically deal with British fleets operating out of Halifax, Bermuda and Jamaica. In the postwar demobilization, however, most of these large warships were decommissioned and placed in reserve, so that the navy's real contribution to coast defense remained in floating batteries and harbor gunboats supporting the forts. But such half-measures were not critical, as no foreign invasion ever threatened in these years.

More serious were disagreements over the Canadian-American frontier extending from Maine to the Rockies and pivoting on the Great Lakes, where American war fleets had prospered during the late war. Because the rapids above Montreal closed the Upper St. Lawrence River and Great Lakes to oceangoing warships, Britain still had to construct ships of war on the Lakes to defend the Canadian shores; the Americans as well had no direct river course from the Atlantic coast to the Lakes. Yet, both countries sought to economize by reducing their respective armed forces on the Lakes, so that in 1817 both nations agreed mutually to dismantle these forces, and the next year they (along with agreeing to fishing rights in the Gulf of St. Lawrence) formalized the Canadian-Louisiana territorial boundary to the Rockies at the 49th parallel. Nevertheless, to stabilize the balance of power in North America, both countries maintained their frontier forts, kept their ships in reserve, and began building canals which by mid-century improved direct water communications between the sea and the Lakes (though for gunboats and supply boats rather than men-of-war). The British naval establishment on the Lakes, however, closed down in 1834, by which time the American force had also withered away. A rebellion in Canada three years later and boundary quarrels from Maine to the Louisiana line kept up Anglo-American tensions, until 1842 when a compromise treaty settled these borders and the passions. The balance of power centered on the Lakes thenceforth declined in importance, and rivalries between the two English-speaking peoples shifted elsewhere.

The weakened state of the Spanish Empire had left the British masters of the Caribbean, but renewal of the Latin American uprisings after 1815 brought nearly overt support of the revolutionaries from the United States, which also wished to dislodge Spain from Florida. The United States in the final years of the Napoleonic period had simply taken over the Gulf coast, from Baton Rouge to beyond Mobile Bay (Spanish West Florida), which along with New Orleans made the United States a Caribbean power to rival the British and Spanish. The United States government felt obliged to pass new neutrality laws in 1817 and 1818, but the people favored the liberal revolts, and American warship captains continued to aid rebel governments by carrying their specie. In order to suppress fresh outbreaks in South America, the Spanish authorities weakened their police forces in Texas, East Florida and the Caribbean. The result was Indian raids into Georgia and the establishment of privateer-pirate bases first at Galveston in 1816 and then in 1817 at Amelia Island off northeast Florida to aid the Latin American republics. Privateers were already operating out of Baltimore and New Orleans, but those of Galveston and Amelia were clearly piratic, attacking even American merchantmen. Spanish-American relations worsened, whereupon the British decided to remain aloof. In November 1817 President James Madison ordered the seizure of both Amelia Island and Galveston, and the next month a frigate and five lesser American warships covered an Army landing at Amelia, thus forcing pirates to abandon their enterprise there. Galveston was not yet taken, but early in 1818 General Andrew Jackson undertook the First Seminole War by crossing into Spanish Florida in pursuit of raiding Seminole Indians. He took the capital, Pensacola, and infuriated the British government by executing one of their merchants who had been assisting the Indians. But he pacified the Indians and by his unauthorized actions hastened the cession of all Spanish Florida to the United States by treaty early in 1819.

The actions of Madison and Jackson eased Spanish-American tensions, helped suppress Gulf coast piracy (also with the enforcement of the neutrality laws), and forced the pirates to shift to the Spanish Main. The treaty had left the Gulf coast from the Sabine River to Mexico in Spanish hands, so that the notorious Laffite band of pirates continued to use Galveston as its base, particularly for raids on the delta of the Mississippi. Other pirates were using islands in the Bahamas and off the coasts of Nicaragua and Venezuela. So the United States government launched an intensive anti-pirate campaign in 1819–20 which had the main effect of finally protecting the American coast. Piracy laws in both years were enforced by naval patrols in and around the Mississippi delta which began capturing pirate vessels. Jean Laffite—with some sentiment toward the Americans, with whom he had helped to defend New Orleans against the British in 1815—in the spring of 1820 abandoned Galveston and shifted to the Mexican coast where the revolutionary spirit was reviving. Simultaneously, American courts began ordering the execution of convicted pirates, while naval patrols entered West African waters to deal with slavers. These actions enraged the Spanish colonials, the pirates and the revolutionary privateers, so that the United States had no choice but to increase its naval strength. Much also depended on the ability of the revolutionary governments to control the activities of the privateers using their flags.

Meanwhile, naval power played a key role in the Spanish American revolutions. The Latin American revolt had intensified in 1815 with the end of the Napoleonic wars and the dispatch from Spain of an expedition of 10,000 troops in 42 transports escorted by 18 warships to pacify the colonies bordering on the Caribbean. But the Spanish navy had been so weakened by the long wars that it could not begin to suppress the revolutionary privateers, let alone provide sufficient support for restoring Spain's authority in Latin America. Initially, during the spring of 1815, this squadron assaulted and took the insurgent position at Margarita Island off Venezuela, going on to blockade and retake Cartagena, the capital of Colombia (New Granada), between September and December, including winning a naval skirmish there in November. But thereafter Spanish naval fortunes waned, for the insurgents began to purchase warships and enlist volunteer crews from Britain, the United States, other European countries and throughout Latin America. These activities placed the former two nations in something of a dilemma. For Britain, though committed to restoring the Royalists in Europe, could use her command of the sea to thwart their pacification of colonial America and thus insure her own trade monopoly over Latin America. The United States, officially neutral, ideologically espoused such causes of democratic self-rule, so joined Britain in treating these conflicts as civil in nature and providing aid only unofficially. Anglo-American aloofness deteriorated, however, as the Spanish position in Latin America weakened after 1817. The revolutions, supported by growing naval forces, centered on two fronts: General Simón Bolívar in northern South America (Colombia, Venezuela and Ecuador) and General José de San Martin in the southern regions (Argentina, Chile and Peru).

Bolívar's campaign for the Spanish Main began at sea and evolved into a continental effort. While in exile in Jamaica in 1815, Bolívar received the services of seven privateers under Luis Brión, a Dutch Curaçao Creole who rose to become admiral over Bolívar's navy, the nucleus of which he had provided. Shifting to Haiti, Bolívar in 1816 mounted a seaborne expedition which retook Margarita Island after one initial failure. Brión's squadron then supported the attack on and capture of Angostura at the mouth of the Orinoco River, after which British sailors and troops began to arrive in Bolívar's camp. Throughout 1817 and 1818 Bolívar's warships blockaded the Spanish coastal positions and fought single-ship duels on the high seas as his armies fought inland, and the Spanish navy at home and in the Caribbean deteriorated. It had countered the insurgents by trying to blockade their base at Margarita, but being reduced to four vessels it had to abandon that task early in 1819. From Margarita, Bolívar's forces carried out amphibious raids and captures—the fleet growing to twenty-seven well-armed vessels during 1818. As the fighting wore on in 1819 most of the provinces of Colombia and Venezuela went over to Bolívar, and the next year a revolution in Spain crippled reinforcement plans for the Spanish forces in America. Early in 1820 Bolívar mounted a seaborne offensive along the Spanish Main, and Brión's fifteen-ship squadron defeated the Spanish squadron at Tenerife. Belated Spanish reinforcements could not halt Bolívar, who in 1821 attacked and took Cartagena by land and sea. His navy closed the blockade and two years later defeated the Spanish warships on Lake Maracaibo, leading to the fall of that key Venezuelan city. The Colombian warships drove the last Spanish troops from their new country in November 1823 to assure Bolívar's victory.

San Martin's campaign in the south resembled Bolívar's in its continental character and the sagacious use of naval forces in support. San Martin realized early that the Spanish naval power that defended the rich province of Peru had to be eliminated. He therefore planned a naval expedition at Buenos Aires to round the Horn and attack Spanish shipping on the west coast of South America. In the winter of 1815–16 such a force of three privateers did just that, destroying much shipping, bombarding and briefly blockading Callao itself. One year later, San Martin crossed the Andes Mountains, defeated the Spanish army and occupied Valparaiso in February 1817. He then set about raising a fleet at Buenos Aires to defend Chile and for an eventual advance on Peru. The small Spanish squadron from Callao then blockaded Valparaiso until discouraged by audacious attacks by British-led Chilean vessels in April 1818. More Chilean ships were purchased, such as a 64-gun former East Indiaman, and were captured; more Anglo-American officers were enlisted; and a naval academy was established, so that in the fall of 1818 a five-ship Chilean squadron was able to break up and capture a Spanish convoy from Cádiz.

Late in that year the fiery Lord Cochrane, formerly of the Royal

Navy, was appointed vice admiral in command of the seven-vessel Chilean navy, improving his fleet for engaging the Spanish squadron at Callao which included eight warships and twenty-seven gunboats. After a skirmish off Callao in February 1819, Cochrane declared the Peruvian coast under blockade, while Chilean privateers attacked Spanish shipping in the Pacific. Failing to lure the Spanish squadron to sea for battle with rockets and fire ships in October, the following June his forces bombarded and took the port of Valdivia, thus clearing the Chilean coast entirely of Spanish garrisons. San Martin now determined to invade Peru by sea, and in September 1820 Cochrane's eight warships escorted his sixteen-transport convoy to their successful landing at Pisco. The fleet then blockaded Callao again, with Cochrane personally leading a boarding party to seize a Spanish 44-gun frigate there in November. San Martin's army finally took Lima in July 1821, and Callao—besieged by land and sea—surrendered two months later. South American independence was virtually assured, for Spain had lost the riches of her most valuable colony.

In 1822–23 the British and American governments, seeing both Spain and Portugal convulsed in revolution at home and abroad, recognized the independence of the Latin American republics. To assure noninterference by the continental monarchs, Canning of Britain and President James Monroe and Secretary of State John Quincy Adams of the United States proclaimed that intervention would not be tolerated. Though this famous policy came to be known as the Monroe Doctrine, its strength rested solely on the ability of the Royal Navy to enforce it. The other European powers generally acquiesced in the edict, except in the realm of suppressing piracy. The new Latin republics began to exert controls over their privateers in these years, so that the obvious pirates in the Caribbean moved from Latin islands to ports in the Swedish, Danish and Dutch West Indies, Spanish Cuba and Puerto Rico, and independent Haiti. Beginning in late 1821, the maritime powers moved to counter these outright murderers and pillagers. The United States created squadrons in the Eastern Pacific and West Indies; the Royal Navy reinforced its units in the Caribbean and off Brazil; a small French naval force operated out of Martinique; the Danes at St. Thomas tried to control the pirates there; Haiti did the same; while American warships blockaded Swedish St. Bart's to achieve similar results. When the Spanish appeared unable and unwilling to act against their pirates, and fearing British seizure of Cuba, United States naval forces in March 1822 occupied Key West Island and demonstrated before Puerto Rico. In the winter of 1822–23 the British threatened to land in Cuba to suppress the pirates, while Commodore David Porter was authorized to convoy vessels of all nations from his base at Key West. Despite the intense tropical heat, the usual diseases and not a little mutual suspicion, British and American forces attacked the pirates at sea and in 1823 were finally assisted by the local Spanish authorities in chasing them onto Cuban territory. By the end of the year, when the Monroe Doctrine was formally announced, major Caribbean piracy had been confined to coastal waters.

Meanwhile, Mexico and Brazil revolted from Spanish and Portuguese rule, while the Spanish were trying in vain to reverse the situation in Peru. In September 1821 Mexico proclaimed its independence, generally succeeded in driving out Spanish ground forces, and was visited by Admiral Cochrane's Chilean fleet that attacked Spanish shipping and coastal posts in the Californias early in 1822. In September 1823 Spain ordered its shipping out of Mexican waters, leaving only the fortress of San Juan de Ulua in Vera Cruz harbor in Spanish hands. Bombarding the port, the guns of the castle forced the town's evacuation and the Mexican government's raising of a navy in the manner of the Chileans to reduce the fortress. Meanwhile, in July 1822, San Martin had handed over all his military strength to Bolívar, who took the next three years to clear Peru of Spanish forces. Cochrane felt his work done and left Chilean service late in 1822, but the Chilean-Peruvian fleet had to blockade Callao during the Spanish reoccupation of it in 1824–25 and ended its operations by taking the Chiloé Islands in January 1826.

Brazil broke from Portugal in 1822 and like Chile and Mexico sought outside help in raising a navy, although two Portuguese frigates and a number of other vessels had fallen into Brazilian hands. With 4700 miles of coastline to defend, the new republic eagerly recruited Portuguese, British, American and other officers and in March 1823 appointed Lord Cochrane as First Admiral of the Brazilian navy. In the meantime, the Portuguese garrisons at Montevideo and Bahian Salvador had been isolated, and in April Cochrane blockaded the Portuguese warships on the coast of Bahia and profited from generally inferior Portuguese leadership. In a 74-gun flagship and leading 8 other vessels, Cochrane frustrated a Portuguese sortie of 17 warships escorting over 70 transports from Salvador to the northern port of Maranhão by capturing some of the transports and the port itself in July and chasing the rest of the convoy all the way to Portugal. Simultaneously, a Brazilian frigate took 18 prizes in Portuguese waters. In 1824 Cochrane helped to quell a rebellion in Brazil, and the next year Portugal accepted Brazilian sovereignty.

Spain was less realistic and painfully tried to salvage something from her disintegrating American empire. Helpless to reverse the situation in Peru, the Spanish hoped to center their efforts on the Caribbean—Cuba, Mexico and Colombia, though the latter two would have to be retaken. Even Cuba was a problem, for anti-pirate operations brought Anglo-

American landing forces into Cuban and Puerto Rican territory in 1824 and 1825, although in August of the latter year Britain, France and the United States jointly renounced any designs to take Cuba. Piracy was thus practically extinguished in the Caribbean, and the Spanish could devote their major energies to recovering Mexico and Colombia. But this proved unattainable. Collecting twenty vessels in the Caribbean and others on the west coast at Acapulco and San Blas, the Mexican navy increased the pressure on the garrison at San Juan de Ulua. Seven vessels from the base at Sacrificios Island below Vera Cruz turned away two Spanish relief forces in October 1825, leading to the castle's surrender the next month. Meanwhile, Colombian privateers were attacking Spanish shipping, and plans were discussed for joint Mexican-Colombian naval operations against Spain, to be joined by the Central American republics which had easily thrown off Spanish rule. The scheme was not realized, but the Latin American pressure continued.

Mexico in the summer of 1826 gave command of its growing fleet to David Porter, recently court-martialed by the United States Navy. Since Havana had become the focus of Spain's attempts to recover her lost colonies, Porter with four vessels harassed Spanish shipping off Cuba late in 1826 until he was chased into Key West by a Spanish squadron. The port had been abandoned as a base by the American squadron in favor of newly acquired Pensacola, so Porter decided to base there himself—a clear violation of American neutrality which Spain protested, but in vain. Returning late in 1827 to Vera Cruz, Porter sent out his warships to augment Mexican privateers attacking Spanish shipping and lost his best vessel, a 22-gun brig, in battle against a Spanish 64 early in 1828. The efforts of Spain achieved nothing more than stalemate. An expedition to recover Colombia in 1827 failed, and though Mexico ended its attacks on Spanish shipping in August 1828, Spain's fortunes did not improve. Porter left Mexican service a year later, just as a Spanish expedition from Havana against Tampico was repulsed by the Mexican troops of General Antonio López de Santa Anna. In the political upheavals of Mexico, Santa Anna took over the government and abolished the too-expensive Mexican navy in 1830. But by then Spain's American empire had been reduced to Cuba and Puerto Rico.

Anglo-American support of the Latin American revolutions had isolated the politics of the great powers from the Western Hemisphere, but it otherwise had little effect on the internal situation in Latin America. Even foreign officers such as Cochrane and Porter had been victimized by the unsettled political intrigue of their adopted causes. Indeed, the political upheavals that have continued to plague these Latin American republics to this day have generally led to dictatorships of strong army officers such as Bolívar and Santa Anna whose major concerns have been internal security and frontier defense. Naval forces they have considered extravagant, and with no maritime populations of any consequence these new nations depended initially on former Spanish and Portuguese officers and then on foreign navies altogether. When Uruguay with Argentine help revolted against Brazil in 1825, the fleet formerly led by Cochrane blockaded Buenos Aires, leading to British mediation which—combined with allied victories on land—in turn led to Uruguayan independence by 1828. Similarly, Peru invaded Bolivia in 1827, supported by a naval squadron which took Guayaquil early in 1829; however by March of the latter year the Bolivians had repelled the invader. And small naval forces figured in the Venezuelan revolution of 1848–49.

But as the Latins warred among themselves, they were vulnerable to naval attack. In fact, to improve their position relative to the Americas, in 1833 the British occupied the Falkland Islands off the coast of Argentina. Five years later, in response to pleas from French nationals living in Mexico, a French squadron of three frigates and lesser craft under Admiral Charles Bandin anchored off Sacrificios and bombarded San Juan de Ulua until it was evacuated. The French then occupied Vera Cruz from April 1838 until Mexico satisfied French demands the following March. Similarly, an Argentine intervention in the Uruguayan civil war of 1843–52 was checked partly by an Anglo-French naval blockade of the River Plate and the occupation of some Uruguayan territory in the years 1845–49. Generally, then, the Latin American republics were isolated by the British navy and yet were protected by the Monroe Doctrine. This dependence placed them somewhat at the mercy of the expanding United States.

## THE CONTINENTAL UNITED STATES

The United States after 1815 declined as a potential maritime power commensurate with the passing of New England's predominance in the Union. To be sure, the American merchant marine by the 1840s rivaled closely that of Great Britain, but it depended upon that nation's capital ships to command the seas in protection of free trade. The United States in fact compared with France as a continental power, employing a large merchant service and second-rank navy. The American Congress in 1813 and 1816 authorized twelve 74-gun ships of the line, all of which were built, but half of which stayed in reserve for a national emergency. Rather, the United States relied—like France and Russia—upon frigates for commerce protection and *guerre de course* and upon gunboats and fortifications for coastal and river operations. As American overseas trade expanded, along with the need for home defense and anti-slaving operations, the United States established naval squadrons throughout the world: the Mediterranean in 1815, the Eastern Pacific 1818, West Indies and Caribbean 1822, Brazil 1826, East Indies 1835, the Home Station 1841, and Africa 1843.

As the French-style planter aristocracy of the South and the frontier-oriented Western men led by Andrew Jackson dominated the national government, American public opinion less and less appreciated the need for a large and expensive navy. Indeed, so suspicious were the politicians of professional naval officers—conservative and aristocratic by nature—that they kept supreme naval authority in the civilian Secretary of the Navy even during the major administrative reforms of 1815 and 1842, refused to create a rank as high as rear admiral (even commodore was temporary and honorary), and allowed the creation of a naval academy in 1845 only because of the demands for education in steam engineering. No real admiralty existed, nor a senior officer like Britain's First Sea Lord, the Admiral of France, or even the United States Army's General-in-Chief. Though extremely busy, the small United States Navy was reduced to minor proportions during the Presidency of General Jackson in the 1830s. Lacking a long naval tradition, the Americans were fully prepared to accept innovations in propulsion and armament. With no real need for a blue-water navy to command the sea, American naval strategy in the early nineteenth century was subordinated to the needs of the Army.

The continental thrust westward, accompanied by a small frontier and militia army, depended logistically on increasingly improved roads, canals (especially the Erie in 1825), rivers and coastal traffic. Especially important was the river steamboat, which dominated internal transportation in the United States during the 1830s and 1840s until challenged by the railroad in the 1850s. The steamer, in fact, hastened the shift of American society westward, for the Mississippi River came to rival the seaports of the Atlantic and Gulf coasts. Cotton from the South moved down the Tennessee and Cumberland rivers to join the Ohio and Mississippi; manufactured goods from the East and the wheat of the Midwest followed the Ohio to the great river thence to New Orleans. Similarly, coastal shipping rounded Key West to supply the Gulf coast as far as Mexico. The Mississippi, then, became the natural highway for the penetration into Louisiana territory; thus the Army, supplied by its own river transports, moved up the tributaries called the Red, Arkansas, Missouri, Platte and Des Moines to build a line of riverbank frontier forts protecting settlers against hostile Indians. The work of the United States Army was thus peacekeeping by pacification, linked with the East by its own system of riverborne logistics. But when mobility was required along the coasts, especially in Florida, Texas and California, the Navy joined in this task. By this rather crude and expedient military strategy, the United States fashioned its continental empire during the nineteenth century. Small wonder, then, that the American people had minimal interest in an oceanic strategy or fleet.

The United States Navy therefore developed in the nineteenth century (in addition to its adherence to coast defense and *guerre de course*) a strategy and doctrine of inshore warfare. Since this evolution was discontinuous—dating back to colonial and Revolutionary times—it was never actually formalized. This was perhaps due to the unconventional and unglamorous nature of inshore fighting, and to American disinterest in formal military doctrines. Nevertheless, along the coasts, rivers and marshes, the Navy joined the Army in combined operations, some amphibious, some dealing with pacification and counter-guerrilla operations, others in blockade and bombardment, and occasional naval battles with fleets of enemy inshore craft. The principal events of this half-century of inshore naval operations between the 1820s and the 1870s were the rivalries with Britain on the Oregon coast and with Mexico on the Gulf and California coasts, the Second Seminole War, the Mexican War and the Civil War.

Though the Army was largely responsible for carrying out the wanton pacification of the native Indians as part of the inexorable westward expansion, the Navy became involved early in the Second Seminole War. When the Florida Seminoles rejected the general removal of Eastern Indians to the trans-Mississippi West by the Army, a virtual guerrilla war developed across most of Florida. Shortly after hostilities began late in 1835, the West Indies Squadron based at Pensacola began to provide support to the Army's operations around Tampa Bay. Early in 1836 Navy vessels cruised the west coast of the Florida peninsula between Tampa and Key West to blockade and interrupt Seminole movements by water as part of the strategy of the senior Army commander, Major General Winfield Scott. The naval aspects of this campaign proved fruitless, for the Seminoles were largely self-sufficient save for arms which could be spirited in from Spanish Cuba aboard small coasters. As the Seminoles moved southward into the Everglades, naval brigades composed largely of Marines made landings on the coast. In order to force all the Indians southward where they could be isolated, naval forces based at St. Augustine joined the Army for the campaign late in 1837. These combined operations brought on much fighting but no clear result, even after Colonel Zachary Taylor's forces crushed the main Seminole force in pitched battle at Lake Okeechobee on Christmas Day. Taylor succeeded to command in Florida and even employed his own naval forces, which hampered Army-Navy cooperation, but pointed up the need for a separate special inshore force to operate on the coasts, rivers and lakes of the Everglades region. In 1839 such a force was organized: the "Mosquito Fleet" (named for a lagoon), comprised of schooners, barges, flat-bottomed boats and canoes under Lieutenant John T. Mc-Laughlin of the Navy. Beginning in the spring of 1840, this fleet of sailors, soldiers and Marines began offensive water operations into the Everglades, culminating in a major expedition in the autumn of 1841. As the last Seminole defenders retreated, McLaughlin's Mosquito Fleet pursued them relentlessly during the first half of 1842 until major resistance ended. Since all the Indians did not submit, total pacification was not completed until 1858. But the Navy had made a major contribution—however makeshift—toward winning the Indian wars.

Just as American settlers drove the Indians from their native soil, simultaneously they penetrated into northern Mexico and attempted to wrest it from the new Latin American country; in the summer of 1835 these Texans revolted and the following March proclaimed their independence. The active fighting of 1835–36 had important naval aspects, for both Texans and Mexicans depended logistically on the neutral port of New Orleans, and the American West Indies Squadron had to insure its country's neutrality. Under the dictatorial presidency of General Santa Anna, who personally led the invasion of Texas, the Mexican navy had virtually ceased to exist, so that the four schooners purchased in the United States to comprise the Texas navy had little opposition in their operations against Santa Anna's waterborne logistics. Unfortunately, they also captured American and British vessels, raising the charge of piracy. In April 1836 the Texas army defeated and captured Santa Anna in the San Jacinto campaign, followed in the summer by a Texas naval blockade of Matamoros and the mouth of the Rio Grande. One year later, three brigs and two schooners of the revitalized Mexican navy blockaded Galveston, captured one of the Texas schooners, and were soon involved with American vessels. Taking advantage of the American preoccupation with the Seminole War and of political unrest in the Mexican province of Yucatan, in 1837 two Texas warships raided that coast and continued their policy of open *guerre de course* in the Gulf of Mexico before the small squadron was run aground off Texas by the Mexicans late in the summer. Stripped of her small fleet, Texas was about to be blockaded again by Mexico when the French suddenly occupied Vera Cruz in 1838–39. The Texans took advantage of this respite to build six sailing warships at Baltimore and to purchase a paddle-wheel steamer, all under a dynamic former American naval officer, Commodore Edwin W. Moore. This force then operated with much success along the Mexican coast and rivers, supported by rebellious Yucatan, from late 1840 to early 1842. During these years, Texas, though bargaining for American statehood, became a sovereign power as the United

States, Britain, France and the Netherlands recognized the Republic.

Mexico steadfastly refused to recognize Texan independence, and in 1842 began to reinforce its navy, quickly hastening a showdown. When it seized several Yucatan warships and purchased two British-manned steamers, the Mexican Navy grew, while an unsympathetic administration under President Sam Houston allowed the naval force of Texas to decline. Nevertheless, Commodore Moore sortied from New Orleans with a 20-gun sloop and 16-gun brig to besieged Campeche, where he joined six Yucatan gunboats late in April 1843. He was seeking an engagement with the Mexican fleet of six vessels, half of which were armed with Paixhans guns, plus auxiliary vessels. Skirmishing with the Mexicans, the Texas squadron entered Campeche, thus raising the siege. The new Mexican squadron commander, Captain Tomás Marín, sent away all but his three Paixhans-armed vessels, filled his depleted crews with soldiers, and daily prepared for battle with Moore's two largest warships. The battle of Campeche finally occurred on May 16, 1843, an erratic gunnery duel in which the Texas sail craft drove off the Mexican steamers, leading eventually to the total abandonment of the siege of Campeche. President Houston, at odds with Moore, branded his cruise an act of piracy and dismissed him from the Navy. The United States then mediated a truce, while Britain and France were committing themselves to the independence of Texas. Fearful of British designs in North America, the American Congress early in 1845 annexed Texas to the Union. Thus another small navy had played its part in the balance of power in the Western Hemisphere, weakening Mexico and contributing to the tension between the continental United States and maritime Great Britain.

Along with the Great Lakes and Texas quarrels, Anglo-American rivalry grew on the Pacific coast of North America from the War of 1812. Other European powers involved initially were Spain and Russia, but neither maintained its claims vigorously. The Russians controlled Alaska and established trading posts as far south as northern California, and in 1821 the tsar tried to exclude foreign vessels from coastal fishing, whaling and sealing to one hundred miles out from the Alaskan shore. Protests from Britain and the United States, plus the proclaimed doctrine of Monroe and Canning, helped induce Russia to make treaties with both countries in 1824–25 granting reciprocal trade and setting Russian territorial claims at the parallel of 54° 40', the southern tip of Alaska. Meanwhile, Spain in the treaty of 1819 over the Florida question had limited its northern imperial border at the 42nd parallel in Upper California, only to lose all its coastal territory to independent Mexico three years later. Between Russian Alaska and Mexican California lay the Oregon country, jointly claimed by Britain and the United States but who in 1818 had agreed to coexist there. British maritime penetration into the Eastern Pacific paralleled their drive into the Western Pacific and led to the creation of a separate Eastern Pacific station at Valparaiso in 1837, although the major port for all maritime carriers and under British protection had become Honolulu in the Hawaiian (Sandwich) Islands. The gradual settlement of traders and farmers from various nations in Eastern Pacific lands, plus occasional visits by warships, did not reach crisis proportions until the early 1840s when accelerated American expansion westward was accompanied by the French thrust into the South Sea Islands.

The shifting of naval forces in the Eastern Pacific to achieve a readjusted balance of power led first to fears of war, then to treaty settlement. In 1840–41 the Canadian boundary dispute, the issue of Texas and disagreements over suppression of the slave traffic combined with the Oregon question to lead to a naval arms buildup in the United States. The United States created (largely from West Indies units) a Home Squadron in 1841 to defend the American coast in event of war and placed its ships in the Pacific on alert. The American commodore there, fearful of a British naval annexation of Mexican Upper California, in 1842 seized the port of Monterey, then withdrew. The next year a British warship captain, apprehensive over the French naval expedition to annex parts of Oceania, proclaimed the British annexation of Hawaii, but was not supported by his government. By that time, American pioneers were pouring into the disputed Oregon country over the Oregon Trail. In 1845 six British warships operated in the coastal waters of Puget Sound and the Columbia River. The Canadian boundary had been settled at the 49th parallel in 1842, and the United States annexed Texas early in 1845, but war appeared imminent over Oregon. Finally, in 1846, the two English-speaking powers agreed to divide the Oregon country, extending the 49th parallel boundary from the Rockies to Puget Sound. Vancouver Island became a British colony in 1849 and was joined to the mainland as British Columbia in 1866, but separate from the provinces of Canada east of the Rockies. Also in 1846 Britain and France made a treaty honoring the independence of Hawaii, thus easing tensions there. Throughout these events, Russia gradually began to roll back its settlements in North America, while Mexico became ever more helpless to administer its distant subjects in Upper California who had revolted successfully early in 1845.

By the beginning of 1846, with Oregon and Texas being brought under the American flag, relations between the United States and Mexico were steadily deteriorating. American settlers had led the Texas revolt and were now claiming the territory beyond the Nueces River as Texan, a claim not recognized by the Mexican government. The

Texans, now as Americans, wanted the vast territory to the Rio Grande, running northwest to tiny El Paso and thence north to Santa Fe, terminus of the overland Santa Fe Trail from Missouri. In addition, American settlers had gained the Oregon lands on the Upper California border and others were playing no small part in the California revolt. More internal discord in Yucatan and along the Gulf of California further weakened the central government at Mexico City. So the Mexican army remained the chief force for internal order and home defense, while the navy consisted of a small force of two steam frigates and three brigs plus light sail craft that had suffered from the attacks of the Texans. The United States, by contrast, was generally unified, save for the slavery issue dividing North and South, its people imperial-minded with a small but seasoned frontier army and growing sail-and-steam frigate and coastal navy clearly superior to that of Mexico. With two great coastlines to defend from the Rio Grande to Yucatan and from above San Francisco to below Acapulco, plus a vast continental territory, Mexico was in no position to wage war on the United States.

## THE MEXICAN WAR

Nevertheless, the Mexican War broke out in the spring of 1846 and quickly assumed the proportions of a land war supported by America's inshore fleet. The armies battled around the mouth of the Rio Grande throughout the second half of 1846, while the American Home Squadron under Commodore David Conner instituted a blockade of the Mexican Gulf coast, operating from distant Pensacola to close the major port of Vera Cruz. In order to achieve an effective blockade, the United States Navy needed command of the sea, which it achieved by default at the opening of hostilities. The Mexican government in the spring of 1846 had decided to fight without a navy, allowing its two steam frigates to be repossessed by their British owners. The rest of the fleet was virtually retired: the three brigs and six schooners in the shallow Alvarado River forty miles southeast of Vera Cruz, and three new schooners at Tampico, some 200 miles north of Vera Cruz. Mexico did make a major effort to enlist privateers by issuing letters of marque throughout the world, using the unprecedented scheme of naturalizing the crews of any Mexican privateer. This thin disguise of Mexico's maritime weakness combined with America's maritime prestige and world opinion against privateering and its practical abuses to defeat this scheme. The one privateer that sailed, a felucca from Algeria, made a single capture, only to be hunted down by the Spanish navy early in 1847. Thus Mexico's feeble naval policy embodied coast defense with fortifications and encouraging—with some success—blockade runners to help supply the army in the field.

American naval efforts therefore aimed at blockade and supporting the invasion of Mexico. The only real difficulty experienced lay in natural hazards of the Gulf: intensely hot weather which helped breed tropical diseases, prostration and dysentery and compounded the difficulties of obtaining and keeping adequate food and water. Pensacola lay one month away by round trip, while sudden tropical storms— "northers"—hit ships on blockade station with great ferocity. Lacking forward bases, therefore, the Home Squadron needed to use the anchorage of Anton Lizardo below Vera Cruz and had to seize coastal points in order to provide rest and provisions. The latter stratagem tended to backfire, however, for the shoreline brought the crews into direct contact with yellow fever and malaria. However, the western coasts of Upper and Lower California did not offer such hazards, and the excellent anchorages there not only provided numerous advanced bases but acted as the key to operations in northern Mexico. By contrast, operations on the Gulf coast—save for Yucatan, which elected to stay out of the war—were but the prelude to an overland campaign to capture Mexico City, deep in the interior, and end the war.

North to south, the Gulf ports that the U.S. Navy blockaded were Matamoros, Soto la Marina, Tampico, Tuxpan, Vera Cruz, Alvarado and Tabasco—all of which lay up rivers or behind sandbars that could be negotiated only by shallow-draft steamers. As such steam schooner gunboats were being purchased and/or constructed and deployed, the blockade continued apace. Matamoros, being on the Rio Grande, was easily occupied early in the war by General Taylor's forces, while Soto la Marina was too far from the major objectives to warrant seizure. Tampico resisted a seaborne expedition in June 1846, as did Alvarado in August, Conner trying to destroy the Mexican squadron there, but in vain. The Mexicans hastily strengthened their coastal defenses at Alvarado and placed them with their small squadron under the overall command of Commodore Marín, so that when Conner made a second attempt on the port in October he was again repulsed. Commodore Matthew C. Perry now reported as pending relief for Conner, who immediately sent him to direct the capture of Tabasco with its Mexican shipping. Late in October, Perry's force took Frontera at the mouth of the Tabasco River and then drove upriver to Tabasco where after some stiff resistance the Mexican squadron fell with the town. Perry then withdrew, leaving two vessels on blockade station; of the various craft taken, a steamer and a schooner were converted to gunboats and incorporated into the Home Squadron. Then, early in November, Conner and Perry led an expedition which took Tampico and its three new gunboats, all of which were transferred into the blockading fleet. The Americans raided up the Pánuco River as far as Pánuco, then ferried some of Taylor's troops down the coast from the Rio Grande to garrison Tampico, which became a forward staging base. In December, when Yucatan briefly threatened to enter the war, Perry occupied the tiny port of Carmen and temporarily extended the blockade to include Yucatan. Awaiting more steamers and plagued by erratic weather, the Home Squadron ended 1846 in general control of the Gulf coast and awaiting the assault on Vera Cruz.

The port of Vera Cruz held the strategic key to the Mexican coast and the approaches to Mexico City; thus its investment became the major naval campaign of the war. General Winfield Scott commanded the Army forces, which included Army transports and Army-built special assault boats, and worked in close harmony with the Navy in planning and executing the landing. The expeditionary force of 12,000 men gathered at Tampico, were combat-loaded at nearby Lobos Island early in 1847, and rendezvoused with the Home Squadron at Anton Lizardo. On March 9 the troops transferred from their transports to the men-of-war, then disembarked into their "surf boats" near Sacrificios Island in the afternoon. Bypassing the castle of San Juan de Ulua, which the heavy ships took under fire, the assault forces landed in successive waves on an undefended beach below Vera Cruz late in the day. The fleet gave them close-in fire support while they established a perimeter on the beach. Next day the sturdy surf boats brought artillery ashore and even towed swimming horses so that the land-sea siege of Vera Cruz could begin. Perry now relieved Conner in command of the fleet and sent heavy naval guns ashore. Despite a sudden norther which wrecked twenty-six transports on the beach, the siege held until both the town and the castle surrendered two weeks later. Scott then sent a column overland to take Alvarado, the Navy under Perry supporting from the sea; the town was easily taken early in April, whereupon the Mexicans scuttled the immobile remnant of their navy in the river. In mid-month Perry's steamers towed his gunboats up the Tuxpan River for the successful investment of that port. Taking everything of military value, Perry then withdrew everything but his blockading vessels. Secure with his coastal base around Vera Cruz, General Scott led his army inland to face Santa Anna and the Mexican army defending Mexico City.

Meanwhile, sparse American ground and naval forces had been wresting northern Mexico from their enemies, which included some unsympathetic Californians. Upon the outbreak of war, the Pacific Squadron had in July 1846 occupied San Francisco and Monterey, which they then strengthened. The new squadron commander, Commodore Robert F. Stockton, ferried the pro-American rebel forces under John C. Frémont to San Diego to operate against the Mexicans between that place and Los Angeles. With naval brigades of sailors and marines, Stockton then occupied Santa Barbara and San Pedro, giving the Americans possession of Upper California's five excellent anchorages, and took Los Angeles as well. In September, however, the Californians at Los Angeles revolted and forced the Americans to reembark. Having great mobility to shift his forces by sea, Stockton spent the next several weeks trying to recover Los Angeles, using San Diego as his prime base. Meanwhile, a small Army expedition under Brigadier General Stephen W. Kearny advanced westward from Missouri, took Santa Fe before pressing on to join forces with Stockton at San Diego, doing so in December after a brief skirmish with Mexican forces. Stockton and Kearny then led a combined Army-Navy expedition of some 600 men overland from San Diego to retake Los Angeles. In January 1847 they accomplished their mission by defeating the Mexicans at the battles of San Gabriel and La Mesa and then accepting the surrender of all Upper California. American forces could then redeploy to the Gulf of California, where two sloops-of-war had been operating against Mexican ports and shipping since late August. Especially successful were succeeding blockades of La Paz, Guaymas and Mazatlán by the vessel under Commander Samuel F. Du Pont. Save for the seizure and occupation of La Paz in April, however, the blockade of the Gulf was difficult to enforce, due to the long major supply route around the Horn to the East coast of the United States.

With General Scott's army fighting its way into Mexico City, the war finally swung to American victory during the spring and summer of 1847. On the Gulf coast, Commodore Perry operated eastward along the coast as far as Carmen in May, followed the next month by an expedition upriver from Frontera which used naval gunfire and a naval brigade to fight its way again to Tabasco, only to evacuate it after yellow fever struck. Blockade duty remained difficult because of the weather and disease, while garrisons ashore were plagued by uncoordinated guerrilla attacks. Nevertheless, Perry maintained the blockade for many more months and even managed to supply the neutral Yucatan government with arms to put down a large-scale Indian uprising. Simultaneously, after a hard campaign, in September 1847 Scott's army captured Mexico City, and peace negotiations were begun. On the West coast, the American naval blockade was extended, using La Paz as the forward base. The Pacific Squadron bombarded and attacked several small coastal points, neutralized Guaymas in October, took and occupied Mazatlán in November, and repulsed a Mexican counterattack in Lower California during the winter of 1847–48. Sealed off from the outside, with only Acapulco still open, its capital city and major settlements occupied, its main army defeated and navy destroyed, Mexico had no choice but to agree to American demands. In February 1848 Mexico ceded all her territory north of the Rio Grande and Gila rivers, including Upper California, to the United States.

The American Empire, fashioned on the decay of the maritime empires of Great Britain (1780s), France (1801), Spain (1819—and, indirectly thereafter, Mexico) and to a lesser extent Russia (1824–67), was purely continental in character. The nationalistic expansionism of the young Republic achieved relentless proportions in the early nineteenth century, having no pity on hapless native Indians or helpless Mexico, from which it extracted by barter an additional parcel of territory south of the Gila River in 1853 to fix finally the present borders of the continental United States. The discovery of gold in California in 1848 hastened the thrust of settlers—and the necessary network of Army frontier forts to protect them—across the continent. The Army reverted to a mere peace-keeping function, still utilizing the rivers for logistics and some transporting, but having to break away to trails, desert and mountains where the rivers ended. The coming of the railroad on a large scale in the 1850s and climaxed by the first transcontinental rail line in 1869 hastened the settlement and pacification of the great Western plains. The Navy also declined after the Mexican War until reforms toward steam began in 1853. But it remained essentially an inshore force committed also to police work: hunting slave-traders, punishing unfriendly Chinese during the Arrow War, and even lending some assistance to the Army as in January 1856 when a sloop of war in Puget Sound used its cannon and a landing party to repel an Indian attack on the coastal settlement there. Secure within its vast borders, the United States had little to fear from its neighbor below the Rio Grande which was convulsed in civil war in the late 1850s, although its neighbor above the Great Lakes and 49th parallel remained troublesome.

The balance of power in the Western Hemisphere continued to rest upon the naval supremacy which underpinned the *Pax Britannica* and the Monroe Doctrine. During the Crimean War (1854–56), an Anglo-French squadron operated against the Russians occasionally from San Francisco as well as Hawaii and Vancouver, and another Anglo-American boundary dispute—over the San Juan Islands in Puget Sound—in 1859 led to the establishment of a British naval base at Esquimalt on the Sound. The Royal Navy, which also had to help pacify British Columbia where gold was discovered during the 1850s, had good reason to fear American expansionism. But British naval supremacy in the Pacific was growing, for in 1859 the Australasian Station was officially established, and in 1862 Pacific squadron headquarters was moved from Valparaiso to Esquimalt. The British were also interested, naturally enough, in constructing a canal across Central America either at Nicaragua or Panama, thus linking up their merchant fleets and naval forces. The United States had similar ideas, and in the late 1840s both countries infiltrated the isthmian regions, the British obtaining rights to the east coast Nicaraguan port of Greytown. As tension mounted, the diplomats sought a compromise and agreed finally in 1850 to share in the eventual construction of—but never to fortify—an isthmian canal. It should be noted that in these tense years 1848 to 1851 the British commander-in-chief in North America and the West Indies Station was none other than Admiral Lord Cochrane, veteran of the Aix Roads operation (1809) and former celebrated leader of the Chilean, Brazilian and Greek navies who certainly inherited the mantle of Nelson in the era of *Pax Britannica*. Yet, apparent American intentions of annexing portions of the Caribbean seemed thinly disguised when a "filibustering" expedition mounted in the United States failed to "liberate" Cuba in 1849–51; an American warship bombarded restive Greytown in 1854; a Spanish-American crisis arose over Cuba the same year; and unsuccessful American filibusterers attempted to conquer Nicaragua in 1856–57 and then Honduras in 1860. Mutual Anglo-American suspicions continued, although in 1859–60 Britain withdrew formally from her holds on Honduran and Nicaraguan territory, and both countries increased their efforts against the illicit slave trade.

American maritime and naval policies in the 1850s generally avoided identification with those of Britain and therefore followed a different course. The gold rush to California stimulated the American fast clipper ship trade from 1848 and helped the American merchant marine to reach its greatest peak—5,151,000 tons to Britain's 5,251,000—in 1855. But then, quite suddenly, the American foreign carrying trade fell off mostly for reasons directly attributable to the British competition. The British government, unlike the American, heavily subsidized private shipbuilders who now began converting to steam propulsion —a change their Yankee counterparts could ill afford. Furthermore, Lloyd's insurance practices discriminated in favor of British shippers, while the railroad began to take some of the American internal trade from coastal vessels. Save for a brief flurry during the Crimean War, then, American maritime trade began a steady decline, crippled severely by a major financial panic in 1857. Regarding merchant craft in time of war, the United States had long depended on privateers as a naval weapon in place of a standing fleet, and thus played no part in the 1856 Declaration of Paris which outlawed privateers. When British warships began searching American-flag slavers in 1858, Southern Congressmen demanded more steam gunboats to defend the Gulf coast against Britain; the unusual interest of the agricultural South in the Navy was due to the desire to protect slavers and was led by Florida Senator Stephen R. Mallory, Chairman of the Senate Naval Affairs Committee. The South thus reflected the attitude of the other sections of the country for a small, defensive inshore navy. The Navy continued to reject any blue-water pretensions and was still slow to adopt steam power fully. Thus when the Home Squadron concentrated off Sacrificios and Vera Cruz to press certain demands on Mexico in the autumn of 1860, it was a hodgepodge of the old and new: one steam and one sail frigate, two steam and three sailing sloops, and four steamers. Then, to further weaken the American position at sea, the Union began to disintegrate politically, and in January 1861 the Home Squadron itself dissolved. America's brief attempt to challenge Britain's maritime superiority in the 1850s thus deteriorated.

# 12
# The American Civil War, 1861–1870

*Nor must Uncle Sam's web feet be forgotten. At all the watery margins they have been present. Not only on the deep sea, the broad bay, the rapid river, but also up the narrow muddy bayou, and wherever the ground was a little damp, they have been and made their tracks.*

—ABRAHAM LINCOLN, 1863

## NAVAL STRATEGY, NORTH AND SOUTH

The American Civil War proved to be a watershed event in the history of navies and of warfare, not to mention its sweeping impact on industrialization, human rights and internal American politics. The secession of eleven Southern states from the Union between December 1860 and June 1861 and their formation into a new nation, the Confederate States of America, reflected the deep divisions between the sections that were not only political and cultural but also economic and imperial. The United States—now including the North, West, and Pacific coast—had aggressively extended both American empire across the continent and economic wealth across the oceans of the world. Northern capital, reinforced by industrial manufacture, maritime shipping, and now the railroads, had arisen to exert control over Southern cotton. As this wealth grew, the South became ever more isolated and conservative, dependent upon the will of Northern financiers who by 1860 threatened absolutely to dominate American politics. Northern men compromised with the South by allowing Negro slavery to survive and to expand into some newly acquired territories, but by 1860 Northern sentiment had so swung against that antiquated institution that Kansas territory, especially, was embroiled in war over it and the largely Northern-officered Navy was finally enforcing the ban on Southern slave imports. In order to preserve its institutions, of which slavery was the heart and symbol, the South chose to form its own country even to the point of war. The remaining states of the Union adhered to their federal government and under the leadership of President Abraham Lincoln acted to restore the seceded states to the Union. The obvious result was war, at first a fairly limited one, but as the fighting continued Lincoln's government realized that success required the utter destruction of the Southern socioeconomic system. This conflict, then, heralded the coming of industrialized total war—the complete and unconditional defeat of an enemy with the first new weapons capable of waging such a fight upon the entire enemy citizenry.

From the beginning, the Union took the offensive, the Confederacy the defensive, the latter seeking only to gain foreign recognition of its independence with the resulting foreign aid necessary for victory. Believing that Great Britain and to a lesser extent France were utterly dependent upon its cotton, the South realistically counted upon British support and possible intervention. Certainly, the Palmerston government would welcome this opportunity to weaken further the already-hurting American carrying trade, while France under Napoleon III stood eager to overturn the Monroe Doctrine and reassert the French imperial presence in the Western Hemisphere. Thus Southern armies had only to protect their frontiers and coasts from Northern invasion and prove the political stability of the Confederate government so that the powers would rally to their side. Northern strategy was consequently placed in the difficult position of defeating the Southern armies, blockading the Southern coast and cotton exports and thus discrediting the rebellious states—all the while observing international law and not antagonizing Britain and France. The difficulty of this task became evident in the first year of the war when the North raised tariffs that hurt Britain, tried to establish a blockade, and so flagrantly violated international law that Britain came to the brink of joining the war against the United States—a distinct possibility, since the British government and textile manufacturers clearly sympathized with the South.

A curious similarity between the Union and Confederacy lay in their common naval tradition, though the North had a clear superiority from the beginning because of its large industrial and maritime complex and existing fleet. In both nations, the army predominated, especially in the South with its planter-aristocracy, while the navies drew upon the same inshore-coast defense-*guerre de course* mentality that dated from the Revolution. Both governments continued the strong civilian control over the navies, and were fortunate enough to have experienced Secretaries, in Connecticut politician Gideon Welles who had administered the clothing and feeding of the Navy during the Mexican War and former Senator Mallory of Florida whose association with naval matters included not only Congressional committee work but inshore service in the Second Seminole War. Neither side had admirals at first, preferring instead the old rank of commodore and the higher but more obscure title of "flag officer." So there was no senior naval officer in either the United States or Confederate States navies and no formal naval staffs to advise each Secretary on naval strategy and policy. Indeed, in both navies, though many officers had wide experience, their initial employment depended largely on enlightened generals with some experience in combined operations; Confederates Robert E. Lee and P. G. T. Beauregard had served on General Scott's staff during the landings at Vera Cruz, where the Northerner George B. McClellan began a career which later included observing the Anglo-French attacks on Sevastopol.

Where the Union and Confederacy differed was in attitudes toward maritime warfare. The North had a thalassocratic tradition and physical plant—forty-two commissioned warships, eight naval shipyards and most of the officers and skilled ratings upon which to mobilize a bluewater navy. The South had no such heritage or plant: two shipyards, seventeen small state vessels and some 200 experienced officers. It also had vital raw materials like wood, iron and coal and skilled carpenters and mechanics, but the Army indiscriminately conscripted the latter and commandeered the South's small rail network which was needed to concentrate building materials at the shipyards. Therein lay the major strategic difference between the belligerents. Effective industrial and manpower mobilization would be key elements in modern total war, and for this the North was eminently more suited. Further, such strategic mobilization and then direction depended upon centralized control, which under Lincoln's firm hand the Federal Union enjoyed, whereas the Confederacy remained true to its name: a number of sovereign states reluctant to centralize. The Confederate government was headed by former U. S. Army officer and Secretary of War Jefferson Davis, who had virtually no experience or interest in naval matters. The Southern naval effort was therefore doomed to makeshift expedients and reliance upon whatever Britain and France might provide.

The rival strategies became apparent from the month that hostilities began, April 1861. The Union would have to command the seas; the Confederacy would have to defend its coastlines. That month General Beauregard bombarded into submission Fort Sumter in Charleston harbor, while seceding Virginia seized the great naval arsenal at Norfolk. This prize plus others gave the South vast numbers of new Dahlgren guns and older-style cannon so vital for coast defense. Simultaneously, Lincoln declared a blockade of the Southern coast, and Navy vessels brought volunteer troops to Washington via Annapolis when Maryland threatened to secede, while a flotilla gathered in the Potomac River to protect the appproaches to the capital. In May and throughout the summer of 1861 both sides fumbled toward their respective objectives. For the North, a temporary strategy board headed by Captain Samuel F. Du Pont of the Navy and General-in-Chief of the Army Winfield Scott independently concluded that the blockade should be implemented by a cordon of advanced bases along the coast (as during the Mexican War) for the coaling of steamers and logistical support in general; the board advocated the seizure of New Orleans to cut off traffic down the Mississippi, while Scott would make that river into a third coast, to be occupied by Union garrisons. Secretary Welles opposed this scheme, which gained the popular label of the Anaconda, since he envisioned the struggle as a mere insurgency and not a total war aimed at strangling the South. By the same token, public opinion in the South favored the total defense of the long 2700-mile coastline from Hampton Roads to the Rio Grande, but Secretary Mallory could only turn to local commanders and state resources for this impossible task. The Confederate government issued letters of marque, and a number of privateers put to sea to claim seventeen Yankee merchantmen before withdrawing in the face of the Union navy by the autumn. Privateering had been so discredited as semi-piracy that Lincoln refused to utilize it, and by 1863 it passed out of existence as a tool of the world's navies. Mallory did, however, launch two ambitious projects: the construction of fast steam frigates in foreign shipyards for commerce raiding, and the conversion of inshore and other craft into ironclad armored gunboats—both projects eventually gaining considerable results. But time was on the side of the North.

Following the repulse of a Union army at the melee known as the first battle of Bull Run in northern Virginia in July 1861, both sides resigned themselves to a long war and started implementing their strategies. Despite Welles's reluctance, the Northern blockade as envisioned by Scott was gradually implemented, though Scott himself at the advanced age of seventy-five (and a general officer since 1814!) retired. As the Union navy took time to construct and convert warships for blockade duty, it received unexpected help from the Confederate government, which placed an embargo on its own cotton exports. Hoping to force British recognition, this diplomatic device instead nearly crippled the Southern economy. Welles's unwillingness to mobilize naval forces on the Western rivers led the Army, under the authorization of General McClellan, to raise its own Western fleet of ironclad and wooden gunboats for later offensive operations. In the East, however, Welles was persuaded by favorable circumstances to begin the cordon encirclement of Confederate seaports. Despite the loss of Norfolk, the Union held nearby Fortress Monroe, easily recaptured Newport

News, and from Monroe launched combined amphibious operations which captured Hatteras Inlet, North Carolina, and Port Royal, South Carolina, in August and November, thereby completely disrupting Confederate coastal traffic as far south as Savannah and giving the Union two key blockading bases. These captures suddenly exposed the weakness of Confederate coast defense and led Secretary Mallory to initiate the outright construction of wooden gunboats for harbor defenses, including 100 small Jeffersonian-type gunboats advocated by Commander Matthew F. Maury.

Such losses also hastened a new overall coast defense strategy being implemented by General Robert E. Lee, commanding in South Carolina, Georgia and East Florida. Lee decided to draw back Confederate troops away from the range of Union naval guns, to abandon indefensible positions along the coast such as islands, and to concentrate available forces inland for employment only at crucial areas wherever the enemy actually landed. Although this stratagem could not stop Union landings, Lee hoped to draw his adversary inland away from naval fire support and there to defeat such expeditionary forces. Though this was a more realistic policy than total coast defense, Lee missed the strategic point that Union coastal operations were not designed—indeed, were not strong enough—to invade the South from the coast, but were merely intended to establish advanced base enclaves for the blockading fleet. So additional places fell to Union forces along the North Carolina and Florida coasts in February, March and April 1862, and in the latter month a major amphibious attack took Fort Pulaski, Georgia, commanding the seaward approaches to Savannah. Thus, unwittingly, Confederate strategic decisions immensely aided the Union blockading effort early in the war.

The success or failure of the blockade depended upon the reactions of Britain, traditional arbiter in international maritime law. The British government, though quick to declare its neutrality, soon found that such a statement did not solve all the legal implications of Lincoln's blockade. To be legal, a blockade had to be effective, and investigating British warships often found Southern ports to be clear of Yankee blockaders. Nevertheless, the British carefully avoided setting any precedents by rashly challenging the blockade, much to the continued displeasure of Confederate diplomats. Then, in November 1861, Captain Charles Wilkes on blockade duty halted the British mail packet *Trent* off Cuba and forced two rebel diplomats on board to surrender. This blatant, unauthorized violation of British neutrality enraged Britain, and although Lincoln wisely repudiated the act and released his prisoners before the end of the year, the Royal Navy prepared for war. Troop reinforcements were hastened to Canada,

Bermuda and the British West Indies, while thirteen warships crossed
the Pacific from the China station; these forces were in position for
fighting by the spring of 1862. The British were also angry with
Mexico, whose recent civil war had so ruined its financial situation
that it refused to repay its European creditors. As a result, a joint
Anglo-French-Spanish expeditionary force occupied Vera Cruz in
December 1861—a violation of the Monroe Doctrine, though the
United States was too busy elsewhere to act. Britain and Spain withdrew the following April, but Napoleon III—anxious to add Mexico
to the French Empire—decided to remain, against the advice of his
expeditionary commander, Admiral J. P. E. Jurien de la Gravière.
France declared war on Mexico, blockaded her Gulf coast, increased
the expeditionary force to 40,000 men, and began a rugged overland
campaign to conquer the country. Hurt by the Confederate cotton
embargo and dependent ultimately upon British sea power, France
elected not to antagonize the United States beyond this breach of the
Monroe Doctrine. But American relations with Britain and France
remained strained throughout 1862.

British actions at sea during the Civil War carefully avoided the
taking of sides, but did aid both Union and Confederacy considerably.
For the North, and with Lincoln's full cooperation, the British moved
to destroy the Atlantic slave trade once and for all. In 1862 an Anglo-
American treaty allowed each nation to let warships search slavers
flying the other's flag, and since the American African squadron withdrew to fight in the war the British could act alone to stop the slave
trade. It did so with great dispatch, also choking off slaving to Cuba
by 1865. But the North was uncooperative regarding neutral waters,
which the warships of its North and South Atlantic and East and
West Gulf Blockading squadrons continued to violate. Not only did
the British build and outfit Confederate cruisers, especially the very
successful *Alabama* commissioned under Captain Raphael Semmes off
the Azores in August 1862, but British merchant steamers ran the
blockade to and from British Bermuda and the Bahamas, the Danish
West Indies (Virgin Islands) and Spanish Cuba; at least five captains
of blockade runners were Royal Navy officers on leave. Their sleek
sail-steamers could easily outrun the slower, fuel-conscious blockaders
by making the short dash between Southern ports and neutral islands.
In this manner, British ships aided the Confederacy, and British arms
and goods supplied the Southern war effort. Northern warships therefore violated neutral waters to try to frustrate these practices; the
West Gulf Squadron even blockaded the neutral Rio Grande River
delta to discourage trade between Matamoros and Brownsville, Texas,
while in the autumn of 1862 Commodore Wilkes led a "flying squadron" that virtually blockaded Bermuda and anchored at Nassau, con-

trary to the orders of local British authorities. Wilkes and other officers continued to seize British merchantmen, and one American warship in May 1863 fired onto the beach at British Eleuthera while engaging a blockade runner. Such illegal acts led to tangled legal cases, but the North got away with them because the Union navy commanded North American waters and because the British were ever sensitive about a possible future war in Europe in which the maritime United States would be the neutral. Thus pro-American precedents were being set by the British recognition of the Union blockade.

Also sensitive to protecting its own commerce, the industrial North insured the security of its trade lanes to Europe. In this respect, the Union was most successful. Realizing that the Confederacy could never have more than two or three commerce raiders active simultaneously around the world, the United States believed convoys to be unnecessary since scattered merchantmen would spread thin Confederate cruiser depredations. This doctrine proved correct, as the five major and several lesser cruisers sank but 261 merchant vessels totaling a mere 110,000 tons during the war. Only one convoy was regularly maintained: the Panama-to-East-coast run of California gold, and it was never attacked. Rebel attempts to outfit privateers in the Pacific never matured, and a Confederate army thrust toward California was repulsed by Union forces in New Mexico in the spring of 1862. Most neutral nations allowed vessels of both navies to use their ports, although Ottoman Turkey returned American favors by closing its ports to the few cruisers of the South. But while Northern wartime shipping remained generally protected, the American merchant marine was nearly destroyed. Its decline since 1855 was accelerated by the war. Lloyd's insurance rates for Yankee vessels soared because of the increased risk, while fear of rebel cruisers discouraged many New England shipowners from even putting to sea. The greatest loss was incurred, however, when these shippers transferred no less than 800,000 tons of Yankee bottoms to neutral foreign registry, including the English which afforded protection by naval power and low insurance. A slow recovery of Northern shipbuilding began as the panic subsided late in 1862, but the merchant marine would never regain its former strength. Still, the war effort continued to be maintained by shipping of all registries, and the Northern naval effort on the high seas concentrated almost totally on blockading the South.

## INSHORE WARFARE, COASTS AND RIVERS

As the two nations mobilized their armies and strategies in the winter of 1861–62, the subtle influence of naval power appeared. Henceforth, all major Union armies in the field were named after rivers, while garrison forces in the Gulf of Mexico were titled the Army of the Gulf. The main force, the Army of the Potomac under General McClellan, would attempt to capture the Confederate capital at Richmond, Virginia, while the armies of the Mississippi, the Ohio, the Cumberland and the Tennessee under various commanders delineated the major areas of Union operations in the West. Whenever these armies won control of their namesake rivers, the South would be seriously humbled. In the East, McClellan planned to utilize his naval superiority by moving down the Chesapeake from the defenses of Washington, basing upon the sea at Fortress Monroe and driving up the James River and the so-called Virginia Peninsula to take Richmond. In the West, General U. S. Grant would depart by land and river from his base at Cairo, Illinois, to attack the forts controlling the Tennessee and Cumberland rivers below their northern junction with the Ohio and Mississippi rivers. A second force in the West would push south from Cairo toward Memphis, beginning to clear the Mississippi. The fact that the North early in the war could mount three separate offensives, plus coastal forays, demonstrates the advantages of attacking from the exterior position with superior numbers of men and amounts of equipment. The Confederacy, which named its main armies after territory, operated from the interior position but with insufficient manpower to meet each thrust, and was further hindered by a vast territory broken by the Appalachian Mountains and served by an inadequate rail network. Furthermore, the rivers in the Confederacy—the defense of which the Navy assumed absolutely no responsibility—favored not internal traffic but invasion from the North. So the simple charge of the Army of Northern Virginia under General Joseph E. Johnston and the Army of Mississippi under General A. S. Johnston was to defend the Tennessee-Virginia frontier from a Union advance by land and river.

McClellan's offensive, known as the Peninsular Campaign, was foiled by the caution and respect for Confederate coast defenses of McClellan himself. Having witnessed the first real ironclad operations in the Crimean War, he had a healthy respect for one of Mallory's new coastal ironclads, this one converted from the captured hull of the former Norfolk-based steam frigate *Merrimac* (now renamed *Virginia*). Late in February 1862 this vessel and five gunboats formed the James River Squadron under Captain Franklin Buchanan and then moved against the Union defenses of Newport News. Though the popularly known *Merrimac* was unsuited for operations beyond the sheltered Hampton Roads, McClellan and his naval commanders believed that the vessel threatened the entire Union blockade, let alone their planned advance on Richmond. McClellan preferred to await the arrival from New York of one of three experimental Union ironclads, the *Monitor,* before attempting to drive up the James. Then, on March 8, Buchanan sallied forth with the *Merrimac* to sink two wooden Union frigates in Hampton Roads. McClellan prepared to evacuate Newport News, but next day the *Monitor* arrived and engaged the *Merrimac.* This monumental first duel between ironclad warships ended in something of a draw, though the *Monitor's* performance saved the other wooden vessels present. But *Merrimac,* refusing entreaties to renew the action, still blocked the James. Thus, strategically, this greatly overrated coast defense vessel by its very existence forced the Union army to make far-reaching changes. McClellan now moved his army by transport to Fortress Monroe, but had to abandon the James in favor of the York River on the north side of the peninsula, at best a swampy and thus inferior approach. Furthermore, the Union navy was so concerned about the *Merrimac* that it refused to transfer ships away from Hampton Roads to support and transport McClellan's army up the York. Without the swift mobility of water transport, McClellan's army bogged down in the mud before a small Confederate force at Yorktown, to which he then stupidly laid siege.

Confederate coast defense policies produced results. Early in March 1862, General Lee was relieved of command of the South Atlantic coast and ordered to Richmond to be President Davis' military adviser. His defense-in-depth strategy on the coast also enabled him to transfer many of those troops to reinforce Richmond. By April Lee had realized the line of McClellan's advance and ordered Johnston's army to shift from northern Virginia to the peninsula. He also sent a force under General T. J. "Stonewall" Jackson to demonstrate in the Shenandoah Valley, whereupon Lincoln withheld part of McClellan's army to defend Washington. In May, Johnston and the rebel army evacuated Yorktown and Norfolk in order to better defend Richmond, leaving the Confederate navy no choice but to blow up the deep-draft *Merrimac* which could not move up the shallow river. The lighter-draft *Monitor* and other Union gunboats then pressed up the James, only to be severely repulsed by shore batteries at Drewry's Bluff. By then, McClellan's army had gone up the York and was scattered in its adjacent swamplands when Johnston struck late in May. McClellan held his position, and Johnston himself was wounded and replaced by General Lee. The Navy ferried reinforcements from Fredericksburg via the Rappahannock River, Chesapeake and York to McClellan, while Jackson marched overland from the valley to reinforce Lee before Richmond. With the Army of Northern Virginia endangering his position on the York, McClellan decided to shift his base south to the James, where the Navy could now support him. Lee stood in

his way, so he had to fight—in the Seven Days' Battles—across the
peninsula in late June. He succeeded, but got no closer to Richmond.
The campaign then ended, a brilliant strategic scheme partially frustrated by one warship.

In the West, the Union army and naval forces enjoyed dramatic
successes over the thinly distributed Confederate forces. In February
1862 Grant and the gunboats of Flag Officer A. H. Foote bombarded
and captured Forts Henry on the Tennessee and Donelson on the
Cumberland, enabling the warships to raid as far south on the Tennessee as northern Alabama and also to press up the Cumberland to
capture Nashville, the key to Tennessee. General A. S. Johnston now
took advantage of the Confederate coast-defense-in-depth strategy to
call up the major garrison forces from Mobile, Pensacola and Galveston
on the Gulf for one massive counterattack on Grant's army. He struck
Grant by surprise at Shiloh on the west bank of the Tennessee early
in April only to be finally repulsed by Union reinforcements and gunboats; the Battle of Shiloh also cost Johnston his life. Simultaneously,
a combined Union Army-Navy force captured Island No. 10 on the
Mississippi in western Tennessee. These events severely weakened the
Confederate coast defenses of New Orleans, now dependent upon
coastal forts and a makeshift force of gunboats. Union forces had
occupied Ship Island off the delta of the Mississippi the previous December, and now, in April, the West Gulf Blockading Squadron under
Flag Officer David G. Farragut easily brushed aside rebel defenses
and took New Orleans. The remnant of the Confederate River Defense
Force then hastened north to inflict a surprise defeat on Union gunboats at Fort Pillow below Island No. 10 early in May. The Union
army rushed its own new Ram Fleet to augment the gunboats on the
Upper Mississippi; between them they destroyed the rebel squadron
at the naval battle of Memphis early in June before steaming down
river as far as Vicksburg, Mississippi. Farragut from New Orleans also
briefly reached that point, but retired below Port Hudson when the
Army could not support him. Without question, the capture of New
Orleans was the most important Union conquest of the war—strangling
Southern commerce on the river and along the Gulf coast.

These stunning Union victories on the Western rivers in mid-1862
had serious repercussions everywhere for the South. Encouraged by
the performance of the *Merrimac,* the Confederate Congress scrapped
its plans for Maury's wooden gunboats and voted funds for ironclads
and batteries for coastal and river defenses. Warship construction
within the Confederacy thus accelerated, some 150 new and converted craft being projected, with 22 armored and 5 wooden vessels
eventually being completed, along with a few conversions. That more

were not was due largely to the dispersal of makeshift shipbuilding facilities well inland on the rivers; also, the yards at New Orleans and Norfolk were lost, and in May Pensacola was abandoned to the blockading forces too. Secretary Mallory and local generals also began experiments with floating (mines) and spar torpedoes and submersibles (submarines, except that they never totally submerged). On its three coastlines, the South had yielded important points within the first eighteen months of the war. On the Atlantic coast, in addition to the Hatteras operations, Flag Officer Du Pont's fleet sank stone-laden hulks off Charleston and Savannah late in 1861, then went on in March 1862 to take the northern Florida ports (Jacksonville, St. Augustine, Amelia Island and Fernandina) and in April Fort Pulaski, Georgia. On the Gulf coast, New Orleans and Pensacola were taken in the spring, Galveston in October, and Farragut was only prevented by inactive superiors from seizing the coastal forts below Mobile. On the Mississippi, Grant was similarly frustrated by his superiors but by July had narrowed rebel control to the narrow strip of river between Vicksburg and Port Hudson. The Confederates could not even mount guerrilla attacks near occupied inland waters without facing strong Union countermeasures: the Army employed its own Ram Fleet and elite Mississippi Marine Brigade with specialized landing craft and floating logistics to help the Navy police the upper Mississippi, while gunboats and transports ferried Union forces on the Tennessee and Cumberland rivers to engage guerrillas. Losing so much territory, the South lost prestige abroad.

The Confederacy could hope for British recognition and intervention only if Lee could crush the Union armies in the East. By his experiences facing the Union navy on the Atlantic coast and in the James River, Lee realized he could not hope to win as long as he operated near the Chesapeake shore. As it was, water transport gave the Northern armies exceptional mobility not only between Washington on the Potomac and Fortress Monroe on the James but on other rivers such as the Susquehanna in Pennsylvania and Maryland and the Rappahannock in Virginia. So he strengthened the shore batteries and fortifications at Drewry's Bluff and around Richmond and Petersburg and moved inland. A new Union army marched southward from Washington while McClellan remained on the peninsula, and Lee with Jackson thoroughly defeated it at the second battle of Bull Run late in August 1862. Lee now resolved to invade the North but being careful to march well inland from Union gunboats, which would navigate up the Potomac to the falls only ten miles above Washington. Lee led the Army of Northern Virginia up the Shenandoah Valley, crossing the Potomac into Maryland early in September. McClellan, by his transports and overland marching, covered the national capital and stopped Lee's army at the Battle of Antietam at mid-month. Lacking reinforcements, Lee could do nothing but retire back into Virginia. When McClellan failed to pursue Lee vigorously, Lincoln relieved his naval-minded general from command. Coinciding with Southern military reverses elsewhere, the Antietam campaign sobered European interventionists. In addition, Lincoln used the occasion to emancipate the slaves, with which the British generally sympathized. The war thus became a moral crusade which the North would conclude only by annihilating the Confederate political and socioeconomic system.

From this time forward, the possibility of British intervention waned, along with any real hope of Confederate victory. Though affected by the blockade, Britain received enough cotton from surpluses, blockade runners, and new sources in Egypt and India to avoid recognizing the South. To be sure, English shipwrights continued to outfit rebel cruisers, but the British government became increasingly sensitive to these practices as Union victories mounted. Palmerston also realized that the Yankee privateering of 1812 could be repeated in a future war, or American-built cruisers outfitted for enemies of Britain. Even in 1863, during an Anglo-Russian crisis, the Russian Baltic Fleet visited New York and its Pacific Fleet went to San Francisco, moves which encouraged Britain to remain neutral and thus not tempt the Americans into seeking a combination with any of Britain's European rivals, now or in the future.

The Confederacy, however, taking advantage of the sluggish Union high command, tried to retrieve its fortunes during late 1862 and the first half of 1863. In the East, Lee soundly defeated two overland thrusts by the Army of the Potomac in northern Virginia—at Fredericksburg in December and Chancellorsville in May. He then retraced his 1862 steps up the Shenandoah Valley across the Potomac well inland from Union gunboats, heading apparently for Harrisburg, Pennsylvania. The Potomac River Flotilla moved up the Chesapeake Bay to the mouth of the Susquehanna; beyond lay the Schuylkill River and the Reading-to-Philadelphia rail line, both of which brought the blockading squadrons their weekly supply of 3000 tons of anthracite coal. However, the excellent Northern rail network was rushing troops from the North into southern Pennsylvania, while the Army of the Potomac also hastened there, intercepting and defeating Lee's army at the Battle of Gettysburg the first three days of July 1863. In the West, the Union slowly tried to cut off the trans-Mississippi states. The United States Navy finally created the rank of rear admiral and gave it to Farragut, who pressed on Port Hudson from New Orleans. Acting Rear Admiral David D. Porter (son of the former American-Mexican commodore) took command of the vessels on the upper river; cooperating with General Grant, Porter besieged Vicksburg by land and water. In July, both Vicksburg and Port Hudson fell, giving the Union absolute control of the Mississippi. On the coasts, the South sent its first admiral, Buchanan, to build up the naval defenses of Mobile and reassigned General Beauregard to command at Charleston. The Union, especially Secretary Welles, had a fetish about capturing Charleston, but when Rear Admiral Du Pont's monitors tried to reduce its defenses in April 1863, Beauregard's guns drove them off. Du Pont's relief, Admiral Dahlgren, fared no better during the summer, the defense of Charleston being the single triumph of Confederate coast defense. But the combined Union victories at Gettysburg and Vicksburg dashed the hopes of the South, and the British government used the occasion to seize two large Laird rams then under construction for the Confederacy in England.

The fact that the South survived for two more years is remarkable and was due to continued Union mismanagement and several inferior generals and to Confederate ingenuity. The blockade got tighter in 1863–64, but some four-fifths of the runners that tried to break through during the war actually succeeded, so difficult was it to maintain a close blockade in the age of steam, even with advanced bases. Worse, Yankee merchants either collaborated with corrupt Union commanders to trade munitions and other goods directly with the South, especially in the Chesapeake Bay-North Carolina Sound area, or traded indirectly by shipping goods to neutral Bermuda, Halifax, Nassau and Havana for passage by blockade runner. The New York-to-Matamoros trade, virtually nonexistent before the war, also thrived and materially aided the South. Irresolute Union generalship led to inaction in Virginia, coupled with a serious Union defeat at Chickamauga in the West in September, a disastrous campaign up the Red River in Louisiana during the spring of 1864, and persistently successful rebel cavalry forays seemingly everywhere. Beauregard's defenses at Charleston included two attacks by Confederate submersibles which sank one and badly damaged another Union warship. The one bright figure for the North throughout these difficulties was General Grant, who drove the Confederate Army of Tennessee from the environs of Chattanooga in November 1863 and to whom Lincoln then gave supreme command of the Union armies the following March.

As Lee's army in Virginia became the prime objective for Union military and naval efforts, the Far West became isolated. The Confederate Trans-Mississippi army command had been virtually independent since the beginning of the war anyway, having its own Texas Marine Department. Texas troops had been drawn back in the defense-in-depth scheme away from the range of naval guns, but they had succeeded in recapturing Galveston early in 1863. The fall of Vicksburg severed the Trans-Mississippi completely from the Richmond government, enabling the district to reap the full benefits of the Matamoros trade. In November 1863 Union forces occupied Brazos Santiago Island near Brownsville and fanned out along the coast to Corpus Christi and Matagorda Bay. This movement failed to affect the repulse of the Red River expedition and proved logistically difficult for any new thrust at Galveston. So the troops were all concentrated at Brazos Santiago during the summer of 1864 where they might at least influence the blockade of the mouth of the Rio Grande.

The Union concern for this region after Vicksburg's fall had less to do with the South than with the apprehension about the French presence in Mexico. In 1863 the French blockaded the Mexican Gulf coast and launched an overland offensive which captured Mexico City in June. Placing the Austrian Archduke Maximilian—formerly Admiral Ferdinand Max of the Austrian navy—on the Mexican throne, the French waged an anti-guerrilla war against the patriots and established a naval blockade of the Mexican Pacific coast in 1864. French warships had bombarded Acapulco early in 1863, then occupied it with landing parties in June 1864. British, French and Russian warships visited San Francisco in 1863–64; the Russians also went to Hawaii, while Anglo-American vessels patrolled from Esquimalt to Valparaiso. A Spanish squadron visited these coasts in 1862–63 and in 1864 occupied the Chincha Islands over a dispute with Peru. Chile and Peru mobilized their small fleets for war with Spain, but British, American and French warships successfully averted any hostilities by the beginning of 1865. These busy activities of the European powers in the Western Hemisphere clearly violated the Monroe Doctrine, so that United States military and naval vigilance over the Western territories and Pacific coasts was maintained even in the midst of the Civil War.

## THE GRAND CAMPAIGN OF 1864–65

At the beginning of 1864, the Union turned to proved practitioners of modern total war, replacing those leaders who had failed to act decisively. By placing Grant in supreme command, Lincoln could now expect a grand strategy for the first time in the war. Grant made his headquarters with the Army of the Potomac and appointed Western veterans to his chief commands. The grand campaign aimed at destroying Lee's army and thus taking the capital city that it was defending. It was a strategy of concentration, Grant's Army of the

Potomac holding down the Army of Northern Virginia while the other army and naval forces swept through the Confederacy destroying Lee's logistics and communications. This meant finally closing the last four major seaports east of the Mississippi—Wilmington, Charleston, Savannah and Mobile; destroying the great granary of central Georgia and its key railhead of Atlanta; and doing the same to the Shenandoah Valley. Not all existing commanders were successful, but as the campaign progressed throughout 1864 competent leaders emerged. Farragut remained in the Gulf and moved against Mobile, defended by forts and a force of coastal ironclads and gunboats under Admiral Buchanan, while Dahlgren tightened the blockades of Charleston and Savannah. General William T. Sherman took supreme command of the Western armies, and while Porter pacified the Mississippi marshes Sherman's forces pressed south from Chattanooga to Atlanta. Opposing him was the greatly weakened Army of Tennessee under Johnston. Grant himself would send his own forces headlong into Lee's army, while other Federal units operated in the Shenandoah and another force moved up the James River peninsula from Fortress Monroe against Richmond. Along with the Army of Northern Virginia, Richmond was defended by General Beauregard's fortifications and the James River Squadron of three new ironclads and several gunboats. This grand campaign went into motion in the spring of 1864.

In Virginia, Grant and Lee displayed their continued respect for naval power as the Wilderness Campaign unfolded. Grant crossed the Rapidan River above Fredericksburg in May and repeatedly attacked Lee's army, but always keeping his rear on the coastal rivers for his logistics. When Lee's army withstood these bloody attacks, Grant merely extended the lines of his much larger army toward the coast, forcing Lee to retreat lest his position be flanked or he be forced to operate near the coast and the Union navy. By this stratagem, which cost him heavily in men (which the Northern draft easily replaced), Grant pressed toward Richmond, hurting Lee who could no longer draw upon the exhausted Confederate manpower supply. Simultaneously, the Army of the James under the incompetent political-general B. F. Butler moved up the James by boat only to be pinned down by Beauregard against a bend in the river called Bermuda Hundred. But Grant pushed around the east side of Richmond, crossed the James to free Butler, and by late June had thrown siege lines around the east and south of Richmond and Petersburg. He established a base at City Point on the James where the Navy could supply and support him. Meanwhile, the feeble Union drive into the Shenandoah had been repulsed, and Lee decided to launch a counterthrust up the Valley for a direct descent on Washington. With two thirds of his army, he faced

Grant at Richmond and sent the other third up the Valley under General Jubal A. Early. Early kept well inland as Lee had done twice before, crossed the Potomac early in July and approached the exposed Northern capital from the northwest. Lee had again successfully threatened Union strategy.

But Union sea power frustrated Lee's last offensive. Grant refused to abandon his lines and dispatched one army corps by water from the James, up the Chesapeake and the Potomac to disembark at the Washington docks the very day that Early attacked the forts on the northwest side of the city. Union gunboats again concentrated in the Potomac and at the mouth of the Susquehanna, while Grant ordered another army corps by sea all the way from New Orleans to Washington via Hampton Roads. Early, outnumbered, had no choice but to fall back though not before raiding into southern Pennsylvania late in July. Grant now created the Army of the Shenandoah from the troops gathered around Washington and ordered General Philip H. Sheridan to use it to crush Early's force and then to burn the Valley crops to the ground. Sheridan fulfilled these orders in the early autumn of 1864, thus destroying a part of Lee's army and its nearest source of food. Rejoining Grant before Richmond and Petersburg, Sheridan's force gave Grant overwhelming superiority. Still, Lee held on during the winter, supported by his active James River Squadron, which, however, was badly battered by Union batteries during a sortie late in January. By then, however, the operations of Sherman, Farragut and Porter had combined with those of Sheridan to begin the progressive starvation of Lee's once fine army.

In the West, Sherman began the Atlanta Campaign in May and by a series of outflanking maneuvers pushed Johnston's army back on Atlanta. Reaching the outskirts of the city, Sherman was attacked boldly by a new rebel commander, General John B. Hood, but in July and August defeated him and took the city. Simultaneously, in August, Farragut's squadron braved floating mine fields to defeat the Confederate flotilla at the battle of Mobile Bay and to bombard the coastal forts there into submission; although the city was not invested, it was now closed to commerce. General Hood, following Lee's example, now thrust northward into Tennessee toward the main Union supply base and rail head at Nashville, while his cavalry actually captured and briefly manned one Union gunboat and five transports on the Tennessee. But Sherman, like Grant, refused to be diverted from Atlanta. Instead, he sent General George B. Thomas to Nashville, which Hood besieged, while Union troops in the North hastened by river and rail to reinforce Thomas. Sherman then burned Atlanta, cut his communications with the North altogether and set off across Georgia, living off the land and applying the torch to whatever supplies his army did not need. Sherman's "march to the sea" in November and December 1864, virtually unopposed, eliminated the last major supply area for Lee's army, while Sherman reestablished his own communications by taking Savannah from the land side and linking up with Dahlgren's offshore fleet. Simultaneously, Thomas sallied forth from his defenses at Nashville and virtually annihilated Hood's army in mid-December. The year finished with the Union victorious nearly everywhere.

The ending of Lee's resistance focused on the closing of the last two ports which supplied him, Charleston and Wilmington. The latter port was especially difficult to close, its defenses being dominated by Fort Fisher at the mouth of the Cape Fear River. The last stronghold for blockade runners, Wilmington was also the base for the runner-turned-cruiser *Tallahassee* which sortied in August 1864 to destroy thirty-three Yankee merchantmen off New York and New England, refueling at Halifax, and then again in November taking six vessels off Delaware. Grant therefore gave Admiral Porter command of the North Atlantic Blockading Squadron and ordered him to take Fort Fisher and thus to close the port. Porter undertook the task in December, but the operation was bungled by his inept Army commander, the troublesome Butler, whom Grant finally removed. Trying again in mid-January 1865, Porter used forty-eight ships and five ironclads to expend 22 tons of ammunition on Fort Fisher preparatory to the successful assault by 10,000 Army, Navy and Marine Corps troops. The Confederacy was falling, its navy virtually finished too. The raider *Alabama* under Raphael Semmes, after sixty-nine captures, was sunk by the steam frigate *Kearsarge* off Cherbourg in June 1864 in the last sailing-ship gunnery duel in history, and by year's end only the new cruiser *Shenandoah* remained at large, operating against Yankee shipping in the North Pacific. In February 1865 General Lee was belatedly given supreme command of Confederate military fortunes, with Rear Admiral Semmes commanding his James River Squadron. But that same month Sherman moved inland into South Carolina, flanking Charleston and forcing its evacuation, while Grant ordered part of Thomas' army by water from Nashville to Cincinnati, thence by rail to Baltimore and again by sea to Fort Fisher. This force captured Wilmington late in February and linked up with Sherman marching into North Carolina. After final battles in North Carolina and Virginia, Grant trapped Lee west of Richmond early in April 1865, forcing his surrender. At the same time a final amphibious assault took the port of Mobile. The Confederacy then collapsed, and all the other Southern military and naval forces soon capitulated.

Union naval policy during the Civil War continued the American inshore tradition though based throughout on undisputed command of the sea. A battle fleet had been unnecessary, though several squadrons and flotillas had been formed to counter the few makeshift Confederate inshore naval units. The blockade initially proposed by Scott and opposed by Welles had taken nearly the entire war to become fully effective, although the last blockade runner entered Galveston over a month after Lee's surrender. Eventually, the four blockading squadrons had employed about 300 naval vessels to capture five times that number of blockade runners. But the blockade was run successfully perhaps 8000 times, or roughly over 80 percent effectiveness if one includes the illicit Yankee trade across the Rio Grande and through Union lines. Still, the blockade was a success, because its very existence discouraged normal trade: untold numbers of merchantmen refused to run the risk of capture, while those which did usually charged disastrous prices and brought in unnecessary luxury items, neither of which helped the Confederate war effort. Furthermore, the so-called Anaconda used many of the same blockaders to harass and help assault Southern coastal and river towns, thereby requiring a major effort at coast defense which the Confederacy could not afford.

Union mobility by water thus provided strategic and tactical back-up for the Northern armies, while Southern naval efforts were isolated and makeshift and rarely utilized in conjunction with land forces. To be sure, the Confederate policy of *guerre de course* indirectly chased nearly half the Union merchant tonnage to foreign registry, but the North prospered from goods carried in these same newly-neutral vessels. The major naval innovations by both sides were technological—in ordnance, armor and steam propulsion, but especially in the revival of attack beneath the waterline. Of the mines, torpedoes, submersibles and rams, the latter made the greatest impression and helped to revive a tactic obsolete since the days of the great galleys. In reality, however, ramming attacks had been largely unsuccessful, and the long-term impact of Civil War naval operations would be in submarine warfare. Amphibious and other inshore activities were significant, but overshadowed by the impressive achievements of the many armies in the field. In sum, Union command of the sea helped to reunify the nation and to reestablish its global naval prestige.

The United States had also asserted sufficient military and naval power to reinterpret international law to suit its own needs—the common attitude of nations commanding the sea during wartime. The Lincoln government had generally adhered to the principles of the 1856

Declaration of Paris which the United States had not signed, leading to the final collapse of privateering as a device of naval warfare and increasing the rule of the effective blockade—though stretching the definition of "effective." The North had firmly adhered to freedom of the seas in principle but had elected to violate neutral shipping whenever contraband was suspected of being carried. Thus the *Trent* affair had symbolized the many Union infringements on free shipping while one cruiser had actually entered the harbor of Bahia, Brazil, in October 1864 to seize the successful rebel raider *Florida*. Such instances, usually repudiated officially, all pointed to a growing reality of total war, namely, that all goods enabled a nation to make war and that therefore the old distinction for contraband items was becoming obsolete. And neutrality itself might even be a fiction in total war, and with it the notion of free trade in wartime. Thus the Civil War signaled the end of more than wooden sailing warships.

## ENFORCING THE MONROE DOCTRINE

The War ended, the United States also asserted firmly, for the first time, its lawful prerogatives in the Monroe Doctrine. To discourage the French project in Mexico, General Grant immediately sent Sheridan with an army to the Rio Grande, and the Navy dispatched a four-ship squadron around the Horn in a show of force. Napoleon III finally yielded to this pressure and to the great expense of the inconclusive guerrilla war, and in 1867 he withdrew from Mexico, forever ending the French pressure on Latin America. Similar American legalism by force was impressed upon the Spanish.

Spain made its last attempt to restore its prestige in Latin America during the 1860s, trying in vain to take advantage of the many quarrels in the Western Hemisphere. From their last toeholds at Cuba and Puerto Rico, the Spanish in 1861 accepted an invitation of the people of Santo Domingo to return, only to be then faced by a bloody insurrection and American protests. Then came the altercation with Peru and Chile in 1864 which suddenly flared up again in September 1865. Spain decided to quit Santo Domingo that year but ignored American protests by blockading Valparaiso and hastening Chilean and Peruvian declarations of war (which were supported by Bolivia and Ecuador). The warring nations fought a number of skirmishes at sea, including an indecisive squadron battle off the Chiloé Islands in February 1866. The American squadron rounding the Horn joined a British force at Valparaiso but neither admiral could persuade the Spanish squadron there to halt its plans to bombard the port. The weak Chilean defenses and privateer-oriented navy were no match for the squadron of Admiral

Méndez Nuñez which destroyed Valparaiso by shelling on the last day of March. With nine warships Nuñez then blockaded Callao, but when he moved in for a bombardment early in May the Peruvians drove him off with severe losses from their English-built artillery and mines, two ironclads and three gunboats. The Spanish ships limped away, five years later using American offices to negotiate a formal peace and thereby thus ending their brief imperial plans.

The years 1864 to 1870 also witnessed a bitter war between aggressive Paraguay and the "triple alliance" of Brazil, Argentina and Uruguay, involving considerable inshore and river fleets. To support its invasion southward, the Paraguayan river steam flotilla with troops on board in June 1865 attacked its Brazilian counterpart at Corrientes, Argentina, on the Parana River, deep in the interior, only to be defeated with heavy losses. From then through October the allied armies and flotillas on the Parana and Uruguay rivers drove the Paraguayans from Corrientes province, after which Brazil reinforced its fleet of thirteen gunboats at Corrientes with four ironclads. Following skirmishing on the rivers early in 1866, in April the allies mounted an invasion of Paraguay by way of the Parana, their armies embarked on Argentine and Brazilian vessels. The army landed and worked overland while the river craft brushed aside mines and fire rafts to lend logistical, sealift and fire support, but the ground forces met a repulse late in September.

Gradually, however, the allied river campaign broke through Paraguay's defenses. In the summer of 1867 ten Brazilian ironclads and the allied army could not press farther upriver due to Paraguayan fortifications and a falling river, so Brazil hastily built shallow-draft monitors which helped the allies to resume their upriver offensive during the winter of 1867–68. In February they captured Asunción, the capital of Paraguay, and while Paraguayan raiders in camouflaged canoes failed to take several Brazilian ironclads the allies cleared the river banks of enemy outposts. By December 1868, when the allies took Angostura, the desperate Paraguayans had to strip their naval crews for home defense ashore, giving the allies absolute command of the rivers. Paraguay scuttled its remaining vessels in June 1869; guerrilla fighting continued; and the next year the United States negotiated a peace settlement.

Spurning offers to annex Santo Domingo and the Danish Virgin Islands in 1867–69, the United States increasingly used the Monroe Doctrine to exert increasing authority over the Americas. Even Britain and Russia were yielding to the reunited American colossus in its obvious sphere of influence. Russia, preoccupied with consolidating her own continental empire in Central and Eastern Asia, abandoned North America altogether in 1867 by selling Alaska and the Aleutian Islands to the United States. This event only increased the British tension over possible American annexation of Canada and British Columbia, anxieties which had been heightened in 1864–66 by Confederate and patriotic Irish Fenian activities along the Canadian-American border. By 1867, up to sixteen British warships had based annually at Pacific squadron headquarters at Esquimalt, and that year Britain gave Canada dominion status within the Empire, thus strengthening its ties with the mother country. Continuing Fenian challenges to Canadian unity and the festering border dispute over the San Juan Islands were then over-shadowed by postwar American demands for British reparations pay-ments to cover damages made by Confederate cruisers built in England, especially those of the *Alabama*. Anglo-American relations again be-came strained, but Britain had no desire to antagonize the United States. Already, power changes in Europe and other events had led to the reduction of imperial forces in North America, so that Britain pre-ferred settlements of lingering problems with the United States. So in 1870–72, by a number of agreements, Britain paid a compromise sum for the *Alabama* claims, ceded by arbitration the San Juan Islands to the United States, put down the Fenian agitation, and joined British Columbia to a finally unified Dominion of Canada. The *Pax Britannica* thus continued in North America, partly because of British respect for American power.

The United States by the 1870s had fashioned its general conti-nental empire and had taken advantage of its own Civil War to emerge as a major industrial power in the world. But it had neither military nor maritime aspirations beyond those of the prewar era. The Grand Army was immediately demobilized and the regular forces returned to the frontier where they supervised the settlement of the continental in-terior and completed the destruction of Indian resistance. Financial investment centered on industrial production and railroad expansion, not on maritime trade. Such oceanic trade flourished, to be sure, but most of it in foreign, particularly British, bottoms. The American merchant vessels that had transferred to foreign flags during the war were refused repatriation by Congress in 1866; financial and labor re-sources shifted away from shipbuilding to the new industrial corpora-tions; progressively higher protective tariffs were instituted; and the government still refused to subsidize American shipowners at a time when Britain was helping her own convert to steam and iron. So the blow to the merchant marine by the Confederate navy combined with these and other factors to accelerate the decline begun after 1855. American merchantmen were therefore inferior to newer British com-petitors and came to be manned increasingly by foreign sailors. Yet this trend was only natural, for the American political center in the 1860s definitely shifted westward as new states entered the Union from West of the Mississippi. New England shipping interests became a political and economic minority, and though the coastal schooner trade grew the American overseas carrying trade steadily decayed.

With no overseas imperial, military or mercantilistic aspirations, not surprisingly the American Congress laid up its fine wartime Navy. By December 1864, when the United States Navy had numbered some 700 vessels mounting nearly 5000 guns, it was—in terms of sheer numbers— the most powerful navy in the world and that very month elevated its most exalted naval officer, Farragut, to the unprecedented American rank of vice admiral. Farragut went on two years later to reach the full rank of admiral, followed by Porter in both ranks in 1866 and 1870. But these were virtually honorary appointments for wartime services rendered, for no other rear admirals achieved these distinctions. And in the autumn of 1867 the demobilization of the Navy began, stripping the force to but 52 vessels in commission and mounting under 500 of the same old guns by 1871. This had been generally an inshore navy anyway, useless outside North American waters, and four major seagoing monitors under construction had been scrapped late in 1865.

Strategically, this naval policy was realistically attuned to American political goals after the war. As usual, cruisers were sent abroad to protect commerce or maintained at home for coast defense, and the old naval stations were reestablished under new names: European (from Mediterranean and African), North Atlantic (Home), South Atlantic (Brazil) and Asiatic (East Indies), while the standing Pacific Squadron was twice divided into North and South squadrons (1866–69, 1872–78). These decisions were all realistic and provided a small but almost adequate-sized navy. Unfortunately, Congress neglected to modernize the old vessels or to authorize new ones, so that sail returned, coal for steam was severely restricted, wood continued over armor, and the old smoothbore cannon were retained. With the usual postwar letdown and desire to economize, the United States thus handicapped its navy.

From 1815 to the beginning of 1870s, the United States grew geographically into a sprawling continental empire, enjoying also until the mid-1850s a superior merchant marine. Its navy had never needed nor had it entertained blue-water aspirations, but had engaged instead in inshore operations in which command of the sea had been virtually automatic. Adequate as this navy was, however, it would never meet future needs if the United States was ever to assume the full dimensions of a modern major power. Isolationistic by habit and temperament, preferring freedom from the global quarrels of the older powers, the United States would never be able to resist the consequences of a shrinking world without a battle fleet. For in 1866 the Atlantic submarine telegraphic cable was laid, and three years later the American continent was joined by a coast-to-coast railroad. On the other side of the world also in 1869 European and Asian sea lanes were shortened by the opening of the Suez Canal. The days of America's splendid isolation were henceforth numbered.

# 13

# The Golden Age of Naval Thought, 1867–1914

*. . . limited war is only permanently possible to island Powers or between Powers which are separated by sea, and then only when the Power desiring limited war is able to command the sea to such a degree as to be able not only to isolate the distant object, but also to render impossible the invasion of his home territory. Here, then, we reach the true meaning and highest military value of what we call the command of the sea. . . .*

—CORBETT

## THE NEW TECHNOLOGY AND MATERIAL STRATEGY

Without discernible interruptions, the *Pax Britannica* continued into the half-century following the American Civil War but with two new paradoxical features: a global cosmopolitanism that promoted unity, and neo-imperialism that bred disunity and the seeds of World War I. The civilization of this half-century, intellectually and culturally perhaps the most dynamic period of Western history since the Renaissance, drew much of its energy from the industrial and democratic revolutions engulfing all peoples. Industry and technology spread from Western Europe to transform Russia, the United States and Japan, though the principles of democracy and socialism—as alternatives to the time-worn monarchies—could only progress whenever the old order collapsed. That lay in the new era and century, but the ideas did spread—as the former era closed—carried by new and rapid forms of communication: steamships, railroads, automobiles, the telephone, telegraph and wireless and primitive aircraft. Global distances shrank accordingly, most dramatically at sea between the respective openings of the Suez and Panama canals in 1869 and 1914. A continuing if naive faith in the Victorian peace enforced by British naval superiority encouraged the free flow of ideas of philosophers, scientists, artists and social thinkers across national boundaries. Insular Britain could thus no longer monopolize the thalassocratic preconditions for cultural vitality, but shared them across the Western world. Witness a cross section of such "global" thought: Freud, Marx, Nietzsche, Darwin, Spencer, Hugo, Mill, Ranke, Einstein, Helmholtz, Proust, Tolstoy, Dostoyevsky, the Curies, the Jameses, Wagner, Tchaikovsky, Rachmaninoff, Stravinsky, van Gogh, Gauguin, Cézanne, Ibsen and Picasso.

But just as advancing technology seemed to bring the peoples of the West closer together, so too did it create the elements of renewed conflict. Increased wealth promoted intense nationalism not only in such newly unified nations as Germany and Italy but in the non-Western peoples exploited by the old and newer powers; indeed, new knowledge in medicine and dietetics conquered the last tropical diseases and stimulated a population explosion on a global scale. The desire for national greatness through economic strength led the powers to reject the doctrine of free trade in favor of closed imperial systems of neo-mercantilism, preferred tariffs and colonial privilege. International competition intensified throughout this era, creating tensions that steadily undermined the edifice of the balance of the European powers. The days of the *Pax Britannica* came to be numbered as rival powers—no longer content to adhere willingly to British rule upon the seas—imitated Britain with their own merchant fleets, colonies and navies. These powers made feeble attempts to perpetuate the old international legalism of the Enlightenment with disarmament conferences at The Hague in the Netherlands in 1899 and 1907 and with the Declaration of London in 1909 which aimed at protecting neutral shippers in time of war. But opposition within Britain itself and elsewhere left the Declaration unratified by any nation, a harbinger of the coming ineffectiveness of international law in total war. New technological weapons would be the final deterrence—or arbiter in war. And the new forces of unrest in the colonies unleashed by the new technology and ideas could never be contained by mere gunboats and imperial police forces, making this half-century the last of undisputed European hegemony in the world.

In no nation did the new technology make a more dramatic impact than Germany, which arose as the major challenge to Britain—despite the fact that Britain perpetuated the delusion that France was still the main threat on the continent until 1900. Germany raced against time and the growth of potentially superior Russia and the United States to become a leading power. Drawing upon a peculiarly rigid class system ruled by feudalistic *Junkers* military aristocrats and *Kaiser* (emperor), Germany mobilized its manpower, raw coal, iron, steel and other metals into a well-organized military-industrial system and borrowed from the British model to fashion an overseas empire and fleet. So impressive did German society become that it soon provided the model for other industrial states. Specifically admired, before 1890, were the peerless political skills of Otto von Bismarck, the industrial success of the Krupp family, the strategic theories of the late Karl von Clausewitz, the general staff organization and military genius of Helmuth von Moltke, the war academies and higher education in general, the military history of Hans Delbrück and the broader framework of German historiography, and the creation of the Imperial German Navy under Albrecht von Stosch and its dynamic growth under Alfred von Tirpitz. Only after 1890 and the new aggressive policies of Kaiser Wilhelm II did Germany begin to appear as a threat to European stability. The new technology enabled Germany and other basically non-maritime-oriented nations to build modern technologically superior navies, but like them Germany remained first and always a continental power with its army as the senior service in matters of policy and strategy.

This technological capacity led to the domination of the material school of strategy over the years 1867 to 1914 in all countries: superior technologically advanced weapons on land and sea would determine victory in diplomacy and war, with the lessons of history to play only a complementary role. The idea of super-warships with improved naval guns, projectiles and armor deciding command of the sea with only perfunctory notice of principles of naval strategy grounded in historical experience appeared as anathema to a number of historian-theorists, notably Captain Alfred Thayer Mahan of the United States Navy and Sir Julian Corbett of Great Britain. Between the publication of Mahan's key work, *The Influence of Sea Power upon History, 1660–1783* in 1890 and of Corbett's excellent *Some Principles of Maritime Strategy* in 1911, these and other men stated and restated the strategic constants of command of the sea. But with their evidence drawn from the age of sail and more recent limited wars, these arguments found subordination by naval planners to the superweapons of the day. Thus, this period is best understood as one continuous arms race of new and better weapons being introduced to control the sea. But, in the realm of naval theory, the debates between material and historical strategists created a golden age of naval thought. The arenas for debate lay in professional associations and journals, academies and war colleges.

The exchange of ideas began to be formalized with the creation of private professional officer societies and the publication of naval and army journals. Britain had pioneered with the Royal United Service Institute in 1831 which started publishing its *Journal* in 1859. The Russians, however, had led the way in naval magazines with the fine *Morskoi*

*Sbornik* in 1848, followed in 1861 by France's *Revue Maritime* (*et Coloniale* till 1892). The best of all the naval journals, after an inauspicious beginning, came to be Italy's *Rivista Marittima;* another minor but eventually improved periodical was Germany's *Marine Rundschau*. The United States Navy combined the interests of its small officer corps in professional, scientific and literary naval matters by establishing the private United States Naval Institute in 1873 which thenceforth published its members' views in its *Proceedings*. These quarterly and monthly journals were augmented late in the century by various naval annuals, especially those edited in England by Thomas Brassey (from 1886) and Frederick T. Jane (from 1897).

All navies had academies for elementary officer education, but the plethora of advanced naval analysis found its highest institutional form in the naval war college. The model for all such advanced schools for senior officers below flag rank, the Prussian War Academy founded in 1810, led eventually to similar army schools in Britain and France during the 1870s. But the major catalyst for advanced strategic thinking, particularly naval, in such institutions was a veteran reformer in naval education, Commodore Stephen B. Luce, who founded the United States Naval War College in 1884. Luce appointed Mahan to the faculty first as lecturer and then as Luce's successor as College president. Mahan's lectures led to his pivotal book in 1890 which enhanced the reputation of the place as the center of America's broad theoretical studies in naval strategy. Building upon British, German and Italian examples, the Naval War College also introduced naval war gaming to its curriculum in order to analyze and test American naval doctrine and plans. Between Luce's College and Mahan's historical theories, naval studies rapidly became an intellectual focus in other navies, although the American Naval War College after 1900 studied less strategy and more narrowly professional subjects. The Russians adopted a similar curriculum for captains and senior lieutenants at their Nikolayev naval academy in 1895, while the British did the same at theirs at Greenwich in 1900, elevating it to an enlarged Royal Naval War College at Portsmouth in 1907. The same year Italy established its School of Naval Warfare, and in 1910 the Germans, who had a small Naval War College at Kiel but combined their higher military studies at the army-dominated War Academy, began to game naval problems. The French, a major naval power deeply concerned with naval theory, established a school of naval war in 1895, but it had only uneven success.

Because rapid technological change fascinated younger officers and confounded conservative and anti-intellectual admiralties and navy departments, these official institutions and organs of expression were regarded as inadequate by some officers. Consequently, they established various national navy leagues to propagandize naval developments, quit the service to expound their views, or awaited retirement to become full-fledged military pundits. Some "young Turks" in the Royal Navy tried to avoid these extremes; led by Captain Herbert Richmond, in 1912 they founded the private *Naval Review* in order to publish and circulate unsigned critical essays. Lesser navies such as those of Austria, Japan and China simply followed or imitated the theories and techniques expounded by the major naval powers.

The analysts of these institutions and privately published works focused strategic arguments around the capabilities of the new weapons. Guilty of technological determinism, the material strategists centered their discussions around the new steam-and-steel warships, specifically the technical questions of armored battleships versus the big guns of other battleships and the underwater torpedoes of smaller vessels. They either ignored the historical arguments or twisted them to serve their own ends. By the same token, the historians like Mahan and Corbett weakened their own cases for relevance by misunderstanding or playing down modern technology. Ironically, since the big-fleet theories of both schools were rarely tested in battle before 1914, the real fighting developed in the colonial areas and was done by gunboats. Still, the battleship symbolized the era.

The tactics of the 1860s, especially confused because of the sweeping technological changes from wood to iron and sail to steam, felt the impact of the American Civil War. For coast defense, the European powers developed their own turreted "breastwork monitors," while on the high seas ironclad-armored battleships ("armored frigates") mounted underwater rams and new rifled ordnance to replace the wooden ship of the line altogether. Instead of a totally armored and thus very expensive vessel, the British and French from 1865 used only a nine-inch belt of armor around the waterline or plates protecting the batteries ("barbettes" or "casemates"). Technological problems postponed the improvement of submersible craft and slowed the universal adoption of breech- over muzzle-loading. In propulsion, special engineering officers appeared, and the simple expansion steam reciprocating engine (17 knots) gradually made way for the horizontal compound engine (18½ knots) of the next decade. In communications, the searchlight complemented signal flags and pennants and evolved into the venetian-blind blinker. Tactically, "squadrons of evolution" rejected the old line-ahead in favor of grouped ironclads in square or oblique attack formations. The reappearance of the underwater ram, gone since galley days, dictated line-abreast tactics for the ram followed by a ship-to-ship gunnery melee at 2000–3000 yards with the turreted guns firing forward throughout the action instead of in broadside.

By contrast, the strategic alignments of the 1860s did not change markedly. Britain and France matched each other's new ironclad squadrons, while Russia—having angered Britain and France by ruthlessly suppressing the Polish uprising—avoided having its Baltic and Pacific fleets trapped in port in the event of war by dispatching them on timely visits to American ports in 1863. Ottoman Turkey crushed a Greek-inspired revolt on Crete in 1866–68, and Austria abolished its naval ministry after its Admiral Max had gone to Mexico as Maximilian. But Austria had greater concerns with the rise of Italy and Germany, when in 1864 Bismarck called for Austrian naval assistance in Germany's attempt to annex the province of Schleswig-Holstein at the expense of Denmark. The small Danish Baltic squadron blockaded the Elbe and Weser rivers, but the Austrians dispatched Commodore Wilhelm von Tegetthoff with a squadron from the Mediterranean to the North Sea. Assisted by three small German craft, Tegetthoff used his two steam frigates to engage three Danish vessels in May 1864 off the British-owned island of Heligoland in the last wooden-sail naval battle in history (plus the *Alabama-Kearsarge* duel in June). Though a draw, the battle was followed by Austrian naval reinforcements which broke the blockade and helped force Denmark to surrender the disputed province. The Germans now began to construct armored coast defense ships, but under army control.

Bismarck's wars of German unification then engaged Austria and France. In 1866 Moltke's Prussian army crushed the Austrian army at Sadowa in the so-called Seven Weeks War, while allied Italy attacked the Austrians in the Adriatic. When an Italian expeditionary force moved against the Austrian island of Lissa, Rear Admiral Tegetthoff used his ironclad rams to sink one Italian ironclad and drive away the other eight on July 20. This ninety-minute battle of Lissa, the first fleet action between ironclads in history, confirmed line-abreast ramming tactics for the ensuing generation of naval tacticians. Tegetthoff at Pola and a gunboat squadron on Lake Garda supported the Austrian army in Italy, but Austria ended the war in October by ceding Venice to Italy. Seriously weakened, Austria gave Hungary its independence under the new dual monarchy of Austria-Hungary in 1867 and allowed the navy of Lissa to deteriorate—despite the dynamic leadership of Tegetthoff from 1868 till his untimely death in 1871 at the age of forty-four. Bismarck then moved to weaken France, initiating the Franco-Prussian War in 1870. The French Navy began the war in July by blockading the German Baltic coast, but Moltke's ground offensive defeated the French Army at Sedan, causing the fall of the French monarchy and the new Republican regime to strip warship crews for the unsuccessful defense of Paris. Such measures frustrated the French blockade and plans for an amphibious expedition in the Baltic. Paris fell in January 1871, France admitted defeat in May, and the new German Empire emerged from the conflict.

European territorial alignments continued basically unchanged over the next four decades, but technological change made the 1870s a period of transition. The armored battleship remained supreme, with the Italians leading in construction under their superb naval designer Benedetto Brin who also served off and on as Minister of Marine, 1876–1898. Italy in 1876 introduced 12,000-ton, 18-knot battleships with unwieldy 17.7" guns protected by British armor: 14 inches of wrought iron (or two 12" plates for 24") and later of homogeneous steel. British and French warships used compound iron and steel armor. These heavy Italian battleships introduced cellular compartmentation with watertight bulkheads, fearing attack below the waterline—not only by rams but by the new 6-knot automotive torpedo developed by the Englishman Robert Whitehead in Austrian service. These torpedos and the defensive compartmentation soon became standard in all major navies. Replacing the sailing-steam frigate, "cruising vessels" (unarmored) and "protected cruisers" (partly armored) began to appear, but as nearly useless compromises of economic and naval needs, especially in France and the United States. Unable to keep pace with the more affluent nations, such minor naval states as Austria, Argentina and the Scandinavians developed small coast defense torpedo boats, forcing Britain and France to imitate them. Naval communications improved with the introduction of the electric arc light for Morse code signals (and spotting torpedoes and mines).

Two widely separated small wars influenced the growing naval arms race late in the 1870s. With German support, Russia in 1871 began to refortify Sevastopol and reopen the Black Sea, leading to the Russo-Turkish War of 1877–78. The Russian navy continued to flourish under the dynamic leadership and reforms of Grand Duke Constantine, with Admiral Popov leading the construction of new ironclads, monitors and torpedo boats for service on the Black Sea and Danube River. The Turks tried to keep pace, but it was the Russians who triumphed, as the Ottoman Empire ever more declined. Using spar torpedoes and mines, the Russian navy supported the army's drive across the Danube and capture of Plevna. More dramatic, in the eastern Black Sea, Lieutenant Commander Stepan Osipovich Makarov used spar and towed torpedoes before the port of Batum, then employed Whitehead torpedoes to sink a 6500-ton Turkish warship. The Ottomans surrendered Batum to Russia at the end of the war and granted independence to Balkan Rumania, Bulgaria, Serbia and Montenegro. In the War of the Pacific, 1879 to 1881, Chile used a formidable small navy with two British-built armored battleships to gain commercial and territorial concessions from Peru and Bolivia. Capturing the Bolivian port of Antofagasta early in the fighting, Chile clamped a naval blockade on the enemy coasts. When the British-built Peruvian ironclad battleship *Huascar* under Rear Admiral Don Miguel Grau attempted to break the blockade throughout 1879, Commodore Galvarino Riveros concentrated the Chilean fleet to pound *Huascar* into submission and kill Grau off Point Angamos, Bolivia, in October. With command of the waters, Chile invaded Bolivia by sea, overran the coast, blockaded Peruvian Callao and in 1880 captured Arica and Pisco by land-sea attack. The major fighting ended in January 1881 when the Chilean army captured Lima; in 1883–84 Bolivia ceded its entire coastline to Chile. Whereas underwater weapons had been decisive in the former war, they were absent in the latter.

Such events helped to define the two major schools of naval thought crystallizing during the 1880s. The "blue-water" philosophy in the Royal Navy used historical arguments and improved guns and armor to advocate command of the sea with battleships. Homogeneous steel (with 5 percent nickel) increased the armor belt from 18″ to 20″ and covered two thirds of the 14,000-ton battleship. Improved 13.5″ guns with longer muzzles mounted in open barbettes gave a better rate of fire and muzzle velocity, aided by steel-encased shells with new powders (eventually smokeless cordite). And new vertical triple-expansion reciprocating engines gave an optimum speed of 18 knots for evading torpedoes. Rejecting the ram altogether, the British countered torpedo boats with 6″ quick-firing guns on the battleships, an escorting flotilla of "cruisers" (formerly armored and protected cruisers, belted steam frigates and corvettes) and "torpedo gunboats."

Opposing this view, the younger, material-oriented officers of the French Navy's *jeune école* (or new school) claimed that this concept of command of the sea had been voided by the torpedo boat, which had made the battleship vulnerable and thus obsolete. Plagued by potential enemies in maritime Britain, continental Germany and Mediterranean Italy, the French Navy suffered a doctrinal crisis during the 1880s exemplified by no fewer than thirty-one different ministers of marine between 1871 and 1902. In general, however, the *jeune école* argument prevailed under the leadership of its spokesmen, Baron Richard Grivel, Gabriel Charmes and Admiral Théophile Aube. Using the first theory of strategic naval bombardment in modern warfare, Aube (naval minister, 1886–87) planned to use his torpedo boats at Cherbourg to attack British seaports, anchored shipping and dockyard installations and his cruisers from Brest to wage *guerre de course* on the high seas, causing economic panic and forcing Britain to terms. Aube went so far as to suspend battleship construction in 1886 and to argue that his torpedo boats would

have to ignore international law in their attack on merchant shipping—
a harbinger of future underwater total war. But France's torpedo craft
proved unreliable and vulnerable in daylight and blind at night during
fleet maneuvers in 1887, undermining the entire edifice of *jeune école*
reasoning.

In fact, battleships remained the yardstick of international power relations in the Mediterranean during the 1880s. In 1881–82 Germany,
Austria and Italy created the Triple Alliance on the continent, but unilateral Italian actions in the middle sea alarmed the French. Following
its leading naval strategist, Domenico Bonamico, Italy pivoted its defenses around a new naval base on the island of Maddalena off the north
coast of Sardinia, established other new bases at Taranto and Gaeta
(near Naples), and heavily fortified the older base at Genoa. When the
Italian battleships concentrated at Maddalena with a German squadron
for a total of ten capital ships in 1889, France retaliated. Already, Admiral Aube had concentrated five French battleships at Toulon to face
Italy and had begun to strengthen the new base at Bizerte, Tunisia, occupied in 1881 largely for reasons of prestige. Now, however, at the end
of the decade, France initiated its first major building program since
1872 of new battleships much superior to Italy's untried "central citadel"
ships and undertook such an effective economic offensive against Italy
that it caused a depression in Italy and related drain on the Italian navy.
By the mid-1890s Italy had little choice but to court the friendship of
France and to abandon any ambitions in the Western Mediterranean.

Beyond torpedo boats to check Britain and battleships to counter
Italy, France strengthened its army to deter Germany and Austria and
even embarked upon a new imperial program. Admiral Aube and the
*jeune école* advocated a global network of bases linked by a French-
built canal across the Isthmus of Panama, and since the Navy had
always administered the colonies the government let it continue in this
role until a new colonial office was established in 1892 to assist. Defense
of the new far-flung colonies, however, remained the Navy's responsibility, so that the Naval Infantry and Marine Artillery had to be posted
abroad. All these expenses proved so great that in the midst of continuing doctrinal battles from 1886 to 1905 the Navy lost interest in
colonial defense, and the *jeune école* so dissociated itself from imperial
concerns as to advocate the sacrifice of both foreign trade and the merchant marine in time of war—an eventuality that would nearly cripple
France after 1914. Without a single dominant doctrine, the French
Navy was engulfed in the same chaos that wracked French politics from
the Boulanger crisis through the Dreyfus affair.

Nevertheless, Britain reacted strenuously in the face of French preparations. The prospect of a swift steam-powered cross-Channel attack

caused repeated "invasion scares" in Britain from 1888, especially as most analysts assumed any modern war would be a short one. French torpedo boats neutralized any thought of a close blockade in such a war, and colonies and merchantmen seemed undefendable in the face of the new machine weapons. Or so reasoned British Army analysts of the "brick and mortar" and "bolt from the blue" schools, which reasoned that the fleet should be kept in home waters for coast defense, backed up by fortifications. They accepted the *jeune école* position that blue-water command of the sea had become obsolete. Unmoved by such views, however, the "blue-water" school prevailed. The Naval Defense Act of 1889 authorized the two-power standard—a minimum battleship strength equal to the combined battleship tonnage (but preferably a 5 to 3 superiority) of its two largest rivals, France and Russia, whose growing mutual friendship was solidified by a defensive alliance in 1894. Then the publication of Mahan's book in 1890 gave historical support to the blue-water school. In truth, Britain's policy was based on quantitative material logic, not on strategic realities. The British had no clear idea during the 1890s for utilizing their battle fleet against France, except for maintaining an open blockade in the Western Approaches and concentrating off Gibraltar—à la Nelson—to keep the French fleet divided. The invasion scares of 1893, 1898 and 1900 were based on ignorance, for the French Navy had no real amphibious plans, policy or tactical doctrine.

But the technological improvements of the 1890s gave cause for alarm. The new 14,000-ton battleships incorporated 12 to 14 inches of face-hardened "harveyed" steel armor and breech-loading 13.5″ guns with steel-capped, explosive armor- and semi-armor-piercing shells; henceforth, one inch of gun caliber had to equal one inch of armor. The broadside returned as one pair of guns in enclosed barbette turrets and just turrets near the center line replaced open barbettes. Quick-firing light guns remained, but intermediate caliber guns began to disappear as long-range (2000–6000 yards) gunnery duels became standard practice. Accuracy of the guns improved materially when Captain Percy Scott of the Royal Navy introduced the doctrine of "continuous aim"—guns locking on enemy targets by means of a gyroscope despite the roll of the ship. With battle speeds of 15 knots, the battleships could now form in column or line-ahead, as in sailing times, replacing the ram, line-abreast, circular and oblique tactical formations altogether. Center-line turreted battleships with broad arcs of fire could now deliver broadside salvos in the tradition of de Ruyter, Suffren and Nelson. The flotilla now included new "armored" or heavy cruisers—which provided the multitudinous duties of its sailing predecessor, the frigate—and the "torpedo boat destroyer" or destroyer to attack torpedo boats or act as such a vessel itself.

Late in the decade, these small craft began to receive the first steam turbine engines in place of reciprocating engines, giving them battle speeds of 30 knots and maximum speeds of 36.5 knots!

Such a battleship-centered fleet mix in Britain aroused outright imitation by other "new" navies, all potential enemies of the Royal Navy, except that most of these also used *jeune école* arguments to give greater attention to cruisers and torpedo boats in the continental manner. Austria-Hungary, Italy, Russia and the United States remained preoccupied with coast defense, with their battleships and torpedo boats in that role. Russia also embraced the strategy of *guerre de course* by creating a "Volunteer Merchant Fleet" of armed merchantmen in 1885. The United States began to break away from coastal forts, monitors and protected cruisers to build new "seagoing coastline battleships" in the 1890s. And as the teachings of its own philosopher Mahan began to have effect, the United States in the 1890s initiated construction of new long-range battleships.

Like America, Germany represented a potential if unrealistic threat to Britain during these years. Indeed, the U. S. Navy was considered conservative and removed from the mainstream of American life, whereas the Imperial German Navy was middle-class and liberal in its origins. Both navies were thus alienated from their armies: the American army in wartime remained largely a militia, nonprofessional force, while the *Junkers*-led German standing army was thoroughly aristocratic, even reactionary. As navies, however, their divorce from the popular government—their individualism—was typical, and both professional officer cadres were drawn largely from national cross-sections of their respective populations and were in reality therefore middle-class, God-fearing and intensely loyal to the point of being apolitical (relative to their politics-oriented sister services). Both the American and German navies were subordinated in military matters to strong civilian control and army seniority. The Americans steadfastly refused to create a senior admiral or admiralty board (like the Army's general-in-chief), with the civilian Secretary of the Navy giving orders. In Germany, a Chief of Admiralty reported to the Kaiser, but the first two chiefs were army generals with army uses for the navy: Albrecht von Stosch from 1871 to 1883 concentrated on coast defense, and Leo von Caprivi from 1883 to 1888 followed the French *jeune école* in promoting cruisers and torpedo boats. With the accession of Wilhelm II in 1888, the navy command was reorganized into three separate offices which further weakened and decentralized it under the vague direction of a Naval Cabinet. Under Bismarck's regime, therefore, the navy had been typically continental, tolerated but rarely promoted by the army.

Suddenly, however, Britain faced a major threat, for in the 1890s

Kaiser Wilhelm II changed everything, and the German army and navy alike became aggressive and expansionistic. Bismarck's cautious diplomacy had come to an end with his dismissal as chancellor in 1890. Continental expansion was advocated by the army with pronouncements of *Drang nach Osten,* and Wilhelm II followed the advice of his pro-Mahan Atlantic-oriented "Fleet professors" for colonies and maritime power in order to rival Britain's achievements, if only for reasons of prestige. Krupp's industries retooled for modern steel warship construction, while home naval defenses were strengthened by the purchase of Heligoland from Britain in 1890 and the completion five years later of the Kiel Canal across the base of the Jutland peninsula. The canal gave German warships easy transit between the North and Baltic seas, thus bypassing the easily blockaded Sound of Denmark. Although the major force behind naval armament was the kaiser himself, his chief agent was the dynamic Admiral Alfred von Tirpitz, a career officer and torpedo specialist whose big-navy attitude combined with his own political machinations to lead to his appointment in 1897 as State Secretary of the Imperial Naval Office.

Utilizing internal political troubles to advantage, Tirpitz promoted anti-British bias to fashion his "risk theory" *(Risikogedanke)* whereby Germany would build such a formidable battle fleet at home that Britain —with her navy scattered to protect her vast global imperial commitments—would never dare risk a naval war with Germany. The German Naval Bill of 1898 called for nineteen battleships in commission, which alarmed the British, who feared such a fleet in alliance with another armada like the French or Russian. Two years later, however, Tirpitz secured a second naval bill which called forth enough battleships to create a fleet that could by itself threaten Britain. The mistake Tirpitz made was the same other material strategists were making, however; with no firm political or strategic goals, the battleships became ends in themselves, prestigious, to be sure, but not integrated into any coherent naval policy that took into consideration the strategic evidence of history. The senior service, the army, under the successors of Moltke continued its Eastern Europe-oriented anti-navy biases and refused to coordinate army-navy planning, despite the warnings of the historian Delbrück and the eminent General Kolmar von der Goltz. Nevertheless, Tirpitz charged ahead to make the Imperial German Navy the second largest in the world.

Britain had no choice but to accept Germany's challenge, with the new Anglo-German naval arms race based on material considerations. Between 1900 and 1905 Britain's battleship inventory increased to some forty 16,000-ton, 18-knot ships mounting four 12″ guns with ranges up to 4000 yards, vessels which Germany now imitated. But new technological developments quickly antiquated even the newest of these ships. Better guns, aimed "continuously" with excellent optics, increased their effective range up to 15,000 yards. The lighter steel armor could now cover the entire vessel, and new turbine engines could give it greater speed. Shipboard electricity and telephones enabled gun directors on the bridge to directly coordinate the turrets for salvo fire. And of major importance, British Captain Henry Jackson and Italian inventor Guglielmo Marconi pooled their work on the wireless to introduce maritime radio into the Royal Navy after successful tests in the fleet maneuvers of 1899. This achievement, promoted also in the Russian navy by physicist Alexander Popov and Admiral S. O. Makarov, not only improved fleet coordination but, of broader import, now enabled all oceangoing ships to maintain contact with the shore—a revolutionary advance in seafaring.

Combining these advances and those of naval architecture especially in Italy and the United States, Britain's new First Sea Lord, Admiral Sir John Fisher, designed and in 1904 laid down the *Dreadnought*. As the prototype for Britain's—and subsequently all nations'—battleships, this all-new battleship type of 18,000 tons had total armoring; mounted only big guns—ten 12" guns in twin turrets, with most along the center line; eliminated secondary armament, save for an anti-torpedo battery of twenty-seven 12-pounder, 4" quick-firers; had five 18" underwater torpedo tubes; and was propelled by steam turbines for a sustained high speed of 21 knots. From its commissioning in 1906, the *Dreadnought* added an entire new dimension to the arms race. Germany, with a new navy, had fewer changes to make and thus quickly conformed to the new weaponry.

Such new proof of material superiority practically killed the threat of the torpedo boat, but simultaneously the *jeune école* embraced the submarine as its new anti-battleship panacea. The submersible had not survived the American Civil War for lack of good engines and underwater stability. Experimention went on, however, in continental France and the United States, both seeking to neutralize British surface superiority. In 1888 the electric storage battery and hydroplanes solved the two basic shortcomings for a true workable underwater boat, and ten years later gyroscopic steering overcame another hurdle. Then, in 1899, France launched the submarine *Narval,* cigar-shaped for better stability and propelled by a triple expansion engine for surface cruising and for recharging batteries for submerged cruising. The cumbersome smokestack in the conning tower was then replaced by the battery-charging internal combustion engine and later the oil-driven diesel engine. Imperfections led to serious mishaps, such as escaping battery gases that could asphyxiate crews while submerged. But suddenly here appeared a warship that could range 500 miles on the surface at 10 knots and cruise submerged at 6½ knots to attack with underwater torpedoes that could move at 30 knots toward targets 800 yards away. Imperfect torpedoes continued to plague torpedo boats and submarines alike, but all navies henceforth pressed sub construction, especially the lesser powers—France, Russia and the United States. Admiral Fisher thus followed suit, as did Tirpitz. But the Germans preferred Mahan's teachings over those of the *jeune école,* simply because the naval high command under Tirpitz was too conservative to accept the revolutionary claims surrounding a new and untried weapon, and as long as no real tactical use could be found for the submarine the Germans gave it lowly status as a defensive torpedo boat. So the *jeune école* failed to convince the Germans, and its prestige even in France waned as the *Dreadnought* mesmerized naval and public opinion throughout the world.

By 1906, the weapons for total war existed, the last important one being the airplane, invented in 1903 by the Wright brothers in the United States. But neither sub nor plane could compete in their primitive states against the technologically perfected battleship. And yet, the arms races of Europe and now also the Pacific would not be resolved until the larger imperial rivalries were somehow settled and the elements of historical strategy fully appreciated.

## THE NEW IMPERIALISM AND HISTORICAL STRATEGY

Strategic thought surrounding the questions of empire fell within the province of the historical school, especially after the publication of Mahan's book in 1890. To be sure, the material school had its effect, but in a more negative sense. Preoccupied with the technological aspects of the arms race, naval analysts gave prime attention to them and either minimized or neglected the doctrinal and tactical aspects of overseas operations. Worse, British superiority in battleships encouraged a smug complacency regarding amphibious and limited warfare, so that it was conducted on an *ad hoc* basis. Lack of staff organization in Britain negated formal interservice coordination; British imperial successes from the previous half-century encouraged conservatism; and general anti-intellectual attitudes stifled an open dialogue. Nevertheless, several officers defied rigid officialdom to join civilian scholars and analysts in considering at least the larger strategic questions raised by historical evidence. Britain as the first and only fully developed maritime empire of the period from 1867 to 1914 set the strategic example for aspiring new empires and sought to enforce the increasingly tenuous *Pax Britannica.*

The naval historians of these years produced the first critical naval histories in modern times and advanced new theories of imperial defense. The British naturally pioneered in this field, by opening up documentary archives and by popularizing naval history in their books, articles and lectures. Most instrumental in initiating the whole subject of naval history was Sir John Knox Laughton, from his first published article on Admiral Suffren in 1867 to the founding of the Naval Records Society in 1893 which began publishing documents from British naval history. The Colomb brothers simultaneously utilized historical data to advance theories on imperial defense: Captain Sir John Colomb of the Royal Marines Artillery in 1867 first pronounced Britain's need for a global network of bases, while Vice Admiral Philip H. Colomb elaborated on the same subject to the point of distorting the evidence in a series of articles in the 1880s published as a book in 1891. Amphibious strategy and tactics received significant if uneven attention from Army officers Major General Sir John Frederick Maurice and Colonels G. F. R. Henderson and Charles E. Callwell and from Major General Sir George G. Ashton of the Royal Marines.

But from 1890—and the subsequent writings of the American Captain Mahan—several brilliant histories of the great age of sail and the more recent applications of sea power received international prominence. Mahan led in the United States, Sir Julian Corbett and Herbert Richmond in Great Britain, and Gabriel Darrieus, René Daveluy and Raoul Castex in France—all naval officers or civilians closely associated with their own national navies. Other nations produced writers who imitated or borrowed heavily from these historians. In general, however, the historical school (*école historique* in France) centered in Britain, where the Society for Nautical Research began publishing its own historical journal, *The Mariner's Mirror,* in 1911.

Mahan was the advocate of imperialism and big navies of the era, though his theories were too often accepted uncritically. By focusing on the British Empire between 1660 and 1815, Mahan resurrected the old beliefs in monopolistic mercantilism and the concurrent need for overseas trade, colonies and navies to protect it all. His analysis of eighteenth-century Britain was essentially correct, but his analogy between that nation of old and the United States of the 1890s was not, for the Industrial Revolution could simply not be compared with the preceding age of agriculture and closed trade. By advancing his belief that "sea power"— trade, colonies and maritime and naval shipping—held the key to national greatness, Mahan convinced his own country and unwittingly induced France, Russia, Italy and Japan to do the same. He offered no alternatives to his formula, so that non-maritime powers eagerly accepted his ideas, while Britain took advantage of his teachings to reaffirm its own imperial strategy. That Mahan was a racist cannot be doubted, for the undeveloped, non-Western regions of the world were the helpless targets of his blatant imperial message. By asserting that battle fleets had determined command of the sea in the past, he provided an additional stimulus for battleship construction at the turn of the century, though his followers failed to note that only *superior* sea power guaranteed imperial greatness. And he ignored modern technology and the larger historical strategic questions of trade protection, amphibious operations, blockade, economic power, international law, and the whole area of limited warfare and colonial pacification.

Where Mahan—and his many popularizers—erred, Corbett generally succeeded, though his major 1911 book on principles of maritime strategy appeared too late to affect the imperial rivalries. Utilizing the critical techniques of a professional historian, Sir Julian clearly codified the major lessons of naval strategy not only from the age of sail but from the few small wars between 1854 and 1905. Like most of his contemporaries, Corbett was unconvinced about the potential effectiveness of commerce raiding cruisers, torpedo boats and crude submarines, and thus like them he minimized the importance of protecting trade. He also criticized the big battleship-big battle determinism and spoke to the more subtle applications of naval power, such as blockade, amphibious operations and the whole relationship of the navy to army objectives.

Most importantly for the imperial question, Corbett expanded upon the incomplete theories of Karl von Clausewitz to formulate guidelines for conducting limited war with naval forces. Clausewitz, wrote Corbett, mistakenly regarded the question of limited war and possible escalation to unlimited or total proportions only in vague continental terms, whereas Corbett believed that true limited war could be waged only by maritime empires. The key to waging limited warfare overseas, Corbett concluded from historical evidence, lay in two factors: deterrence and geographic isolation. With overwhelming strategic forces such as the British home fleets, the prospect of an unlimited counterstroke would deter other powers from threatening the island homeland. This achieved command of the sea, which, extended across the waters to threatened territories such as those on the Asian periphery, would lead to absolute isolation of the disputed area from outside interference by enemy navies. Once an area such as Malaya, Korea, Madagascar or New Zealand was isolated by naval forces, the area's outside routes for supply and reinforcement would be completely severed, and the area could be expeditiously conquered and pacified by ground forces. Britain as an island nation had generally understood these things, as dramatically shown in the isolation and conquest of Canada in the Seven Years War, though her ignorance of it in the American Revolution had cost her the thirteen American colonies (a fact at which Mahan also hinted). In varying degrees, the imperial powers of the late nineteenth century learned the sagacity of these principles, but through trial and error rather than by doctrinal foresight and planning.

The imperial policies behind the *Pax Britannica* before and after 1861 were reflected in the writings of Corbett, Mahan and others, with Britain always the leader and later imperial powers the imitators. The Western powers in general utilized naval units to suppress the last vestiges of piracy, slavery and smuggling throughout the undeveloped regions of the world, but also used their naval and imperial ground forces to occupy and colonize most of these same areas. The capital ship for policing remote waters remained the inshore steam gunboat, an outgrowth of the Crimean War and the importance of which peaked with the 1000-ton (and smaller) river and coastal sloops, monitors and gunboats of the 1890s. As the maritime colonial powers began to clash in these distant waters, however, cruisers and finally battleships were dispatched abroad —to protect colonies, sea lanes, bases and trade in general and to deter possible attack on any of these imperial vitals. When this happened, at the turn of the century, such disputed territories and their adjacent waters—Africa, Asia, Latin America and the Pacific—became part of a general global balance of power.

British imperial policy in these years underwent dramatic changes induced largely by the invasion scares resulting from the new technology. The fear of steam warships crossing the Channel to invade Britain led the British Army to focus defenses at home and thus to weaken the British naval presence abroad. Consequently, from 1861 a coast defense mania swept the country, leading to the construction of fortifications on the British coasts, the reduction of overseas garrisons, and the increasing reliance upon the larger colonies such as Canada and Australia to defend themselves. The arguments of the Colombs for an overseas network of garrisoned coaling stations went unheeded until the late 1880s when the new imperial rivalries and the larger warships required more substantial naval bases abroad, especially in the Mediterranean. Nevertheless, continuing hysteria over a possible cross-Channel invasion kept major British fleet units concentrated at home, placing an unusually heavy burden upon the gunboats and understrength naval and colonial commands abroad. These demands were particularly acute as Britain under prime ministers William E. Gladstone and Benjamin Disraeli extended the British Empire with new colonial acquisitions. The rise of new imperial powers finally forced Britain to relinquish its absolute maritime supremacy and to seek allies abroad to help continue the *Pax Britannica*. Throughout the last four decades of the century, therefore, Britain struggled, area by area, to preserve the imperial order against growing rivals.

In the Mediterranean, Britain tried to balance the growing imperial strength of France and Italy and to maintain the political integrity of the shaky Ottoman Empire against these powers and Russia. When Turkey proved unable to control its vassal khedive (viceroy) of Egypt, Ismail, whose army and navy (with several former American Confederate naval officers) pushed down the Red Sea into the Sudan in the late 1860s, Britain took over control of the new Suez Canal in 1875 and seven years later bombarded Alexandria from the sea and created a virtual protectorate over Egypt. When the subject Greeks challenged Ottoman authority in 1886, Britain helped blockade Greece; the Turks alone suppressed another Greek uprising in 1896–97. France led by premier Jules Ferry in 1881 used its navy to bombard and occupy Bizerte and Sfax in Tunisia, followed by outright French annexation of the country under the guise of a protectorate alongside French Algeria. Italy in 1882 pushed down the Red Sea to annex Eritrea and parts of Somaliland and Ethiopia and was driven out of Ethiopia by its army in 1896. Spain and France both applied pressure on Morocco, but by 1900 Britain enjoyed firm control over Mediterranean sea lanes from its naval bases at Gibraltar, Malta and Alexandria.

In North America, Britain faced a growing "new navy" of the United States in the 1880s which began to shift from a coast defense to an offensive stance. In 1890 Captain Mahan could envision a possible war with Britain to be decided by an American fleet concentration off New York and an amphibious assault on Nova Scotia as part of an invasion of Canada. But the U. S. Navy experimental "squadron of evolution" of 1889 grew into the seagoing North Atlantic Squadron in 1897 to pose as a potential threat to British transatlantic communications. The economic thrust of the United States and Russia into the Pacific had caused British anxieties for Canada's western defenses, especially during Russia's war with Turkey in 1877–78 and with the establishment of an American coaling station at Pearl Harbor, Hawaii, in 1887 and of the Puget Sound Naval Base at Bremerton, Washington, opposite the British base at Esquimalt, British Columbia. Such fears proved unrealistic, however, especially as the focus of Anglo-American tensions remained in Latin America.

The Caribbean Sea continued to be a British lake, patrolled by warships from Bermuda and Jamaica, but the U. S. Navy—counter to public opinion—from the late 1860s actively sought a base of its own in this "American middle sea." Britain and the United States cooperated to eradicate slavery from Spanish Cuba in 1869, where a war scare erupted between Spain and the United States in 1873–74 before a British warship arrived to stabilize the situation. In the 1880s the French failed to build a canal across the Colombian Isthmus of Panama, and threatening

American warships angered Santo Domingo and supported an unsuccessful scheme for a canal across Nicaragua. In the 1890s, however, the Spanish suppression of Cuban rebels and two German warships forcing concessions from Haiti combined with Mahan's writings to stimulate American imperial designs in the Caribbean. The U. S. Navy's weakness had been dramatized by the victory of the Chilean fleet over Peru in 1879–81, by the Chilean navy's suppression of a dictatorial takeover attempt in 1891 and by the subsequent diplomatic break between Chile and the United States over an incident involving American sailors on liberty in Valparaiso—finally settled in 1892. A similar navy-led revolt in Brazil in 1893–94 failed, with an American naval force standing by for possible intervention at Rio de Janeiro. Immediately thereafter, Britain and the United States nearly ruptured their relations over a boundary dispute between Venezuela and British Guiana, until diplomatic maneuvering ended the war scare early in 1897. By then, the imperial fever had aroused the American people, not against mighty Britain but against poor old Spain.

The Spanish-American War of 1898 developed from American desires to free Cuba from Spanish rule and from the big-navy expansionism of Captain Mahan and Assistant Secretary of the Navy Theodore Roosevelt. When the American battleship *Maine* arrived off riot-torn Havana to protect American lives there early in the year, it and 260 of its crew were blown up by a mysterious submarine mine. The incident and others led to an American declaration of war in April. The U. S. Navy implemented long-standing strategic war plans and turned over strategic direction to a Naval War Board that included Mahan. Neither side contemplated attacking the other's homeland, though the hysterical American public caused substantial naval forces to be tied down to coast defense. The American offensive, relatively swift, clumsy and almost comical, quickly destroyed Spanish naval power. On May 1 Commodore George Dewey—with four cruisers basing at British Hong Kong —easily destroyed the seven old Spanish warships at Manila Bay in the Philippines, despite notoriously poor gunnery. Meanwhile Admiral Pascual Cervera with four armored cruisers and three destroyers slipped into Santiago Harbor on Cuba's south coast, only to be blockaded there by the American squadron of Commodore W. S. Schley. The main American fleet of four new battleships under Rear Admiral W. T. Sampson then arrived and seized the fine harbor of Guantánamo Bay forty miles to the east as an advanced base. Late in June the fleet supported a ragged amphibious assault on Daiquiri and Siboney, twenty miles above Santiago. When these troops gained the high ground over Santiago, Cervera had no choice but to attempt a breakout. On July 3 the Spanish ships cleared the harbor and ran westward, only to be destroyed or beached by Sampson's ships in pursuit. Expeditionary forces then took Puerto Rico late in July and Manila in August. Spain capitulated and ceded its remaining empire to the United States: Puerto Rico, the Philippines and Guam in the Marianas. Cuba became a virtual American protectorate, as Britain saw its strategic dominance over the Caribbean challenged.

In sub-Saharan Africa, the British had few European rivals between the mid-1860s and mid-1880s as they extended their empire over several primitive peoples and used gunboats to police coasts and rivers against slavers and to protect British lives and property. In West Africa, Palmerston's anti-slave strategy led to the annexation of Lagos in 1861, followed by the seizure of Elmina from the Dutch ten years later, war against the Ashanti tribes in 1873–74 and concurrent policing of the Gold Coast alongside the French in Senegal and the Germans in the Cameroons. In South Africa, where diamonds were discovered in 1867, the British fought native wars against the Kaffirs, Basutos and Zulus and battled the Dutch-descended Boer farmers in open war, 1880–81. In East Africa, in addition to a brief punitive expedition into Ethiopia (Abyssinia) in 1867–68, the British between 1862 and 1883 crushed Arab slave trading from Zanzibar and used cruiser sweeps and a naval blockade to stop it along the entire coast. Isolated slaving continued and required naval patrols by the European powers and British military intervention in Nyasaland, but after fifteen nations in 1890 agreed to suppress slavery in concert it was gradually eradicated (Brazil gradually abolished the practice between 1871 and 1885, the last large nation to do so).

The most intense new imperial rivalries erupted in the mid-1880s and focused on Africa for the next two decades, but the British navy still controlled its peripheral waters from the bases at Gibraltar, the Falkland Islands, Simonstown in South Africa, Aden and India. British colonial forces suppressed the Ashantis and annexed Nigeria in the west in the 1890s, tightened controls over South Africa after the discovery of gold there in 1886, and sent gunboats up the Nile to help suppress a fanatical Arab uprising and capture Khartoum in 1884–85 and then assist General Sir Horatio Kitchener to conquer the Sudan, 1896–98, especially at the decisive Battle of Omdurman. The pacification of Uganda followed. Belgium signaled the coming of new rivals in 1877 by initiating the conquest of the Congo. Germany burst upon the imperial scene in 1883–85 by colonizing Tanganyika in East Africa, Southwest Africa and the Cameroons and Togoland in West Africa; marines and warships kept the natives pacified. Later light cruisers were used to help put down a last fanatical uprising in German East and Southwest Africa in 1904–08. France made Madagascar into a protectorate in 1882, used naval bombardments and landings against rebellious natives in 1885 and 1894–95 before turning the island into a colony in 1896 and using the army to pacify it over the next ten years. France and Britain offset Italy's foray into the Red Sea with tiny protectorates there, while Spain moved into West African Guinea and Rio de Oro in 1902 and 1907.

The European balance of power embraced Africa, though all frontier clashes were resolved by diplomacy and strong British shows of force. In East Africa, the British occupied the coast of Kenya in 1887 to thwart further German expansion, and three years later a great power compromise endorsed the French reign in Madagascar, transferred North Sea Heligoland Island from Britain to Germany, and allowed Britain to establish a protectorate over Zanzibar. Between 1896 and 1899 Britain used its navy to subdue the natives there and destroy the last vestiges of East African slavery. In 1898 Kitchener's army forced the French withdrawal from Fashoda on the Nile, but the next year the two Dutch republics of South Africa tried to throw off British suzerainty and courted German assistance. This Boer War (1899–1902) caught Britain unprepared for a major limited war, but its command of the sea enabled a rapid sealift of troops and supplies from England to Durban and the blockade of German contraband at Delagoa Bay in neighboring Portuguese Mozambique from 1900. The Boers initially drove British ground forces back on Ladysmith, where they were besieged before being relieved by reinforcements and three naval brigades supported by naval gun carriages fashioned by Captain Percy Scott. The British counterattack and Kitchener's scorched-earth policy and civilian concentration camps finally defeated the Boer armies, but such excesses of imperialism forced Britain to give South Africa dominion status. With the increasing liberalization of colonial rule throughout most of Africa, the balance of African colonial spheres stabilized. In the last analysis, however, only Britain really profited from the great wealth of its holdings in Africa; the other countries used theirs largely for purposes of national prestige.

British domination of the Indian Ocean littoral continued to act as a strategic buffer against possible Russian expansion. Imperial forces kept the northern Indian frontier pacified, between an expedition into Bhutan in 1865 and a 1903–04 drive into Tibet. British control over the Persian Gulf continued with the Trucial System, treaties with Persia and increased intervention in Muscat and Bahrain to suppress the Arab slave trade. Ottoman Turkey used the fleet of Kuwait to bombard and take Qatif and to help Turkey annex Hasa and Yemen in 1871. To offset Turkish pressure and protect the growing British steam-driven trade in the Gulf, Britain in the 1880s established a protectorate over Bahrain and instituted regular Navy patrols and in the 1890s extended the Trucial System to include Muscat, Qatar and Kuwait. Britain thus brought maritime order to the Persian Gulf, frustrated large-scale gun running and slaving and countered real or imagined Turkish, French and Russian threats there before 1905. By then, the Gulf had become but another arena of the European power balance, and the British profited politically and commercially from their administration of the Trucial System.

The Southeast Asian flank of this Indian Ocean defensive network required British intervention against slavery, piracy and general lawlessness which grew into outright occupation. From Singapore and south Burma, the British responded to French interference in Burma in 1885–86 with a riverborne expedition up the Irrawaddy and the annexation of Burma. Malay piracy in the 1870s brought British naval intervention and eventual control over the entire Malay peninsula, while British and American colonists in nearby Sarawak and North Borneo asked for British annexation, obtained in 1888. The Dutch controlled the adjacent East Indies and western New Guinea (Papua), finally pacifying the last native uprisings throughout the islands by 1908. Moro pirates from the southern Philippines faced Spanish gunboats in a prolonged anti-pirate campaign from the 1860s, but it was U. S. Navy gunboats and Army forces that generally pacified the Moros during the first decade of the new century. Farther south, the British Australasian Squadron and colonial naval brigades put down the last Maori native uprising in New Zealand in the 1860s, and the establishment of British protectorates over the south coast of New Guinea and the southern Solomon Islands in the 1880s and 1890s provided a strategic shield for the growing colony of Australia.

The imperial surge of the late nineteenth century also led to a scramble for relatively worthless islands in Pacific Oceania. In the South Pacific, the British occupied the Fijis (1874), Gilberts and Ellices (1892) and Tonga Islands (1900), while the French made Tahiti and the Society Islands a colony (1880). Britain and France jointly administered the New Hebrides. In 1884–85 Germany claimed the Marshall Islands and part of New Guinea. Germany, United States and Britain claimed Samoa, but after a savage hurricane which ravaged the warships of all three nations in Apia Harbor in 1889 they agreed to neutralize Samoa as an independent country. Over the next decade, however, the agreement was abrogated, Britain withdrew, and the other two powers divided Samoa between them. In 1898–99, with the American victory over Spain, the United States obtained Guam in the Marianas, occupied uninhabited Wake Island, and annexed the Hawaiian Islands at the invitation of the native government. Possession of the Hawaiian and Aleutian groups gave America predominance in the North Pacific. Simultaneously, Spain sold the Carolines and other Marianas islands to Germany. By 1900, the Pacific spheres of influence had been stabilized, with each policed by occasional warships and small colonial and native garrisons.

Major imperial rivalries in the Orient involved Britain, France, China and Indochina (Vietnam, Laos and Cambodia). Manchu China, still resisting Westernization, did not end the bloody Taiping Rebellion until 1864 and then only under the leadership of American and British soldiers of fortune. Neither could China control its own pirates without the naval forces of seven Western nations led by British Admiral Sir Henry Keppel in 1867–69. Anti-Western riots required the presence of Western warships, especially off Tientsin in 1870, so that China during the 1870s began to purchase the obsolete vessels of Western nations and to set up coastal arms factories at Shanghai, Foochow and Tientsin, largely with French assistance. But the weak Manchu leadership kept the Chinese Navy divided between northern and southern commissioners who drew from a Sea Defense Fund (established in 1875) to purchase ships and guns. The dynamic northern commissioner from 1870 to 1895, Li Hung-chang, built up his own Peiyang fleet, created a naval academy, and fortified Port Arthur to offset Japan. The several southern commissioners over these years tried to use their Nanyang fleet to protect the coast from the Yangtze River to the Gulf of Tonkin thus running afoul of the French. The French naval conquests in Indochina in 1858–61 increased their involvement there, leading to a French naval expedition up the Red River to capture Hanoi and face the Chinese "Black Flag" pirates behind Hué in 1873. China then helped the natives of northern Vietnam to close trade on the Red, leading to another French naval expedition to take Hanoi in 1883. When it was severely punished by the Black Flags, the force of three ironclads and two gunboats under Admiral A. A. P. Courbet bombarded Hué in July and forced new concessions, including a Chinese agreement to withdraw its forces in 1884. But resulting fears for her southern frontier led China into war with France.

The Sino-French War of 1884–85 failed to arrest French incursions into Indochina and seriously weakened China. Chinese arms on land initially defeated the French; their wooden vessels and fire rafts could not begin to challenge French armorclad and torpedo launches, nor would Li Hung-chang send any of his warships from the north to assist the Nanyang fleet. On August 23, 1884, Admiral Courbet with eight vessels in twelve minutes virtually annihilated the Chinese squadron of eleven wooden craft at the Ma-wei anchorage of Foochow, then destroyed the dockyard. In October Courbet blockaded and bombarded the coast of Formosa and in February 1885 destroyed a five-ship Nanyang fleet relief expedition. British pressure failed to discourage the French, who captured Langson in northern Vietnam, Keelung and the Pescadores Islands, though their army was crushed outside Langson. The imperialistic Ferry government in France fell, and the peace treaty reestablished the prewar *status quo,* but in 1887 France created the colony of French Indochina from Vietnam and Cambodia. The independent Siam intervened in Laos against French and Chinese alike, whereupon French warships anchored off Siamese Bangkok to force the cession of Laos and western Cambodia into French Indochina in 1893. With mobility by sea, the French Navy controlled this colony in the same manner as Navy and Army colonial leaders kept North Africa and Madagascar pacified. The presence of British naval forces at Singapore and Hong Kong guaranteed Chinese integrity from further French pressure, but the rise of Japan created more complex difficulties.

Japanese anti-Western attitudes and internal rivalries exposed serious weaknesses, but Japan moved decisively to correct its deficiencies. Civil war between the ruling Tokugawa shogunate and the rival Satsuma and Choshu clans in the 1860s brought on a Franco-American naval bombardment of Choshu Shimonoseki and a British shelling of Satsuman Kagoshima in 1863. The next year British Admiral A. L. Kuper in one of the Royal Navy's last active 101-gun first-rate ships of the line led nine British, three French, one American and four Dutch ships—some with rifled cannon—in the reduction of the forts of Shimonoseki and the occupation of Yokohama. The Satsuma and Tokugawa both yielded to these actions to grant more concessions to the West. The civil war did not end, however, until 1868 when the rebel clans defeated government forces led by Dutch-trained Kamajiro Enomoto at the naval battle of Hakodate. Admired by the victors, Enomoto was appointed as the first vice admiral of the new Imperial Japanese Navy, separated from direct army control in 1872. Throughout these wars and after, the Japanese obtained Western warships, naval engineers and professional instruction at home and abroad in a concerted effort to adopt Western technology. Britain dominated Japanese naval development with a naval mission in Japan during the 1870s, during which the new government of the "Meiji restoration" subdued the last Satsuma revolt. So unified, Japan could now join in the imperial expansion of the West.

Though resentful of her strong dependence on Britain, Japan borrowed whatever naval techniques and advisers were necessary to counter neighboring Russia and China. A gradual strategy of defensive expansion led to a punitive though temporary expedition against Chinese Formosa in 1874, the occupation of the Bonin Islands with American concurrence the next year, and the seizure of the Ryukyu Islands (principally Okinawa) in 1879, giving Japan a favorable strategic position opposite Chinese Shanghai. Russia's establishment of a naval base at Vladivostok in 1874 led Japan the next year to occupy the Kurile Islands in the north, agreeing to Russia's possession of the large adjacent island of Sakhalin. From this island defense perimeter, Japan turned toward its ancient target, Korea, whose internal political chaos had led to French and American naval bombardments and landings at Kanghwa forts guarding the entrance of the Han River in 1866 and 1871. With covetous eyes on Chinese Korea, Japan expanded its Army and Navy. In the 1880s the Army became pro-German, and the Navy replaced its British advisers with French and German officers; French naval designer Emile Bertin convinced Japan to adopt the *jeune école* scheme of building cruisers and torpedo boats. The Army dominated strategy, however, while the Navy expanded the defensive perimeter by occupying the Volcano Islands (notably Iwo Jima) in 1891. Japanese pressure against Korea mounted as Japan grew ever more anxious about China and Russia.

Russian eastward expansion across Asia helped to turn the Orient into a major area of imperial conflict. Ever worried, Britain made war on Afghanistan in 1878–80 when that country dared to court Russia. The new pro-British Afghan government failed to discourage the Russians from conquering adjacent Merv in 1884, after which, however, Russia looked to the Pacific. When in the 1880s Russian forces tried to obtain exclusive rights over Wonsan Harbor in northeast Korea, the British occupied Port Hamilton in southern Korea until the Russians withdrew. China, beset by the French war in Indochina, simultaneously submitted to Russian demands around the Amur River and both countries agreed to withdraw their forces from Korea. China remained too hopelessly divided to resist foreign pressures, its navy separated in four parts. Only the Peiyang fleet of Li Hung-chang remained strong, reorganized in 1888 with two powerful 7400-ton battleships from Germany, making nine modern vessels concentrated at the new Port Arthur base under Admiral Ting Ju-ch'ang. Anglo-American advisers had only limited successes in teaching the stubborn Chinese, whose naval strategy consisted only of traditional coast defense with strong fortifications and inshore warships. Japan, recognizing Chinese weaknesses, decided to settle the question of which Eastern power would dictate the future of Korea and act as a bulwark against further Western imperialism.

The Sino-Japanese War of 1894–95 followed amphibious landings by both armies near Seoul and a naval skirmish in which the Japanese sank a Chinese gunboat and drove off a cruiser at Inchon (Chemulpo). Both sides then ferried troops on transports to Korea, the Chinese via the Yalu River, the Japanese via Inchon and Pusan. Admiral Ting used the Peiyang fleet to protect the coast near his bases of Port Arthur and Weihaiwei on the Liaotung and Shantung peninsulas, while Admiral

Sukenori Ito's Japanese fleet roamed the Yellow Sea and bombarded both bases in August 1894. When Ting escorted a convoy of reinforcements for the Chinese army retreating from Pyongyang toward the Yalu, Ito attacked him in the battle of the Yalu River on September 17— two Chinese battleships and ten cruisers against a dozen better-armed Japanese cruisers. Steaming in line-ahead, Ito's fleet bludgeoned Ting's ships in ragged line-abreast, then maneuvered into two divisions to split the Chinese units and send some of them into panic flight. Losing five cruisers, the Chinese fled to Port Arthur just before the Japanese army crossed the Yalu into Manchuria and landed on the Liaotung peninsula for an overland descent on Arthur. Ting broke through Ito's blockade to reach Weihaiwei before Arthur fell in November, only to be blockaded at Weihaiwei by Ito and an army expeditionary force. In February 1895 Japanese torpedo boats sank a Chinese cruiser, while the larger ships bombarded Weihaiwei and its trapped fleet. Admiral Ting committed suicide, his own torpedo boats failed in a last breakout attempt, and Weihaiwei surrendered on the 12th. When the Japanese overran Manchuria and threatened Peking, China submitted.

The postwar settlement directly involved the Western powers who could accept the cession of Chinese Formosa and the Pescadores Islands to Japan but not mainland Port Arthur. Russia led France and Germany in preventing that from happening and so gave Russia more time to complete the Trans-Siberian Railroad to Vladivostok. In 1896–98 Russia even obtained from China the right to route the track across Manchuria and the outright cession of Port Arthur for the Russian Pacific Fleet. The helpless Manchu dynasty still had nine German-built cruisers, but these were insufficient to challenge Russia, which now threatened Korea. Japan responded however by incorporating the seventeen captured Chinese vessels into its own navy and ordering 12"-gunned 12,000 to 15,000-ton battleships from Britain and armored cruisers, destroyers and torpedo boats from Britain, Germany, France and Italy. Modeling its admiralty, tactics and training closely on the British, Japan determined to create a first-class navy to prevent another diplomatic humiliation at the hands of the Russian-led Western powers.

In 1897–1900 the Western Pacific emerged as an area of strategic rivalries equal to that of Europe, with the *Pax Britannica* succumbing to six naval nations acting unilaterally. The general victim was China: Russia extended its control from Arthur to Dairen and the Liaotung peninsula and pressed into north Korea. Germany occupied Tsingtao and leased Kiaochow Bay. France moved into Kwangchow Bay. Britain secured Weihaiwei and extended Kowloon, near Hong Kong. The United States conquered and annexed the Philippine Islands, but feared for the integrity of China and its own trade position there. So in 1899 the

United States initiated its "Open Door policy" to prevent the economic dismemberment of China, a noble-sounding appeal that the other powers had to accept in principle. The policy gained time for the *Pax Britannica* and for Britain's economic penetration into the fertile Yangtze basin and provided stability in China while America fought the Philippine insurrection (1899–1902) and began the pacification of the Moro tribes. Where the Manchus could do nothing against the West, the fanatical Boxer Rebellion tried by besieging the Western legations in Peking in 1899–1900. For the last time in the Orient the Western powers followed British leadership by accepting the command of Vice Admiral Sir Edward H. Seymour over some thirty warships from Great Britain, Germany, Russia, France, Japan, the United States, Italy and Austria. Repulsed from a landing attempt at the Taku forts at the mouth of the Peiho River, Seymour's fleet bombarded them into submission early in 1900. Then in July and August 18,000 troops assaulted and took Tientsin, drove up the Peiho and fought their way into Peking. The Boxers crushed, Russia immediately occupied all of Manchuria and collected a huge indemnity payment from crippled China. Anxious over Russian expansion, Japan moved to fill the strategic vacuum now developing with the collapse of the British *pax*.

By 1900 the imperial and limited wars of four decades had been absorbed into the larger strategic struggle now developing not only in Europe but on a global scale. Whatever lessons were to be gleaned from these many activities would now be submerged by the naval arms race dominated by the *Dreadnought*. If general war was to be avoided, a new balance of power would have to be constructed, the object of a new system of naval alliances.

## NAVAL ALLIANCE SYSTEMS

The Anglo-German confrontation over battleship construction from 1900 required general British strategic realignments that affected power relations everywhere in the world, but these could not prevent the steady plunge of the powers into the catastrophe of World War I. In the first three years of the twentieth century Britain finally perceived Germany to be the real threat to European and thus global stability and the *Pax Britannica*. The two-power fleet standard originally aimed at France and Russia was therefore replaced with a battleship construction program to counter Tirpitz's "risk theory" of building two thirds (38) of British battleship strength. Tirpitz believed Britain would not risk war against such a fleet because of heavy British fleet commitments abroad, enabling Germany to dictate policy on the continent and in the colonial sphere. But Tirpitz underestimated Britain's adaptability to such a threat.

Under the dynamic leadership of Admiral Sir John Fisher, Second Sea Lord from mid-1902 and First Sea Lord from Trafalgar Day (October 21), 1904, the Royal Navy began to replace its old battleships with dreadnoughts and instituted important reforms in administration, personnel and gunnery. And with the conclusion of active imperial pacification operations, gunboat construction ended in favor of the battleship and its flotilla. Most importantly, however, the British initiated a diplomatic policy aimed at reducing tension abroad, ending Britain's virtual political isolation, and thus enabling major fleet units to be reconcentrated at home against Germany. Especially from the fleet redistribution scheme of December 1904, the British naval legions began to return to the strategic center of the Empire.

In the Western Hemisphere, Britain accepted the assertiveness of the United States and henceforth fostered friendly relations. Under the dynamic leadership of naval-minded President Theodore Roosevelt (1901–09), the U. S. Navy became a blue-water battleship fleet dedicated to eliminating all European navies from the Caribbean and protecting both seaboards. Virtually his own Secretary of the Navy, Roosevelt promoted battleship authorizations from Congress, utilized an advisory General Board of senior admirals under Dewey, modernized gunnery and used submarines to complement coastal fortifications, created the Atlantic and Pacific fleets in 1906 and 1907, and in the latter year concentrated all sixteen battleships in the Atlantic Fleet, making it the largest single battle force in the world at the time. Cruisers led the Pacific Fleet and the smaller Asiatic Fleet created in 1910.

With shared suspicions over Germany in the Caribbean, Britain gradually turned over its policing to the United States, including in 1900–01 the right to build and fortify a canal across Panama. When Colombia stalled this American plan, in 1903 Roosevelt engineered and supported a quick and successful revolution in Panama. To guard the Canal, built over the years 1904 to 1914, Roosevelt established fleet bases at Culebra off Puerto Rico and (by lease from Cuba) at Guantánamo Bay in 1903, the same year that German warships bombarded the coast of Venezuela over fiscal difficulties. Needing economic order in Latin America to keep out the Germans and promote American profits, Roosevelt instituted his own corollary to the Monroe Doctrine by declaring the exclusive American right of intervention there. Between 1905 and 1916 therefore the Navy landed Marines and Army troops in several chaotic Caribbean nations to restore economic and political order. Roosevelt consciously courted British favor, as anti-German feeling mounted in the United States. As a result, Britain between 1904 and 1906 (officially by 1911) withdrew its North American squadron from Bermuda, closed the base at Jamaica, abandoned St. Lucia altogether, and downgraded and turned over the major fleet installations at Halifax and Esquimalt to the Canadian government. Henceforth, Britain would depend upon the U. S. Navy—by 1905 the third largest navy in the world—to protect its dominions in the Western Hemisphere and to insure maritime stability there.

But American naval expansion, becoming global, would soon rival the Royal Navy in overall strength. Both the U. S. Navy and Army began—ever so haltingly, devoid of realistic institutional changes— to reform along European lines, while the Navy became the tool of impressing the other powers of American independence of the British naval strength that had so long protected North America. But American fears of primarily Germany led to numerous unilateral shows of naval force: the entire Atlantic battle ("Great White") fleet circumnavigated the globe via Japan in 1907–09, visited British and French ports in 1910–11 and the Mediterranean in 1913, while one division of battle-ships called at ports in Germany, Sweden and Baltic Russia in 1911. Such anxieties, as over a potential German landing in strife-torn Mexico, helped cause American interventions there between 1914 and 1917. An incident involving an American naval shore party at Tampico in April 1914 prompted President Woodrow Wilson to order the occupa-tion of Vera Cruz taken by force by naval and Marine landing parties. After the dispute was settled, the Mexican civil war spilled over onto American soil in 1916, followed by an American overland expedition into Mexico. After the outbreak of war in Europe in 1914, many Ameri-can admirals presumed that Germany would defeat Britain and then cross the Atlantic to stake out an empire in the Western Hemisphere, a fear fed by German diplomatic moves. So the United States planned to fight Germany alone, and in 1915 new naval authorizations provided for new battleships and battle cruisers to command local American waters against the German High Seas Fleet. Without advanced bases along its Eastern seaboard like Canadian Halifax and British Bermuda, the Americans maintained a strong unilateral and independent strategic naval stance for deterring Germany or for fighting its fleet on the open sea.

The sudden rise of Japan as the fourth ranking naval power in the world alarmed both Britain and the United States, but both preferred Japanese to Russian supremacy in the Far East and devised their diplomacy accordingly. In 1902 Britain allied formally with Japan and agreed to intervene in any Russo-Japanese conflict only if a third party —France and/or Germany—joined Japan's enemy. Both powers en-dorsed the American "open door" in China, Manchuria and Korea, a further anti-Russian statement which the United States informally sup-ported by basing its own warships at British Hong Kong and Japanese ports. The Americans used such Chinese ports as Chefoo near British Weihaiwei on the Shantung peninsula, established the Yangtze River Patrol of three former Spanish gunboats at Shanghai, and—much to Russian displeasure—stationed a gunboat at the port of Newchang on the Manchurian Liaotung peninsula. The Anglo-Japanese alliance enabled Britain to recall its heavy fleet units from Asia, leaving Japan to Russia's vigorous reaction. Reneging on an agreement with China in 1902 to evacuate Manchuria, Russia the next year challenged the "open door" and threatened to intervene in Korea. American Admiral Robley D. Evans then concentrated three battleships, two monitors and several cruisers at Chefoo, but Russia strengthened its naval defenses in Asia to thwart Japan. Hastening seven of its twenty-seven battleships to Port Arthur and cruisers and destroyers to there and Vladivostok, with prefabricated submarines going across the Trans-Sib Railway to the latter place, Russia prepared for war with Japan—a smaller and weaker power in the eyes of the Western world.

The Russo-Japanese War of 1904–05 assumed maritime proportions from the outset, with Japan having the distinct strategic advantage. Geographically, athwart Russian communications between its two Asiatic ports, Japan had merely to control these waters and support the Army's transfer to Manchuria. As in antiquity, Japanese naval policy remained subordinate to the Army, but command of the Yellow Sea served this strategy perfectly. Furthermore, the main Russian fleet lay in the distant Baltic, with another element in the Black Sea, whose outlets—the Skaggerak and Dardanelles—were controlled by the British navy. The only possible shortcut between Kronstadt and the Far East, the Northeast Passage, had been closed in 1902 when the tsarist government had stupidly stopped Admiral Makarov's new icebreaking efforts there as unwanted competition to the Trans-Sib Railway.

So before Russia could dispatch more reinforcements to Asia, Japan launched a sneak torpedo boat attack against Port Arthur on February 8, 1904, and one of its cruiser squadrons destroyed two Russian cruisers off Inchon (Chemulpo). Then Japan declared war officially. The main Japanese fleet of six new battleships with escorts led by Admiral Heihachiro Togo mined and blockaded the entrance to Port Arthur, enabling the Army to land at Inchon and drive toward the Yalu. Admiral Makarov took command at Arthur, only to be lost when his flagship struck a mine and sank with all hands in April. In May the first Japanese army crossed the Yalu and a second landed above Port Arthur on the Liaotung peninsula, but Togo's supporting fleet lost two of its six battleships to Russian mines. Then, in July, the inept Russian viceroy for the East, Admiral Evgeni Alexiev, ordered Admiral Wilhelm Vitgeft and his six old battleships to break out of Togo's blockade. Togo intercepted Vitgeft in the battle of the Yellow Sea on August 10 and completely routed him, killing Vitgeft with a lucky hit on the bridge of his flagship. Japanese warships sank one Russian cruiser in this action and another out of Vladivostok, the others escaping back into their own or neutral ports. The latter refuge meant internment for the duration, a rule of international law strictly enforced by the American battleships and monitors at Chinese Chefoo and Shanghai. Russian warships far away in the Red Sea began to seize neutral vessels, mostly British, prompting the British and Americans to apply diplomatic pressure and the British to close the Suez Canal, Dardanelles and all their own ports to Russian shipping. Russia had no choice but to transfer its naval crews ashore to help in the defense of Port Arthur against the Japanese Army, while a relief army hastened thence from Eastern Europe via the Trans-Sib.

To save Port Arthur, Russia then made the desperate decision to dispatch its main fleet from the Baltic on an 18,000 mile voyage as a relief force. Lacking its own merchant marine and raw coal, the Imperial Russian Navy contracted with a private German steamship company to provide fuel en route and arranged to round Africa while another part of the fleet obtained permission to pass through the Suez Canal. Admiral Zinovi Petrovich Rozshestvensky led the "Second Pacific Squadron"—a hodgepodge of aging and new inferior battleships and escorts—out of the Baltic in October 1904, only to succumb to totally unreasonable fears of Japanese torpedo boats in the North Sea by bombarding a group of helpless British fishing trawlers at Dogger Bank. British diplomats thereafter harassed Russian coaling efforts along the way, assisted by the tropical heat of Africa and coal dust which lowered morale already plagued by political malcontents within the fleet. The two Russian squadrons rendezvoused off French Madagascar, only to be threatened by unsuccessful mutinies on two ships early in 1905. Rozhestvensky passed Singapore in April and was joined at Camranh Bay, French Indochina, by another squadron from the Baltic. By then, however, Port Arthur had fallen, and Rozhestvensky had to reshape his course for Vladivostok via the Tsushima Strait, where Togo lay waiting for him.

On May 27, 1905, Togo's compact, well-disciplined and well-gunned four battleships, eight cruisers, twenty-one destroyers and sixty torpedo boats ensnared the dispirited and exhausted Russian fleet at the Battle of Tsushima. Twice crossing Rozhestvensky's line—"capping the T"— Togo's gunners sank three Russian battleships and during the night and following day sank five more and captured the remaining two (one with the wounded Rozhestvensky on board). In addition, the Japanese sank one and captured two coastal ironclads, captured and sank seven cruisers, and sank five destroyers and two torpedo boats. Japan thus sent 146,900 tons of Russian naval shipping to the bottom and captured some 40,000 tons more. Of the surviving four Russian cruisers, three escaped to Manila, only to be interned by the Americans, and the other managed to reach Vladivostok. The Japanese lost but three torpedo boats in probably the most stunning naval victory of modern times. A new Russian army had gathered at Harbin to check a northward Japanese offensive into Manchuria, and Vladivostok held on, sending out patrols of thirteen American-built submarines. But Tsushima had shaken Russian society and the Navy, where mutinies now erupted, most dramatically aboard the Black Sea battleship *Potemkin;* its successful mutineers surrendered the vessel to the Rumanian government and went into exile. Mutually exhausted, Russia and Japan concluded peace in September 1905 at the American naval base at Portsmouth, New Hampshire, with Theodore Roosevelt mediating.

Postwar great power arrangements in the Pacific left Japan generally supreme as a buffer between a retrenching Russia and an active United States. Satisfied that Russian pressure on India had been checked by British special status in Persia, Afghanistan and Tibet and that the seventh-ranked Russian navy had been neutralized, Britain concluded a more permanent alliance with Japan late in 1905 and withdrew its last major fleet units from the Far East. Russia surrendered Port Arthur and southern Sakhalin Island to Japan, along with all claims to Korea, control over which Britain and the United States handed to Japan. All the powers in 1905–07 ceased their imperialistic ventures in China and accepted the "open door," while the enfeebled Manchu dynasty went through its final death throes, 1908–12. Taking advantage of American President William Howard Taft's "dollar diplomacy," the Manchus in 1911 involved American shipbuilders in a Chinese naval revival, but this collapsed the next year with the creation of the new Republic of China. The United States and Japan accepted their mutual spheres of influence in the Pacific, but antagonisms mounted after 1905 over American immigration policies and the naval arms race. Japan sought naval self-sufficiency, commissioning its last battleship in a British shipyard in 1910 and hoping to build a battleship fleet 70 percent that of America's. The United States Navy stopped admitting Japanese midshipmen to its Naval Academy in 1906, made an impressive "good will" visit to Japan with the Atlantic-based "Great White Fleet" in 1908, and evolved a strategic "Orange Plan" for eventually fighting Japan. The fleet would base at Bremerton, San Francisco and Pearl Harbor for any campaign westward, although its forward bases at Guam in the Marianas and at Subic Bay and Manila in the Philippines remained woefully inadequate for such a war. American fears of Germany, however, kept the battleships concentrated in the Atlantic and required that conflict with Japan be carefully avoided.

With the Japanese fleet allied (by renewed treaty in 1911), the American fleet basically friendly and the Russian fleet neutralized, Britain also reduced its strategic requirements in the Mediterranean by accommodating the fifth- and sixth-ranked naval powers, France and Italy. The new French battleships in 1902 suddenly lost importance with the return of the *jeune école* to control, now championing submarines. More significant, Britain and France finally realized their mutual strategic needs for countering the Triple Alliance of Germany, Austria-Hungary and Italy and in April 1904 concluded the *Entente Cordiale*. They initiated military conversations and agreed that Britain should have absolute control over Egypt and that France be allowed to expand from Tunisia and Algeria over Morocco. This antagonized imperialistic Germany, as did American pro-Anglo-French naval shows of force during several diplomatic crises over Morocco in 1904–05. An American squadron of six battleships and eight cruisers demonstrated in the middle sea in May 1904, and the following year another American battleship squadron visited British Gibraltar while President Roosevelt arbitrated a Franco-German dispute over Morocco in favor of France. Italy proved to be no real threat at sea, for despite its alliance with Germany, it had lost the naval race with France, concluded new understandings with that nation in 1902, and begun to counter the small navy of its reluctant Austro-Hungarian ally. But the appearance of German naval units in the middle sea from 1905 converted the region into but one more theater of general European balance of power.

By the end of 1905, British naval diplomacy had succeeded in re-concentrating the major fleet units at home and for the next four years focused on anti-German aims, especially in the Mediterranean. Spain in 1907–08 sided with the *Entente Cordiale* over Morocco and contracted for three new British-built battleships. Simultaneously, the *Entente Cordiale* and Franco-Russian alliance grew into a Triple Entente against the Triple Alliance, with Britain settling its differences with Russia over the Persian Gulf. More difficult was Britain's desire to shore up Ottoman Turkey, "the sick man of Europe," against covetous neighbors Austria, Russia, Italy and especially Greece. When a local naval race between Turkey and Greece commenced in 1908, Britain provided an admiral to direct the Ottoman fleet. But Britain's most strategic change involved the abandonment of the two-power standard. Because the U. S. Navy had become so powerful, Britain could not hope to build a battleship fleet the equal of the next two, Germany's and America's. So in April 1909, thanks largely to the work of Rear Admiral J. R. Jellicoe, the Admiralty decided to build a battle fleet 60 percent larger in dreadnoughts than Germany's. From this time forward, any British thought of war against the United States was simply rejected, naval conversations with the French were accelerated, and all plans for naval war were made with Germany generally in mind.

Between 1909 and 1912 tensions mounted as the alliances grew ever more firm. Russia, intervening with Britain in a Persian revolution, initiated a new dreadnought, cruiser and destroyer construction program, which included the world's first minelaying submarine, and streamlined its admiralty under a dynamic new Minister of Marine, Vice Admiral Ivan K. Grigorovich. France planned to concentrate its six new dreadnoughts at Brest against Germany, but instead based them at Toulon to deter the growing fleets of Italy and Austria. In 1911 France finally landed an expeditionary force at Fez to conquer anarchy-ridden Morocco, and Britain countered the dispatch of a German gunboat thence by diplomatic pressure, while France agreed to cede part of the French Congo to Germany. In Britain, an administrative upheaval led to the resignation of Admiral Fisher as First Sea Lord and the appointment of Winston Churchill as First Lord of the Admiralty. The British, anxious over the Balkan question, dispatched a naval mission to Greece, awkwardly matched by the British advisers in the Ottoman navy. Then Italy determined to grab Libya, the last surviving North African state under nominal Ottoman control, and use it as a buffer against further French expansion. The Italo-Turkish War of 1911–12 demonstrated the effectiveness of the Italian navy led by the reform-minded naval minister Rear Admiral P. L. Cattolica. Calling up its naval reserves, the Italian fleet bombarded the Adriatic coast at Preveza and shelled and captured the Libyan port cities of Tripoli, Tobruk and Benghazi. Moslem Arab guerrilla tactics led to an Italian naval blockade of the Libyan coast, angering France and Britain. The British-led Ottoman fleet retreated behind the Dardanelles, and in the spring of 1912 the Italian navy captured Rhodes and the Dodecanese Islands. When the Italian army overran Libya, Turkey submitted and ceded Libya, Rhodes and the Dodecanese to Italy.

Virtually defenseless, the Ottoman Empire now received Franco-Russian guarantees for the integrity of the Dardanelles and Black Sea against Italy and Austria, but this did not affect the Balkan enemies of Turkey. In the First Balkan War, 1912–13, the armies of Greece, Bulgaria, Serbia and Montenegro overran European Turkey while the Greek navy controlled the Aegean. The imposed great power settlement carved up these lands to the victors, created the new nation of Albania and ceded Crete to Greece. Bulgaria unsuccessfully waged the Second Balkan War in 1913 against her former allies for more territory. Possession of the Aegean islands, taken by the Greek navy in the First war, remained in dispute. So Turkey and Greece vied to purchase battleships in Britain and America, succumbing to the same battleship hysteria that had already engulfed other such unlikely naval powers as Brazil, Chile and Argentina. Turks and Greeks alike ignored their British advisers who insisted such deep-draft vessels would be next to useless in the shallow inlets of the Aegean. Nevertheless, the strategic realignments in the Mediterranean bore importantly on the general European power balance.

Ultimately, in fact, the Mediterranean and Balkan problems drew the powers into war. Germany promoted Triple Alliance advances into the middle sea and even began to replace British advisers in Turkey with its own. The Alliance had Italy's six fast dreadnoughts (promoted by naval writer Giovanni Sechi) and the four of Austria-Hungary, whose Imperial Navy improved with many torpedo boats and submarines under the reform-minded Admirals Count Rudolf Montecuccoli and Francis Ferdinand. In mid-1913, at German insistence, Austrian and Italian naval leaders held joint contingency discussions for war, and two large German warships were placed at their disposal. The Triple Entente moved to check increased German penetration into the Mediterranean in 1912 and 1913. The British and French navies reformed under Fisher's successors and Churchill on the one hand and naval minister Théophile Delcasse and Augustin Boué de Papeyrère on the other. The French fleet and part of the British definitely redeployed to the middle sea, although the Russian navy remained plagued by mutinies and uncompleted construction. But the real arms race involved only Britain and Germany, whose time ran out in June 1914 when a Serbian terrorist in Balkan Bosnia assassinated the Austrian Archduke Francis Ferdinand. Austria demanded redress from Serbia and upset the delicate balance of power in Europe, setting in train the rapid diplomatic deterioration that began World War I.

Between 1906—the *Dreadnought* and the fleet's recall—and 1914, Britain had exploited the naval alliance system to achieve her traditional strategic aims. At the end of 1906, strategic concentration had been achieved: sixteen battleships in the Channel fleet at Dover, twelve in the Atlantic fleet at Gibraltar and eight in the Mediterranean—a system still intact eight years later. Tirpitz's risk theory had therefore failed; the High Seas Fleet was outnumbered by Britain's home forces. In doctrine, therefore, the British "blue-water" school had triumphed over the "bolt from the blue" and *jeune école* schools; the offensive battleship would command the seas, whereas coastal defenses and torpedo-laden vessels could not. And to augment the battle line Admiral Fisher had introduced the battle cruiser, a heavy vessel strong in guns like the battleship but fast and weak in armor like the cruiser. Unfortunately, as events were to prove, the "capital ship" alone could not exert command of the sea without applying the strategic lessons of history. And all historical evidence was either ignored or twisted to fit material arguments, while the nagging questions regarding tactics would only be solved in the crucible of battle. By 1914 and the end of the *Pax Britannica* the dreadnought had become the supreme superweapon and strategic panacea of the technological age—a false distinction that only two world wars would expose.

# BOOK SIX

## Era of the Total Wars

*By maritime strategy we mean principles which govern a war in which the sea is a substantial factor. Naval strategy is but that part of it which determines the movements of the fleet when maritime strategy has determined what part the fleet must play in relation to action of the land forces; for it scarcely needs saying that it is almost impossible that a war can be decided by naval action alone.*

—CORBETT

World Wars I and II, the result and manifestation of the last surge of great-power nationalism mixed with the new imperialism and uncontrolled arms race, seriously interrupted but did not stifle the growing spirit of global cosmopolitanism of the late nineteenth and early twentieth centuries. The powers that went to war in 1914, then regrouped in 1918–1922 and finally resumed the conflict on an even greater scale from 1939, were playing out the last contradictions of the old European-directed political order. Failing to reckon with the full implications of industrialized total war, the European powers—and Japan in the early 1940s—turned to the traditional forms of armed conflict to achieve the traditional goals of national greatness—imperial territorial gain, economic wealth and self-sufficiency, and military prestige. Rampant nationalism in these years was perhaps not unusual in such relatively new great powers as Germany and Japan, but it was equally rife in France, Britain, Russia, America and the lesser states.

What such tradition-bound powers, old and new, failed to accept was that the new cosmopolitanism found fresh expression among emergent countries, classes and philosophies which resented the old European hegemony and which took advantage of the holocaust to undermine the old order. The leading revolutionary figures of this new thrust were V. I. Lenin in Russia and Woodrow Wilson in the United States, while in India the Hindu Mahatma, M. K. Gandhi, was scarcely less important. All sought to replace the antiquated imperialism and nationalistic global hegemony of the European great powers by appealing to universal human needs for freedom and equality. Though generally unsuccessful in these years because of the stubborn refusal of the old order to submit, these appeals were sufficiently strong to fill the vacuum left when Europe finally exhausted itself—after 1945. The era of the total wars, of uncontrolled nationalism and weapons technology carried to the extreme, acted as a tragic transition period from the stabilized tensions of the *Pax Britannica* to those of the *Pax Americana*.

The United States occupied a unique role in this transition, for as war engulfed the Western powers only the North American colossus was left unscathed by the terrible violence. Geographic insularity combined with the long American democratic tradition and America's brief experience in thalassocratic expansion to make the United States the refuge of Western culture and hope in the years between 1914 and 1945. The Americans entertained the naive belief that a great power could remain neutral and indeed isolated in the century of total and global war and cosmopolitanism, but twice, in 1917 and 1941, they reluctantly and belatedly accepted their responsibilities as a great power and came to the rescue of Europe. In this way, the United States somewhat resembled the position of Britain in the wars of the French Revolution and Napoleonic periods; not only was American prosperity and soil not violated by the two world wars, but scientific, technological and industrial progress continued on an even greater scale.

Despite the American thrust into the Pacific, however, United States foreign policy had always been isolationistic—save for geographic and economic expansion within the Western Hemisphere—so that the Americans intervened in Europe only after allied Anglo-French survival was actually threatened. American reluctance to intervene militarily on behalf of China kept the United States free of active involvement there as long as Japan did not jeopardize the balance of the powers in the Pacific. So the attempt of the new empires, Germany, Italy and Japan, to assert their hegemony over Europe and Asia respectively, had to be met by Britain and France—and the uncertain assistance of internally shaky Russia—but without the concerted involvement of the United States. The tragedy lay in the fact that the European powers believed they could continue their nationalistic and imperialistic rivalries with the same relative ease as they had in the nineteenth century. The industrial age did not oblige them, leading to massive total war for which they were unprepared. Not learning from the bloodbath of 1914–18, Europe committed virtual suicide by renewing the struggle in 1939. The world had changed, the level of violence having been magnified to unprecedented and unanticipated proportions by weapons of incredible destructiveness.

Total war in the industrial age demanded rigid centralized controls in order to mobilize entire national populations and economies for breaking the will of the enemy citizenry. Recognition of the need for such centralization came only slowly after 1900 and without any firm direction in any of the powers. Alarmed by its relative unpreparedness for the Boer War, Britain in 1902 had created its Committee of Imperial Defense, but interservice rivalry soon compromised much of its effectiveness as a centralized controlling body; Admiral Fisher viewed Britain's defensive needs in global, imperial terms and distrusted the Army General Staff whose major concern remained home defense and the possibility of sending a wartime cross-Channel expeditionary force to France. Fisher went further and refused to develop a similar modern staff organization for the Navy. The Committee by 1911 had decided on defensive plans for the Empire, with considerable naval autonomy for Australia, New Zealand and Canada, but it did not succeed in unifying Army-Navy planning. Neither did the prime minister and his cabinet. In Germany, the Army General Staff, model of all staff organizations, had developed viable war plans, but only for a land war in Europe. Both German diplomatic and naval leaders remained ignorant of Army plans, with the kaiser and the prime minister unable to unify defense planning. In the United States, the Army's General Staff was very loose, while the Navy had to battle political and traditional service conservatism just to get a Chief of Naval Operations by 1915; otherwise, unity of command and planning rested only with the President. The same was generally true of the other powers.

What total war demanded, from 1914 on, was civil-military-economic command and control at the very top, and so after war came, expert management executives from industry had to be employed to mobilize strategic raw and industrial materials for total war. Jealous of their established constitutional authority—during the two wars and in the long interval between them—statesmen, generals and admirals resisted the creation of permanent military-industrial complexes for directing national policy. As a result, centralized control in the years 1914 to 1945 remained temporary and makeshift, while real unity of command depended upon dictatorial chiefs of state and their powerful industrial managers as aides: in Germany Walter Rathenau, Erich Ludendorff, Adolf Hitler and Albert Speer; in Britain David Lloyd George and Winston Churchill; in the United States Woodrow Wilson, Bernard Baruch and Franklin D. Roosevelt; in France Georges Clemenceau; and in Russia Joseph Stalin.

The pre-World War I ascendancy of the material school of strategy, with its advocacy of super machine weapons as the final arbiter in war, logically pointed to new realities that would develop in an industrialized total war, but such hints of the future devastation were met only by traditional legalistic rationales. Clausewitz had argued from the experience of the Napoleonic wars that total war required that the whole enemy country be overwhelmed, and in 1899 a Polish-Russian economist-military pundit named Ivan S. Bloch in a six-volume study of war predicted that the new superweapons—machine guns, heavy artillery, military railroads—would lead to a stalemate. If each side had them, he reasoned, neither would be able to overwhelm the other, and both would therefore bludgeon each other into impotence. The traditional reaction of the political statesmen to such prophecies was to convene peace conferences at The Hague, but these did not succeed in stopping the mounting arms races. The traditional response of the military men was to seek overwhelming victory by a swift overland offensive at the beginning of the war, the Germans with their Schlieffen Plan, the French with their Plan XVII. As for war at sea, Fisher borrowed the arguments of Mahan and Corbett to claim that his dreadnoughts would crush the German fleet in a pitched battle early in the war, a view Tirpitz had followed in his risk theory when he assumed the British home fleets would be understrength. All of these strategic assumptions rested largely on conjecture, and even the brief experience of the Russo-Japanese War proved little that was conclusive. What no one could know was that Bloch's contention was indeed correct, that is until new superweapons, notably the submarine and airplane, would enlarge the battlefields and undermine the old faith in international law among nations. Equally important, the materialists erred seriously in minimizing the tried and true principles of strategy to be gleaned from history. There were to be no shortcuts in modern total war.

## SHIPS AND SEAFARING

The naval weapons for total war, imposing as they appeared, did not fundamentally change through the contemporary era of the world wars. Save for the aircraft carrier, the warships that comprised the major navies in 1914 did not change markedly by 1945, when the long hostilities finally came to an end. In fact, not only did warship categories remain standardized among battleships, cruisers, destroyers and sub-marines, but each individual vessel belonged to a specific class of its warship type. With such standardized classes of ships, the major navies introduced the practice of painting numbers on each hull, along with the ship's name. In addition, in some navies, each type vessel was given an abbreviation.

The battleship (or superdreadnought) of the world wars remained the index of naval power throughout most of the era, from the five ships of British 30,000-ton *Queen Elizabeth*-class of 1913 to the two 64,000-ton *Yamato*-class battlewagons of Japan and four 45,000-ton American battleships of the *Iowa* (BB-61)-class by 1944. The tactical aspects of battleship war did not change: the range of the gun remained the major factor in naval warfare, balanced by defensive armament and speed. The battleship gun of first 13.5″ and 14″ and then 15″ in the *Queen Elizabeth*s, 16″ in the *Iowa*s and 18.1″ in the *Yamato*s naturally had varying maximum effective ranges, but the larger calibers could reach 35,000 yards or about twenty miles. Defensive armor—inches of steel thickness—roughly paralleled the gun calibers (13″ in the armor belt of the *Queen Elizabeth*), but the Americans set the "all or nothing" trend of again placing heavy armor only over the vital parts of the ship. The concentrated salvos of eight to twelve large-caliber naval guns in double, triple, and/or quadruple turrets thus gave these battleships their punch—not only in relatively flat broadsides but in high-trajectory plunging fire. Speed also became a crucial factor for maneuvering into line-ahead or column battle formation. Geared and electric steam turbine engines had become standard, but the need for higher-pressure steam and high super heat to achieve battleship speeds in excess of 21 knots could not be provided by boilers fired by coal. So oil was introduced with the *Queen Elizabeth,* giving her 25 knots, and soon replaced coal altogether. Improvements in marine engines over these years led to a technological ceiling of about 32 knots in the *Iowa*. Hence, the speedier superdreadnoughts came to be known as "fast battleships."

Naval weaponry thus centered around the need to support and en-hance the firepower of these heavy-gunned "capital ships." To give the battle line additional firepower and better armed reconnaissance, Ad-miral Fisher had introduced a new ship-type, the battle cruiser, in 1907. Armed like a battleship Fisher's *Invincible*-class battle cruiser displaced 17,400 tons and mounted eight 12″ guns, but the side armor was thinned to 7″ or that of a cruiser to give the battle cruiser speeds up to 26.5 knots. Speed, Fisher reasoned, was the armor of the battle cruiser; it could run away from the killing salvos of the battleships. The Germans quickly designed their own battle cruisers, but with complete 12″ armor belts and 11″ guns. The battle cruiser proved vulnerable and uneconomical in World War I, however, and was replaced after the war by the aircraft carrier, whose longer-range scout planes provided better "eyes" for the fleet. The brief presence of the battle cruiser, however, led to the removal of the last intermediate-caliber guns from the battleships and the regular assignment of 27- to 45-knot destroyers to the battle fleet to launch torpedo attacks against approaching battle cruisers. The World War I British destroyer of 1500 tons and World War II American destroyer of 2050 tons carried respectively six and ten 21" torpedo tubes plus four 4.7" and five 5" quick-firing guns. The demise of the battle cruiser had no effect on the need for the well-named multi-purpose destroyer, whose torpedoes, guns and depth charges could be used against surface ships, aircraft and submarines. The other ship type for escorting battleships, and for multitudinous independent work, was the standard cruiser. With speeds, armament and duties comparable to those of the destroyer, the heavy cruiser grew in these years from 7100 tons with 6" guns in World War I to the World War II vessel of 14,000 tons with 8" guns; in this category also was the interwar German "pocket battleship" of 12,000 tons with 11" guns and a speed of 26 knots. The light cruiser, scaled down from these dimensions, eventually evolved into an antiaircraft gun platform. The submarine, also considered a fleet auxiliary for scouting as well as attacking, led to anti-submarine tactical countermeasures, anti-torpedo bulkheads and bulges in battleships, and new weapons such as the depth charge. Throughout the world wars, therefore, at least until 1942, the battleship reigned supreme on the seas, supported by its flotilla or escort of battle cruisers (then aircraft carriers), heavy and light cruisers, destroyers and submarines.

But the range of the battleship gun did not increase markedly over these years, whereas the radius of action of the fleet submarine and of shipborne aircraft did. As a result, sub and carrier as new weapons systems promised to replace the naval gun—a future denied as long as possible by tradition-bound battleship admirals. The trials with seaplanes, balloons and submarines between 1903 and 1913 had naturally been unimpressive because of technical limitations. But during World War I, defensive coastal submarines were augmented by those of long-range, oceangoing capability, and at war's end turret-mounted scout planes on battleships and cruisers and water-launched seaplanes were augmented, then superseded, by aircraft carriers. In carriers, Britain's 20,000-ton *Furious* of 1916 incorporated the same basic features of all subsequent carriers to the American 27,000-ton *Essex* (CV-9)-class of 1943. The aircraft complement grew from ten planes on the *Furious* to over ninety on the latter, their round trip ranges increasing from only a few miles to over 500. Plane types were initially divided between scouts and torpedo-droppers, but in the 1920s the scouts started to carry bombs, while fighters were added for defensive purposes. In World War II, carriers with their improved aircraft, aerial bombs, torpedoes and rockets finally replaced the naval gun and battleship in the naval arsenal.

What the carrier did to battle fleets, the submarine did to merchant warfare. The basic design of the sub or U-boat (the German name being *Unterseeboot,*) did not change, though the size did over these years: 400 to 2800 tons, making 17.5 to 20 knots on the surface under diesel power, 7 to 9 knots submerged under electric power, though the Germans in 1944 introduced the air-intake-exhaust schnorkel (invented five years before by the Dutch navy) which allowed diesel power underwater for over 17 knots. Torpedoes vastly improved from a maximum range of 1000 yards at 18 knots in 1914 to 5000 yards at 46 knots by 1945. Carriers and submarines alike flirted with multi-missions but with uneven results: the carrier *Furious* mounted torpedo tubes, the American *Lexington* (CV-2)-class carried 8" guns, and in World War II some aerial mines were laid by carrier planes; the French submarine *Surcouf* mounted twin 8" guns and carried a seaplane, as did the Japanese I-class subs; and submarines proved very useful at laying mines. The question of whether the carrier and submarine could completely drive the battleship and its escort surface ships from the seas lay with surface fleet's countermeasures that could be developed against each. The latter effort consequently characterized whole new aspects of naval tactics over this period.

The heavy technical demands made by these new weapons, like those on land (and land-based aircraft), helped to strengthen the material school of strategy. Yardsticks of naval power in strategic decisions, international agreements and war gaming reflected a capital-ship mentality, in which gun ranges and technical considerations predominated in the search for the Mahanian "big battle" to decide command of the sea. Admiral Fisher with his dreadnought and battle cruiser inventions reflected this predilection, as did proponents of the new carrier and submarine.

To understand the technical intricacies of the new weaponry, experts were needed. This led to ever-increasing specialization in naval training and personnel assignments. In officer classes, the new improved technology began to appear after senior flag officers had risen to the highest commands through the older battleship hierarchical channels; their conservatism thus often accounted for much of the early ineffective utilization of the new weaponry. Junior officers had to decide on careers in the older capital ships or in air or subs at the risk of choosing unsuccessful specialties, like those who went into rigid airships. The common enlisted rating generally profited from the new technology, which required well-trained (and well-treated) skilled technicians, while the advent of oil over messy coal made life at sea more bearable. The quality of officers and ratings thus improved with the level of naval education, and the naval profession became ever more attractive. Discipline remained rigid, but the old abuses at last disappeared.

The last vestiges of the older navies faded away as war at sea shifted from daylight battles to round-the-clock, all-weather operations. Radio electronics improved to the point where in World War II surface ships, aircraft and subs could be detected by radar and sonar, their movements recorded and transmitted over vast distances of water by radio. Radio messages could be similarly intercepted and decoded by new cryptography machines. Coastal operations called forth new overseas mobile logistical vessels, the last large monitors and coast artillery, specialized amphibious transports and assault craft, minelayers and minesweepers, and a new swift motor patrol-torpedo (PT) boat.

As technician specialists concentrated on mastering both the old and new machines, their faith in them grew, to the minimization of studying the strategic constants of the past. In many respects, given the awesomeness of the industrial-technical-scientific revolution, this preoccupation is understandable. But, when the strategic realities manifested themselves in wartime, the old problems of achieving command of the sea reappeared: trade protection, amphibious warfare, defense against invasion, and the need for powerful continental allies among the major contenders, Britain and Germany. Like Pitt before him, Winston Churchill more than any other person would reapply historical strategy and techniques. Only then did absolute command over the Atlantic and Pacific oceans become possible.

# 14
## World War I, 1914–1918

*The idea that the weapon should determine the strategy to be used is based on the implied assumption that strategy and destruction are synonymous. This simply is not true. Naturally, strategy will be influenced by the availability of weapons, but strategy should use destruction only when there is no other way of gaining or exercising control.*

—HENRY E. ECCLES, 1968

## BRITISH AND GERMAN STRATEGY

For one hundred years, Europe had not been plagued by a general war, so that the powers plunged into this fray in July and August of 1914 on the assumption that it would be a short war. After Austria-Hungary's declaration of war on tiny Serbia, the opposing alliances followed suit, save for Italy. France, Russia and Britain cemented their entente as a formal Alliance arrayed against the German and Austrian coalition which came to be known as the Central Powers. Italy, despite her recent joint plans to cooperate with Austria, had been arming against that nation and now declared her neutrality rather than face the growing Anglo-French fleet in the Mediterranean. Ottoman Turkey, correctly suspicious of Russian designs to take the Dardanelles and even Constantinople, signed a secret alliance with Germany. Abroad, Japan honored her alliance with Britain and declared war on the Central Powers. The isolation-minded United States remained neutral and called upon the belligerents to respect the rights of neutral shippers as enunciated in the 1909 Declaration of London. But such matters as neutrality and international law were luxuries of a bygone era, as neutral Belgium discovered when Germany opened the war by executing its Schlieffen Plan—overrunning Belgium in order to invade and defeat France. The standing armies and navies were similarly inadequate to meet the demands of total war, so that the mobilizations required the calling up of all reserves (the best naval reserve systems were the Royal Naval Volunteer Reserve, created in 1903, and the U. S. Naval Reserve, formalized in 1915) and eventually mass conscriptions of men and industries. As the armies clashed on the Western front, Ivan Bloch's predictions of stalemate came true, and the powers showed little imagination in seeking alternate strategies to win. Victory upon the sea soon became crucial, and World War I spread into a furious naval struggle primarily between Britain and Germany.

German naval strategy at the beginning of World War I was based on so many miscalculations as to virtually nullify the striking power of the High Seas Fleet throughout the war. Defensively, Tirpitz's fleet lay in the strongest of positions; from the Heligoland Bight, minefields, coastal submarines and cruiser patrols protected the naval bases at Wilhelmshaven and Cuxhaven, the ports of Bremen up the Weser River and Hamburg up the Elbe, and the North Sea entrance to the Kiel Canal, while the naval base at Kiel commanded the Baltic coast of Germany. By 1912, when Admiral Prince Heinrich, the kaiser's brother, was fleet commander, the Germans had simply assumed the British would follow their ancient historical practice of instituting a close blockade of their continental enemy's coast, which would enable the Germans to use their inshore weapons to the full. But when the war broke, the British did no such thing. Whereas the French ports of Cherbourg, Brest and Toulon had always threatened vital British imperial sea lanes, the German North Sea ports lay too far from these to enjoy any such strategic distinction, so that the British Admiralty in 1912 had decided to institute an open blockade not of German ports but of the North Sea itself, from the distant bases of Scapa Flow in the Orkney Islands and Cromarty and Rosyth in Scotland.

A healthy British respect for Germany's inshore defenses of mines and torpedoes also contributed to the British decision to neutralize the German fleet passively rather than by seeking the decisive battle preached by Mahan (who, incidentally, died late in 1914). Totally committed to Mahan's battleship mentality, the German naval staff had no alternate strategic plan to the decisive battle, and—despite Tirpitz's frantic urgings for a decisive fleet sortie—the kaiser and naval staff refused to pit their 15 dreadnoughts and 5 battle cruisers against the 24 British dreadnoughts and 6 battle cruisers. And time worked against Germany, with only 8 capital ships building to Britain's 17 more. The British fleet concentration in the North Sea had handily frustrated Tirpitz's risk theory, and now—in August 1914—the Germans quickly discovered that they had greatly overestimated the importance of their battle fleet and had underestimated the shrewd strategic flexibility of their maritime foe.

The Imperial German Navy was further inhibited by the predominance of the Army in policy and strategic decision-making. Opposed to the war because of unpreparedness, the Navy remained oriented Westward toward the Atlantic and the British enemy, unlike the Army which sought expansion into Eastern Europe—a divergency of war aims that never changed. The Army had not informed the Navy of the Schlieffen Plan, so the fleet had no prepared plans to support the Army's drive through Belgium. That thrust gave Germany the use of occupied Antwerp and the naval bases of Ostend and Zeebrugge, but Tirpitz and the Navy had never seriously considered mounting an overseas invasion of England so had no contingency plans, joint Army-Navy or just naval, for utilizing these new gains. Confident that it would crush the British Expeditionary Force crossing the Channel to reinforce the French Army, the German Army even rejected using the fleet to attack the British Army's transports. But even had the Navy more influence in grand strategy, its own doctrinal rigidity discouraged innovative strategic thinking. It was committed to battleships, around which its disjointed administrative and operational structure had evolved. Superior vessels with superb gunnery, optics, armor, and day and night tactics had led to no other alternative but a blue-water fleet, so that the possibility of a continental naval policy along *jeune école* lines had never been contemplated. Rapid improvements in submarines for long-range operations did not lead to any new commitment to a sub-centered navy; Germany went to war with only twenty-five U-boats—and these for coast defense and fleet reconnaissance—and had made no provisions for major new construction. Consequently, the battle fleet would languish, and morale would deteriorate, complicated by a widening breach between the new Prussianized officer caste and the poorly treated enlisted men.

As the German admirals were realizing their strategic plight, Vice Admiral David Beatty led five British battle cruisers with destroyers and cruisers in a lightning naval raid on the German cruiser patrol in Heligoland Bight on August 28. The British force overwhelmed the German, sinking three German light cruisers and a torpedo boat before running back out to sea. Before the first month of the war ended, then, the basic character of blue-water fleet operations by both navies in the North Sea had been determined: passive naval patrols and lightning raids.

British naval strategy, traditionally predominant over Army thinking, for the first time since Marlborough's day was subordinated to continental objectives. The reason was not fear of invasion, though that possibility continued to bother a great many British generals after 1905, when the "bolt from the blue" group had been thoroughly overridden by the "blue-water" Navy men who guaranteed that Britain's command of the sea would protect British shores. Even should a small German raiding force attempt to land, Admiral Fisher believed that coastal submarines would frustrate its success. Although steam had bridged the Channel, Corbett and others had pointed out that a surprise invasion would be virtually impossible with the advent of the wireless; enemy fleet movements could be announced by radio. Finally, as the Spanish and French had learned in the age of sail, command of the sea was an absolute prerequisite to amphibious invasion. If Germany meant to invade England, reasoned the British Admiralty, it would have to seek battle with the British fleet, which is precisely what the British wanted. For this very reason, in fact, Germany never contemplated invasion, thus eliminating any real possibility of a decisive battle. But to deter any possible German invasion schemes, the British fleet stood ready, along with a home army.

From 1904 to 1911 Admirals Fisher and Arthur K. Wilson, his successor as First Sea Lord, had advocated a traditional maritime strategy in event of war, placing the British Expeditionary Force ashore on the German coast, probably in the Baltic, to divert substantial German forces fighting along the French frontier. But the generals refused to consider this possibility, having no amphibious doctrine for landing against a defended beach. Instead, the Army's planners advocated the transfer of the entire Army to France to tip the balance against the massed German army. In 1911 the issue had come to a head in the Committee of Imperial Defense, with the result that the continental strategy prevailed and the Fisher-Wilson admirals were replaced by others more congenial to the new strategy, notably the new civilian First Lord of the Admiralty, Winston Churchill. Fisher's uncompromising attitudes and refusal to develop an adequate naval staff system left the Navy at the mercy of the newly strengthened and pro-Army committee—led by the energetic Maurice Hankey, formerly of the Royal Marines—and also left both Army and Navy devoid of any joint plans for possible amphibious operations in the future. When war came, the Navy ferried the British Expeditionary Force across the Channel and then protected its vital seaborne lines of communication.

Beyond supporting this continental strategy, the prime strategic mission of the Royal Navy became commerce warfare—protecting incoming merchant shipping and strangling that of Germany. For the first time in British history, shipping became absolutely essential to Britain's survival; two thirds of the food needed for feeding the population was imported, and British industry depended upon raw materials from the outside. Mahan and Corbett had concluded from the days of sail that *guerre de course* had always failed to counter Britain's blue-water command, arguing that the tremendous volume of merchant trade would make an effective comprehensive attack on it by surface raiders well nigh impossible. Furthermore, with the development of the wireless, enemy cruisers could not long survive undetected, and they depended also on fueling bases, whereas in past wars wind had given raiders unrestricted freedom. Privateering had been abolished in 1856 (save for a few Confederate raiders in the 1860s), and modern raiders had not the time to warn victims and take off their crews because of the latter's radio distress calls summoning fleet units. The commerce raider seemed doomed in modern war.

Defense of commerce could best be achieved, reasoned the Mahan-Corbett school, by strong naval concentrations at terminal points of trade routes, where enemy raiders might be expected to lie in wait for their prey. The Admiralty ruled out convoy as too slow and easily detected both by enemy agents prior to sailing and by enemy cruisers seeing the collective smoke at sea. Though both Mahan and Corbett had doubts about their conclusions on convoy, they agreed that dispersed shipping would enable enough merchantmen to get through to support the war effort; in any case, absolute protection had never been possible anyway. The British Admiralty adopted these attitudes and in 1913 had decided to arm merchantmen as a final precaution. What the British failed to realize, however, was that in total war the old legalism of the eighteenth and nineteenth centuries would not deter a modern power like Germany from adopting a policy of unrestricted *guerre de course,* ignoring the old rules of warning victims and rescuing their crews and even sinking neutral shipping bound for Britain. Some fears existed over the possibility of armed German merchantmen disguised as neutrals acting as raiders, but only Admiral Fisher seems to have anticipated in 1912–14 the future use of long-ranging submarines as commerce raiders. By the outbreak of war, the British had totally underestimated the naval threat to their oceanic trade.

British plans for offensive trade war also rested upon apparent historical evidence drawn from Mahan and Corbett. Germany, not being a true maritime power and thus probably not dependent upon overseas imports, would suffer no more than had France of old. Blockade, to be sure, would be instituted, but with the primary purpose of forcing the German High Seas Fleet to seek battle in order to break it. But in 1912, because of the inshore torpedo craft and shore-based scout planes and Zeppelin airships, along with the extreme difficulty of capturing an advanced island base along the North Sea coast, the Admiralty had decided on a distant blockade of the North Sea rather than the traditional close blockade. Not only did this eliminate any real possibility of a decisive battle, but it raised difficult legal questions about neutral shipping to the Central Powers. Most overseas trade reached Germany by way of the neutral ports of Dutch Amsterdam and Rotterdam, thence by the Rhine and Maas rivers to the industrial Ruhr basin.

In World War I, the major neutral shipper to Central Powers and Allies was the United States, so that neither coalition wanted to offend this important supplier of industrial and raw materials and foodstuffs. For Britain, the problem was most acute, having in 1856 and 1909 accepted in principle the freedom of neutral trade whether to a belligerent nation directly or via another neutral port. But Britain's strategic antecedents long predated the tranquil *Pax Britannica,* and by 1914 the Admiralty had no serious reservations about its exercising its ancient rights of searching and seizing neutral vessels trading with the enemy. As the old notion of neutrality in total war died, so too did the trappings of neutral rights. The trade of Scandinavian neutrals to Germany proved virtually impossible to stop in the distant Baltic and at best difficult along the inshore waters of the North Sea, save by alert cruiser patrols. Abroad, the old practices of running down enemy raiders and squadrons and capturing enemy colonies would be easier. But Germany, hardly a maritime colonial empire, could be defeated only by economic victory in the North Sea. Mahan and Corbett agreed with the British Admiralty on the matter of somehow preventing enemy commerce at all costs.

In addition to such difficulties, the Royal Navy's general strategic superiority was threatened by tactical sterility reflected in the key naval leaders, Churchill and Fisher, who returned to his former post as First Sea Lord late in 1914. Fisher's great naval reforms and capital ship creations had included telling warnings about the future of aircraft in war, submarines as commerce raiders, and the need for amphibious craft and training. But Fisher had no use for staff, including the Naval War Staff created by Churchill in 1912, and was violently intemperate with those who disagreed with his point of view, including the much younger Churchill. Worse, though he admired the work of Corbett and Richmond, Fisher had no use for history as an analytical tool, and therefore virtually ignored tactical studies, depending instead on the technical awesomeness of the floating behemoths he had created. Anti-intellectual, like most naval officers of his time, Fisher personified the material school which worshiped the intrinsic value of super machine weapons. By contrast, Churchill astutely read history and was chagrined to discover upon taking office in 1911 that he was virtually alone in the naval service in this respect; Corbett's epic book published that year was largely ignored by professional officers. Nevertheless, Churchill also overlooked much historical evidence by accepting a continental rather than a maritime strategy and by rejecting the efficacy of convoy in wartime. And he flew in the face of modern technology to press for close blockade and to deny the submarine threat.

In fleet tactics, embodied in the Grand Fleet Fighting Instructions and Battle Orders, both Fisher's and Churchill's conservatism stood out; all cruising and fighting had to be done in rigid line-ahead formations, the commanding admiral asserting absolute control over the fleet in an effort to "cap the T" of the enemy line: the concentration of broadside fire on the vulnerable head of the enemy's column. No flexibility or personal initiative could be allowed subordinate admirals, nor exposure of the line to enemy destroyer torpedo attacks, nor pursuit of a retreating enemy fleet which might use torpedoes and mines, especially near its bases. The old formalism had returned; Nelson's spirit but not his teachings survived. And this rigid caution passed down from Churchill and Fisher to fleet commanders Jellicoe and Beatty. In the matter of aircraft the British high command gave only belated attention—in 1912–14—to building airships and seaplanes. Instead, the big gun battle would determine command of the sea. But even such an engagement had its ominous side. Tactical training had been minimized before the war, night tactics all but ignored, and no coordination of gunnery and tactics pressed. And the longer the German High Seas Fleet refused battle, the more entrenched would this tactical sterility become within the British Grand Fleet.

The first months of the war in the North Sea developed into the same general stalemate that characterized land operations on the Western front. In August 1914 the Germans swept through Belgium into France, and the British Expeditionary Force crossed the Channel to help stop the thrust. A hasty British attempt to relieve Antwerp failed, but neither was the British Army pinned down against the sea—as Fisher had feared (and which would occur in 1940). The Allies stopped the German offensive at the Battle of the Marne early in September, whereupon both sides tried to outflank the other, appearing as a "race to the sea" throughout the autumn. The carnage finally ended with the armies in two parallel systems of trenches by the end of 1914, with the British ground forces on the French left and next to the sea. The professional core of the British Army had been slaughtered, so that Britain mobilized its manpower at home and throughout the Empire to reinforce its Army on the Western front. While merchant ships were not convoyed, troop transports were: the two-hour crossing from Dover and Folkestone to Calais and Boulogne, covered by a new destroyer patrol at Dover which offset German destroyers raiding from Belgian Ostend and Zeebrugge; the longer night run from Portsmouth to Le Havre screened by anti-submarine craft; and the first Canadian army units being escorted across the Atlantic by a capital-ship screen.

The British Grand Fleet at Scapa Flow and Rosyth stood ready to thwart any sortie by the High Seas Fleet, but was suddenly threatened by bold German U-boats. In September and October subs sank two cruisers off Scotland and three old cruisers patrolling off the Dutch coast. A German minelayer used mines to sink a British cruiser off Harwich in August, and two months later other German mines sent a dreadnought to the bottom off northern Ireland. Admiral Jellicoe in October moved the Grand Fleet to the west side of Scotland while anti-submarine defenses were developed at Scapa. Admiral Fisher wanted to mine Heligoland Bight to similarly harass the Germans, but prewar backwardness in undersea tactics found the Royal Navy with inadequate numbers of minelayers and notoriously unreliable mines. Instead, the Germans stepped up their harassing operations by initiating battle cruiser raids to bombard the east coast of England, at Yarmouth in November and Scarborough in December, both to cover minelaying vessels and the latter to lure British fleet units in the minefield. Off Scarborough, in fact, the two main fleets narrowly missed a general engagement, frustrating the British Admiralty (which had broken the German codes), as did nuisance reconnaissance raids by high-flying German Zeppelins based in Belgium. Primitive British naval aircraft could not attain those altitudes, but did destroy three of the airships by air raids on their bases.

But the fleets heightened their efforts to trap advance scouting units, Admirals Sir John Jellicoe and Friedrich von Ingenohl using their respective battle cruiser squadrons under Admirals Sir David Beatty and Franz von Hipper to accomplish the feat. On January 24, 1915, the two battle cruiser forces engaged at Dogger Bank, Beatty's five against Hipper's four plus cruisers and destroyers. Confused signals, the rigid tactics and Beatty's fear of imagined German mines and submarines prevented a general rout, but his guns sank one and badly damaged another of Hipper's battle cruisers. The kaiser, alarmed by his losses, relieved Ingenohl from command and forbade further sorties that would unnecessarily risk his capital ships.

From the Battle of Dogger Bank for over a year the main fleets remained stalemated while both sides endeavored to decide the issue on land. The German fleet, now commanded by Admiral Hugo von Pohl, remained at anchor behind the Heligoland defenses as a fleet-in-being. Sowing mines—from U-boats and new minelayers after mid-1915—the Germans hoped to whittle down the Grand Fleet so that a decisive battle between equal fleets would eventually be possible. Also, the kaiser wanted to save his precious capital ships for possible bargaining strength at the peace table. Meanwhile, German submarines and minecraft (sweepers and layers) attempted to break the blockade, while the German Army hammered away on the Western front. The British fleet stood watch over the North Sea—the battleships from Scapa Flow, the battle cruisers from Rosyth—while rejecting any risky foray into the dangerous inshore waters of Germany (including Admiral Wilson's plan to take and hold the island of Heligoland). The daily cross-Channel flow of men and material was guarded, sustaining the futile and bloody offensives of the Allies trying to break the entrenched German Army on the Western front.

With such a stalemate on land and sea, the Royal Navy initiated proposals to revert from the new continental strategy to the tried and true maritime strategy of assailing the enemy's periphery by amphibious assault. Fisher had always advocated such a program, and in the frustrating latter days of 1914 Churchill followed history to adopt the same position. With the main German army held down in Flanders, the logical move was to transform the Eastern front into a powerful offensive. The chief vehicle would naturally be the Russian army, the catalyst an Allied assault on the Central Powers either in the Baltic or the Eastern Mediterranean-Black Sea region.

The Baltic Sea, long dominated by the Russians, provided the most direct route by sea into Germany but was offset by diplomatic and geographic difficulties. Diplomatically, the Allies wanted to keep Sweden, Denmark and Norway neutral for economic and strategic reasons. Scandinavian trade was vital to the Allies, even though Germany was obtaining iron ore from the pro-German Swedish government. Strategically, Denmark as always dominated the entrance to the Baltic and when war broke out her navy mined the Belts (as did the Germans) and the western side of the Sound, making the passage hazardous for ships of war. The Germans could, in addition, pass their warships through the Kiel Canal into the Baltic, although they had long since decided to make this front a passive one until victory was achieved in the West. The Allies were equally unprepared to mount significant operations in Baltic waters, but in August the Russian army swept into East Prussia, only to be stopped cold in the Tannenberg campaign late in the month by Generals Paul von Hindenburg and Erich Ludendorff. The Russian navy also began the war energetically in these parts, due largely to its vigorous Baltic commander, Vice Admiral Nicolai von Essen, who sowed 2200 mines at the entrance to the Gulf of Finland to protect the approaches to Kronstadt and Petrograd (St. Petersburg) and who planned both to deliver an ultimatum to the Swedish fleet at Karlskrona and to use his predreadnoughts to lure the German fleet into his minefields. The Russian tsar vetoed these schemes as too risky, even though von Essen's excellent mines put out of action four of Admiral Prince Heinrich's eight cruisers supporting the German army in Latvia by January.

In addition, Russian minelayers and submarines were joined in October by two British subs under the aggressive Lieutenant Commander Max Horton, basing at Reval on the Gulf of Finland.

With the prospect of this well-led Russian Baltic Fleet being supported by the British, Admiral Fisher moved to introduce a scheme for a British naval offensive into the Baltic. Already, between August and December, Churchill had wanted to provoke a German fleet sortie and battle by seizing a German island—if not Heligoland as Admiral Wilson wanted, then Borkum or Sylt at either terminus of the short German coast, or even, as others suggested, at Zeebrugge. When these proposals were rejected as too risky in January 1915, Fisher resurrected a prewar scheme to place an Anglo-Russian amphibious force on the Pomeranian coast only ninety miles from Berlin, ignoring Churchill's objection that a close blockade of Heligoland Bight—from an advanced captured island base—was a prerequisite. With the help of the historian Corbett, Fisher in January proposed that the entire Grand Fleet enter the Baltic to support a Russian assault, closing the Heligoland Bight and Wilhelmshaven fleet anchorage with (admittedly inferior) British mines. The government rejected the plan, however, largely because of the uncertainties of trying to negotiate the narrow and tricky Sound, along with the unfeasibility of closing the Bight to a possible German fleet sortie while the British fleet was away in the Baltic. Had the plan carried, the Germans may well have sent heavy units into the Baltic to engage the Grand Fleet, and Russian inshore operations would have probably been effective. But the Russian army, ever active, remained an unknown factor, hardly worth the risk of Britain uncovering her command of the North Sea for the project.

The Baltic now became a strategic backwater, attended by the death of von Essen in the spring, and Anglo-Russian sub and mine forces fell back on the Gulf of Riga to help contest the German advance on land. During the summer and autumn of 1915, Commander Horton led Anglo-Russian subs in a Baltic offensive that sank a German cruiser and sixteen merchant ships and damaged a battle cruiser. But then the theater bogged down into a stalemate on land and sea, with political revolutionary discontent spreading through the Russian armed forces.

## THE MEDITERRANEAN AND COMMERCE WARFARE

If Russia could not be converted into a major front through the Baltic, then the only alternative was through the Mediterranean, a theater which grew into a major avenue both for Allied strategy on the Eastern front and for Allied merchant shipping. Only by maintaining command over the middle sea could the Allies contain the Central Powers and thus inhibit their naval operations beyond—in the South Atlantic, South Pacific and Indian oceans. Italy had declared its neutrality, and Turkey secretly allied with the Central Powers and in November 1914 declared war on the Allies. So Anglo-French naval forces in the Mediterranean focused on containing Austria-Hungary and Turkey and their limited fleets and in remaining mobile enough to concentrate outside this sea, especially in the Atlantic, to protect Allied commerce.

In late 1914 and early 1915, the Allies exerted their command over the Mediterranean though not without some difficulty. The two German heavy ships at Austrian Pola eluded Allied naval forces in August to shell the French Algerian coast and escape to Turkey, where they aided materially in closing Allied communications with Russia via the Black Sea. The French fleet under Admiral Boué de Lapeyère sealifted important Algerian ground forces to the continent and bottled up the Austrian battleships of Admiral Anton Haus at Pola, lifting Haus's blockade of Allied Montenegro. But when the French tried to support the Montenegrans by sea over the winter and spring, Austrian U-boats damaged a French battleship and sank a heavy cruiser near the Strait of Otranto and caused the French to retire to Pylos for a distant blockade of the Adriatic. The Austrian army retreated from its thrust into Serbia and Russian Poland, covered by three Danube River monitors, but was saved by German reinforcements.

With the German and Austrian fleets generally contained, however, the British in late 1914 could implement traditional maritime strategic prerogatives: control of global trade routes and seizure of German colonies. British imperial forces easily captured defenseless Pacific Samoa, African Togoland, the Cameroons and Southwest Africa, but inadequate amphibious doctrine led to their repulse at Tanga, German East Africa. British and Russian cruisers and a Japanese battle cruiser escorted Indian and "Anzac" (Australia and New Zealand) troop convoys across the Indian Ocean to the Middle East, while the three German raiding cruisers operating in these waters enjoyed only brief success before being sunk or blockaded in East Africa. In this way, along with war risk insurance policies, the British frustrated German surface *guerre de course* strategy early in the war.

The one major enemy overseas threat, the German China Squadron of Vice Admiral Count Maximilian von Spee, required fleet action. Training at Ponape in the German Carolines at the outbreak of war, this fleet of two heavy and three light cruisers found itself cut off from its base at Tsingtao by the Japanese navy. The Japanese besieged and took Tsingtao in November 1914 and easily overran the German Palau, Marianas, Caroline and Marshall island groups, obliging Spee to operate in South American waters. Avoiding Anglo-Japanese forces hastening across the Pacific, the German squadron sank two British heavy cruisers at the battle of Coronel off the coast of Chile on November 1 and then rounded the Horn into the South Atlantic. The British Admiralty hastened Vice Admiral Sir Doveton Sturdee with two battle cruisers and seven cruisers from Britain to defend the Falkland Islands, where they met and destroyed Spee's squadron on December 8. The battle of the Falkland Islands, the last pure gunnery action in history fought without fear of torpedoes or aircraft, ended Germany's policy of waging *guerre de course* with surface ships, and in February 1915 Germany turned to the U-boat as its prime merchant raider.

Before Germany could build enough U-boats for this purpose, though, the British attempted to decide the war by a strategic offensive via the Middle East and Eastern Mediterranean. British imperial forces occupied Turkish Basra in the Persian Gulf late in 1914 to protect the now-vital oil interests there and to support an abortive campaign up the Tigris River into Mesopotamia throughout 1915. Failing to take Baghdad, the British even had a new monitor and two gunboats captured by the Turks. Anglo-Russian forces cooperated in Persia, while the Turks pressed on Russian Black Sea ports and the British Suez Canal. German Admiral Wilhelm Souchon used his German battle cruiser and light cruiser and Turkish cruisers and destroyers to bombard Sevastopol and Novorossisk in the autumn of 1914, and the sultan proclaimed a Holy War throughout the Middle East. British forces strengthened the defenses of the Canal—reinforced by French warships from Indochina and Syria—to break up a Turkish overland offensive which tried to cross the Canal on pontoons in February 1915. Britain annexed Cyprus, France controlled the coast of Palestine, and Russia battled Turkey on the Caucasus frontier to keep the Canal secure for the duration. With such activity in this region, First Lord Churchill decided to mount a major offensive in Europe from the East.

Churchill hoped to create a viable second front in the Eastern Mediterranean, just as Fisher had planned to do in the Baltic, and he pushed the enterprise through the British War Cabinet in January. Churchill planned on an Allied naval drive through the Dardanelles, Sea of Marmara and Bosporus to invest Constantinople and open a fresh and much-needed supply route to Russia. Such a feat would also relieve the Caucasus and Mesopotamian fronts, outflank Austria-Hungary, and hopefully encourage the neutral Balkan states of Greece, Rumania and Bulgaria to join the Allies. Unfortunately, the strategic potential of this brilliant design—maritime strategy at its finest—was partly compromised by political factors: it encouraged France to increase its annexation plans for Ottoman Syria and Palestine, Italy to join in the expected spoils of victory by declaring war on Austria (but not Germany) in May 1915, and Russia to demand the outright postwar annexation of the Dardanelles and Constantinople itself. Traditional British support of the Ottoman buffer against Russia in the middle sea now led to British reluctance to ask for Russian naval cooperation from the Black Sea side. Indeed, Russia, which had also proposed such an operation, used its Black Fleet of five battleships, two seaplane carriers and old destroyers under Admiral A. A. Eberhardt to blockade the coast of Anatolia, support the Caucasian front and now bombard the entrance of the Bosporus. But mutual Anglo-Russian suspicions and Russian ground commitments against the Germans and Austrians restricted Russian cooperation during the campaign to a naval demonstration off the Bosporus and a minefield planted there partly by the world's first mine-laying submarine, the *Krab*.

Churchill's enthusiasm over such a Mediterranean strategy, flatly opposed by Admiral Fisher, suffered from tactical weaknesses. Generally unsupported by historical precedents, Churchill assumed that warships alone (with small Marine landing parties) could reduce strong coastal fortifications, in this case those commanding the Dardanelles which had been strengthened following an Anglo-French naval bombardment in November 1914. Churchill also underestimated the effect of the new underwater weapons against battleships, for the Germans had laid sixteen minefields across the Chanak Narrows connecting the Dardanelles with the Sea of Marmara. Basing at Lemnos, the Anglo-French fleet from mid-February to mid-March 1915 shelled both sides of the Dardanelles and was reinforced to include the new *Queen Elizabeth*, twelve other British and four French battleships, a battle cruiser and many cruisers, destroyers and crude, makeshift minesweepers. Led by Vice Admiral John de Robeck, this force attempted to run the Narrows, only to have six predreadnoughts strike mines; three went down quickly, another being disabled by shore artillery. Within grasp of his objective, de Robeck hastily retired. Then Churchill decided to transform the effort into a major amphibious assault against the Gallipoli peninsula on the European side of the Dardanelles. His error now lay in attempting an operation for which no tactical doctrine, specialized weapons or techniques had been developed. These shortcomings, plus the countermeasures of the Central Powers, doomed the operation from the outset.

The Gallipoli campaign, centered on the assault of April 15, 1915, violated every principle of combined operations that might have been gleaned from history. The Allies did not enjoy local command of the sea because of ineffective minesweeping trawlers and the presence of Turkish destroyers and German and Austrian U-boats. The Navy and Army never solved the issue of unity of command, either from London or locally, where ground and naval commanders displayed uneven qualities and lack of aggressiveness. The element of surprise had long been lost, and the diversionary tactics of two feints and one landing on western Cape Hellas did not fool the defenders led by Generals Liman von Sanders of Germany and Mustapha Kemal of Turkey. Logistical mistakes required that the transports from England be unloaded and reloaded at Alexandria, wasting an entire month and preventing a much-needed rehearsal. For covering fire, the naval gunners had no training or experience for close-in pinpoint fire and showed it by their ineffective barrage. Inadequate naval and aerial reconnaissance led to ignorance of the water currents and landing beaches. Admiral Fisher had produced motorized armored landing barges and steam launches for his Baltic venture, but with its cancellation these were not made available for the Gallipoli operation. Instead, 200 large and hundreds of small makeshift assault craft assumed the burden of landing the 80,000 British, French, Anzac and Indian troops in the face of heavy fire from the 30,000 defending troops.

The Gallipoli assault failed from the first. Sloppy and unsteady ship-to-shore movement left the troops pinned down or slaughtered along the water's edge, thus creating serious delays in bringing up supplies and more men. Then the commanders failed to exploit their beachhead aggressively. Instead of systematically probing weaknesses in the Turkish lines to gain the high ground ahead of enemy reinforcements, the troops dug in on the beach, while the floating reserves were not committed. So the Turks rallied behind Kemal and fought desperately and successfully to blunt the assault on the first day. Nothing changed over succeeding days, except that an enemy destroyer sank another old British battleship and enemy U-boats began to arrive. Bitter disputes between Churchill and Fisher led to the recall of the *Queen Elizabeth* and Fisher's resignation in May as First Sea Lord—never to return, despite subsequent efforts by the Navy to gain his reappointment. But Churchill soon followed him into retirement as the scapegoat for the failure at Gallipoli. Late in May the submarine *U-21,* steaming from the North Sea to Austrian Cattaro, sank two more predreadnoughts off Gallipoli before joining in the general Austro-German U-boat assault on Allied Mediterranean shipping. British subs sank two Turkish battleships and lesser vessels in the Sea of Marmara, and a new surprise Anzac landing on the west coast of Gallipoli in August failed to break the stalemate. Then, in October, Bulgaria joined the Central Powers and overran Serbia and Montenegro, creating a new front before Salonika in neutral Greece and requiring French and Italian warships to evacuate the Serbian and Montenegran armies from the mainland to Corfu. The Allies had no choice but to evacuate Gallipoli, which they did in an unusually masterful withdrawal between late November 1915 and early January 1916. The Gallipoli fiasco had discredited amphibious operations in general and done nothing to alter the strategic stalemate in Western Europe.

Indeed, the entrance of new belligerents into the fighting led to much bloodshed but little else in 1915 and 1916. Despite massive battles at Verdun and the Somme, the Western front did not move, while in the East a Russian offensive crippled Austria-Hungary and brought in Rumania as an Ally, but to no avail. In the Middle East, the Russians drove to Trebizond on the Black Sea before being stopped and lost a brand-new dreadnought to an operational mishap, and the British expeditionary force on the Tigris became trapped and had to surrender to the Turks. Italy declared war on Germany in August 1916 but concentrated its efforts against Austria at the Alps and in the Adriatic. The underwater mines and subs of both sides in the Mediterranean forced the battleships to remain in port at Italian Taranto and Brindisi, British Malta, French Algerian Bizerte and Austrian Pola, although the Allies did use theirs for protecting merchant shipping. Austrian saboteurs, mines, light vessels and naval aircraft from Cattaro, Pola and Trieste countered Italian supremacy and coastal raids in the Adriatic by sinking three Italian battleships in 1915–16. But the Adriatic, like the Italian front, remained a strategic backwater of the war, crucial only as the outlet for German and Austrian fleet U-boats operating against Allied sea lanes to Gallipoli, Salonika and Suez.

As for Germany during 1915–16, the U-boat had begun to prove its worth as a commerce raider, although the prewar niceties of international law embodied in the Declaration of London exerted a powerful check on its full destructive capability. The Austro-German sub offensive in the Mediterranean proved to be so effective during 1916—sinking over one million gross tons (average vessel 3000 tons) that year—that the British began to divert much of their Far East merchant shipping from the Suez route to the Cape. Allied countermeasures against the U-boat in the middle sea were so ineffective that the Central Powers boats closely observed prize rules; they warned each merchantman and took off its crew before sinking it—usually with the deck gun in order to conserve torpedoes. In the Atlantic, however, the proximity of British naval bases made such legalities suicidal, so that only unrestricted submarine warfare—without any warning or thought of the crews—would work. The German Naval Staff, already cool toward this new weapon because it diverted strength from the blue-water fleet, rejected such proposals early in 1915 also for fear of diplomatic repercussions from neutral shippers. Predictably, then, the United States protested the sinking of the British passenger liners *Lusitania* and *Arabic* in May and

August, whereupon the German government in September closed down all U-boat operations in the Western Approaches, English Channel and North Sea in favor of the less-sensitive Mediterranean. When the successes there reconvinced the kaiser and his Naval Staff of the efficacy of unrestricted underwater *guerre de course* in March 1916, its resumption brought about the sinking of the cross-Channel steamer *Sussex,* the usual American protest, the same decision of the kaiser to withdraw his best U-boats from British waters, and his discharge of Admiral Tirpitz. President Wilson in fact had unknowingly saved the Allies with his protests, for an all-out U-boat offensive might well have aggravated serious Allied shortages in war materials in mid-1916 sufficiently to win the war for the Central Powers.

The Allied blockade of the Central Powers succeeded more from diplomatic than tactical devices. The British, less sensitive to American protestations than were the Germans, gradually abandoned their lip service to the Declaration of London in favor of enforcing Orders-in-Council to restrict neutral trade to the continent. The Royal Navy thus mined the Strait of Dover to stop, search and detain neutral vessels and confiscate partial or entire cargoes as contraband of war. British antisub countermeasures in 1915–16 were too halfhearted to blockade or stop the U-boats which tried to create their own blockade of the British Isles. The British simply left the initiative with the U-boat, which had relative freedom beyond British coastal waters to attack non-escorted merchant shipping. Instead of adopting convoy on the high seas, the British armed their merchantmen—often a very successful measure, had them fly neutral flags and maneuver in zigzags, while well-gunned decoy merchant "Q-ships" made several sorties with uneven results. The Navy regularly patrolled only inshore waters, using armed trawlers, yachts, torpedo boats, subs and shore-based aircraft in addition to anti-mine nets and towed explosive paravane sweeps.

The Admiralty preferred to deal offensively with the U-boat, however, by sending out sporadic hunt-and-kill patrols of destroyers armed with depth charges, but this seldom worked because of the great expanse of water, the mobility of the subs, the scarcity of destroyers and the difficulty of underwater detection even with primitive hydrophones. Airplanes and airships occasionally bombed U-boat bases, and early in 1916 British fleet units in the North Sea successfully countered several bold forays by German minesweepers and surface raiders. In the Mediterranean, the French and Italians could not cooperate and lacked any antisub expertise, using ineffective defensive nets and cruiser patrols at the Strait of Otranto. But the Royal Navy gave little advice there, preferring to send battleships (some Allied forty by the end of 1915!) with their large and costly retinue of escorts and service ships to the middle sea. Some antisub reforms early in 1916 made a few improvements, but still the U-boats ran through the straits of Gibraltar and Otranto with relative impunity.

On balance, the commerce war between February 1915 and mid-1916 seesawed back and forth. Germany started the offensive with only twenty-one boats in 1915, but its increased construction gradually broadened the effort as Allied antisub tactics failed to keep pace. Throughout 1915, for instance, German subs sank 748,000 tons of British merchant shipping at the cost of only twenty boats. In addition, mines claimed another 77,000 tons and surface raiders 29,000. Only six Central Powers boats sank ninety-two merchantmen during the autumn in the Mediterranean, and *U-35* under Lieutenant Commander Lothar von Arnauld de la Perière alone accounted for most of the many sinkings there throughout 1916. During the first half of 1916, enemy subs and mines claimed nearly half a million tons of Allied merchant shipping plus two old battleships and two cruisers (one with Lord Kitchener on board) at the cost of thirty-four boats. To be sure, both sides suffered, with the civilian populations of the Central Powers starting to hurt far more than those of the Allies. The Royal Navy steadfastly maintained command of the North Sea against the German surface fleet, but missed the key strategic point that the real threat lay underwater. Instead of centering its strategy on the long and unglamorous method of economic strangulation and defeat of the U-boat, the British Admiralty preferred to regard its blockade as an inducement to force the German High Seas Fleet into a decisive battle. That battle came, but it altered very little, for the final victory at sea would be determined by the success or failure of the submarine.

## ANGLO-AMERICAN COMMAND OF THE SEA

The stalemate on land and sea by mid-1916 led both the Allied and Central Powers to seek new solutions to break it. On land, fresh assaults on all fronts displayed a remarkable lack of strategic and tactical imagination and led only to mounting devastation and bloodshed. They merely proved the prewar arguments of Bloch that modern machine weapons only tended to neutralize one another. And at sea, the fleet action off Jutland demonstrated the same fact, so that the commerce war finally impressed itself on the conservative admiralties that the stalemate would only be broken in that quarter. The ultimate German decision for all-out unrestricted submarine warfare would force America's entry into the war, giving the Allies just enough manpower to break the deadlock on the continent and additional naval power to enable them to realize the maritime goals of their basically continental strategy. But the lessons and their implementation took over two more years to learn, making 1916–18 an unprecedented period of intensive warfare at sea.

The opposing battle fleets ended their relatively passive roles as each side sought to make active use of them. Admiral Sir John Jellicoe, an able administrator and conservative tactician, used the Grand Fleet to dominate the North Sea, though with standing orders never to risk his precious battleships against German torpedoes or mines. In March 1916 his cruisers bombarded the Sylt Island radio station and the airship drome at Tondern, while the continuous patrols kept the Fleet busy. Jellicoe looked to the day when he could engage the Germans in a traditional line-ahead action, to achieve tactical concentration by capping the enemy T. But his formalist training precluded initiative by his subordinates and any preparations for night action, while he had not remedied the armor weaknesses of his battle cruisers. His counterpart, Vice Admiral Reinhard Scheer, the new commander of the German High Seas Fleet, instituted a vigorous program of tactical training and raids aimed at whittling down British fleet strength. In April his battle cruisers bombarded Lowestoft, England, and early in May he refused to be lured out by Jellicoe whose units again shelled Sylt Island and Tondern. When the heavy spring weather precluded the use of airships for fleet reconnaissance, Scheer decided to attack British shipping to Norway in the Skagerrak. When Scheer sortied on May 30, Jellicoe did the same, with the result that on the next day the two great fleets collided off the Jutland peninsula in the long-awaited battle.

The Battle of Jutland (or Skagerrak) opened late on May 31, 1916, between opposing battle cruiser forces which tried to lure one another into the jaws of their respective dreadnought lines. Vice Admiral David Beatty had 6 battle cruisers, 4 new dreadnoughts, 14 light cruisers, 27 destroyers and 2 seaplane carriers; Vice Admiral Franz von Hipper had 5 battle cruisers, 5 light cruisers and 30 destroyers. Running south, the two lines commenced firing about 3:30 P.M. at 16,500 yards and closed to 13,000 yards. The superior gunnery of the Germans outperformed that of the British, with the flash from several hits igniting the magazines of 2 battle cruisers, sending both to the bottom. Two destroyers on each side were sunk, but as Beatty's dreadnoughts closed he saw Scheer's battle line approaching. Turning about at 4:45, Beatty tried to lure Hipper north into the main force of Jellicoe, but keeping his superior ignorant of developments. The running gunnery duel then merged into a general engagement that involved Jellicoe's 24 dreadnoughts, 3 battle cruisers, 8 armored cruisers, 12 light cruisers, 51 destroyers and one minelayer and Scheer's 16 dreadnoughts, 6 predreadnoughts, 6 light cruisers and 31 destroyers. Poor visibility neutralized the planes from Jellicoe's one seaplane carrier (another had been inadvertently left behind), while fear of German subs (18 of them were in British waters) and torpedoes influenced Jellicoe. Even so, Jellicoe absorbed Beatty's force at 6:00 and slammed into Hipper's van, seriously damaging 3 German light cruisers. Jellicoe then capped the German "T" by swinging eastward to silhouette Scheer's ships against the setting sun and cutting off his possible retreat back to his base in Germany.

But German tactics quickly frustrated Jellicoe's excellent tactical position. The devastating gunnery exchange at 12,000 yards in this "Windy Corner" claimed a British battle cruiser and cruiser and put four German battle cruisers out of action. Then, about 6:35, Scheer executed what the British considered impossible: a battle turn of 180°. Without melee tactics, the British squadron commanders could not pursue, and Jellicoe held his course. When Scheer tried to break through at 7:00 he found his "T" still capped and encountered murderous fire from the British broadsides. The well-drilled German ships executed another brilliant battle turn at 7:20, covered by their torpedo-firing destroyers which caused Jellicoe's light cruisers to turn away. By sunset at 8:19 the two fleets were running southward on parallel tracks, Jellicoe between Scheer and Germany. Scheer now determined to pass through Jellicoe's rear during the night and conveyed his plan by radio to the German Admiralty, which concurred. British intelligence radio listeners intercepted these messages, but failed to inform Jellicoe. At 11:00, as the destroyers continued to trade blows, Scheer began his move, witnessed by British ships in the rear which did not inform Jellicoe. By twilight at 2:00 A.M. on June 1 Scheer had escaped, which Jellicoe did not learn for two more hours, by which time he had no choice but to return to base. Nothing had changed strategically, while the Germans tactically had sunk three battle cruisers, three cruisers and eight destroyers to their own losses of one predreadnought, one battle cruiser (scuttled), four cruisers and five destroyers. The British had lost 6800 out of 60,000 men, the Germans 3100 out of 45,000.

The duel at Jutland had demonstrated the futility of material strategy. No dreadnoughts had been lost by either side, but neither had the torpedo been decisive. Little tactical imagination had been displayed by any senior admiral, save for Scheer's battle turns, while the battle cruiser had displayed fatal weaknesses. More armor protection would only make it into a battleship, whereas its scouting function had achieved few results. The new experimental aircraft carrier seemed to offer more promise for the future as "the eyes of the fleet." The British had won the battle in the strategic sense, since they still held command of the North Sea, but they had suffered a psychological blow to their naval prestige. Scheer made a last important sortie in August for a bombardment of the Sunderland coast, but Jellicoe's approach to within thirty miles caused Scheer to retire. The High Seas Fleet resumed its status as a fleet-in-being and awaited new dreadnoughts under a remarkably misdirected building program that seemed to ignore the outcome of Jutland. The Grand Fleet also received new construction but prepared to move from Scapa Flow to Rosyth and the Firth of Forth in order to better prevent another German fleet sortie. This continued vigil—necessary because of the failure to destroy Scheer at Jutland—required valuable destroyers that could not be diverted to antisubmarine duty. The expensive battle fleets would not fight again.

The performances of the Central Powers navies at Jutland and Gallipoli did have the strategic effect of sealing off Russia from direct outside help, meaning that the Eastern front would hold only as long as the Russian army could continue its exhausting campaigns. Though the Russian summer offensive of 1916 virtually took Austria out of the war, the Mediterranean theater remained stalemated and both the Black and Baltic seas closed to Allied shipping. With the Dardanelles closed, Admiral Alexander Kolchak, the new commander of the Russian Black Sea Fleet, began to plan and rehearse an attack on the Bosporus but it never took place. The German High Seas Fleet kept the Baltic Fleet neutralized at Kronstadt, but in midyear the British opened up a new supply route via the Arctic. Some 600 Allied merchantmen initially reached Kola on the Barents Sea and Archangel on the White Sea, there joined by British antisub cruisers and minesweepers. But inadequate rail facilities led to the stockpiling of these supplies in port, and the Germans increased their U-boat operations during the winter of 1916–17 to continue the isolation of Russia. Then, in March 1917, a revolution swept over Russia and replaced the tsarist regime with a shaky democratic government which tried mightily to stay in the war. But as long as the German army kept hammering away at Russia and German U-boats, mines and heavy ships kept the Baltic and Black seas closed, Britain could never readopt any peripheral strategy to relieve Russia. Knowing this, the Germans realized the best way to insure the blockade and ultimate defeat of Britain, Russia and France lay in the resumption of unrestricted submarine warfare.

Support for unrestricted U-boat operations against Allied and neutral shipping gradually gained strength within German strategy-making circles throughout the remainder of 1916. U-boat operations, reduced during the summer, intensified in September in the Channel, North Sea and Western Approaches and as far away as Iberia, the Russian White Sea, Iceland and North America. Allied and neutral merchant ship losses tripled to a monthly average of 94,000 tons during the last third of the year. Admirals Scheer and Henning von Holtzendorff, the aged

Chief of Naval Staff, argued for unrestricted operations, predicting that the 150 U-boats available by February (82 in the North Sea, of which 36 were at sea simultaneously) could humble Britain within six months. The Army, encouraged by its summer victories and throwing off its fears of Dutch and Danish military intervention on the Western front from such a U-boat offensive, now supported it and fell back on a new Hindenburg line early in 1917 just to make sure. An additional risk involved Scandinavian underwater weapons, namely Dutch coastal torpedo boats and Danish mines in the Sound, soon to become a major U-boat route in place of the mine-infested North Sea. Yet the Navy had more consuming if unstrategic reservations over any increased U-boat activity. The conservative bureaucracy led by Tirpitz's successor as naval minister, Admiral Eduard von Capelle, feared that the organizational and promotional hierarchy based on the battle fleet would be usurped during and after the war by the glut of submarine officers. And since Britain was to be humbled within six months, both Capelle and Holtzendorff refused to authorize a new and massive U-boat construction program. The government used this timetable—and the exaggerated sinking reports of its U-boat commanders—to decide in January 1917 for unrestricted submarine warfare, effective February 1.

British and American naval capabilities figured importantly in the overoptimistic projections of the German leaders. Though British shipping losses mounted and antisub countermeasures remained inadequate, the Royal Navy after Jutland understood clearly that the commerce war held the key to victory. The British people threw out the government of Lord Asquith in the autumn as evidence of their frustration, and Admiral Jellicoe—now convinced the sub had become the final arbiter—was elevated to the post of First Sea Lord in order to prosecute a vigorous antisubmarine policy. Admiral Beatty succeeded to command of the Grand Fleet. Antisub tactics did not improve or even change at once, but at least the Admiralty created a specialized Antisubmarine Division in December. As long as the Germans believed that the British would not change, the former's strategy seemed wise. And indeed the innovations of early 1917 achieved little: special transit zones and "dazzle" painting of merchantmen to confuse U-boat aiming, strengthened coastal patrols whereas most U-boats operated beyond them at 50 to 300 miles out, the arming of all merchantmen to replace the Q-ship and such desperate experiments as the unsuccessful attempts to train sea lions and sea gulls in sub detection! But in April alone the Central Powers sank nearly 870,000 tons of Allied and neutral vessels. As suspected, the United States responded by declaring war that same month. But the German Army could not conceive how the Americans could raise, equip and train an expeditionary force for service in France in 1917. The German Navy doubted whether the Americans would have enough transports to bring an army to Europe—in 1917 or ever—and correctly assumed that the U.S. Navy had been emphasizing capital ship over antisub construction so as to be a negligible factor against the U-boat.

So the decision for victory lay in the ability of the German Navy to strangle Britain with an unrestricted U-boat campaign before Britain overcame its antisub tactical deficiencies and before the United States could sealift a modern army to the Western front. Six months seemed like more than enough time, but the Germans badly miscalculated the ability of both the Royal and United States navies to overcome doctrinal conservatism and achieve the tactical flexibility to check the U-boat and thus prolong the war until an American army could be mobilized and committed to battle.

German smugness and naval conservatism also hurt the new German strategy. A lingering belief in the efficacy of surface *guerre de course* led early in 1917 to the breakout of three merchant cruisers on successful raiding cruises, and destroyers from Zeebrugge continued to plague Allied shipping in the Channel. Organizationally, the high command simply refused to reform its rigid staff system to allow the overall coordination of the U-boat offensive; when the U-boat chief, Commodore Hermann Bauer, recommended in April that a command sub be stationed off the Western Approaches to coordinate U-boat operations by radio (like the later wolf packs of World War II), he was not only turned down but relieved of command. So the boats of the North Sea and Flanders could not be coordinated—a major administrative flaw. In the High Seas Fleet, the austere officer corps mistreated its crews—already plagued by food shortages and the post-Jutland inactivity—so that enlisted morale in the fleet plummeted as the better officers and ratings began to transfer to the U-boat arm. Growing discontent then led to several mutinies in the fleet during the summer of 1917, an inexcusable consequence since the battle force provided the basis of the Navy's manpower as well as minesweeping in support of U-boat operations. At least Holland and Denmark remained neutral, but the German U-boat strategy of counterblockade would never be fully implemented before its own six-month deadline—by which time the British and Americans would be working in concert.

The United States in fact demonstrated remarkable strategic and tactical flexibility in meeting the U-boat onslaught. True, the administration of Woodrow Wilson had followed a unilateral course of heavy-ship construction—embodied in the Naval Act of 1916—generally to deter Germany in the Atlantic and Japan in the Pacific. And certainly the Americans, sensitive to the British Orders-in-Council violating neutral

American rights, remained somewhat aloof from the Alliance by becoming only an "Associated Power." But any lingering Anglophobia went into eclipse as Wilson mounted a great moral crusade for world democracy, beginning with the salvation of Britain and France from the Central Powers. Completing American defenses of the Panama Canal with the purchase of the Danish Virgin Islands early in 1917, Wilson rejected the fears of several admirals who forecast a German victory and who thus wanted a two-power battleship standard against Germany and Japan. Instead, he adhered to the recommendations of Admiral William S. Sims, ranking American naval officer in Europe, and Captain William V. Pratt in the Navy Department to accept the new British emphasis on antisubmarine construction. And since American shipyards could not build both battleships and destroyers, Wilson opted for the latter and postponed capital ship construction for the duration. More immediately, however, the U. S. Navy hastened many of its available lighter warships to British and French ports for employment as subchasers. When properly utilized, these vessels would make a significant contribution to Allied commerce protection.

Simultaneously with the American entry into the fighting in April 1917, the British finally decided to adopt convoy—probably the most fateful decision of the naval war. Prewar and early wartime arguments against convoy had stressed their invitation to attack, their congestion in port, and their illegality in neutral ports. But local convoys from Holland, Norway and France since mid-1916 had had some success, and now statistics revealed that—especially with American destroyers— the Allies had enough warships to escort merchant convoys. Despite anti-convoy conservatism in the Royal and U. S. navies, several key officials now pressed for it: the energetic new prime minister, David Lloyd George, Sir Maurice Hankey of the War Cabinet, Admirals Beatty and Sir Rosslyn Wemyss and Captain Herbert Richmond, leader of the "young Turks" and an adviser to Lloyd George. As the "black fortnight" of April 17–30 witnessed record U-boat successes, Admiral Jellicoe and the Admiralty reluctantly decided to initiate two experimental escorted convoys to Britain. They sailed in May: 17 merchantmen from Gibraltar at 6½ knots, and 12 from Hampton Roads at 9 knots. Both arrived safely, save for one straggler sunk from the latter convoy. Consequently, the Allies gradually and successfully instituted a regular convoy system over all their sea lanes, leading Admiral Sims to champion convoy in the U. S. Navy, whose Atlantic units were now integrated into the British command and doctrinal system.

Britain reformed its war-making machinery to lead the Allies in this new and vigorous antisubmarine strategy. Lloyd George appointed Churchill to be Minister of Munitions and Sir Eric Geddes first to the new post of Navy Controller—to handle logistics and leave the admirals to concentrate on operations—and soon after to be First Lord of the Admiralty. Never very keen on convoy, Jellicoe was relieved as First Sea Lord late in the year by Wemyss. In the Mediterranean, Allied leaders met at Corfu to reform commerce protection and welcomed the arrival in April of a Japanese squadron of one light cruiser and 8 (later 12) destroyers to assist. In the British Isles, British and American naval aircraft operated from coastal stations in reconnaissance and attack roles against U-boats, also attacking their bases in Flanders. Beatty and Captain Murray F. Sueter improved the British naval air arm by pushing torpedo plane development over the unpredictable seaplanes, catapult-plane towed lighters and 2 experimental aircraft carriers. New mines drove many U-boats from the Strait of Dover and Heligoland Bight to transit into the North Sea via the long Kiel Canal-Danish Sound route. But the convoy offered the most effective tactical device. Even one escorting warship forced the U-boat to remain submerged, throwing off its aim at zigzagging or fast merchant ships. British code-breaking and general intelligence kept U-boat movements under surveillance, while the wireless advised convoys accordingly. Finally, ample numbers of Allied destroyers and subchasers combined with mounting merchant ship construction to counter the U-boat. By 1918, 6 to 8 warships escorted each convoy of 15 to 25 merchantmen between New York, Hampton Roads and Nova Scotia and Allied ports in Europe.

The convoys *always* got through, leading to the relatively swift German admission of failure in the commerce war. German U-boat numbers peaked at 139 (55 at sea simultaneously) in September 1917, including new larger 1870-ton "U-cruisers." From 869,000 tons of merchant shipping sunk in April, these losses declined to 600,000 tons in May and then with convoy to under 175,000 tons (68 vessels) in September. With targets difficult to locate or attack, the German Admiralty early in the autumn shifted its U-boats away from the open ocean of the Western Approaches to the coastal English Channel and Irish Sea. Allied sinkings of U-boats never exceeded ten in any month, but the U-boat had been neutralized in the North Atlantic, and the brief U-boat redeployment succeeded only until the Allies shifted more patrol craft, seaplanes, airships and mines into their threatened coastal waters. In addition, improvements in British minesweeping techniques began to neutralize German mining efforts late in the year. The trend continued in 1918. German tonnage warfare avoided Canadian and American troop convoys altogether in order to sink six million tons of Allied and neutral shipping between February 1917 and January 1918, but convoys and escort forces increased to such proportions that the U-boats rarely attacked them. Allied admirals could not believe the deterrent value of the convoy and mistakenly tried to measure their success in numbers of U-boats sunk. But the Germans replaced most U-boats lost with an equal number of new boats (roughly eighty during 1918). What they could not replace were the experienced U-boat captains and crews lost at sea. By the summer of 1918 the convoys—now extended to coastal waters— had beaten the U-boats, and though they switched back to the Western Approaches for surfaced night attacks and as far afield as North America they could not halt the flow of growing Allied shipping.

The battle fleets of both sides tried to augment the commerce war. Admiral Scheer used High Seas Fleet units to sink two Anglo-Scandinavian convoys in the North Sea in October and December 1917 and to sweep British mines. Admiral Beatty merely added a battleship squadron as convoy backup and in January 1918 made the momentous decision not to provoke a fleet action but rather to subordinate all Grand Fleet activities to the antisubmarine campaign. An unpopular decision in both the Royal and U. S. navies—the latter contributed 4 dreadnoughts to the Grand Fleet in December—it nevertheless recognized strategic realities. In April 1918 Beatty shifted his 34 battleships, 9 battle cruisers and their flotillas from Scapa Flow to Rosyth, and though it failed to intercept an uneventful sortie by Scheer's 19 dreadnoughts and 5 battle cruisers later in the month the Grand Fleet continued to command the North Sea. In addition, Allied naval aircraft controlled the air and British mines closed the Heligoland Bight to U-boats in February, forcing all U-boats to transit via the Sound and Skagerrak. Then, in March, the Allies followed an American proposal to begin the laying of a mine barrage across the 240 miles of the North Sea between the Orkney Islands and Norway—evidence of continuing doubts about the efficacy of convoy. By October, when Norway closed its waters to U-boats, 56,000 American and 15,000 British mines had been sowed, but claimed only half a dozen U-boats. To close the English Channel to German destroyers and U-boats, Admiral Sir Roger Keyes in early 1918 strengthened British patrols and minefields, added searchlights to illuminate the Dover Strait at night, and tried—unsuccessfully— to close Zeebrugge and Ostend with sunken ships during blocking expeditions in April and May. By September, however, 24 of the 43 U-boats based in Flanders had been lost, and the survivors quit the Channel altogether.

Though the Allies tightened their command over the North Sea and Channel, German control of the Baltic Sea helped to take Russia out of the war. Allied ground offensives on the Western and Eastern fronts achieved little during 1917, after which a German thrust along the Gulf of Finland took Riga in September, and High Seas Fleet units cleared Russian mines and supported the amphibious capture of Oesel, Moon and Dago islands in October. Then, as the German fleet controlled the approaches to Kronstadt and Petrograd in November, the Bolsheviks and frustrated Kronstadt sailors overthrew the Russian democratic government and moved to conclude an armistice with the Central Powers. The British ordered their Baltic subs scuttled and looked on helplessly as the Communists signed an armistice in December. The High Seas Fleet, having survived Jutland, remained as a fleet-in-being to deter any possible British naval sortie into the Baltic. The Russian collapse relieved pressure on Germany elsewhere, for the Austrians stubbornly resisted Italian attacks, and even the Balkan front changed little with the entrance of Greece into the war as an Ally. The German Army led by Ludendorff wanted to convert the surrendered Russian Black Sea Fleet into a viable force in that quarter following the occupation of Sevastopol in April 1918. But it was frustrated by the scuttling of several vessels by order of Lenin and even more so by the German Navy's refusal to divert its energies away from the North Sea. Even so, Ottoman Turkey now had nothing further to fear from Russia, although its armies and river gunboats lost Jerusalem and Baghdad to fresh land-river British drives in the Middle East.

These events helped to transform the war into a relentless moral crusade during 1918. The original imperialistic motives were submerged in the growing ideological struggle between Wilsonian democracy and Leninist communism and the global popular disgust with the meaningless bloodshed of the European powers. Unsuccessful mutinies erupted in the French Army in the spring of 1917, the Austro-Hungarian Navy in October and the following February, as they did in the German and Russian fleets. Finland threw off Russian domination late in 1917, only to be crushed in April in a civil war ended partly by German amphibious landings in Finland. To destroy the decadent German, Austrian and Ottoman empires, the Allies tightened their blockade of the Central Powers and centralized their leadership into virtual dictatorships to win the war. Under Lloyd George, Wilson and Georges Clemenceau, a Supreme War Council and British-dominated Allied Naval Council directed the final campaigns. Ground forces were unified under the supreme command of French Marshal Ferdinand Foch in April, just as American Army and Marine Corps divisions began to arrive in France. The British combined their army and naval air squadrons in the Royal Air Force that month, supported by the Allied air forces. Only the French and Italian navies—prewar rivals—refused to cooperate in the Mediterranean. Germany consolidated its leadership behind General Ludendorff, and in August Admiral Scheer took over supreme naval command, succeeded as High Seas Fleet commander by Hipper. But Germany could not break the Allied armies—now reinforced by fresh American troops—on the Western front during the spring and summer and had to fall back before the Allied counterattack in July and August.

At sea, the Central Powers tried desperately to hold, but failed everywhere except in the Baltic. In the Mediterranean, convoy triumphed by midsummer, and the Allies spent five months laying a mine barrage across the Strait of Otranto. The new aggressive commander of the Imperial Austrian Navy, Rear Admiral Nikolaus Horthy de Nagybánya, tried to break the barrage in June with his four dreadnoughts, only to lose one and turn back in the face of an Italian torpedo boat attack. In the Aegean, a Turko-German surface force passed out of the Dardanelles in January to sink two British monitors off Imbros before being driven back by mines and air attacks which sank a cruiser. Turko-German ground forces had better success in pushing back the British from Armenia and the Black and Caspian sea coasts, but this front had become a strategic backwater. Admiral Scheer in September relegated the surface fleet to supporting the U-boats in the North Sea and the Army in the Baltic, and the next month obtained the kaiser's approval for a new U-boat construction program. But this desperate measure came much too late as the Central Powers retreated and collapsed everywhere during the autumn. In October, the Austro-Hungarian Empire fell apart into the revolutionary republics of Poland, Czechoslavakia, Hungary and Yugoslavia. The tottering dual monarchy transferred the fleet to Yugoslavia and its Danube flotilla to Hungary, and on November 1 two Italian frogmen sank the flagship dreadnought of the Austro-Yugoslav fleet with a mobile mine at Pola. The Balkan republics signed an armistice, and Allied warships occupied all their Adriatic ports. Simultaneously, British offensives in the Middle East took Turkey out of the war.

Virtually alone, Germany desperately tried to salvage what it could. When the German Army and U-boats evacuated Ostend and Zeebrugge in mid-October, Allied forces occupied these key bases. On the 20th, President Wilson demanded and got—as a prerequisite to armistice—the cessation of the unrestricted submarine campaign. Scheer recalled his U-boats and reassigned them to the High Seas Fleet to help it lure the Grand Fleet into one last battle. On the 26th a liberal government replaced imperial rule, spreading fear throughout the officer class and relief among the enlisted men. Scheer, Hipper and the reactionary naval high command now rebelled against the new regime by preparing their final sortie as a virtual suicide mission to salvage German honor. The 80,000 sailors of the High Seas Fleet rejected such madness by a general mutiny on the 29th as the ships rendezvoused at Wilhemshaven for the sortie. Four years of mistreatment by arrogant junior officers fed their efforts, forcing Hipper to cancel the operation the next day. The sailors refused to sail anywhere and gradually merged their mutiny with the political revolutionaries that helped to overthrow the kaiser on November 9. The new German democratic republic signed the armistice—or virtual surrender—two days later.

British sea power had finally eliminated its major naval rival and kept it neutralized through internment of the High Seas Fleet at Scapa Flow later in November. The Anglo-American command of the Atlantic had defeated the U-boat and blockaded the German economy with telling effect, indirectly with Fisher's dreadnought fleet and directly by antisub convoys and destroyers. Final victory overlooked the material deficiencies of the battle fleets and tended to minimize the potential power of the submarine and aircraft, while the Gallipoli debacle had thoroughly discredited amphibious tactics and strategy. Happily for the victors, however, British naval conservatism had yielded to expedient innovations to win absolute command of the sea. Germany's naval conservatives by contrast changed little from Tirpitz through Scheer and could never bring themselves to accept the U-boat as the prime naval weapon of a continental power. The High Seas Fleet had preserved the coasts of Germany from invasion and given a creditable performance at Jutland, but it never really evolved beyond the role of a passive fleet-in-being. Even the sinking of over 7,600,000 tons of British and over 3,000,000 tons of other Allied and neutral shipping could not convince the German admirals of their doctrinal errors. And, finally, the Germans simply did not have the experience and confidence in naval matters enjoyed by their enemy.

Aside from the reassertion of British supremacy at sea, however, the "Great War" had settled none of the great power issues that had led to war in 1914. Britain and France were imposing an intolerable victor's peace on Germany, while—equally alarming—the United States and Japan now resumed their naval arms race in the Pacific. The armistice of 1918 therefore would remain just that, unless somehow a system of naval arms controls could eliminate the possibility of the resumption of total war.

# 15
# Naval Armistice and Arms Control, 1919–1940

*A state which adopts the policy of constructing a Navy composed primarily of submarines consciously renounces the struggle for sea power. . . .*

—ADMIRAL HERMANN BAUER,
German Navy, 1931

## THE POSTWAR BALANCE OF POWER

The devices by which the great powers sought to turn the armistice of 1918 into a permanent condition of international stability and peace were unique, yet firmly rooted in the antebellum legalism of the *Pax Britannica*. They were, namely, formal international organization and a system of naval arms controls. That both failed to prevent the resumption of total war in 1940–41 reveals the naiveté of the powers in their underlying political assumptions. International political unity embodied in the League of Nations came about after the revitalization of the prewar global cosmopolitanism in the wartime idealism of Woodrow Wilson. But without the full participation of all the powers, notably the United States, Soviet Russia and Weimar Germany, such a system could only be at best imperfect. Rather, the treaties ending World War I represented the same traditional notions about European global hegemony and power balances, when in fact the national empires of Europe had been mortally wounded by the disaster of 1914–18. The failure of the League's members to enforce their own rules against aggression while vainly attempting to achieve economic self-sufficiency seriously compromised the powers in their postwar reconstruction programs. Furthermore, rising nationalism within European colonial and power preserves undermined imperial order everywhere; the end of the European overseas empires had been hastened by the heavy costs of the war.

473

The new attempt at naval arms control between the great powers did succeed as long as all the signatories were willing to abide by the warship limitations agreed upon. Cloaked in the misnomer of outright "disarmament," the various international naval conferences in the 1920s and 1930s in fact attempted only to reduce international tensions by establishing naval building holidays and ratios. Actual disarmament of modern machine weapons was not possible, for such machinery could not be separated from the totality of industrial civilization, a fact which the powers seemed to realize. Yet the weapons they chose to limit were not those which were revolutionizing warfare, the submarine and airplane, but rather the same prewar index of naval power, the battleship. The submarine would probably have had to have won the war by defeating Britain in order to be accepted fully as a major weapon after the war, while the smaller naval nations clung to it as their only alternative to big surface fleets. The airplane was still too limited technically to warrant controls, but the powers appreciated its potential by limiting aircraft carriers. So the wartime belligerents found not peace in their armistice and postwar treaties, but merely a breathing spell during which to prepare for the final agony of resumed total war.

The armistice of 1918–19 in itself did not resolve the great power struggles of the time, and three more years passed before relative order could be reestablished between the powers. The final disposition of the German fleet by the Allies and the establishment of the League involved many difficulties. The Russian Civil War led to great power interventions around the Russian periphery as the democracies attempted to help overthrow the Bolshevik regime. Rampant nationalism and religious strife turned the Middle East into a bloody arena of internal warring and power rivalries following the collapse of the Ottoman Empire. Finally, in the Pacific, the United States and Japan resumed their naval arms race with capital ship construction that threatened to lead to open war— placing Great Britain in an embarrassing position, since she was allied to both Pacific powers and was too exhausted economically from the war to participate in this new building race. Only the convening of the Washington Naval Conference in 1921–22 halted the Pacific power struggle, leading to a decade of relative quiet throughout the world.

Great Britain and the United States cooperated in the dismemberment of Germany's navy, but remained otherwise antagonistic over the growth of American naval might which challenged British supremacy at sea. Allied disputes over the disposition of the surrendered High Seas Fleet evaporated on July 21, 1919, when the skeleton crews of that fleet simply scuttled their ships while still interned at Scapa Flow: 400,000 tons of war shipping, including fifteen dreadnoughts. But then President Wilson at the peace conference at Versailles demanded that Britain endorse the principle of freedom of neutral shipping in time of war, which the British regarded as an American economic attack on the Empire and thus refused to accept. Wilson also pressed for and got a League of Nations, while his naval advisers urged the creation of an international League navy. But none of the powers could accept the idea of subordinating their fleets to such a force, and the American Congress refused to join the League at all. The Versailles Treaty of October 1919 thus lacked any real element of collective security without American participation, and though the United States cut back many of its grandiose naval building programs so offensive to Britain, the two great maritime victor nations remained at cross-purposes and continued to act unilaterally. France tended to side with Britain as European powers ever fearful of Germany; Britain remained allied with America's rival, Japan; and all the powers simply excluded Bolshevik Russia from any postwar discussions.

The Communist revolution in Russia had not only alarmed the other powers, but provides one of the few instances of political activism in naval history. The Kronstadt sailors, especially of the cruiser *Aurora*—still enshrined at Leningrad (Petrograd), were rewarded for their part in the revolution with the creation of a powerful Naval Commissariat within the unified defense structure and then, early in 1918, with the Socialist Worker-Peasant Red Fleet. But such leftist activity among sailors proved exceptional, stemming more from injustices within the old navy than from political activism—not unlike the German naval mutiny. Counterrevolutionary naval officers were also active. Admiral Horthy threw out a Communist government and a Rumanian army from Hungary in 1919 and then became national regent. Russian Admiral Kolchak of the Black Sea Fleet seized power there late in 1918 to help bring on the Russian Civil War. And, finally, in March 1921 the Kronstadt sailors again mutinied, this time against their rigid Communist masters, and had to be severely crushed. Sensitive to internal dissension, the new Soviet government also had to reckon with the new Baltic republics of Finland, Poland, Lithuania, Estonia and Latvia, especially since the former wartime Allies decided to support these new nations with active military and naval aid.

Despite the strong anti-Communist attitudes of President Wilson, First Lord Geddes and Admirals Wemyss and Beatty, and the imperial territorial designs of the Allies on Russian territory, their warweary peoples refused to allow any systematic or full intervention. Nevertheless, between 1918 and 1921, the Allies made halting attempts to support the anti-Bolshevik forces during the Russian Civil War. In the Far East, Allied ground forces and warships occupied Vladivostok and British naval gunners helped Admiral Kolchak capture Omsk and briefly man his twenty-one-gunboat flotilla on Lake Baikal until he was defeated and executed. Then the Allied forces evacuated Vladivostok, although Japan did not leave northern Sakhalin until 1925. In South Russia, the British supported the White Russians against the Reds on the Black and Caspian seas with landing forces, aircraft and gunboats in order to protect their oil-rich Middle East holdings. After France and Italy failed to police the Black and Caspian seas respectively, the British withdrew and with the French and Americans helped evacuate the Whites as they were driven back on the coast by a Red offensive. In North Russia, Allied warships occupied Murmansk and Archangel in mid-1918 and sent a small flotilla up the Dvina River. One year later fourteen British and American gunboats, shipped by rail from Murmansk, joined twenty-five Finnish patrol boats to seize control of Lake Onega, while British gunboats and monitors supported an offensive up the Dvina. Stranded in this unpopular war by White defections and Red victories, a battalion of Royal Marines refused to fight on the Onega front, and Britain led the general Allied withdrawal. On these three distant fronts, therefore, the Allies achieved little more than to antagonize the Soviet regime.

On the Baltic front, however, the wartime Allies made a determined effort to resist the Bolsheviks because of their threat to the new Baltic nations. In addition, the Allies retained a large force of unsurrendered German troops as a buffer against the Bolsheviks until they began to seek their own territorial objectives. The British committed considerable naval forces to the Baltic, generally commanded by Rear Admiral Walter H. Cowan and reinforced by French warships and a small but spirited new Estonian Navy under Rear Admiral Juhan Pitka. The U. S. Navy generally confined its operations to civilian food relief. Operating out of Copenhagen, Finnish Helsinski (Helsingfors), Estonian Tallinn (Reval), Latvian Liepaja (Libau) and Riga, Lithuanian Memel and Polish Danzig, the Allied navies sought to control the Gulf of Finland and blockade the Russian Baltic Fleet (Soviet Activated Squadron) at Kronstadt under Comrade A. P. Zelenoy. The Red Russian ground and sea forces, personally commanded by Joseph Stalin, defended the Lake Ladoga front and other approaches to Petrograd-Leningrad. While the armies seesawed across Baltic lands, the Allies and Soviet Russia waged an undeclared naval war from November 1918 into 1920.

Allied strategic mobility at sea aided materially in preserving the independence of the Baltic States, but failed utterly—as elsewhere—even to weaken the Soviet regime. In response to a Soviet ground offensive during the winter of 1918–19 which captured Estonian Narva, Latvian Riga and Lithuanian Vilna, Anglo-Estonian units harassed the coast and captured two modern Russian destroyers; Estonia created a squadron on Lake Peipus; the Poles drove the Russians out of Vilna; and German-Latvian forces retook Riga and Liepaja. In mid-1919 Admiral Cowan supported an Estonian counterattack on land by using Allied vessels in the Gulf of Finland to bombard the coast, support landings and sweep mines. In June, Cowan's torpedo boats sank a Russian cruiser, and in August, covered by a diversionary carrier air strike, they charged straight into Kronstadt roadstead to sink the two Russian battleships and a depot ship there, losing three of their eight to a Russian destroyer. In May the Estonians captured the entire Bolshevik gunboat flotilla on Lake Peipus, and in October Anglo-Estonian vessels, including one 7200-ton monitor with twin 15″ guns, supported a successful White Russian offensive toward Petrograd. The Reds held, but lost three destroyers to Allied mines. Late in the year the Germans made a final bid to take over Riga and Liepaja, only to be driven back by Allied fleet units, Latvian troops and a river flotilla, in addition to which the Allies instituted a blockade of German Baltic ports. The coming of winter cold and ice, discontent and isolated mutinies in the British fleet and Allied indecision finally led to a general withdrawal. In 1920 Soviet Russia made peace with Finland, Estonia, Latvia and Lithuania, but carried on the war with Poland until 1921 when Anglo-French naval units rushed supplies to Danzig and enabled the Poles to repulse the Russians and conclude peace.

Postwar national boundaries in continental Europe reflected the Wilsonian self-determinism accepted at Versailles and were partially influenced by naval patrols. The dismemberment of the Austro-Hungarian Empire and territorial annexations of the Dalmatian coast, Zara and Fiume by Italy between 1919 and 1924 required Allied naval patrols in the Adriatic to assure the political integrity of Yugoslavia. Britain also kept gunboats on the Danube River till 1925, keeping normal trade open. This self-determination frustrated several Allied wartime deals to carve up the Ottoman Empire in the form of mandates that eventually led to independent Middle Eastern states. Britain obtained a mandate over Mesopotamia as the state of Iraq, which had to be pacified in 1920, and the Trucial System and Aden protectorate enabled the British to control the waters around Saudi Arabia, although Egypt obtained its virtual independence in 1922. On the Levantine coast, Britain received the mandate over Palestine and Transjordan, and France took over Syria and Lebanon on the same basis.

A Turkish nationalist movement led by Mustapha Kemal resisted further dismemberment of the country, however, resulting in much bloodshed between 1919 and 1922. Moslem Turk-Christian Greek antagonism prompted Anglo-Greek and Italian landings at Smyrna and Adalia respectively, and the arrival of American battleships with escorts in 1919. When the Greeks then mounted an offensive across Anatolia and Greek warships attacked the coast, the Allies kept the Dardanelles open and early in 1920 occupied Constantinople for defensive purposes. The Italians held Adalia, the French tried to take over Cilicia, and in June Admiral de Robeck used five British battleships and some seaplanes to occupy the eastern shore of the Sea of Marmara and drive back Kemal's army. But during the winter of 1920–21 Kemal negotiated French and Italian withdrawals, obtained rapport with Russia by ceding the port of Batum to it, and profited from the strict neutrality enforced by the naval patrols under American diplomat-Admiral Mark L. Bristol. Then, during the summer of 1921, Kemal stopped a new Greek offensive and drove it back on Smyrna where a disastrous fire and reprisals killed tens of thousands of refugees. The offshore Anglo-American naval units, hampered by logistical and diplomatic limitations, could do little to save the victims. The Greek invasion crushed, the diplomats finally concluded peace in 1923, creating the Republic of Turkey which included European Thrace and neutralizing the straits. Allied warships then withdrew from the Black Sea.

British supremacy at sea enabled the Royal Navy to police all European and South Asian waters, especially in containing Russia—however unnecessary this was, due to total Bolshevik preoccupation with internal matters. In addition to the relatively successful neutralization of the Baltic and Black seas, the British still held the Strait of Gibraltar, Suez Canal, Bab el Mandeb and Persian Gulf. In India, torn by warring Moslems and Hindus, British troops and air forces enforced stability to thwart Russia, especially westward to the Persian Gulf. They pacified a restive Afghanistan in 1919, but yielded to a Russian naval demonstration on the Caspian Sea to withdraw from Persia (Iran) in 1920–21. The Russians also withdrew, leaving that region generally stabilized. By the same token, British forces ended their intervention efforts in the Russian Civil War everywhere. The Anglo-Japanese alliance insured the containment of the new Soviet state in the Far East, but it also created serious tensions with Britain's wartime American ally.

Japanese-American rivalry had been postponed during World War I, but Japan continued to press upon the relatively helpless new Republic of China. Japan had not only occupied Germany's Pacific islands and Chinese base at Tsingtao but had violated early American neutrality in the Philippines, operated its naval vessels as far eastward as the Galápagos Islands and Gulf of California, and in early 1915 had issued "Twenty-one Demands" to China for territory and virtual political submission. As long as China had remained neutral, Japan had had to keep its warships out of Chinese waters, while the neutral American Yangtze gunboat patrol could continue and American diplomatic maneuvers enforced the "open door." Then, in 1917, following a warlord and Manchu upheaval, both China and the United States declared war on the Central Powers, and Japanese warships returned. To quiet Japan, the Americans vaguely recognized its "special interests" in China and kept their major warships out of the Pacific altogether. The end of the war and massive Japanese intervention in Russia signaled the renewal of the Japanese-American naval arms race, in addition to which the powers at Versailles mandated Germany's Pacific islands to Japan. Britain could do nothing in the Far East, for postwar naval retrenchment under the "Geddes axe" of First Lord Geddes' special committee recommendation of 1921 reduced Royal Navy strength outside of Europe. Alarmed by these new strategic realities, Britain's Pacific and Indian ocean colonies—Canada, India, Australia and New Zealand—in 1921 demanded that the mother country replace the Japanese alliance with a new settlement involving the United States as a friendly party.

The United States government, equally tired of the arms race and anxious to reduce tensions with Japan, in 1921 convened the Washington Naval Conference of the five largest naval powers. The United States, Britain and Japan—with France and Italy as minor participants— froze the strategic *status quo* in the Pacific, placed a ceiling on capital ship construction, and recognized the political and territorial integrity of China (the latter with four other nations). The powers agreed not to build new fortifications on their island possessions or mandates in the Pacific, except for British Singapore, American Pearl Harbor and the Japanese home islands, and to respect each other's zones of maritime control: Britain in the South Pacific, Japan in the Central Pacific, France in Indochina, and the United States in the Hawaiian, Aleutian and Philippine island groups. In battleships and battle cruisers, virtually all construction was to cease and a ceiling ratio of $5:5:3:1.67:1.67$ was to be established. Specifically, the five naval powers agreed to limit their capital ship tonnage to vessels under 35,000 tons mounting 16″ guns and totaling 500,000 tons each for Britain and the United States; 300,000 tons for Japan; and 167,000 tons each for France and Italy. These agreements, which superseded the Anglo-Japanese alliance, were to last for ten years, at the end of which another conference was to convene to consider renewal.

The Washington settlements, instead of achieving actual disarmament as many people naively believed, represent the first successful attempt at arms control in history. The shortcomings lay in the type of weapons that were not limited and in the eventual failure of all the powers to perpetuate the compromises of the meeting. But since the senior naval policy makers of all the powers regarded the battleship as the index of naval might, the conference indeed succeeded in checking the arms race and thus extending to the Pacific the same general armistice that prevailed in Europe. Unfortunately, however, France refused to consider any limitation to her ground forces as long as her wartime allies Britain and America would not guarantee her frontier against a possibly resurgent Germany. Aviation was in such a primitive state that any curtailment of military aviation would necessarily require the inherent halting of overall developments in commercial aeronautics, a possibility repulsive to all these modern industrial nations. But in the naval sphere, aviation was to be at least controlled by imposing the same 5:5:3 ratio on aircraft carriers if not their planes; in general, carriers were to be limited to 27,000 tons, with tonnage ceilings of 135,000 tons each for Britain and America; 81,000 for Japan; and 60,000 for France and Italy. The other potentially revolutionary naval weapon, the submarine, received no such restriction. Britain, trying to avert the repetition of its near-defeat by Germany's U-boats, worked to outlaw subs altogether. But France, traditionally a continental nation dependent upon such inexpensive coast defense and *guerre de course* vessels, would have none of it and was supported in large measure by the United States, whose naval planners saw similar uses for the sub in any future war with Japan. So no action was taken on the submarine. Battleships naturally required escorts, but the only restrictions placed were to limit cruisers to 10,000 tons and 8" guns. Carriers were also limited to 8" guns, but no attention was given the multi-purpose destroyers. Though the admirals of each country bemoaned these reductions to their operating fleets, they now in fact were unknowingly prevented from expending more funds on the questionably effective battleships while gaining valuable time and freedom to develop the weapons that would eventually dominate future total naval warfare—the airplane and submarine.

The arms races and armed conflict of the early twentieth century thus ended everywhere by the close of 1922, and all that remained was to enforce the various agreements. Throughout the 1920s enforcement proved successful in the Pacific and nearly impossible in Europe. The Treaty of Versailles created a Control Commission of British, French, Italian and Japanese officers to insure that Germany in no way attempted to rearm, but the lack of staffing, clever German evasiveness and the American refusal to sign the treaty all combined to undermine the efforts of the Commission, which deluded itself by closing down its naval unit in 1924 with the statement that the German Navy was effectively disarmed. Attempts by the League of Nations to enforce anything similarly proved fruitless, for the American absence added to the British and French retrenchment to encourage covert German violations of the Versailles disarmament dictates throughout the 1920s.

By contrast, in the Pacific the mutual attitudes of the Washington signatory powers precluded any violation of the non-fortification agreements. Despite repeated warnings from the Navy, the American government did nothing significant to improve the naval facilities in the Philippines, Guam or Wake, while the British allowed Hong Kong's defenses to languish. The Japanese, though refusing to allow any inspection by foreign nations, did absolutely nothing to fortify or develop the mandated islands for military uses during the decade. Despite foreign apprehensions to the contrary, Japan enjoyed an era of relative tranquillity under the new Prime Minister Admiral Tomosaburo Kato and the men who succeeded him upon his death in 1923. Kato regarded the Imperial Japanese Navy as a deterrent force and thus kept it at the treaty strength. The British and American governments were simply not disposed to build up to treaty levels, so that Japan during the 1920s never felt threatened by either or even both powers.

The spirit of naval arms control established at Washington continued until and after the scheduled renewal conference held in London in 1930. Between 1925 and 1928 Germany agreed at Locarno to respect neighboring national frontiers; Britain, the United States and Japan met at Geneva, but failed in their intention to limit cruiser, destroyer and submarine strengths; and the major powers agreed at Paris to outlaw war, but without the necessary corollary of enforcing the agreement. Despite the wild idealism of the latter endeavor, the naval powers met again in 1930 to make some hard agreements for extending naval arms controls. Though Japan had built to Washington treaty limits, and had but one ocean to patrol against the two oceans concerning both Britain and America, Japanese pride had been rankled by the inferior ratio assigned the Imperial Navy, and opposition against treaty extension mounted in the person of old Fleet Admiral Togo of Tsushima fame and a rising militant group of Army and Navy officers.

Nevertheless, the first effects of the worldwide Great Depression of 1929–30 were forcing Japan to retrench economically and to enable Admiral Kato's successors to carry on at the London Conference. Capital ship (including carriers) ratios were generally maintained, with a ratio of about 10:10:7 being established for cruisers for Britain, the United States and Japan respectively. (France and Italy again were negligible participants). Most importantly, parity in submarines was granted across-the-board. In the face of a combined Anglo-American effort to abolish subs altogether, each of which had been far outdistanced in sub construction since 1922 by France, Japan and Italy, the latter powers used familiar arguments for coast defenses to achieve parity and substitute limitation with vague statements about submarines observing international law in time of war. In fact, the powers returned to the same ambiguities and loopholes of the 1909–16 period, wanting the restricted use of subs, but lacking necessary controls. The London treaty would expire at the end of 1936, when another conference would again consider renewal.

The attempt at naval arms control ultimately failed for the same reason that the armistice arrangements of 1918–22 collapsed: several of the powers became impatient at such restrictions which ran counter to new policies of national expansion. Ideologically, the ascendance of fascist regimes in Italy (1922), Japan (1931) and Germany (1933) combined to neutralize the League of Nations and all the treaty arrangements so laboriously worked out after World War I. And France and Italy, still in mutual fear of each other, refused to compromise. Neither the League members (including Soviet Russia which joined in 1932) nor the United States had the desire to try to enforce League or treaty stipulations when Japan conquered Manchuria in 1931, Italy invaded Ethiopia in 1935, Germany reoccupied the Rhineland in 1936, and civil war broke out in Spain the same year. In 1933 Japan quit the League and late the next year repudiated the terms of the Washington and London treaties—to be effective two years hence. Germany, a member since 1926, left the League also in 1933 and two years later denounced the Treaty of Versailles. Italy remained a member of the League as late as 1937, but its belligerence had long since made the League into a mockery. Still gripped by global economic depression, the other powers could do little but complain, begin their own belated rearmament, and seek some kind of new alliance system and balance of power. In the end, however, unilateral national security replaced international trust.

The last attempts at naval arms control sought much and gained virtually nothing. A world disarmament conference met at Geneva over 1932–34 seeking to check weapons of land warfare, but the several international crises led to its collapse. Great Britain, understandably alarmed both by the apparent apathy and inability of her former allies to help her check the growing aggressiveness of especially Germany, entered into a separate naval arms agreement with that country and in so doing repudiated the Versailles arrangements. The Anglo-German Naval Treaty of 1935 allowed Germany to build a navy 35 percent the size of the total naval forces of the British Empire in all classes of warships, except subs. Of all things—in view of the near-victory of the U-boats in 1916–17—the British allowed the Germans parity in subs! In December 1935, Britain, the United States, Japan and France convened at London again to arrange a continuation of the 1930 ratios, but Japan demanded parity in all warship classes, an intolerable objective to the Anglo-American delegates which resulted in the Japanese withdrawal from the meeting early in 1936. Nevertheless, Britain, America and

France agreed among themselves to certain "qualitative" (ship characteristics) limitations on new warships, most of which survived till 1938 and some of which remained binding as late as 1942. The last piece of naval arms control, a special protocol which prohibited unrestricted submarine attacks on unarmed shipping in time of war, was agreed upon at London in early November 1936 by Britain, America, Japan, Italy and France, by Germany two weeks later and by Russia the following February. But again, enforcement depended totally upon the signatories to obey it.

In the last week of 1936, Japanese obedience to the limitations of 1922 and 1930 ended, and, despite continuing overtures for international agreement, naval rearmament went forward unabated in Japan and throughout Europe.

## THE INTERWAR NAVIES AND EMPIRES

The art of naval warfare and of colonial pacification resumed after 1918 as if no world war had taken place. Machine weapons, embodied in the strategic bomber and superdreadnought, kept the material school of strategy in the forefront, due partly to an imperfect appreciation of how command of the sea had helped to end the war. The massive armies preoccupied the continental nations as always, as these sought panaceas in the defensive Maginot Line or the offensive tank-air-infantry *Blitzkrieg*. Italian General Guilio Douhet, the foremost material strategist, even reasoned that land-based bombing planes would bomb European military, industrial and urban centers into submission, while the armies and navies remained stalemated. In fact, however, strategic bombers were but a long-range extension of continental artillery which could lay down a barrage for advancing armies and apparently sink advancing warships—just as American General Billy Mitchell's planes dramatically did in tests off the American East Coast in 1921. But Douhet had little to say about the Pacific, where the aircraft carrier evolved into the long-range extension of the naval gun to support amphibious operations, sink other warships and develop its own antiaircraft defenses. Yet, neither the carrier nor submarine could dislodge the battleship in these years as the nucleus of blue-water fleets.

The notion of command of the sea did not change, and the same strategic arguments persisted, but on a much lower-keyed intellectual level. One reason lay in the fact that no naval theorists really matched the impressive material arguments of Douhet or the so-called "geopoliticians" who argued that control of the "heartland" of Central Europe would ultimately neutralize the sea powers. Mahan had died in 1914 and Corbett in 1923, leaving Admirals Richmond and Raoul Castex of France to advance their theories and incorporate the newest technology. Conservative battleship admirals thus returned to the old prewar anti-intellectualism, their naval war colleges and fleet maneuvers looking to another Jutland and virtually ignoring the promise of airplane and submarine. Only Castex envisioned the renewed use of the sub as a commerce raider as in World War I, while Admiral William A. Moffett led a group of American naval aviators outside the battleship navy to theorize that the fast carrier had replaced the battleship as the backbone of blue-water navies. The technical limitations of subs and planes were also part of the reason, so that they were both regarded as fleet reconnaissance and secondary attack elements during the 1920s and 1930s. The memory of Gallipoli discredited amphibious operations in Europe, but the U. S. Marine Corps foresaw their utility in any war across the Pacific against Japan. No navy made any real progress in logistics, and most further centralized their command structures. The only real progress occurred in improvements to existing weapons and in several complementary inventions at the tactical level.

The newer technology and naval treaty limitations in fact hastened the decline of the battleship. The weight restrictions imposed by the treaties demanded economy through qualitative improvements to warship hull design: better steel and lighter alloys, arc welding instead of rivets, and fewer but larger boilers. In propulsion, after 1930 high steam pressures and temperatures were produced from geared turbines, although the Germans used high-speed diesel engines and several navies adopted hydraulic machinery for auxiliary power. Armor did not change, whereas fire control got better. Antisub defenses included underwater bulges on the larger surface ships and the introduction of "asdic" ("sonar" from 1943) echo-acoustical sounding devices for sub detection, but virtually nothing was done to extend wartime convoy techniques. Antiair defenses centered on increased warship speeds and semiautomatic 5″ guns and large machine guns ("pom poms"). Radio assisted importantly in sub and aircraft detection and interception, but shipborne radar in the late 1930s was the most revolutionary development of these years. By bouncing pulsed transmissions of radio microwaves off solid objects, the Germans with the 80cm band could detect surface ships at twenty miles, and British, Americans and French used the 10cm band to detect aircraft up to a hundred miles. By 1941, Anglo-American radar sets could detect ships also, range for gunnery purposes, and enable closely coordinated cruising formations even at night. Radio-direction finders and radar-radio fighter plane direction also developed apace. Other isolated naval research initiated aerial bombsight and rocket devices and improved upon the wartime achievements in cryptography.

Surface ships reached their maximum efficient displacements for high-speed operations under the treaty restrictions. The slower battleship and faster battle cruiser merged into the fast battleship, beginning in the mid-1930s with the two 31.5-knot French *Dunkerques,* although the few surviving battle cruisers like Britain's *Hood* retained their old deficiencies. Main turreted batteries generally mounted 14" to 16" guns (or 11" in the two German *Scharnhorst*s to 18.1" in the two Japanese *Yamato*s). Heavy cruisers tended to exceed their 10,000-ton limit, but still had to sacrifice armor to keep down their weight and yet to mount eight to ten power-driven 8" guns and make at least 32 knots. Somewhat smaller light cruisers had less armor but twelve to fifteen 6" guns for speeds (for Italy at least) as high as 41 knots. Equally swift destroyers bristled with 5" guns, antiaircraft and other machine guns and torpedo tubes, while submarines—limited to 2000 tons in 1930—stayed small also because of high-speed diesel engines, arc welding and high tensile steel. Motor torpedo boats of 20 to 35 tons with highest speeds between 35 and 50 knots remained in the French and Italian navies until Britain, Germany and the United States renewed their construction after 1935. These and such lesser vessels as gunboats and mine warfare craft improved fleet capabilities, but only did aviation really alter naval tactics significantly.

The aircraft carrier dominated naval aviation in these years, though the rigid dirigibles competed until several tragic crashes put them out of business. Britain led with experimental carriers in the 1920s, after which the United States and Japan settled on the construction of the 30-knot fast carrier displacing between 20,000 tons (the American *Enterprise,* 1938) and 30,000 tons (the Japanese *Shokaku,* 1941), plus a few larger ones allowed by the 1922 treaty. Gradually, the flush-deck design with lowered smokestacks gave way to the full wooden flight deck with "island" superstructure for bridge and stacks. Later British carriers incorporated the armored flight deck to withstand land-based air attacks, but at the price of additional weight and reduced oil capacity limiting cruising range, and reduced aircraft stowage limiting plane complement. As "the eyes of the fleet," the carriers emphasized scout-planes, which doubled as dive-bombers, and these were largely replaced in the late 1930s by battleship- and cruiser-mounted catapult float planes, multi-engine seaplanes and land-based patrol bombers. The scout-dive-bomber evolved into an attack plane alongside the torpedo-bombing plane, with both escorted by defensive fighter planes. Finally, antisub air operations were left to the multi-engine non-carrier planes and eventually also non-rigid blimps. The tactical relationship between carrier and battleship was not settled during these two decades, beyond the broad agreement that they should be mutually supporting.

In general, only the U. S. Navy and Royal Navy remained blue-water forces aimed at winning command of the sea, with the other navies being continentalist, interested primarily in coast defense and support of armies and land-based air forces—Germany, France and Italy in European waters; Japan, China and Holland along the periphery of Asia; and Russia on her long Eurasian coastlines.

British naval policy at the Admiralty remained very conservative and material-oriented although the "young Turks" led by Admirals Richmond (who retired in 1930) and K. G. B. Dewar promoted new ideas at the war colleges, and some gradual reforms occurred, thanks to such men as Admiral Lord Chatfield, who was Beatty's flag captain at Jutland and rose to be First Sea Lord, 1933–39. Staff centralization and improvement followed bitter wartime weaknesses with a new Naval Staff College founded by Wemyss in 1919, a new interservice Chiefs of Staff Committee led by Hankey four years later, a Tactical School at Portsmouth in 1924 and the Imperial Defense College under Richmond in 1927. But any service unification was frustrated by the Royal Air Force's refusal to return the Fleet Air Arm to the Navy's full control until 1937. Preoccupied with Jutland and the big battle, especially as it might be fought against Japan, the British minimized strategic studies, ignored the unsolved problems of trade defense save for a smug complacency in the abilities of asdic, rejected amphibious maneuvers because of Gallipoli until 1938, and simply did not develop or appreciate naval aviation or submarines. The battle fleet Fighting Instructions remained thoroughly formalist, though some attention was given to night tactics and destroyer action. Admiralty anti-intellectualism repressed the critical *Naval Review* until 1926, but this could not prevent experimentation at sea, as when Admiral Richmond used his Eastern Fleet to try combined operations off Bombay in 1924 and Admiral Chatfield utilized the carriers of his Mediterranean Fleet in the early 1930s for torpedo air strikes, fleet antiair defenses and at-sea refueling. Convoy was finally accepted again in 1937, but the British simply assumed that they would again command the sea in any future war and resume their 1914 continental strategy of sending the Army and strategic air forces to the aid of France.

The British Empire strategically resembled the pre-1914 situation with the important difference that the Pacific possessions could probably not be defended against an aggressive Japan. Politically, also, Ireland obtained its independence after a five-year civil war in 1921; ten years later Britain granted semi-autonomous "Commonwealth" status to Canada, South Africa, Australia and New Zealand; and over these decades Egypt, Palestine, Iraq and India began to enjoy increasingly liberal home rule. Encouraging these dominions to develop their own defenses, Britain drastically reduced its overseas garrisons in order to concentrate on Europe and the Mediterranean. The British agreed that France should control the Western Mediterranean, and Britain should dominate the rest, including the sea routes to India via Gibraltar, Malta, Alexandria, Aden, Simonstown in South Africa, Trincomalee on Ceylon, Singapore and Hong Kong. Britain planned to meet any Japanese attack by holding Singapore with its 15" coastal guns until fleet reinforcements could be dispatched from the home squadrons. This strategy depended upon peace in Europe, a growing unlikelihood as Germany and Japan cemented their alliance in the late 1930s. As the British inability to defend their Far Eastern possessions became evident, the latter could only turn to the United States for possible assistance.

Britain's wartime ally, France, had even less interest in naval reforms or even naval construction, a reluctance which embroiled the French Navy in serious political struggles from 1924. Subordinated to a rather passive Superior Council of National Defense in 1921 and an ever-dominant Army, the Navy even lost its air arm to a new independent Air Ministry for four turbulent years, 1928–32. French postwar naval doctrine followed the prewar arguments, with the traditionalists advocating battleships, especially when Germany and Italy began building them in 1931, and the more material-minded of them like Admiral Daveluy following *jeune école* thinking for coast defense against Germany and Italy. The reform-minded Naval Ministry of Georges Leygues from 1917 to 1933 tried to accommodate these needs and treaty limitations by first confining construction to *jeune école* fast cruisers, torpedo boats, destroyers and subs and then four new battleships. Historical strategist Admiral Castex tried to resolve these doctrinal dilemmas in a five-volume work on strategic theory between 1929 and 1939 and as commandant of the School of Naval Warfare and Center for Higher Naval Studies and founder of the unified College of Higher National Defense Studies. But real rearmament did not begin until 1938 when Admiral J. L. X. François Darlan led the initiation of a general construction program which included two carriers. This would prove to be too little and too late for France to develop a respectable continental fleet against both Germany and Italy.

The French overseas empire compounded many of the problems surrounding French naval doctrine and strategy. Not only did France need to defend its vital possessions along the North African coast, but it had responsibilities for much of tropical Africa, Madagascar, Somaliland, mandated Syria and Lebanon, Indochina and several islands scattered throughout the world. In the Mediterranean, Franco-Spanish forces completed the pacification of Morocco in the Riff War of the early 1920s and later mop-up operations. To counter Italy in North Africa and complement Bizerte, France built the new naval base of Mers-el-Kebir at Algerian Oran and erected the Mareth defense line across southeastern

Tunisia. Adjacent Casablanca and Dakar remained as French African bastions on the Atlantic coast, but the French depended utterly on British naval protection in the Middle East. The far-flung Asian islands and French Indochina created such impossible strategic demands that Admiral Castex recommended the abandonment of North Africa, the Middle East, Indochina and possibly Madagascar in the face of any major attack. However realistic, such a viewpoint offended French honor and prestige, leading the Navy to sacrifice additional material effort from the prime European arena to these strategically unimportant regions. France, the continental power, at her peril resisted the growing independence movements in these areas to persist in her dreams of imperial grandeur.

Italy also returned to its basic prewar strategic stance, save for the fact that the fascist regime of Benito Mussolini—an inlander from Piedmont—had little sympathy for the needs of the Navy and stifled any new construction and much-needed administrative reforms until 1926. Naval Minister Admiral Thaon de Revel and the new Institute of Naval War, founded in 1921, unsuccessfully fought Mussolini's separate air force of 1923 which embraced the Navy's rather considerable air arm. Consequently, the admirals could not get the aircraft carriers, offensive torpedo planes, adequate reconnaissance planes and defensive fighters that they badly needed. The Washington treaty forbade new battleships, but Italy competed with France in fast cruisers, destroyers and torpedo boats and from 1930 in new replacement battleships. The Italians generally outclassed the French in the Mediterranean, but their admirals— very pro-British from the wartime experience—looked only to protecting the sea route to Libya and took no interest in distant operations, trade protection, sealift of war materials, counterblockade techniques, *guerre de course*, night fighting tactics or foreign technological progress in asdic and radar. Trapped within the Mediterranean, Italy's navy did little to prepare for the war toward which Mussolini drifted during the 1930s.

The Italian Empire also remained confined to the middle sea, save for Mussolini's extension of it into East Africa. France held the Western Mediterranean and tried unsuccessfully to build up the Yugoslav Navy to counter Italy in the Adriatic. During a diplomatic incident with Greece in 1923 Italian naval forces bombarded and briefly occupied Corfu, after which Mussolini wrested disputed Fiume from Yugoslavia and gained virtual control over Albania's economy and military, which included the fortification of Valona on the east side of the Otranto Strait. Mussolini used the "Italian Aegean Islands" (Rhodes and the Dodecanese) to seek Middle Eastern oil, brutally pacified restive Libya and in the 1930s decided to conquer Ethiopia as part of a new Roman-type North African Empire. Directly antagonistic to Britain and France, Mussolini's preliminary moves prompted the reinforced British Mediterranean Fleet to shift from exposed Malta to Alexandria and Eastern units to Aden to block both ends of the Red Sea. When Italy invaded Ethiopia in October 1935 and the League of Nations imposed retaliatory economic sanctions on Italy, Britain refused to enforce them or close the Suez Canal without full French support and use of their bases at Bizerte and Toulon. Also, any war with Italy would weaken the Anglo-French navies now needed to check Japan and Germany, especially after the latter denounced the Locarno pact and reoccupied the Rhineland in March 1936. Two months later the Italian Army completed the conquest of militarily backward Ethiopia but at the complete sacrifice of British friendship. Mussolini turned to court Germany and in April 1939 occupied and annexed Albania. But should war come, Mussolini lay in a vulnerable strategic position, for 70 percent of Italy's imported raw materials had to pass through British-held Suez and Gibraltar. He would require the naval help of the Germans, whom his admirals detested.

Germany, which did not turn fascist until Hitler's takeover in 1933, similarly regarded the Navy as outside the mainstream of national life. Save for the abortive Kapp putsch of 1920, the Navy remained apolitical and loyal to the Weimar and Nazi governments, both of which subordinated naval activities to the continental army. Restricted by Versailles to a few old surface ships for coast defense, the Germans used clandestine means to develop U-boats and aircraft through private industry. A naval war college course also developed illegally, but the former Allies had neither the will nor the means to enforce the Versailles dictates. Severely criticized for its blue-water aspirations under Tirpitz, the Navy planned only for mine warfare and coast defense in the Baltic against Poland and France. But with the administrative reform of the Navy in 1928 under its new Commander in Chief, Admiral Erich Raeder (Hipper's chief of staff at Jutland), the Weimar Navy began to follow the writings of Vice Admiral Wolfgang Wegener for a *guerre de course* fleet in the *jeune école* tradition. New torpedo boats, then cruisers and finally three 11,000-plus-ton, 28-knot, 11"-gunned "pocket battleships" preceded new U-boat construction under Hitler. As *Führer,* Hitler controlled all German defenses and followed Mussolini in creating a separate Air Force *(Luftwaffe)* which absorbed and downgraded naval aviation. From 1934 Hitler saw France and Russia as the enemy and so countered French battleship construction with the two *Scharnhorst*s and two 42,000-ton, 31-knot, 15"-gunned *Bismarck*s, all of them driven by fast turbines. Anxious for British neutrality, Hitler concluded the Anglo-German naval pact of 1935 and promised his admirals as late as 1938 that he would avoid a conflict with Britain at all costs.

The empire of the Third Reich remained oriented to the continent of

Europe, and even the likelihood of war with Britain kept the Navy's strategy devoted to a *guerre de course* philosophy. Surface ship construction, culminating in the Z-Plan in the winter of 1938–39, aimed at thirteen battleships, four carriers, thirty-three cruisers and many destroyers by 1944 to raid enemy shipping individually and in small "task forces"—a concept with which the Germans had experimented for several years. U-boat construction—267 subs under the Z-Plan—would be used by their commander, Commodore Karl Doenitz, in massed, radio-coordinated "wolf packs" in a World War I-style "tonnage war" to blockade the British Isles. Unfortunately for Germany, its limited shipbuilding facilities and oil reserves were divided in equal priority between battleships and subs with inadequate quantities of each to eliminate the mass of merchant tonnage. Furthermore, modern technology had already neutralized the surface raider, but Hitler continued to support his prestigious battleships. The Navy manned all coastal fortifications, but did nearly nothing to develop marines, service forces or amphibious tactics, although fleet units did participate in the seizure of Lithuanian Memel in March 1939. Hitler continued to ignore the warnings of Admiral Raeder about the lack of German naval preparedness for a war with Britain, and in April 1939 he abrogated the Anglo-German treaty of 1935. By this time, both nations lay in the grip of another arms race, so that Hitler made another unexpected diplomatic shift by signing a nonaggression pact with Soviet Russia. The unpredictable dictatorships were pushing Europe toward the resumption of total war.

Communist Russia followed continental Germany and Italy in using the Navy for coast defense but also seeking a prestigious small surface fleet, while the Mahan-influenced former tsarist officers yielded to a Red-inspired naval strategy of *guerre de course (molodaia shkola)* based on the submarine. To exploit Russia's vast interior position against the Germans in the Baltic, Anglo-Turkish forces in the Black and the Japanese in the Pacific, the erratic Five-Year plans for economic recovery assisted the completion of the White Sea Canal which in 1933 connected the White, Baltic and Caspian seas via a system of lakes and rivers, and the Northern Sea Route gradually developed to the Far East from 1927. The Baltic Fleet remained as the principal arm of the "Naval Forces of the Red Army" with one battleship, eight cruisers, a light minefield, an eight-boat submarine barrier, seaplanes and coastal fortifications commanding the Gulf of Finland and the approaches to Kronstadt and Leningrad. Light naval forces comprised the Black, Northern and Pacific fleets. In 1933–35 dictator Joseph Stalin, confronted with the menace of Germany, concluded alliances with France and Czechoslovakia, restored traditional naval ranks, and initiated new cruiser, destroyer and submarine construction for a balanced fleet. In 1938 the bloody Stalinist purge of former tsarist officers and his own enemies deprived Russia of its ablest naval officers. Yet, the next year he ordered his new Naval Commissar Admiral Nikolai G. Kuznetsov to lay down a surface fleet of coastal battleships, cruisers and even carriers to be covered by land-based aircraft. Though designed as a deterrent force, such a navy would never have the real prestige of a powerful Red Army. Russia's vacillating interwar naval doctrine thus resembled Hitler's, and both were baptized in the Spanish crisis.

The opposing forces of the Spanish Civil War (1936–39), the pro-Communist "Republican" (or "Loyalist") government and the pro-fascist "Nationalist" forces of General Francisco Franco, received most of their outside assistance by sea. The Spanish Navy, torn internally by the civil issues, nevertheless remained under general Republican control to blockade Franco's main Nationalist Army in Morocco during the summer of 1936. Alarmed by reports of Republican terrorism, the democracies refused aid to the government, whereupon Russia dispatched "volunteers" from the Black Sea to Barcelona and other east coast ports. But Franco used a troop airlift and dissension within the Republican Navy to break the blockade in September and establish himself in southern Spain, with access to the sea at Seville and Cádiz. Germany hastened two pocket battleships and other ships plus air and army "volunteers" to support Franco, who began to develop his own navy which blockaded Republican ports in November. This effort succeeded in hindering Russian merchant ships en route to Spain, a weakness that taught Stalin the efficacy of surface warships. Early in 1937 Britain led France, Germany and Italy in the creation of a four-power naval patrol to thwart intervention in Spain, but the belligerents' aircraft occasionally attacked these vessels, leading to British protests and the bombardment of the Republican port of Almeria by the German pocket battleship *Deutschland* in May. Worse, Italian subs operating out of Naples and Majorca in August began sinking ships bound for Republican ports, leading to Anglo-French antisub measures that finally stopped the practice early in 1938. Germany and Italy then quit the nonintervention patrol and aided Franco so successfully that they could withdraw their major naval units altogether. Early in 1939 Franco's forces took Barcelona and Madrid, ending the war in a victory for fascism. At least Anglo-French warships had acted in concert for the first time since World War I, and the British pressured Portugal to end aid to Franco and renew her traditional alliance with Britain in 1939.

In Asia, China remained at the center of the endless political rivalries of the great powers for fifteen years after the Washington conference guaranteed the "open door." In that treaty year of 1922 a British gunboat rescued President Sun Yat-sen at Canton in the growing civil strife between Nationalists, Communists and warlords that threatened the life of the young republic. Renewed Chinese piracy between Hong Kong and Shanghai led to British-escorted coastal convoys, and Yangtze bandits brought on gunboat patrols by the British, Americans, Japanese and French. The general vulnerability of Western and Japanese lives, property, enclaves and legations to the political chaos of the country could only be met by interventions of the powers, as early in 1927 when no fewer than twenty-one cruisers plus lesser vessels from seven nations concentrated at Shanghai with a 40,000-man Anglo-Indian landing force to protect their interests. In March British and American warships engaged Nationalist Chinese forces to cover the evacuation of foreigners from beleaguered Nanking, and a year later Japan placed an expeditionary force ashore at Tsingtao. Whereas Britain and America only policed troubled waters in China, Japan and Russia had more grandiose designs. In 1924 Russia annexed Mongolia and five years later began to fight Nationalist forces over the railway in Manchuria; in October 1929 five Soviet gunboats sank three Chinese gunboats on the Amur River. And Japan had even greater interests in Manchuria.

Japan, gradually becoming fascistic and dictatorial between 1931 and the rise to power of General Hideki Tojo in 1941, focused its revived expansionism on China. Dominated by its Army warrior class, Japan planned to create a "Greater East Asia Co-Prosperity Sphere" centered on the Asian mainland, with the Imperial Navy in support. Japanese air forces remained separate and basically tactical; the Army's aviation was trained during the 1920s by the French, the Navy's by a British naval mission. In 1931 Japan suddenly invaded and occupied Manchuria, and the next year Japanese warships and carrier planes covered a landing of troops at Shanghai until an Anglo-American naval force arrived and the United States Fleet concentrated at Hawaii, pressuring the Japanese to withdraw. But the League of Nations could not prevent the establishment of a Japanese puppet state in Manchuria—the consequence of the Great Depression and the general apathy of world opinion toward intervention. Japan then quit the League, abrogated its treaty commitments and in 1936 allied with Nazi Germany against Soviet Russia. The next year Japan invaded China to begin the second Sino-Japanese War. The German-trained Chinese Nationalist Army of Chiang Kai-shek resisted stubbornly, but could not prevent the seizure of Shantung and Peking; Shanghai and Nanking fell after a barrage from naval guns and carrier planes. Despite the shelling of two British gunboats by Japanese artillery and the sinking of the American gunboat *Panay* by naval aircraft on the Yangtze in December 1937, neither nation actively intervened. The next year Japanese river craft, aircraft and troops pressed up the Yangtze to take Hankow in October, the same month that an amphibious assault took Canton. Then, as the ground war stalemated at the foothills of the Himalayas, Russia fought an un-declared war on the Mongolian-Manchurian frontier during 1938–39 that decisively checked the Japanese in that quarter.

Japanese naval policy remained defensive throughout these events. Centralized under an Imperial Headquarters in 1937, the Navy retained its ancient mission of transporting and supporting the Army and pro-tecting its lines of communication to Asia, also the forward bases at Port Arthur, Dairen and Formosa. With Japan's strategy oriented to the continent, the islands of the Pacific became mere appendages and were consequently never fortified during the 1920s and 1930s: the Kuriles, Bonins, Volcanos, Ryukyus, Marianas, Carolines and Marshalls. Should the Western navies, particularly that of the United States, intervene, they would be whittled down in day and night attacks by Japanese subs and destroyers—both with superior torpedoes, by "flying squadrons" of cruisers and carriers with dive- and torpedo-bombers, and by land-based planes and seaplanes from the mandated islands, where airfield construction slowly began in 1934. Once the approaching American battle fleet had been scaled down, the traditional line of battleships would engage the enemy in the Western Pacific in the manner of Tsushima. Despite the arguments of Admiral Isoroku Yamamoto and others against such a conservative reliance on battleships, the Imperial Japanese Navy did not plan for long-range blue-water operations and did not even begin at-sea refueling of major warships until 1941. It developed superior optics and star shells for night actions, but had no radar and remained deficient in tactical, antiaircraft and offensive carrier techniques. Even as a continental navy, it lacked a balanced doctrine: amphibious and river practices were impressive in support of the Army, but no attention was ever given commerce defense or *guerre de course,* with Japan's excellent subs being employed as fleet vessels.

The European powers, becoming increasingly preoccupied with Ger-many, gradually came to depend on American leadership in balancing Japanese power in the Pacific. Britain's communications between Trin-comalee in Ceylon and Hong Kong improved markedly with the opening of Singapore's new base facilities in 1938, but the French in Indochina could do nothing when the Japanese in 1939 took Hainan Island in the Gulf of Tonkin and the French-claimed Spratly Islands in the South China Sea. The only outside communications of Chiang Kai-shek lay from Kunming overland by rail to French Haiphong and by automobile on the British Burma Road, making both potential Japanese targets. The Dutch in the East Indies tried to do more, since the Royal Nether-land Navy was usually concentrated in the Far East to police the islands, operating out of Batavia and British Singapore. In response to

Japan's thrust into China in 1937, Holland concentrated three (two brand-new) of its four light cruisers plus destroyers, subs and mine vessels in the Indies and two years later authorized three new 28,000-ton battle cruisers to counter Japan's heavy cruisers. The United States planned to defend the Philippines with the Asiatic Fleet and fixed fortifications around Manila Bay (and at Guam and Wake) until the main fleet units could sortie to their relief from Hawaii—the essence of the "Orange Plan." But both the Asiatic Fleet and coastal guns remained woefully understrength, as the United States attempted to adopt a realistic unilateral strategy throughout these years.

The United States retreated from its European wartime involvement almost as suddenly as it had entered it and concentrated its naval power in the Pacific. The United States Fleet, created in 1922, was comprised of the twelve newest battleships in the Pacific and the six older ones in the Atlantic, but beyond this the Americans remained rigidly isolationistic—despite the warnings of the Navy's General Board and naval publicists like Hector C. Bywater and William Howard Gardiner. The naval economy practiced by both the prosperity and depression Presidential administrations of the 1920s and 1930s kept the U. S. Navy from growing to full treaty strength and from maintaining peak efficiency, but left it strong enough to continue policing the Caribbean and to deter Japan. A "special service squadron" of very old cruisers and gunboats operated out of Panama to support Marine Corps landings and naval shows of force in troubled Mexico, Haiti, the Dominican Republic, Panama, Honduras, Cuba, Nicaragua, Costa Rica and El Salvador, complemented by British units and on two occasions by Canadian warships. No foreign power, however, intervened in the Chaco War between Bolivia and Paraguay in 1932–35. The American government rested its continental defenses and those of Hawaii and the Canal Zone on wartime railway and fixed guns and antiaircraft guns and the warships existing at the time of the Washington treaty. President Franklin D. Roosevelt in 1933 decided to concentrate on domestic affairs, to end the interventions in Latin America and—particularly through the Congressional campaign of Carl Vinson—to provide funds to improve fleet upkeep and to build closer to treaty strength. But he steadfastly refused general naval rearmament until 1938 and the wake of the *Panay* incident, hoping mightily to avoid antagonizing Japan.

American interwar naval policy reflected the U. S. Navy's firm belief that it would eventually fight Japan, even though inadequate funding— until after 1938—prevented the practical application of the new theories for fighting a war across the vast Pacific. If any one officer dominated these years, it was Admiral William V. Pratt, former wartime planner who attended and supported the Washington and 1930 London arms conferences, held the presidency of the Naval War College in 1925–27 and all the major battle fleet commands, and was Chief of Naval Operations, 1931–33. The Jutland-battleship mentality continued to dominate official American naval thought, but Pratt replaced the simple battleship war gaming at the War College with studies of amphibious operations, logistics, war plans and international relations, all fundamental for the war against Japan. These reforms did not survive his tenure at the College, but other elements of the fleet pursued several of them. The U. S. Marines, used as regular infantry during the war, built upon their pre-war base defense mission to fashion a new role of advance base landing assaults from the theories of island-hopping of its Lieutenant Colonel Earl H. Ellis. Amphibious doctrine improved rapidly after the creation of the Fleet Marine Force in 1933, first in maneuvers and tactical manuals, then with close support aircraft, tracked amphibious landing craft and attack transports over 1938–41. The fast aircraft carrier, though ostensibly a reconnaissance vessel, emerged as an offensive strike weapon through the administrative leadership of Admiral William A. Moffet and the operational direction of Admiral Joseph Mason Reeves. The latter, under the direct command of Admiral Pratt, first used carriers with dive- and torpedo-bombers effectively in independent offensive attack operations in the fleet problem of 1929. Thereafter, the naval aviators ignored the Jutland school to develop their own formulae for fast carrier operations to fight the Japanese fleet, and had several new carriers built during the 1930s for such trials. Commerce warfare received little attention, for American cruisers were seriously weakened qualitatively by treaty economy measures, and submarines were earmarked for scouting and attacking surface warships. The large sub of the 1920s yielded to an all-purpose boat of some 1400 tons in the 1930s which could cruise 12,000 miles, dive faster, lay mines, torpedo ships and sink merchantmen or provide shore bombardment with a 5″ deck gun. Nearly nothing took place in the crucial area of logistical doctrine until 1940 when base facilities began to be expanded at Pearl Harbor and battleships began to refuel at sea (carriers in 1939).

The U. S. Navy expected a war with Japan, that it would begin with a sneak attack, and that Hawaii was the mostly likely target—so that several fleet maneuvers took place in the 1930s anticipating such an attack. Indeed, in 1939–40 the Japanese initiated new base construction in the Marshall Islands and moved a new fleet into the mandates to operate from Kwajalein in the Marshalls, Saipan in the Marianas, and the Palaus and especially Truk in the Carolines. Japan continued to fight in China and created a new fleet in the Kurile Islands which could watch Russia, but fleet activities in the Central Pacific were clearly directed against the United States.

From the summer of 1939, however, the attention of the Western world focused on Europe, where the breakdown of the Versailles arrangements and the postwar treaties threatened to result in renewed total war.

## ANGLO-GERMAN WAR

Europe's plunge back into war followed the continued aggressiveness of fascist Germany and Italy and the appeasement policies of Britain and France, the virtual isolation of Soviet Russia and the dogged neutrality and noninvolvement of the United States. Hitler's policies led to a new system of alliances throughout Europe from 1935: France and Russia against the "Axis" of Germany, Italy and distant Japan, with Hitler's armed diplomacy annexing Austria and Czechoslovakia in 1938–39. Russia then made its nonaggression pact with Hitler, but France and Britain prepared for war and guaranteed the integrity of Poland after Hitler seized Lithuanian Memel in March 1939. In the Mediterranean, Turkey sided with the Anglo-French camp, having accepted naval parity with Greece in 1930, refortified the Dardanelles from 1936, and in the spring of 1939 annexed Syrian Alexandretta just as Mussolini conquered Albania, an action which brought Anglo-French guarantees of Greek security. Miscalculating that the Allies would not protect Poland any more than they had Czechoslovakia, Hitler invaded Poland in September 1939. Britain and France declared war, though all the other powers proclaimed their neutrality, a luxury that only delayed their inevitable absorption into the totality of this modern war. The delay was made possible by the simple fact that World War II began as a decidedly limited conflict primarily between Britain and Germany.

Both of these powers, despite their recent buildups, had to rely on emergency measures to wage war upon the sea, but the same World War I strategic relationships in the North and Baltic seas resumed. From Scapa Flow—poorly defended and only accepted as the main base over Rosyth one year before—the majority of Britain's 7 battleships, 2 battle cruisers, 4 aircraft carriers, 17 cruisers, 35 destroyers, 16 submarines and many lesser craft in home waters joined the Royal Air Force in dominating the North Sea. The Germans avoided the immediate wartime blockade by sending 2 pocket battleships and 39 U-boats to sea as commerce raiders just prior to the invasion of Poland, leaving one pocket and 2 regular battleships, 8 cruisers and 34 destroyers blockaded along the North Sea coast but equally free to control the Baltic. But, unlike in World War I, the Germans had no intention of developing another blue-water high seas fleet. The British Western Approaches had been weakened by the release of two Royal Navy bases in southern Ireland to the new Irish republic earlier in the year, but the French Navy had a raiding force of 2 new battleships, one carrier, 3 cruisers and 10 destroyers at Brest. Allied maritime communications in the Mediterranean and South Atlantic enjoyed—with Italy's neutrality—absolute security behind a total of 6 battleships, one carrier, 45 cruisers, 72 destroyers and 57 submarines. But such overwhelming superiority at sea could do little to check Hitler's *Blitzkrieg* into Poland.

The German thrust also involved Russia, as the armies of each carved up helpless Poland within one month and then sought to dominate the Baltic. While German fleet units blockaded Polish ports (though several Polish destroyers and submarines escaped from Gdynia to England), German merchant ships operated out of Russian Murmansk and a Russian river flotilla supported the Red Army's drive up the Dnieper River to Pinsk and destroyed the Polish flotilla on the Pripet River. The Russians then virtually annexed Estonia, Latvia and Lithuania and established Baltic Fleet units at their ports. When Finland refused Russia the use of its naval bases at Hango in the Gulf of Finland and Petsamo in the Arctic, in late November Russia invaded Finland. Isolated from outside help by the Germans in this "Winter War," Finland threw up a defense line in the south, concentrated its small navy at Turku (Abo) to protect communications to neutral Sweden, and used mines and subs to attack Russian shipping in the Gulf. The Russians countered with minesweepers and their own subs (supplied by German surface ships) and amphibious assaults that took several Finnish islands in the eastern Gulf. Russia's ground offensives into Finland failed in December, but succeeded two months later. Finland capitulated in March 1940, ceding Viborg and the adjacent territory as far as Lake Ladoga and leasing Hango to Russia. When Russia annexed more lands to the Ukraine three months later and created a new Danube River flotilla to defend them, the two aggressors had settled into a precarious balance of power in Northern Europe. Russia could then accelerate its own military preparations, and Germany could concentrate on the Allies.

Following the fall of Poland, the conflict became a "phony war" as Hitler unrealistically waited for Britain and France to recognize his conquest and make peace. To avoid further antagonizing them, he refrained from attacking the French Maginot Line or the British Expeditionary Force which had arrived to augment it, kept his powerful *Luftwaffe* out of British skies, and even placed severe operating restrictions on his few active commerce raiders. Hoping to placate France, Hitler forbade his warships to attack French shipping for several weeks. And knowing British sensitivity to international law, he ordered his U-boats to observe the strict protocols of the 1936 submarine convention to warn unarmed merchantmen before attacking them. But when the *U-30* mistakenly and without warning sank the British passenger liner *Athenia* on the first day of the war, the Allies naturally assumed that Germany intended to prosecute unrestricted submarine warfare as in 1917–18. And as subsequent victims radioed for help, Hitler progressively lifted the restrictions on his boats. But Hitler's naval strategy of *guerre de course* still had impressive results. The *U-29* sank the British carrier *Courageous* in the Irish Sea in September, and the next month Lieutenant Commander Gunther Prien took his *U-47* inside the harbor defenses of Scapa Flow to sink the battleship *Royal Oak* with nearly 800 of its crew. German ships, subs and planes sowed ground-magnetic and moored-contact mines off the British coast which claimed 114 merchant ships, 15 minesweepers and 2 destroyers in the first six months of the war. Hitler's surface raiders had less success. In December, after sinking several merchantmen, the pocket battleship *Graf Spee* was mauled by 3 British and New Zealand cruisers in the battle of the River Plate and had to be scuttled off neutral Montevideo, Uruguay, to avoid internment or destruction by more British fleet units converging on the area. Similar fears also caused the termination of a brief sortie into the North Atlantic by the battleships *Scharnhorst* and *Gneisenau.*

Perplexed by Allied adamancy and countermeasures, Hitler interfered with Admiral Raeder by altering his naval program. He cautiously restricted any unnecessary risk to his few heavy surface ships as raiders, cut back the priorities of the prewar Z-Plan to only subs, and thwarted the implementation of new additional authorizations for U-boat construction. Nevertheless, Admiral Doenitz, directing U-boat operations from shore and first experimenting successfully with group "wolf pack" tactics late in 1939, could boast of his boats sinking, between September 1939 and March 1940, a total of 222 merchantmen aggregating 765,000 tons, at the cost of 18 of his original 56 boats. Surface raiders, mines and aircraft claimed another 181 merchant ships totaling nearly 540,000 tons. And Hitler discovered the fallacy of his adherence to international law when in February the British destroyer *Cossack* ignored that law to enter neutral Norwegian waters and liberate some 300 British prisoners from the German supply ship *Altmark.* With each Allied success, Hitler's impatience mounted.

In fact, Britain and France were determined to frustrate Hitler in every possible way, and the "phony war" gained them invaluable time to press new construction and try to overcome serious tactical deficiencies. But neither navy displayed much strategic innovativeness at the outset, neither the French Navy under Admiral Darlan whose government merely assumed that the economic blockade would defeat Germany, nor the Royal Navy under the reappointed First Lord of the Admiralty Winston Churchill and First Sea Lord Admiral Sir A. Dudley P. R. Pound which recommitted old errors. The renewed reluctance to adopt defensive convoys led to the same World War I preference for offensive hunt-and-kill operations. Convoys were adopted, but only in small sizes, dispersed in the open ocean and escorted by vessels poor in asdic, depth charges and antiaircraft guns. The convoys were further confined to the environs of the British Isles with limited escorting from Freetown in West Africa, from Nova Scotia and in the Mediterranean. The British reinstituted mine barrages in the Dover Strait (successful) and between Scotland and Ireland (unsuccessful) and prepared to repeat the North Sea mine barrage (to have equal lack of success as in 1918) and to aerially mine the mouths of Germany's rivers (with some success). The Royal Navy was not prepared to deal with German magnetic mines or surfaced U-boat night attacks, both of which had been employed in 1918 by the Germans. The unproved Q-ships took to the sea with absolutely no effect. Finally, in the crucial areas of amphibious warfare and naval aviation, the British also erred. They actually closed down their tiny training office of combined operations, and the Fleet Air Arm was so deficient in equipment from its interwar subordination to the Royal Air Force that it had to depend on that service for much antisub work. The Navy's air arm did not develop real antisub techniques, and the RAF would not commit enough land-based bombers to attack German anchorages.

Still, the energetic Churchill sought a viable maritime strategy to turn the German flank just as he had sought to do in World War I. The original continental stance had placed the British Army in France in a passive role as part of the "phony war," while Churchill urged the cultivation of continued Italian neutrality to keep the Mediterranean quiet. This meant the Baltic would be the logical place to strike Germany, and Churchill and his admirals envisioned a fleet sortie thence to cut Germany's iron ore trade with Scandinavia, create a new front and perhaps convince Russia to join the Allied cause. But as the plan gained momentum at the Admiralty late in 1939, serious reservations began to surface, especially from Admiral Pound. Without adequate air cover—which the RAF could not provide at such extreme ranges—the fleet would be at the mercy of the *Luftwaffe* as well as of U-boats, mines and coast artillery. As the project was gradually abandoned early in 1940, Churchill and the admirals considered plans to ignore Norwegian neutrality by occupying the sources of Scandinavian ore near Narvik and/or mining Norwegian waters to stop German shipping.

The niceties of international law thus evaporated just like the precarious naval arms controls of the interwar years as the powers again faced the harsh necessities of total war. The British could not respect Norwegian neutrality if Germany was to be blockaded in the Baltic, and since German *guerre de course* required advanced bases for the resupply of its U-boats, German agents were laying the basis for this use of ports in neutral Spain. The Axis powers of course had nothing but contempt for neutrality, as Norway, Denmark, the Netherlands and Belgium were soon to discover in Northern Europe, while Mussolini in the Mediterranean and the Japanese militarists in the Far East grew anxious to reap the benefits of Allied unpreparedness. The United States repealed its neutrality laws in late 1939 in order to supply the Allies, and Soviet Russia could only hope that Hitler would refrain from turning eastward until its rearmament was completed. Total world war finally resumed in the spring of 1940 as Hitler's *Blitzkrieg* overran Western Europe.

# 16
## World War II,
## 1940–1945

*History has conclusively demonstrated the inability of a state with even a single continental frontier to compete in naval development with one that is insular, although of smaller population and resources.*

—MAHAN

## THE AXIS OFFENSIVE

The total warfare of 1918 resumed from the spring of 1940 as if no long interlude had occurred, but in fact Hitler, Mussolini and Tojo represented the last attempt of authoritarian dictatorships to restore European (and Japanese) political hegemony along traditional imperial lines. The totality of the new democratic and communistic ideologies introduced by Wilson and Lenin found relentless champions in Roosevelt and Stalin, while the old war-horse Churchill in a very real sense superintended over the sacrifice of the old and mighty British Empire as it initially bore the brunt of the Axis onslaught. Modern machine weapons also promised—but only promised—to transform the face of war, though not until the B-29 very-long-range bomber, V-2 interrange rocket and airborne atomic bomb could be produced and utilized in really great quantities. The limitations of the technology of the early 1940s thus denied the use of any such strategic panaceas, so that the antagonists relied on the same continental and maritime strategies of their many predecessors in history. For the Allies, this meant winning command of the sea—but now also its air.

The dictatorships enjoyed the same strengths and weaknesses of every major despotism in history, only they were compounded by the new technology. Isolated egotists sensitive to any criticism, the fascist strong men by their overcentralized control not only thwarted staff work and effective coalition cooperation, but stifled their scientists and engineers from producing enough new machines of war. All supported continental objectives and strategies, kept their armies (and new air forces) as the senior service and failed to appreciate fully their navies. In Germany, Hitler personally ran everything through the Supreme Command of the Armed Forces, a weak staff body which included only a few naval officers, and the Naval War Staff got only whatever Admiral Raeder could get for it from Hitler. Hitler so hindered his scientists that he did not press for jet aircraft, the strategic rocket or submarine schnorkel breathing device until 1943. In Italy, Mussolini and the Army similarly dominated the Supreme Command, under which an efficient but overcentralized and unimaginative naval department functioned. In Japan, Emperor Hirohito generally followed the advice of Tojo's Supreme War Council, to which the Naval General Staff contributed a junior voice. Soviet Russia was run by Stalin through the Red Army, to which the independent Commissariat of the Navy (created in 1937) was subordinate, and in 1941 Stalin reassigned only recently removed political commissars to each fleet unit —so suspect did the Navy remain to him.

The democracies again centralized in wartime but with sufficient flexibility to encourage Allied cooperation, good staff work and scientific creativity. And both Great Britain and the United States enjoyed sufficiently dynamic and naval-experienced heads of state to develop an effective maritime strategy in combination with a suspicious continental Russia and the new strategic air forces. Winston Churchill, First Lord of the Admiralty in 1911–15 and 1939–40, in April and May 1940 succeeded to supreme command in Britain as head of the new War Cabinet, Prime Minister, head of a central committee of scientists and virtually his own First Lord. Franklin Roosevelt, Assistant Secretary of the American Navy from 1913 to 1920 and President since 1933, as Commander-in-Chief created the Joint Chiefs of Staff to direct the war and the Office of Scientific Research and Development to create new weapons. Such strong political leaders occasionally meddled in strategic and scientific planning, but generally relied on their generals, admirals and air marshals who cooperated through the Allied Combined Chiefs of Staff and with an expanded military-industrial-scientific complex directed by experienced industrial and scientific managers. This Anglo-American system thus developed long-range programs which produced a host of new devices, especially for the war at sea: radars, radios and loran for navigation; high-frequency radio direction finders, sonar and magnetic airborne detectors to help locate enemy ships and planes; new aircraft and warships, such as the tractored amphibious landing craft (notably the Dukw); antiaircraft guns and the radio-detonated proximity fuse on antiaircraft shells;

antisub, barrage and aircraft rockets; and finally the atomic bomb. Operational research applied mathematics to achieve statistical analyses of field problems. The greatest hindrance to applying these weapons lay in the tactical conservatism of admirals and generals and their interservice rivalries and anti-civilian biases. But since time favored the Allies, adopted they eventually were.

Between April 1940 and June 1941 the old weapons held the line as Germany and Italy tried to conquer all Western Europe, and Japan to conquer China before Russia and America became involved. Initially, Hitler outflanked Britain in the North Sea by brazenly crossing the Skagerrak in the face of the British Home Fleet at Scapa Flow to invade Norway by sea and air in April 1940 using surface fleet units, twenty-five of Doenitz's U-boats and a newly expanded logistical organization. Norwegian coastal guns and torpedoes sank a German heavy cruiser, but Allied warships and expeditionary forces hastening thence could not dislodge the bridgehead. They did, however, make the Germans pay dearly. In addition to damage inflicted on several fleet units, a British sub forced a light cruiser to be scuttled, Norwegian batteries and British dive-bombers sank another light cruiser, and on April 10 and 13 five British destroyers and then the battleship *Warspite* with nine destroyers and a seaplane combined to sink ten German destroyers and one U-boat at Narvik fjord. All Norway was in German hands by the end of May, Denmark had fallen in one day (April 9), and Sweden stood neutral but isolated. U-boats and surface raiders, covered by the *Luftwaffe,* could now virtually avoid the North Sea to prey on Allied and neutral shipping in the North Atlantic. Whereupon British forces occupied Iceland on May 10.

Encouraged by these northern successes, Hitler now thrust his *Blitzkrieg* westward to take France out of the war. Starting on May 10 the German armies and tactical air forces swept across helpless Holland and Belgium, outflanking the Maginot Line and trapping Franco-Belgian troops and the entire British Expeditionary Force against the Channel at Dunkirk. With the German Navy still battered or committed in Scandinavia, it did not participate in this offensive, so that the French Atlantic Fleet units escaped to the Mediterranean and the small Dutch fleet to England. The *Luftwaffe* aerially mined Allied harbors in April and May, but failed completely to defeat the RAF and the beachhead at Dunkirk, from which some 338,000 Allied troops were evacuated by 861 vessels of the Royal and French navies and private owners between May 28 and June 4. German planes, coastal U-boats and torpedo boats did sink 243 craft, the largest 6 British and 3 French destroyers, but without a real surface fleet and air superiority the Germans could not command the Channel. Italy declared war on June 10, and four days later the Germans took Paris. French naval authorities defended their bases from landward attack as long as possible, enabling Allied vessels to evacuate another 192,000 British and Polish troops plus French warships to England and North Africa. In the meantime, the British lost the carrier *Glorious* and 2 destroyers to the battleships *Gneisenau* and *Scharnhorst,* but not before one of the destroyers and a sub inflicted sufficient damage on both vessels to force them back into the yards for extensive repairs. Italian land-based air strikes forced Anglo-French Mediterranean fleet units to pull back out of range to Gibraltar and Alexandria. But France surrendered to Germany on June 24, giving Hitler key U-boat bases on the Biscay coast to outflank the Western Approaches.

To counter the sudden imbalance in the middle sea and to enable strategic concentration in the Western Approaches à la Kempenfelt and Nelson, the British in June redeployed Home Fleet units to Gibraltar as Force H under Admiral Sir James F. Somerville. At Alexandria lay the Mediterranean Fleet of Admiral Sir Andrew B. Cunningham and the voluntarily inactive exiled French force of one battleship, 4 cruisers and 3 destroyers. When the other French fleet units in northwest Africa proved less cooperative, Force H battleships sank or disabled 3 French battleships at Algerian Mers-el-Kebir on July 3–4; one battleship and 5 destroyers escaped to Toulon. Similarly, four days later, a British carrier and lesser vessels damaged the lone French battleship at Dakar. Unimpressed by the 6-battleship, 105-submarine Italian Navy, Admiral Cunningham used 3 battleships and one carrier with escorts to interrupt Italian communications to Libya and drive back Admiral Angelo Campioni's 2-battleship, 18-cruiser force off Punto Stilo on the Italian Calabrian coast in early July. And an Australian cruiser sank an Italian cruiser north of Crete to help maintain Allied maritime communications. The British had offended French honor by their actions, but France had lost the services of its Navy anyway. The Germans occupied Paris and northwest France, and—by the terms of the "armistice"—a collaborationist government controlled southern France from Vichy, including the remaining fleet units under Admiral Darlan. The French survivors of Dunkirk followed the leadership of General Charles de Gaulle as the "Free French" in England, where their few surviving warships came under British control and the direct command of Admiral Émile Muselier, an undistinguished officer whom Darlan had forced into retirement in 1939. Neither Vichy nor "Free" regimes could really control their far-flung vessels which gradually found their way into the Allied war effort.

Britain, virtually alone, now hastened warship construction, especially of destroyers, to counter the U-boat offensive and prepare to withstand a German cross-Channel invasion attempt. In July 1940 Admiral Doenitz from his new headquarters in France initiated his wolf pack tactics with his U-boats operating through the new Norwegian and French ports. Between June and September his boats sank an average of over 450,000 tons of merchant shipping per month, leading Britain to seek material aid from the United States. President Roosevelt responded in September by transferring fifty World War I-vintage destroyers to Britain in return for the use of British Commonwealth naval and air installations in Newfoundland, Bermuda, British Guiana and the British West Indies. The United States also increased its neutrality patrols in the Western Atlantic and interned several French warships in the French West Indies. But the American government and people were neither willing nor able to give direct assistance to Britain as Hitler laid his invasion plans.

Ironically, Hitler perpetuated his delusions for a negotiated peace until mid-July when he finally authorized Operation Sea Lion. None of the German armed services were enthusiastic about a cross-Channel invasion, with the Navy flatly opposing it in favor of maritime blockade. But the Army took on the project as a virtual river-crossing, with the Navy providing the pontoons and the *Luftwaffe* air cover. None of the services had any real amphibious doctrine or experience; no interservice cooperation developed; the Navy did not have full command of the operation; and the *Luftwaffe* even built its own landing prahms. Indeed, so battered had the Navy been in Norway that it could not begin to command the Channel. *Luftwaffe* chief Hermann Goering accepted the multiple tasks of winning command of the air, interdiction of British land and maritime communications, pre-landing barrage and close air support. So the scheme, despite the buildup along the French coast and mounting British anxieties, was impossible from the beginning, and even before July ended Hitler secretly decided to postpone Sea Lion indefinitely and to invade Russia one year hence. Goering's planes could hammer Britain into submission, but even if that failed the defeat of Russia should convince the British of the futility of further resistance. In reality, Hitler surrendered the strategic initiative, for the RAF turned back the *Luftwaffe* in the Battle of Britain over southern England during August and September, and both air forces commenced their strategic bombing campaigns. On September 17 Hitler officially cancelled Sea Lion, ten days later completed his formal "Axis" with Italy and Japan, and lost the great momentum of the summer *Blitz*.

Though Hitler had failed to break Britain by direct means, he turned to his Navy and Italian partners during the autumn of 1940 to strangle the British in the Atlantic and Mediterranean while he planned for the invasion of Russia. Italian subs joined U-boats in the Atlantic, while seven disguised German auxiliary cruisers and the pocket battleship *Admiral Scheer* successfully attacked Allied shipping in the North and South Atlantic and Indian oceans without being sunk. The German Navy pressed for an active front in the Mediterranean, especially to drive the British from Gibraltar and keep them out of Crete, while Mussolini in September and October invaded Egypt from Libya and Ethiopia, and attacked Greece from Albania. But Franco refused the essential Spanish cooperation for attacking Gibraltar, and the Greek and British armies and air forces repulsed Mussolini—effectively destroying Hitler's faith in him and any real possibility of cooperative Axis planning. And the Royal Navy frustrated Italo-German designs in the middle sea and South Atlantic. In the latter quarter, Vichy French naval forces and diplomatic pressure protected West African Dakar from an Anglo-French naval attack in September, but Churchill had the Free French occupy the Cameroons to help protect Freetown and made plans to occupy the Spanish and Portuguese Canary, Madeira and Azores island groups should Gibraltar fall. Franco's stand made that unnecessary, and British sea lanes to India remained protected by warships operating from South African Simonstown, West African Freetown, the Falkland Islands and Gibraltar. And that base plus Malta and Alexandria enabled the British navy to counterattack against the Italians in the Mediterranean and force Hitler to come to their rescue.

During the autumn, winter and spring of 1940–41, therefore, Cunningham's reinforced Mediterranean Fleet and Somerville's Force H commanded the middle sea while Anglo-Greek ground and air forces counterattacked in North Africa and the Balkans. Cunningham occupied Crete and on November 11 sent Swordfish torpedo-bombers from the new carrier *Illustrious* to attack the main Italian fleet anchorage at Taranto. The twenty-one planes caught the Italians by surprise, sank or bottomed three of their six battleships and got away with only two planes lost. This first dramatic demonstration of offensive carrier air power caused the Italians to remove their fleet units from Taranto to Naples. British warships shelled the Italian army retreating through Albania, and small British forces were able to capture the Italian armies in Egypt, Libya and Ethiopia during the first five months of 1941. In January planes from Malta severely damaged an Italian battleship; in February warships bombarded Genoa and other Italian coastal points; and on March 28–29 Admiral Cunningham with three battleships, one carrier, several cruisers and destroyers defeated a smaller Italian force under Admiral Angelo Iachino off Cape Matapan, southern Greece, sinking three cruisers and two destroyers at the cost of one airplane shot down and a cruiser damaged.

The Italian Navy continued to transport and support the Army in

the Balkans and North Africa, to lay mines around Malta and along
the Italian coast as barriers, to sweep enemy mines, and to operate
submarine and light surface forces against Allied war and merchant
shipping, but the fleet had been effectively neutralized by the British.
Removed to Spezia, the fleet belatedly began to convert a liner into
a carrier and to improve its torpedo planes, without both of which it
could never effectively challenge British heavy fleet units. Worse, oil
shortages nearly immobilized the Navy by midyear. By contrast, the
British Mediterranean Fleet had adopted a new standard fleet tactical
formation: battleships, carriers, cruisers and destroyers in a single
mutually supporting, antiaircraft circular formation. The old line-ahead
of Trafalgar, Tsushima and Jutland thus became obsolete in the face
of enemy air attack.

Without a surface fleet to command the Mediterranean, the Axis
powers could not conquer its periphery, but the German-led land and
air offensives begun in early 1941 nearly succeeded. Land-based
Italian and German air attacks pounded Malta and the ships passing
through it between Gibraltar and Alexandria. They damaged and sank
warships and merchantmen alike, but never with sufficient effect to
discourage the British from continuing to operate through Malta.
German planes based in the Italian Aegean Dodecanese Islands early
in the year dropped aerial mines in the Suez Canal, temporarily closing
it. But the British convoyed men and material around the Cape of
Good Hope to the Red Sea, enabling them in the spring to regain
East Africa and, with Free French help, to drive pro-German troops
from Iraq, Syria and Lebanon. The Italian Navy convoyed the new
German army under General Erwin Rommel to North Africa without much interference, until the night of April 15 when four British
destroyers attacked and sank a convoy of three Italian destroyers and
three (of five) transports with their German troops near Kerkenah
Banks off the Tunisian coast, losing one of their own number. Rommel
mounted an offensive in North Africa, but could not dislodge the
British troops at Tobruk in eastern Libya, reinforced by sea with an
Australian division. Holding in all these places, the British, however,
yielded to a new German ground-air offensive which overran Yugoslavia and Greece in April. The Royal Navy evacuated Allied troops
from the continent and enabled the small Royal Hellenic Navy to
escape to Alexandria. Neither could the Allies hold Crete, which the
Germans took by airborne assault in May, although British naval forces
prevented German reinforcements from reaching Crete by sea until all
Allied troops could be evacuated by the Navy. Both sides suffered
heavy losses in the battles for Greece and Crete, heavy German air
attacks and Italian subs and motorboats sinking five British cruisers

and six destroyers and damaging a great many more warships, including a carrier and three battleships.

The German attack on British communications gradually improved during early 1941, but enemy resistance and Spanish neutrality effectively delayed Hitler as he prepared his major effort against Russia. Goering's aircraft on Crete and Rommel's tanks before Tobruk threatened to close and even capture the Suez Canal, Alexandria and the oil-rich Persian Gulf area. But heavy losses suffered in the airborne assault on Crete persuaded Hitler to abandon a similar plan to take Malta, which stubbornly resisted continuous Axis bombings. After refusing to help attack Gibraltar, Spain also closed the Canary and Cape Verde islands to German raiders, but Franco did allow U-boats to refuel at Spanish ports. From St. Nazaire and other French Atlantic ports, Doenitz waged his "tonnage warfare" against British shipping in what came to be known as the Battle of the Atlantic. He concentrated his wolf packs in the least-protected but most heavily traveled oceanic areas, especially the Northwest Approaches, to sink almost half of the four million tons of Allied merchant shipping lost during 1940. Such attacks were indiscriminate of cargo carried, so that many really essential war materials got through. Furthermore, U-boat commanders found Doenitz's tight shore-based controls from Brest (later Lorient) too restrictive, for they preferred to attack independent, unescorted vessels. Escorted convoys cost the Germans twenty-three boats during 1940 which could not be replaced until the new construction program of mid-1940 yielded new boats.

British antisub countermeasures did not begin to show significant results until major reforms were instituted early in 1941. At that time, the British discontinued their Q-ship efforts and finally shelved their offensive antisub operations in favor of more strongly escorted convoys. In February and March screening destroyers battled back to sink or capture Germany's three leading U-boat skippers, Lieutenant Commanders Guenther Prien, Otto Kretschmer and Joachim Schepke, the leading World War II merchant killer with over 265,000 tons to his credit. Inadequate Allied antisub air patrols left a "black pit" for unfettered U-boat operations in the mid-North Atlantic beyond the range of planes operating from British and Canadian coastal airfields. But in April, the RAF's Coastal Command was turned over to the Navy for coordination of antisub operations, while airfields were established in Iceland. U-boat sinkings of merchantmen, peaking at nearly 700,000 tons in April, dropped to 500,000 tons in May, at the end of which the first convoy was escorted all the way across the Atlantic, and sinkings dropped further in June. Strong escorts and aircraft seemed to be the proper British answer to Doenitz's tonnage strategy, provided that enough ships and planes became available to counter the new U-boats.

Hitler's stubborn refusal to abandon the surface raider helped weaken the underwater campaign, and Allied aircraft and heavy fleet units—coordinated by radio—generally succeeded in neutralizing these ships during the first half of 1941. Shifted from their North Sea ports to Brest, these battleships and cruisers were subjected to an air-sea blockade by the RAF, minelayers and subs. Lacking advanced bases, these raiders could not stay at sea long, as between January and March when the *Scharnhorst* and *Gneisenau* under Admiral Gunther Lütjens sank twenty-two merchantmen in the North Atlantic, only to be chased back into Brest by British aircraft which then seriously damaged them. Then, in May, a Swedish cruiser alerted the British Admiralty to Lütjens' sortie from the Baltic with the sleek new battleship *Bismarck* and heavy cruiser *Prinz Eugen*. Intercepted by the new battleship *Prince of Wales* and the battle cruiser *Hood* on May 24, the *Bismarck* with an opening salvo blew the *Hood* and 1500 men to bits (like her predecessors at Jutland) and then drove away the *Prince of Wales*. But now British fleet units converged on the force in the North Atlantic, so that Lütjens sent the *Prinz Eugen* on to Brest and set *Bismarck*'s course for the same place. On the 27th, Swordfish torpedo planes from the carrier *Ark Royal* of Force H combined torpedo hits with those from shadowing destroyers at night to slow down the *Bismarck*. Next morning the battleships *King George V* from Scapa and *Rodney* from convoy duty arrived and reduced the *Bismarck* to a flaming hulk; she was sent to the bottom with Lütjens and 2300 of her crew by torpedoes from a cruiser. German auxiliary cruisers operated in the Pacific and Indian oceans, until a British cruiser sank one in May. The *Admiral Scheer* returned from a successful cruise there early in the year, but after the loss of the *Bismarck* Hitler kept his precious battleships at Brest, where RAF bombers continued to attack them.

But the overall German successes encouraged Japan to renew its flagging war against China. With the French collapse, Japan pressured Britain to close the vital Burma Road and attacked Vichy French Indochina while establishing airfields there to operate against Chinese communications and bases during the summer of 1940. Later in the year and early in 1941 Churchill reopened the Burma Road; a Chinese Communist offensive weakened the Japanese in North China; a Vichy French cruiser and four sloops defeated the stronger navy of Japan's ally Siam off the Koh Chang archipelago; and in April Japan concluded a nonaggression pact with Russia. The United States, not as obliging, determined to check Japanese ambitions in the Far East. In the summer of 1940 President Roosevelt put a crimp on the

Japanese war machine by halting the export to Japan of strategic chemicals, lubricating oil, aviation fuel and equipment and scrap iron and steel. In the autumn, American Asiatic Fleet vessels left northern Chinese ports for good, and the United States Fleet followed its last war game by concentrating as a deterrent force at Pearl Harbor in Hawaii. American aid increased to China via the Burma Road, leading Japanese planners to accelerate their preparations to fight the Western powers. The primary strategic objective was war materials to defeat China—now the vital oil, gasoline and rubber of Southeast Asia, notably in British Malaya and the Dutch East Indies. The Imperial Navy planned to follow its traditional policy—ferrying and escorting the Army invasion flotillas to conquer these regions, which would include the adjacent naval bases along such new lines of communication: Manila, Hong Kong and Singapore. Seizure of the Philippines would thus bring in the United States alongside Britain and Holland.

Since swiftness and surprise were crucial for any Asian *Blitz,* the Japanese Combined Fleet could not wait passively for the American Battle Fleet to steam into Japanese waters for the decisive battle, although naval and air installations were finally being constructed on the Pacific islands in 1940–41 to thwart any American advance. Also, since large numbers of fleet units and land-based naval air forces were necessary for the advance into Southeast Asia, they could not be spared for a naval battle. Needing a new strategy to deal with the American fleet, Admiral Isoroku Yamamoto, Combined Fleet commander, developed a very bold one indeed. Always a naval air advocate, he planned to use Japan's six fleet carriers to sink the American battleships and carriers in a surprise air raid on their anchorage at Pearl Harbor. To this end, in April 1941 he created an independent carrier force, the First Air Fleet, and charged Commander Minoru Genda with devising suitable carrier tactics. For weapons, Genda led the development of aerial torpedoes for the shallow waters of Pearl Harbor, with the torpedo and bombing planes to be escorted by Japan's new Zero fighter. For operating formations, Genda realized—from his own tests and from British experiences in the Mediterranean and against the *Bismarck*—that carriers had rendered the old battle-line formalism obsolete. So he formulated two carrier cruising formations —a defensive box of carriers together in mutual support, and separate offensive squadrons of two carriers each, these several hundred miles apart to converge their planes over the target fleet. Though both formations suffered from inadequate antiaircraft screens of destroyers only, they represented the first original naval tactics based on the striking power of independent carrier forces. How soon they would be employed against the United States depended largely on developments in Europe.

Responding both to Japanese aggressiveness and to the German U-boat onslaught against Britain, the United States in 1940–41 mobilized its own war-making capability to protect its own national interests and to shore up the holding actions of Great Britain and China. In the summer of 1940, along with the destroyers-for-bases deal which both helped Britain and strengthened America's Atlantic defenses, Congress authorized new naval construction for a "two-ocean navy" and the following February created the administrative machinery for it, the Atlantic and Pacific fleets. During the winter of 1941, Anglo-American joint staff discussions were held, while the fifty destroyers plus ten Coast Guard cutters were turned over to the Royal Navy for antisubmarine warfare. Whenever the United States entered the fight, the planners agreed, Hitler should be stopped and defeated first, then Japan. To this end, during the spring the Roosevelt Administration initiated the "Lend Lease" of war materials to Britain and obtained the use of British shipyards for American warships. American air bases opened in Bermuda, Newfoundland and Greenland (with exiled-Danish permission); the American Defense Zone—agreed upon with the Latin American states earlier—was extended beyond local coastal waters; and patrolling United States warships began to provide information on German U-boat movements to the Royal Navy. Hitler wanted to avoid a confrontation with America, but his frustrated sub commanders proved difficult to control, as on May 21 when one of them sank the American freighter *Robin Moor* in the South Atlantic. Six days later Roosevelt declared an "unlimited national emergency" for his country.

By early June 1941, the United States government—despite considerable opposition from a large segment of the American public—was all but officially committed to the war against Germany, and Hitler would soon bring in Russia. Repercussions of these events in the Far East would hasten the opening of hostilities there. During the latter half of 1941, therefore, World War II would become global.

## GLOBAL WAR

From the summer of 1941 till the spring of 1943 the Soviet Union and the United States reeled under the German and Japanese attacks on them, but doggedly held on in alliance with Britain to turn back the Axis offensives in virtually two separate wars. The continent-oriented Axis powers had to be contained by Anglo-American supremacy at sea, and the main German Army blunted by the Red Army. Significantly, joint Allied strategic planning proved far superior to any Axis cooperation. Churchill and Roosevelt generally unified their efforts, supported ultimately by the exiled French, Dutch and Poles, the Commonwealth nations and most of Latin America in both oceans. Stalin viewed the capitalist democracies with grave suspicion, particularly in light of the interventions of 1918–20, and he remained convinced that Anglo-American delays in mounting a second front against Hitler in the West were deliberately designed to weaken the Russian Communist state in the wake of the German onslaught. Nevertheless, the Russians grudgingly cooperated in Europe and remained neutral in Asia, where China became the major continental Ally.

By contrast, the Atlantic and Pacific Axis powers—save for occasional blockade-running merchantmen and subs—cooperated hardly at all and thereby missed at least three golden opportunities. In the Indian Ocean, no major joint effort was ever made against Allied sea lanes (including one quarter of Anglo-American aid to Russia via the Persian Gulf); although German and Japanese subs operated there, the German U-boat captains finally quit cooperating with the Japanese because of atrocities committed by the latter against some of their victims. In the waters of North America, a joint submarine blockade could have paralyzed Allied shipping there and even closed the Panama Canal, as the Americans fully expected, but no such effort was made. Finally, almost half of the Allied Lend Lease aid to Russia went to Vladivostok via the North Pacific from American West Coast ports, but the Japanese so thoroughly honored their nonaggression pact with Russia that they allowed these Russian merchantmen to pass through the Pacific war zones unhindered. Such was the nature of the fascistic dictatorships—strange bedfellows with their own specific, separate and selfish war aims.

Russo-American entry into World War II took place between Hitler's invasion of Russia on June 22, 1941, and the Japanese attack on the American Battle Fleet at Pearl Harbor the following December 7. In July the U. S. Navy landed Marines in Iceland to relieve the British there and began to escort all shipping to and from that strategic island, thus releasing many Anglo-Canadian escort vessels. The same month, the United States, Britain and the Dutch government-in-exile froze Japanese assets, choking off virtually all foreign oil exports to Japan and thus acting as an ultimatum to Japan to back down in Asia from lack of oil or fight the Western maritime powers to get Indonesian oil. In August the Allies formalized their staff agreements to defeat Hitler before Japan, and their navies began to pool information, especially in amphibious and antisubmarine warfare. During the autumn, United

States naval convoy chores reached halfway across the Atlantic to waiting British escorts and even protected a British troop convoy from Halifax around Africa to the Middle East. The United States also extended Lend Lease to Russia and forbade Axis U-boats to operate in the defensive zone of the Western Hemisphere. Beginning to shoot back, Hitler's U-boat commanders missed an American destroyer in September, damaged one and sank another in October, and sank an American tanker early in December. The Americans began to arm their merchantmen so they could enter the war zone, ended their Yangtze Patrol and transferred the last warships in China to the Philippines. Encouraged by German successes and promises of victory, Japan occupied Saigon and Camranh Bay in French Indochina and decided to conquer Southeast Asia, beginning with the attack on Pearl Harbor. The United States thereafter declared war on Japan, whose German and Italian allies honored their treaty commitments by declaring war on the United States.

Axis and Allied strategies then followed conventional continental and maritime practices. The Germans simply tried to conquer Russia and with Italy aimed to isolate Britain in the Atlantic and Mediterranean until Russia surrendered. The Japanese similarly planned to overrun Southeast Asia and finally China and to form a defensive perimeter in the Central Pacific to contain the United States until Hitler brought on the Russian collapse and forced Britain to terms. The Axis navies operated in support of their respective armies' objectives. The Anglo-American Allies adopted a maritime strategy reminiscent of Pitt's system of the 1750s. The Royal, Commonwealth and U. S. navies would keep open the sea lanes, protecting shipping, eliminating enemy fleet units, and blockading both continents to supply major continental armies in both theaters, namely those of Russia and China. When their navies had won general command of the seas and their air forces command of enemy air spaces, by which time their continental allies ought to have broken the Axis armies, the Anglo-American coalition would land their own armies to tip the balance on land. The crucial factor in the strategies of both sides was time. If the Axis could not win in 1941 or 1942, the tremendous output of American industry would be able to recoup the early losses and mobilize totally against the gradually strained Axis economies.

Everything hinged on Russia's ability to stop Hitler, whose attack took Stalin by complete surprise and drove back the Red Army on a wide front from Poland to the Crimea in the summer and autumn of 1941. The navies of both played only minor roles as Hitler tried to *blitz* his way into the key cities of (north to south) Leningrad, Moscow and Kiev before the onset of the terrible Russian winter. Against

Leningrad, German and Finnish torpedo boats, mines and subs helped
the armies overrun the Baltic states, damage two Russian cruisers and
sink nine destroyers in the Gulf of Finland as the Russian Baltic Fleet
joined in the defense of besieged Leningrad. A German force which
included the battleships *Tirpitz* and *Admiral Scheer* moved into the
Gulf, where the *Luftwaffe* sank a Russian battleship and old cruiser.
But the Russians moved their ships up the Neva River to provide
artillery support and naval brigades ashore. Leningrad held, as did
the Lake Ladoga region, against the German-Finnish attackers. Against
Kiev, the Germans overran the Ukraine before being stopped at Rostov
on the Don River, at Sevastopol and just beyond Kerch in November.
Neutral Turkey kept the Dardanelles closed and Italian ships out, so
that the weak and inexperienced Russian Black Sea Fleet could easily
attack Axis shipping and the Axis Rumanian port of Constanta, supply
Sevastopol (and Odessa before its fall) and support an amphibious
assault at Feodosia which retook the Kerch peninsula in December.
But the *Luftwaffe* sank five destroyers and many other units of this
fleet, partly the result of ineffective Russian naval aviation subordinated
to the Army's air arm. Against Moscow, the German drive simply
bogged down before a tenacious defense, overstrained German logistics,
a counterattack by Siberian reinforcements and then the winter mud,
cold and snow. Hitler had been stopped just at the moment the United
States officially entered the war.

With one quarter of Allied aid to Russia going by sea to Murmansk
and Archangel on the Barents and White seas (half via the North
Pacific, the rest through the Persian Gulf), the Battle of the Atlantic
gradually shifted to the North Atlantic, though not intensively until
early 1942 when Hitler realized the extent of Allied convoys on this
route. Doenitz's tonnage campaign for 1941 roughly equaled the previous year's successes: U-boats claimed over two million of the four
million-plus tons of Allied merchant shipping sunk by Axis vessels,
mines and planes. But between June and December 1941, 27 German
and 13 Italian subs were lost, leaving Germany with 91 operational
U-boats (but another 158 working up) by the beginning of 1942. Such
losses could not be sustained if more merchant tonnage was not sunk;
in other words, Allied shipbuilding and uneven defensive measures
were maintaining enough of a balance to keep the war effort alive.
Also, the surface raiders never recovered from the *Bismarck* episode:
British and Australian cruisers sank 2 auxiliary cruisers in November,
and the RAF made Brest so unsafe that the German Navy in February
dramatically ran the *Scharnhorst, Gneisenau* and *Prinz Eugen* up the
Channel under *Luftwaffe* cover to North Sea ports where they could
be used against the convoys to North Russia. The *Tirpitz* and *Admiral*

*Scheer* were consequently shifted to Norway, where they joined *Luft-waffe* and U-boats to increase the *guerre de course* campaign.

Such a redeployment actually gained time for the Allies in the Mediterranean, for the Axis onslaught of late 1941 seriously weakened Allied sea power everywhere. A British ground offensive in North Africa against Rommel in November and December succeeded in re-lieving the landward threat to the Suez Canal, but a simultaneous offen-sive by German and Italian subs led to sinking of the carrier *Ark Royal* and the battleship *Barham* during November, and the serious damaging of the battleships *Queen Elizabeth, Valiant* and *Malaya* in December. The Japanese carrier attack on Pearl Harbor that month sent five American battleships to the bottom, and land-based Japanese air from French Indochina sank the British battleship *Prince of Wales* and battle cruiser *Repulse* off the Malayan coast. With virtually no capital ships in the Mediterranean, only a few carriers available in the Pacific and Indian oceans, and remaining strength concentrated in the North Atlantic, the Allies had to utilize their strained naval forces carefully and judiciously to maintain a creditable defensive on all the fighting fronts during the winter and spring of 1942.

The Japanese offensive succeeded in its original strategic objective of conquering Southeast Asia and establishing a defensive perimeter across the Central Pacific; it even sank seven Anglo-American capital ships in December, but failed to locate and destroy the fast carriers of the American Pacific Fleet. Absent from Pearl Harbor at the time of the air raid by Yamamoto's six carriers, these American carriers became the main Allied striking force of that fleet under Admiral Chester W. Nimitz, while the United States declared unrestricted sub-marine warfare against Japan. But neither carriers nor subs could pre-vent Japanese amphibious forces from overrunning American Guam, Wake and the Philippines, British and Commonwealth Hong Kong, Singapore, the Gilbert and northern Solomon islands, New Britain and Rabaul in the Bismarcks, and most of New Guinea, along with the Dutch East Indies, between December 1941 and May 1942. American PT boats helped delay the Japanese in the Philippines, and between the Japanese landings in Borneo and Celebes in January and the assault on Batavia, Java, in March, an Allied force of American, British, Dutch and Australian warships fought a series of sacrificial actions. The battle of the Java Sea on February 27 culminated this effort, when Admiral Takeo Takagi used four Japanese cruisers and thirteen destroyers to sink two Dutch cruisers (of a five-cruiser Allied force) and five of ten Allied destroyers led by Dutch Admiral Karel Doorman. Yamamoto's carriers returning from Pearl Harbor struck Port Darwin in northern Australia, while the Japanese Army overran

British Burma and Malaya. The Imperial Navy then thrust into the Indian Ocean to take the Andaman Islands, raid the British Ceylonese bases of Trincomalee and Colombo (where they lost many planes to some RAF veterans of the Battle of Britain), sank the British carrier *Hermes,* two cruisers and a destroyer, and caused the British Eastern Fleet to retire to bases in East Africa.

Though the Japanese had generally established their defensive perimeter, they wanted to add a few outposts and there ran afoul of the surviving American carriers. Throughout early 1942 these vessels, usually commanded by Admiral William F. Halsey, Jr., raided Japanese island positions in the Central and South Pacific and even sent sixteen Army bombers to strike Japan itself in April. The Japanese determined to dislodge the last Allied defenders from southern New Guinea and the southern Solomons, whereupon they could cut American-Anzac communications and counter the Allied sub offensive from Australian ports. But the Americans, having broken the Japanese naval codes, concentrated the carriers *Lexington* and *Yorktown* with escorts under Admiral Frank Jack Fletcher in the Coral Sea to stop them. Admiral Takagi's cruisers escorted landing forces which occupied Tulagi in the Solomons on May 3, but on the 7th and 8th Fletcher's task force engaged the Japanese carriers *Shokaku* and *Zuikaku* in the Battle of the Coral Sea—the first all-carrier battle in history. Though inferior to the Japanese Zero fighters, Fletcher's F4F Wildcat fighter pilots inflicted heavy losses on them, while the SBD Dauntless dive-bombers seriously damaged the *Shokaku* and sank an escorting light carrier. Japanese carrier planes hit the *Lexington,* forcing it to be scuttled, but Takagi now abandoned his designs to take Port Moresby, New Guinea. The same month a British amphibious operation took the Vichy French port of Diego Suarez in northern Madagascar. These operations kept vital Allied Eastern sea communications open across the southern Indian and Pacific oceans.

The surviving American carriers led Admiral Yamamoto to seek the neutralization of Pearl Harbor by taking Midway Island, from which his land-based Navy planes could then bomb the American Pacific Fleet base. But again American knowledge of the intercepted Japanese codes enabled Admiral Nimitz to concentrate his three available carriers at Hawaii to give Yamamoto the battle he so earnestly desired; until the American carriers were all eliminated, Japan would not enjoy command of the sea—and the air over Hawaii. Executing a highly complex plan of lure and deception, Yamamoto unwisely split up his great armada in order to accomplish his purpose. Early in June 1942 two Japanese light carriers, supported by 7 cruisers and 12 destroyers, moved into Aleutian waters to bombard the naval base at

Dutch Harbor, and 18 submarines took station north and west of Hawaii in order to attack the American carriers when they sortied north to defend the Aleutians. But Nimitz had already sent his carriers to sea, not to protect the less important Aleutians, but to contest Yamamoto's main thrust toward Midway. Fletcher led the *Yorktown,* Admiral Raymond A. Spruance the *Enterprise* and *Hornet,* with land-based air and subs to cooperate; the last few battleships had been sent back to California. Yamamoto further separated his 7 battleships (plus one light carrier, 4 cruisers and 12 destroyers) from the 4 fast carriers, *Kaga, Akagi, Soryu* and *Hiryu* (plus 2 battleships, 3 cruisers and 12 destroyers), thus eliminating the possibility of mutual anti-aircraft support. Once these forces defeated the American fleet, the amphibious attack could be made on Midway from 12 transports (supported by yet 2 more battleships, another light carrier, 2 seaplane carriers, 7 cruisers and 29 destroyers). This separation of units and missions—fleet battle and amphibious assault—compromised Japanese tactics and enabled Nimitz to concentrate his available strength against the chief threat, Yamamoto's 4 attack carriers.

The Battle of Midway, one of the most decisive actions in naval history, took place on June 4, 1942. Japan's four fast carriers, guided by the mistaken information that the remaining American naval strength was en route to the Aleutians, went into their standard but poorly escorted defensive square formation for attacking shore installations and began striking Midway as part of the pre-landing barrage. The Japanese carrier planes were thus armed with general bombs rather than torpedoes and the armor-piercing variety of bombs for use against ships. During the early morning, American Army, Navy and Marine Corps land-based planes from Midway located the carriers, but all missed with their bombs and were either shot down or driven off by defensive Japanese fighters. Then Japanese reconnaissance planes located part of the American fleet, whose carrier planes were now searching for Yamamoto's carriers. The Japanese now began to rearm and refuel their planes for a fleet action, though they could not disperse their carriers according to doctrine as long as they had to attack Midway too. At mid-morning, their launch carefully timed by Admiral Spruance and his staff, the American TBD Devastator torpedo-bombers from *Hornet* and *Enterprise* made contact with the enemy, but because they had become separated from their fighter escort were practically all shot down. However, as this was happening, the SBD Dauntless dive-bombers from all three American carriers chanced upon the Japanese carrier force—undetected, no less. Diving out of the sun, these planes hit *Kaga, Akagi* and *Soryu* just as their aircraft were being armed and fueled on deck; by noon all were in a sinking condition. Another attack later in the day also finished the *Hiryu,* but since so many planes had been on board all four carriers refueling, most of their valuable pilots merely jumped overboard and were rescued by their escorts. A later American strike sank a heavy cruiser, while a last Japanese flight managed to locate and disable the *Yorktown,* which was then finished off three days later by a Japanese sub. Deprived of his fleet cover, Yamamoto had no choice but to abandon the Midway operation, though his northern forces did occupy desolate Attu and Kiska islands in the Aleutians.

Though Japanese carrier strength had been whittled down to rough parity with the Americans—some five each—the victories of the Coral Sea and Midway could not relieve Axis pressures elsewhere during the spring of 1942. Germany's spring offensives took Sevastopol and the Kerch peninsula in the Black Sea, and in North Africa Rommel captured Tobruk and pressed into Egypt, while Axis and Allied planes traded blows around Malta and its vital convoys. In March British commandos destroyed the big French dry dock at St. Nazaire, but the Allies had less success against Doenitz's U-boats. The simultaneous need for Doenitz to blockade the American East Coast and to cut the heavy Allied use of the "Murmansk run" overtaxed his 125 boats during the first half of the year. To be sure, his subs between January and June claimed no fewer than 585 merchantmen totaling over three million tons, in addition to another 400 vessels of one million tons sunk by aircraft, mines and surface ships. But Germany and Italy lost 21 and 7 subs respectively in the process, and as the Americans ever so gradually developed coastal convoys and antisub forces Doenitz followed his usual practice of shifting his boats to safer areas: from the United States East Coast to the Caribbean in the late spring, then to the mid-Atlantic during the summer. By that time, the first new prewar Allied naval construction had become available, giving the Allies opportunities to make limited counterattacks.

Allied strategic differences reflected their own pressing needs and historical biases. Russia wanted a second front established in the West by an Anglo-American assault on the coast of France to relieve its armies in the East; traditionally continent-oriented American generals agreed on such a direct approach. But the British, steeped in the maritime strategy of the Pitts, Barham and Churchill—now termed the "indirect approach" by the British military pundit B. H. Liddell Hart —preferred to postpone such a project until Hitler's "Fortress Europe" had been isolated by Allied command of the seas around and the air over Europe and reduced by the Red Army. Also, the harsh experience of Dunkirk was accented in August by a disastrous Anglo-Canadian commando raid on the French coast at Dieppe, creating grave doubts about a major amphibious landing until the Anglo-Americans had overwhelming strength. Rommel's North African offensive threatened the Allies in the Middle East, and Doenitz's U-boats caused the Allies to cut back their Murmansk convoys during the summer. And within the Allied Combined Chiefs of Staff was the outspoken Commander-in-Chief of the United States Fleet and Chief of Naval Operations, Admiral Ernest J. King, a superior administrator and strategist who personally directed the American antisub effort in the Atlantic and unrelentingly insisted on a full American effort against Japan. Unlike his British First Sea Lord counterpart, Admirals Pound and (from late 1943) Cunningham, King got relatively little interference from his chief of state, though he upset the British.

All these elements led to several key Allied strategic decisions in mid-1942: postponement of the cross-Channel attack, victory first in the Mediterranean and a separate American war in the Pacific, despite British disbelief that the United States could wage two simultaneous wars. Stalin's second front for the time being came in the form of Lend Lease convoys and Anglo-American strategic air forces which bombed Germany and drew valuable *Luftwaffe* units away from the Eastern front. Anglo-American maritime strategists thus had their way in first seeking command of the sea in 1942 and 1943 before returning in force to the continent.

All Allied operations in the European theater depended on the success of the convoys in the Battle of the Atlantic, but the U-boat *guerre de course* prevailed through the first months of 1943. Doenitz's boats and other Axis weapons claimed over 800,000 tons of merchant shipping in both June and November 1942 and over 600,000 tons in each of the intervening months and in the following March. But Doenitz's tonnage warfare avoided the crucial well-escorted convoys with their most important cargoes in favor of easier targets in increasingly broad operating areas, as from Hitler's decision in June 1942 to attack Brazilian shipping which hastened that nation's declaration of war and cooperation in Allied antisub efforts. Though the Murmansk route had been temporarily closed, foul weather, uncoordinated *Luftwaffe* units and only partly effective surface raiders weakened the commerce war from Norway. And new U-boats, their "milch cow" supply subs, acoustical torpedoes and wolf pack tactics could not offset Allied counterattacks. At last Hitler virtually suspended all German surface ship operations and replaced Raeder with Doenitz as his naval commander early in 1943.

For the Allies, Admiral King championed defensive convoys over offensive hunter-killer operations until enough antisub vessels were available for them and such new weapons as the forward-fired depth charge and escort carrier could be proved. Air operations with convoys had been originally limited to merchant-ship-launched planes and an occasional escort carrier such as the prototype, the British *Audacity,* which was sunk by a U-boat late in 1941. Shore-based patrol bombers and lighter-than-air blimps of the RAF and U. S. Navy and Army Air Forces covered American, Canadian, Icelandic and British waters, but still left the "black pit" air gap south of Greenland empty of aerial cover. The many new escort carriers and destroyers began to close this gap, so that in March 1943 the Americans turned over all convoy escort duty to Britain and Canada in order to shift to offensive hunter-killer operations with the new American Tenth Fleet, created in May under King's direct command. While these forces operated from the United States, Admiral Sir Max Horton sent hunter-killer groups into the Western Approaches, and Allied bombers began an air offensive against U-boats in the Bay of Biscay. So, between June 1942 and May 1943 the Germans lost 165 U-boats—in May alone 41—and the Italians 29 more. And German merchant sinkings could not offset Allied mass-produced Victory and Liberty merchant ships. Admitting defeat in the North Atlantic, Doenitz withdrew his boats from that quarter late in May to reconsider his strategy.

As Allied supplies got through, Soviet Russia initiated its first counterthrust with the Red Army, supported by warships, naval infantry and a slowly recovering naval air force. Russian destroyers, subs and torpedo boats protected Murmansk in the Kola Inlet and attacked German shipping off Norway until met by a concerted German anti-sub effort there in April 1943. Russian naval aircraft and coastal craft frustrated German naval and amphibious attacks in the Gulf of Finland from September 1942, helped lift the siege of Leningrad in January 1943 and then attacked Axis merchantmen in the Baltic until the Germans instituted convoys and defensive patrols which sank ten Russian subs and erected an enlarged mine barrage to close Kronstadt. Following a German summer and autumn drive along the Volga and Don rivers and Black Sea coast which forced the Russian Fleet from Novorossisk to smaller ports like Batum, the Russians launched a brilliant counterattack in November 1942 which captured the entire Axis Army before Stalingrad the following February. German and Russian naval forces parried around Novorossisk during the winter, but remained stalemated throughout the spring. Such Russian successes forced Hitler to divert reinforcements to the Eastern front from the Mediterranean, enabling the Anglo-Americans to implement their peripheral strategy there.

The Atlantic Allies now moved to regain North Africa by a pincers movement closing in from East and West Africa. In the East, a British amphibious assault took Vichy French Madagascar in September and October 1942, while the British Army stalled Rommel's offensive before El Alamein, only sixty miles from Alexandria. Then, late in October, the British Eighth Army under General Bernard L. Montgomery counterattacked at El Alamein and drove Rommel from Egypt. On November 8, an Allied army under American General Dwight D. Eisenhower supported by naval forces under Admiral Cunningham landed in Morocco and Algeria. Craftily eluding U-boats, American troop convoys and escorting fleet units ferried the assault forces from the United States to land at four places for the investment of Casablanca, while British vessels supported an American landing at Oran and an Anglo-American landing at Algiers—both mounted from England. Defending Vichy French naval, air and ground forces resisted unsuccessfully for two days, then, led by Admiral Darlan, surrendered and went over to the Allies. The sudden intrusion of Allied reinforcements into the Mediterranean gave the Allies final command of that sea, enabling Allied expeditions to seize Bougie and Bône in eastern Algeria days later and to establish airfields to contest the air over land and water. Because of the Darlan defection, the Germans dissolved the Vichy government and occupied the rest of France, but not in time to prevent the French from scuttling their surviving fleet units at Toulon. Rommel withdrew before the Allied pincers into Tunisia by the end of the year and managed to counter Allied blows, but Allied air and sea power isolated his army there. The Axis armies in North Africa surrendered in May 1943, thus reopening the supply route to the Persian Gulf and Russia via the Suez Canal—a much more convenient route than around South Africa.

Allied maritime strategy in the Pacific reflected the American control under Admirals King and Nimitz, though not without the opposition of continental strategists who preferred to concentrate the Allied effort against the Japanese in China, Southeast Asia and the Philippines. But neither Allied-Chinese forces in the China-Burma-India theater nor American-Commonwealth forces under American General Douglas MacArthur in Australia and southern New Guinea could be spared adequate forces from the other fronts to adequately contest the major Japanese armies and their air forces. Japan was most vulnerable at sea, because of the long lines of communications to island bases throughout the vast Pacific. So the U. S. Navy mounted a major *guerre de course* sub effort from Hawaii and Australia against Japanese shipping, a tonnage war that was effective since Japan had no adequate policy of commerce protection and never really developed one. Conversely, Japan missed a real opportunity to attack American shipping by continuing to use its subs in fleet and Army support. To further insure Allied sea routes to the Anzac countries, Nimitz collected his still-meager fleet units and one Marine Corps division to take Tulagi and Guadalcanal islands in the southern Solomons on August 7, 1942. Japanese fleet units and naval air forces at Rabaul responded immediately, beginning a six-month battle of attrition over the possession of Guadalcanal. Throughout most of the campaign, American forces held only the airfield and beachhead and commanded the adjacent air and sea in daylight when convoys brought in supplies and men, whereas the Japanese held the rest of the island, reinforcing it during the night under cover of air and surface ship attacks. As time went on, this otherwise unimportant island became the focus of the war in the Pacific for both sides.

The Guadalcanal campaign raged from August 1942 to February 1943, with each side reluctantly exposing its precious heavy surface units and veteran naval aviators piecemeal as necessity dictated. Planes from airstrips on Rabaul and Guadalcanal and from carriers tangled daily, with the cumulative effect of gradually costing Japan her best pilots, who were not rotated home to train new air groups, unlike the Americans who were. The several naval battles similarly wore away fleet strength on both sides, but to Japan's disadvantage, since her industrial base would take at least one year longer than that of the United States to replace ships lost. The three American carriers supporting the initial landings at Guadalcanal were foolishly withdrawn by an overcautious Admiral Fletcher on August 8, whereupon Admiral Gunichi Mikawa came down from Rabaul to penetrate the Guadalcanal roadstead with seven cruisers; shortly after midnight on the 9th his force sank one Australian and four American cruisers and a destroyer in the battle of Savo Island. Two weeks later, three carriers led a Japanese fleet sortie from Truk into the battle of the Eastern Solomons (August 22–25) with American carriers, whose planes sank one Japanese light carrier and destroyed ninety enemy aircraft. The American submarine *S-44* sank a Japanese heavy cruiser in August, but Japan's *I-26* crippled the carrier *Saratoga* and in September *I-19* sank the carrier *Wasp*. In the middle of October, American and Japanese cruisers clashed in the battle of Cape Esperance, costing Japan one cruiser lost and two severely damaged, but two Japanese battleships with cruisers and destroyers bombarded the airfield on Guadalcanal. Admiral Yamamoto now determined to launch a massive air-sea attack to take Guadal, but Admiral Nimitz countered by placing the aggressive Admiral Halsey in command in the South Pacific.

The issue came to a head quickly, with the Americans led by Halsey managing to frustrate Yamamoto's scheme. In the battle of the Santa Cruz Islands, October 26–27, 1942, the small carrier forces again traded blows. The Americans shot down 100 more Japanese carrier planes and put the carrier *Shokaku* out of action for nearly a year, while the Japanese forces sank the carrier *Hornet* and seriously damaged the carrier *Enterprise*. In mid-November reinforcement attempts by both sides led to the prolonged and decisive Naval Battle of Guadalcanal from the 12th to the 15th. During the first night, surface forces slugged it out, leaving two of five American cruisers and four destroyers sunk and two Japanese cruisers sunk and the battleship *Hiei* so badly damaged that it was sunk next morning by *Enterprise* planes. On the 14th American planes also sank two more Japanese cruisers and seven transports, so that Yamamoto rushed the battleship *Kirishima* with four cruisers plus destroyers into the fray. In the final night action, the new American battleships *Washington* and *South Dakota* met and sank the *Kirishima,* credit going largely to the radar-directed guns of the *Washington* against a ship without radar. Unbeknownst to the Americans, this victory gave them command of the seas around Guadalcanal by convincing Yamamoto to evacuate Japan's portion of the island. The Japanese retreat was masterfully disguised, with Japanese fleet and air units sinking one American cruiser and badly damaging three others in the battle of Tassafaronga, November 30, and sinking another in the battle of Rennell Island on January 29–30, 1943. The next week the Japanese successfully evacuated Guadalcanal. Halsey's inspired leadership had resulted in the first permanent dent in Japan's defensive perimeter, but more importantly, Japanese fleet and pilot losses compounded the disaster of Midway.

Having placed the Japanese squarely on the defensive in the South Pacific, the Americans with Commonwealth participation strengthened their positions there and in the North Pacific during the spring of 1943. Land-based Army, Navy and Marine Corps bombers and fighters from Guadalcanal and New Guinea whittled down Japanese naval air strength at Rabaul and adjacent installations and shipping. In March, Army bombers sank four Japanese destroyers and seven of eight troop transports in convoy in the battle of the Bismarck Sea; American PT boats sank the last transport. And in April American fighters robbed Japan of its foremost naval commander and strategist by shooting down Admiral Yamamoto on a flight between Rabaul and Bougainville. In the North Pacific, Japan tried to hold on to Attu and Kiska islands while Japanese planes from Paramushiro in the Kuriles and American planes from Dutch Harbor and other bases in the central Aleutians battled to control the air. The foul weather hampered all operations, and the indecisive cruiser battle of the Komandorski Islands in March settled nothing except that it helped convince the Japanese to supply Attu and Kiska only by sub. In May an American amphibious assault took Attu, and two months later the Japanese executed another carefully disguised evacuation, this time from Kiska. Allied North Pacific routes to Russia and South Pacific routes to Australia were now secure.

As the spring of 1943 drew to a close, the limited Allied offensives had succeeded in throwing the Axis back on the defensive. The U-boat had been successfully checked, North Africa taken, the South Pacific and Indian Ocean held, and Russia saved from the German onslaught. These successes, often undramatic battles of attrition, bought invaluable time for American war industry to reach the production levels whereby it could feed, arm and generally supply the Allied nations and provide the huge quantity of superior weapons for the all-out offensives against the Axis powers across the globe.

## ALLIED COUNTEROFFENSIVE

Despite Russian frustration over the continuously delayed cross-Channel attack to open a Western front, several Allied strategic conferences during 1943 guaranteed that the assault would come in the spring of 1944. In the meantime, the Anglo-American navies would test their new post-Pearl Harbor weapons by winning command of the Atlantic and Pacific oceans to blockade both Germany and Japan, while their strategic air forces began the reduction of both countries and their armies took Italy out of the war and prepared for the assault on Hitler's "Fortress Europe." Serious differences between Stalin and Churchill continued as both now looked to postwar political arrangements in Europe. Stalin would guarantee his western frontier against a resurgent Germany by establishing Russian hegemony over Eastern and Central Europe. Churchill would frustrate such an eventuality by sending the Anglo-American armies into the Italian and/or Balkan peninsulas via the "soft underbelly" of Europe to liberate Central Europe ahead of the Red Army. But Roosevelt held the bargaining power with superior American arms and industry and compromised American moralistic goals to generally side with Stalin's position. Fascism, after all, was the enemy, not the Russian Ally. The Americans decided to support Churchill in the Mediterranean only, after which the carefully rationed amphibious craft would be redeployed for the cross-Channel attack. Stalin could liberate Eastern Europe, the Murmansk run would be reopened, and the Americans would undertake their own offensive against Japan's defensive perimeter in the Pacific, instead of through Burma as Churchill wanted. And time decidedly favored the Allies, whose industrial output in mid-1943 beat that of the Germans and Japanese by a full year.

To supply Russia and stockpile men and material in England for the cross-Channel attack, the Allies had to win the Battle of the Atlantic. After the German battleships *Tirpitz* and *Gneisenau* and ten destroyers raided the outpost at Spitzbergen in September 1943, the Allies moved up to neutralize the last German surface raiders in Norway. British midget subs damaged the *Tirpitz* at her anchorage later that month, and planes from five carriers immobilized her the following March, while the *Scharnhorst* attacked a convoy in December only to be sunk by the battleship *Duke of York* and torpedoes from escorting cruisers and destroyers. Allied bombers closed U-boat operations in the Bay of Biscay, and the neutral Portuguese government assisted by leasing the Azores Islands for Allied seaplane, land-based patrol bomber and naval operations. British subs turned from the neutralized German surface raiders to attack German merchant shipping and U-boats in the North Atlantic late in 1943 and were joined by British escort carrier groups. The renewed Murmansk convoys were heavily escorted, forcing Doenitz to shift his U-boats into the mid-Atlantic. There they ran afoul of the U. S. Tenth Fleet's new offensive hunter-killer groups of escort carriers and destroyer escorts. These forces under Admiral King's direction mounted new TBF/TBM Avenger torpedo-bombers; sonobuoys, aircraft searchlights and airborne microwave radars for sub detection; and aerial rockets, faster-sinking depth charges and homing torpedoes. The Allies also utilized quantitative analysis techniques (operations research) to institute larger convoys, three-sub wolf packs (for the Pacific) and systematic aerial mining procedures. Doenitz's own innovations—massproduced prefabricated U-boats, acoustical torpedoes and schnorkel underwater breathing devices to avoid having to surface—would not begin to be ready until mid-1944. Consequently, Allied monthly merchant losses never exceeded 210,000 tons after July 1943, while Doenitz lost 167 U-boats between then and May 1944—faster than Germany could build new ones. Thus did the Allies win command of the Atlantic sea lanes, prerequisite to the cross-Channel attack.

Russia tied down the main German armies by mounting its general counterattack following the great tank battle of Kursk, 300 miles south of Moscow, in July 1943. To keep the Murmansk-Archangel supply routes open, Russian subs attacked German shipping in northern Norway, requiring the Germans to extend their antisub measures thence during the summer, and Russian destroyers and subchasers assisted incoming Allied convoys. The Northern Sea Route also stayed open for occasional reinforcements from the Pacific. Crossing the Dnieper during the latter half of 1943, the Red Army then liberated Smolensk and Kiev and the western Ukraine early in 1944. Throughout these operations, the Black Sea Fleet under Admiral L. A. Vladimirskij added more ships and planes to operate on the left flank. In September 1943 it assaulted and retook Novorossisk, naval infantry going ashore in 120 landing boats behind cutters which cleared the minefield, and under cover of naval air and coastal gunfire linked up with the army behind the city. Covered by the Azov Flotilla of Admiral S. G. Gorshkov, the same force established a bridgehead on the Kerch peninsula in early November, but was checked by stiff German resistance. Taking advantage of the Russian winter offensive, the Fleet bypassed the Crimea to retake Nikolayev and Ochakov in March and Odessa in April 1944, assaulting across the Kerch Strait to regain Sevastopol in the Crimea in May. Light Russian warships, naval aircraft and subs could then blockade and attack the Axis bases at Rumanian Constanta and Bulgarian Varna and Burgas. By June, Russian fleet units were relieving Axis pressure in the Black and Baltic seas, and the army had kept the *Wehrmacht* sufficiently occupied on the Eastern front to enable the Anglo-American allies to regain the Mediterranean.

While Admiral Cunningham's minesweepers battled subs and planes to clear a path for Allied convoys between Gibraltar and Suez in May 1943, General Eisenhower built up his forces in North Africa to take Italy out of the war. Allied bombings and a threat of amphibious assault led to the Italian surrender of Pantelleria Island in June, after which the 2500 invasion craft for Sicily collected from Britain, America, North Africa, Malta and the Middle East. Well-rehearsed and preceded by days of aerial bombing from North African-based aircraft, the assault of July 10 inaugurated such new amphibious craft as the Dukw, LST, LCI, LCT and LCVP. A silent approach did not effect the planned surprise, and the non-naval tactical air support left much to be desired, but general Axis resistance proved to be lighter than expected—partly the result of an Allied ruse. A sub had planted a body with bogus papers off the Spanish coast seen by German agents who then caused the diverting of important minelayers to Greece and a panzer division to Sardinia, expected landing points. The Allied armies raced across Sicily, but could not prevent the escape of Axis troops across the Strait of Messina in August.

Mussolini's government fell late in July, and the successor regime agreed to an armistice early in September which the Germans would not honor and instead set up Mussolini as a puppet in the north. That month the British crossed into Italy while the Americans assaulted Salerno below Naples, the Germans evacuated Corsica and Sardinia, and British forces landed on several Italian Aegean islands. A German air strike sank one Italian battleship before that fleet surrendered to the Allies at Malta, and on October 13 Italy declared war on Germany. The Germans halted the Allied overland advance and retook the Aegean islands, whereupon the Allies in January 1944 landed north of Rome at Anzio only to be trapped there in Gallipoli fashion by the Germans. Allied antiair and antisub measures thwarted Doenitz's and Goering's spring attacks in the middle sea, and in May the Italian stalemate ended with an Allied breakout that liberated Rome on June 4. Anglo-Italian naval patrols in the Adriatic supported Yugoslav partisans, but the major Allied effort was shifted back to the English Channel. The Mediterranean campaign had tested amphibious techniques and troops alike and seriously weakened Germany in the classic maritime strategic manner.

The turn of the tide in the Mediterranean and Atlantic enabled the British to strengthen the Indian Ocean front. Admiral Lord Louis Mountbatten, who had directed the British amphibious recovery early in the war, in 1943 became Commander, Southeast Asia, and pressed for an amphibious assault from the Bay of Bengal to relieve Allied ground forces in Burma. But the requirements for landing craft in the Mediterranean confined his amphibious activities to coastal operations in Burma from December 1943. He did obtain considerable heavy British fleet units after the neutralization of the German battleships and the Italian fleet, along with surface ships of the reunified French National Navy (in June 1943) and American Pacific Fleet units on loan. Consequently, the Eastern Fleet under Admiral Somerville returned from East Africa to Ceylon in 1943 for operations against a U-boat offensive from a new German sub base at Penang in Japanese Sumatra and for attacks on several Japanese islands. Doenitz's shift away from closely guarded sea lanes in his tonnage war brought him some successes in the Indian Ocean before being contained by Allied countermeasures. And during the spring and summer of 1944 Mountbatten directed several carrier-surface bombardments of Sumatra, Java and the Andaman Islands. These were only nuisance raids against a Japan which was losing the air over China to Allied planes and the North China countryside to Mao Tse-tung's Communist forces but holding off Chiang Kai-shek's Nationalist armies in the South. Also, mounting numbers of Allied warships enabled French and Italian cruisers to help patrol the Central Atlantic and Russia to obtain the loan of several older Anglo-American vessels and later some surrendered Italian warships. Yet, the most impressive concentration of Allied war shipping lay in the Pacific, where the United States determined to wrest command of the sea from Japan.

The American offensive in the Pacific during 1943–44 exploited quantitative and qualitative superiority from the strategic exterior position. With their weakened fleet centrally based at Truk in the eastern Carolines, the Japanese could not utilize their normally advantageous interior position to meet the three simultaneous thrusts the Allies now sent against them. Admiral Nimitz controlled all Pacific warships and the offensives from the South Pacific (Third Fleet) under Admiral Halsey and the Central Pacific (Fifth Fleet) under Admiral Spruance, while General Douglas MacArthur attacked from the Southwest Pacific using Nimitz's warships on loan (Seventh Fleet) under Admiral Thomas C. Kinkaid. The awkward command relationship had resulted from interservice distrust and fundamental doctrinal differences of the Navy's maritime strategists Admirals King, Nimitz and Spruance and the Army's continental strategist MacArthur, who had tremendous political influence, though not enough to concentrate the whole offensive in his theater. For assaulting the islands of the South Pacific, the north coastal enclaves of New Guinea and the coral atolls of the Central Pacific, new amphibious techniques had to be worked out during the actual battles, primarily under the direction of Admirals Richmond Kelly Turner and Daniel E. Barbey and Marine General Holland M. Smith. If the Japanese fleet elected to fight, fleet tactics had to be developed around the many new fast battleships and carriers. The naval aviators of Admiral John H. Towers developed fleet doctrine around the new *Essex*-class carriers and their new F6F Hellcat fighters—proved at sea in 1944 under the command of Admiral Marc A. Mitscher. But Admiral Spruance, last of the formalist battleship admirals, resisted adopting the melee-type tactics of the carriers until forced by the circumstances of battle. So inferior had the Japanese fleet become by this time, however, that even faulty tactics could not seriously jeopardize the American advance. Finally, the submarines of Admiral Charles A. Lockwood heightened their *guerre de course* war of attrition against Japanese sea lanes.

During the summer and autumn of 1943 the three-pronged Allied Pacific offensive went into motion. To first neutralize the great Japanese naval and air base at Rabaul, Halsey and MacArthur worked up the Solomon Islands and New Guinea coast respectively between June 1943 and March 1944, beating off all Japanese air and naval attacks. As Halsey's landing forces took the central Solomons in the summer and fall, his covering forces of cruisers, destroyers and PT boats used radar and superior tactics to fight four night actions which sank one Japanese cruiser and several destroyers and troop transports at the cost of a cruiser and destroyer. On November 1 Halsey's troops landed at Bougainville in the northern Solomons, drawing many Japanese cruisers to the target area. On the 2nd his covering forces sank one of four Japanese cruisers at the battle of Empress Augusta Bay, and three days later a few carrier planes from the *Saratoga* dramatically damaged six of seven Japanese cruisers anchored at Rabaul. Halsey's land-based planes frustrated Japanese naval air forces and from Bougainville began regular strikes against Rabaul. Then, on November 20, Spruance used carrier and battleship cover to land the Marines at fanatically defended Tarawa and Makin atolls in the Gilberts which fell after heavy fighting. Mistakes were made in amphibious and carrier tactics, but the lessons were quickly learned and generally corrected. In December MacArthur jumped from the New Guinea coast to take Cape Gloucester at the opposite end of New Britain Island from Rabaul, while Halsey's forces went on to occupy Green and Emirau islands in February and March 1944. Rabaul had been encircled and isolated from outside help, and Japan's outer defenses pierced in three places.

The sudden success of the new mobile American amphibious-carrier force demonstrated the fallacy of Japan's defensive perimeter and created a new strategic option for the Allies in the winter and spring of 1944. Fortified as "unsinkable carriers" to whittle down the advancing American fleet, Japan's Pacific islands had in fact no mobility against the many fast carriers and land-based Army bombers. They thus offered no refuge as fleet bases for Japan's heavy fleet units, which hastily abandoned Rabaul and Truk before the American approach. This being the case, Admiral Nimitz decided to bypass both those bases and lesser ones, keeping them neutralized by land-based planes from the islands his forces did take. Airfields could be rapidly repaired and enlarged by naval Construction Battalion ("Seabees") and Army engineers. Even while Rabaul was being encircled, in January and February 1944 Nimitz sent Spruance's Fifth Fleet into the Marshall Islands. Admiral Turner's amphibious forces landed and took Kwajalein and Eniwetok under the barrage of his older prewar battleships and escort carriers. Admiral Mitscher's Task Force 58 of eleven fast carriers provided strategic cover, the eight new fast battleships—with no other work to do—giving additional antiaircraft protection along with the Hellcat fighters. Breaking away from the beaches and refueling at sea by fast fleet tankers, Task Force 58 in February headed westward to destroy Japanese land-based air at Truk and in the distant Marianas Islands. MacArthur occupied the Admiralty Islands and Hollandia in New Guinea in March and April as Army planes and the fast carriers destroyed Japanese air in New Guinea and the Palau Islands. From new anchorages in the Marshalls and Admiralties, the Pacific Fleet could now look to the capture of the Marianas and MacArthur to northwest New Guinea, after which the three prongs of the offensive could join together.

Japan could do little with an understrength fleet and a virtually useless policy of trade protection against Lockwood's subs from Hawaii and those operating out of Australia. The Americans replaced malfunctioning torpedoes with new electrical ones copied from German designs and even operated in several German-style wolf packs to sink most of the 3,500,000 tons of Japanese merchant shipping lost during 1943 and the first half of 1944. American subs operated as far as Japanese home waters and even sowed mines off the Chinese coast. Japanese merchant ship construction, like that of its warships, could not begin to offset these losses, while the Imperial Japanese Navy—regarding convoy escort as defensive and unglamorous—never developed sophisticated antisub techniques, using only the oldest and least effective destroyers plus some escort carriers and too few new frigates after mid-1943—even after a special escort command was created that November. A Japanese staff proposal for a defensive mine barrier between Japan and Borneo was delayed because the mines were being harbored for possible use against an increasingly worrisome Russia. As time ran out, Japan would have no choice but to commit its still-inferior fleet and undertrained carrier pilots for the protection of its inner defenses.

By June 1944 Japan and Germany stood alone against the combined might of the Allies. Russian manpower with American equipment had turned back the German armies, and now Russian industry was beginning to recover. Chinese manpower, unevenly effective, was now to be augmented by American B-29 strategic bombers and substantial British support on the Burma front. Allied sea power had regained command of Atlantic, Mediterranean and Central and South Pacific waters, with escort and fast carriers and land-based planes neutralizing Doenitz's U-boats and Japanese naval air power. Allied amphibious doctrine, perfected through much experience, had taken Italy out of the war and regained the key areas of the South and Central Pacific. The full weight of American and Allied industry and manpower could now be employed to spearhead the assault on Hitler's Fortress Europe and to begin the air-sea blockade of the Japanese Empire.

## ANGLO-AMERICAN COMMAND OF THE SEA

The final Allied offensives of the war, from the summer of 1944 to the summer of 1945, produced a fanaticism on the part of the Axis powers that delayed, but could not prevent, their eventual collapse. Indeed, the presence of the new Anglo-American-Canadian bridgehead in Normandy and the American capture of the Marianas Islands in June and July 1944 were such sufficient recognition of coming Axis defeat that late in July they induced several high-ranking German officers to make an unsuccessful attempt on Hitler's life and the highest Japanese statesmen to overthrow the Tojo regime. But Allied war aims mitigated against any real possibility of a negotiated end to the hostilities, for early in 1943 Roosevelt had promoted the war aim of "unconditional surrender," meaning that the Nazi and Japanese militarist leaders had no alternative but to fight to the finish. Indeed, the Russo-

German conflict had taken on the dimensions of a religious struggle—between communism and fascism—so that Hitler could expect no quarter from Stalin. And the American crusade in the Pacific fully aimed at eliminating the Japanese state and humbling or even destroying its "divine" Emperor, making the Japanese resistance religious, even suicidal.

With their conventional weapons losing the fight, their economies being strangled by the Allied air-sea blockades, and with American and British strategic bombers starting to mercilessly pound their industrial centers, the Germans and Japanese placed their faith in new secret weapons—guided missiles. In June Germany began launching V-1 buzz bombs from France at southern England, followed in September by V-2 interrange ballistic missiles from the Low Countries. During the autumn Japan unleashed its human-guided projectiles, *kamikaze* planes and *kaiten* submarine-torpedoes, followed in the spring by *oka* (or *baka*) piloted bombs, suicide torpedo boats and even swimmers. Fortunately for the Allies, these weapons came too late or appeared in such a piecemeal fashion that effective countermeasures could be devised. As for Allied secret weapons, the atomic bomb headed the list of new developments that would reduce the Axis efforts into relative insignificance.

No Axis secret weapon, as with the older dreaded U-boat and *Luftwaffe* fighter, could stay the Red Army's steady advance into Central Europe from the east during the summer and fall of 1944. In the south, Russian ground forces combined with Black Sea Fleet units to take the German-held Rumanian port of Constanta late in August, the last land-sea operation on that front, with Rumania and Bulgaria abruptly changing sides by the time the Red Army crossed the Danube early in September. During the autumn the Germans retreated from Greece into Yugoslavia. In the north, the Russians took Finland out of the war with a massive overland offensive throughout the summer and weakened the German mine barrier in the Gulf of Finland by steady air strikes and torpedo boat attacks which sank several light German surface ships. The collapse of Finland jeopardized German Army units along the southern coast of the Gulf and Lake Peipus, but naval vessels in both waters helped prolong the defense until Red Army units outflanked them. Russian forces took most of the Baltic islands and their subs broke through the German mine barrier to attack enemy shipping. Still, German destroyers and torpedo boats controlled Baltic waters, avoiding or sweeping British-laid aerial mines and successfully evacuating most German troops from Estonia and Latvia during the autumn. Anglo-Russian air strikes finally neutralized the last heavy German surface units, RAF bombers sinking the *Tirpitz* in northern Norway in November and forcing those in the Baltic to be converted into antiaircraft platforms. Simultaneous with these drives, the Red Army pushed into

Poland and Hungary, meeting virtually no resistance in the air and reduced resistance on the ground, as Germany shifted many forces away to fight on the newly created Western front.

The Allied landing at Normandy on June 6, 1944 (D-Day), caught the Germans unprepared. Field Marshal Rommel had only begun to lay mines and set up anti-beaching obstacles along the "Atlantic Wall" and was even confused by an Allied feint off Calais, while Doenitz lost 13 of his 36 defending U-boats which succeeded in sinking only 2 frigates, one corvette and an empty transport of the massive 4000-vessel Allied armada that crossed the Channel on that and succeeding days. The well-rehearsed assault—the greatest in modern times—placed over 175,000 men ashore, and was covered by Allied air forces in England and an Anglo-American-French fleet under Admiral Sir Bertram Ramsay which included 6 battleships, 15 cruisers, one monitor and many destroyers and rocket-launching craft for gunfire support. The Allied Expeditionary Force was commanded by General Eisenhower, with actual landing operations being directed from the amphibious command ship (AGC) *Ancon*. Since the assault took place between the heavily defended ports of Cherbourg and Le Havre, depriving the Allies of docking facilities, two artificial roadsteads—called "Mulberry" and largely the idea of Churchill—had to be fashioned from sunken hulks, though one was demolished several days after D-Day by a ferocious late spring storm. Nevertheless, the assault was an unqualified success and enabled the Allies to develop a formidable permanent bridgehead, which engulfed Cherbourg by the end of June, prior to the breakout across Western Europe in late July and August.

In order to further carve up the German Army defenses in France, the supporting gunships entered the Mediterranean where they reinforced Allied units to reach a strength of 5 battleships, some 20 cruisers, 9 escort carriers and a great many destroyers; these craft supported Franco-American landings in southern France on August 15. Both Allied fronts formed a pincers in August and September to recover or isolate all French seaports, thus ending the last U-boat presence near the Western Approaches and the last *Luftwaffe* threats in the Western Mediterranean, liberating Paris and sending the Germans in full retreat—simultaneous with the Allied advances in Italy and on the Eastern front.

The Germans' reaction to these Allied thrusts into their rear was sufficient to slow, but not to reverse the Allies. U-boat sinkings of merchant shipping declined to new wartime lows, around 50,000 tons in each of the autumn months, and Hitler strengthened his missile and ground defenses as his armies fell back on the homeland. The Allied advance had been so swift, however, that the logistical strain was slow-ing down the offensive, and the approach of winter further inhibited continental operations. If, however, Eisenhower could punch through the northern German defenses the Allies would have the Scheldt and Antwerp as forward bases, enabling them to overrun the V-2 missile sites. But the Germans crushed an Anglo-American airborne drop at Arnhem in Holland in late September, and the advancing ground forces did not reach the Scheldt for another month. On November 8 a British amphibious assault took Walcheren Island, though the rest of the month was consumed by Allied minesweepers clearing the Scheldt before Antwerp could become operational. Hitler then turned his V-2s on Antwerp, increased the attacks of his new schnorkel-equipped U-boats on Allied shipping, and in mid-December sent a massive armor spearhead into the American lines in Belgium and Luxembourg aimed at taking Antwerp. In this "Battle of the Bulge," however, the Allies repulsed his drive and in January 1945 renewed their offensive. Simultaneously, the Russians launched a general winter offensive all along the Eastern front, supported by devastating Allied air bombings of German targets, and in February Turkey and other Middle Eastern states finally declared war on Germany.

The end of Hitler's empire then came swiftly, though the U-boats increased their monthly sinkings to around 100,000 tons through April, and the German escort forces successfully controlled the Baltic for the evacuation of German forces from this theater in order to surrender on the Western front rather than to the dreaded Russians. In the east, most of the surviving German heavy surface ships succumbed to aerial bombs, and in the west Eisenhower's armies crossed the Rhine on naval landing craft in March. Hitler committed suicide on April 30, leaving the final task of surrender to his successor, Admiral Doenitz, who took Germany out of the war finally on May 8.

Japan's resistance promised to be longer and even more fanatical given the great distances and the relative strength of the unbeaten Japanese armies in China and the homeland. The "Mobile Fleet" of 450 planes on 9 fast carriers plus 5 battleships with escorts had moved to a new interior position at Tawi Tawi in the secluded Celebes Sea to counter Nimitz's and MacArthur's drives into the Western Pacific. This preoccupation left Admiral Mountbatten relatively free to mount offensives in the Indian Ocean. From Trincomalee and Colombo, Ceylon, the Eastern Fleet's surface ships, subs and aircraft extended Allied control over the Bay of Bengal during the second half of 1944. They drove German and Japanese subs from Penang to new and safer bases at Soerabaja and Batavia, cut vital Japanese seaborne logistics between Singapore and Rangoon, mined enemy waters by air, and supplied a new and steady Sino-American-British ground offensive into Burma.

Without amphibious craft, however, Mountbatten could not undertake a seaborne offensive into Malaya, leaving the Japanese free to use the excellent base facilities at Singapore and to mount an effective offensive against southern China and Allied air bases there during the autumn. With Japan tenaciously contesting its continental imperial possessions, the main Allied thrust had to come from the Pacific.

Fooled by MacArthur's jumps up the New Guinea coast to Wakde and Biak in May and June 1944 as the principal Allied advance, the Japanese committed their land-based air prematurely, losing much of it to Army planes, and were thus surprised when the United States Fifth Fleet descended on the Marianas in mid-June. When American Marines stormed ashore at Saipan on June 15 (the same time that the great Normandy bridgehead was being established on the other side of the world), Japan had little choice but to use its fleet to try to dislodge the invaders. From Pearl Harbor, Admiral Nimitz spread out his huge Pacific Fleet to support this assault and the anticipated naval battle: Lockwood's submarines scouted the waters between Saipan and Tawi Tawi, while Spruance used Turner's amphibious vessels and 125,000 troops to take Saipan, supported by 7 older battleships, 11 cruisers, 8 escort carriers and many destroyers and covered by Mitscher's 15 fast carriers, their almost 1000 planes and screen of 7 fast battleships, 10 cruisers and 60 destroyers—the most powerful purely naval force ever assembled to that time! Admiral Soemu Toyoda, Combined Fleet commander in Tokyo, ordered his mobile force under Admiral Jisaburo Ozawa to take the 9 carriers from Tawi Tawi via the Philippines to a point 500 miles west of Saipan and to shuttle his 450 planes between the carriers and Guam and Tinian near Saipan, attacking the American fleet en route.

Spruance learned of the Japanese fleet sortie from his subs and dispersed his ships accordingly: the transports moved 200 miles to the eastward, the gunfire support ships formed a battle line on the west side of Saipan, and the fast carriers initially went westward in search of Ozawa on June 18. Lockwood's subs lost contact with the Japanese fleet, which Spruance then concluded—from his experience at Midway— would approach in two parts. Tactically trained as a battleship-oriented formalist and obsessed with the false notion that enemy surface ships could actually outflank his fast carriers, whose planes had an operating radius of 250 miles, the nonaviator Spruance rejected the advice of aviator Mitscher to send Task Force 58 westward to find Ozawa and instead recalled the carriers to remain offshore. On June 19, the Battle of the Philippine Sea began with Ozawa's planes shuttling in from their distant carriers, only to be annihilated by Mitscher's Hellcat fighters in the "Marianas Turkey Shoot," while Lockwood's subs caught up with

Ozawa's ships and attacked; *Albacore* mortally damaged the new carrier *Taiho,* and *Cavalla* sank the veteran *Shokaku.* The battle ended late on the 20th when Task Force 58 managed to get close enough to the retiring Ozawa to sink the carrier *Hiyo* with aerial torpedoes. The Japanese thus lost the battle, Saipan Island and three carriers, but not their fleet.

The American victory at the Philippine Sea forced open Japan's defenses. Marines and Army troops completed the conquest of Saipan Island and assaulted and took adjacent Guam and Tinian during July and August. All three islands were then converted into airfields for the new B-29 bombers, which began operating against Tokyo and other Japanese cities in November. MacArthur completed his drive up the north coast of New Guinea by the end of July, at which time the American Joint Chiefs of Staff yielded to his insistence on the liberation of the Philippines—a political promise he had made to the Filipinos upon the evacuation in early 1942. Strategically, this decision was generally sound, for the object of both Pacific drives was to reach the "Luzon bottleneck"—the narrow funnel between Luzon, Formosa and China through which all Japanese shipping had to pass from the oil-rich East Indies to the homeland. As preludes, on September 15 MacArthur's forces easily occupied Morotai in the Celebes area, and the same day Nimitz's Marines assaulted the fiercely contested Peleliu in the Palau group of the western Carolinas.

What was faulty about the American preparations to assault the Philippines—at Leyte Island in mid-October—lay in command relationships. Since the Philippines were in the Southwest Pacific theater, MacArthur commanded the operation, augmenting his Seventh Fleet with more ships from the Central Pacific; his strategic covering forces, however, were the fast carriers of what was now designated the Third Fleet under Admiral Halsey, who took his orders only from Nimitz and not MacArthur. This violation of unity of command symbolized the mutual suspicions between the Army and Navy, the latter fearing with good reason that MacArthur considered its warships expendable. The arrangement was all the more regrettable in light of the elaborate Japanese plans for the defense of the Philippines. Japanese naval construction now yielded three new carriers, but the "Marianas Turkey Shoot" had eliminated the last trained pilots for any of the carriers. Admiral Toyoda therefore planned to lure Halsey's fast carriers away from the beaches with four of Ozawa's nearly planeless carriers from Japan and to hasten two battleship forces from Borneo and Singapore to strike the shipping off Leyte in Halsey's absence. If this defensive strategy failed, the new *kamikaze*s were to be committed.

The Battle for Leyte Gulf, the last traditional sea battle in history, began with fast carrier and land-based air strikes on Japanese defenses early in October and reached its climax with the repulsing of the Japanese fleet sorties near the end of the month. On October 13 Halsey's carrier strikes on Formosa enticed Toyoda to commit his land-based naval air forces prematurely to action. Toyoda lost hundreds of planes (over 650 by the landing date) in savage air battles with the fast carrier fighters. On October 20 the first elements of 200,000 Army troops stormed ashore at Leyte, and the Japanese implemented their elaborate plan. Admiral Ozawa with his "Northern Force" of carriers, two half-battleships and escorts headed south from Kure in Japan, while Admiral Takeo Kurita and the "Center Force" of five battleships, twelve cruisers and several destroyers from Singapore headed for San Bernardino Strait via Palawan and the Sibuyan Sea, and the "Southern Force" of two battleships, one cruiser with destroyers under Admiral Shoji Nishimura (joined by a three-cruiser force from Japan) left Borneo via the Sulu Sea for Surigao Strait.

To bar the Japanese forces' passage through both straits and their concentration off Leyte, the Americans set new defensive positions. Kinkaid's Seventh Fleet old battleships, cruisers, destroyers and PT boats formed a line across Surigao Strait and virtually blew Nishimura's battleships *Yamashiro* and *Fuso* out of the water during the night of October 24–25. After two of Lockwood's subs sank two and disabled a third of Kurita's Center Force cruisers off Palawan, Halsey launched carrier air strikes against this force in the Sibuyan Sea during the 24th, sinking the superbattleship *Musashi* but losing the light fast carrier *Princeton* to a land-based bomber. Still, Kurita pressed on through San Bernardino Strait which he found uncovered, for Halsey had bitten for Ozawa's bait and had headed north after Ozawa's Northern Force without coordinating his movements with the Seventh Fleet at the beaches. After dawn on the 25th Halsey found the Northern Force off Cape Engaño, Luzon, and began sinking *Zuikaku* and the three lighter carriers. But simultaneously the Center Force suddenly appeared off Leyte-Samar and began shooting up American shipping, joined by the first land-based *kamikaze*s. In the melee, the Japanese sank two escort carriers, two destroyers and a destroyer escort before Kurita suddenly headed out to sea to engage what he thought was Halsey's fleet (really more escort carriers) instead of completing his task, which was basically a suicide mission. Kurita then ran back through San Bernardino Strait during the night before the returning Halsey could cut him off, though Halsey's planes did manage to sink one cruiser the next day. The beachhead at Leyte had been saved, despite the shortsightedness of Halsey and the divided command system that had victimized the American operation, and the Japanese surface fleet ceased to be a major strategic factor, even as a fleet-in-being.

Allied military, naval and air power spent the late autumn and winter of 1944–45 hammering away at Japan's Southeast Asian defenses and closing the Luzon bottleneck to begin the blockade of Japan. The intensive operations of late 1944 had forced Japanese merchant shipping into the restricted operating areas of Asian coastal waters from Singapore to the Tsushima Strait, thus providing easy targets for the many Allied submarines. By contrast, the radarless Japanese subs had so failed to support the surface fleet off the Marianas that all had been recalled during the late summer to be equipped with radar, only to fail again at Leyte and to be wasted thereafter supplying Army garrisons on bypassed islands. (The Japanese Army even took a turn at building its own subs.) Japan's convoy escort force, even with planes equipped with radar or magnetic detectors, still failed to stop the Allied submarine attrition of merchant shipping—some 2,000,000 tons lost to all causes, but mostly subs, between July and December. Indeed, American submarines sank four of Japan's five escort carriers between December 1943 and November 1944, in which latter month the *Archerfish* sank the giant 68,000-ton fast carrier *Shinano* out of Tokyo Bay and *Sealion* sank the battleship *Kongo* off China, and in December *Redfish* sank the new carrier *Unryu* in the East China Sea. Since mid-1943, British and Dutch subs had operated from Ceylon, but during the summer of 1944 they began basing at Fremantle, Australia, with the Americans—the shorter-range British boats to deploy in the Gulf of Siam and the southern Java Sea, the Dutch to patrol the waters of the East Indies, thus releasing the long-range American subs to cruise to the Philippines.

Savage *kamikaze* attacks could not prevent MacArthur's army from securing Leyte and taking Mindoro (south of Luzon) in December, then leapfrogging up to Lingayen Gulf on western Luzon with an amphibious assault in January 1945 which pushed inland to liberate Manila in February. Simultaneously, Allied forces pressed deeper into Burma, supported by several flotillas of British landing craft and gunships off Arakan, reopening the Burma Road in late January. That same month Third Fleet fast carriers swept through the South China Sea sinking merchant shipping, while the four fast carriers of the new British Pacific Fleet attacked Japanese oil refineries in Sumatra. Though the fighting continued on the ground in the Philippines for several months, the United States fleets operating out of Leyte-Samar and Subic Bay-Manila were able to close the Luzon bottleneck by the beginning of March, and the Japanese ended their attempts to run oil from Southeast Asia to the homeland. The blockade had begun.

With the Southeast Asian areas cut off from the Japanese homeland, their bypassed garrisons tried valiantly but unsuccessfully to repel Allied mopping-up attacks. On the mainland, a Japanese offensive in southern China began in January 1945 by taking several American airfields before being checked by the Chinese finally in May, while in March the Japanese eliminated the French government of Indochina and totally occupied the colony. The Burma front was defended tenaciously, especially against the British-Indian-African amphibious assaults mounted from Chittagong against several Burmese islands in January and then worked down the coast during the spring. When a British amphibious assault force arrived off Rangoon on May 2, it found the Japanese had evacuated three days before in fear of a British overland advance. The Japanese retreat into Thailand (Siam) now became general. In the outlying islands such as the Bismarcks, the Solomons and New Guinea, Australian ground forces began the mop-up, while Japanese troops throughout Indonesia fell back on Java, Sumatra and Borneo, the latter island being assaulted and occupied in various key places by Australian and American forces between May and July. In the meantime, Allied surface ships and subs swept through Indonesian waters, bombarding coastal positions and sinking all manner of Japanese shipping, including a light cruiser east of Java by an American sub wolf pack in April, one heavy cruiser in the Malacca Strait by British escort carrier planes and destroyers in mid-May and another in the Banda Strait by a British submarine early in June. Allied command of Indonesian waters enabled the British-led surface ships and subs to plunder interisland convoys, sweep mines from anticipated invasion areas (notably Singapore), bombard coastal positions and even send midget subs into Singapore late in July to damage a Japanese heavy cruiser there. So meager had Southeast Asian targets become that Allied submarine headquarters in the Southwest Pacific were moved from Fremantle to Subic Bay in May, where greater pressure could be applied to the main effort against the Japanese home islands.

Air-sea blockade of the island empire became the Allied strategy for finishing Japanese resistance in 1945, although Allied leaders decided to apply three other stratagems to assist, each, however, proving to be relatively superfluous. The need for a continental army had always been a main feature of maritime strategy, and China had not provided that force sufficiently; although the Chinese Communists had virtually neutralized the Japanese Army in North China, the Nationalists were not able to stop the Japanese offensive in South and Central China until May, so that the American landings in January had been at Luzon, bypassing Formosa and the Chinese coast. But now, at the Allied conference at Yalta in February, the Russians promised to redeploy their

Army from Europe (three months after Germany's defeat) to the Far
East to fight the considerable Japanese armies in Manchuria. The second
stratagem, largely the U. S. Army's, called for a massive Normandy-type
amphibious invasion of Japan in the autumn of 1945. Third, if it was
ready and tested, the atomic bomb would be used. But these devices
were merely added weight to the crushing air-sea blockade of Japan
during the spring and summer. Japan's economy and war machine would
be absolutely destroyed: by strategic B-29 bombers from the Marianas
blanketing Japanese industrial centers with incendiary bombs and mining Japanese coastal waters with aerial mines; by medium bombers and
fighters from forward island bases at Iwo Jima and Okinawa, both to
be taken by amphibious assault; by submarines encircling Japan; and
by fast carrier air strikes and shore bombardments against the remnants
of the Japanese fleet and coastal defenses. Japan's only viable defense
lay in the *kamikaze,* which though ultimately unsuccessful made the
Allies pay dearly for their efforts.

Assaults on Iwo Jima and Okinawa in February and April 1945 respectively proved difficult against the fanatical Japanese resistance from
every quarter, but American forces nevertheless overcame it. Command
of the sea became absolutely essential, and both beachheads could be
isolated from any outside interference save for *kamikaze*s. That isolation
was due to the mobility of the fast carriers, again renamed Task Force
58 under Mitscher and which were now totally supplied by at-sea
logistical replenishment groups operating out of several of the many
distant captured island bases. Again part of Spruance's Fifth Fleet, the
carriers ranged along the Asian periphery attacking even Japanese ports
and the fleet anchorage at Kure, though constantly plagued and damaged
by *kamikaze*s. A welcome addition in March came in the form of 4
fast carriers of the British Pacific Fleet, giving Mitscher some 16 carriers at all times. The *kamikaze*s sank several smaller ships off Iwo, but
Admiral Turner still landed and supported the Marines who conquered
the island in the severest fighting of the Pacific War. The Okinawa
operation was similar, though on a larger scale, with Turner landing
183,000 Army and Marine troops from the amphibious units of Spruance's nearly 1500 vessels during the first week of April. In addition to
the usual *kamikaze*s, the Japanese even dispatched their superbattleship
*Yamato,* one light cruiser and 8 destroyers on a suicide mission against
the invasion beach. Mitscher's carrier bombers and torpedo planes intercepted these ships and sank them all, save 4 of the destroyers. *Kamikaze* attacks from land bases and fierce Japanese Army resistance on
Okinawa dragged on till late June. The struggle cost the United States
over 750 planes and 36 light vessels plus several hundred others dam-

aged. But American carrier and land-based planes destroyed perhaps 8000 Japanese planes in the air and on the ground, enabling the Fifth Fleet to complete its ring of island bases around Japan.

While the B-29s pounded Japanese cities, their aerial mines and American submarines closed Japanese waters. During March, April and May the B-29s dropped five types of aerial mines—two of them, subsonic and pressure, unsweepable—into the Tsushima Strait between Japan and Korea, in the main shipping routes along Honshu and Kyushu, all major harbors and the Inland Sea. During June and July most of the 12,000 aerial mines of the campaign were sown, virtually halting all Japanese coastal shipping, while Navy planes from Okinawa were helping to mine South Korean waters. The last preserve of enemy shipping, the Sea of Japan, closed in June when a wolf pack of nine American subs entered it via the well-mined Tsushima Straits to sink twenty-seven merchantmen inside of seventeen days before escaping out via the northern La Pérouse Strait, losing one of their number to a patrol boat depth charge attack. More subs operated in the Sea of Japan over the next two months, but found targets exceedingly scarce. The reason was that, by the end of July, the mines and subs had clamped a totally effective blockade of all major Japanese ports. No ship could move in or out of any harbor, and the Japanese were powerless to sweep the mines. Of the 1,600,000 tons of Japanese merchant shipping sunk during 1945, about three quarters of it succumbed to the mine blockade. The strategic bombers between March and August nearly finished what was left of Japanese urban industry, so humbling Japan that starvation would soon face the Japanese civilians and home army girding for the expected invasion. In addition to millions of militia forces, in June and July Japan withdrew its last 3000 *kamikaze*s, 5000 other planes and 3300 suicide boats to meet that attack.

As Japanese officials debated surrendering in accordance with an ultimatum issued by Allied leaders meeting at Potsdam in July new fury descended on the home islands. The American-British fast carrier armada, again redesignated the Third Fleet, under Halsey, began projecting naval power against strategic targets in Japan—the first instance in history of strategic bombardment on a massive scale from the sea. In addition to bombing industrial and transportation targets in Tokyo and other cities, the 1200 carrier planes struck the anchored Imperial fleet at Kure on the Inland Sea on July 24 and 28, sinking three battleships and three cruisers and severely damaging two of Japan's newest but immobilized carriers. Japan had only a few long-distance submarines with which to retaliate, and one of them, the *I-58,* managed to sink the unescorted American heavy cruiser *Indianapolis* in the Philippine Sea early in August. Third Fleet battleships and destroyers even shelled coastal industrial targets at point-blank range, and several typhoons ravaged the Japanese coast. Finally, between August 6 and 9, three sudden events convinced the Japanese government to surrender earlier than expected from the air-sea blockade alone: two United States B-29s dropped atomic bombs on Hiroshima and Nagasaki on the 6th and 9th respectively, and Soviet Russia declared war on Japan on the 8th— three months to the day of the German surrender (as agreed at Yalta).

The unexpected Russian attack had a profound impact on Japan, whose major armies in China had not been defeated in the field and thus had resisted all the surrender talk. The Red Army's mechanized thrust changed such obstinance, driving from Outer Mongolia, the Amur River region and Vladivostok through Manchuria and into North Korea in just one week, ferried and supported by the 8 monitors, 11 gunboats and 52 armored cutters of the Amur Flotilla. The Soviet Pacific Fleet of 2 heavy cruisers, 79 destroyer types and subchasers, 78 subs, 204 torpedo boats and over 1500 land-based naval aircraft plus naval infantry operated mostly from Vladivostok but also from Sovetskaya Gavan farther north and Petropavlovsk on Kamchatka to eliminate the northern outposts of the Japanese Empire. Initially, the Russians had determined to assume a defensive stance in their coastal regions, except for the thrust into Korea, but the virtual collapse of Japanese resistance in Manchuria led them to assume a makeshift offensive into southern Sakhalin and the northern Kuriles. Torpedo boats raided North Korean Pacific ports in preparation for several landings, only one of which met any resistance: on August 13, the same day that U. S. Third Fleet carrier planes made a heavy raid on Tokyo, Russian naval infantry assaulted and took the port of Chongjin without opposition, but then absorbed a Japanese counterattack on the ground before major air and sea reinforcements enabled a general advance inland over the next three days.

The Japanese government yielded to the Potsdam ultimatum on August 15, but resistance did not cease in this second Russo-Japanese war until the 19th. As Russian forces pushed overland on Sakhalin Island, amphibious assault forces landed without opposition at several points along the coast. The only major assault in the Kuriles took place on the 18th at Shimushu Island, but defending Japanese guns sank several landing craft and held the attacking forces to a small beachhead perimeter. Then the defenders joined the general Japanese capitulation by surrendering on the 23rd. The next day Paramushiro Island surrendered, and the Russians airlifted troops into Pyongyang, North Korea, whereupon the fighting ceased, and on succeeding days the Russians occupied all of the Kuriles and Sakhalin Island and Korea north of the 38th parallel. An airborne force also occupied the former Russian naval bases at Dairen and Port Arthur. Soviet amphibious operations had been successful if uneven, combining equally with the atomic bomb to hasten Japan's surrender by several weeks.

Japan's official surrender on September 2, 1945, on the deck of the American battleship *Missouri* in Tokyo Bay came primarily as the result of the air-sea blockade of over three years of fighting. American command of the sea and air had made an amphibious invasion unnecessary in this greatest naval war in history. Once Japan's offensive had been blunted at Midway and Guadalcanal in 1942, the Americans had won invaluable time during which to build and train a new fleet to replace the one lost at Pearl Harbor and after. In the meantime, the long-range American attack submarines mounted their growing *guerre de course* campaign against the Japanese merchant fleet, exemplified by such successful subs as the *Flasher* which alone sank 100,000 tons of enemy shipping and the *Tautog* which claimed twenty-six vessels; in all, the subs accounted for more than half of the some 8,500,000 tons of Japanese shipping lost. (Mines and planes sank the rest.) By the summer of 1943, when the new fleet began to arrive in the Pacific, it was an entirely new conception from the battleship-centered one of prewar years. Spearheaded by the Fast Carrier Task Force which seized and held command of the air and sea, the new amphibious forces could land Fleet Marine Forces ashore at various islands with relative impunity. From the newly won islands, the naval blockade and strategic bombardment closed off and defeated Japan in 1945. The naval battles of the Philippine Sea and Leyte Gulf, fought against inferior Japanese fleets, were almost anticlimactic, as were the atomic bombs and the Russian attack. The American logistic establishment, and its careful protection, proved vital to Allied success, in contrast to Japan's feeble efforts in both commerce protection and submarine *guerre de course*. Completely subordinated to a continental strategy in China, the Imperial Japanese Navy had assumed blue-water pretensions in an impossible attempt to maintain command of the vast Pacific waters. Even the more than 2400 *kamikaze* pilots who perished failed to delay the inevitable defeat.

World War II in Europe also witnessed probably the last traditional application of naval power in a massive worldwide war. The Anglo-American navies, with a superior industrial base and favorable geographic insularity, successfully neutralized the Italian and German surface fleets and early prevented any Axis invasion ever being mounted against the British or American homelands. But the U-boats had presented the same strategic problems in this war as in 1914–18, making the Battle of the Atlantic the key to the Allies' turning from the strategic defensive to the offensive, not possible until mid-1943 when Anglo-American industry produced advanced techniques and many new weapons. German and Italian subs claimed over 2800 merchant ships totalling nearly 14,500,000 tons but at the cost of no fewer than 781 German U-boats and a few Italian boats. As the escort carriers and land-based patrol planes neutralized the U-boats, so too did aviation lead in the blockade and bombing of Hitler's Europe, establishing the essential command of the sea and air prerequisite to amphibious assaults in North Africa, Sicily, Italy and France. Still, the principal Allied striking arm remained the Red Army, until 1944 armed and equipped mostly by long-suffering Allied transatlantic convoys and the unmolested North Pacific merchantmen. The Russian Navy, though crippled early in the fighting, recovered sufficiently to assist in the counteroffensives of 1943–45. Churchill's Mediterranean strategy, whatever its motive, did follow the ancient British maritime strategic practice of the indirect approach to whittle down enemy strength on the continental periphery prior to a major landing as at Normandy. From command of the sea followed continental invasion.

The Anglo-American atomic bomb and German V-2 rocket revolutionized warfare, but not to the often-mistaken end that all the naval lessons of World War II were rendered obsolete. True, battleship actions and fleet battles—even with carriers—lay in the past, but any future naval requirements short of atomic warfare would embrace the same techniques and weapons that had been used in this last great sea war.

# BOOK SEVEN

## Pax Americana

*. . . Russian policy is really to push down southward and command what every writer and every thinking man from the most ancient times knows perfectly well is the great thing to possess, namely, "the command of the seas," and Russia, in my opinion, is determined upon possessing the "command of the seas."*

—CAPTAIN BEDFORD PIM,
Royal Navy, 1884

As devastating as were the total wars of 1914–45 and the weaponry which they bequeathed to the future, the global cosmopolitanism which they had interrupted now resumed, to fashion a genuinely new era in human affairs which can be labeled—in the strategic realm at least—the *Pax Americana*. A better label or complete definition is not yet possible for lack of historical perspective, but at the midway point (1973) between the end of the world wars era (1945) and the start of the twenty-first century (2001) one can discern the essential features of this age. A technologically based Western-oriented *Weltanschauung* has engulfed the world, awakening common human purpose to minimize if not eradicate the traditional dilemmas caused by political and economic divisiveness. Aerospace technology has led to rapid global communications via the jet-propelled aircraft (1945), commercial television (1948) and the orbital communications satellite (1965), and has propelled man beyond his own planet into space (1961) and even to the surface of the moon (1969), in addition to sending un-manned probes to the other planets of the solar system. Equally sig-nificant, rampant scientific industrialism led to the initiation in the 1960s of common efforts to check its excesses, both to the natural en-vironment and to human beings. The outstanding example is the sudden awareness that the unchecked pollution and exploitation of the oceans and fresh-waterways will destroy them ecologically and thus eventually also the human race. The overpopulation of the world, made possible by modern science and medicine, has led to the general awareness of limi-tations in natural resources, food and energy sources—the traditional and principal causes of imperialism and war.

The realization—in the wake of the atomic bomb and its successor weapons—that total war is no longer politically viable or humanly acceptable further binds together humanity to prevent its repetition. A new worth of the individual has thus emerged to challenge the older assumptions of imperial rule, industrial exploitation, economic and ideological conflict, and even the demands of nationalism. A new human vitality—not unlike that of the former thalassocracies—is being forged on a global scale, but only as the older biases and values are gradually —and ever so painfully—supplanted.

The generations of the *Pax Americana* have therefore witnessed the demise of the old European global hegemony, the emergence of post-war superpowers in the United States and Soviet Russia, a host of newly liberated former colonial states and new power centers in Western Europe, Japan and the People's Republic of China. The excessive nationalism of the powers gradually passed as their world-wars leaders left power: Roosevelt in 1945, Stalin in 1953, Churchill in 1955 and de Gaulle in 1969. Their successors—joined by the last great wartime leader, Mao Tse-tung in the early 1970s—have matured with an aware-ness of the new global and strategic realities that limit traditional forms of imperialism, overt revolution and war. Great power diplomacy has thus increasingly sought to restrict the exuberant and dangerous nationalism of the emerging smaller nations, through bilateral coopera-tion, the forum of the United Nations created formally in 1945 and through the international policing efforts primarily of the U. S. Navy. Like its predecessors of Minos, Athens, Rome, Venice, Holland and Britain, the United States found itself the only surviving maritime power capable of maintaining order upon the seas, enforcing inter-national law, and leading multilateral efforts to check piracy (especially hijacking at sea and in the air) and smuggling (arms and drugs) and in promoting weather reporting and rescue at sea. By its formidable military strength at sea and in the air, the United States has balanced the continental powers of Russia and China and policed the oceans of the world. Strategically, then, the era can be aptly regarded as the *Pax Americana*.

As other nations have come to share American maritime prosperity, the oceans have assumed universal importance as not only avenues but sources of food and minerals. Since 1945 entire new fields of sea science and oceanic technology have arisen: underwater exploration and drilling for oil and gas; aquaculture ("sea farming") and general fishing; oceanography and marine biology; submersible craft, plus scuba and skin diving; underwater archeology and deep-water salvage; the recovery of early American manned spacecraft at sea; and even the possible domestication and military utilization of the pilot whale and especially the dolphin. But water pollution by American oil and chemical companies, overfishing by Russia, Japan and the Scandinavian countries and underwater weapons systems of the Russians and Americans have led to the need for restraints. International law has continued to promote free use of the seas, but the old 3-mile coastal limit of national territorial jurisdiction has gradually been extended to 12 miles and even claims of 200 miles by especially Brazil and Ecuador, whose gunboats have tried to enforce them. Such laws depend upon enforcement, with the United States and secondarily Russia having the only sizable navies to do it. In 1963 both nations banned underwater nuclear testing and seven years later prohibited nuclear and other massive weapons on the ocean floor ("seabed") beyond the 12-mile limit. But agreements by all nations using the oceans are necessary in this global age, initiated at the United Nations Conference on the Law of the Sea in 1958 and the unofficial *Pacem in Maribus* ("Peace in the Oceans") conference which met at Malta in 1970. As in the past, however, international agreements depend upon the willingness of the participants to live up to them and especially upon the acquiescence of the great powers which are capable of commanding the seas.

Unfortunately, the breakdown of the wartime Alliance, the final collapse of the British and other European empires, and the growing ideolgical rift between the democratic-capitalistic United States of America and the communistic Union of Soviet Socialist Republics resulted in the Cold War which dangerously delayed mutual understanding and cooperation at sea or anywhere else. Both powers had been traditionally strategic continentalists, save for America's reliance upon the British naval shield, which simply evaporated in 1947. United in their anti-fascist crusade, neither superpower could immediately and realistically resolve postwar political boundaries and spheres of political, economic and strategic influence and thus created two armed camps during the late 1940s and 1950s which included Western Europe in the "Free World" camp and "Red" China in the "Communist bloc." This bipolar balance of power, heightened by the nuclear arms race, gradually disintegrated during the late 1950s and 1960s with the postwar recoveries and autonomous policies of Western Europe, China, Japan and the "Third World" developing nations in Africa, Latin America, the Middle East, South and Southeast Asia. Joined by economically and socially oppressed elements within American and Russian societies, these new nations inaugurated a "revolution of rising expectations" to advance the larger global cosmopolitanism and human rights movements. This effort by the "have-not" peoples against the "have" undermined the brief bipolarity of the 1950s and helped expose the strategic fallacy of the Russo-American Cold War, a fact dramatically demonstrated also by the Cuban missile confrontation of 1962. Soviet-American distrust and antagonism thus gradually diminished during the 1960s and culminated in the Strategic Arms Limitation Treaty (SALT) of 1972.

As in the political sphere, strategic thought has also been reluctant to throw off its assumptions rooted in the era of the total world wars. The material strategists prevailed for over twenty years with their faith in the panacea of super machine weapons, fed by the false notion that strategic bombing had largely decided the outcome of World War II rather than the Herculean efforts of the United States and Royal navies and the Red Army. In fact, however, the nuclear-armed land- and carrier-based bombers, now capable of strategic bombardment, destroyed the last real distinctions between land and sea long-range artillery in the 1950s, at which time the intercontinental ballistic missile (ICBM) appeared, guaranteeing the eventual doom of the manned strategic delivery system. The hardened missile silo and missile-launching submerged submarine of the 1960s, plus the possibility of orbiting satellite weapons, created a "balance of terror" between Russia and America, both having the separate capability of annihilating the human race in a nuclear war many times over ("overkill"). Nevertheless, material strategists—typified by Herman Kahn and Robert S. McNamara in the United States—persisted in the belief of the viability of nuclear war by using computers, electronic war gaming and mathematical and economic analysis and games theory. Hoping for "damage limitation" in such a war, they ignored or minimized the inevitable massive destructiveness of a nuclear exchange to the transportation, communications and electrical power systems, much less social institutions, upon which modern society (and its weapons) depend for survival. They also seemed to forget the basic historical fact that the nations devastated by World Wars I and II had been able to recover only with the full economic aid of a major nation unscathed by the devastation, namely the United States, a refuge that would obviously be absent after any third world war.

The predominance of material strategists in the major powers thus characterized their defensive stances. The *ad hoc* military-industrial management complexes of the two world wars thus became formalized, the modern superweapons having to be rigidly controlled in the delicate balance of terror. Expensive weapons had to be made "cost effective" by specialized "organization men" with their bureaucratic staffs of experts and advisers, and military men blended into the political decision-making process to guarantee the optimum use of these weapons. Such a hierarchical rigidity has perhaps been a key element in checking the outbreak of a nuclear World War III, but it has also had a stifling effect on the creative energies of the American and Russian people—and on their military and naval officers. Bureaucracy is by nature conservative, lethargic and self-perpetuating merely for its own ends, but survives as long as national public opinion can be convinced to accept and support it. Also, world opinion has been no small factor in reacting to the decisions of the two bureaucratic superpowers. The blind obedience of the American and Russian peoples that sustained the Cold War leaderships of the late 1940s and 1950s began to wane as the new realities became evident in the 1960s, partly the result of the new global cosmopolitanism which is antithetical to rigid authority but also because of the generally narrow and unimaginative strategic thought and policies of the "cold warriors" that led to confusion and loss of public confidence in them.

Historical strategy did indeed initially seem obsolete in the nuclear age, but not to the thinkers who quietly examined and discussed it. Indeed, the vast post-1945 literature on the phenomenon of war was merely a continuation of academic discussions of the 1930s embodied in such relatively new professional fields as military and diplomatic history and international relations. In most cases, the historical strategic analysts had been trained or had written in that decade and tended to be less impressed by nuclear weapons and machine-computed intellectual tools than were the material strategists. Stressing the continuity of historical experience as preached by their teachers Corbett and Mahan, these thinkers harkened back not only to Clausewitz but even to Themistocles in appreciating the traditional uses of maritime and imperial strategy and limited warfare, hence the efficacy of naval power. In this respect they have not been original in their theories, but by keeping active much thought on the importance of command of the sea, blockade, commerce warfare, amphibious operations and naval diplomacy they have provided alternatives for the nuclear determinism once it proved inadequate during the 1960s.

Significantly, few of the historical strategists have been active officers or policy advisers during the course of their writings, which have been counter to the anti-intellectual conservatism of their nuclear-dominated armed forces. But as retired officers, university professors and professional writers they have taught at war colleges, participated in the "think tank" activities of their material strategy colleagues, and generated much service discussion in their several professional journals. Among the leading historical pundits have been, in the United States, Admirals John D. Hayes and Henry E. Eccles, Professors Bernard Brodie, Robert E. Osgood, Oskar Morgenstern, Theodore Ropp and Anthony E. Sokol (formerly Austro-Hungarian Navy), and writers Herbert Rosinski (former German naval war college professor), Hanson W. Baldwin and George E. Lowe (both formerly U. S. Navy); in Russia Admirals V. A. Alafuzov and K. A. Stalbo and writers N. P. V'iunenko and D. I. Kornienko; in Germany, Admiral Friedrich Ruge; and in Britain, Admirals Sir Herbert Richmond (who died in 1953), Sir Anthony Buzzard and Sir Peter Gretton, Captain Stephen W. Roskill, Professors P. M. S. Blackett and L. W. Martin, and writer Sir Basil Liddell Hart. Interestingly, several army general officers have also shown a genuine appreciation for historical strategy, limited war and navies: British Field Marshal Viscount Montgomery of Alamein, American Generals Douglas MacArthur, Maxwell Taylor and James Gavin, and French General André Beaufre. Supporting the analyses of these individuals have been the treatises of many traditional historians, of which the present work is an example.

The historical strategists had little impact on political policies until the inadequacies of material nuclear strategy began to become evident. For Britain, Russia and the United States respectively, the eye-opening events were the Arab-Israeli crisis of 1956, the Cuban blockade of 1962 and the Vietnam War of 1965–73. Gradual buildup of limited war forces followed but without any systematic strategic rationales. National leaders, overawed by nuclear weapons, tended to see only irrelevance in the past and the more-lasting maritime principles expounded by Mahan and Corbett. One glaring example of ignorance was their neglect of Corbett's warning that limited war by a maritime power should be undertaken only when the battlefield can be geographically isolated—in modern parlance, interdicted—from outside supply and reinforcement by command of the sea. This proved possible in the British and American limited wars during the early 1950s in Malaya and Korea, peninsulas bordered mostly by water, but could never be possible in the one-coastline divided country of Vietnam on the continent of Asia; the United States paid dearly for its ignorance of this fact in the protracted Vietnam War. But as nuclear weaponry has become obviously useless in conflicts short of general war, the historical strategic arguments gain in acceptance.

Below the nuclear arena, therefore, the naval weapons of the *Pax*

*Americana* have differed but little in their tactical roles from their predecessors; indeed, many veteran warships of World War II themselves have far outlived their originally expected longevity. Roles and missions of the basic warship types have not changed, save for the complete replacement of the battleship with the carrier and the advent of missilery. Modern nucleonics have made large-scale overseas invasions unlikely, but defense against underwater ballistic missile attack has required ever more sophisticated antisubmarine weapons systems. The ballistic missile sub and to a lesser extent the attack carrier have new missions of strategic bombardment, both being capital ships, the former for general war, the latter for limited war. But the increasing inadvisability of nuclear war has tended to remove missile subs from the equation of normal naval strategy and tactics and into a separate political status, while fear of escalation into such a conflict has acted as a check on the use of tactical nuclear weapons on carrier planes, antisub forces and patrol craft (and ground and air forces). Nevertheless, American and Soviet admirals seem to be thinking in unrealistic terms about another potential sea war, so that fleet tactical attack functions and defensive techniques tend to blend with the missilery of the nuclear realm. The attack carrier is defended by escorting vessels with surface-to-air (SAM) antiaircraft missiles, homing torpedoes and antisub rockets (ASROC). Carrier fighters use air-to-air missiles (AAM), carrier attack planes aerial bombs and air-to-surface missiles (ASM). Antiship surface-to-surface sub and shipborne "cruise" missiles (SSM) have replaced the naval gun except in shore bombardment. Offensive and defensive mine warfare craft and systems have grown in sophistication but unchanged in mission and delivery techniques. Attempts to counter the intercontinental and interrange ballistic missiles (ICBM, IRBM) in flight in the form of antiaircraft guns and missiles, notably the antiballistic missile (ABM) missile, have proved prohibitively expensive and tactically doubtful in effectiveness. Nuclear deterrence has thus depended on offensive missiles, with the rest of the missile inventory being employed in traditional naval missions.

Naval operations have been revolutionized by developments in propulsion and communications. Ship propulsion machinery has progressed into improved diesel engines and steam and gas turbines and the advent of nuclear reactors to replace conventional boilers in providing steam power. The latter system, only gradually replacing oil, provides virtually unlimited cruising range at sustained high speeds (over 35 knots). Communication improvements have included more sophisticated radar and sonar, magnetic sub detectors, electronic countermeasures (ECM), navigational devices, radios using fixed antennae and communications satellites for short- and long-range circuits, and computers (dating from the U. S. Navy's IBM Naval Ordnance Research Computer, Norc, in 1954). Jet engines have gradually replaced most piston-engines on carrier fixed-wing aircraft; the multi-engine land-based long-range patrol plane (usually piston-driven) has supplanted the seaplane altogether; and the helicopter has emerged as a workhorse of multitudinous benefits. For warships, larger and heavier missiles, engines, aircraft and electronic equipment have meant increased displacements: the American nuclear carrier *Enterprise* 76,000 tons and the Soviet V/STOL carrier *Kiev* 45,000 tons; the American *Salem*-class and Russian *Sverdlov*-class heavy cruisers 17,000 and 15,500 tons respectively; the helicopter carriers of the *Iwo Jima* and *Moskow* classes 17,000 and 15,000 tons; the American guided missile nuclear-powered cruiser *Long Beach* and frigate *Truxton* 14,000 and 8000 tons each; American and French ballistic missile subs over 7000 tons; the large British "County"-class destroyers 5500 tons; with lesser specialized escort ships so large as to blur the former distinctions between light cruisers and destroyers.

Enlarged ship sizes and concurrently greater speeds have led to the development of revolutionary alternative concepts in fundamental ship design which minimize or eliminate altogether both the resistance of the waves to ship's hull and the skin friction due to the movement of the wetted surface. One is the hydrofoil, whereby the hull is lifted out of the water on small submerged wings as it speeds forward to some 50 knots. The Russians produced the first hydrofoil warships—inshore patrol craft and subchasers—in 1965. The other and more exciting invention is the hovercraft (air cushion vehicle; ground effect machine; surface skimmer), in which the vehicle rides on a cushion of air a few feet off the ground or water at speeds of over 80 knots at sea (but up to 300 miles per hour over monorails on land). Largely a British invention, the first experimental naval patrol hovercraft joined the Royal and United States navies in the late 1960s, but the type has endless possibilities especially as an amphibious vessel which can virtually ignore traditional natural obstacles. Experimentation in all facets of seaborne operations promises eventually to liberate the major navies from many traditional technological limitations—in the use of spacecraft for navigation, the increased placing of improved alloys such as aluminum and plastics in ship fittings or entire vessels (like the Royal Navy's all-plastic minehunter launched in 1972), new hull designs like the catamaran, strengthened deep submergence vehicles, vertical takeoff and landing aircraft (V/STOL) and maybe even new uses for wind and sails. Given the accelerating pace of modern science and technology, major scientific breakthroughs can be expected henceforth in ship and aircraft design, assigning many old *and* new weapons systems to hasty obsolescence and causing naval planners to weigh ever more carefully their strategic priorities in building new weapons of exceedingly high cost.

Still, new technical weaponry has not significantly changed the functions of navies, a hard fact learned again by all fleets in the tumultuous early years of the *Pax Americana,* during which the much-vaunted superweapons failed to offer strategic panaceas in a rapidly changing world. Men—as always—and not machines have remained the final arbiters in harnessing the sea for peaceful advantage or defensive purpose. Joined by women naval personnel on board larger American warships in the early 1970s, seamen now enjoy the best health, pay, training and general living and working conditions of any sailors in history.

## IMPERIAL COLLAPSE AND COLD WAR

The Russo-American Cold War developed as the direct result of the collapse of European hegemony in the world, but especially of the inability of Great Britain to maintain the strategic balance of power on the continent of Europe and to police the global sea lanes. The demise of the empires of Italy, Germany, Japan, Britain, Holland and France between 1943 and 1954 left political and economic vacuums to be filled either by the two new superpowers or the emerging small nations. Though cloaking their diplomatic policies in ideological rhetoric, the United States and the Soviet Union restored balance of power relationships in Europe and the Far East and returned to the historic practices of establishing spheres of influence. Instead of colonies, this type of imperialism assumed economic and ideological dimensions that led to involvement in limited "wars of national liberation" and ultimate ideological failure as the emerging former colonial peoples avoided American democracy and Russian communism in favor of unilateral courses. Under the umbrella of self-neutralizing nuclear weapons, the United States assumed the historical maritime strategic stance of the whale (eagle?) and Russia the historical continental posture of the elephant (bear?).

At first, the naval weapons that had survived World War II helped to demobilize the great armies but also fell victim to the awesomeness of atomic weapons, either in tests or by comparative obsolescence. The Japanese fleet was totally scrapped, while several German and Italian vessels avoided this fate by going into the Russian Navy, especially the newest U-boats which taught the Russians much. Under its nuclear monopoly, the United States further tested two atomic bombs in the Marshall Islands in July 1946 which sank or gutted two American fast carriers, one Japanese and three American battleships, one German and two American cruisers, an American sub and a destroyer. The ubiquitous mines could not be disposed of quite so easily, the Germans not ending their minesweeping operations until 1971 and American mines continuing to sink an occasional Japanese vessel even after that. The United States yielded its atomic monopoly to Russia in 1949, and both countries developed the hydrogen bomb in the early 1950s. But the Red Army defended the "iron curtain" across Central Europe and American land-sea-air power projected conventional power across the oceans of the world. The weapons of World War II thus continued to meet real strategic needs while the powers continued to explore and debate the utility of nuclear weapons.

The United States, despite its rapid postwar demobilization and reluctance to become oceanic policeman, had to look to its maritime posture which seriously deteriorated during the late 1940s. The unification of the armed forces—Army, Navy and a separate Air Force—under Secretary of Defense James V. Forrestal in 1947 led to a fierce interservice rivalry for the retrenched budget which favored nuclear weapons. Fearing obsolescence to new Air Force strategic bombers, the Navy under the leadership of Admiral Forrest P. Sherman (Nimitz's wartime planning officer) nevertheless survived and late in 1949 sent its first nuclear-armed attack planes to sea aboard its newest carriers. Postwar 1947 force levels were set at 15 fast attack carriers and 100 diesel-powered submarines. So the carrier gained a limited role as a nuclear deterrent, joined in the early 1950s by several cruisers and subs mounting Regulus surface-to-surface nuclear-tipped guided missiles. The similarly threatened U. S. Marine Corps turned to dispersed amphibious operations using the newly improved trooplifting helicopter from carrier and assault vessel decks. The American merchant marine, never a serious commercial competitor to the continental railroads, highway trailer trucks, canal-river barges of the Mississippi Valley or intracoastal oil tankers, lost its wartime inventory to the reserve "mothball" fleets, or by sale or gift to needy allied maritime nations in 1946–48. Most remaining American shippers escaped high maritime and longshoreman union wage and employment guarantees by shifting their registries to Panama, Liberia or Honduras, which would provide the necessary trade and profits. But these flag reductions hurt the American strategic posture dependent upon such vessels for sealift and logistical backup for its military forces during times of crisis. And the trained mercantile manpower followed the ships to the foreign registries. The new unified Military Sea Transportation Service of 1949 thus had too few and too old reserve supply ships, and the government refused to provide expensive new ones. Cutbacks in warships and overseas base facilities also reflected the false sense of security offered by nuclear weapons. The United States thus had no systematic preparations for fulfilling its new strategic missions and could respond to emergency situations only as they arose—a dangerous, shortsighted non-policy typical of the isolation-bound American people whose free strategic security behind two ocean barriers had in fact come to an abrupt end.

Soviet Russia had even less interest in maritime enterprises than its new enemy. Stalin reunified his armed forces under Red Army control in 1947 including a larger but still inferior land-based strategic air force. Russia's economic strength lay in the newly conquered "satellite" states of Eastern Europe and the interior regions of Russian Eurasia, all made more accessible to the industrial centers by an ever-growing railroad system and postwar improved inland waterway network of rivers and canals that connect Russia's five seas—the White and Baltic in the north, the Caspian, Sea of Azov and Black in the south—with traffic to and from the Russian Pacific coast going via the Trans-Sib Railway and Arctic Northern Sea Route. With such a strategic interior position, the Red Navy in the immediate postwar years adopted the same prewar stance of an active defense, but incorporated several tactical lessons of World War II. Stalin remained the chief proponent of this policy, even restoring the independent Navy Commissariat in 1950 (abolished again upon his death in 1953), though the major uniformed figure was Admiral Kuznetsov, wartime Navy commander-in-chief till 1947 and again 1950–55. This "fortress fleet" included all the familiar continental naval elements of inshore mines and torpedo craft, land-based naval aircraft, coastal fortifications and naval infantry for coast defense and submarines for commerce warfare. But Stalin sought more balance by building new and larger cruisers and destroyer leaders and by projecting for a few aircraft carriers. In addition to the older coastal regions, new Russian territorial gains from the war required such a buildup. The Baltic Sea returned to absolute Soviet control with the acquisition of the Karelian Isthmus to protect Leningrad, the absorption of Estonia, Latvia, Lithuania and East Prussia and its new ice-free Russian fleet base at Baltiisk (replacing Kronstadt), and the control and use of the ports of occupied Poland and East Germany. The Black Sea also came under Russian control with the absorption of Rumania and Bulgaria—with their ports—into the Soviet bloc. Russian naval defenses there were augmented by the Danube River Flotilla of patrol boats, minelayers and amphibious troops. Russia's Pacific defenses included all of Sakhalin Island, the Kuriles and Port Arthur, jointly operated with China, plus a very large river flotilla on the Amur River. From these coastal regions Russia's small merchant fleet, including several wartime American Lend Lease Liberty ships, operated into the oceans. But the Navy still remained an adjunct to the Army, its geographic outlets dominated by foreign powers at the Danish Sound, Turkish Dardanelles and Japanese Tsushima and La Pérouse straits.

The other European nations became minor naval powers generally dependent on the two superpowers for postwar recovery. The United States by disposing of its wartime merchant fleet over 1946–48 to Scandinavia, France, Holland and Italy restored their economies, and by its Cost-Sharing Ship Construction Program of the early 1950s provided them with light warships. Only Great Britain retained an independent blue-water naval posture, but in 1946–48 the new permanent Ministry of Defence cut back the Royal Navy's ships, planes and bases to give priority to the strategic bombers of the RAF. Without a nuclear role, the Navy in 1949 concentrated in qualitative research for its carrier-centered and antisub fleet, developing the angled deck, steam catapult and mirrored landing system for its carriers—improvements quickly imitated by the U. S. Navy. But in 1951 the British navy accepted the reality that it too had to depend on the American fleet in time of war. The United States and Britain supplied light surface ships and subs to several new or older underdeveloped nations; several of their light antisub carriers found their way eventually into the navies of France, Holland, Brazil, India, Argentina, Spain and Canada. By the same token, Russia eventually supplied smaller naval vessels to its satellites and to neutral powers like India and Indonesia.

The immediate Cold War issues focused on Russia's consolidation of its defensive frontiers during 1945–46. In addition to the assimilation of Eastern and parts of Central Europe into the Soviet sphere, the Russians made territorial and maritime demands on Iran and Turkey for control of the Dardanelles, for a Mediterranean base and for more influence in the Persian Gulf. Counteracting these moves, Britain began moving warships and troops into these regions, also to the Adriatic to sweep mines and support the Greeks against Communist guerrillas only to be taken under fire by Albanian shore batteries in May 1946. But Britain, economically prostrate from two world wars, could no longer restore the balance of power in these waters, and had to request first American assistance, then outright American leadership. Following the advice of Secretary Forrestal, President Harry Truman used naval demonstrations to help influence the Russians to stop their demands on Turkey and Iran. The battleship *Missouri* visited Istanbul (formerly Constantinople) and Athens during the spring of 1946, followed by the new carrier *Franklin D. Roosevelt* with its 123 planes during the summer, both relying on their mobile logistics rather than a base network, though the British made theirs available. American naval power redeployed to the Atlantic during 1946, nine attack carriers and three battleships, leaving six carriers and one battleship in the Pacific by the end of the year.

Europe's postwar economic plight became so severe that early in 1947 the British decided to quit both Greece and Turkey, and the new American Secretary of State, General George C. Marshall, advised Truman to go to the aid of all Europe, but especially Britain, Greece and Turkey. The Russians had counted on Western Europe's reliance on Polish coal, Rumanian oil and Hungarian wheat for its economic recovery, but in March 1947 Truman announced his "doctrine" to provide American economic aid and military equipment to Greece and Turkey and any other countries threatened by communism, followed in June by the Marshall Plan of massive American foreign aid to Europe. While Forrestal's warships demonstrated around European waters, Marshall's economic planners took the offensive by mobilizing the American merchant marine to transport vast quantities of grain and coal from the United States and oil from the Middle East to help the European economies recover. When Russia and her new satellites were invited to join this American-directed effort, Russia not only declined, but used Czechoslovakia's acceptance as part of the pretext to crush the few vestiges of independence left in that country early in 1948. America's large maritime effort to provide merchantmen for the economic and military sealift to Western Europe, supported by Anglo-American naval power, began to have immediate success. By 1948, Russian-American animosities had hardened, with Truman following a policy of "containment" of international communism—the work of George F. Kennan, along with Marshall and Forrestal—and Stalin cautiously probing for ways by which to dislodge the Americans from establishing an anti-Russian solidarity in Western Europe. And to reinforce the great success of the Marshall Plan, in June 1948 the U. S. Navy established the Sixth (Task) Fleet in the Mediterranean—a task force of two carriers, two or three cruisers, at least nine destroyers, and an attack transport with 1000 Marines embarked. Simultaneously, an American naval force was also stationed permanently in the Persian Gulf.

The American- and Soviet-led blocs quickly crystallized during 1948–49. When Communist Yugoslavia bolted from the Russian alliance in June 1948, Communist supply lines to the Greek guerrillas were severed, and the Greeks used American arms to crush the guerrillas by late 1949. Also in June 1948 the Russians blockaded "Western" Allied overland traffic through eastern Soviet-occupied Germany to the American, British and French sectors of Berlin. The Allies responded by stopping all trade with East Germany and instituting an airlift of cargo planes which frustrated Soviet designs within a year. Then, in April 1949, these Allies joined formally into the North Atlantic Treaty Organization (NATO): the United States, the United Kingdom, France, Canada, Belgium, the Netherlands, Luxembourg, Denmark, Norway, Iceland (independent since 1943), Italy and Portugal. Two years later Turkey and Greece joined, while neutral Sweden, Finland, Yugoslavia and Spain remained friendly, Spain even leasing naval and air bases to the United States in 1953. The political restoration of Germany also began, but in two separate parts belonging to the opposing camps. The creation of NATO effectively checked Russian expansionism in Europe and the Middle East, the general NATO deterrent based on superiority in the air and at sea rather than on the ground against the formidable Red Army. General Eisenhower, who became Supreme Allied Commander in 1950, simply never had enough troops from the economically strained NATO nations, so he relied on the American strategic air forces for nuclear intimidation and Allied naval forces to contain the Russians on the flanks of the European peninsula. The Supreme Allied Naval Commander—from 1951 always the commander of the U. S. Atlantic Fleet based at Norfolk, Virginia—controlled the Royal Navy-centered fleet units in the North Sea and the augmented U. S. Sixth Fleet in the Mediterranean. For their part, the Russians strengthened their "iron curtain" across Europe and looked elsewhere to test Allied strength.

Beyond Europe, the collapse of the old European empires offered many opportunities for superpower involvement, but these emerging peoples doggedly resisted further great power encroachments. The Latin American nations joined in the Organization of American States in 1947–48 and remained preoccupied with their endless internal turmoils. In the Middle East, Jewish Israel was formed after Britain's withdrawal in 1948 and then had to fight its Arab neighbors during 1948–49 to preserve its political integrity. Arab Egypt became a republic under Gamal Abdel Nasser in 1953–54 and pressed for British withdrawal from the Suez Canal, though the British hold on the Persian Gulf and the Trucial System did not change. North African Libya became independent in 1951 and two years later granted the United States and Britain rights to military bases there. In South Asia, Britain lost the heart of its Empire in 1947 when it granted independence to Hindu India and Moslem Pakistan, and a year later to Burma and Ceylon (Sri Lanka). During all these political dislocations, Anglo-American naval patrols provided a modicum of control. More importantly for the Cold War, Britain wisely promoted the friendship of her former colonies —often in the loose Commonwealth association—and all shared Britain's traditional desire to deter Russian economic and political incursions.

Southeast Asia created special problems due to the collapse of the Japanese Empire, the Chinese civil war and the determination of France and Holland to restore their colonies. The United States and Britain respectively granted independence to the Philippines (1946) and Malaya (1948), but would not withdraw their forces until political order was restored and the native Communist rebels crushed. American aid helped the Filipinos put down the Hukbalahaps by 1954, and between 1948 and 1954 the British and Malays waged a larger war against Communist guerrillas. While the British sealed off the Kra Isthmus from outside reinforcement in the Corbett manner, British ships bombarded enemy coastal positions, their planes provided tactical air support, and helicopters airlifted British, Malayan, African and Gurkha troops to defeat the guerrillas, though terrorist activities continued until 1960. Thailand (Siam) remained independent, while the Indonesian principalities of Sarawak, North Borneo and Brunei became British crown colonies at their own request in 1946. But the other Indonesians under Achmed Sukarno had to fight a five-year war against Dutch and British troops before the Dutch East Indies could become the Republic of Indonesia in 1950. Anglo-French-Chinese Nationalist forces alike battled the nationalist-Communist Vietminh forces of Ho Chi Minh in French Indochina in 1945–46 until the French assumed the burden alone. Laos and Cambodia accepted virtual independence within the new French Union in 1949 but the North Vietnamese fought on. French naval forces helped to pacify the Mekong River delta in the south in 1945–46, then based a new river fleet at Saigon to concentrate on the Red River in the north. As "river assault divisions," these forces used American-built landing craft, former Japanese junks, French river launches and occasional destroyer escorts or converted aviation tenders to battle crude Vietminh mines and ambushes in this largely ground-fought war which dragged on into the 1950s.

The Cold War in East Asia reflected the political vacuum left by the Japanese collapse. The United States filled it in the Western Pacific, establishing General MacArthur as Supreme Allied Commander over Japan, permanent naval bases there, at Okinawa and in the Philippines and a "trusteeship" over the hard-won Pacific islands. Russia could do little to challenge any of these moves, even agreed to evacuate Manchuria and shared Port Arthur and Dairen with the Chinese. But China remained wracked by civil war during the late 1940s between the Nationalists of Chiang Kai-shek and the Communists of Mao Tse-tung. American air and naval forces helped the Nationalists reoccupy the cities and ports of North China in 1945–46, with U. S. Marines guarding the rail lines between the cities as the Communists regained control of the countryside and even frustrated several American landings along the coast. Reluctant to become involved in this war, both the United States and Russia withdrew their forces from China in 1946–47 as Chinese Communist fortunes gradually improved. Early in 1949 Mao's forces captured Peking, then swept across the Yangtze and down the coast, driving Chiang's forces from the continent in December to Formosa, Hainan and several lesser offshore islands. In Korea, the Russians and Americans had occupied the peninsula jointly, divided at the 38th parallel, in 1945 and then had gradually withdrawn their forces. By the beginning of 1950, however, the Russians decided to test America's containment policy in Asia by instigating a North Korean attack on South Korea. In February 1950 Russia allied with Red China, which took Hainan Island in the Gulf of Tonkin in April, but which probably had no influence on Russia's Korean decision. The North Koreans crossed the 38th parallel on June 25, 1950, but the Russians had miscalculated, for two days later President Truman—with United Nations approval (possible because of the timely absence of the Russian delegation)— ordered the Seventh Fleet to support South Korea and to interpose itself in the Formosa Strait both to protect Chiang and to prevent any attempt he might make to return to the mainland. United Nations ground, air and sea forces would then go to Korea. With American forces returning to the continent to thwart another Russian parry, the Chinese Communists had good cause for alarm.

The Korean War (1950–53), the first real limited conflict of the Cold War and initial proving ground for the Russo-American struggle, proved frustrating for all participants, who were unable to practice their respective arts of war perfected during World War II. The United States, traditionally Army-oriented and now oversold on strategic bombing, found the thought of using nuclear weapons both politically risky—out of fear of escalating the struggle into a global World War III—and morally repulsive and therefore had to turn to the traditional weapons of maritime strategy so recently under political attack as obsolete: naval blockade and sealift, amphibious operations and the use of a conventional and relatively small ground army and tactical air forces. The new wrinkle was fighting for limited objectives, namely for only containing Communist aggression and not fighting for total victory, the full implications of which were painfully learned during the tenure of General MacArthur's command in the first year of the fighting. Still, the United States prosecuted its forced maritime strategy only halfheartedly. It pulled many World War II warships and Liberty and Victory merchant ships out of mothballs to meet the emergency. New construction was authorized for amphibious and mine warfare craft and aircraft carriers, but no new merchant fleet was laid down, while the projected new *Forrestal*-class attack carriers were built with a primarily nuclear deterrent capability in mind. Worse, the United States refused to accept its new strategic status as a maritime power by utilizing its belligerent rights under international law to institute a naval blockade. It did so through the United Nations against North Korea in July 1950, but rejected the pleas of MacArthur and Admiral Sherman to do the same against Red China when that country entered the war in November, following the dubious legalistic reasoning that the war was not declared and that it violated the old American belief in freedom of the seas. The United States thus failed to utilize the full extent of its ability to command the sea with a blockade that would have stopped trade to China by sea and taxed Russia's ability to supply China over the Trans-Sib Railway.

The Communists were also frustrated. Although Russian personnel did supervise the mining of Wonsan Harbor with Russian mines in July and August to prolong American minesweeping techniques, the miscalculation that America would not fight meant that the North Koreans could not be allowed to drive the Americans into the sea (as well they might have done in August) for fear that American recovery might be possible only with nuclear weapons. The Russians no doubt had apprehensions about the Chinese intervention early in the war because it ultimately meant that the Chinese would assume the larger direction of the war. Mao's Chinese could not exploit their superior guerrilla tactics in the mountainous, positional terrain of Korea and thus could rely only on their massive manpower. Before long, all three major powers and the United Nations accepted the inevitable realization that the fighting should be as limited as practicable and that the ultimate goal be a return to the *status quo antebellum*.

As the North Koreans drove into South Korea during the summer of 1950, the U. N. forces formed a defensive perimeter around Pusan and exploited the maritime advantages of their peninsular position to counterattack. South Korean, British, Australian and New Zealand naval forces operated on both sides of the peninsula below the 37th parallel and Anglo-American fast carriers shifted between west and east to strike North Korean targets and lines of communications above that parallel. Then, on September 15, the U. S. Seventh Fleet under Admiral C. Turner Joy landed General MacArthur with one Army and one Marine division at Inchon, supported by three fast and two escort carriers, to outflank the North Koreans just as Allied forces broke out from the Pusan perimeter. The pincers drove the Communists back into North Korea, after which U. N. forces landed at Wonsan on the east coast in October, the general offensive driving toward the Yalu River. With the seeming victory and the unification of Korea at hand, Allied fleet units began to withdraw.

But the new and still unsettled Chinese regime of Mao Tse-tung would no more tolerate any alien army on its Yalu River border than would Russia in Central Europe (or, for that matter, would have the United States along the Rio Grande), and at the end of October the Red Chinese began sending troops across the Yalu. The Red Chinese government could ill afford to weaken its effort at internal consolidation by the liquidation of its buffer in North Korea, where an unfriendly government might provide an avenue for the return of Chiang Kai-shek's Nationalists, whose troops both MacArthur and Chiang wanted, but were not allowed to use in the Korean War. The Chinese Communists were sensitive to all their borders, and in October began the rapid conquest of Tibet on the south. At sea, they were generally successful in eradicating the age-old problems of Chinese piracy, and they allowed the British to retain Hong Kong as their entrepôt to the West, but they repeatedly clashed with Japanese fishermen over territorial fishing rights. Red China had no real navy to speak of and was relatively powerless against the limited blockade imposed by Nationalist vessels. But her army and Russian-trained air force drove MacArthur out of North Korea during November, many U. N. units having to be evacuated by sea. Early in 1951 the Allies recovered and reestablished the front around the 38th parallel, whereupon MacArthur was relieved of command in April for criticizing his superiors who would not allow him to bomb air and supply bases inside Manchurian China. Mao's government had restored its North Korean buffer and forced the United States to reassess its goals and strategy.

By 1951 both the United States and the Soviet Union had achieved a stalemate everywhere in the world and now sought to strengthen it without seeking further gains. The United States allied with Australia and New Zealand (ANZUS), began to rearm Japan and West Germany as anti-Russian buffers and restrained its military leaders from further offensives into North Korea. Russia organized its satellites in Europe, crushed East German uprisings in 1953 and carefully avoided further involvement in Korea. The Red Chinese worked to isolate that conflict by honoring certain Allied sanctuaries: the bases and air-sea operating areas in Japan, South Korea and even the Sea of Japan. The Allies did the same by staying away from Chinese waters and air space. Exploiting their command of the seas around North Korea, though, Allied naval forces blockaded the coast, used Wonsan Harbor as an advanced base, and swept enemy mines, while the fast carriers of Task Force 77 attacked Communist supply routes in North Korea. American naval jets were so inferior that they required cover from Air Force fighters against Russian-built Mig interceptors, but Navy-Marine close air support clearly excelled along the battle line, and battleship and destroyer fire assisted importantly along the coast. Despite the strategic limitations, Admiral J. J. Clark used his four Seventh Fleet fast carriers from May 1952 to the end of the war in July 1953 to knock out the great Suiho Dam complex on the Korean side of the Yalu, heavily damage industrial targets and pound enemy rear areas with his "Cherokee strikes," all of which helped force the Chinese to accept the armistice. The Seventh Fleet had atomic bombs by 1953, but never even contemplated using them.

The political and military settlements of 1953–54 generally stabilized great power relationships in the Far East and ended the first phase of the Cold War. The new administration of President Eisenhower made Nationalist China on Formosa an Allied bastion against Red China and refused to provide the French with an atomic strike from First Fleet carriers against Vietminh forces besieging the French garrison at Dien Bien Phu, French Indochina, in 1954. When that fortress surrendered in May, France quit Indochina altogether by granting outright independence to Laos, Cambodia and Vietnam, the latter being divided —by international agreement at Geneva—into North and South at the 17th parallel. The U. S. Navy helped the French evacuate North Vietnam and then increased its own support of South Vietnam. The armistices at the 17th and 38th parallels seemed transitory, like the nuclear arms balance, for the ideological struggle between democracy and communism and the anti-colonial revolts against European over-lordship were mounting. To meet so many challenges and create a viable *Pax Americana,* American command of the sea remained essential.

## NUCLEAR BALANCE AND CONFRONTATION

The decade following the Korean and Vietnam settlements and the first operational deployment of thermonuclear weapons was one of nuclear superpower competition, improved delivery systems and continuing political dislocations—not only in the demise of the old European empires, but in the beginning disintegration of the superficially monolithic "free world" and "Communist" blocs. The "Western" alliance system became the stronger of the two with several improvements: West Germany's admission into NATO in 1954–55; the creation of the European Economic Community (Common Market) in 1958; the founding of the Southeast Asia Treaty Organization (SEATO) of the United States, Britain, France, Australia, New Zealand, Thailand, Pakistan and the Philippines in 1954–55; and the forging of a Central Treaty Organization (CENTO) over 1955–59 among Britain, Turkey, Pakistan and Iran, all of which made unilateral defensive treaties with the United States. Though French intransigence weakened NATO and SEATO and though Cuba went Communist in 1959–61, American Presidents Eisenhower (1953–61) and John F. Kennedy (1961–63) asserted firm if uneven leadership over the Western nations. The "Eastern" bloc had less success following the death of Stalin in 1953 and the rise to power of Nikita Khrushchev in Russia by 1956. The Soviet government organized its European satellites under the Warsaw Pact of 1955—Russia, East Germany, Poland, Czechoslovakia, Hungary, Rumania, Bulgaria and Albania—but had to suppress riots in Poland and a general uprising in Hungary in 1956. This seeming Russian weakness and Khrushchev's apparent desire to peacefully "coexist" with the West led to Chinese Communist separatism from 1957 and a final break in 1960. Russia then recalled its technical advisers from China, which grew increasingly militant toward the United States and neutral India and in 1961 won over Albania to its side. Thus the brief Communist monolith melted away even as the Western alliances appeared to strengthen.

Nevertheless, the Cold War went on, with the United States leading in technological weaponry. Nuclear energy was harnessed for ship power plants under the aegis of Admiral Hyman G. Rickover, first in the submarine *Nautilus* in 1955 and the carrier *Enterprise* in 1961. The Navy tried to share the offensive nuclear attack role of the Air Force with an unsuccessful jet seaplane patrol bomber and the very successful 60,000-ton *Forrestal*-class carriers from 1955 using long-range A3D strike aircraft, the same year that Admiral William F. Raborn, Jr., began to develop the Polaris solid-fuel ballistic missile. With this weapon system, launched underwater and navigated by extremely accurate inertial guidance systems, the Navy fought off Air Force attempts to obtain operational control to fashion this ultimate offensive deterrent of the Cold War—alongside the land-based missile, over which it had the advantage of mobility and the ability to hide. Converting 5 of the first teardrop-shaped high-speed *Skipjack*-class nuclear-powered attack subs into "Polaris" boats, the Navy commissioned and deployed the first in 1960, the 5900-ton *George Washington* (SSBN-598), armed with 16 A-1 Polaris missiles with ranges up to 1400 miles. Five specially designed Polaris subs of the 6900-ton *Ethan Allen*-class followed in 1961–63, each with A-2 Polaris missiles with a range of 1700 miles. Then, between 1963 and 1967, 31 Polaris subs of the 7300-ton *Lafayette*-class joined the fleet, mounting A-2 and 2900-mile-ranged A-3 missiles. With unlimited cruising ranges, these vessels were based at New London, Connecticut; Charleston, South Carolina; Holy Loch, Scotland; Rota, Spain; Pearl Harbor; and Apra Harbor, Guam. American sea-based missiles on 41 boats thus ringed Soviet Russia by the mid-1960s.

The Soviet Union, although superior in numbers of conventional attack subs, responded only slowly to the American missile challenge. The Russians of course pioneered with the missile-launched Sputnik heavy payload satellite and the hardened ICBM, but had greater difficulty reducing such large payloads to fit their subs. Finally, however, during the 1960s, the Russians placed 2 to 4 guided or ballistic surface-launched missiles on several of their conventional boats and inaugurated nuclear power and the teardrop hulls in some 100 new boats, each displacing upwards of 3500 tons with up to 8 ballistic missile tubes. The Russians finally matched the Polaris boat in 1968 with the "Y" class ("Yankee I"-NATO designation), armed with 16 Sawfly underwater missiles with initial ranges to 1500 miles. Lesser boats carried the shorter-ranged Sark and Serb missiles, 375 and 1250 miles respectively. Practically a decade behind the United States in the development of ICBM subs, the Russian Navy thus posed its greatest threat in conventional torpedo-armed attack boats, especially the 150 1000-ton diesel-powered medium-ranged "W" class boats and 15 modified "R" class boats of the 1950s, the 60 2000-ton diesel ocean-going attack boats of the "Z" and "F" classes during the late 1950s and early 1960s, and the 35 "G" and "J" conventional boats and 50 "Q" coastal-mining subs of the 1960s—a grand total of some 375 subs of all types by 1970!

American and NATO naval efforts thus concentrated on antisub warfare (ASW) and antiaircraft (AAW) protection against land-based Russian aircraft. The United States between 1953 and 1963 continued to build *Forrestal* and larger attack carriers with their heavy defensive jet fighters, converting most of the older *Essex*es to ASW work with piston-driven S2F Trackers and HSS helicopters, while Britain completed four new attack carriers and France two. Following the last battleships into retirement, antiaircraft guns yielded to surface-to-air missiles on all surface ships. Joining ASW carriers and their escorts were seaplanes, land-based patrol planes and hunter-killer subs, both diesel and nuclear-powered, in the British and French navies as well as the American. For amphibious operations, the U. S. Navy led the other two and lesser Western navies by utilizing the helicopter on board special assault carriers ("commando," British) to provide vertical trooplift envelopment complementary to conventional landing craft. The U. S. Marines officially adopted this new doctrine in 1955 and six years later centered their air-sea assault on the Fast Amphibious Force of one helicopter carrier and four LSDs (landing ship, dock—carrying helicopters, landing craft and Marines). Unable to match such a surface capability, the Russians in 1957–61 turned to a *jeune école* philosophy—surface-to-surface tactical guided "cruise" missiles (capable of being nuclear-tipped) on board cruisers, destroyers, subs and patrol boats of the *Komar* and *Osa* classes: the Strela with ranges up to 112 miles, its successor Shaddock to 248 miles, and the 12-18 mile short-ranged Styx. Phasing out their cumbersome surface-to-surface

Regulus missile, the United States and allied navies had to rely on carrier aircraft until they could develop their own similar tactical missiles.

Not surprisingly, missiles and nuclear weaponry led to highly rigid political-military controls and a preoccupation with this dimension of potential conflict. In the United States, the Defense Department was streamlined in three reorganizations between 1953 and 1965 and overcentralized under Secretary of Defense Robert S. McNamara, 1961–68. As virtual deputy commander-in-chief to the President and with his own staff of "whiz kid" economics and management experts, he bypassed the uniformed Joint Chiefs of Staff to give direct orders to Polaris boat commanders and those of the Air Force's Strategic Air Command, a necessity imposed by the nature of atomic weapons. Internally, the U. S. Navy followed these trends by centralizing authority in the Chief of Naval Operations, electronically simulating its war gaming at the Naval War College from 1957, giving Admiral Rickover virtual dictatorial authority over the nuclear power program, and in 1962 creating its own "think tank" of experts, the Center for Naval Analyses, the logical outgrowth of operations research. Such changes were followed and influenced by the British, whose RAF (Bomber Command) was centralized under defense minister Duncan Sandys (1957–59) and a Unified Ministry of Defence in 1964. Russia did the same, Marshal Grigori Zhukov (1955–57) controlling the Long Range Air Force and Strategic Rocket Forces.

The emphasis on strategic air forces led to attempts in all three nations to downgrade seaborne strategic and tactical forces. That these were unsuccessful was due to the ICBM boats, persistent demands for warships in limited war situations and the dogged leadership of three dynamic navy chiefs—Admiral Arleigh A. Burke, American Chief of Naval Operations from 1955 to 1961; Admiral Sergei G. Gorshkov, Soviet Commander-in-Chief of the Navy from 1955 into the 1970s; and Admiral Earl Mountbatten, British First Sea Lord 1955 to 1959 and thereafter Chief of Defence Staff. The sheer expense of especially aircraft carriers led to the criticism of them: in 1963 the demand for a superior American carrier fighter resulted in McNamara's driving Burke's brilliant successor, Admiral George W. Anderson, out of office; in Britain Sandys' 1957 Defence White Paper ended carrier construction; and in Russia Stalin's successors ended the independent naval ministry and fostered the return to a sub-centered fleet over a balanced fleet which might have included carriers. Especially in the United States, nuclear proponents under Secretary of State John Foster Dulles and then McNamara placed primary faith in nuclear deterrence through such doctrinal slogans as "massive retaliation," "counterforce" and "controlled thermonuclear war." But late in the 1950s military theorists like Bernard Brodie and Henry Kissinger began to recognize the utility of non-nuclear conventional forces, and between 1957 and 1963 American strategists evolved "balanced forces" capable of a "controlled and flexible response" to diplomatic crises. But the strategic material determinism exemplified by McNamara, Sandys and Zhukov resisted real non-nuclear development—until actual political realities demanded it.

The strategic balance focused on Europe during the 1950s, where NATO and the Warsaw Pact alliance remained precariously stalemated. The former controlled the Danish Sound, North Sea and North Atlantic, and the Russians confined their surface navy to the Baltic and even returned Arctic Porkkala to Finland. The West continued to use its nuclear weapons to deter the Red Army on the continent, where the Russians erected the Berlin wall in 1961 after a series of Cold War diplomatic crises. NATO vessels also patrolled the Mediterranean, where the Suez crisis of 1956 involved the Russian-backed Arab world led by Egypt and the Anglo-French-supported Israelis. When Nasser nationalized the Suez Canal, with Israel desiring free access to Eilat on the Red Sea Gulf of Aqaba, England, France and Israel in October launched an attack on Egypt without consulting the former two nations' major NATO ally, the United States. Neutralizing Egyptian naval units in the Eastern Mediterranean and Red seas, the allies mounted an amphibious invasion from Cyprus, Malta and Marseilles to take Port Said and the Canal. Anglo-French carriers, a French battleship and other escort and bombardment ships supported airborne-seaborne landings in the delta of the Nile early in November. World opinion and U.S.-U.N. pressure forced a cease-fire, but the war had intensified the Cold War. Under a new "Eisenhower doctrine," the U. S. Sixth Fleet escorted Israeli merchantmen through the Gulf of Aqaba, demonstrated off Jordan in 1957 and the next year landed Marines at Beirut, Lebanon, to prevent the institution of Communist government there. When Iraq, which quit the Western alliance in 1959, attempted to annex Kuwait in the Persian Gulf in 1961, two British carriers and Marine Commandos intervened. So conventional Anglo-American naval forces prevented Middle Eastern states from actively siding with the Soviet Union—a tactical lesson not lost to the Russians.

Western policy in the Mediterranean did, however, discredit the NATO powers there and hastened the collapse of the French Union in Africa. Tunisia got its independence in 1956, but allowed France to retain its military bases. In 1961 Tunisian forces attacked the French garrisons, whereupon a French carrier-cruiser force fought its way into Bizerte, only to be withdrawn after U.N. mediation the next year, leaving the French in control only of their air bases there. A

French Army mutiny failed to save Algeria, which got its independence in 1962, and Franco-Spanish-American forces withdrew from Morocco between 1955 and 1964. The British joined the French in granting independence to their colonies in tropical Africa, though generally maintaining economic and some military ties: British Ghana and Nigeria in 1957 and 1960, French Madagascar (Malagasy Republic) in 1960, the Belgian Congo in 1960, British Tanganyika and Zanzibar in 1961 and 1963 (combined into Tanzania, 1964) and British Kenya in 1963. These movements were far from bloodless, but the wars were generally internal and not against the European powers or part of the Cold War struggle. Racially torn South Africa left the Commonwealth in 1961 but guaranteed Britain's use of Simonstown in time of war. Otherwise, these nationalistic wars and states successfully resisted the meddling of the Cold War antagonists.

Similarly, the Far East situation reflected wars of national liberation that were only fortuitously connected to the Russo-American confrontation. Russia even gave up Port Arthur in the mid-1950s to Red China, while Britain steadily reduced its naval commitment east of Suez. This left the United States to enforce the Korean and Vietnamese armistices and to contain communism to mainland China and to begin the gradual development in 1954 of "self-defense forces" in Japan. The Seventh Fleet protected the Nationalist Chinese on Formosa and tried to minimize the skirmishing between the two Chinese governments in that region. The Red Chinese Navy, headed by former Army marshal Admiral Hsiao Ching-kuang from 1950 into the 1970s, began growing into a respectable coast defense force after 1953 with Russian submarines, destroyers, subchasers, minesweepers, torpedo boats and naval advisers who in 1956 helped China begin the construction of over twenty "W"-class medium attack subs. This fledgling navy, however, could deal only with minor navies and not the American. On one occasion in 1954 Red Chinese torpedo boats sank a Nationalist destroyer escort, but later lost two planes to a two-carrier American force that moved in following the destruction of a British airliner by Chinese fighters. Early in 1955 American Seventh Fleet units led by no fewer than five carriers effortlessly evacuated Chinese Nationalists from the disputed offshore Tachen Islands, and in the summer of 1958 a Communist attempt to blockade Nationalist Quemoy Island with artillery bombardments was thwarted by American warships escorting troop convoys to Quemoy. By 1960, when the Russians withdrew their aid to Red China, the Seventh Fleet kept one attack carrier off Japan, one off the Philippines and one off Formosa and Okinawa and was committed to the defense of Nationalist Formosa and the Pescadores, especially Quemoy and Matsu—as the warring Chinese factions continued to spar with raids and shellings. Admiral Hsiao's navy was sufficiently established, however, to continue its growth through home construction of existing types plus thousands of motorized junks and several hundred land-based naval fighters and torpedo-bombers. Another invasion threat of Quemoy in March 1962 ended with the usual American naval concentration and effective Nationalist retaliation in the air.

American forces also had to police the sea lanes of South and Southeast Asia as the new nations there flirted with Russian and Chinese communism. India, relying on British naval aid, tried to remain neutral and expelled the colonial Portuguese from Goa and Diu in 1961, but after China attacked the Indian border the next year India began to seek active military assistance from Russia. This move offended the United States, which was allied with Pakistan, India's antagonistic but weak neighbor. In South Vietnam, American advisers replaced the French after 1954, and five years later the United States increased its aid against the growing militancy of Communist North Vietnam under Ho Chi Minh and of the Communist Pathet Lao in Laos. The Kennedy administration used Seventh Fleet units in 1961–62 to help the South Vietnamese Navy patrol its coast against Communist guerrillas, while ground forces assisted Laos and Thailand. In Indonesia, Sukarno in 1957 began harassing the Dutch in their last Asian colony of West New Guinea, leading in 1960 to the dispatch of Holland's one carrier with three destroyers to the region but with no marked success. Sukarno demanded that the Dutch leave New Guinea and in 1962 stepped up his infiltration, though in January Dutch naval vessels sank one of three Indonesian torpedo boats trying to land guerrillas. By August, the retrenching Netherlands agreed to Sukarno's demands and began to withdraw. Emboldened by this success, in December Sukarno turned on Malaya, whose anti-Communist struggle had only finally ended two years before. The emerging Federation of Malaysia, officially proclaimed in 1963 and comprising Malaya, North Borneo, Sarawak, Sabah and Singapore, appealed to Britain, which sent one commando carrier with its Marines to preserve the Malaysian frontier near the last protectorate of Brunei, Borneo. Aside from these minor naval and advisory efforts against insurgents in South Vietnam and Malaysia, by 1963 Southeast Asia was relatively tranquil.

The same was true of Latin America, save for American intervention in Guatemala in 1954, until Fidel Castro turned Cuba into a pro-Russian Communist state and made the Caribbean into a Cold War battle front with the Cuban missile crisis. American and several Latin American warships made anti-guerrilla patrols in 1959–61, culminating in an abortive American-supported anti-Castro amphibious assault at the Bay of Pigs on Cuba's south coast in April 1961 that failed for lack of naval and air support. The next year American reconnaissance planes discovered that the Russians were erecting interrange ballistic missiles in Cuba, leading President Kennedy to meet the challenge of Chairman Khrushchev. Dismissing the advice of his military advisers to invade Cuba or bomb the missile sites and thus possibly trigger a nuclear World War III, he decided to use indirect means, thereby giving the Soviet Union a chance to understand American determination and thus to back down.

After obtaining the support of NATO and the Organization of American States to "quarantine" Soviet flag and chartered vessels from taking more missiles into Cuba, Kennedy on October 24, 1962, ordered the reinforced Atlantic Fleet of 183 ships, including eight aircraft carriers and over 30,000 embarked Marines, into Caribbean waters, where they were joined by token naval units from Argentina, Venezuela and the Dominican Republic. With absolute command of the sea, the United States thus added a new aspect to international law in the nuclear age, namely, the use of limited coercive force to interdict alien weapons deployment dangerous to American and hemispheric security and to the delicate equilibrium of the global balance of power. No actual force had to be used, although American antisubmarine units forced six Russian submarines to the surface in waters adjacent to the quarantine. Kennedy personally directed the strategic aspects of this blockade, while Secretary McNamara interfered with Admiral Anderson and the established Navy chain of command to deal with the tactical aspects. But, on balance, the operation was an unqualified success. The two superpowers had come to the brink of nuclear war, whence Khrushchev realized his miscalculation and agreed to withdraw Russian missiles and bombers from Cuba, and Kennedy agreed to end the blockade. In mid-November, after American warships observed the withdrawal, the quarantine was lifted, and the crisis ended. Both sides had relearned the efficacy of the traditional uses of naval power in diplomacy and political strategy.

The Cuban confrontation conclusively demonstrated the folly of nuclear saber-rattling as a tool of international rivalry and convinced the superpowers to cooperate in promoting arms control. In April 1963 a telecircuit "hot line" was opened between the Kremlin and the White House, followed in July by the Limited Nuclear Test Ban Treaty that ended testing in the atmosphere, space and underwater (leaving only underground). Antarctica and outer space were denuclearized altogether in 1959 and 1966, and the Geneva Disarmament Conference began to consider overall arms control in 1962. Many of the fears of both sides about a possible "missile gap" evaporated with the advent of highly accurate intelligence-gathering earth satellites that eliminated the guesswork from the arms race, and two new superpower leaders emerged in the mid-1960s to hasten the reduction of Russo-American tensions, Lyndon B. Johnson and Leonid I. Brezhnev. The need became all the greater with the increased quantity and quality of ICBMs. The U. S. Navy began replacing its A-1 and A-2 Polaris missiles with the A-3 and the more accurate C-3 Poseidon, each housing the multiple independently targeted reentry vehicle (MIRV) of some ten to fourteen separate H-bomb warheads. Deployment of the Poseidon began in 1971. Russia, which shifted its primary naval targets from American carriers (with their A3D bombers) to Polaris boats in 1964, kept pace by increasing the range of its Sawfly ICBMs to 3500 miles by the 1970s. Underwater sub detection proved difficult, and the defensive ABM system expensive and doubtfully effective, so that offensive deterrence seemed to be the key to the arms race and any arms controls.

Russia and the United States had additional pressures from new nuclear nations. Great Britain developed its own nuclear weapons in the 1950s and the next decade purchased A-3 Polaris missiles for its five new *Resolution*-class ICBM subs to augment NATO's nuclear deterrent. West Germany and Italy also depended on American technology, all the NATO powers rejected the Multilateral Nuclear (naval) Force in the early 1960s, and in 1960 France bolted from the NATO defensive system. Developing its own nuclear weapons, France laid down four *Redoutable*-class nuclear subs each with sixteen Polaris-type ICBMs ranging to 1250 miles for service in the 1970s. China also exploded its own nuclear devices in the 1960s and considered nuclear-powered missile subs. To check the further spread of nuclear weapons, the United States and Russia with some sixty other countries signed the Nuclear Non-Proliferation Treaty in 1968. China and France avoided all nuclear arms controls, and Japan, West Germany, India and Israel continued to be apprehensive about them. Nevertheless, the two superpowers forged ahead with the Seabed Treaty of 1970 prohibiting nuclear weapons on the ocean floor and with the abolition of chemical-biological weapons the next year.

But the most important step toward nuclear arms control was the Strategic Arms Limitations Talks (SALT) initiated in November 1969 and held at neutral Vienna and Helsinki. These culminated in a Russo-American arms limitation treaty in May 1972 in which the United States sacrificed its lead in nuclear weapons—if "lead" is an appropriate notion after "overkill" has been reached—in favor of parity, although holding superiority in H-bombs within its MIRV missiles. The two-part agreement limited each nation to 100 defensive

ABMs around Washington and Moscow and another 100 at another site and froze the number of land-based ICBMs and ICBM-launching subs. This meant 42 Russian and 41 American ballistic missile subs by the mid-1970s (or ultimately no more than 62 and 44 respectively), a majority of American missiles being MIRV-tipped, plus some 1000 land-based American ICBMs and 1600 for Russia, the MIRV giving the United States a lead of 5700 to 2500 H-bomb warheads. All this was exclusive of less-important manned strategic bombers and tactical nuclear weapons. (American B-52 bomber bases became so vulnerable to Soviet missile subs that early in 1972 the B-52s were redeployed throughout the continental United States.) Older weapons will be replaced as they age and become outdated by new technology, even if the new weapons happen to be "qualitatively" superior; China and France can be expected to continue on their own paths; and either signatory could easily violate or abrogate this first SALT agreement.

Strategically, America and Russia had at last officially acknowledged the universal danger of nuclear weapons and their lack of utility in international competition and military rivalry. The possibility of nuclear war was importantly reduced, at least for the five years of this initial pact, with each superpower seeking to impose its policy goals at lower levels, using traditional strategic and tactical tools, not the least of which is conventional naval power.

## RUSSO-AMERICAN NAVAL RIVALRY

The revealed unviability of nuclear Cold War, especially between the Suez and Cuban crises of 1956 and 1962, along with American carrier and submarine developments and the defection of Albania, convinced the Soviet Union to undertake blue-water naval construction to challenge the U. S. Navy's supremacy in the *Pax Americana*. The historic role of command of the sea thus remained with conventional naval forces and not ICBM vessels as the Russo-American rivalry reached into the maritime sphere in the 1960s. Nevertheless, the U. S. Navy has remained an offensive maritime force and the Red Navy a continental fleet subordinated to the Army. The United States has enjoyed at-sea logistical mobility, an overseas network of bases, amphibious and general surface superiority and a sophisticated balanced limited war fleet centered around its attack carriers. The Navy has thus become the senior service in the United States, forming the basis of a traditional maritime strategy, with the U. S. Army being reduced to a professional limited war force alongside the smaller Marine Corps and land-based tactical Air Force. The huge Red Army and Chinese People's Army can only be contained by nuclear forces, so that American defensive policy has gradually become ocean-oriented and committed to reducing the risks of escalation into the nuclear sphere. Russia has followed the precedents of many continental forebears in trying to transcend its geographic priorities and limitations by imitating America's blue-water strategy. Much of the Cold War of the 1960s and 1970s, if indeed it still deserves that designation, can thus be understood as two superpowers trying to appreciate the ramifications of these strategies.

The United States in the 1960s evolved its strategy from the "flexible military response" of the Kennedy-Johnson-McNamara administrations to the "Nixon Doctrine" hammered out from 1969 by President Richard M. Nixon and his defense adviser Henry Kissinger. Both "Strategic Offensive Forces" (nuclear armed) and "General Purpose Forces" have operated in four numbered fleets—the First (renamed Third in 1973) in the Eastern Pacific, the Second in the Atlantic and Caribbean, the Sixth in the Mediterranean and the Seventh in East Asia—from a global network of bases: Yokosuka, Japan; Subic Bay, Philippines; Okinawa; Pearl Harbor; Puget Sound-Bremerton, Washington; San Francisco-Alameda and San Diego, California; Newport, Rhode Island; New London, Connecticut; Charleston, South Carolina; Mayport, Florida; Norfolk, Virginia; Guantánamo Bay, Cuba; Rota, Spain; and Gaeta, Italy, until replaced in 1972 by Piraeus, Greece, along with the naval and port facilities of numerous allies. The Caribbean and Latin America in general have continued as an American strategic preserve, with the U. S. Navy augmented by the small British, Canadian, Dutch and Latin American navies containing Russian intrusions and the spread of Castro's Communists there. A massive American amphibious intervention in the Dominican Republic in 1965 was the last such measure before the lessening of Cold War tensions, although the U. S. Navy from late 1969 has had to watch Russian surface operations from the Cuban naval base at Cienfuegos. Abroad, the United States has promoted its naval allies in NATO and the Far East to help enforce the *Pax Americana,* especially as its own merchant and naval vessels are aging and not replaced rapidly enough.

Soviet Russia, with no such allies, during the 1960s determined to extend its maritime capabilities against the United States, enjoying the material advantage of brand-new and thus qualitatively superior merchant and naval vessels. But its continental preoccupations have required the suppression of satellite revolts, as in Czechoslovakia in 1968 and Poland two years later, and large troop concentrations against NATO in Central Europe and especially in the Far East against China, where border clashes have become commonplace. Committed to coast defense and the protection of commerce, the conventional forces of the Red Navy have operated in four area fleets: the Baltic based at Kaliningrad, the Northern at the only ice-free port of Severomorsk (near Murmansk), the Black at Sevastopol, and the Pacific at Vladivostock. These forces are deployed into three concentric "blue belt" defense zones, the coastal waters out to 150 miles and covered by land-based naval air, an intermediate zone up to another 150 miles offshore and partially covered by long-range planes, and the open sea dominated by far-ranging subs. From such a basically defensive posture all Soviet naval strategy has been fashioned. Tactically, the Russians have pioneered in surface-to-surface antiship cruise missiles, but have otherwise imitated American techniques modified to Russian needs. The small Naval Infantry, reactivated in 1964, was still integrated into the Army for short-range amphibious operations. Russian admirals have advocated seaborne invasion but lack the long-range blue-water sealift, logistical and assault capability and a large balanced fleet with fire and air support, service and auxiliary backup prerequisite for commanding the sea and air. A few antisub helicopter carriers began to appear in the late 1960s, followed by a prototype medium-size carrier for the 1970s. But all these surface vessels lack combat experience, rely on non-nuclear power plants and short-range V/STOL aircraft, and do not have real overseas bases.

In fact, the Russian Navy suffers from the same strategic limitations of all continental navies. Its surface ships can show the flag and act as a "fleet-in-being," but are trapped by unfavorable geographic outlets. The missile ships are a threat to enemy surface ships and subs should a limited sea war somehow recur, in which the killer subs would provide the greatest danger as a *guerre de course* and antisub force. But all remain targets of the considerable American surfaceantisub fleets. As an inshore navy, the Russian fleet has been most formidable, employing minecraft, land-based air, torpedo boats, destroyer escorts, gunboats, coast artillery and missiles, Naval Infantry and cruisers capable of commanding coastal waters. The political factor is also a considerable hindrance. Like Colbert and Tirpitz before him, Admiral Gorshkov must abide by the wishes of the Party and Army chiefs, while political commissars preach the rigid Communist party line on board each warship. The Russian naval elite—like the tsar's and Hitler's—remain outside the mainstream of Russian political life, as it did in the mutiny of 1921, and enforces Spartan-like discipline and living conditions on its enlisted crews, most of which are conscripted. Such a closed and tightly controlled society is hardly conducive to the creation of the kind of freewheeling thalassocratic society prerequisite to blue-water greatness. But the Russians keep up appearances and have fumbled accordingly in many spheres of maritime activity.

Among the other major navies, those of Britain, China and France have continued to command the most respect and not only because of their own nuclear arsenals. The Royal Navy has shrunk during this period, giving up its last heavy cruisers and attack carriers to concentrate on ASW and escort ships for NATO, including 20,000-ton multi-purpose "through deck cruisers" armed with V/STOL fighters, helicopters, ship-to-air missiles and French-built Exocet ship-to-ship missiles for the 1970s. Whereas Britain surrendered most of its peacekeeping responsibilities to the U. S. Navy, France has maintained a small and independent balanced fleet which has carriers for use in the Atlantic and Mediterranean. Also independent has been China's naval development from 1964 when Admiral Hsiao began to develop a respectable inshore navy in three fleets: the North Sea Fleet from the Yalu to Shantung, guarding Peking; the East Sea Fleet facing Formosa and guarding Shanghai; and the South Sea Fleet, from Swatow to the Gulf of Tonkin and centered on Canton. Strategically and tactically akin to the Russian Navy, the Chinese have added to the normal inventory of continental naval weapons hydrofoil torpedo boats and a sixty-vessel amphibious force for short-range sealift. Though subordinated to Army control, the Navy has nevertheless extended its range of operations into the Indian Ocean littoral, especially East Africa.

Beyond the construction of both strategic and conventional warships, the naval rivalry between the United States and the Soviet Union has been concentrated not so much in actual confrontations that might risk war between them as in supporting underdeveloped emerging nations in the Middle East, Asia and Africa in hopes of gaining their support —for political, ideological, economic and related strategic reasons. The most potentially explosive situations have been those in which nations so supported by either side have been at war with one another, notably Israel and Egypt, India and Pakistan, and North and South Vietnam, conflicts in which the combat-tried United States has been more willing to be actively involved, while the Russians have been content to focus on foreign aid and military advisers in limited roles. In areas not actively disputed, like the Indian Ocean, Russia and to some extent China have been more active, seeking to gain naval base facilities or anchorages to extend the range of their seagoing ships—areas generally being abandoned by Britain and France and which could be centers of active rivalry should the United States take up the challenge. Finally, across the seven seas, American and Russian ships and naval planes have jockeyed with each other in perpetual but dangerous games of intimidation, surveillance and submarine detection. The "theaters" of naval rivalry during the last third of the twentieth century are thus the open ocean (between subs and antisub forces), Latin America, the Mediterranean, the Middle East, the Indian Ocean (including East Africa and the Persian Gulf), Southeast Asia and the Western Pacific.

In the open ocean, the cat-and-mouse sub-antisub game of detection and potential destruction endlessly continues, by the early 1970s each superpower having some 100 nuclear-powered subs (plus some 300 Russian and only 35 American conventional boats). Detection has remained the key and most difficult problem, though both sides have assistance from orbiting surveillance and navigational satellites. The Americans have led, however, with infrared sensors in their satellites and patrol planes; two vast fixed deep ocean listening nets of sonar cables known as Caesar and Sossus; the sonars, sonar buoys, hydrophones, transducers, large-aperture towed arrays of surface ships and shipborne ASW planes; floating detection robot platforms; and a new ocean-bottom suspended array system. The chief difficulty of all these is separating the "signature" of subs from natural noises in the ocean, leading to such false contact reports as in 1970 when most of the Argentine Navy put to sea only to intercept two copulating whales! Soviet sub sorties from the four Russian fleet areas can be more easily tracked by patrol planes, but once "lost" in open waters they are more difficult to relocate. Total oceanic surveillance being impossible, the U. S. Navy began to replace its special hunter-killer ASW task forces of antisub carriers and depth-charge-armed destroyers of the 1950s and 1960s with new techniques and weapons in the 1970s. Antisub helicopters and new S-3 aircraft have been assigned to the regular attack carriers and their escorts, armed with the Mark 46 homing torpedo, and "hunter" subs seek out deep-diving enemy subs. In addition, the Americans place hopes in a new multi-purpose 15,000-ton V/STOL-armed "sea control ship" like the British "through deck cruiser" to escort surface ships. The smaller Russian surface fleet can never begin to match these multitudinous systems, but the Russians are nevertheless pioneering in underwater and acoustical research with some 200 oceanographic research vessels.

In Latin America, Russian warships began regular visits in 1969 and promise to continue for the foreseeable future. Operating from Cuban Cienfuegos, Russian and Cuban vessels maneuver close to American territorial waters, but the Caribbean remains virtually an American lake in the same manner that the Black Sea is Russian. Furthermore, militant communism has waned in Latin America, whose countries pursue generally independent policies, save for annual joint ASW maneuvers with U. S. Fleet units.

The Mediterranean is the prime area of Soviet-American rivalry, with the Americans enjoying greater mobility than the Russians, whose first squadron entered the middle sea in 1963. NATO forces have operated from Gibraltar, Malta (independent since 1964), Italian Gaeta and the Piraeus, while the Russians have utilized anchorages off Spanish Alboran Island (near Gibraltar), in the Tunisian Gulf of Hammamet, Salum Bay near Alexandria, and near Greek Kithira Island (ancient Kythera). Despite certain diplomatic limitation rights of passage through the Turkish Dardanelles, the Russian Navy has sought Arab help in establishing Mediterranean bases. In addition to auxiliary base facilities at Egyptian Port Said and Syrian Latakia, the Russians erected naval bases at Alexandria and two other Egyptian ports during the 1960s only to be expelled from that country in 1972 though still retaining rights of visit. Without airfields for its TU-16 ("Badger" to NATO) medium reconnaissance bombers which shadow the U. S. Sixth Fleet, the Russians must construct antisub carriers with V/STOL planes while their diplomats look for a permanent base, possibly at Malta or Algerian Mers-el-Kebir, finally abandoned by the French Navy in 1968. Independent Communist Yugoslavia and pro-Chinese Albania (with its naval base at Valona) are of no use to the Russians and of little or no use to NATO. In addition to watching the Russians, NATO had to intervene in strife-torn Cyprus after a Turkish naval demonstration in 1964, but otherwise has been preoccupied with the running Arab-Israeli conflict.

The Arab-Israeli "Six-Day War" of June 5–10, 1967, affected the Mediterranean balance of power by its demonstration of pro-Western Israel's superiority in all arms. While Israel's air forces destroyed or humbled those of Egypt, Syria, Iraq, Lebanon and Jordan and its armies conquered Arab territory up to the Suez Canal and the River Jordan, its fifteen-vessel navy of destroyers and PT boats took the Egyptian Red Sea base of Sharm el-Sheikh and forced the Egyptians to block and close the Suez Canal and abandon Port Said in favor of Alexandria. Israeli ASW vessels drove off a twelve-submarine Egyptian sortie against the coast, and the destroyer *Elath* (or *Eilat*) and two PT boats sank two of Egypt's PT boats off Sinai. The powers became involved when a Russian Black Sea squadron entered Alexandria, and the Israelis severely damaged an American reconnaissance vessel. The powers helped bring on a cease-fire, freezing the battle positions and the closure of the Canal. In October Egyptian *Komar* torpedo boats used Styx missiles to sink the *Elath* off Port Said—the first instance in history of a warship being sunk by surface-to-surface missiles. Henceforth, the Russians kept a strong fifty-vessel squadron with at least a helicopter carrier and cruiser in the middle sea to counterbalance the two-to-three-attack carrier-centered U. S. Sixth Fleet. The Israelis have strengthened their armed forces with American aid, especially F-4 Phantom II fighters, and purchased French-built Sa'ar-class 40-knot-plus PT-missile boats, each armed with eight new Gabriel surface-to-surface missiles. To protect its incoming oil tankers from fedayeen Arab guerrillas in the Red Sea, in 1972 Israel sealifted commandos to seize two unoccupied islets near the Strait of Bab el Mandeb. Oil has also been a prime cause of the continued American and Russian naval presence in the Eastern Mediterranean and Middle East, for although both countries have much of their own oil, their European and Japanese allies and satellites depend upon Middle Eastern oil. And just as the Russians have begun limited carrier construction, NATO and the Americans have been active: in 1968 a new NATO maritime air command of American, British and Italian reconnaissance aircraft systematized aerial surveillance; in 1970 the reinforced Sixth Fleet demonstrated against a Syrian attack on Jordan; in 1971 the first of a new class of American 40-knot gunboats began to tail Soviet surface ships doing the same thing to larger American units; and in the early 1970s the first American surface-to-surface missiles (Standard, then Harpoon) began to deploy.

African nationalism in the tropics by contrast has avoided superpower military involvement in a balance of lesser powers deeply rooted in racial and ancient anticolonial issues. To wage internal wars, protect frontiers and deter attacks, the African nations have relied on British, French, American, Russian and Chinese aid and construction to create respectable inshore navies. For instance, in the Biafran secessionist war (1967–1970), Nigeria used Russian-built PT boats to blockade and assault the coast of Biafra and patrol the Niger and other rivers. Pro-Russian Guinea had eight Russian-built patrol boats to help repel a Portuguese-sponsored landing of rebels in four amphibious craft at Conakry in 1970 and has been since protected by a small Russian naval presence. Portugal, the first and last European imperial nation, under its president Admiral Americo Thomaz in the 1960s and 1970s, has created the strongest navy in Africa—destroyers, fast frigates, submarines, river and amphibious craft—to police the coast of Angola and Mozambique against rebels and the black nations and in general support of apartheid-based South Africa and Rhodesia. The apartheid policy has so isolated the latter two countries from the rest of the world that South Africa has had to build its own rather formidable coastal navy. Black Africa by contrast has had to rely on Royal Navy assistance to stabilize the several new frontiers. In 1964, for example, the British air- and sealifted troops and commandos into Tanzanian Dar es Salaam, Kenya and Uganda and used naval demonstrations the next four years as part of a U. N. arms embargo against the Portuguese (in Mozambique), Rhodesians and South Africans. Inland Zambia has relied on Britain's aid for inshore vessels, while Tanzania has accepted Chinese naval aid for a naval base at Dar es Salaam. Somalia, independent since 1960, turned to the Russians for a new port at Berbera on the Gulf of Aden and a dozen PT boats, occasionally warring with Ethiopia and Kenya. The Russians have tried to exploit the political chaos around Bab el Mandeb following the British withdrawal from Aden in 1967 by establishing an anchorage at Socotra Island and taking over Port Sudan from the Sudanese. But Sino-Russian incursions into Africa have been uneven, while the racial tensions promise continual intra-African strife.

The East African power balance directly affects the political situation in the Indian Ocean littoral, also fraught with local rivalries and great power incursions. When Britain announced in 1966–68 that it would withdraw from the Persian Gulf and other areas east of Suez by the end of 1971, Iran decided to shift closer to the Western alliance. Motivated also by Russian favoritism toward Egypt and naval aid to Iraq for operating on the Gulf, Iran sought—and got—from Britain four new 1200-ton frigates armed with surface-to-air missiles and eight 50-knot and four 60-knot new British hovercraft with trooplift capability, supported by an air force of American F-4 fighters and Italian- and American-built helicopters and an army which includes hundreds of British-made tanks. For strategically placed bases, the naval base at Khurramshahr opposite Iraqi Basra has been enlarged, a hovercraft base constructed farther down the Gulf at Kharg Island, and a new base established at Bandar Abbas, commanding the Strait of Hormuz, where three small offshore islands were seized by the Iranian Navy in November 1971. Such a superior inshore fleet has more than offset the retiring British force of one frigate and five minesweepers to protect not only Iran but the Gulf coastal states of Kuwait, Saudi Arabia, Bahrain, Qatar, Oman and the Union of Arab Emirates—the latter the successor to the former Trucial System. In addition, however, independent Bahrain late in 1971 concluded an agreement for the United States to establish a permanent naval base on the island only to abrogate it two years later after the Arab-Israeli war, whereupon the United States in 1974 shifted to a joint naval facility with Britain on Diego Garcia in the Chagos Islands. In 1973 Russia was beginning to build a naval base at Umm Qasr on the Iraqi Persian Gulf coast. Iran has thus become the key to Western defenses and oil investments in the Middle East, offering stability in the midst of an otherwise divided and chaotic Arab world. But both American and Russian facilities in the region remain subject to the ever-changing whims of these politically sensitive Arab nations.

Key to the Indian Ocean of course remains the subcontinent of India, where Russia, the United States and China have tried to exploit the serious divisiveness between India and Pakistan. Though stubbornly neutral, India in the mid-1960s began accepting naval aid from Russia which included a major base at Visakhapatnam and frigates, subs and inshore craft to augment India's one carrier, two cruisers, minesweepers and other vessels. Pakistan, with one cruiser and five destroyers and strategically vulnerable with its two territorial parts separated by India, still bombarded Dwarka on the western Gulf of Kutch in an inconclusive war with India in 1965. Russia then reinforced India with *Osa*-Styx missile boats, and Pakistan obtained subs from Italy and France. Then, in December 1971, the East Pakistan secession as the state of Bangladesh from West Pakistan expanded into a second war with India. The Indian Navy blockaded both belligerent coasts, the carrier *Vikrant* bombing and closing the East Pakistani port of Chittagong and the *Osa* missile boats helping to sink one and damage another Pakistani destroyer and sink two minesweepers during the Indian operations against Karachi. Holding absolute command of the sea, India guaranteed the independence of Bangladesh and the defeat of Pakistan, though a sub of the latter managed to sink one Indian frigate. The Indian blockade also helped to frustrate Chinese attempts to help Pakistan, and American and Russian heavy fleet units immediately demonstrated in the Indian Ocean. Russia then stationed a 20-ship force in this ocean, using anchorages off Socotra and the Seychelles Islands. Britain in 1970, however, had modified its decision to withdraw from these waters by stationing a token naval force at Singapore and developing those Anglo-American naval facilities at Diego Garcia. The British also retained several other islets in the Indian Ocean, though granting independence to Mauritius in 1968, and the United States accepted Australia's invitation to develop a joint naval base at Cockburn Sound near Fremantle. The Indian Ocean thus promises to grow as a key area of great power rivalry.

In the Western Pacific, the U. S. Navy has effectively controlled all international waters from its ring of bases around Asia supporting the Seventh Fleet and has clashed only with the coastal forces of local navies. Russian ships and aircraft from Vladivostok have shadowed American vessels, and by 1973 the Chinese navy had become the third largest in the world, though decidedly defensive. The coastal navies of Japan, South Korea and the Nationalist Chinese on Formosa depend totally on American naval protection. Beyond the continuing clashes around Formosa, the major incidents have involved North Korea's attempts to frustrate American surveillance of its coasts. In January 1968 one North Korean subchaser and four PT boats overhauled and seized the lightly armed and unresisting "spy ship" *Pueblo* off Wonsan Harbor, prompting an ineffective American task force sortie into the Sea of Japan which in turn prompted a Russian squadron to appear. Similarly, in April 1969 North Korean aircraft shot down a U. S. Navy EC-121 land-based patrol "electronic intelligence plane" ninety miles off the North Korean coast after it had violated Korean air space, and a follow-up demonstration by a four-carrier American task force accomplished nothing. As with the growing rivalries in the Indian Ocean, however, Western Pacific naval activities were subordinated during the decade 1963–73 to events in Southeast Asia.

The creation of Malaysia as an independent nation in 1963 encouraged Sukarno of Indonesia to continue his expansionistic policies against it, only to be checked in a confrontation with Anglo-Malaysian-Anzac-Gurkha forces (1963–66). When Indonesian guerrillas and troops penetrated into North Borneo and attempted joint operations with pirates in the Malacca Strait, a British fleet of two attack carriers, escorts, commandos, minesweepers, subs and eventually two hovercraft operated from Singapore to control the seas, isolate the battlefield and support and supply the troops. The considerable Indonesian Navy which included one Russian-built heavy cruiser, fourteen "W"-class subs and twelve *Komar* missile boats, among other vessels, did not interfere. The British observed Indonesian territory and air space as sanctuaries and avoided bombing jungle targets for fear of hitting innocent natives, thus winning their support. By the end of 1964, with Indonesia obviously losing, its regulars were committed, and Sukarno turned from Russia to court China. But the Commonwealth sent in troop and ship reinforcements early in 1965, and Sukarno attempted a Communist takeover, whereupon his generals undertook a coup which unseated him and led to an anti-Communist bloodbath during the autumn. (Singapore split off from Malaysia, but it was a separation of convenience over ethnic and commercial matters). The Indonesian infiltration dragged on until August 1966 when the new government made peace with Malaysia. The British withdrew, and the Malaysian and Indonesian navies turned to the task of suppressing the pirates who had been very active throughout the decade.

Unlike the sagacious British handling of the Indonesian confrontation, the United States' response to renewed North Vietnamese pressure against South Vietnam was politically ill-conceived, strategically unsound and tactically disjointed. The administrations of Presidents Eisenhower, Kennedy and Johnson all shored up several Asian nations under the Military Assistance Program, especially with military advisers in the

Laotian and Vietnamese guerrilla wars of the late 1950s and early 1960s, while the five inshore squadrons of the Royal Thai Navy used American-built patrol boats and amphibious craft to police the long Gulf of Siam coast. Erroneously convinced from the Korean and Cuban experiences that the local Vietnamese struggle was linked to the Kremlin-led mono-lithic Communist bloc of the 1950s, the United States responded to intensified guerrilla attacks in 1963–64 with massive aid lest all South-east Asia fall (the "domino" theory). And instead of focusing on the political questions raised by the main enemy, the indigenous National Liberation Front (Vietcong) of the South, the Americans viewed the crisis as primarily a military problem to be directed against North Viet-nam, Russia and China, who were supporting the Vietcong. Strategically, therefore, the McNamara regime attempted to direct the military effort as closely as it did the missile effort against Russia, which meant a material strategy. Heavy military hardware was thus employed—naval support, aerial bombardment and finally troops—in uneven doses as part of the prevailing limited war doctrine of "controlled escalation" or "graduated response" of the early 1960s. Instead, this shortsighted strategy led to "gradualism" whereby the Vietnamese Communists were able to prepare adequate defenses and countermeasures for each gradual increase of American material force.

The Vietnam War (1965–73) exposed American ignorance of mari-time strategy. Unlike the nineteenth-century British and their philosopher Corbett's teachings, unimaginative American strategists failed to recog-nize the prime military goals from the outset: total isolation of the battlefield by interdicting all enemy supplies by air attack and naval blockade and virtual total pacification and occupation of South Vietnam by ground forces. Since the country is not an island or peninsula like Malaya or Korea and thus not "interdictable," overland communications could never be cut by air bombing, and the United States and South Vietnam could never raise enough ground forces to occupy the long Laotian and Cambodian frontiers and thus prevent logistic and troop infiltration unless the United States decided to fight a major ground war in Asia. Furthermore, the World War II myths of strategic morale bombing led to attempts at intimidation by the bombing of selected targets in North Vietnam. Only the Navy was well-suited to meet its tasks: the long-term command of the waterways of and to South Viet-nam, sealift and coastal support and naval blockade of the North—which was kept restricted until the very last months of the war. Conse-quently, the American armed forces tried to develop tactical doctrines on the foundations of an overall faulty strategy, and not surprisingly only the Navy fully succeeded. American participation went through three general stages: gradual involvement during 1964 and early 1965, gradual intervention and escalation between 1965 and 1968, and gradual disengagement 1968 to early 1973.

The gradual American involvement consisted of a series of naval incidents in addition to increased material aid and advisers. Overriding the advice of the Joint Chiefs, Secretary McNamara in February 1964 ordered American destroyer patrols into North Vietnamese waters, while South Vietnamese PT boats carried out commando raids against the North, and U. S. Navy and Air Force jets flew reconnaissance for Thai and Laotian air strikes on Laotian guerrillas near the North Vietnamese border. Fighter "flak suppressing" escorts joined after two Navy planes were shot down during the summer, and Seventh Fleet strength in the Gulf of Tonkin grew to four attack carriers plus one antisub carrier and escorts. On the night of July 30 South Vietnamese PT boats raided two North Vietnamese islands in the Gulf, and on August 2 counter-attacking enemy PT boats mistakenly engaged the American patrol destroyer *Maddox* which sank one and drove off the rest with the help of a carrier strike. The next night another raiding force from the South struck the North coast, leading to another confused encounter on the 4th during which carrier planes sank two more North PT boats. President Johnson used this "Gulf of Tonkin incident" to justify retaliatory carrier strikes which sank twenty-five North Vietnamese PT boats at their bases and destroyed the oil storage depot at Vinh. In September United States destroyers and North Vietnamese PT boats again skirmished, followed the next month by renewed South Vietnamese PT-commando raids. Vietcong guerrillas in the South finally attacked American advisers, leading Johnson to order carrier strikes north of the 17th parallel in February 1965 and the commitment of American ground forces.

The gradual intervention and escalation of the conflict involved Anzac, South Korean and Thai as well as South Vietnamese armed forces under general American command—till 1968 Admiral U. S. G. Sharp at Pearl Harbor and General William C. Westmoreland at Saigon. The three American armed services lacked overall philosophies for such an unglamorous limited war, to the requirements of which they gave low equipment priorities. Their roles and missions overlapped and thus remained confused, fostering worse-than-usual interservice rivalries and competition. The Army viewed the struggle in Mao Tse-tung's terms as a problem for "counterinsurgency" but abandoned Clausewitzian notions of breaking the enemy's will in favor of ridiculous body-count statistics during halfhearted "search and destroy" patrols; took over the Marine Corps' vertical envelopment idea with "airmobile" divisions airlifted in helicopters, meaning that the Army had to build its own air force; and Regular Army units even found themselves operating as Marines in the waterways of the Mekong delta region. The Air Force stayed out of the tactical airmobility business altogether; refused to risk its B-52 bombers over North Vietnam against strategic targets (until very late in the war) but used them for—of all things—tactical air support with dubious effect in the South; and did not provide adequate close support until —as during the Pacific war and Korea—it used Navy and Marine techniques. The Marines were employed in positional Army-type operations near the 17th parallel ("Demilitarized Zone," DMZ) as during World War I and Korea instead of remaining a seagoing shock force. The Navy in its water element exercised its usual functions of commanding the sea, providing overall logistical sealift and amphibious mobility and naval bombardment of coastal targets North and South, while a good deal of its early strategic bombardment of the North with carriers was executed by piston-driven tactical A-1 Skyraider planes, which were thus kept from their more effective role of close air support in the South. The same was true of the one battleship employed. Also, the Navy often had to protect its own "riverine" forces in Army areas. Small wonder then that the armed forces had no better solution to the Vietnam problem than their equally confused civilian managers.

In the war of interdiction and supply, however, the Navy eventually completed all its assigned tasks. In addition to secondary coastal bases, Navy Seabees constructed major base facilities at Camranh Bay and Vung Tau in South Vietnam and Sattahip, Thailand, while the Military Sea Transportation Service called on its last mothballed Liberty and Victory ships to help meet the vast logistical requirements. Navy and Coast Guard river craft, monitors, helicopters, hovercraft, cutters and "Swift Boats" helped the South Vietnamese Navy's Junk Force and River Force cut off enemy waterborne supply along the coast and in the Mekong delta (Operations "Market Time" and "Game Warden"). Admiral Elmo R. Zumwalt extended this successful campaign to the Cambodian coast and inland "Parrot's Beak" sanctuary on the upper Mekong ("Sea Lords") during 1968–70, augmented by an Allied ground offensive thence during the spring of 1970. The Mobile Riverine Force similarly used new assault support patrol boats (ASPR) to clear the approaches to Saigon in the Rung Sat area in 1967–69, backed by off-shore helicopter carriers and bombardment forces. Gradually, successful anti-shipping patrols were extended up the North Vietnamese coast ("Sea Dragon") to the 20th parallel in 1966–68 with battleship, cruiser and destroyer fire and mining. Similarly, Task Force 77 carriers on "Yankee Station" struck selected North Vietnamese targets ("Rolling Thunder") during these years, their jets fighting off Russian-built Mig fighters but suffering heavily from Russian-made SAM missiles. The often politically interrupted naval air strikes, like those of the Air Force, had great success, especially in 1967 when they used deadly accurate television-guided air-to-surface Walleye glide bombs. Hanoi and Haiphong remained as sanctuaries, for fear of Russian and/or Chinese intervention to protect their freighters supplying the North. By the same token, Allied planes and ships assiduously avoided the Chinese border and air space, though the targeting was gradually extended to near the Chinese border in August 1967. Similarly, naval blockade was also absolutely forbidden.

Gradual disengagement followed from McNamara's growing realization of the uselessness of his "controlled escalation," the powerful Communist Tet offensive across the 17th parallel early in 1968, and violent anti-war sentiment in the United States. President Johnson gradually eliminated all bombing of the North throughout 1968 while seeking a negotiated settlement. His successor, Richard M. Nixon, continued the American withdrawal ("Vietnamization") as part of the Nixon Doctrine and the negotiations. The Doctrine, first officially enunciated in July 1969 and largely the work of Henry Kissinger, finally recognized the need for a maritime strategy by withdrawing American ground forces from the mainland of Asia, leaving such fighting to allied troops while the United States provides material aid and commands the sea and air. With most of the waterways successfully interdicted, the U. S. Navy in 1969–70 turned over some 825 inshore and river craft to the South Vietnamese Navy, a once faction-ridden service that had been stabilized by Commodore Tran Van Chon. American air strikes shifted to Laos and the still-open "Ho Chi Minh Trail" to keep up the pressure during the negotiations. The United States meanwhile achieved *rapprochement* with Russia and China, so that when North Vietnam launched a massive assault across the 17th parallel in the spring of 1972 the Nixon administration clamped an aerial mining blockade on Haiphong and six other harbors and ordered the most intensive bombing effort of the war, including planes from six carriers, against the North, this time including Hanoi and Haiphong. When the negotiations stalled late in the year, another aerial attack was launched. The settlement was finally reached in January 1973, freezing the *status quo*.

The ultimate success of the Nixon-Kissinger Doctrine—a maritime strategy—depends largely on a coalition of Asian states allied to the United States. The SEATO alliance, undermined by the partition of Pakistan, is no real counterpart of NATO, and the nine-nation Asian and Pacific Council (ASPAC) formed in 1966 lacks real unity, its members—South Korea, Formosa, the Philippines, Malaysia, Thailand, South Vietnam, New Zealand, Australia and Japan—still dependent on American leadership. One thing is certain: unless these countries industrialize, they will remain economically backward and isolated, with little impact on the power balance in Asia. The one power among them that is of great power status already is Japan, which the United States hopes will assume a greater military role in the East, but which the other nations view with misgivings due to bad memories from World War II, and which is rearming only cautiously and reluctantly. Her growing Maritime Self-Defense Force and reacquisition of Okinawa (from the United States in 1972) are only a beginning. If and when Japan rearms to full great power status, her strategy will probably be patterned on that of the United States—a limited nuclear deterrent against Russia and China, her Pacific rivals, and an enlarged surface navy capable of helping the U. S. Navy patrol Eastern sea lanes, especially to the Persian Gulf, the source of most Japanese oil. Until that happens the United States Navy must bear the burden of implementing the Nixon-Kissinger Doctrine—with its string of bases around the periphery of mainland Asia from Guam to Australia, its maritime strategy of surface forces policing the sea lanes, and its limited strike fleets built around carriers and Marine-loaded amphibious ships ready to assist Allied nations, but only after most careful consideration and with the Vietnam debacle ever in mind.

The involvement of the superpowers in the affairs of lesser nations was conclusively demonstrated in the October 1973 Arab-Israeli war, waged largely with weaponry supplied by the great powers and which involved not only the balance of power in the Middle East but the availability of Arab-controlled oil resources to all nations. Though primarily a land and air struggle, the war at sea again favored Israel's small but enterprising navy. To avoid detection by Arab planes, Israeli missile boats operated under cover of night. They fired Gabriel missiles to sink several Syrian missile boats lying amid cargo vessels (some of which were also hit) of neutral nations at Latakia and Tartus. The Israeli vessels also bombarded the coasts of Syria and Egypt before the cease-fire ended hostilities. During this October war, the reinforced Mediterranean fleets of the United States and the Soviet Union stood by, an American carrier force demonstrated in the Indian Ocean to match the Soviet naval presence there, and Bahrain ordered the U. S. Persian Gulf force out of its newly leased base there. The balance of power had thus been maintained in the Middle East, although the superpowers must develop alternate energy sources if they are ever to be free from their utter dependence on Arab oil.

For the remainder of the century, unlike the watershed SALT agreement checking nuclear escalation, limited wars will continue, as in the previous century. As long as the United States practices a maritime strategy, keeps its merchant and naval fleets well-equipped with new and many vessels, and continually studies the historical evidence of practicing such a strategy, it will enforce the *Pax Americana*. If it fails to do these things, the Soviet Union may indeed—by default—develop a superior oceanic strategy and navy. Despite its doctrinal public arguments that the new technological weaponry has enabled its missile-armed forces to neutralize the American navy, continental Russia is simply no match at sea for a strong and determined balanced American navy. Except in waters actually contiguous to Russia, the United States will continue to command the seas for the foreseeable future.

# Epilogue
# World War III

*. . . no empirical science, consequently also no theory of the Art of War, can always corroborate its truths by historical proof; it would also be, in some measure, difficult to support experience by single facts. If any means is once found efficacious in War, it is repeated; one nation copies another, the thing becomes the fashion, and in this manner it comes into use, supported by experience, and takes its place in theory, which contents itself with appealing to experience in general in order to show its origin, but not as a verification of the truth.*

—CLAUSEWITZ

"Command of the sea" will continue to be a constant of historical maritime strategy as it has been in the past, up to the moment that a thermonuclear World War III breaks out—if it does. History continues to instruct in broad, strategic principles as well as in a continuum of development at lesser levels—tactical, administrative, logistical, material and command. Such general patterns of history, dependent always on geography, deserve summary notice here, especially as they reflect the preconditions and prerequisites for the emergence of thalassocracies and show why continental states have been prevented from such an evolution. By their several past examples, maritime- and non-maritime-centered national experiences suggest alternative courses of action for the future. And finally, stepping outside the strictures of his profession, the historian—or this one at least—can borrow from the political scientists, defense theorists and gamesmen to offer a "scenario" of a hypothetical World War III based on *current possibilities*. This last should at the very least round out the history of navies, since no historian likely to survive such a nuclear holocaust will have either the facts or the motivation to write the full naval history of World War III.

A very general evolutionary pattern of thalassocratic growth emerges from the histories of the Minoans, Athenians, Venetians, Dutch, British and possibly the Americans, remembering always that each experience was unique in timing and details. First, from a favorable geographical position on an extensive coastline, the desire to trade fish, agricultural and manufactured goods for economic growth led to overseas merchant shipping. Second, the need for economic and thus political security to protect these vessels from pirates and rival maritime traders led to arming the merchantmen, then outfitting several as privateers or building a few cruisers especially for fighting. Third, a developing mercantilistic nation required a rudimentary navy of coastal gunboats to help defend the seaports and a fleet of cruisers and other warships to systematically protect shipping and to attack that of an enemy in wartime; this might be termed the *guerre de course* phase. Fourth and most crucial, shifting from the defensive to the offensive, the maritime nation acquired overseas colonies or trading stations both for raw materials and for markets, built and maintained a permanent superior navy of capital fighting ships designed to actively police the trade routes, to protect the merchant shipping and overseas stations, and to seek out and destroy the enemy's warships and merchant vessels in wartime battle and/or blockade. In other words, it achieved the ability to command the sea through a maritime strategy. Economically and militarily, it had become an integrated maritime empire, and it imposed order upon the seas—*pax*—with its navy in order to preserve its prosperity. It also supported the exploration of uncharted regions of the world both for profit and new knowledge. Finally, the vitality and affluence at work during this long process culminated in a golden age of enlightened government, human rights, high culture and artistic achievement. Usually seeking at least one major continental ally to help contain its jealous enemies, this thalassocracy enforced its *pax* by active "cold," limited and even total wars, leading it eventually to dominate world politics. This exalted status was usually lost only when emerging rival maritime powers and/or nearby continental enemies defeated the thalassocracy, aided by its internal decay caused partly by the greed and corruption of succeeding generations. Ultimately receding in grandeur and power, it then lived on the memories of its past glories.

By contrast, continental powers with long, exposed frontiers on land often aspired to thalassocratic greatness but usually never could get beyond the *guerre de course* stage, the fate of the Persians, Spartans, Phoenicians and Carthaginians, Arabs, Turks, Byzantines, Vikings, Spanish, Portuguese, French, Germans, Italians, Japanese and Russians. Alexander and Rome are very special cases of overland world conquest which thus absorbed all the seaports, but both had to borrow heavily from the conquered Greeks at sea. The geographic preoccupation with landward economies and defenses fostered autocratic, army- and/or church-dominated political systems that neither desired nor could afford equally strong armies and navies. Whatever cultural achievements such nations fostered, they rarely reached heights comparable to the thalassocracies in democratic government, free economic enterprise or intense artistic creativity. Many such nations tried to do these things by going to sea and even came close to such heights, but never quite succeeded, in the last analysis because of constant wars stemming largely from the heavy demands imposed by their geographic exposure and internal pressures. The industrial and technological revolutions of the past two centuries have enabled virtually all nations with any coastline to build more warships than previously, but technology can also be used to thwart thalassocratic growth as well as encourage it, of which the fascist and communist dictatorships are prime examples. Perhaps, by the twenty-first century, Russia's expansion upon the seas and exploration of space will modify the rigid Soviet system, but the geographic and political barriers are most formidable.

The last third of the twentieth century is unique, like any period in history, so that actual parallels are misleading, but the current *Pax Americana* does strongly resemble the *Pax Britannica* of a century ago. The American industrial capitalistic system dominates world markets, while American democratic government (for all its shortcomings) and material affluence provide the model for developing new nations, though the current level of American culture is more debatable. Strategically, the United States applies an oceanic maritime system that in any other time would have deserved the label imperial. The ballistic missile submarines are the chief agent for deterring nuclear aggression, while the surface navy enforces freedom of the seas and protects America's allies with their valuable bases. The anomalies in this system—by no means strange to earlier maritime states—are a disinterested and thus uninformed public about oceanic matters; conservative, apolitical admirals whose public relations and image still lag behind those of the generals; a professional naval and lay distaste for limited wars; a fleet of warships overaged because of governmental and public neglect; a dangerously deteriorating merchant fleet (though foreign flag carriers remain predominantly pro-American); and a quite normal Navy tendency to become alarmed, even panicky, over Russian naval and maritime growth—the type of alarm that a century ago generated unrealistic French "invasion scares" in Britain.

The United States Navy will, for the foreseeable future, strengthen its twofold capability of deterring nuclear war and policing the seas. If it is to become the focus of a new American maritime strategy, however,

American defense planners will have to choose to reduce Army and Air Force appropriations, since until the 1970s those two services had equal funding for increasingly expensive but questionable strategic roles and missions. And the sheer expense of individual weapons systems with their cost overruns means that quantitative as well as qualitative choices will have to be made constantly, for no nation—and least of all the United States—exists on weapons alone. For the Navy, new naval weapons of the 1970s reflect the strategic concepts of the 1960s. Extending the range and power of the Polaris-Poseidon ballistic missile subs is the new *Trident*-class sub of twenty-four MIRVed missiles with ranges up to 4500 miles (Undersea Launched or Sub-Launched Ballistic Missile System, the ULMS or SLBM), while serious consideration is being given to removing all ballistic missiles from land to the sea aboard attack carriers and specially designed surface ships (the Ship-Launched Missile System, SLMS, or Ballistic Missile Ship, BMS, and possibly even a sea-based anti-ballistic-missile missile system, SABMIS). More secure because of the difficulties of detection and cheaper than hardened silos, the latter "sea-based option" forces could be armed with the new MIRVed Minuteman III missile now on land. The growth of the Russian surface fleet may lead to a new dual-purpose American sub with improved 6000-mile Poseidon ballistic missiles (ExPo), the maneuverable re-entry vehicle (MaRV), and antiship submarine tactical missiles (STAM) to attack ships as well as strategic targets.

To command the seas for normal surface, air and ASW operations, the U. S. Navy will deploy each of four nuclear-powered carriers in special very mobile task groups, two in the Atlantic, two in the Pacific; the new F-14 Tomcat fighter will augment, then replace, the veteran F-4 Phantom II on all attack carriers. New destroyer escorts and frigates with newer electronic interception systems, surface-to-air missiles and manned helicopters will protect surface ships from missile or submarine attack, while the Navy is pressing forward with its own surface-to-surface tactical antiship "cruise" missiles. New amphibious assault vessels and logistics ships will provide increasing mobility with Marine Corps teams embarked, and new V/STOL carriers and planes will give added protection in the air. New PT boats for inshore work are needed; minelaying is being progressively downgraded (probably a mistake); and minesweeping is being left ever more to smaller allied navies (never depend on an ally!). The technological breakthroughs in propulsion are revolutionizing naval operations, with fast-starting gas turbine engines, nuclear power, hydrofoils and hovercraft systems becoming available for increasing numbers of ships by the end of the century. If the Navy gets most of these things, it will surely retain command of the seas.

The present oceanic challenger, Soviet Russia—in the historical pattern of maritime and continental rivalries—has imitated Anglo-American maritime developments and has even contributed significant advances of its own to naval science. Ship for ship, many of its vessels are newer, faster and better than their American counterparts, like those of many of its continental predecessors over their maritime competitors; indeed, Russian oceanic trade, fishing and research are downright superior. But the Soviet Navy is still a parade fleet or "fleet-in-being," untried in battle and unrisked even in limited wars, and Russian diplomacy still remains too clumsy to make it an effective tool. Part of this diplomatic weakness is due to the unattractiveness of communism and Russian militarism to emerging nations. Indeed, any Russian East African bases will probably prove to be as relatively useless as were France's and Germany's colonies in the nineteenth century and for the same reasons. For Russia is not a thalassocratic nation, nor does it employ a maritime strategy; the superior Red Army instead maintains a stranglehold over Central Europe and nervously patrols the long Chinese frontier. An ever stronger U. S. Navy can only force a Russia with naval delusions to commit even greater expenses on its own navy for really peripheral needs—a serious drain on any continental economy that must lead to continuing doubts by the Soviet's Party leadership, the predominant Army and the average consumer. Except in the nuclear arena, Russia remains the elephant to the American whale.

The Soviet Navy will continue to match American strategic capabilities and to maintain a scaled-down version of the American surface fleet. In ballistic missile subs, the 16-missile Yankees are being joined by 12-missile Deltas (or Yankee II) and a new 16-missile sub, both with missile ranges to 4000 miles. The accuracy of their missiles has been improved significantly by a stellar inertial guidance system aligned in flight on certain stars, and all are multiple-tipped (multiple re-entry vehicle, MRV). Matching the more sophisticated independently targeted MIRV of the Americans will take more time to develop. Nuclear power is being placed in increasing numbers of Soviet submarines, but the Russians continue to produce new diesel-electric boats for coast defense and will take longer than the Americans to equip their surface ships with nuclear engines. Instead, their pioneering work in gas turbines will be exploited. Russian ASW techniques will improve, along with their mine warfare weapons and surface-to-surface "cruise" missiles, with the major air element still provided by land-based naval bombers.

The Soviet Navy is developing a limited blue-water capability with at least one medium-size V/STOL carrier and new guided AAW missile cruisers as escorts, but it is doubtful whether these will ever seriously match the American attack carrier weapon system in quality or quantity. Amphibious vessels and the Naval Infantry will be increased, but largely for development around the periphery of Russia. The Russian fleets will thus remain defensive, relying upon the submarine both to provide strategic deterrence and to threaten American surface ships and subs, thereby defending the homeland from missile or amphibious attack. Russian diplomacy will continue to seek overseas facilities where the surface navy can "show the flag," but whether Russia will ever develop the logistical mobility and base network typical of a true blue-water navy is extremely doubtful. Of course, this analysis may be incorrect, especially if the United States creates power vacuums upon the seas by allowing its navy to deteriorate—an unlikely possibility.

Whatever the American and Russian navies do will depend upon the policies and decisions of their respective governments. Both countries have had such notoriously bad luck with some of their allies—the United States with France and South Vietnam, and Russia with China and Egypt, for example—that both may tend to be drawn ever closer in resolving their differences. Both nations have traditionally fostered isolationistic tendencies, and the new economic power centers of Western Europe and Japan offer formidable challenges in the 1970s and beyond. America and Russia may thus seek to progress from the initial SALT agreements of 1972 to reduce their—and others'—armaments and thus to compete more effectively in the economic sphere, thereby solving manifold internal problems. New reconnaissance satellites may force them to further limit land-based missiles, unless the latter have mobility as on railroads, while increasingly effective offensive weapons may lead to a total ban on ineffective and expensive defensive systems altogether. Russia will compete economically on the high seas, while the American Merchant Marine Act of 1970 insures America's desires to compete there as well with more and newer merchantmen. Indeed, such common interests and problems, along with the worldwide desire to reduce the chance of nuclear war, may drive the two superpowers into mutual economic dependence and—not inconceivably—into a defensive alliance by the end of the century, as in 1941 and as ancient rivals Britain and France did at the beginning of the century. Such a prospect, now less farfetched than ever, may well convince the United States to adopt a full-blown maritime strategy and the Soviet Union to be content with its defensive naval posture. Conversely, though, third parties like China or Israel could conceivably increase Russo-American tensions and even create a Sarajevo-like crisis to trigger a nuclear exchange.

Though rigid controls in any shooting situation between the United States and Soviet Russia are earnestly desired by both parties, such would be virtually impossible to enforce during the few minutes necessary for either side to gain the strategic advantage of the first strike, so that World War III—if it happens—will probably be a total thermonuclear war. Launching all their pre-targeted missiles, the subs should have little difficulty in obliterating every major city and port even if only relatively few of their missiles or warheads penetrate any anti-missile defenses. The qualitative edge of the U.S. Navy in ASW will enable its hunter subs, carrier planes and escort ships to sink many but surely not all of the numerous Russian subs and probably not before the latter have fired most of their missiles. Immediately, however, Soviet antiship attack subs and missile ships will sink as many American subs and surface ships as they can locate, despite defensive countermeasures. Manned bombers and land-based missiles will be launched on their one-way trips before their bases and silos are destroyed by the sub-launched missiles. Outside of the ballistic missile submarines, therefore, conventional naval forces will play an insignificant role. Amphibious forces, logistical ships, convoys and inshore craft will have virtually no function at all, for literally within, say, ninety minutes of the initial "button-pushing" the major political, transportation and communications centers will be wiped out, along with the important industrial and fuel complexes. Oil-burning vessels and all aircraft will be immobilized without more fuel, with most nuclear-powered ships being sunk. Any merchant and naval vessels already at sea that happen to survive this holocaust will return to gutted ports, there to drop anchor for the last time. If it matters, the United States will probably, militarily, have gotten the better of the short war, with the underdeveloped Third World nations escaping most of the direct destruction, if not the global fallout of radiation. But nobody will "win" World War III, for industrial civilization as we have known it will have ceased to exist.

Post-World War III civilization, whatever of it survives, will have to start all over again. Somehow, food will have to be produced, then goods traded on whatever vessels (sail?) can be fashioned; such craft will have to be protected from outlaws and pirates bent on their own survival, and so the need for armed warships, etc., etc. We will be back where the Minoans started, and the process will begin again. . . .

# Bibliography

By the nature of this broad overview, secondary works provided most of the information, save for much primary and oral research the writer has done as part of his specialized work in twentieth-century naval history. In addition to books (naval and more general), several key dissertations, some theses and many articles have been consulted, along with newspaper items from the most recent years. Most sources consulted were in English, not surprisingly since maritime Britain has dominated the field of naval history, only sharing its lead with American scholarship since World War II—an obvious reflection of the strong national maritime and naval pursuits of both countries. Where non-English-language sources were necessary, the writer tended to rely on translators.

Works listed here reflect only those actually used in the writing of this book, so that this should not be considered as a definitive bibliography of the field. The literature of naval and maritime history is vast, but is catalogued best in Robert G. Albion, *Maritime and Naval History: An Annotated Bibliography,* 4th ed., Mystic, Conn., 1972. Other useful English-language bibliographies are:

Higham, Robin. *A Guide to the Sources of British Military History.* Berkeley; London, 1972. Listing of books, articles, private manuscripts and documents, official papers, British libraries, military booksellers and professional journals.

International Commission on Maritime History. *Bibliographie de l'Histoire des Grandes Routes Maritimes,* 4 vols. Lisbon, 1967–to date. Published first in the quarterly *Boletim Internacional de Bibliografia Luso-Brasileira* of the Calouste Gulbenkian Foundation, Volumes II (the United States) and IV (Great Britain) are in English, Volumes I (France, Denmark, Germany and Poland) and III (Spain and Portugal) are in French.

Manwaring, G. E. *Bibliography of British Naval History: Bibliographical and Historical Guide to Printed Manuscript Sources.* London, 1930, 1969.

Millett, Allan R. and B. F. Cooling. *Doctoral Dissertations in Military Affairs.* Manhattan, Kans., 1972. English language dissertations only; annual supplements in the journal *Military Affairs,* which also contains a bibliography of articles in each issue.

National Maritime Museum. *Catalogue of the Library,* 2 vols. Greenwich, 1968, 1970.

[Naval History Division]. *United States Naval History: A Bibliography,* 6th ed. Washington, 1972.

General sources are listed here first, then specific sources as they were first used in the writing of the book, though naturally many sources cover broad periods of time, overlapping in the chapters. Sources are otherwise listed alphabetically by author, being annotated only where the title fails to convey the subject matter. Abbreviations used for the *United States Naval Institute Proceedings* and the American *Naval War College Review* are *USNIP* and *NWCR* respectively.

## GENERAL WORKS and BOOK ONE.
## COMMAND OF THE SEA—AND THE ALTERNATIVES

Albion, Robert Greenhalgh and Jennie Barnes Pope. *Sea Lanes in Wartime: The American Experience, 1775–1945,* 2nd enl. ed. Hamden, Conn., 1968.

Allison, R. S. *Sea Diseases: The Story of a Great Natural Experiment in Preventive Medicine in the Royal Navy.* London, 1943.

Anderson, R. C. *Oared Fighting Ships, From Classical Times to the Coming of Steam.* London, 1962.

Anderson, Romola and R. C. *The Sailing Ship: Six Thousand Years of History.* New York, 1963.

Archibald, E. H. H. *The Metal Fighting Ship in the Royal Navy, 1860–1970.* New York, 1971.

————. *The Wooden Fighting Ship in the Royal Navy, 897–1860.* London, 1968.

Ballard, G. A. *Rulers of the Indian Ocean.* London, 1927.

Barraclough, Geoffrey. *An Introduction to Contemporary History.* New York, 1964. Recent history, 1890s to 1960s.

Barzun, Jacques, Paul H. Beik. George Crothers and E. O. Golob. *Introduction to Naval History.* New York, 1944.

Basch, Lucien. "Ancient Wrecks and the Archeology of Ships." *The International Journal of Nautical Archeology and Underwater Exploration,* I (1972), 1–58. An overview of the field.

Bass, George F., ed. *A History of Seafaring based on underwater archeology.* London, 1972.

Brodie, Bernard. *A Guide to Naval Strategy,* 5th ed. New York, 1965.

———— and Fawn Brodie. *From Cross-bow to H-Bomb.* New York, 1962. A short history of weapons.

Colomb, P. H., Vice Admiral. *Naval Warfare: Its Ruling Principles and Practice Historically Treated.* London, 1899.

Corbett, Julian S. *Some Principles of Maritime Strategy.* London, 1911, 1972.

Creswell, John, Captain, R.N. *Generals and Admirals: The Story of Amphibious Command.* New York, 1952.

Daly, R. W. "Russian Military and Naval Doctrines." Unpublished course narrative, U. S. Naval Academy. From the Scythians to the Revolution. See his "Russia's Ancient Ally: the Sea," *USNIP,* 98, no. 8 (August 1972), 60–67, for an example.

Dupuy, R. Ernest, Colonel USA (Ret), and Colonel Trevor N. Dupuy, USA (Ret). *The Encyclopedia of Military History.* New York, 1970.

Eccles, H. E., Rear Admiral USN (Ret). "Strategy," rev. essay. *Selected*

*Readings in Evolution of Strategy Theory.* Washington: mimeographed, 1968.

Fergusson, Bernard. *The Watery Maze: The Story of Combined Operations.* New York, 1961.

FitzGerald, C. P. *The Southern Expansion of the Chinese People.* London, 1972.

Gardiner, Leslie. *The British Admiralty.* London, 1968.

Hampshire, A. Cecil. *The Royal Marines, 1664–1964.* n.p. [1964].

Harrison, Richard Edes, and the Editors of *Fortune. Look at the World: The FORTUNE Atlas of World Strategy.* New York, 1944.

Hasslöf, Olof, *et al.,* eds. *Ships and Shipyards; Sailors and Fishermen: Introduction to Maritime Ethnology.* Copenhagen, 1972.

Hay, David and Joan. *No Star at the Pole: A History of Navigation from the Stone Age to the 20th Century.* London, 1972.

Hearnshaw, F. J. C. *Sea-Power and Empire.* London, 1940.

Huçul, Walter Charles. "The Evolution of Russian and Soviet Sea Power, 1853–1953." Ph.D., University of California at Berkeley, 1953.

Hyatt, A. M. J., ed. *Dreadnought to Polaris: Maritime Strategy Since Mahan.* Toronto, Ont., 1973.

Jameson, William. *The Most Formidable Thing: The Story of the Submarine from its earliest days to the end of World War I.* London, 1965.

Jane, Fred. T. *The Imperial Russian Navy: Its Past, Present, and Future.* London, 1899.

Knox, Dudley W. *A History of the United States Navy.* New York, 1948.

Kuykendall, Ralph S. *The Hawaiian Kingdom, 1778–1854: Foundation and Transformation.* Honolulu, 1947.

Landström, Björn. *The Ship: An Illustrated History.* Garden City, [1961]. Primitive to nuclear-powered vessels; all types.

Lewis, Michael. *The History of the British Navy.* Baltimore, 1957.

Lloyd, Christopher. *The Nation and the Navy: A History of Naval Life and Policy.* London, 1954. The British navy.

Macintyre, Donald, Captain, R.N. (Ret), and Basil W. Bathe. *The Man of War.* London, 1968. History of the warship.

McFee, William. *The Law of the Sea.* New York, 1950.

Marder, Arthur J. "From Jimmu Tennō to Perry—Sea Power in Early Japanese History." *American Historical Review,* LI, no. 1 (October 1945), 1–34.

Mitchell, Mairin. *The Maritime History of Russia, 848–1948.* London, 1949.

Nef, John U. *War and Human Progress.* New York, 1963.

Phillips-Birt, Douglas. *A History of Seamanship.* London, 1971.

[Pierce, P. K., Lieutenant Commander, USNR]. *Riverine Warfare: The U. S. Navy's Operations on Inland Waters,* rev. ed. Washington, 1969.

Potter, E. B. and Chester W. Nimitz, eds. *Sea Power: A Naval History.* Englewood Cliffs, N.J., 1960.

Potter, Pitman B. *The Freedom of the Seas in History, Law, and Politics.* London, 1924.

Robison, S. S., Rear Admiral, USN (Ret), and Mary L. Robison. *A History of Naval Tactics from 1530–1930.* Annapolis, 1942.

de la Roncière, Ch. and G. Clerc-Rampal. *Histoire de la Marine Française.* Paris, 1934. History of the French Navy.

Ropp, Theodore. *War in the Modern World,* rev. ed. New York, 1962. Since 1415.

Rose, J. Holland. *Man and the Sea: Stages in Maritime and Human Progress.* Cambridge, 1935. A catchall, but mostly exploration.

Rosinski, Herbert. *Power and Human Destiny.* New York, 1962. "Power" and "tension" as alternatives to "peace" and "war" through historical examples.

Roskill, S. W., Captain, R.N. (Ret). *The Strategy of Sea Power.* London, 1962. Historical overview with emphasis on Britain.

Russell, Sir Herbert. *Sea Shepherds: Wardens of our Food Flocks.* London, 1941. History of convoy.

Semple, Ellen Churchill. *Influences of Geographic Environment: On the Basis of Ratzel's System of Anthropo-Geography.* New York, 1911.

Stafford, Edward Perry, Commander, USN. *The Far and the Deep.* New York, 1967. History of submarines with bibliography.

*Svenska Flottans Historia,* 3 vols. n.p., 1942–45. A huge history of the Swedish Navy and thus Scandinavia in general.

Tavernier, Bruno (tr. by Nicholas Fry). *Great Maritime Routes: An Illustrated History.* Paris, 1970.

Taylor, E. G. R. *The Haven-Finding Art.* New York, 1971. History of navigation.

Tolkowsky, Samuel. *They Took to the Sea: A Historical Survey of Jewish Maritime Activities.* New York, 1964. Overstated.

Toussaint, Auguste (tr. by June Guicharnaud). *The History of the Indian Ocean.* Chicago, 1967.

Vagts, Alfred. *Landing Operations: Strategy, Psychology, Tactics, Politics, From Antiquity to 1945.* Harrisburg, 1946.

Weigley, Russell F. *The American Way of War: A History of United States Military Strategy and Policy.* New York, 1973.

Whitehouse, Arch. *Amphibious Operations.* Garden City, 1963. A history.

Williams, Neville. *Contraband Cargoes: Seven Centuries of Smuggling.* London, 1959.

Woodward, David. *The Russians at Sea: A History of the Russian Navy.* New York, 1965.

## BOOK TWO. THE EARLY THALASSOCRACIES, 2000 B.C.–A.D. 1415

Adams, John, to Richard Rush, October 19, 1815. Adams papers, letter 148, on microfilm reel 122. Courtesy of John J. Kelly, Jr. A summary of international maritime law from 1075 to 1270.

Adcock, F. E. *The Greek and Macedonian Art of War,* Berkeley, 1962.

———. *The Roman Art of War Under the Republic.* New York, 1963.

Arrian (tr. by Aubrey de Sélincourt). *The Life of Alexander the Great.* Baltimore, 1958.

Ashe, Geoffrey, *et al. The Quest for America.* New York, 1971. The debate over prehistoric maritime contacts between Eastern and Western hemispheres.

Balcer, Jack M. "From Confederate Freedom to Imperial Tyranny: A Study of the Restrictions Imposed by Athens on the Political Self-Determination of the Members in the Delian Confederacy, 478–431 B.C." Ph.D. dissertation, University of Michigan, 1964.

Basch, Lucien. "Phoenician Oared Ships." *The Mariner's Mirror,* 55 (1969), 139–162, 227–245, 381–382.

Basham, A. L. *The Wonder That Was India*. New York, 1954. Early navies of India briefly recounted.

Berlitz, Charles. *Mysteries from Forgotten Worlds*. Garden City, 1972. Mounting prehistoric and archeological evidence for a possible antediluvian thalassocracy and related maritime communications.

Bibby, Geoffrey. *Looking for Dilmun*. New York, 1969.

Boardman, John. *The Greeks Overseas*. Baltimore, 1964. Ancient Greek migrations and colonizations in the Mediterranean world.

Breasted, James Henry. *A History of Egypt*. New York, 1905; 1964.

Brooks, F. W. *The English Naval Forces, 1199–1272*. London, 1932; 1963.

Caesar, Julius (tr. by Jane F. Mitchell). *The Civil War*. Baltimore, 1967.

Carter, John M. *The Battle of Actium: The Rise and Triumph of Augustus Caesar*. London, 1970.

Cary, M. and W. H. Warmington. *The Ancient Explorers*. London, 1929; Baltimore, 1963.

Cassidy, Vincent H. *The Sea Around Them: The Atlantic Ocean, A.D. 1250*. Baton Rouge, 1968.

Casson, Lionel. *The Ancient Mariners*. New York, 1959. A history of seafaring in the ancient world.

———. *Ships and Seamanship in the Ancient World*. Princeton, 1971.

Chambers, D. S. *The Imperial Age of Venice, 1380–1580*. London, 1970.

Charlesworth, M. P. *Trade-Routes and Commerce of the Roman Empire*. 1926; New York, 1970.

Cipolla, Carlo M. *Guns, Sails and Empires: Technological Innovation and the Early Phases of European Expansion, 1400–1700*. n.p., 1965.

Clark, Frederick William. *The Influence of Sea-Power on the History of the Roman Republic*. Menasha, Wisc., 1915.

Culican, William. *The First Merchant Venturers: The Ancient Levant in History and Commerce*. London, 1966.

Diehl, Charles. *Byzantium: Greatness and Decline*. New Brunswick, N. J., 1957.

Edwards, I. E. S., *et al.*, eds. *The Cambridge Ancient History*, 3rd ed., Vol. I, Pt. 2: *Early History of the Middle East*. Cambridge, 1971.

Eickhoff, Ekkehard. *Seekrieg und Seepolitik zwischen Islam und Abenland: Das Mittelmeer unter Byzantinischer und Arabischer Hegemonie (650–1040)*. Berlin, 1966. Byzantine-Arab naval rivalry in the Mediterranean.

Fahmy, Aly Mohamed. *Muslim Sea-Power in the Eastern Mediterranean From the Seventh to the Tenth Century A.D.* London, 1950.

Fisher, Sir Geoffrey. *Barbary Legend: War, Trade, and Piracy in North Africa, 1415–1830*. Oxford, 1958.

Gomme, A. W. "A Forgotten Factor of Greek Naval Strategy." *Journal of Hellenic Studies*, 53 (1933), 16–24. A treatise on the interrelationships between Greek armies and naval squadrons.

Gordon, Cyrus H. *Before Columbus: Links Between the Old World and Ancient America*. New York, 1971.

———. *The Common Background of Greek and Hebrew Civilization*. New York, 1965. Argues for a common Semitic heritage.

———. *Ugarit and Minoan Crete*. New York, 1966.

Green, Peter. *Armada from Athens*. New York, 1970. The disastrous overseas expedition against Syracuse during the Peloponnesian War.

———. *The Year of Salamis, 480–479 B.C.* London, 1970.

Herman, Zvi (tr. by Len Ortzen). *Peoples, Seas and Ships.* New York, 1967. Ancient seafaring peoples.

Herodotus (tr. by Aubrey de Sélincourt). *The Histories.* Baltimore, 1964. The Persian invasion of Greece.

Hourani, George Fadlo. *Arab Seafaring in the Indian Ocean in Ancient and Early Medieval Times.* Princeton, 1951.

Hutchinson, R. W. *Prehistoric Crete.* Baltimore, 1962.

Irwin, Constance. *Fair Gods and Stone Faces.* New York, 1963. Argues for global-ranging seafarers in early times.

Johnstone, Paul. "Stern First in the Stone Age?" *The International Journal of Nautical Archaeology and Underwater Exploration,* II, no. 1 (March 1973), 3–11. Earliest Mediterranean seafaring.

Jones, Gwyn. *A History of the Vikings.* London, 1968.

Jordan, Borimir. "The Administration and Military Organization of the Athenian Navy in the Fifth and Fourth Centuries B.C." Ph.D., University of California at Berkeley, 1968.

Kienast, Dietmar. *Untersuchungen zu den Kriegsflotten der Römischen Kaiserzeit.* Bonn, 1966. The Roman imperial navy from Augustus through the fourth century A.D.

Laing, Donald R., Jr. "A New Interpretation of the Athenian Naval Catalog, IG 112, 1951." Ph.D., University of Cincinnati, 1965.

Landström, Björn. *Ships of the Pharaohs.* London, 1970.

Lane, F. C. "Venetian Ships and Shipbuilding of the Renaissance." Ph.D., Harvard University, 1934.

Lewis, Archibald R. "England as an Atlantic Maritime Power,. 1100–1350 A.D." Unpublished paper, Medieval Academy Annual Meeting, Chapel Hill, N.C., 1971.

————. *Naval Power and Trade in the Mediterranean, A.D. 500–1100.* Princeton, 1951.

————. *The Northern Seas: Shipping and Commerce in Northern Europe, A.D. 300–1000.* Princeton, 1958.

Lo, Jung-pang. "The Emergence of China as a Sea Power during the Late Sung and Early Yüan Periods." *Far Eastern Quarterly,* XIV (August 1955), 489–503.

Luce, J. V. *Lost Atlantis: New Light on an Old Legend.* New York, 1969. Connects the Atlantis legends with ancient Minos, focusing on its collapse to volcanic eruption.

Ma Huan (tr. by J. V. G. Mills, ed.). *Ying-Yai Sheng-Lan* ["The Overall Survey of the Ocean's Shores"]. Cambridge, 1972. Contemporary accounts of Cheng Ho's voyages, early 1400s.

Marinatos, Spyridon. "Thera: Key to the Riddle of Minos." *National Geographic,* 141, no. 5 (May 1972), 702–726.

Marlowe, John. *The Golden Age of Alexandria . . . 331 B.C. to . . . 642 A.D.* London, 1971.

Meiggs, Russell. *The Athenian Empire.* Oxford, 1972.

Meirat, Jean. *Marines antiques de la Mediterranée.* Paris, 1964.

Mellersh, H. E. L. *The Destruction of Knossos: The Rise and Fall of Minoan Crete.* New York, 1970.

Merker, Irwin Loeb. "Studies in Sea-Power in the Eastern Mediterranean in the Century Following the Death of Alexander." Ph.D., Princeton University, 1958.

Miller, J. Innes. *The Spice Trade of the Roman Empire, 29 B.C. to A.D. 641.* Oxford, 1969.

Miller, Molly. *The Thalassocracies: Studies in Chronography II.* Albany, 1971. Sixth-century B.C. Aegean.

Morison, Samuel Eliot. *The European Discovery of America: The Northern Voyages,* A.D. *500–1600.* New York, 1971.

Morrison, J. S. and R. T. Williams. *Greek Oared Ships, 900–322* B.C. Cambridge, 1968. Uses archeological evidence to clear up many problems about ancient Greek naval history.

Moscati, Sabatino (tr. by Alastair Hamilton). *The World of the Phoenicians.* New York, 1968.

Mylonas, George E. *Mycenae and the Mycenaean Age.* Princeton, 1966.

"The Near East and the Aegean in the Second Millennium B.C." American Historical Association session, New York, December 1971.

Needham, Joseph. *Science and Civilisation in China,* Vol. 4, *Physics and Physical Technology,* Pt. III: *Civil Engineering and Nautics.* Cambridge, 1971. Ancient Chinese seafaring.

Ormerod, H. A. *Piracy in the Ancient World.* 1924; Chicago, 1967.

Page, D. L. *The Santorini Volcano and the Desolation of Minoan Crete.* London, 1971.

Renfrew, Colin. *The Emergence of Civilisation: The Cyclades and the Aegean in the Third Millennium* B.C. London, 1972. Argues for the unique development of Minoan and Greek civilization, as opposed to Gordon's view. Much on seafaring.

Riley, Carroll L., *et al.,* eds. *Man across the Sea: Problems of Pre-Columbian Contacts.* Austin, 1971.

Rodgers, W. L., Vice Admiral, USN (Ret). *Greek and Roman Naval Warfare.* Annapolis, 1937, 1964.

———. *Naval Warfare Under Oars, 4th to 16th Centuries.* Annapolis, 1939, 1970.

Sallust (tr. by S. A. Handford). *The Jugurthine War; The Conspiracy of Cataline.* Baltimore, 1963.

Sasson, Jack M. "Canaanite Maritime Involvement in the Second Millennium B.C." *Journal of the American Oriental Society,* 86, no. 2 (April–June 1966), 126–138.

Säve-Söderbergh, Torgny. "The Navy of the Eighteenth Egyptian Dynasty." *Uppsala Universitets Årsskrift 1946: no. 6.* Uppsala, 1946.

"The Search for Sunken Ships." *Surveyor* (August 1971), 22–28. Underwater archeology for the ancient Mediterranean.

Shepard, A. M. *Seapower in Ancient History.* Boston, 1924.

Snodgrass, A. M. *The Dark Age of Greece: An Archeological Survey of the Eleventh to the Eighth Centuries B.C.* Edinburgh, 1971.

Southworth, John van Duyn. *The Age of Sails.* New York, 1968.

———. *The Ancient Fleets.* New York, 1968.

Spencer, George Woolley. "Royal Leadership and Imperial Conquest in Medieval South India: The Naval Expedition of Rajendra Chola I, *c.* 1025 A.D." Ph.D., University of California at Berkeley, 1967. Includes a good overview of maritime activities in India and Southeast Asia, 2000 B.C. to A.D. 1100.

Starr, Chester G. "The Myth of the Minoan Thalassocracy." *Historia 3* (1954–5), 282–291.

————. *The Roman Imperial Navy, 31 B.C.–A.D. 324.* Ithaca, 1941.

Thiel, J. H. *Studies on the History of Roman Sea-Power in Republican Times.* Amsterdam, Holland, 1946.

Thompson, Edgar K. "Swiss Naval Wars." *Mariner's Mirror,* 59, no. 1 (February 1973), 99. 1300–1550 A.D.

Thucydides (tr. by Rex Warner). *The Peloponnesian War.* Baltimore, 1954.

Vegetius, [Flavius Renatus] (no tr.). "Military Institutions of the Romans." n.p., n.d. Book V of this classic work deals with the navies of imperial Rome.

Warmington, B. H. *Carthage.* Baltimore, 1964.

Watson, William. *Early Civilization in China.* New York, 1966.

Weir, Michael. "English Naval Activities, 1242–1243." *Mariner's Mirror,* 58, no. 1 (February 1972), 85–92.

Wheeler, Sir Mortimer. *Civilizations of the Indus Valley and Beyond.* New York, 1966.

Wiel, Alethea. *The Navy of Venice.* London, 1910.

Wilcken, Ulrich. *Alexander the Great.* 1931; New York, 1967.

Wilson, W. R., Captain, USN (Ret). "The Sea Battle of Dannoura." *The American Neptune,* XXVIII, no. 3 (July 1968), 206–222.

Yadin, Yigael. *The Art of Warfare in Biblical Lands,* 2 vols. New York, 1963.

## BOOK THREE. THE OCEANIC AGE, 1415–1730

Albion, Robert Greenhalgh. *Forests and Sea Power: The Timber Problem of the Royal Navy, 1652–1862.* 1926; Hamden, Conn., 1965.

Anderson, R. C. "The First Dutch War in the Mediterranean." *Mariner's Mirror,* 49, no. 4 (November 1963), 241–265.

————. *Naval Wars in the Baltic during the Sailing Ship Epoch, 1522–1850.* 1910; London, 1969.

————. *Naval Wars in the Levant, 1559–1853.* Liverpool, 1953.

————. "The Thirty Years' War in the Mediterranean." *Mariner's Mirror,* 55 (1969), 435–451, and 56 (1970), 41–57.

Bamford, Paul W. *Fighting Ships and Prisons: The Mediterranean Galleys of France in the Age of Louis XIV.* Minneapolis, 1973.

————. *Forests and French Sea Power, 1660–1789.* Toronto, 1956.

Battick, John Francis. "Cromwell's Navy and the Foreign Policy of the Protectorate, 1653–1658." Ph.D., Boston University, 1967.

Beck, Horace P. *The American Indian as a Sea-Fighter in Colonial Times.* Mystic, 1959.

Bensusan, Harold Guy. "The Spanish Struggle Against Foreign Encroachment in the Caribbean, 1675–1697." Ph.D., University of California at Los Angeles, 1970.

Boxer, C. R. *The Dutch Seaborne Empire, 1600–1800.* New York, 1965.

————. *The Portuguese Seaborne Empire, 1415–1825.* New York, 1969.

Bradford, Ernle. *The Sultan's Admiral: The Life of Barbarossa.* New York, 1968.

Brandel, Fernand (tr. by Siân Reynolds). *The Mediterranean and the Mediterranean World in the Age of Philip II,* 2 vols. London, 1972–73.

Corbett, Julian S. *Fighting Instructions, 1530–1816.* London, 1905; New York, 1967.

Creswell, John. *British Admirals of the Eighteenth Century: Tactics in Battle.* Hamden, Conn., 1972.

De Meij, J. C. A. *De Watergeuzen en de Nederlanden, 1568–72.* Amsterdam, 1972. The Sea Beggars.

Earle, Peter. *Corsairs of Malta and Barbary.* Annapolis, 1970.

Ehrman, John. *The Navy in the War of William III, 1689–1697.* Cambridge, 1953.

Elliot, J. H. *Imperial Spain, 1469–1716.* New York, 1963.

———. *The Old World and the New, 1492–1650.* Cambridge, 1970.

Elridge, F. B. *The Background of Eastern Sea Power.* Melbourne, 1948. The navies of the Far East throughout history.

Gardiner, C. Harvey. *Naval Power in the Conquest of Mexico.* Austin, 1956. Cortez's inland fleet.

Geyl, Pieter. *The Netherlands in the Seventeenth Century.* London, 1961.

Goslinga, Cornelis Ch. *The Dutch in the Caribbean and on the Wild Coast, 1580–1680.* Gainesville, Fla., 1971.

Haley, K. H. D. *The Dutch in the Seventeenth Century.* London, 1972.

Hansen, H. A. "The Sound Trade and the Anglo-Dutch Conflicts, 1640–1654." Ph.D., University of California at Los Angeles, 1947.

Hess, Andrew C. "The Battle of Lepanto and its Place in Mediterranean History." American Historical Association unpublished paper, Boston, December 1970.

———. "The Evolution of the Ottoman Seaborne Empire in the Age of Oceanic Discoveries, 1453–1525." *American Historical Review,* LXXV, no. 7 (December 1970), 1892–1919.

Hoffman, Paul Everett. "The Defense of the Indies, 1535–1574. A Study in the Modernization of the Spanish State." Ph.D., University of Florida, 1969.

Huizinga, J. H. (tr. by Arnold J. Pomerans). *Dutch Civilisation in the Seventeenth Century, and other essays.* London, 1968.

Jamieson, Alan. "The Tangier Galleys and the Wars against the Mediterranean Corsairs." *American Neptune,* XXIII, no. 2 (April 1963), 95–112.

LeGuin, Charles A. "Sea Life in Seventeenth-Century England." *American Neptune,* XXVII, no. 2 (April 1967), 111–134.

Lisk, Jill. *The Struggle for Supremacy in the Baltic, 1600–1725.* London, 1967.

Mallett, Michael E. *The Florentine Galleys in the Fifteenth Century.* Oxford, 1967.

Marcus, G. J. *A Naval History of England,* Vol. I: *The Formative Centuries.* London, 1961. To the end of the American Revolution.

Monk, W. F. *Britain and the Western Mediterranean.* London, 1953.

Moore, Ronald Oury. "Some Aspects of the Origins and Nature of English Piracy, 1603–1625." Ph.D., University of Virginia, 1960.

Moses, Norton H. "The British Navy and the Caribbean, 1689–1697." *Mariner's Mirror,* 52, no. 1 (February 1966), 13–40.

Natharius, Edward William. "The Maritime Powers and Sweden, 1698–1702." Ph.D., Indiana University, 1959.

Oakeshott, Walter. *Founded Upon the Seas: A Narrative of Some English Maritime and Overseas Enterprises during the period 1550 to 1616.* Cambridge, 1942.

Ollard, Richard. *Man of War: Sir Robert Holmes and the Restoration Navy.* London, 1969.

Parry, J. H. *The Age of Reconnaissance.* New York, 1963. Covers the entire period of European exploration.

————. *The Spanish Seaborne Empire.* London, 1966.

Peckham, Howard H. *The Colonial Wars, 1689–1762.* Chicago, 1964. In North America.

Petersen, Charles W. "England and Danish Naval Strategy in the Seventeenth Century." Uncompleted Ph.D., University of Maine.

Pierson, Peter O'Malley. "A Commander for the Armada." *Mariner's Mirror,* 55 (1969), 383–400. The appointment of the Duke of Medina Sidonia.

Pilgrim, Donald George. "The Uses and Limitations of French Naval Power in the Reign of Louis XIV: the Administration of the Marquis de Seignelay, 1683–1690." Ph.D., Brown University, 1969.

Powell, J. R. *The Navy in the English Civil War.* Hamden, Conn., 1962.

Powley, Edward B. *The English Navy in the Revolution of 1688.* Cambridge, 1928.

————. *The Naval Side of King William's War.* London, 1972. Covers the years 1688–1690.

Richmond, H. W. *Statesmen and Sea Power: The Navy as an Instrument of Policy, 1558–1727.* London, 1946, 1953. The British navy.

Rogers, H. C. B., Colonel. *Troopships and Their History.* London, 1963. The British trooplifting transports from the mid-seventeenth to the mid-twentieth centuries.

Saunders, Roy. *The Raising of the Vasa: The Rebirth of a Swedish Galleon.* London, 1962.

Scheina, Robert Lewis. "Mass Labor: The Key to Spanish Maritime Construction in the Americas during the Sixteenth Century." *Mariner's Mirror,* 58, no. 2 (May 1972), 195–202.

Schurz, William Lytle. *The Manila Galleon.* 1939; New York, 1959. Spanish maritime commerce to the Philippines, 1565–1815.

Teneti, Alberto (tr. by Janet and Brian Pullan). *Piracy and the Decline of Venice, 1580–1615.* London, 1967.

Vere, Francis. *Salt in Their Blood.* London, 1955. A popular account of the Dutch navy during the seventeenth century and in World War II.

Williamson, James A. *The Age of Drake.* London, 1938.

Wilson, Charles. *The Dutch Republic.* New York, 1968.

————. *Profit and Power: A Study of England and the Dutch Wars.* London, 1957.

## BOOK FOUR. BRITISH EMPIRE AND THE WORLD WARS, 1730–1815

Arthur, Charles Burton. "The Revolution in British Naval Strategy, 1800–1801." Ph.D., Harvard University, 1966. An overstated case for St. Vincent's close blockade of France.

Bird, Harrison. *Navies in the Mountains: The Battles on the Waters of Lake Champlain and Lake George, 1609–1814.* New York, 1962.

Brown, Wilbur S., Major General, USMC (Ret). *The Amphibious Campaign for West Florida and Louisiana, 1814–15.* Tuscaloosa, 1969.

Coggins, Jack. *Ships and Seamen of the American Revolution.* Harrisburg, 1969.

Darrieus, Gabriel, Captain, F.N. (tr. by Philip R. Alger). *War on the Sea.* Annapolis, 1908. Napoleon and sea power.

Forbes, Eric G. "Who Discovered Longitude at Sea?" *Sky and Telescope,* 41, no. 1 (January 1971), 4–6.

Glover, Richard. "The French Fleet, 1807–1814; Britain's Problem; and Madison's Opportunity." *Journal of Modern History,* 39 (September 1967), 233–252. Napoleon's naval construction that forced the British to overextend their wartime fleet.

Graham, Gerald S. *Sea Power and British North America.* Cambridge, 1941. The demise of mercantilism after the American Revolution.

Gruber, Ira D. "Admiral, Lord Howe and the War for American Independence." Ph.D., Duke University, 1961.

Hayes, Frederic H. "John Adams and American Sea Power." *American Neptune,* XXV, no. 1 (January 1965), 35–45.

Howarth, David. *Trafalgar: The Nelson Touch.* New York, 1969.

Jackson, Melvin H. *Privateers in Charleston, 1793–1796.* Washington, 1969.

Kelly, John J., Jr. "The Struggle for American Seaborne Independence as Viewed by John Adams." Ph.D., University of Maine, 1973.

Kennedy, Ludovic. *Nelson's Band of Brothers.* London, n.d.

Knox, Dudley W. *The Naval Genius of George Washington.* Boston, 1932.

Kulsrud, Carl J. *Maritime Neutrality to 1780.* Boston, 1936.

Lester, Malcolm. "Anglo-American Diplomatic Problems Arising from British Naval Operations in American Waters, 1793–1802." Ph.D., University of Virginia, 1954.

Lewis, Emanuel Raymond. *Seacoast Fortifications of the United States: An Introductory History.* Washington, 1970.

Mackesy, Piers. *The War in the Mediterranean, 1803–1810.* Cambridge, Mass., 1957.

Mahan, Alfred Thayer. *The Influence of Sea Power upon History, 1660–1783.* Boston, London, 1890; New York, 1957.

———. *The Influence of Sea Power upon the French Revolution and Empire, 1793–1812,* 2 vols. Boston, 1892; New York, 1968.

———. *Naval Strategy.* Boston, 1911.

———. *Sea Power in its Relations to the War of 1812,* 2 vols. Boston, 1905; New York, 1968.

Marcus, G. J. *The Age of Nelson: The Royal Navy in the Age of its Greatest Power and Glory, 1793–1815.* New York, 1971. Volume II in an ongoing history of the British navy.

Masefield, John. *Sea Life in Nelson's Time,* 3rd ed. Annapolis, 1972.

Nasatir, Abraham P. *Spanish War Vessels on the Mississippi, 1792–1796.* New Haven, 1968.

Oglesby, J. C. M. "War at Sea in the West Indies, 1739–1748." Ph.D., University of Washington, 1963.

Parry, J. H. *Trade and Dominion: The European Overseas Empires in the Eighteenth Century.* New York, 1971.

Robertson, Sir Charles Grant. *Chatham and the British Empire.* London, 1946.

Rush, N. Orwin. *The Battle of Pensacola, March 9 to May 8, 1781.* Tallahassee, 1966.

Saul, Norman Eugene. "Russia and the Mediterranean, 1797–1807." Ph.D., Columbia University, 1965.

Stout, Neil R. *The Royal Navy in America, 1760–1775.* Annapolis, 1973.

Syrett, David. "The Methodology of British Amphibious Operations during the Seven Years and American Wars." *Mariner's Mirror,* 58, no. 3 (August 1972), 269–280.

Tunstall, Brian. *William Pitt, Earl of Chatham.* London, 1938.

## BOOK FIVE. PAX BRITANNICA, 1815–1914

Allin, Lawrence C. "The *U.S. Naval Institute Proceedings* as a Vehicle of American Naval Thought, 1873–1900." Uncompleted Ph.D., University of Maine.

Baker, Maury Davison, Jr. "The United States and Piracy during the Spanish-American Wars of Independence." Ph.D., Duke University, 1946.

Ballard, G. A. *The Influence of the Sea on the Political History of Japan.* London, 1921.

Bartlett, C. J. *Great Britain and Sea Power, 1815–1853.* Oxford, 1963.

Bauer, K. Jack. *Surfboats and Horse Marines: U. S. Naval Operations in the Mexican War, 1846–48.* Annapolis, 1969.

———. "The United States Navy and Texas Independence: A Study in Jacksonian Integrity." *Military Affairs*, XXXIV, no. 2 (April 1970), 44–48.

Baynham, Henry. *Before the Mast: Naval Ratings of the 19th Century.* London, 1971.

Belknap, George E., Rear Admiral, USN. "The Home Squadron in the Winter of 1860–61." *Papers of the Historical Society of Massachusetts,* XII: *Naval Actions and History, 1799–1898.* Boston, 1902, pp. 75–100.

Berghahn, Volker R. *Der Tirpitz-Plan.* Düsseldorf, 1972.

Bernath, Stuart L. *Squall Across the Atlantic: American Civil War Prize Cases and Diplomacy.* Berkeley, 1970.

Bidwell, Robert Leland. "The First Mexican Navy, 1821–1830." Ph.D., University of Virginia, 1960.

Bigelow, John. *France and the Confederate Navy, 1862–1868.* New York, 1888.

Billingsley, Edward Warner. *In Defense of Neutral Rights: The United States Navy and the Wars of Independence in Chile and Peru.* Chapel Hill, 1967.

Boatner, Mark Mayo, III, Lieutenant Colonel, USA. *The Civil War Dictionary.* New York, 1959.

Bourne, Kenneth. *Britain and the Balance of Power in North America, 1815–1908.* Berkeley, 1967. Includes navies.

———, and Carl Boyd. "Captain Mahan's 'War' with Great Britain." *USNIP*, 94, no. 7 (July 1968), 71–78. Mahan's war plans for a possible war with Britain in the 1890s.

Brainard, Alfred P. "Russian Mines on the Danube." *USNIP*, 91, no. 7 (July 1965), 51–56. The Russo-Turkish War of 1877–78.

Braisted, William Reynolds. *The United States Navy in the Pacific, 1897–1909.* Austin, 1958; New York, 1969.

———. *The United States Navy in the Pacific, 1909–1922.* Austin, 1971.

Bright, Samuel R., Jr. "Confederate Coast Defense." Ph.D., Duke University, 1961.

Brodie, Bernard. *Sea Power in the Machine Age.* Princeton, 1941. Covers the years 1814 to 1940.

Brooke, George M., Jr. "The Role of the United States Navy in the Suppression of the African Slave Trade." *American Neptune*, XXI, no. 1 (January 1961), 28–41.

Buhl, Lance Crowther. "The Smooth Water Navy: American Naval Policy and Politics, 1865–1876." Ph.D., Harvard University, 1968.

Buker, George Edward. "Riverine Warfare: Naval Combat in the Second Seminole War, 1835–1842." Ph.D., University of Florida, 1969.

Busch, Briton Cooper. *Britain and the Persian Gulf, 1894–1914.* Berkeley, 1967.

Cecil, Lamar J. R. "Coal for the Fleet That Had to Die." *American Historical Review,* LXIX, no. 4 (July 1964), 990–1005. Logistics of the Russian fleet voyage from the Baltic to Tsushima.

Challener, Richard D. *Admirals, Generals, and American Foreign Policy, 1898–1914.* Princeton, 1973.

Chapin, John E. "Impact of the Civil War on Maine Shipping and Shipbuilding." M. A. thesis, University of Maine, 1970.

Clowes, Sir William Laird. *Four Modern Naval Campaigns: Historical, Strategic, and Tactical.* London, 1902; 1970. Limited wars between 1866 and 1894.

Cornwall, Peter George. "The Meiji Navy: Training in an Age of Change." Ph.D., University of Michigan, 1970. Late nineteenth century Japan.

Cullen, Charles W., Lieutenant Commander, USN. "From the Kriegsacademie to the Naval War College: The Military Planning Process." *NWCR,* XXII, no. 5 (January 1970), 6–18. War colleges of the late nineteenth century.

Dallett, Francis James. "The Creation of the Venezuelan Naval Squadron, 1848–1860." *American Neptune,* XXX, no. 4 (October 1970), 260–278.

Daly, R. W. *How the Merrimac Won: The Strategic Story of the C.S.S. Virginia.* New York, 1957. That vessel's impact on McClellan's Peninsular Campaign.

Falk, Edwin A. *From Perry to Pearl Harbor: The Struggle for Supremacy in the Pacific.* Garden City, 1943. Japanese naval power from the 1850s to the 1940s.

Field, James A., Jr. *America and the Mediterranean World, 1776–1882.* Princeton, 1969. Includes the Mediterranean Squadron.

Fox, Grace. *Britain and Japan, 1858–1883.* Oxford, 1969. Naval relations included.

———. *British Admirals and Chinese Pirates, 1832–1869.* London, 1940.

Gebhard, Louis A. "The Development of the Austro-Hungarian Navy, 1897–1914: A Study in the Operation of Dualism." Ph.D., Rutgers University, 1965.

Gilbert, Benjamin Franklin. "Naval Operations in the Pacific, 1861–1866." Ph.D., University of California at Berkeley, 1951. Navies of all nations in the Pacific then.

Gough, Barry M. *The Royal Navy and the Northwest Coast of North America, 1810–1914.* Vancouver, 1971.

Gowing, Peter Gordon. "Mandate in Moroland: The American Government of Muslim Filipinos, 1899–1920." Ph.D., Syracuse University, 1968. Much background on Spanish naval pacification operations, then that by the United States.

Graham, Gerald S. *Great Britain in the Indian Ocean: A Study of Maritime Enterprise, 1810–1850.* Oxford, 1967.

———. *The Politics of Naval Supremacy: Studies in British Maritime Ascendancy.* Cambridge, 1965. Heaviest on the nineteenth century.

Grenville, John A. S. and George Berkeley Young. *Politics, Strategy, and American Diplomacy: Studies in Foreign Policy, 1873–1917.* New Haven, 1966. Much on the U. S. Navy.

Hagan, Kenneth J. "Admiral David Dixon Porter: Strategist for a Navy in Transition." *USNIP,* 94, no. 7 (July 1968), 139–143.

——. *American Gunboat Diplomacy and the Old Navy, 1877–1889.* Westport, Conn., 1973.

Halpern, Paul G. *The Mediterranean Naval Situation, 1908–1914.* Cambridge, Mass., 1971.

Hayes, John D., Rear Admiral, USN (Ret). "Sea Power in the Civil War." *USNIP,* 87, no. 11 (November 1961), 60–69.

——. "Stephen Bleecker Luce." *NWCR,* XXII, no. 1 (September 1969), 75–79.

Heffernan, John B. "The Blockade of the Southern Confederacy: 1861–1865." *The Smithsonian Journal of History,* II, no. 4 (Winter 1967–1968), 23–44.

Henson, Curtis Talmon, Jr. "The United States Navy and China, 1839–1861." Ph.D., Tulane University, 1965.

Hollyday, Frederic B. M. *Bismarck's Rival: A Political Biography of General and Admiral Albrecht von Stosch.* Durham, 1960. Early years of the Imperial German Navy.

Hough, Richard. *First Sea Lord: An Authorized Biography of Admiral Lord Fisher.* London, 1969.

——. *The Fleet That Had to Die.* New York, 1958. Tsushima.

——. *The Potemkin Mutiny.* New York, 1961.

Hovgaard, William. *Modern History of Warships.* London, 1920; Annapolis, 1971. The period 1860 through World War I.

Howeth, L. S., Captain, USN. *History of Communications-Electronics in the United States Navy.* Washington, 1963. Mostly the early years.

Huntington, Samuel P. *The Soldier and the State: The Theory and Politics of Civil-Military Relations.* New York, 1957. A historical view of the American situation.

Jane, Fred. T. *The Imperial Japanese Navy.* London, 1904.

Jenrich, Charles H. "The Papal Navy." *USNIP,* 89, no. 9 (September 1963), 74–79.

Johnson, Franklyn Arthur. *Defence by Committee: The British Committee of Imperial Defence, 1885–1959.* London, 1960.

Johnson, Ludwell H. "Commerce Between Northeastern Ports and the Confederacy, 1861–1865." *Journal of American History,* LIV, no. 1 (June 1967), 30–42.

Johnson, Robert Erwin. *Thence Round Cape Horn: The Story of United States Naval Forces on Pacific Station, 1818–1923.* Annapolis, 1963.

Jornacion, George W. "The Time of the Eagles: United States Army Officers and the Pacification of the Philippine Moros, 1899–1913." Ph.D., University of Maine, 1973. Includes Naval operations.

Kajima, Morinosuke. *The Emergence of Japan as a World Power, 1895–1925.* Tokyo, 1968.

Kelly, J. B. *Britain and the Persian Gulf, 1795–1880.* Oxford, 1968.

Kelly, Patrick James. "The Naval Policy of Imperial Germany, 1900–1914." Ph.D., Georgetown University, 1970.

Kiralfy, Alexander. "Japanese Naval Strategy." Edward M. Earle, ed. *Makers of Modern Strategy.* Princeton, 1941; New York, 1966, pp. 457–484. Mainly 1894–1942.

Laing, E. A. M. "Naval Operations in the War of the Triple Alliance, 1864–70." *Mariner's Mirror,* 54, no. 3 (August 1968), 253–279.

Langley, Harold D. *Social Reform in the United States Navy, 1798–1862.* Urbana, Ill., 1967.

Lass, William E. *A History of Steamboating on the Upper Missouri River.* Lincoln, Neb., 1962.

Lee, H. I. "Mediterranean Strategy and Anglo-French Relations, 1908–1912." *Mariner's Mirror,* 57, no. 3 (August 1971), 267–285.

Livermore, Seward W. "The American Navy as a Factor in World Politics, 1903–1913." *American Historical Review,* LXIII (July 1958), 863–879.

Lloyd, Christopher. *The Navy and the Slave Trade.* New York, 1949. The British navy, but others to some extent.

Long, David F. *Nothing Too Daring: A Biography of Commodore David Porter, 1783–1843.* Annapolis, 1970.

Makaroff [*sic*], S. J. [*sic*], Vice Admiral, I.R.N. (tr. by Lieutenant John B. Bernadou, USN). "Discussion of Questions in Naval Tactics." *Notes on Naval Progress.* Washington, 1898.

Marder, Arthur J. *The Anatomy of British Sea Power: A History of Naval Policy in the Pre-Dreadnought Era, 1880–1905.* New York, 1940.

———. *From the Dreadnought to Scapa Flow: The Royal Navy in the Fisher Era, 1904–1919,* Vol. I. London, 1961.

*La Marina Militaire Nel Suo Primo Secolo di Vita, 1861–1961.* Rome, 1961. History of the Italian Navy.

McCleary, John William. "Anglo-French Naval Rivalry, 1815–1848." Ph.D., Johns Hopkins University, 1947.

McIntyre, W. David. *The Imperial Frontier in the Tropics, 1865–75.* London, 1967. The British.

Merli, Frank J. *Great Britain and the Confederate Navy.* Bloomington, Ind., 1970.

Miller, Harry. *Pirates of the Far East.* London, 1970. Heaviest on the nineteenth century.

Morgan, William Abraham. "Sea Power in the Gulf of Mexico and the Caribbean during the Mexican and Colombian Wars of Independence, 1815–1830." Ph.D., University of Southern California, 1969.

Naval History Division. *Civil War Naval Chronology, 1861–1865.* Washington, 1971.

———. *The Texas Navy.* Washington, 1968.

Nish, Ian H. *The Anglo-Japanese Alliance: The Diplomacy of Two Islands, 1894–1907.* London, 1966.

Norton, Gary. "The Mississippi Marine Brigade, 1862–64." Uncompleted M. A. thesis, University of Maine.

O'Gara, Gordon Carpenter. *Theodore Roosevelt and the Rise of the Modern American Navy.* Princeton, 1943; New York, 1969.

Osborne, Milton E. *The French Presence in Cochinchina and Cambodia: Rule and Response (1859–1905).* Ithaca, 1969.

Padfield, Peter. *Aim Straight: A Biography of Admiral Sir Percy Scott.* London, 1966.

Parnell, Charles Lavelle, Lieutenant, USN. "Gunboats in the Desert." *USNIP,* 94, no. 11 (November 1968), 74–90. The British on the Nile, 1898.

Patterson, Andrew, Jr. "Mining: A Naval Strategy." *NWCR,* XXIII, no. 9 (May 1971), 52–66. Nineteenth and twentieth centuries.

Paullin, Charles Oscar. *American Voyages to the Orient, 1690–1865.* Annapolis, 1910–11; 1971.

Perry, John Curtis. "Great Britain and the Imperial Japanese Navy, 1858–1905." Ph.D., Harvard University, 1961.

Pocock, R. F. and G. R. M. Garratt. *The Origins of Maritime Radio*. London, 1972.

Preston, Antony and John Major. *Send a Gunboat! A Study of the Gunboat and Its Role in British Policy, 1854–1904*. London, 1967.

Preston, Richard A. *Canada and "Imperial Defense": A Study of the Origins of the British Commonwealth's Defense Organization, 1867–1919*. Durham, 1967.

Price, Marcus W. "Blockade Running as a Business in South Carolina During the War Between the States, 1861–1865." *American Neptune*, IX (1949), 31–62.

Priestley, Herbert Ingram. *France Overseas: A Study of Modern Imperialism*. New York, 1938. Includes the French Navy.

Prucha, Francis Paul. *The Sword of the Republic: The United States Army on the Frontier, 1793–1846*. [New York], 1969. Includes the waterborne support and river fortification network.

Pullar, Walter S., Lieutenant Colonel, USMC. "Abe Lincoln's Brown Water Navy." *NWCR*, XXI, no. 8 (April 1969), 71–88. The Civil War on the inland waters.

Rawlinson, John L. *China's Struggle for Naval Development, 1839–1895*. Cambridge, Mass., 1967.

Reynolds, Clark G. "The Civil and Indian War Diaries of Eugene Marshall, Minnesota Volunteer." M. A., Duke University, 1963. Includes waterborne pacification operations against Confederate guerrillas and the Sioux Indians, 1862–66.

———. "The Great Experiment: Hunter's Horizontal Wheel." *American Neptune*, XXIV, no. 1 (January 1964), 5–24. The leading challenger to the screw propeller.

——— and William J. McAndrew, eds. *1971 Seminar in Maritime and Regional Studies*. Orono, Me., 1972. Oceanic history and strategy in the nineteenth and early twentieth centuries.

Ropp, Theodore. "Anacondas Anyone?" *Military Affairs*, XXVII, no. 2 (Summer 1963), 71–76. Origins of the Union Civil War strategy.

———. "Continental Doctrines of Sea Power." Earle, ed. *Makers of Modern Strategy*, pp. 446–456. Mainly the French Navy.

———. "The Development of a Modern Navy: French Naval Policy, 1871–1914." Ph.D., Harvard University, 1937.

Ross, J. O'C. *The White Ensign in New Zealand*. Wellington, 1967. The Royal Navy in New Zealand, including the Maori wars.

Rossell, H. E. *Historical Transactions, 1893–1943: "Types of Naval Ships."* n.p., 1945.

Sandler, Stanley. "A Navy in Decay: Some Strategic Technological Results of Disarmament, 1865–69 in the U. S. Navy." *Military Affairs*, XXXV, no. 4 (December 1971), 138–142.

Scheina, Robert L. "Seapower Misused: Mexico at War 1846–48." *Mariner's Mirror*, 57, no. 2 (May 1971), 203–214.

Schonberger, Howard B. *Transportation to the Seaboard: The "Communication Revolution" and American Foreign Policy, 1860–1900*. Westport, Conn., 1971.

Schonfield, Hugh J. *The Suez Canal in Peace and War, 1869–1969*. Coral Gables, 1969.

Schurman, D. M. *The Education of a Navy: The Development of British Naval Strategic Thought, 1867–1914*. Chicago, 1965.

Seager, Robert, II. "Ten Years Before Mahan: The Unofficial Case for the New Navy, 1880–1890." *Mississippi Valley Historical Review*, XL, no. 3 (1953), 491–512.

Selby, John. *The Paper Dragon: An Account of the China Wars, 1840–1900.* New York, 1968.

Sokol, Anthony E. *The Imperial and Royal Austro-Hungarian Navy.* Annapolis, 1968.

Soley, John C., Lieutenant, USN. "The Naval Brigade." *Military Historical Society of Massachusetts*, XII [1890], 245–268. Early landing forces in the U. S. Navy.

Spector, Ronald Harvey. " 'Professors of War': The Naval War College and the Modern American Navy." Ph.D., Yale University, 1967. The formative years, 1884–1914.

Sprout, Harold and Margaret. *The Rise of American Naval Power, 1776–1918.* Princeton, 1939, 1967.

Sprout, Margaret. "Mahan: Evangelist of Sea Power." Earle, ed. *Makers of Modern Strategy*, 415–445.

Steinberg, Jonathan. *Yesterday's Deterrent: Tirpitz and the Birth of the German Battle Fleet.* London, 1965.

Still, William N., Jr. *Confederate Shipbuilding.* Athens, Ga., 1969.

———. *Iron Afloat: The Story of the Confederate Ironclads.* [Nashville], 1971.

Stokesbury, James Lawton. "British Concepts and Practices of Amphibious Warfare, 1867–1916." Ph.D., Duke University, 1968.

Stoll, Ronald M., Midshipman, USN. "A Ship There Was, But It Flew the White Ensign." Undergraduate research paper, United States Naval Academy, 1966. The British navy in the Boer War.

Taylor, George Rogers. *The Transportation Revolution, 1815–1860.* New York, 1951. Land, sea, canal, river, etc.

Turk, Richard Wellington. "Strategy and Foreign Policy: The United States Navy in the Caribbean, 1865–1913." Ph.D., Fletcher School of Law and Diplomacy, 1968.

Utley, Robert M. *Frontiersmen in Blue: The United States Army and the Indian, 1848–1865.* New York, 1967.

Vale, Brian. "The Creation of the Imperial Brazilian Navy, 1822–1823." *Mariner's Mirror*, 57, no. 1 (January 1971), 63–88.

———. "Lord Cochrane in Brazil. I. The Naval War of Independence, 1823." *Mariner's Mirror*, 57, no. 4 (November 1971), 415–442.

———. "Lord Cochrane II: Prize Money, Politics and Rebellion, 1824–25." *Mariner's Mirror*, 59, no. 2 (May 1973), 135–159.

Ward, W. E. F. *The Royal Navy and the Slavers.* London, 1969.

[Webber, Richard H., Lieutenant, USNR]. *Monitors of the U. S. Navy, 1861–1937.* Washington, 1969.

Wells, Tom Henderson, Commander, USN. *Commodore Moore and the Texas Navy.* Austin, 1960.

———. *The Confederate Navy: A Study in Organization.* University, Ala., 1971.

White, Donald G., Ensign, USNR. "The Misapplication of a Weapons System: The Battle Cruiser as a Warship Type." *NWCR*, XXII, no. 5 (January 1970), 42–62.

Williamson, Samuel R., Jr. *The Politics of Grand Strategy: Britain and France Prepare for War, 1904–1914.* Cambridge, Mass., 1969.

Willock, Roger, Colonel, USMCR. *Bulwark of Empire: Bermuda's Fortified Naval Base 1860–1920*. Princeton, 1962.

———. "Gunboat Diplomacy: Operations of the North America and West Indies Squadron, 1875–1915." *American Neptune*, XXVIII, no. 1 (January 1968), 5–30, and XXVIII, no. 2 (April 1968), 85–112. The British.

Wiswall, F. L., Jr. *The Development of Admiralty Jurisdiction and Practice Since 1800: An English Study with American Comparisons*. Cambridge, 1970.

Woodward, E. L. *Great Britain and the German Navy*. Oxford, 1935. The Anglo-German naval rivalry, 1898–1914.

Worcester, Donald E. *Sea Power and Chilean Independence*. Gainesville, Fla., 1962.

Wyckoff, Don P. "The Chilean Civil War, 1891." *USNIP*, 88, no. 10 (October 1962), 58–63.

## BOOK SIX. ERA OF THE TOTAL WARS, 1914–1945

Albion, Robert Greenhalgh. "Makers of Naval Policy, 1798–1947," 2 vols. Unpublished manuscript, Washington, 1950.

Anderson, Edgar. "An Undeclared Naval War: The British-Soviet Naval Struggle in the Baltic, 1918–1920." *Journal of Central European Affairs*, XXII (April 1962), 43–78.

Andrade, Ernest, Jr. "The Ship That Never Was: The Flying-Deck Cruiser." *Military Affairs*, XXXII, no. 3 (December 1968), 132–140. Aspects of the 1930 London naval conference.

———. "Submarine Policy in the United States Navy, 1919–1941." *Military Affairs*, XXXV, no. 2 (April 1971), 50–56.

———. "United States Naval Power in the Disarmament Era, 1921–1937." Ph.D., Michigan State University, 1966.

Ansel, Walter. *Hitler and the Middle Sea*. Durham, 1972. German strategic designs on the Mediterranean, 1940–41.

———. *Hitler Confronts England*. Durham, 1960. The German mobilization and plan to invade England in 1940.

Auphan, Paul, Rear Admiral, F.N. (Ret), and Jacques Mordal. (tr. by Captain A. C. J. Sabalot, USN [Ret]). *The French Navy in World War II*. Annapolis, 1959.

Barker, A. J. *The Bastard War: The Mesopotamian Campaign of 1914–1918*. New York, 1967. Includes river operations.

Bauer [Hermann], Admiral [G.N., Ret] (tr. by Lieutenant H. G. Rickover, USN). *The Submarine*. Berlin, 1931; Newport, 1936. World War I impact of submarines.

Baxter, James Phinney, 3rd. *Scientists Against Time*. Boston, 1946. American scientific-weapons research and development, World War II.

Beitzell, Robert. *The Uneasy Alliance: America, Britain and Russia, 1941–1943*. New York, 1972.

Belote, James Hine. "The Development of German Naval Policy, 1933–1939." Ph.D., University of California at Berkeley, 1954.

Bennett, Geoffrey. *Cowan's War: The Story of British Naval Operations in the Baltic, 1918–1920*. London, 1964.

Berg, Meredith William. "The United States and the Breakdown of Naval Limitation, 1934–1939." Ph.D., Tulane University, 1966.

Berg, Sigval M., Jr., Midshipman, USN. "A Period of Crucial Development,

1920–1940." Undergraduate research paper, United States Naval Academy, 1967. Interwar American submarines.

Bidlingmaier, Gerhard. *Seegeltung in der Deutschen Geschichte.* Darmstadt, 1967. Sea power in modern German history.

Buell, Thomas B., Lieutenant Commander, USN. "Admiral Raymond A. Spruance and the Naval War College." *NWCR,* XXIII, no. 7 (March 1971), 30–51 and no. 8 (April 1971), 29–53.

Bulkley, Robert J., Jr., Captain, USNR (Ret). *At Close Quarters: PT Boats in the United States Navy.* Washington, 1962. World War II.

Burdick, Charles B. *Germany's Military Strategy and Spain in World War II.* Syracuse, 1968.

———. " 'Moro': The Resupply of German Submarines in Spain, 1939–1942," *Central European History,* III, no. 3 (September 1970), 256–282.

Bureau of Supplies and Accounts [USN]. *Special Report on Operations and Organization of the German Naval Supply System During World War II.* Washington, 1953.

Burns, Richard Dean. "Inspection of the Mandates, 1919–1941." *Pacific Historical Review,* XXXVII (November 1968), 445–462.

———. "Regulating Submarine Warfare, 1921–41: A Case Study in Arms Control and Limited War." *Military Affairs,* XXXV, no. 2 (April 1971), 56–63.

Bush, Vannevar. *Pieces of the Action.* New York, 1970. Direction of American scientific-weapons activity in World War II.

Caldwell, Robert C., Major, USMC. "The Role of the Tracked Amphibian in Modern Amphibious Warfare." *NWCR,* XXII, no. 5 (January 1970), 68–99.

Christman, Albert B. *History of the Naval Weapons Center, China Lake, California,* Vol. I: *Sailors, Scientists, and Rockets.* Washington, 1971. Early rocket and missile research.

Clark, Admiral J. J., USN (Ret) with Clark G. Reynolds. *Carrier Admiral.* New York, 1967. Autobiographical account of American naval aviation, 1925–1953.

Davis, George T. *A Navy Second to None: The Development of Modern American Naval Policy.* New York, 1940.

Douglas, Lawrence H. "Submarine Disarmament, 1919–1936." Ph.D., Syracuse University, 1970.

Dreyer, Sir Frederick C., Admiral, R.N. *The Sea Heritage: A Study in Maritime Warfare.* London, 1955. Autobiographical.

Duroselle, Jean-Baptiste. "Le conflict stratégique anglo-american de juin 1940 à juin 1944." *Revue d'Histoire Moderne et Contemporaire,* X (July–September 1963), 161–184. Traces roots of American continental strategic tradition.

Dyer, George Carroll, Vice Admiral, USN (Ret). *The Amphibians Came to Conquer: The Story of Admiral Richmond Kelly Turner,* 2 vols. Washington, 1972. American amphibious leadership, World War II.

———. "Naval Amphibious Landmarks." *USNIP,* 92, no. 8 (August 1966), 50–60. 1920s to middle of World War II.

Enders, Calvin W. "The Vinson Navy." Ph.D., Michigan State University, 1970.

Fergusson, Bernard. *The Watery Maze: The Story of Combined Operations.* London, 1961. British amphibious operations, World War II.

Frank, Willard Chabot. "Sea Power, Politics and the Onset of the Spanish War, 1936." Ph.D., University of Pittsburgh, 1969.

Fuchida, Mitsuo and Masatake Okumiya. *Midway, The Battle That Doomed Japan.* Annapolis, 1955.

Garthoff, Raymond L. "Soviet Naval Operations in the War with Japan—August, 1945." *USNIP*, 92, no. 5 (May 1966), 50–63.

Genda, Minoru, General, JASDF (Ret). "Tactical Planning in the Imperial Japanese Navy." *NWCR*, XXII, no. 2 (October 1969), 45–50.

Gilbert, Nigel John, Lieutenant Commander, R.N. "British Submarine Operations in World War II." *USNIP*, 89, no. 3 (March 1963), 73–81.

Gordon, Arthur, Commander, USNR (Ret). "The Day the *Astral* Vanished." *USNIP*, 91, no. 10 (October 1965), 76–83. An aspect of German-American quasi-war, 1941.

Grant, Robert M. *U-Boats Destroyed: The Effect of Anti-Submarine Warfare, 1914–1918.* London, 1964.

Greenfield, Kent Roberts, ed. *Command Decisions.* Washington, 1960. World War II.

Golovko, Arseni G., Admiral, Soviet Navy. (ed. by Sir Aubrey Mansergh; tr. by Peter Broomfield). *With the Red Fleet.* London, 1965. Autobiographical; the Northern Fleet in World War II.

Grenfell, Russell, Commander, R.N. *The Art of the Admiral.* London, 1937. Naval strategy from 1900 to 1937.

Gretton, Sir Peter, Vice Admiral, R.N. *Winston Churchill and the Royal Navy.* New York, 1968.

Groeling, Dorothy Trautwein. "Submarines, Disarmament and Modern Warfare." Ph.D., Columbia University, 1935.

Hayes, John D., Rear Admiral, USN (Ret). "Admiral Joseph Mason Reeves. USN (1872–1948)." *NWCR*, XXIII, no. 3 (November 1970), 48–57 and XXIV, no. 5 (January 1972), 50–64.

Herwig, Holger H. "Admirals *versus* Generals: The War Aims of the Imperial Germany Navy, 1914–1918." *Central European History*, V, no. 3 (September 1972), 208–233.

Hezlet, Sir Arthur, Vice Admiral, R.N. *The Submarine and Sea Power.* London, 1967. The twentieth century.

Higham, Robin. *The Military Intellectuals in Britain: 1918–1939.* New Brunswick, N. J., 1966.

Historical Section, Office of the Chief of Staff of the Royal Italian Navy. *The Italian Navy in the World War, 1915–1918.* Rome, 1927.

Holmes, W. J. *Undersea Victory: The Influence of Submarine Operations on the War in the Pacific.* Garden City, 1966. American and Japanese.

Hood, Ronald Chalmers, III. "The Crisis of Civil-Naval Relations in France, 1924–1939: No *Concorde* Between Them." M. A., University of Maine, 1972.

Horn, Daniel. *The German Naval Mutinies of World War I.* New Brunswick, N. J., 1969.

Isely, Jeter A. and Philip A. Crowl. *The U. S. Marines and Amphibious War.* Princeton, 1951. Through World War II.

Ito, Masanori, with Roger Pineau. *The End of the Imperial Japanese Navy.* New York, 1962.

*Jane's Fighting Ships, 1919.* London, 1919; New York, 1969.

Kennedy, Malcolm D., Captain. *The Estrangement of Great Britain and Japan, 1917–35.* Berkeley, 1969.

Koginos, Manny T. *The Panay Incident: Prelude to War*. Lafayette, Ind., 1967.

Kumao, Baron Harada (tr. by Thomas Francis Mayer-Oakes). *Fragile Victory: Prince Saionji and the 1930 London Treaty Issue from the Memoirs of Baron Harada Kumao*. Detroit, 1968.

LeMasson, Henri. *Navies of the Second World War: The French Navy*, 2 vols. Garden City, 1969. Prewar period too.

Lenton, H. T. *Navies of the Second World War: Royal Netherlands Navy*. London, 1967. Prewar period too.

Lewis, Wallace Leigh. "The Survival of the German Navy 1917–1920: Officers, Sailors and Politics." Ph.D., University of Iowa, 1969.

Lockwood, Charles A., Vice Admiral, USN (Ret). *Down to the Sea in Subs*. New York, 1967. Autobiographical; 1900 through World War II.

Lott, Arnold S., Lieutenant Commander, USN. *Most Dangerous Sea: A History of Mine Warfare, and an Account of U. S. Navy Mine Warfare Operations in World War II and Korea*. Annapolis, 1959.

Louis, William Roger. *British Strategy in the Far East, 1919–1939*. Oxford, 1971.

Lundeberg, Philip K. "The German Naval Critique of the U-boat Campaign, 1915–1918." *Military Affairs*, XXVII, no. 3 (Fall 1963), 105–118.

———. "Undersea Warfare and Allied Strategy in World War I." *The Smithsonian Journal of History*, I, no. 3 (Autumn 1966), 1–30 and no. 4 (Winter 1967), 49–72.

Macintyre, Donald, Captain, R.N. (Ret). "Shipborne Radar." *USNIP*, 93, no. 9 (September 1967), 70–83. Prewar and World War II development in all navies.

Marder, Arthur J. *From the Dreadnought to Scapa Flow: The Royal Navy in the Fisher Era, 1904–1919*, Vols. II–V. London, 1965–1970.

———. "The Influence of History on Sea Power: The Royal Navy and the Lessons of 1914–1918." *Pacific Historical Review*, XLI, no. 4 (November 1972), 413–443.

———. "The Royal Navy and the Ethiopian Crisis of 1935–36." *American Historical Review*, LXXV (June 1970), 1327–56.

———. "Winston is Back: Churchill at the Admiralty." *The English Historical Review*. Supplement 5, 1972.

Martienssen, Anthony. *Hitler and His Admirals*. New York, 1949.

Maugeri, Franco, Admiral, Italian Navy. *From the Ashes of Disgrace*. New York, 1948. The Italian Navy before and during World War II.

Maund, L. E. H., Rear Admiral, R.N. *Assault From the Sea*. London, 1949. British amphibious warfare in World War II.

McHugh, Francis J. "Gaming at the Naval War College." *USNIP*, 90, no. 3 (March 1964), 48–55.

Milkman, Raymond H. "Operations Research in World War II." *USNIP*, 94, no. 5 (May 1968), 78–83.

Monroe, Elizabeth. *Britain's Moment in the Middle East, 1914–1956*. Baltimore, 1963.

Moorehead, Alan. *Gallipoli*. London, 1956.

Morison, Samuel Eliot. *History of United States Naval Operations in World War II*, 15 vols. Boston, 1947–62.

———. *Strategy and Compromise*. Boston, 1958. Allied strategic decisions.

Morton, Louis. "War Plan *Orange*: Evolution of a Strategy." *World Politics*, XI, no. 2 (January 1959), 221–58.

O'Connor, Raymond, ed. *The Japanese Navy in World War II*. Annapolis, 1969. Articles by former Japanese naval officers.

Okumiya, Masatake, Lieutenant General, JASDF (Ret). "For Sugar Boats or Submarines?" *USNIP*, 94, no. 8 (August 1968), 66–73. Japanese interwar development of the mandated islands.

Oyos, Lynwood E. "The Navy and the United States Far Eastern Policy, 1930–1939." Ph.D., University of Nebraska, 1958.

Piterskij, N. A. [Rear Admiral, Soviet Naval Reserve]. *Die Sowjet-Flotte im Zweiten Weltkrieg*. Oldenburg, 1966. The Soviet Navy in World War II.

Preston, Richard A. "The R.C.N. and Gun-Boat Diplomacy in the Caribbean." *Military Affairs*, XXXVI, no. 2 (April 1972), 41–44. The Canadian navy in the early 1930s.

Raeder, Erich, Grand Admiral, German Navy. *My Life*. Annapolis, 1960.

Reynolds, Clark G. "Die Entwicklung des Flugzeugträgers in Amerika, 1919–1945." *Marine Rundschau*, 60, no. 6 (December 1963), 337–48. Development of the aircraft carrier in the United States.

———. *The Fast Carriers: The Forging of an Air Navy*. New York, 1968. Anglo-American-Japanese carrier development, prewar and World War II; emphasis on attack carriers in the Pacific.

———. "Hitler's Flattop—The End of the Beginning." *USNIP*, 93, no. 1 (January 1967), 41–49.

———. "Sea Power in the Twentieth Century." *Journal of the Royal United Service Institution*, CXI (May 1966), 132–39. An interpretative updating of Mahan.

———. "Submarine Attacks on the Pacific Coast, 1942." *Pacific Historical Review*, XXXIII, No. 2 (May 1964), 183–93. Japanese.

Ropp, Theodore. "The Modern Italian Navy." *Military Affairs*, V (Spring 1941), 32–48 and (Summer 1941), 104–116. Early twentieth century.

Roscoe, Theodore. *United States Submarine Operations in World War II*. Annapolis, 1949.

Roskill, Stephen. *Naval Policy Between the Wars*, Vol. I: *The Period of Anglo-American Antagonism, 1919–1929*. London, 1968.

———, Captain, R.N. *The War at Sea, 1939–1945*, 3 vols. London, 1954–62. The Royal Navy in World War II.

Ruge, Friedrich, Vice Admiral, F.G.N. (tr. by Commander M. G. Saunders, R.N.) *Der Seekrieg: The German Navy's Story, 1939–1945*. Annapolis, 1957.

Sachar, Howard M. *The Emergence of the Middle East: 1914–1924*. New York, 1969. Includes the naval aspects of confrontation.

Saville, Allison Winthrop. "The Development of the German U-Boat Arm, 1919–1935." Ph.D., University of Washington, 1963.

Schilling, Warner R. "Admirals and Foreign Policy, 1913–1919." Ph.D., Yale University, 1953. United States.

Schofield, B. B. *British Sea Power: Naval Policy in the Twentieth Century*. London, 1967.

Socas, Roberto E. "France, Naval Armaments and Naval Disarmament: 1918–1922." Ph.D., Columbia University, 1965.

Spigai, Virgilio, Vice Admiral, Italian Navy. "Italian Naval Assault Craft in Two World Wars." *USNIP*, 91, no. 3 (March 1965), 50–59.

Sprout, Harold and Margaret. *Toward a New Order of Sea Power: American Naval Policy and the World Scene, 1918–1922*. Princeton, 1943; New York, 1969. Global postwar naval realignments.

Sweetman, Jack. *The Landing at Veracruz: 1914*. Annapolis, 1968.

Toland, John. *The Rising Sun: The Decline and Fall of the Japanese Empire, 1936–1945*. New York, 1970.

Tolley, Kemp, Rear Admiral, USN (Ret). "Our Russian War of 1918–1919." *USNIP*, 95, no. 2 (February 1969), 58–72.

Trask, David F. *Captains & Cabinets: Anglo-American Naval Relations, 1917–1918*. Columbia, Mo., 1972.

Tuleja, Thaddeus V. *Statesmen and Admirals: Quest for a Far Eastern Policy*. New York, 1963. The Pacific area, 1931–41.

Turnbull, Archibald D. and Clifford L. Lord. *History of United States Naval Aviation*. New Haven, 1949. To 1941.

Von der Porten, Edward P. *The German Navy in World War II*. New York, 1969.

Walter, John C. "The Navy Department and the Campaign for Expanded Appropriations, 1933–1938." Ph.D., University of Maine, 1972. United States.

Watt, Donald C. "Stalin's First Bid for Sea Power, 1933–1941." *USNIP*, 90, no. 6 (June 1964), 88–96.

Wheeler, Gerald E. *Prelude to Pearl Harbor: The United States Navy and the Far East, 1921–1931*. Columbia, Mo. [1963].

———. "William Veazie Pratt, U. S. Navy: A Silhouette of an Admiral." *NWCR*, XXI, no. 9 (May 1969), 36–61.

White, Donald G., Ensign, USNR. "The French Navy and the Washington Conference." *NWCR*, XXII, no. 3 (November 1969), 33–44.

Wilds, Thomas. "How Japan Fortified the Mandated Islands." *USNIP*, 81, no. 4 (April 1955), 400–407. Pre-World War II.

Williams, Ann. *Britain and France in the Middle East and North Africa*. London, 1968. Twentieth century.

Winton, John. *The Forgotten Fleet: The British Navy in the Pacific, 1944–1945*. New York, 1969.

Woodward, David. "The High Seas Fleet—1917–18." *Journal of the Royal United Service Institution*, 113 (August 1968), 244–250. Germany.

## BOOK SEVEN. PAX AMERICANA. AND EPILOGUE: WORLD WAR III

Abel, Elie. *The Missile Crisis*. New York, 1966. Cuba, 1962.

Ackley, Richard T., Commander, USN (Ret). "The Soviet Navy's Role in Foreign Policy." *NWCR*, XXIV (May 1972), no. 9, 48–65.

Alden, John D., Commander, USN. "A New Fleet Emerges: Combat Ships." *Naval Review, 1964*. Annapolis, 1963.

Allen, Scott, Lieutenant Commander, USN. "China: Nuclear Dragon." *USNIP*, 98, no. 6 (June 1972), 43–49.

Auer, James E., Lieutenant Commander, USN. "Japan's Maritime Self-Defense Force: An Appropriate Maritime Strategy?" *NWCR*, XXIV, no. 4 (December 1971), 3–20.

Baker, R. K. "Tropical Africa's Nascent Navies." *USNIP*, 95, no. 1 (January 1969), 64–71.

Baldwin, Hanson W. "After Vietnam—What Military Strategy in the Far East?" *The New York Times Magazine* (June 9, 1968), 36–37 and *passim*.

———. *Strategy for Tomorrow*. New York, 1970.

Barber, James A., Commander, USN. "The Nixon Doctrine and the Navy." *NWCR,* XXIII, No. 10 (June 1971), 5–15.

de Bazelaire, Yves, Rear Admiral, F.N. "The French Navy." *Naval Review 1965.* Annapolis, 1964, 118–137.

Beavers, Roy, Commander, USN. "The End of an Era." *USNIP,* 98, no. 7 (July 1972), 18–25. Shifting power balances and naval requirements.

Bird, Thomas C., Lieutenant Commander, USN. "British East of Suez Policy: A Victim of Economic Necessity." *NWCR,* XXII, no. 8 (April 1970), 54–70.

Blixt, Melvin D., Captain, USN. "Soviet Objectives in the Eastern Mediterranean." *NWCR,* XXI, no. 7 (March 1969), 4–27.

Borgese, Elisabeth Mann. "The Prospects for Peace in the Oceans." *Saturday Review* (September 26, 1970), 15–22.

Bradley, David. *No Place to Hide.* Boston, 1948. Early A-bomb tests.

Breyer, Siegfried (tr. by Lieutenant Commander M. W. Henley, R.N.). *Guide to the Soviet Navy.* Annapolis, 1970.

Brittin, Burdick H., Captain, USN. "Piracy—A Modern Conspectus." *USNIP,* 91, no. 5 (May 1965), 71–81.

Brodie, Bernard. *Strategy and National Interests: Reflections for the Future.* New York, 1971.

————. *Strategy in the Missile Age.* Princeton, 1959, 1965.

Bull, Hedley. "The New Balance of Power in Asia and the Pacific." *Foreign Affairs,* 49, no. 8 (July 1971), 669–681.

Bussert, J. C., Master Chief Sonar Technician, USN. "The Navy Gap in the Seventies." *USNIP,* 98, no. 6 (June 1972), 18–26. Partly fiction.

Cagle, Malcolm W., Commander, USN and Commander Frank A. Manson, USN. *The Sea War in Korea.* Annapolis, 1957.

Cagle, Malcolm W., Vice Admiral, USN. "Task Force 77 in Action Off Vietnam." *USNIP,* 98, no. 5 (May 1972), 66–109.

Carlson, Verner R., Major, USA. "Rebuilding Norway's Navy." *USNIP,* 92, no. 1 (January 1966), 55–65.

Casey, Ralph E. "Political and Economic Significance of the World's Merchant Marines into the 1980s." *NWCR,* XXI, no. 8 (April 1969), 4–13.

The Center for Strategic and International Studies. *Soviet Sea Power.* Washington, 1969.

Christol, Carl Q. and Charles R. Davis (and Quincy Wright). "Maritime Quarantine: The Naval Interdiction of Offensive Weapons . . . to Cuba, 1962." *American Journal of International Law,* 57 (July 1963), 525–565.

Cliff, Donald K., Lieutenant Colonel, USMC. "Soviet Naval Infantry: A New Capability." *NWCR,* XXIII, no. 10 (June 1971), 90–101.

Cohen, Paul. "The Erosion of Surface Naval Power." *Foreign Affairs,* 49, no. 2 (January 1971), 330–349.

Colestock, Edward E., Rear Admiral, USN (Ret). "A Naval Appreciation of Brazil." *Naval Review 1967.* Annapolis, 1966, pp. 160–179.

Collins, Frank C., Jr., Commander, USN. "Maritime Support of the Campaign in I Corps," *USNIP,* 97, no. 5 (May 1971), 156–179.

Colvin, Robert D., Commander, USN. "Aftermath of the *Elath.*" *USNIP,* 95, no. 10 (October 1969), 60–67. Trends in PT boats.

Cottrell, Alvin J. and R. M. Burrell, eds. *The Indian Ocean: Its Political, Economic, and Military Importance.* New York, 1972.

Cox, Donald V., Rear Admiral, USN. "The Sea Control Ship System." *USNIP,* 98, no. 4 (April 1972), 113–115.

Coye, Beth F., Lieutenant Commander, USN, *et al.* "An Evaluation of U. S. Naval Presence in the Indian Ocean." *NWCR,* XXXIII, no. 2 (October 1970), 35–52.

Craft, James Pressley, Jr. "The Role of Congress in the Determination of Naval Strategy in Support of United States Foreign Policy 1956–1966." Ph.D., University of Pennsylvania, 1969.

Crowe, William James, Jr. "The Policy Roots of the Modern Royal Navy, 1946–1963." Ph.D., Princeton University, 1965.

Cummings, E. J., Captain, USN. "The Chinese Communist Navy." *USNIP,* 90, no. 9 (September 1964), 64–73.

Cunliffe, Marcus, ed. *The London Times History of Our Times.* New York, 1971. An overview, 1945–70.

Davies, John Paton. "The U. S. Invented the 'Imbalance of Power.' " *The New York Times Magazine* (December 7, 1969), pp. 50 and *passim.*

Davis, Vincent. *The Admirals Lobby.* Chapel Hill, 1967. USN, twentieth century.

"Details of Indo/Pakistani War Reported in *Marine Rundschau." USNIP,* 99, no. 3 (March 1973), 127–128.

Dewenter, John R. "China Afloat." *Foreign Affairs,* 50, no. 4 (July 1972), 738–751. The Chinese Navy.

Eccles, Henry E., Rear Admiral, USN (Ret). *Military Concepts and Philosophy.* New Brunswick, N. J., 1965. Contemporary.

———. "Suez 1956—Some Military Lessons." *NWCR,* XXI, no. 7 (March 1969), 28–56.

Eller, Ernest McNeill, Rear Admiral, USN (Ret). *The Soviet Sea Challenge: The Struggle for Control of the World's Oceans.* n.p., 1971.

Emery, S. W., Jr., Lieutenant (j.g.), USN. "The Merchant Marine Act of 1970." *USNIP,* 97, no. 3 (March 1971), 38–43.

Fairhall, David. *Russian Sea Power.* Boston, 1971.

Fall, Bernard B. *The Two Viet-nams: A Political and Military Analysis.* New York, 1963.

Feis, Herbert. *From Trust to Terror: The Onset of the Cold War, 1945–1950.* New York, 1970.

Field, James A., Jr. *History of United States Naval Operations: Korea.* Washington, 1962.

Fontaine, André (tr. by Renaud Bruce). *History of the Cold War: From the Korean War to the Present.* New York, 1969.

Freitag, Robert F., Captain, USN. "The Effect of Space Operations on Naval Warfare." *Naval Review 1962–63.* Annapolis, 1962, pp. 173–195.

Galvin, John R. *Air Assault: the Development of Airmobile Warfare.* New York, 1969. World War II through Vietnam.

Garrett, William B., Lieutenant Commander, USN. "The U. S. Navy's Role in the 1956 Suez Crisis." *NWCR,* XXII, no. 7 (March 1970), 66–78.

Gorshkov, Sergei G., Admiral of the Fleet, Navy of the U.S.S.R. "The Development of Soviet Naval Science (Excerpts)." *NWCR,* XXI, no. 11 (February 1969), 30–42.

Gretton, Sir Peter, Vice Admiral, R.N. (Ret). *Maritime Strategy.* New York, 1965.

Gullion, Edmund A., ed. *Uses of the Seas.* Englewood Cliffs, N. J., 1968. An overview, naval and non-naval.

Hagan, Kenneth J. and Jacob W. Kipp. "U.S. and U.S.S.R. Naval Strategy," *USNIP,* 99, no. 11 (November 1973), 38–44.

Hale, Richard W. "The Fledgling Navies of Black Africa." *NWCR*, XXIV, No. 12 (June 1972), 42–55.

Halperin, Morton H. *Limited War in the Nuclear Age.* New York, 1963.

Hankinson, David K., Commander, R.N. (Ret). "HMS *Centaur* at Dar es Salaam." *USNIP*, 95, no. 11 (November 1969), 57–66.

Harllee, John, Rear Admiral, USN (Ret). "Patrol Guerrilla Motor Boats." *USNIP*, 90, no. 4 (April 1964), 70–79. Inshore vessels.

Harrigan, Anthony. "Inshore and River Warfare." *Orbis*, X, no. 3 (Fall 1966), 940–946.

Hayes, John D., Rear Admiral, USN (Ret). "Patterns of American Sea Power, 1945–1956: Their Portents for the Seventies." *USNIP*, 96, no. 5 (May 1970), 337–352.

———. "Sea Power and Sea Law." *USNIP*, 90, no. 5 (May 1964), 60–67. The Cold War aspects.

Herrington, Arthur C. "U. S. Navy Policy." *NWCR*, XXII, no. 1 (September 1969), 4–13.

Hessler, William H. "Blue Water Around Red China." *USNIP*, 89, no. 2 (February 1963), 27–39.

Hewlett, Richard G. and Francis Duncan. *A History of the United States Atomic Energy Commission,* Vol. II: *Atomic Shield, 1947–1952.* University Park, Pa., 1969.

Hezlet, Sir Arthur, Vice Admiral, R.N. (Ret). *Aircraft and Sea Power.* New York, 1970. Twentieth century, but used for the Cold War.

Hooper, Edwin Bickford, Vice Admiral, USN (Ret). *Mobility, Support, Endurance: A Story of Naval Operational Logistics in the Vietnam War, 1965–1968.* Washington, 1972.

Hoopes, Townsend. *The Limits of Intervention.* New York, 1969. High-level American planning during the Vietnam War.

Huan, Claude, Lieutenant Commander, F.N. "The French Submarine Force." *USNIP*, 92, no. 2 (February 1966), 42–53.

Hunt, George P. "The Four-Star Military Mess." *Life* (June 18, 1971), 50–68.

*Jane's Fighting Ships, 1969–70.* London, 1970.

Joshua, Wynfred. *Soviet Penetration into the Middle East,* rev. ed. New York, 1971.

Kaul, R., Lieutenant Commander, I.N. (Ret). "India's Russian Navy." *USNIP*, 96, no. 8 (August 1970), 38–45.

———. "The Indo-Pakistani War and the Changing Balance of Power in the Indian Ocean." *USNIP*, 99, no. 5 (May 1973), 172–195.

Kotsch, W. J., Captain, USN. "The Six-Day War of 1967." *USNIP*, 94, no. 6 (June 1968), 72–81.

Laforest, T. J., Captain, USN. "Strategic Significance of the Northern Sea Route." *USNIP*, 93, no. 12 (December 1967), 56–65.

Littauer, Raphael and Norman Uphoff, eds. *The Air War in Indochina.* Boston, 1972.

Little, Ivor C., Commander, SAN. "Sea Trials for South Africa." *USNIP*, 98, no. 12 (December 1972), 78–83.

Lowe, George E. *The Age of Deterrence.* Boston, 1964. The nuclear arms race and strategic theory, 1953–64.

———. "The Case for the Oceanic Strategy." *USNIP*, 94, no. 6 (June 1968), 26–34.

———. "The Only Option?" *USNIP,* 97, no. 4 (April 1971), 18–26. The Nixon Doctrine as oceanic strategy.

MacDonald, Scot. *Evolution of Aircraft Carriers.* Washington, 1964. Twentieth century, but used for post-World War II aspects.

Margaritis, C., Vice Admiral, Hellenic Navy. "The Future Roles and Problems of Small Countries' Navies." *NWCR,* XXIV, no. 5 (January 1972), 35–40.

Martin, L. W. *The Sea in Modern Strategy.* New York, 1967.

Masson, Philipe and J. Labayle Couhat. (tr. by G. G. and K. K. Sick). "The Soviet Presence in the Mediterranean: A Short History." *NWCR,* XXIII, no. 5 (January 1971), 60–66.

MccGwire, Michael, ed. *Soviet Naval Developments: Context and Capability.* Halifax, 1973.

McCleave, Robert E., Jr., Major, USA. "The National Defense Requirement For a U. S.-Flag Merchant Marine." *NWCR,* XXI, no. 12 (June 1969), 64–79.

McClintock, Robert. "The American Landing in Lebanon." *USNIP,* 88, no. 10 (October 1962), 65–79.

———. "Latin America and Naval Power." *USNIP,* 91, no. 10 (October 1965), 30–37.

———. "The River War in Indochina." *USNIP,* 80, no. 12 (December 1954), 1303–11. The years 1945–54.

McCutcheon, Keith B., Lieutenant General, USMC. "Marine Aviation in Vietnam, 1962–1970." *USNIP,* 97, no. 5 (May 1971), 122–155.

McDevitt, Joseph B., Rear Admiral, USN. "Current International Law Problems of the Navy." *NWCR,* XXII, no. 9 (May 1970), 41–49.

McDonald, David L., Admiral, USN. "Carrier Employment Since 1950." *USNIP,* 90, no. 11 (November 1964), 26–33.

McKnew, Thomas W. "Four-Ocean Navy in the Nuclear Age." *National Geographic,* 127, no. 2 (February 1965), 145–187.

Merdinger, Charles J., Captain, USN. "Civil Engineers, Seabees, and Bases in Vietnam." *USNIP,* 96, no. 5 (May 1970), 254–275.

Moulton, J. L., Major General, Royal Marines (Ret). "The Defense of Northwest Europe and the North Sea." *USNIP,* 97, no. 5 (May 1971), 80–97.

———. "The Indonesian Confrontation." *Naval Review 1969.* Annapolis, 1969, pp. 143–171.

Murphy, Frank M., Captain, USN. "Seapower and the Satellites." *USNIP,* 95, no. 11 (November 1969), 75–83. Warsaw Pact navies.

Murphy, R. P. W., Lieutenant, USNR, and Colonel Edwin F. Black, USA. "The South Vietnamese Navy." *USNIP,* 90, no. 1 (January 1964), 52–61. The early years, to 1963.

Naval History Division. *Keeping the Peace.* Washington, 1966. Cold War naval operations.

"New Nuclear Strategy for America?" *U. S. News and World Report* (April 13, 1970), 32–34. The sea-based missile option.

*The New York Times. The Pentagon Papers.* New York, 1971. High-level planning and prosecution of the American intervention in the Vietnam War, 1964–68.

———. *United States Foreign Policy in the Nixon Administration.* New York, 1971.

Paolucci, Dominic A., Captain, USN (Ret). "The Development of Navy Strategic Offensive and Defensive Systems." *USNIP,* 96, no. 5 (May 1970), 204–223. The period 1945–70.

Parson, Nels A., Jr. *Missiles and the Revolution in Warfare.* Cambridge, Mass., 1962.

Petersen, Charles W. "The Military Balance in Southern Africa." C. P. Potholm and Richard Dale, eds., *Southern Africa in Perspective.* Glencoe, Ill., 1972, 298–317.

Petersen, Henrik M., Captain, Royal Danish Navy. "Maritime Denmark." *USNIP,* 94, no. 1 (January 1968), 37–49. Cold War naval buildup.

Petrov, Victor P. "Soviet Canals." *USNIP,* 93, no. 7 (July 1967), 32–44.

*Polaris Fleet Ballistic Missile Weapon System Fact Sheet.* [Washington], June 1, 1966.

Polmar, Norman. *Soviet Naval Power: Challenge for the 1970s.* New York, 1972.

Popham, Hugh. *Into Wind: A History of British Naval Flying.* London, 1969. Used for post-1945 aspects.

Porath, Reuben, Lieutenant Commander, IDFN. "The Israeli Navy," *USNIP,* 97, no. 9 (September 1971), 33–39.

Prina, L. Edgar. "The Navy First Used Think Tanks During World War II," *Armed Forces Journal* (September 28, 1968). Mainly the 1960s.

Ramage, Lawson P., Vice Admiral, USN. "The Military Sea Transportation Service." *NWCR,* XXI, no. 9 (May 1969), 4–11.

Ravenal, Earl C. "The Nixon Doctrine and Our Asian Commitments." *Foreign Affairs,* 49, no. 2 (January 1971), 201–217.

Reynolds, Clark G. "The U. S. Navy in Doubt: Disarmament and Technology After World War II." Canadian Forces College *Extension Bulletin,* No. 17 (February 15, 1969), 12–20.

———. "Youth and the U.S. Navy." *USNIP,* 99, no. 7 (July 1973), 26–33.

Roberts, Chalmers M. *The Nuclear Years: The Arms Race and Arms Control, 1945–70.* New York, 1970.

Rogers, Robert B., Commander, USN. "Trends in Soviet Naval Strategy." *NWCR,* XXI, no. 11 (February 1969), 13–29.

Rosecrance, R. N. *Defense of the Realm: British Strategy in the Nuclear Epoch.* New York, 1968.

Ruge, Friedrich, Vice Admiral, GFN (Ret). "The Reconstruction of the German Navy, 1956–1961." *USNIP,* 88, no. 7 (July 1962), 52–65.

"Russia: Power Play on the Oceans." *Time* (February 23, 1968), 23–28.

Saar, C. W., Commander, USN. "Offensive Mining as a Soviet Strategy." *USNIP,* 90, no. 8 (August 1964), 42–51.

Schneider, Mark Bernard. "SABMIS and the Future of Strategic Warfare." *USNIP,* 95, no. 7 (July 1969), 26–34.

Schratz, Paul R. "A Commentary on the *Pueblo* Affair." *Military Affairs,* XXXV, no. 3 (October 1971), 93–95.

Schreadly, R. L., Commander, USN. "The Naval War in Vietnam, 1950–1970." *USNIP,* 97, no. 5 (May 1971), 180–209.

———. "Sea Lords." *USNIP,* 96, no. 8 (August 1970), 22–31. Waterborne interdiction in the Mekong delta, Vietnam War.

"Seapower in the Space Age." *Air Force/Space Digest* II, no. 4 (April 1966) [entire issue].

Sharp, U. S. G., Admiral, USN. "Report on Air and Naval Campaigns Against North Vietnam and Pacific Command-Wide Support of the War,

July 1964/July 1968." *Report on the War in Vietnam (as of 30 June 1968)*. Washington, 1969.

Sherrill, Robert. "SCRAM, SCAD, ULMS and other aspects of the $85.9-billion defense budget." *The New York Times Magazine* (July 30, 1972), pp. 7 and *passim*.

Sherwood, [M.] Lee. "The Seventh Fleet in Limited War: From Theory to Practice." Undergraduate research paper, University of Maine, 1969.

Sick, Gary G., Lieutenant Commander, USN. "Russia and the West in the Mediterranean: Perspectives for the 1970s." *NWCR*, XXII, no. 10 (June 1970), 49–69.

Simpson, Howard R. "Offshore Guerrilla War." *NWCR*, XXII, no. 2 (October 1969), 17–20. Surface-to-surface missile boats.

Smith, Robert H., Captain, USN (Ret). "ASW—The Crucial Naval Challenge." *USNIP*, 98, no. 5 (May 1972), 126–141.

Sokol, Anthony E. *Sea Power in the Nuclear Age*. New York, 1961.

"Soviet Union: Reaching for Supremacy at Sea." *Time* (January 31, 1972), 28–33.

Spanier, John W. *American Foreign Policy Since World War II*, 4th rev. ed., New York, 1971.

Steel, Ronald. *Pax Americana*, rev. ed. New York, 1970.

Stewart, James, Lieutenant Commander, R.N. (Ret). "East of Suez." *USNIP*, 92, no. 3 (March 1966), 41–51. British policy.

———. "The Suez Operation." *USNIP*, 90, no. 4 (April 1964), 37–47. The 1956 affair.

Swarztrauber, S. A., Commander, USN. "River Patrol Relearned." *USNIP*, 96, no. 5 (May 1970), 120–157. River warfare, Vietnam.

Symington, Stuart, Senator. "Laos: The Furtive War." *World* (August 29, 1972), 34–37. American involvement, 1964–72.

Theberge, James D. *Soviet Seapower in the Caribbean: Political and Strategic Implications*. New York, 1972.

Uhlig, Frank, Jr. "Some Speculations on the Navy at the End of the 1970s." *NWCR*, XXIV, no. 9 (May 1972), 9–15.

"U. S. Naval Operations Against North Vietnam, August 1964–November 1968." *Naval Review 1969*. Annapolis, 1969, pp. 359–363.

Valentine, Andrew J., Commander, USN. "R̩: Quarantine." *USNIP*, 89, no. 5 (May 1968), 38–50. Cuban missile crisis and blockade.

Van Horssen, D. A., Lieutenant Commander, USN. "The Royal Thai Navy." *USNIP*, 92, no. 6 (June 1966), 77–83.

Vito, Albert H., Jr., Captain, USN. "Developing the Fleet's Aircraft." *USNIP*, 92, no. 9 (September 1966), 69–77. Post-1945.

Waskow, Arthur I., ed. *The Debate over Thermonuclear Strategy*. Boston, 1965.

*Weyer's Warships of the World, 1969*. Annapolis, 1968.

Wettern, Desmond. "The Royal Navy and the Continuing Commitments." *USNIP*, 97, no. 8 (August 1971), 18–25.

Windchy, Eugene G. *The Tonkin Gulf*. New York, 1971. In August 1964.

Xydis, Stephen George. "The American Naval Visits to Greece and the Eastern Mediterranean in 1946—Their Impact on American-Soviet Relations." Ph.D., Columbia University, 1956.

Much material on the post-1945 period was derived from standard press accounts and numerous interviews and conversations with many U. S. Navy and Marine Corps officers, former midshipmen students and colleagues during and since the writer's years on the faculty at the U. S. Naval Academy (1964–68) and as coordinator of the U. S. Naval Institute's Distinguished Visitor Program (1967–69).

Unavailable dissertations and recent books too late to be utilized in the present work:

Beck, Horace. *Folklore and the Sea.* Middletown, Conn., 1973.

Chowdharay-Best, G. "The King's Chambers." *Mariner's Mirror,* 60, no. 1 (February 1974), 92–96. Early international law.

Dennis, Michael F. H. "The Role of Navies in Limited War." Ph.D., University of Minnesota, 1971.

Glover, Richard A. *Britain at Bay: Defence Against Bonaparte, 1803–14.* New York, 1973.

Gorshkov, S. G., Admiral of the Fleet, SN. "The Gorshkov Papers." *Morskoi Sbornik* (1972–73), tr. and reprinted, *USNIP,* 100, nos. 1–11 (January–November 1974).

Guilmartin, John F. "Changing Technology and Mediterranean Warfare at Sea in the Sixteenth Century." Ph.D., Princeton University, 1971.

Herwig, Holger H. "The German Naval Officers Corps: A Social and Political History, 1890–1918." Ph.D., State University of New York at Stony Brook, 1971.

Howse, Derek and Michael Sanderson. *The Sea Chart.* London, 1973. Historical survey.

Jenkins, E. H. *A History of the French Navy.* London, 1973.

Lane, Frederick C. *Venice: A Maritime Republic.* Baltimore, 1973.

May, W. E. *A History of Marine Navigation.* London, 1973.

Seno, Sadao, Commander, JMSDF. "A Chess Game with No Checkmate: Admiral Inoue and the Pacific War." NWCR, XXVI, no. 4 (January–February 1974), 26–39.

Violette, Aurele J. "Russian Naval Reform, 1855–1870." Ph.D., Ohio State University, 1971.

# Index

*Place names indexed only when relating to specific naval action.*

625

632                                    *Index*

642 *Index*